Centre de Sciences Humaines (Centre for Social Sciences and Humanities): Created in 1990 and based in New Delhi, the CSH is part of the network of research centres of the French Ministry of Foreign Affairs. The Centre's research work is primarily oriented towards the study of issues concerning the contemporary dynamics of development in India and South Asia. The activities of the Centre are focused on four main themes, namely: Economic growth and sustainable development, International and regional relations, Institutional structures and political constructions of identity and Urban dynamics.

Centre de Sciences Humaines, 2, Aurangzeb Road, New Delhi- 110011, India, Tel: (91) 11 3041 00 70, Fax: (91) 11 3041 00 79
E-mail: infos@csh-delhi.com
Website: http://www.csh-delhi.com

Institut Français de Pondichéry (French Institute of Pondicherry): Created in 1955, the IFP is a multidisciplinary research and advanced educational institute. Major research works are focusing on Sanskrit and Tamil Languages and literatures—in close collaboration with the Ecole Française d'Extrême-Orient—ecosystems, biodiversity and sustainability, dynamics of population and socio-economic development.

Institut Français de Pondichéry, 11, Saint Louis Street, PB 33
Pondicherry 605001, Tel: (91) 413 2334 168
Fax: (91) 413 2339 534
E-mail: ifpdir@ifpindia.org

EASTWARD BOUND

India's New Positioning in Asia

ISABELLE SAINT-MÉZARD

MANOHAR

CENTRE DE SCIENCES HUMAINES

2006

Contents

Acknowledgements

The present volume is a revised version of a PhD thesis written between 1997 and 2001 at the *Institut d'Etudes Politiques* in Paris. As in any such long work, there are a great number of persons who helped me in various ways. I therefore restrict myself to those who were involved with my work in the closest way, and start by acknowledging the constant support of my supervisor, Christophe Jaffrelot, during and after the submission of the thesis. David Camroux, Jean Luc Domenach and Jean Luc Racine allowed me to have a better understanding of my research topic.

I acknowledge the great help offered by the successive teams at the Centre de Sciences Humaines (CSH). The CSH hosted me during my two-year fieldwork in Delhi and supported the publication of the thesis. I am particularly thankful to Frederic Grare who was director of the Centre from 1999 to 2002.

Many a scholar at Jawaharlal Nehru University, the Institute of Defense Studies and Analysis, and the Centre for Policy Research gave incomparable insights into my subject. Among them, G.V.C. Naidu stood out for his constant availability and willingness to share. Many thanks to Mukul Asher at the National University of Singapore for making my field trip there so much easier.

Finally, I thank Professor Wong Siu-lun, director of the Centre of Asian Studies at the University of Hong Kong, as well as my colleagues M.G. Curley and N.D. Thomas from whom I learnt so much as a post doctoral scholar.

ISABELLE SAINT-MÉZARD

GATT	General Agreement on Trade and Tariffs
GMS	Greater Mekong Sub-Region
ICCR	Indian Council for Cultural Relations
IDSA	Institute for Defence Studies and Analysis (India)
IISS	International Institute for Strategic Studies (Singapore)
ISRO	Indian Space Research Organization
ISEAS	Institute for South-East Asian Studies (Singapore)
IMF	International Monetary Fund
IOR-ARC	Indian Ocean Rim—Association for Regional Cooperation
JETRO	Japan External Trade Organization
MGC	Mekong-Ganga Cooperation
MITI	Ministry of International Trade and Industry (Japan)
MTCR	Missile Technology Control Regime
NAFTA	North American Free Trade Area
NAM	Non-Aligned Movement
NIC	Newly Industrialized Countries
NRI	Non-Resident Indians
NNWS	Non-Nuclear Weapon State
NWS	Nuclear Weapon State
NPT	Non-Proliferation Treaty
OECD	Organization for Economic Cooperation and Development
SAARC	South Asian Association for Regional Cooperation
SAFTA	South Asian Free Trade Area

SAPTA	South Asian Preferential Trading Arrangement
SEATO	South-East Asian Treaty Organization
SEANWFZ	South-East Asian Nuclear Weapon Free Zone
SIA	Singapore International Airlines
SICCI	Singapore Indian Chamber of Commerce and Industry
SLORC	State Law and Order Restoration Council
SPDC	State Peace and Development Council
UMNO	United Malays National Organization
UNCTAD	United Nations Commission for Trade and Development
UNDP	United Nations Programme for Development
WTO	World Trade Organization

Introduction

Conceptualizing East Asia

At first glance, there appears to be a dividing line separating India and its East Asian neighbours today, in spite of the fact that they all belong to the Asian continent. Indeed, countries in the Indian sub-continent are considered as falling under South Asia, a regional unit extending up to Myanmar's western borders and, therefore, adjoining East Asia. In order to understand what lies behind today's cut-off point, it may be useful to look back at the historical emergence and development of the East Asia concept, to identify the point in time when the idea that India and East Asia belonged to two different areas within Asia first appeared. It would also be helpful to discover when these concepts were first formulated and imposed by the Europeans, and when they were appropriated by the concerned parties themselves. Evidently, these issues must be considered within a more global reflection on the very idea of Asia. In short, an attempt will be made to understand how the concept of 'Asia' was broken up into geographical subsets that led to the 'separation' of India from its eastern neighbours. Taking a look at the past is indispensable in order to understand the relations currently prevailing between India and East Asia, for as the political expert and historian Pekka Korhonen affirms, 'In a study of regional integration, geographic metaphors are crucial, because they define so clearly which country belongs to a certain group and which country does not'.[1]

India was once a major cultural and religious pole, exerting its influence over all its neighbours, now seen as 'Central Asia' or 'East Asia'. The spread of Buddhism and Hinduism went hand in hand with India's highly developed trade relations with China and South-East Asia. To the Graeco-Romans, the Indian sub-continent and its neighbours in East Asia belonged to the same world, and was so for most of recorded History.[2] The proof can be found in the generic use of the Latin term *India,* for several centuries, to denote all the known and unknown territories beyond the Indus River. In fact, the term was even understood sometimes as including certain regions of the African continent. An increasing number of 'Indies' were added to the European vocabulary in the thirteenth and fourteenth centuries as Europeans applied the term *India* to the new lands discovered further East. Hence, products like pepper were described as being of Indian origin whereas they could just as easily have been imported from regions situated beyond the sub-continent. The same held true for the silk imported from China, which passed through the land routes that crossed through the Indo-Greek kingdoms in northern India.

While most of Asia was known as *India* throughout the entire European Middle Ages, there were sub-divisions designated by expressions such as 'India within the Ganges', 'India beyond the Ganges', 'Farthest' or 'Upper India', 'Greater India', 'Middle India' and 'Little India'. The distinction made fairly early on between India before the Ganges (*India intra Gangem*) and India beyond the Ganges (*India extra Gangem*) demarcated a particular entity corresponding more or less to what would later be called the Indian sub-continent or South Asia. In his thirteenth-century travel writings, Marco Polo situated the province of Abyssinia in 'Middle India', whereas 'Greater India' extended from Malabar to Kesh-Makran (on the Iranian coast) and 'Little India' covered eight kingdoms, from Chamba (in South Vietnam) to Motupalli in Andhra Pradesh.[3] 'Upper India' could extend right up to Northern China (*Cathay*) and the more general term of 'East Indies' (*India Orientalis*) tended to include all the islands, from Australia to Japan and beyond.[4] After 1492, the expression *India Orientalis* also made it possible to distinguish these regions from the New World territories that Christopher Columbus, in his confusion, had also called the Indies.

This terminology remained in use throughout the sixteenth and seventeenth centuries. All the territories East of the Indus were still called *India* and geographical maps of *India Orientalis* showed the entire region from India to today's South-East Asia.[5] It was only in the beginning of the eighteenth century that European cartographers started to distinguish an Indian entity that was separated from the rest of the Asian continent. In 1710, the British cartographer, Herman Moll, drew a small map showing all of India on a single page—the first of its kind presenting the sub-continent as a separate unit. Herman Moll redrew the map in 1726 and entitled it *India Proper, or the Empire of the Great Mogul.* This representation of 'India Proper' reflected the growing awareness, in England, of the specific identity of the subcontinent. It also manifested the desire to leave behind the confusion that reigned until then with regard to the use of the term *India* for all of Asia.[6] From the second half of the eighteenth century, the mapping of these territories became a corollary to the colonial enterprise. Indeed, the growing military and political domination of the subcontinent by the British was accompanied by the determination to master its geographical representation, in as scientific and accurate a manner as possible—in short, mapping was an exercise in political control.[7] This enterprise eventually led to the 1799 *Map of Hindustan,* drawn by James Rennell, the first real representation of India in its entirety.

In spite of these initial distinctions, India remained fully integrated within a larger Asian area, increasingly structured by European expansionism. In fact, the trading activities of the European East India Companies that expanded rapidly in the seventeenth and eighteenth centuries spread from the Cape to the Pacific. What the European missionaries and merchants called the East Indies corresponded to a vast region embracing all of the East African and Asian coasts, with the Indian peninsula being granted pride of place.[8] A trading junction of prime importance, India enjoyed intense commercial relations with South-East Asia in the eighteenth and nineteenth centuries. During the first two decades of the nineteenth century, the subcontinent offered a base from which unofficial empires were built to expand trade and influence in the Middle East, East Africa and coastal China.[9] In the second half of the nineteenth century, India gradually became the base for British economic and military penetration in Asia. Colonies in Penang, Singapore and Malacca were governed from the subcontinent until 1867. After the Third Anglo-Burmese War in 1885, Rangoon was turned into a province of the Indian Empire and remained one till 1937. The British domination of South and South-East Asia led to an integration of these two areas within the same geopolitical unit, until the Second World War broke out.

While it had been formulated quite a while ago in the West, the concept of Asia remained foreign to the continent's inhabitants, as did the feeling of belonging to the same geographical unit. Western geographical concepts did not establish themselves in Asia until the massive arrival of the Europeans, in the nineteenth century. That was when the first 'Asianist' thinkers emerged—Okakuzo in Japan, and Tagore and Vivekananda in India—and developed their theories on Asian unity and the spiritual ethos of the people of the continent.

Asia was, therefore, a concept that was imported from the West, and that only really began to be appropriated in the beginning of the twentieth century. In this regard, the 1904–5 Russo-Japanese War played a decisive role, as it led to the emergence of the idea of an Asian identity, including the Arab, Persian, Indian, Chinese and Japanese cultures. In 1907, an Asian Friendship Association was established in Tokyo. It drew Chinese, Korean, Vietnamese, Filipino and Indian students, determined to understand how Japan managed to negotiate its relations with the West. However, modernized Japan considered itself to be outside Asia and was scarcely sensitive to the idea of the regeneration of the continent. During the 1930s, Japanese foreign policy orchestrated the metaphor of Asia to legitimize resistance to Europe's colonial powers. The sole objective of the discourse on the 'liberation of Asia' was to support the constitution of a Japanese sphere of co-prosperity. Nonetheless, the fact remains that the slogan 'Asia for the Asians' would have caught the imagination of many. Hence, the Indian nationalist, Rash Bihari Bose, went to Japan in the hope of obtaining support for his revolutionary activities.

In the 1930s, some of the Indian nationalist elite started hoping that the ideals of Asian solidarity would work as a mobilizing ideology to fight against the colonial powers.[10] Following the Second World War, India became Asia's standard bearer and intensified its initiatives in favour of the emancipation of the continent's inhabitants. One of India's most significant pan-Asian initiatives was to organize an Asian Relations Conference in 1947. This event constituted the first appearance of Asia in international politics. At the same time, this vast gathering of Asian nations, which took place even before they had attained their independence, heralded fundamental tendencies that were to work toward the sub-division of the continent. Japan did not attend the conference, a sign that reflected its demarcation from the continent. The Arab world was under-represented and proved itself to be far from involved in the project for Asian unity. The Arab League and Middle Eastern nations simply seemed not to consider themselves as Asian.[11] Hence, the conference emerged as a South and South-East Asian gathering.[12] It thereby revealed a dividing line between an essentially Moslem Middle Eastern Asia and an East Asia that covered the Indian subcontinent as well at the time.

However, even within East Asia, the concept of Asian unity did not receive unanimous support from the countries that were supposed to be part of it. The small South-East Asian States revealed their joint apprehension of being absorbed by one of the Big Two—China and India. For its part, China endeavoured not to allow India establish itself as the Asian leader. These discrepancies between the Asian nations emerged during the diplomatic campaign conducted by New Delhi for setting up an Economic Commission for Asia, along the lines of the European Economic Commission.[13] When India won its bid in the United Nations toward the end of 1946, the delegations of the Philippines, China and Korea demanded to be included in the Commission under the denomination of the Far East,[14] rather than Asia. That is how the Shanghai-based United Nations Economic Commission for Asia and the Far East was born in June 1947.

Despite these developments, the Western perception of the 1950s still relied on the concept of *India orientalis*, although the designation of South-East Asia henceforth started to be more frequently used.[15] The idea of South-East Asia that was forged in the course of the nineteenth century gained in popularity during the Second World War. Indeed, in 1943, the British established their South-East Asian Headquarters in Ceylon, in order to organize their defence against the advance of the Japanese army in Asia.[16] The sense of the term remained within the post-war collective imagination of the West. India and the region corresponding to contemporary South-East Asia therefore still belonged more or less to the same conceptual unit, bringing together poor and under-developed countries that were in need of American aid. This extensive South-East Asian area was circumscribed in opposition, on the one hand, to an essentially Arab and more prosperous Middle East and, on the other, to Central Asia and Siberia, which were included within the Soviet sphere. Socialist Asian countries constituted a separate group, whereas Japan considered itself—and was considered—as being totally apart.[17] This Western perception more or less corresponded with the conceptions of the Asian peoples themselves, as they were revealed during the Asian Relations Conference in 1947. The concept of South Asia therefore did not exist and, because of this, the nations of the Indian subcontinent belonged to the South-East Asian unit.

This South-East Asian area, broadly speaking, found institutional expression in the Colombo Plan for Co-operative Economic and Social Development in Asia and the Pacific, a loose organization for co-ordinating economic aid among the countries in the region.[18] India still played a central role in the region. When Japan joined the Colombo Plan, it was interested basically in India, which was supposed to offer great development potential. The two states had already established relations on several fronts. Indeed, New Delhi was one of the first capitals in Asia to have renewed diplomatic relations with Japan, in 1952. A few years later, in 1958, India became the first country to receive a loan in Yen while South-East Asian countries were endeavouring to deal with the difficult issue of obtaining compensation from Japan. But Nehru's dreams of Asian integration were put to the test of the Cold War in the 1950s. The Conference of the Colombo powers that brought together Sri Lanka, Myanmar, India, Indonesia and Pakistan took place for the first time in April 1954 and revealed that the confrontation between the two blocks had already instituted divisions between the Asian states.[19] Toward the end of the 1950s, it became clear that the erstwhile faith in Asian solidarity and the great traditions of harmony and synthesis did not suffice to found a regional project.[20]

The caesura between India and South-East Asia therefore emerged clearly in the mid-1950s and deepened further in the course of the 1960s. The border clash with China in 1962 was seen as a bitter failure that called into question the interest and commitment of India's elite with regard to Asia. India's vision of the outside world became increasingly confined to its contentious relations with Pakistan and to two associated fixations: the Kashmiri imbroglio and the support extended by the West to Islamabad. Finally, the polarization of the Cold War succeeded in dividing Asia. India increasingly turned toward the Soviet block while several East Asian states except for the Indo-Chinese peninsula, chose the pro-American option. The notion of Asian unity went to pieces because of the distorted perceptions induced by the Cold War. In the 1960s, regional cooperation in the name of Asia dissolved into the promotion of South-South cooperation and the Non-Aligned Movement (NAM). In 1961, New Delhi was included in Prime Minister Ikeda's South-East Asian visit, a tour that was the first instance of the new economy-oriented Japanese diplomacy. But the Japanese delegation was disappointed with Prime Minister Jawaharlal Nehru's attitude, which made him lean toward non-alignment and show little interested in proposals of economic cooperation. Relations between India and Japan gradually became strained. From the 1960s onwards, Tokyo sided with the Western security system, while New Delhi pursued its non-aligned principles. However, the distance between the two countries was essentially the result of India's increasingly introverted economic policy choices.[21]

South-East Asia, for its part, slowly began to get structured when the Association of South-East Asian Nations (ASEAN) was formed in 1967, with Indonesia, Malaysia, the Philippines, Singapore and Thailand as its founding members. Political neutrality was affirmed officially as a smokescreen for a pro-Western sensibility that put India at odds with the Association. The ASEAN countries dissociated themselves from their Indian neighbour and imposed a stricter definition of South-East Asia. It was, therefore, hardly surprising to witness the emergence of the notion of South Asia in the 1960s, almost by default. In the 1970s, the Cold War continued to exacerbate ideological differences, and crystallized over the Indochina conflict. But perhaps differing economic performance demarcated the various Asian sub-regions far more clearly. By virtue of their rapid development, the ASEAN states hitched on to the 'fast-growing-economies' train driven by Japan and South Korea. The concept of the 'Western Pacific' then emerged, designating this part of Asia, with extraordinary growth rates. In the international collective imagination, the dividing line between India (with its fairly autarchic economic system) and its eastern neighbours (well-integrated in the prosperous and newsworthy Pacific zone) became very clear thenceforth. In the process, the notion of Asia was lost in the triumphant geographical concept of the Pacific. This hybrid concept tended to cover an economic unit characterized by its dynamism and, hence, grouped together countries along the perimeter of the Pacific Ocean—both Asian and American. Even the Economic Commission for Asia and the Far East changed into the Economic Commission for Asia and the Pacific. In 1980, a Pacific Economic Cooperation Council (PECC) was created, accompanied by the euphoric rhetoric of the Pacific Age. India, which conformed to an essentially politico-strategic apprehension of international relations on its part, seemed indifferent to the importance of the economic dynamics structuring its eastern neighbourhood at the time. Its negligence led it to decline an invitation extended by the ASEAN in 1980 to participate in its conference as a dialogue partner. New Delhi contented itself with working with its immediate neighbours to set-up the South Asian Association for Regional Cooperation (SAARC), in 1985. South Asia thenceforth gained an institutional dimension. The caesura with South-East Asia was consummated.

However, the end of the 1980s witnessed a change in the Pacific metaphor, to the benefit of the re-emergence of the Asia concept.

Indeed, the United States dissociated itself from trans-Pacific cooperation, as it felt threatened by the success of the Western Pacific Asian economies. The emergence of expressions like 'Asian Tigers' and 'Asian Dragons', and the craze for the so-called 'Asian' economic model testified to the rebirth of the concept of Asia. But above all, it was when China entered centre-stage, with its free-market-oriented economic policy, that the complementary metaphors of the Pacific and Western Pacific seemed to have become somewhat obsolete. The concept of the Asia-Pacific was then preferred, as it made it possible to include the entire Chinese mainland. This change in the international collective imagination found institutional expression in 1989, with the establishment of the Asia Pacific Economic Cooperation (APEC) group. The regional project, supported by the United States, was essentially economic in nature.

The refocusing on Asia continued during the 1990s. In fact, the idea of the Pacific suffered a fresh assault when, in 1991, the Malaysian Prime Minister, Mahathir Mohammad, came up with the idea of the East Asian Economic Caucus (EAEC). Far more restrictive, this scheme of regional organization included the ASEAN, China, Japan and South Korea, and advocated a new regional unit, corresponding to East Asia. Traditionally, the East Asia concept referred rather to the Chinese cultural sphere—essentially China, South Korea and Japan. But during the 1980s, the various Japanese leaders who toured South-East Asia tended to extend the concept to include this region as well.[22] Unlike the 'Western Pacific', the notion of East Asia had not only an economic content, but also a strong political connotation. In fact, it excluded Asia's 'white' economic powers—Australia and New Zealand—and asserted its position as an alternative to the American APEC scheme. Interestingly, the East Asia concept promoted by the EAEC project came to win its first official recognition with the establishment of the Asia-Europe Meeting (ASEM), in March 1996. This development in the debate opposing different regional versions of Asia proved of considerable symbolic importance. As Pekka Korhonen demonstrated, the creation of the ASEM illustrated the extent to which East Asia—particularly South-East Asia—had managed to monopolize the 'geographical metaphor' of Asia. With the result that the geographic area covered by the Asia concept had shrunk, in a way. In fact, in the period following the Second World War, the western borders of Asia tended to be situated near Pakistan or Afghanistan, in political or economic terms. India therefore belonged more or less to the same functional unit as its East Asian neighbours. But in the post-Cold War world, these borders seemed to have moved toward Myanmar—as if the regional concept of Asia had to be expurgated, per force, to form a viable and relatively homogeneous unit. It goes without saying that in the process of 'refocusing' the 'Asia' concept, the Indian subcontinent found itself relegated to a peripheral status. The proof lies in the research studies of the 1990s, which often tended to view what was merely a part for the whole. One only has to look at the number of works that used the generic term of 'Asia' although they essentially dealt with East Asia alone.

In short, Asia is a fluctuating idea, whose definition varies according to the actors, the issues and the periods of time under consideration. Hence, the term 'East Asia' will be used for the purpose of the present work, defined as including the ASEAN[23] and North-East Asian countries: Japan, South Korea and China. This meaning corresponds to the version of Asia supported by Malaysia, since the early 1990s. From this viewpoint, the choice of the 'East Asia' region seems far more appealing than that of the Asia-Pacific. In the first place, the metaphors of Asia and East Asia are making a strong comeback and, contrary to the various imagined communities based on the Pacific, these metaphors stem from a political rationale, not just economic issues alone. Moreover, East Asian nations have played a critical role in shaping the new Asian region, as reflected by the fact that the terms of Asia and East Asia have so often been amalgamated in recent times. The paradox, therefore, is that the process of redefining contemporary Asia has been monopolized by just a single part of Asia, excluding India, in spite of India being one of the countries that has contributed the most, both culturally and intellectually, to shaping the Asian concept. A study of the relations between India and East Asia will, therefore, help in reflecting on India's place in this 'new Asia'.[24]

At this juncture, the vague and vast nature of the notion of East Asia must be pointed out. Choosing to deal with the relations between India and East Asia on the whole may seem ambitious in view of the immensity and diversity of the region envisaged. From a methodological point of view, however, it is difficult to carve out geographical, economic or political sub-units or to use any 'level of aggregation' smaller than that of East Asia. As Philippe Hugon explains, the ASEAN cannot really be thought of *in abstracto* and 'insofar as regionalization has been largely induced by industrial poles and commercial and financial networks, with the effects of contagion and interdependence that come in their wake, Japan, South Korea and China have had to be included in East Asia'.[25] Our methodological approach will be, rather, to put the emphasis on the ASEAN, while taking into account the Japanese pole and the newly industrialized countries (NICs), especially South Korea. As for China, it will remain in the background and will be considered only insofar as its impact on relations between India and East Asia is concerned. Sino-Indian relations are a separate subject by themselves, but in the framework of the present study, they constitute just one of the parameters of India's 'Look East' Policy.

The Indian Opening up to East Asia

The Asian miracle of the 1980s left India on the periphery of the 'new Asia'. New Delhi chose to content itself, then, with its close partnership with the Soviet Union. In fact, India's traditionally westward-looking elite seemed decreasingly sensitive to its eastern neighbourhood after Nehru's demise, with the exception of Japan. It was only under Indira Gandhi's second government that India's interest in East Asia reawakened. Such renewed interest in India's eastern neighbourhood was concomitant with efforts toward opening up the economy. On her return to power in 1980, Indira Gandhi supported the reformers and, in September–October 1981, left on a two-week tour of South-East Asia. The year 1984 seemed to mark a fresh start in Indo-Japanese relations, when Japanese Prime Minister, Nakasone, came to India on an official visit, the first of its kind in twenty-three years. The same year, Rajiv Gandhi took over from his late mother and breathed fresh life into the economic reform process. He visited Japan three times, in 1985, 1987 and 1988. Japanese aid, which had stagnated until then at around ¥ 30 billion per annum, doubled in 1986. In December 1988, relations with China received a fresh boost with Rajiv Gandhi's historic visit to Beijing. Between 1986 and 1989, the young Prime Minister also worked toward a greater rapprochement with the ASEAN. Unfortunately, the Association was no longer interested in India's overtures. In any case, the spirit of reform died in 1987 and Rajiv lost the elections in the fall of 1989. The coalition governments that followed until the spring of 1991 were too fragile to initiate durable economic reforms.

A complete change seemed to have taken place in 1991. Although tenuous, the coalition government led by the Congress Prime Minister P.V. Narasimha Rao gave a lasting boost to the policy of opening up to East Asia by launching the 'Look East' policy. At this juncture, it is important to understand what triggered the Look East policy as well as the specific context in which it was launched. India was particularly disconcerted at the new international scenario that emerged after the two major crises of the Gulf War and the collapse of the Soviet Union. Indian diplomacy was not ready to face such international upheavals and was, therefore, slow to react. Due to the stands it had taken during the first Gulf War, New Delhi had alienated the sympathy of the Arab countries and lost its stature within the NAM. Furthermore, the downfall of its erstwhile Soviet partner constituted no less than a black hole in India's foreign policy. The disintegration of the USSR basically implied an end to the political support India enjoyed in the Security Council and the loss of a source of low-cost arms and technology. At the same time, one of the founding principles of India's foreign policy—non-alignment—was called into question in a world that had become unipolar. The fear of American hegemony rose as Washington increased pressure against New Delhi on various fronts, while remaining strongly inclined toward supporting India's hostile neighbour, Pakistan.

At the beginning of the 1990s, the predominant feeling in India was that the country was under the threat of being marginalized in a world that appeared increasingly structured by economic dynamics and regionalist trends. The consolidation of the ASEAN, the growing integration of Europe and the intensification of negotiations for the creation of free trade areas in North America (NAFTA)[26] as well as in the Asia-Pacific (APEC), strengthened New Delhi's fear with regard to the formation of exclusive regional blocks. As for the SAARC, the only organization for regional cooperation to which India belonged, it was in no position to constitute a viable alternative in terms of regional integration. Moreover, at a time when it had to reconsider its position in the world, India fell prey to major macroeconomic problems. In the spring of 1991 the country was close to asphyxiating and eventually suffered an unprecedented balance of payments crisis, largely engendered by the Gulf War. Its foreign exchange reserves had fallen to a level where they could only cover two weeks of imports. With the support of the IMF, the new government resolved to implement a structural adjustment plan in July 1991. The reform policy consisted of deregulating, privatizing and globalizing an economy that until then had been a bastion of state planning and control. The reform measures announced were rapidly implemented and the collapse of the Soviet Union only accelerated the process. Indeed, the demise of India's preferential bilateral agreements with the USSR led to the disappearance of a Rupee-trade zone that used to account for approximately a quarter of Indian exports. The budget prepared by Finance Minister Manmohan Singh in February 1992, triggered the second phase of the liberalization programme in the fields of international trade and exchange rates.

With economic liberalization underway, the influx of foreign exchange became of vital importance, along with access to the markets of prosperous countries and an increase in transfers of technology. Thus, New Delhi realized that enhanced relations with centres of economic growth had to be a top-priority on its international agenda. Parti-cularly sensitive to the importance of external relations, Prime Minister P.V. Narasimha Rao understood that it was imperative for India to resort to economic diplomacy. In other words, India's foreign policy had to place itself at the service of the country's new economic and technological interests, with the primary objective of changing India's image abroad and promoting its economic potential. It was in this context that the Look East policy was launched, for the one region in the world that embodied prosperity and economic success was East Asia. But New Delhi had to catch up on the mounting delay caused by its negligent attitude toward the region. India also had to assume certain humility *vis-à-vis* wealthy neighbours it had long looked down on. However, the idea of benefiting from the surplus capital of these Asian economies far surpassed these considerations, all the more so since the East Asian states themselves seemed highly interested in India's new open policy.

Against this backdrop, the main subject of this work is to analyse the developments in India's position with regard to the contemporary East Asian region since the early 1990s. This general question is addressed in nine chapters, reflecting the various facets of the Look East policy as well as the stakes raised by India's opening onto the East Asian region. The first chapter presents the policy, explaining how it was conceived in New Delhi and how it was received in East Asia, while highlighting the impetus for such policy thrust towards India's eastern neighbours. The second chapter observes the evolution of trans-national flows—especially in terms of trade and investments —between India and East Asia from the early 1990s to the 1997

Asian crisis. Then, the third chapter exposes the various difficulties faced by the Look East policy, including the impact of the Asian crisis on the new links forged between India and East Asia. In the fourth chapter, the ideological underpinnings of the Look East policy are exposed, in particular India's attempts at participating in the contemporary definition of an Asian identity. The fifth chapter observes how India has performed in terms of institutional integration, while the sixth chapter focuses on the nature of the cultural and religious links between India and East Asia. Finally, the last three chapters concentrate on the strategic and defence dimensions of India's Look East policy. They show that while India was fairly alienated from its eastern neighbours in the early 1990s, it had by the early 2000s substantially enhanced its profile in the Asian strategic equation.

NOTES

1. Pekka Korhonen, *Japan and Asia Pacific Integration: Pacific Romances, 1968–96*, London: Routledge, 1998, p. 3.
2. While India was well known to the Greeks as a rich land, its Eastern neighbourhood remained unknown for several centuries. In the fifth century BC, Herodotus wrote, 'Asia is inhabited up to India; further east, the country is uninhabited and no one knows anything about it.' The conquests of Alexander the Great in the fourth century considerably enriched European knowledge of India. They also opened up major trade routes and enabled extensive cultural exchanges. See Susan Gole, *India within the Ganges*, New Delhi: Jayaprints, 1983, p. 24.
3. The story of Marco Polo's voyages was written in 1299 when he was a war prisoner in Genoa. This account constituted the principal source material of cartographers during the two following centuries (Gole, *India within the Ganges*, p. 34).
4. The terms *India Intra Gangem* and *India Extra Gangem* appeared in the tenth map of Asia attributed to Ptolemy's work, *Geographia*. This map of Asia was printed in 1490 for the first time, in Rome. The maps attributed to Claudius Ptolemy (first century AD) survived till the Middle Ages and exerted considerable influence on early European cartographers (Gole, *India within the Ganges*, pp. 24–6).
5. Pekka Korhonen, 'Monopolizing Asia: the Politics of a Metaphor', *Pacific Review*, vol. 10, no. 3, 1997, pp. 347–65.
6. Gole, *India within the Ganges*, p. 64.

7. Jackie Assayag, *L'Inde: Désir de Nation*, Paris: Odile Jacob, 2001, pp. 51–88.
8. Holden Furber, *Rival Empires of Trade in the Orient, 1600–1800*, Delhi: Oxford University Press, 1990, p. 7; James Mills, *The History of British India and Orientalism*, Oxford: Clarendon Press, 1992.
9. C.A. Bayly, *Indian Society and the Making of the British Empire*, Cambridge: Cambridge University Press, 1988.
10. Christophe Jaffrelot, 'L'Inde et l'Asiatisme', D. Camroux and J.L. Domenach (ed.), *L'Asie Retrouvée*, Paris: Seuil, 1997, pp. 229–49.
11. Birendra Prasad, *Indian Nationalism and Asia*, Delhi: B.R. Publishing Corporation, 1979, p. 214.
12. In this, it echoed the initial preferences of its organizers. In fact, when the issue of which countries should be invited first came up, one school of thought maintained that it would be preferable to limit the conference to South-East Asia, as these nations formed 'one region from the security and economic viewpoints and because they were more closely allied with India than the others'. It was finally decided that invitations would be sent to all Asian countries, viz., Middle Eastern countries and Egypt as well. But the expansion of the area covered was linked to a more pragmatic argument: psychologically, the greater the number of invitees, the greater would be the impact of the event (Asian Relations, *Report of the Proceedings and Documentation of the First Asian Relations Conference*, New Delhi, March–April 1947, New Delhi: Asian Relations Organization, 1948, pp. 4–5).
13. In 1946, the United Nations established the Economic Commission for Europe in order to distribute American aid.
14. In the original French text, *Far East* is translated as 'Extrême-Orient' and *East Asia* as 'Asie orientale'.
15. Korhonen, 'Monopolizing Asia', p. 356.
16. For the historical formation of the term South-East Asia: Donald K. Emmerson, ' "Southeast Asia": What's in a Name?', *Journal of Southeast Asian Studies*, vol. 15, no. 1, 1984, pp. 1–25.

    It is difficult, historically, to identify the emergence of the concept of South-East Asia. It came into current usage during the nineteenth century, but remained vague for a long time. In the nineteenth century, the term could be used to include a large part of India and China. In the 1920s, South-East Asia could be either South Asia or East Asia, depending on the authors. For instance, Heine-Geldern built the region along cultural lines that included Assam, areas of East Bengal, the Andaman and Nicobar Islands and Formosa.
17. Korhonen, *Japan and Asia Pacific Integration*, pp. 43–4.
18. The South-East Asia Treaty Organization (SEATO), established on

8 September 1954, also corresponded to a particularly broad interpretation of the region involved. While the United States, France and Great Britain were the signatories on the Western side, the concept of South-East Asia also included Australia, New Zealand, Pakistan, the Philippines and Thailand.

19. Sisir Gupta, *India and Regional Integration in Asia*, Bombay: Asia Publishing House, 1964, p. 51. The conference powers met in November 1956 for the last time.
20. Werner Levi, *The Challenge of World Politics in South and Southeast Asia*, London: Prentice-Hall, 1968.
21. Arjun Asrani, 'India-Japan Relations', Foreign Service Institute, *Indian Foreign Policy, Agenda for the 21st Century*, New Delhi, Foreign Service Institute: Konark Publishers, vol. II, 1998, pp. 344–6.
22. Korhonen, *Japan and Asia Pacific Integration*, p. 187.
23. Brunei joined the five founding members—Indonesia, Malaysia, the Philippines, Singapore and Thailand—in 1984, Vietnam in 1995, Laos and Myanmar in 1997, and Cambodia in 1999.
24. Karoline Postel-Vinay, *Le Japon et la Nouvelle Asie*, Paris: Presses de Sciences Po, 1996.
25. Philippe Hugon, Introduction to 'La régionalisation Comparée en Afrique Sub-Saharienne et en Asie de l'Est', *Revue Tiers Monde*, no. 155, July–September 1998, pp. 489–90.
26. The NAFTA (North American Free Trade Area) brings together the United States, Canada and Mexico.

CHAPTER 1

India's Look East Policy

1.1 An Outcome of India's Economic Liberalization

The decision to initiate reforms in the Indian economy was taken in a situation of emergency. Nevertheless, the balance of payments crisis in 1991 simply triggered a process that had already been emerging for several years. Hence, the IMF's proposals converged with the views of the Indian reformers, rather than being simply imposed on the country. As Isher Judge Ahluwalia put it, a state of mind favouring reforms already existed.

The change in course was the direct result of the balance of payments crisis, although several discussions and debates had been held since the end of the 1970s on the need for change, viz., at around the time when China had begun to change its own economic policy.[1]

In other words, a certain 'Look East' could be found well upstream of the economic liberalization policy itself.

AN ECONOMIC OPENING UP STIMULATED BY THE EAST ASIAN GROWTH MODELS

India was well aware of the economic ascendancy of Japan since the 1960s. Rather, it was the discovery of the success achieved by the Newly Industrialized Countries (NICs) and several ASEAN economies that played a role in calling India's development choices into question. Indeed, right up to the 1950s, India enjoyed a considerable edge over most East Asian countries. Fifty years later, the political class, the business communities and a large part of the intelligentsia realized how far India had fallen behind the same countries. As Prime Minister Narasimha Rao himself acknowledged, India was very impressed when South Korea was admitted to the OECD, in 1996.[2] Manmohan Singh, the Finance Minister under the Rao government, kept comparing India with this small North-East Asian country during the first half of the 1990s. It is true that when the two countries gained independence in 1947, India could boast of being far more advanced in its industrial development than most East Asian states. However, in the 1960s and then, in the 1970s, South Korea achieved an annual growth rate of ten per cent, while India remained static at the 'Hindu' growth rate of three per cent per annum. Before the Asian crisis almost ninety per cent of the Korean population fell under the ambit of the middle class. In India, the percentage of the population living below the poverty line still remained at least at forty per cent.

In this regard, while the Look East policy stemmed from economic reforms, as we shall see later, it also existed well before the reform process. J.N. Dixit, the former Foreign Secretary, admitted that the success of the East Asian economies played a role in the choice made by Indian decision-makers in the early 1990s to opt for liberalization: 'The illustrative influence of the modernization of the Chinese economy, and the economic performance of the members of ASEAN and others such as South Korea and territories such as Taiwan gave an impetus to the process.'[3] It was, indeed, a surprising change in the Indian state of mind, given that the country suffered from a superiority complex for many years, and refused to even entertain any comparisons with a 'small country' like South Korea. Furthermore, China's economic upswing undoubtedly played a major role in the decision to opt for liberalization, especially as China stood out as the closest to India in terms of its size and complexity.

In short, in the early 1990s, the idea that India had missed the East Asian growth train became more or less accepted. The series of reforms that was launched in 1991 therefore provided an opportunity to catch up with these economies. International financial institutions gave an additional incentive to emulate the East Asian growth miracle, with their reports constantly comparing India's performance with that of its Eastern neighbours. Moreover, an Indian high official, Satyam Kaji, was the Vice-President for the East Asia region in the World Bank since the early 1990s. The latter, who played a decisive role in the institution's publication on the Asian miracle, did not stop highlighting the experience of its neighbours to India. In April 1995, during a conference of Indian financiers in Bombay, he asserted that if the country could replicate the same kind of commitment that East Asian countries had exhibited, an 'Indian miracle' would inevitably take place.[4]

The group of decision-makers that came into power in June 1991 was fully conversant with the mechanisms that had contributed to the prosperity of the tiger and dragon economies. They felt the urgency of the situation and were concerned about the need to ensure that the country was not left on the periphery of the 'Asian miracle'. Prime Minister Narasimha Rao, who had been the Minister for External Affairs under Indira Gandhi from January 1980 to July 1984 and, under Rajiv Gandhi from 1988–9, knew East Asia well. His several visits to the region in the 1980s enabled him to witness the changes occurring there. Narasimha Rao entrusted the Finance portfolio to Manmohan Singh, the former Secretary-General of the South Commission in Geneva. Thanks to the number of study visits he had undertaken, Dr Singh had a clear view of how far back his country had fallen and took a critical look at the course of India's development.[5] But as the main architect of India's reforms, he was also determined that his country would catch up with the growth taking place in Asia.[6] Another high official from an international institution, Montek Singh Ahluwalia, was included in the team of reformers. He had worked with the World Bank earlier, one of the best possible positions for understanding South-East Asian growth.

Not only did the observation of the tigers play a role in triggering the reform process, but it also contributed to it. All through the 1990s, several Indian experts and policy-makers felt that the NICs' experience of development provided many examples that could be emulated. They were obviously aware of the fundamental differences between India and these economies, which were small countries for the most part, often with just a single language, culture and identity, and a homogeneous population. In short, the total opposite of India. Moreover, to explain the difference in economic growth, Indian analysts referred to the different development options adopted in the past—self-sufficiency and import substitution in India's case; economic liberalization and export promotion in the case of several East Asian countries. However, all along the 1990s, the promoters of India's economic liberalization kept looking toward East Asia. For instance, in his annual report on the country's economic performance for the year 1996, the Finance Minister stated officially that the development experience of East Asian countries served as an inspiration for India, in particular in its decision to open up to foreign investors.[7]

Hence, Indian reformers found inspiration in the way different East Asian States managed the opening up of their economies. In 1993 for example, the office of the Economic Advisor to the Commerce Minister requested Price Waterhouse, a management consultancy, to carry out a comparative analysis of investment promotion zones in Indonesia, Malaysia, Thailand and China.[8] Another example can be found in the budget prepared in 1997 by the Finance Minister, P. Chidambaram, which reduced import rates by engaging to align them with those of the ASEAN by 2000. His avowed objective was to ensure that India would become 'as competitive as any other Asian country by 2000'.[9] In another field, Kishan S. Rana, a former diplomat, was of the opinion that in order to promote India's economic interests abroad, it was necessary to adopt strategies similar to organizational models existing in Asia such as in Taiwan, South Korea or Japan. However, Singapore was the favourite example. The diplomat felt that like the city-state, New Delhi needed to establish specific fora for the promotion of trade and the expansion of foreign trade, in order to complement the duties of a highly overburdened Commerce Minister.[10]

The interest in Asian development models transcended political divides and changes in government. In July 1996, the new Minister of External Affairs of the United Front government, I.K. Gujral, asserted during a visit to South-East Asia, 'The conviction in India is growing among our leaders, the intelligentsia and even in popular perception that we could profit from the successful growth and developmental experience and model of South-East Asia and ASEAN'.[11] He also proposed frequent interaction between Indian and East Asian decision-makers to discuss macro-economic policies, social prog-rammes and capital and resource mobilization techniques, especially in the infrastructure field. I.K. Gujral's proposal therefore constituted an official acknowledgement of the effectiveness of the East Asian growth model and India's desire to emulate it. What is more, it may even express India's admiration for the East Asian experience of state interventionism. It is true that since the early 1990s, a number of analysts argued that the East Asian development model was based on selective state intervention. With ambitious projects in several sectors, from infrastructure to sustained social programmes, East Asian states were acknowledged as the great architects of an economic growth that was also based on policies promoting high savings and investment rates. Even the champions of the market economy model came to recognize the advantages of public interventionism. For instance, the World Bank published a report in 1993, praising the intervention of Asian governments that helped stimulate development.[12] So perhaps the reason why Indian reformers and senior officials were so fascinated with the East Asian growth model in the early 1990s was that they wanted to maintain a strong state apparatus in the context of economic liberalization.

In no case did the Indian state conceive of liberalization as a loss of power in decision-making or economic management. In its view, if India was allowing market forces free play, this did not imply that it had been reduced to a secondary role. In fact, it was not a matter of exclusivity—the state or the private sector—but, rather, of a complementarity between the two. The perception of the Indian state with regard to its role in the liberalization process was clearly formulated by A.N. Ram, a diplomat specializing in economic issues:

> The very process of 'liberalization' and 'deregulation' stems from a recognition that economic activity in developing countries would have to be guided both by the market and the state. It is for the state to decide the extent, the nature and the content of liberalization.[13]

In the same way, the market determined to what extent and in which fields it could substitute for public intervention. The public and the private sectors were, therefore, supposed to contribute harmoniously to the country's socio-economic makeover. The senior official concluded that, 'It, therefore, becomes necessary for us to understand and explain to our partners abroad that in the new dispensation, the state's role has neither withered away nor shrunk; it has merely been redefined to meet the challenges arising out of 'globalization' and 'liberalization'.

In other words, the Indian state conceived of liberalization not as a loss of power, but as a redefinition of its functions. Hence, to promote the economic reform process, the state sought to work in partnership with the Indian private sector. The long criticized arrogance of the administration was no longer a viable attitude, as the reform programme called for close cooperation between the Indian government and business circles. The Chambers of Commerce and Industry started playing a more active role in the work of the various ministries. Large delegations of businessmen began to accompany political leaders during their official visits abroad. When he was at the head of the Ministries of Commerce and then Finance, P. Chidambaram even took inspiration from the Japanese model of close collaboration between the public and private sectors. For example, he attempted to launch a joint initiative by the government and chambers of commerce and industry by creating a fund for promoting Indian trademarks.[14]

Initially, the liberalization inevitably led to a reduction in direct state control over economic activities. For example, when the licensing system was gradually dismantled, private economic actors gained by increasing their room for manoeuvre. Nevertheless, the Indian state remained a vital player in economic activities, especially when these transcended domestic boundaries. Its diplomatic arm provided it with its own lever in international economic relations. In the process of the Indian economy becoming globalized, diplomacy became a favoured tool of action for the state. In a way, liberalization increased the state's importance in defending and promoting national economic interests at the international level. The state's role and functions found themselves redefined, particularly in the field of foreign policy, where the preeminence of commercial and financial concerns led to the application of economic diplomacy principles.

INDIA'S NEW ECONOMIC DIPLOMACY

Former Foreign Secretary Muchkund Dubey once defined economic diplomacy as 'the conduct of foreign policy in the economic field'.[15] This interpretation came to include various dimensions in the early 1990s. The first one was to ensure that the legal framework of world trade was in favour of India's national interests, and it was the Ministry of Commerce's job to participate actively in multilateral negotiations. Another important aspect of economic diplomacy was that of highlighting and promoting the country's potential abroad, especially in the most dynamic growth centres. That was a task that the Ministry of External Affairs had to accomplish. Indeed, capital shortages constituted a major constraint for Indian development efforts. New Delhi therefore had to attract foreign investment, an arduous task given the level of international competitiveness in the matter. Hence, the country had to position itself in capital-surplus economies by projecting the image of an attractive destination. But existing stereotypes were not advantageous for India, which had long pursued a highly restrictive policy with regard to foreign investments. Indian diplomacy also had to convince the developed world of the durability of its reforms, prevent foreign investors from becoming sceptical about India's political stability and highlight the abundant opportunities it offered for economic cooperation. In short, the Ministry of External Affairs had to promote the idea that India was emerging as a future economic giant. It was at this stage that economic diplomacy came into play. Indeed, in several ways, it was an operation in public relations that aimed at changing India's image internationally.

The new economic diplomacy constituted a major reversal in comparison with the traditional principles of India's foreign policy. In fact, diplomatic circles had long put economic issues on the backburner, placing them below purely political or strategic issues in importance. Priorities underwent a sea change in the early 1990s at the instigation of Muchkund Dubey. The latter held the post of Foreign Secretary under Prime Ministers V.P. Singh and Chandra Shekhar and, during the first six months of P.V. Narasimha Rao's prime ministership. Indeed, Dubey anticipated the preeminence of economic issues in foreign policy fairly early and proceeded, therefore, to strengthen the Ministry's economic division. It is to be noted that in 1990, he added an economic coordination cell to this division, whose task it was to consult other ministries in matters concerning foreign investment projects.

With the coming into office of the reformers' team and at P.V. Narasimha Rao's behest, the Ministry of External Affairs was officially charged with handling economic diplomacy.[16] Until then, there had been a considerable organizational handicap in the promotion of India's economic interests abroad. The commercial sections in Indian embassies fell under the Ministry of Commerce. Thus, they were somewhat neglected by a Ministry whose priority was to implement economic policy at the national level and participate in multilateral negotiations within the GATT framework (General Agreement on Tariffs and Trade), as well as in the World Trade Organization. Thus, at the end of 1991, a note from the Prime Minister strongly recommended the Ministry of External Affairs as well as its diplomatic missions to concentrate on the economic and technological aspects of India's foreign relations. The embassies redirected their work toward the promotion of Indian exports and the improvement of the image of India's economy. They were also directed to work at attracting the attention of foreign investors to India's potential. Heads of Mission abroad were made directly responsible for the conduct of economic and trade relations with the country to which they were accredited. Diplomatic staff also received special training on economic issues.

Within the Ministry itself, the Economic Division was further strengthened, as one of its duties was to ensure that India's commercial interests were promoted internationally. Supported by a new Investment Promotion Unit, established in 1993, the Division provided India's diplomatic missions abroad with a continuous flow of information on the progress achieved in implementing the reforms. It also facilitated the organization of trade shows and exhibitions, as well as seminars on India's economic policies. Moreover, the Ministry of Foreign Affairs was thenceforth associated more closely with decisions on the country's economic policy.[17] Through its Principal Secretary and the Cabinet Secretary, Prime Minister Rao ensured that the Ministry was effectively included in the government's economy-related work, in particular in fine-tuning procedures related to Indian exports, foreign investments or the acquisition of new technologies. For the first time, the Foreign Secretary participated as a member, rather than merely a guest, in two institutions that debated economic issues at the highest level: the High Committee of Secretaries for the Economic Policy and the Foreign Investment Promotion Board (FIPB).

In many respects, the official launch of the economic diplomacy revealed that the perceptions of the Indian state about international politics had undergone a paradigmatic change. As the analyst Ramesh Thakur put it, India's foreign policy had until then operated essentially in a realist framework, in which the state was the main actor on the international scene, with its armed forces as its primary tool and national security as its main objective.[18] But the changes launched at the end of the 1980s showed that the Indian state started to acknowledge the primacy of economic power over strategic objectives. In fact, economic instruments and the control of multilateral institutions proved more effective that military force in exerting international influence. Against a background of economic globalization and the general trend of market reforms, there was no choice but to accept that, thenceforth, power was increasingly defined in terms of economic performance rather than geostrategic calculations. Here, once again, the influence of East Asia on changing perceptions in India must be stressed. After all, hadn't the Asia-Pacific started playing a greater role in world affairs specifically because of its economic dynamism? In short, Indian decision-makers realised that economic success played a growing role in defining the status of a state in the international arena. In other words, it would be India's prosperity that would give credibility to its claim to being a major world power.

IMPLEMENTING THE LOOK EAST POLICY

In the framework of economic diplomacy, priority areas were chosen, East Asia being the first among them, as it was seen as the driving force behind world growth at the time. Japan and South Korea,

Singapore, Malaysia and Thailand—all these countries were considered potential investment sources and new markets to be tapped. By intensifying trade and financial exchanges with these economies, India could even hope to be swept along in their dynamism. Thus, Prime Minister Narasimha Rao's government launched the 'Look East' policy. It goes without saying that the Look East policy was spurred, above all, by economic motivations. It was in many respects the external policy extension of the domestic economic liberalization process. Hence, the Ministry of External Affairs, along with the Ministries of Finance and Commerce orchestrated the opening up of the Indian economy to East Asia. Within the Ministry of External Affairs, the economic cells worked the hardest to promote the rapprochement with East Asia.

The initiation of the Look East policy certainly stemmed from a consensus that had built up among a large section of India's elite, which was convinced of the need to strengthen links with the countries of the 'Asian Miracle'. Nonetheless, it was Prime Minister Narasimha Rao, who gave concrete directions for the reorientation of India's policy toward its eastern neighbourhood. In order to grow economically closer to South-East Asia, India's strategy worked on two levels. It endeavoured to improve its relations both at the multilateral level, with ASEAN and, at the bilateral level, with each of the Association's member states. At Narasimha Rao's request, the Foreign Secretary, the primary official of the Ministry of External Affairs, took direct charge of South-East Asian countries. The region formerly fell under a lower level official, the Secretary, East, J.N. Dixit therefore found himself heading the Southern Division, as of the second half of 1992, while at the same time wielding direct control over the Economic Division.[19] There could be no better manifestation, in organizational terms, of the economic rationale behind the diplomatic opening up to South-East Asian countries. As for India's partnership with ASEAN, it was primarily handled by the Multilateral Economic Relations Cell, a sub-unit of the Economic Division. In other words, India's approach of ASEAN was also determined by commercial and financial motivations, whereas the Association, as such, did not initially have any economic underpinnings. But as suggested by the testimony of Kamlesh Sharma, Deputy Secretary Economic Relations, Ministry of External Affairs, Indian diplomatic perceptions of South-East Asia seemed, thenceforth, to be part of an essentially profit-oriented paradigm: 'A positive aspect of ASEAN is their involvement with each other's growth and India has now perceived this clearly. ASEAN is at the heart of our reworked strategy.'[20]

The changes wrought in institutions handling bilateral cooperation also testified to the new drive toward East Asia. A Joint Commission was set-up in 1990 with Thailand, in 1992 with Malaysia and in 1996 with South Korea as well as Indonesia. New Delhi even opened a High Commission in Brunei Darussalam in 1992.[21] In the case of Japan, the government endeavoured to reactivate existing networks. It was essentially the Ministry of Finance that attempted to add new dynamism to economic relations with Tokyo. Manmohan Singh soon contacted his Japanese counterparts, almost as soon as Narasimha Rao nominated him to the post.[22] The Minister of Finance was probably helped in his task by his former post as Chairman of the Committee for Indo-Japanese Studies, a group that had been formed as far back as in 1958 with the objective of promoting relations in all fields between the two countries. The Committee was formed under the Indian Planning Commission and worked as a forum of interaction for eminent persons who were nominated as members by the government. Furthermore, the Deputy Secretary, Ministry of Finance, N.K. Singh, became the contact point for structuring and strengthening relations with Japan. He had earlier headed the Economic Section at the Indian Embassy in Tokyo and was believed to have a large number of contacts in Japanese economic power structures. Montek Singh Ahluwalia, Secretary, Economic Affairs Department, Ministry of Finance, urged the Ministry of External Affairs to use its embassy in Tokyo to gain a foothold in the Japanese business network.

Apart from institutional changes, the Look East policy also led to a multiplication of politico-economic delegations to East Asia. The most important protagonists of these missions were the Prime Ministers and the Ministers of External Affairs, Finance and Economic Affairs. But in accordance with the desire for partnership with the private sector, political leaders were accompanied by large business delegations. And, while the Indian government representatives always met their political counterparts, they also endeavoured to contact business communities in East Asia, directly. Their interventions were essentially devoted to the presentation of India's liberalization measures and were aimed at giving an impetus to bilateral trade. In this regard, one of the major objectives was to get investors interested by highlighting the opportunities available in priority sectors for the development of the national economy: the transport infrastructure (road and rail networks, port infrastructure), power and telecommunications.

Indian diplomats flew to and fro across East Asia during the first two years of reforms. Sometimes, to ensure that their visits had a greater impact and to underscore the economic dimensions of their missions, Indian diplomats were willing to show greater flexibility with regard to certain political or strategic issues, as was the case in North-East Asia. When Prime Minister Rao visited Tokyo in June 1992, at the invitation of his counterpart, K. Miyazawa, he took the opportunity to meet the most senior decision-makers in the field of economic affairs: the head of MITI, the Minister of Finance and the heads of the five main Japanese economic organizations. Narasimha Rao also devoted two days of his visit to one-to-one meetings with the Chairmen of Japan's most important multinationals. Although his agenda was basically oriented toward economic relations, it was not possible for him to ignore the bilateral differences that existed with regard to the nuclear issue, all the more so as Japan was searching to play a more active international role at the time, focusing on disarmament. India, whose status as an undeclared nuclear power was more or less acknowledged, found itself in a rather awkward position in view of Tokyo's policy. However, Indian diplomacy could hardly allow itself to hurt the sensibilities of a country that it had identified as a major source of investment and technology transfer. Thus, in order to show that India did pay attention to Tokyo's concerns, Prime Minister Rao agreed to start an informal bilateral dialogue on the nuclear issue. Apart from the USA, Japan was the only country with which New Delhi had agreed to conduct such a dialogue.[23]

Prime Minister Rao's visit to South Korea in September 1993 was another good example of the diplomatic reorientation called for by India's economic concerns. Until then, New Delhi had endeavoured to follow an even policy with regard to both North and South Korea. But during his Seoul visit, the first ever visit by an Indian Head of Government to South Korea, Prime Minister Rao affirmed clearly that this policy was over. India's approach to the two states would henceforth be dictated by her commercial interests.[24] As a corollary, the visit engendered a notable change in perceptions, with the Korean business community 'suddenly' becoming aware of the existence of India and, in particular, the process of economic liberalization taking place there.[25]

As for India's newly-established links with Taiwan, they showed to what extent India's relations complied with its economic imperatives henceforth. New Delhi, which did not recognize Taiwan as a separate political entity, increasingly regretted the absence of trade relations with this prosperous economy in the early 1990s. In spite of China's extreme sensitivity on the issue, Indian officials established their first informal contacts with their Taiwanese counterparts in Tokyo, Hong Kong and Geneva. In order not to upset Beijing, New Delhi guaranteed that these contacts would remain unofficial. However, it was assiduous in promoting economic cooperation with Taiwan. The decision to open a Taiwanese commercial office in Bombay was taken very quickly in 1992. In October the same year, the Ministry of External Affairs' Economic Division hosted a major seminar for promoting investments in the island.[26] Then, in September 1994, a delegation from the Centre for Policy Research, a think tank close to the Indian government, visited Taipei and met several officials representing the economic departments of the Taiwanese authorities.[27] Finally, an Indian non-governmental commercial representation was established on the island in 1995.

There were frequent interactions between senior Indian officials and their South-East Asian counterparts. Their joint membership of the Non-Aligned Movement (NAM) enabled them to relaunch bilateral relations fairly quickly. In September 1992, at the NAM Summit in Jakarta, Narasimha Rao had a private meeting with Mahathir and Goh Chok Tong, the Prime Ministers of Malaysia and Singapore respectively, as well as with President Soeharto of Indonesia. Moreover, soon after being promoted to the post of Minister of Finance in April 1991, Manmohan Singh chose Singapore and Malaysia for his first visits abroad, a truly symbolic choice. As for Narasimha Rao, he personally visited most South-East Asian countries between 1993 and 1995. The Prime Minister visited Thailand in April 1993 and made concrete efforts to give an impetus to trade relations, along with his Thai counterpart. In fact, the two Prime Ministers agreed on the need for high-level political orientations for the intensification of bilateral commercial ties and, to this end, identified several sectors for future cooperation. In September 1994, Rao visited Singapore, a state that no other Indian Prime Minister had visited officially for twenty-six years, before going on to Vietnam. His Vietnam visit led to the establishment of working groups to accelerate the strengthening of economic ties.[28] In August 1995, Rao visited Malaysia, accompanied by a large business delegation. No less than five MoUs were signed in the presence of the two Prime Ministers, concerning both the protection of bilateral investments as well as cooperation in the highway construction and satellite communication sectors.[29] On this occasion, the Malaysian Prime Minister affirmed that the quality and level of bilateral economic relations would constitute a milestone for evaluating the state of Indo-Malaysian relations. The priority given to economic relations could not be substantiated any more clearly.

The coming into power of new governments did not lead to a slowdown in India's diplomatic ballet in South-East Asia. In July 1996, the Minister of External Affairs, I.K. Gujral, visited Jakarta. Just a month later, in August 1996, he also visited Singapore and Malaysia. In Kuala Lumpur, he met the Minister of Finance, Anwar Ibrahim, and they jointly identified sectors of Malaysian expertise that were of interest to India, including port infrastructure and power. All in all, after 1991, most visits by Indian leaders to East Asia appeared to have been directly related to the new objectives of India's economic diplomacy. Above all, they were aimed at promoting the opening up of the Indian market and at laying strong foundations for a rapid increase in trade.

1.2. East Asian States' Interest in India's Overtures

In most cases in East Asia, states stimulated and supported economic growth. They also benefited greatly from such policies. These powerful and interventionist states played their roles in forging close collaboration with the business circles in their countries.[30] In fact, major industrial groups often had very close ties with the state, whether in Thailand, where the royal family was the owner of the country's biggest industrial group, or in Indonesia and Malaysia where national enterprises proliferated or even in South Korea where the *chaebols* belonged to the state for many years. The wave of liberalism may well have traversed East Asia in the early 1980s, bringing deregulation and opening up to market forces in its wake, but Asian states remained primary players in economic processes. Thus, states in East Asia played a pre-eminent role in stimulating trade flows toward India. Indeed, there was a convergence between India's opening up and the trade-related concerns of several East Asian governments. The latter's foreign policies also gave priority to economic issues, particularly, access to foreign markets and raw material supplies. The diplomatic policies of the region's states, aimed at protecting economic growth, therefore saw prospects for fruitful cooperation in India's liberalization. The number of visits to India by East Asian political leaders increased in the 1990s. These visits were clear signals for their respective business communities, aimed at changing perceptions and drawing attention to the vast emerging market that was India. Finally, it must be noted that the interest of East Asian decision-makers in India's overtures was further sparked by the fact that relations between New Delhi and Beijing had warmed somewhat, as witnessed by the visit to India by Premier Li Peng in December 1991 and that of Narasimha Rao to China in September 1993. Relations between these two giants even began to come into the fold of economic diplomacy. When the Indian Vice-President, K.R. Narayanan, met President Jiang Zemin in October 1994, the two statesmen decided not only to continue the process of normalization, but also to give a fresh impetus to bilateral economic cooperation.

JAPAN: BEYOND OFFICIAL AID, BUT HOW FAR?

The magnitude and constancy of Japanese official aid marked the government's desire to remain engaged in the Indian economy. In April 1991, when India's balance of payment was at its lowest, Tokyo was the first capital to intervene. Japan, which first announced that it would convene an extraordinary meeting of the India Aid Consortium, finally preferred to short-circuit the institution by announcing, on 25 April 1991, a 150 million Yen aid package to India, to be disbursed immediately, with a further 350 million to be disbursed in May that year.[31] The short-term debts contracted by Indian banks and financial institutions with Japanese banks were extended at the request of the Japanese Minister of Finance.[32] Tokyo maintained its support to New Delhi through the IMF, the World Bank and the Asian Development Bank. Generally speaking, Japan was India's primary bilateral donor for almost ten years. Between 1988 and 1995 (except for 1990), India was one of the ten highest beneficiaries of Japanese aid and, in 1991, it was among the five highest. The share of official Japanese aid in the total foreign aid received by India was not just high, but also rose during the first half of the 1990s.[33] In terms of engagement, Japanese official aid accounted for 4 per cent of the total foreign aid granted to India in 1985–6. The figure rose to 20 per cent in 1991–2, 31 per cent in 1993–4 and 38 per cent in 1995–6. In terms of disbursement or use, Japan accounted for 5 per cent of the total aid credited to India in 1985–6, 17 per cent in 1991–2 and 25.4 per cent in 1995–6. However, from the Japanese point of view, India's share in the total amount of its foreign aid remained quite low. In 1992–3 for example, India was the sixth highest beneficiary of Japanese aid in the world, but received only 3.4 per cent of the total amount of such aid. Interestingly, Japan's Official Development Aid (ODA) lay emphasis on Indian infrastructure, power, transport and irrigation. These orientations were not surprising, given the fact that the lack of infrastructure in India had been identified by Japanese investors as a major obstacle to their entry in the market. Japanese governmental aid could therefore have been aimed at preparing the Indian environment in order to attract Japanese investors.[34]

In fact, in Japan, it was the state agencies which proved to be the most interested in India's economic liberalization. In 1992, for the first time, the Ministry of International Trade and Industry (MITI) proposed direct consultations related to the reform policy with officials from the Indian Ministry of External Affairs. These annual or biannual meetings that took place in addition to the activities of the Joint Commission were an important indication of Japan's interest in India's liberalization. The subjects broached essentially concerned technology transfers and infrastructural investments. In 1994, the Economic Cooperation White Paper by the MITI devoted an entire chapter to India, for the first time. India was characterized as one of the 'three emerging markets' to which Japan needed to pay attention. Like Vietnam and China, India was described as 'Asia's new frontier'.[35] The expression selected was quite important as it led one to believe that in its new perspective, Japan was ready to include India in its regional environment, in the same capacity as China and Vietnam. The head of the MITI and Prime Minister to-be, Ryutaro Hashimoto, paid an official visit to India in January 1995.[36] It was the first visit by a Minister of the MITI to India and there was no better signal to arouse the interest of the Japanese business community. At the same time, Hashimoto announced the implementation of seven initiatives aimed at strengthening economic ties with India. Among these were a USD 1 million loan for Japanese companies investing in the country and the establishment of a second branch of the Japan External Trade Organization (JETRO), in Bombay. These initiatives came as clear indications of the Japanese government's commitment to the boosting of bilateral trade. They also contained a clear message for the Japanese business community, signalling that Tokyo considered India as a new partner in its international trade relations.

In 1996, a MITI study group composed of representatives of the corporate sector along with officials and experts on India was formed to assess Japan's investment prospects in the country. In its conclusions, the Committee's report stated that it was advisable for Japan to expand its relations with India in the framework of its larger Asian policy.[37] The MITI report departed considerably from previous official studies—the Ishikawa Mission in July 1992 and the Yamashita Mission in March 1994—which laid a far greater emphasis on the conditions to be fulfilled to avail of greater Japanese investments. More balanced in nature, the 1996 MITI report opined that it was not solely up to the Indian government to create a favourable atmosphere for investments, but that it was also the responsibility of the private sector. It also emphasized that Japan's support for India's economic reform process was important not only for bilateral relations, but also for stable development in Asia. The series of initiatives undertaken by the MITI in 1992–6 tend to show therefore that it was first and foremost Japan's state agencies which endeavoured to include India in the regional sphere of activities of the Japanese business community.

SOUTH KOREA AND SOUTH-EAST ASIA: A NEW-FOUND INTEREST IN THE INDIAN MARKET

Since the early 1990s, China had exerted a considerable pull on foreign investment flows. As a result, the capital-surplus economies of East Asia were largely engaged in their vast neighbour's market. In such a context, many decision-makers in the region found much to commend in India's liberalization, for it gave them the opportunity to diversify their investment destinations—in other words, not to venture everything on a China whose political development remained far from foreseeable. The Indian economy offered valuable export prospects for these countries, which were constantly in search of new markets. All the more so since at the time that reforms were the order of the day in India, the Asian tigers and dragons were deeply concerned by the recession that had hit their biggest trade partners in the West and in Japan. To this was added the competition raging between the ASEAN countries and NICs to enter into new markets. The fear of falling behind in the race for an emerging market led to additional competition, much to India's benefit.

During his September 1993 visit to South Korea, Prime Minister Rao had invited his interlocutors to send trade delegations to India to familiarize themselves with the changes brought about by the liberalization process. In fact, the following year, Seoul sent a large delegation to India, composed of representatives of its principal Ministries. In February 1996, the Korean President, Kim Young Sam, paid an official visit to India, accompanied by his Trade and Industry Ministers as well as around forty businessmen. Interestingly, changes in Sino-Korean relations were a factor in South Korea's new interest in the Indian economy. Indeed, when Seoul reestablished its diplomatic ties with Beijing in 1992, the Korean business community rushed toward the Chinese market. Bilateral trade went up from USD 500 million to USD 10 billion and, in less than a year and a half, investments in China rose to USD 150 million. However, the high levels of involvement in the Chinese market went hand in hand with certain apprehensions at government level, more so in early 1994, when differences between Beijing and Seoul came out in the open. The enthusiasm of the business community with regard to the Chinese market suffered, with the result that India—a far more reassuring country in many respects—increasingly became the favoured destination in the new directions adopted by Korean investors.[38]

South-East Asian states also showed a marked interest in the opening up of the Indian market. Whether it was Singapore, Malaysia or Thailand, each of these states had their own specific motivations and, therefore, deployed their own strategies in this regard. In Thailand's case, the country proclaimed its new Look West policy, i.e. a reorientation of its external relations toward India and Africa.[39] In fact, Thailand was concerned about maintaining its competitiveness in the face of increasing international competition and, hence, was endeavouring to forge close partnerships with countries that could potentially provide low labour cost operations or that were rich in natural resources. The Thailand Investment Board therefore drew the attention of its private sector to India, describing it as a potential destination for Thai capital. The Thai authorities also endeavoured to make the business community aware of the opportunities available in India's infrastructural, textile and agricultural sectors.

Just like the NAM, the G-15 acted as a channel for interactions between decision-makers, thereby enabling ties with Malaysia and Indonesia to be tightened. New Delhi was in charge of organizing the G-15 Summit in December 1993. But the event was cancelled at the last minute, as the required quorum was not present. It must be noted that the only two Heads of Government to maintain their visit to India were the Prime Minister of Malaysia, Mahathir Mohammad, and the Indonesian President, Soeharto. In the absence of the G-15, bilateral consultations were an adequate motivation for these two South-East Asian leaders to visit India. Mahathir and Soeharto demonstrated their goodwill toward New Delhi by agreeing to return in March 1994, to attend the deferred G-15 Summit. Mahathir's visit at the end of 1993 gave him the opportunity to sign technical cooperation agreements aimed at promoting joint ventures in the private sector between the two countries.[40] Railway construction, telecommunications, the rubber industry, vocational training techniques and the air-conditioning industry were some of the sectors selected for cooperation between these countries in order to strengthen bilateral trade relations. In December 1996, Mahathir Mohammad paid a state visit to India, accompanied by a delegation composed of approximately forty businessmen. For Kuala Lumpur, the palm oil trade was a rather delicate domestic policy issue, which also entered into the negotiations held in New Delhi. In fact, Malaysia was the primary exporter of palm oil in the world and India was one of its primary buyers. To ensure that Indian imports continued, Kuala Lumpur agreed to grant New Delhi civil engineering projects. A barter system was established to this end, through which the two countries maintained a 'deposit account'. The parties that benefited from the agreement in India were public sector enterprises like HMT, IRCON, BHEL and Larsen and Toubro.[41] Bharat Heavy Electricals (BHEL), for example, was involved in several power plant construction projects in Malaysia.

'INDIAN FEVER' IN SINGAPORE

Singapore proved to be the East Asian state that welcomed India's Look East policy with the greatest enthusiasm. However, no two partners could be as far removed from each other from the viewpoint of UNDP indicators. On the one hand, there was a tiny state with just three million inhabitants and a per capita income of USD 15,730 in 1992, and on the other, a giant in demographic terms with 880 million inhabitants with a per capita income of no more than USD 310. Nevertheless, government agencies of the tiny city-state were the ones which, above all, welcomed India's liberalization and undertook to mobilize the private sector. Thus, in his National Day Speech in 1993, Prime Minister Goh Chok Tong affirmed that he intended to inject a 'mild Indian fever' in Singapore's business community. Besides, 1993 was also the year that marked the start of Singapore's ambitious regionalization programme, aimed at giving the national economy a fresh impetus. For over twenty years, Singapore's growth had relied basically on two factors: the inflow of a large volume of foreign investment and the development of physical, commercial and financial infrastructure that was both sophisticated and efficient. But the city-state feared that the small size of its population and territory could, over the long run, affect the growth of its domestic economy. The regionalization programme launched in 1993 was therefore aimed at building an economy that was more outward-looking in order to strengthen the city-state's domestic economy and competitiveness. In other words, the aim was to take advantage of Singapore's special skills and expertise to invest in the region's growth areas.

The regionalization programme was the reason for the prominent role played by state agencies, as emphasized by two Singaporean economists, Mukul Asher and Ramkishen S. Rajan: 'It is important to keep in mind that Singapore's commercial thrust towards India (as in the case of Singapore's commercial thrust towards enhancing its external economic relations), is largely led by the government's pragmatic considerations. Designated Statutory Boards and Government-linked companies play a primary implementing role in these activities.'[42]

The Singapore Trade Development Board (STDB) was indeed the government body put in charge of playing a crucial entrepreneurial role to trigger the regional expansion strategy. In May 1993, the institution organized a 'regionalization forum' and proposed to introduce a new phase of cooperation between the public and private sectors, in order to implement the regionalization programme. In other words, the STDB offered substantial support to the private sector, both by identifying investment opportunities and helping them forge joint ventures, and by conducting feasibility studies. Hence, Singapore's investments were channelled toward the areas targeted by its public authorities.

The regionalization programme identified the Indochinese peninsula, Myanmar, China and India as the new growth frontiers.[43] Among the countries selected, India offered special advantages from Singapore's point of view. In fact, the city-state's government was somewhat anxious about the dynamism of the business communities in the other NICs—such as South Korea, Taiwan and Hong Kong—which had already invested heavily in China, the ASEAN countries and the Indochinese peninsula. In contrast, the city-state's enterprises preferred the familiar environment of the ASEAN economies, especially Malaysia and Indonesia. Fearing that Singapore's economy may lose its competitive edge, the government endeavoured to incite its domestic firms so that they would venture into the new emerging economies in the region. In this context, Singapore considered that it had a trump card to play in India, a more or less virgin market where few Asian investors were present. In other words, while competing NIC economies were focusing on China and South-East Asia's emerging markets, Singapore espied an opportunity in playing a pioneering role in India. Moreover, this tiny state, highly conscious of its vulnerability and limitations in terms of natural and human resources, had great expectations from the vast Indian economy and its abundant labour. The constant catchphrase about the potentially huge middle class of the Indian market could not fail to attract a country that was precisely looking for new markets. Finally, Singapore was concerned about reducing risks by diversifying its investment destinations. China was an inordinately attractive pole, but India's opening up could provide a balance—at least, so it hoped.

From 1991 to 1996, contacts between Singapore's officials and New Delhi multiplied. The range of sectors covered for future cooperation—from art and culture to human resources, including, naturally, both trade and investments—was proof of the ambitions harboured by the protagonists and showed the convergence of political will in Singapore and New Delhi, with both states aiming at mobilizing their private sectors. Bilateral contacts were actually established right from the time the reform process started in India. Indeed, the policy-makers involved in India's liberalization chose Singapore as a regional centre to disseminate information in the entire Asian region. Prime Minister Goh Chok Tong was thus one of the very first Heads of Government to be informed of the liberalization policy by the Minister of External Affairs, Madhav Sinh Solanki. The visit was a prelude to a conference organized jointly by the Indian government and the Singapore Trade Development Board

(STDB), in October 1991.[44] The Minister of External Affairs, Wong Kan Seng, then paid a visit to India as early as in December 1991. In March 1992, the Deputy Prime Minister and Minister of Commerce and Industry, Lee Hsien Loong, paid a five-day official visit to India, accompanied by a large delegation. The idea of an industrial corridor between Tamil Nadu and Singapore was envisaged. In early February 1993, B.G. Georges Yeo, Minister of Information and the Arts and Second Minister of External Affairs, visited India, accompanied by a delegation of decision-makers in the fields of art and culture, as well as commerce and industry.

In January 1994, Prime Minister Goh Chok Tong was the guest of honour at India's Republic Day celebrations.[45] He came with a very large delegation including the Ministers of External Affairs, Trade and Industry, several senior officials, around forty CEOs and a large media team. The visit was aimed at forging a strategic economic alliance with India, in other words, launching coordinated actions by the two governments and their business communities to form joint ventures in several fields, such as tourism, civil aviation, telecommunications, real estate and freeway development, shipping, harbour infrastructure and financial services. Moreover, three MoUs were signed, relating to tourism, shipping and double taxation exemptions. As for Prime Minister Rao, he visited Singapore in September 1994 and his discussions primarily dealt with trade.[46] Similarly, a dozen agreements were concluded between Indian and Singaporean companies. Still in his capacity as Prime Minister, Goh Chok Tong returned to India in January 1995. This time, he was the guest of honour at the centenary of one of India's main trade organization, the Confederation of Indian Industries (CII). This second visit in less than a year testified to the close relations between the decision-making circles of the two countries. An agreement for cooperation in Science and Technology was signed. The Minister of Finance, Manmohan Singh, then visited Singapore in September 1995 and met Prime Minister Goh Chok Tong as well as Senior Minister Lee Kuan Yew. The latter returned the visit in January 1996, at the Prime Minister's invitation. In June 1996, the Minister of Finance, P. Chidambaram, visited Singapore and met the Prime Minister, the Deputy Prime Minister as well as the Ministers of Finance and Information. Clearly, the continual coming and going of the officials of the two states testified to their joint desire to increase socio-economic interactions in the most diverse sectors and at the earliest.

THE CONFEDERATION OF INDIAN INDUSTRIES: A TRADE ORGANIZATION IN PARTNERSHIP WITH THE POLITICAL LEADERSHIP

To complete our observation of the pre-eminence of the state agencies in Asian economic interactions, we shall take the viewpoint of a business actor of primary importance—the CII. The strategies of the CII in India and East Asia show that even in the eyes of the Indian business community, state institutions still played an essential role in economic developments. In fact, the Confederation established ten or so representative offices whose priority objective was to develop close relations with the political and economic decision-makers of the target region. In East Asia, representative offices were opened in Oṣaka and Singapore in the early 1990s. The networking strategy that CII implemented with East Asian decision-makers was essentially aimed at sensitizing them to India's liberalization, to keep them informed of the latest developments and to pressurize them to persuade their business communities to take interest in the Indian market.[47] These overseas offices therefore served as intermediaries between the Indian and East Asian governments. For institutional and political actors in East Asia, these offices were full-time interlocutors guaranteeing certain continuity in the economic dialogue, thereby making it possible to mitigate the effects of India's political instability. With regard to the Indian political leaders, CII was most expeditious in taking advantage of the new creed concerning the need for cooperation between the state and business circles. The Confederation therefore worked in close partnership with the government, particularly in the field of external trade relations.[48] In other words, the Confederation established itself as a major stakeholder helping the Indian state to implement its new principles of economic diplomacy.

Consequently, the Confederation came to be closely involved in the Look East policy. The Prime Minister of Malaysia, Mohammad Mahathir, the ASEAN Secretary General, Dato Ajit Singh, the Prime Minister of Singapore, the Deputy Prime Ministers of Thailand, Vietnam and South Korea, decision-makers all, soon joined the close interpersonal network that CII gradually built. Since 1994 at least, the members of the cell specializing in Singapore—the CII-Singapore Core group—met the Prime Minister of the city-state personally at least once a year. In this regard, the CII served as a go-between for the Indian government in relation to the city-state's decision-makers.

In fact, in the early 1990s, the CII Chairman, S. Bhargava, himself several times underlined the pivotal role that his organization was playing in the development of close relations between Singapore and India. In the process, the CII became quite close to the Singapore Trade Development Board (STDB) and the Economic Development Board (EDB), two of the most important trade bodies of the city-state's government.

In order to successfully build its network of decision-makers, CII was not content with the work carried out by its representative offices abroad. It participated actively in major regional or world economic summits, in addition to organizing them. In October 1996 for example, the Confederation organized a session of the World Economic Forum in New Delhi. In early 1997, it hosted the eighth edition of the Entrepreneurs Conferences of the Asia Society, on the theme 'Towards the Free Market: Sustaining Reforms in India and Asia'. What is more important, the Confederation welcomed many Asian decision-makers on this occasion, notably George Yeo, Minister of Information and the Arts of Singapore, N. Akrasanee, Minister of Trade of Thailand and Vo Van Kiet, Prime Minister of the Socialist Republic of Vietnam.[49] The Confederation also launched the cycle of Partnership Summits, a series of annual conferences convened in a different Indian city each time, an example of its networking strategies. These events never failed to bring together a large number of foreign decision-makers, many of them from East Asia. The first edition of this cycle of conferences was held in 1995 in Calcutta, at the time of the commemoration of CII's centenary. To mark this dual event symbolically, who best to choose as the guest of honour than Goh Chok Tong, who was without a doubt one of the personalities who had most been seen in India at the time.[50] In its enthusiasm, the CII even decided to designate 6 January as 'Singapore Day', in commemoration of the visit by the city-state's Prime Minister! CII's involvement in the implementation of the Look East policy can, therefore, clearly be seen here.

The CII's activities in partnership with the Indian and East Asian governments show that an unprecedented network had been built between state leaders and representatives of the private sector, in order to intensify trade relations between India and East Asia. There were many different combinations and partnerships between actors of different types. In East Asia for example, Indian political leaders endeavoured to establish contacts both with their political counterparts and with the business community. Business organizations like CII considered, for their part, that governments had to be their primary interlocutors and therefore endeavoured to build a network of political decision-makers in East Asia. And when East Asian political leaders visited in India, in their turn, they were accompanied, most of the time, by large private sector delegations and met Indian political actors as well as representatives of the business community. However, one must not forget that in these new complementarities between governments and business circles, public agencies retained the leadership role, both in India and in East Asia. Trade delegations were a corollary of the diplomatico-economic activities that remained, above all, the prerogative of the states.

1.3 The Impetus for the Look East Policy: Catching up with the Regionalization of the World

In the early 1990s, India started to suspect the European Union and North America of harbouring protectionist proclivities through new regional trade arrangements. It thus strove to develop relations with alternative partners—the East Asian countries, in this instance. But the latter had become part of APEC, a loose grouping at the time, but one from which New Delhi was also excluded. In this respect, APEC was perhaps the biggest challenge to India's Look East policy. Since it feared being isolated from all the major regional groupings that were being formed in the world, India embarked on an active race for regional integration. In so doing, the Look East policy took on a constructive dimension and became a vehicle for different regional projects in East Asia.

India's Marginalization from the Major Regional Blocks

With the economic reforms underway, India acquired a keener perception of regionalization trends the world over and was consequently concerned about the possible marginalization of its economy.[51] Regional trade agreements had been proliferating since the 1980s. According to the WTO, about ninety-eight regional agreements were notified with the GATT under Article XXIV between

1947 and 1994. Practically half of them emerged during the last decade, between 1984 and 1994. In the first instance, the renewed interest in regional cooperation was attributed to the stalemate that the Uruguay Round multilateral trade negotiations seemed to have reached in the early 1990s. However, the positive conclusion of these negotiations and the creation of the World Trade Organization (WTO) in 1994 did not in any way alter the enthusiasm for regional cooperation. So much so that at the start of the 1990s, the world economy appeared to be on the way to splintering into three regional blocks, dominated by the European Community, the United States and, possibly, Japan.

New Delhi closely observed the formation and consolidation of these three regional poles. To start with, the process of European integration made substantial progress, especially in 1990, when the member countries decided to harmonize their monetary and fiscal policies for the year 1996. The Common Market became a reality in 1993. To that could be added the prospect of a medium term integration of former East European socialist economies. As for the United States, they started promoting transcontinental regionalism, essentially to compensate for the stagnation of the GATT negotiations. They signed a Free Trade Agreement with Canada in 1989. The agreement paved the way for the formation of NAFTA in 1993, associating Canada, Mexico and the United States. The group's members considered setting up a free trade area in a ten-year timeframe. The agreement also provided for free capital flows and the drawing up of common rules concerning intellectual property rights. The United States' long-term ambition through NAFTA was to create a pan-American free trade area. Hence, the entire South American continent could potentially be involved in the project.

Because the United States and some European economies were among its primary economic partners, India started to have misgivings about the development of a so-called 'North-Atlantic regionalism'. From New Delhi's point of view, the European Union and NAFTA did not seem very compatible with the multilateral and non-discriminating regime guaranteed by the WTO. In other words, the consolidation of these two regional groups in the West was seen as an unwelcome trend in the context of India's efforts to open up its economy to the world market. Reflecting India's concerns, Bhagwati and Srinivasan, two well-known Indian economists, warned that the world trade system could, in the short term, split into broad blocks around

Europe, NAFTA, and Asia. They added that if India did not manage to join one of these three blocks, it would face discrimination in terms of trade flows and investments.[52] Indeed, the EU accounted for about 26 per cent of Indian imports and absorbed 28 per cent of its exports.[53] But India was not a significant trade partner for the Union. Thus, it felt insecure in trade negotiations with Brussels. Similarly, New Delhi did not have much bargaining power *vis-à-vis* NAFTA. And within the North American group, the United States was India's primary trade partner, accounting for eighteen per cent of its exports and fourteen per cent of its imports. But the United States did not consider New Delhi an important partner at that time, and was much more enthusiastic about the East Asian economies.

In accordance with their recent enthusiasm for transcontinental regionalism, the United States actively supported the formation of a forum for the Asia-Pacific Economic Cooperation (APEC), especially in the early 1990s. Established in 1989, during the Canberra Ministerial Summit, APEC aimed at drastically reducing tariff and non-tariff barriers, as well as defining a code of conduct for transnational investments and for human resource flows between member countries. Thus, at the Bogor Summit in November 1994, APEC economic leaders adopted the objective of free trade in the Asia-Pacific by 2010 for developed countries and by 2020 for the less developed countries. The following year, at the Osaka Summit, the participants drew up a plan of action to give concrete shape to the commitments made in the Bogor Declaration. The member countries agreed to take action, on an individual level, to liberalise their economies and facilitate trade and investments. This came as the first case of concerted unilateral liberalization at the regional level, outside the framework of the GATT multilateral negotiations. At the same time, APEC members acquired greater room for manoeuvre and flexibility in achieving the objectives that had been fixed. By the mid-1990s therefore, APEC came to project the attractive image of the 'largest market in the world'.[54]

From the time the APEC concept was on the drawing board, New Delhi had formally communicated its interest in being associated with the group and in participating in its activities. Despite its many applications, it did not succeed in becoming a member throughout the 1990s. Nevertheless, it closely observed changes in APEC's relations with countries outside the group. Given that it was not a member, at the very least, India did not want to be penalized because of its exclusion. This was a great concern, especially since the group included most of the East Asian countries with which New Delhi wished to strengthen its economic relations. In other words, the Look East policy could be indirectly affected by the possible formation of an exclusive and protectionist block in the Asia-Pacific region. Thus, decisions taken within APEC and their possible discriminatory effects on trade flows with non-member economies had to be monitored closely.

The specific features governing APEC's procedures and general objectives were formalized on the basis of the notion of open regionalism.[55] At first glance, this concept could be considered to be contrary to the allegedly closed regionalism represented by the European model, which was accused of promoting exclusive economic liberalization for a protected market. Open regionalism, on the contrary, excluded all trade initiatives likely to lead to a free trade area or a customs union, since such measures were considered discriminatory by nature.[56] Hence, open regionalism was related to a process that was essentially supported by market forces and a unilateral economic liberalization by states, with formal institutional arrangements playing a minor role. Theoretically, therefore, APEC's open regionalism was meant to be in harmony with the economic multilateralism of the GATT and the WTO. Consequently, at the Bogor summit in 1994, APEC members clarified that the regional cooperation promoted within the group would be in tune with the WTO's multilateral principles. At the Osaka summit in November 1995, they set out to confirm APEC's compliance with multilateral liberalization and even suggested an accelerated implementation of liberalization commitments made during the Uruguay Round negotiations. In accordance with the WTO and GATT commitments, APEC's liberalization measures therefore had to follow the logic of the Most Favoured Nation treatment, as per GATT's Article I. By virtue of this fundamental multilateral principle, no country should suffer *vis-à-vis* another, from advantages or disadvantages that might not be simultaneously extended to all the other countries. In other words, any trade concession granted to a member of the multilateral trade system must be automatically applied to all the other members. In theoretical terms, therefore, the liberalization measures instigated within APEC also had to benefit non-member signatories of the WTO. In this sense, open regionalism and its related non-discrimination principle were, in fact, in harmony with the WTO's multilateral spirit.

And, *a priori*, New Delhi would have few reasons to fear that APEC would discriminate against it, commercially, in the Asian region.

Yet, the open regionalism doctrine promoted by APEC was not unambiguous.[57] At the Osaka Summit, divergent views emerged with regard to the general application of the Most Favoured Nation clause to non-member countries. Asian States, including Japan, upheld the non-discriminatory approach towards countries that were outside the group. But the United States proved to be more inclined to operate on the basis of reciprocity or conditionality. In other words, Washington did not intend to allow non-member countries to benefit from APEC's liberalization measures, without them offering some compensation.[58] From the American perspective, the latter should benefit from free trade only on the condition that they too adopted equivalent liberalization measures. This major disagreement was further aggravated by APEC's vague and equivocal nature. Indeed, the group did not lay down any guidelines for the implementation of open regionalism, a concept that was vaguer than could be imagined. Besides, the concerted mechanism of unilateralism began showing its limitations at the Subic Bay Summit held in the Philippines, in 1996. Many Asian Development Bank and OECD experts expressed concern over the absence of any system of guarantees for the extension of liberalization measures to non-member countries.[59] Moreover, the APEC's statement of intent concerning the application of free-trade benefits to non-members had nothing unique about it. In fact, all regional blocks offered similar clauses, at least in theory. In practice, however, there was no mechanism guaranteeing that member countries would choose to liberalize unilaterally. In the mid-1990s, APEC's evolution over the medium term therefore appeared to be quite vague. Countries as large as the United States were likely to continue to influence the group's decisions concerning the conditional handling of the Most Favoured Nation clause with regard to countries outside the group. In practice, APEC's open regionalism could as well be considered a 'void concept'. The concern expressed by countries excluded from the group, such as India, was thus justified.

This concern was further reinforced by two major decisions that were taken at the Osaka Summit concerning non-member countries. In the first instance, the participants at the forum felt it necessary to set-up a dispute mediation section. Even though the declaration of the Osaka Summit explained that this initiative would respect the rights and obligations of the WTO principles, there was some concern in India about the compatibility between regional dispute-resolution mechanisms and the WTO's dispute-resolution body.[60] The guarantee of the primacy of WTO forums over those of regional organizations was quite rightly a concern for countries that had been excluded from any major regional grouping. Secondly, the Osaka Summit came to an agreement according to which all APEC economies could consider granting all the group's members the benefits of a reduction or elimination of tariff or non-tariff barriers, on a voluntary basis, as a result of sub-regional arrangements. This decision concerned the sensitive issue of coordination between sub-regional groups and mega-groups. In fact, the APEC covered NAFTA, ASEAN and the agreement for strengthening economic relations between Australia and New Zealand.[61] However, these groups practised preferential trade arrangements while APEC put forward the principle of non-discrimination. Although no firm commitment was made, exclusive preferences operating within ASEAN or NAFTA could be extended to all APEC members, on certain conditions. This major contribution to open regionalism within the Asia-Pacific region would nonetheless have a fairly significant negative effect on the trade interests of non-member countries. Thus, the risk of discrimination would become even greater.

Consequently, despite all the rhetoric that was intended to be reassuring, open regionalism did conceal the risk of trade discrimination. It must be pointed out that such discrimination could even be involuntary. Indeed, APEC functioned as an important forum for the coordination of economic policies and for the drawing up of rules, standards and procedures concerning trade activities between member economies.[62] Unless they were kept scrupulously informed, countries outside the group would necessarily be handicapped by their lack of knowledge about APEC's trade harmonization and facilitation programmes. The multiple ambiguities within APEC and its concept of open regionalism did not escape the scrutiny of Indian observers. As a result, experts like Muchkund Dubey, the former Foreign Affairs Secretary, recommended that pressure should be maintained for becoming a member of the group. But this proposal highlighted another difficulty inherent in open regionalism, which was well formulated by Jagdish Bhagwati.[63] Indeed, the Indian economist held the view that when a group reached a substantial size, it could decide to no longer accept any new members because its own well-being would start declining. And in fact, it was India that seemed to be paying the price, in this hypothesis. One of the reasons evoked for rejecting New Delhi's application was, indeed, related to the size of the Indian economy and the imbalance its integration would entail within the group.

India's feeling of exclusion was all the more profound, as the only regional group to which it belonged was not very satisfactory. SAARC was formed in 1985 and, right from the beginning, it aimed at promoting economic cooperation. However, the group made very little progress over the years. It is true that most of its members—Bangladesh, Nepal, Bhutan and the Maldives—belonged to the category of Least Developed Countries. As for India, it had long remained wary of the project. Thus, in 1992, intra-regional trade only accounted for three per cent of the overall trade of SAARC member countries.[64] In 1993, the SAARC members attempted to revive the process of cooperation and adopted various measures to initiate preferential trade agreements. The SAPTA regime, approved in May 1995, enabled member countries to import goods at tariffs that were ten per cent lower than those imposed on imports from countries outside SAARC. Member states also decided to work together to eradicate poverty from the region and promote the socio-economic development of their peoples. Despite its great ambitions, the SAPTA initiative presented many limitations. The scope of the preferential trade arrangement envisaged proved to be limited as far as the creation of trade flows between South Asian economies was concerned. It was calculated that SAPTA would, at best, raise their overall trade by 0.3 per cent over a period of two to three years.[65] Hence, New Delhi could not expect SAARC to become a significant regional block, or to have much economic influence over the global trade system. In any case, SAARC was also handicapped by the political conflict between India and Pakistan.

In an insightful analysis, some economists from the *Indian Institute of Foreign Trade*, a research institute that acts as an adviser to the government in New Delhi, gave their appraisal of India's situation concerning the international economic scenario:

> The world trading system is in the process of splintering into trade blocs in spite of the successful conclusion of the Uruguay Round of Multilateral Trade Negotiations. No trading bloc in South Asia is likely to have enough of an economic clout to counteract this phenomenon of trading blocs causing a market entry problem to a country like India. This calls for a closer relationship with regional trading blocs on a bilateral basis. Thus a closer relationship with ASEAN is a pre-requisite for India.[66]

Similarly, another government adviser, Sanjeev Reddy, affirmed that a close relationship with ASEAN was essential for India to survive in an environment increasingly turned towards trade regionalization.[67] Placed in the context of the regionalization of the world, the Look East policy thus clearly illustrated India's concerns faced with the risk of its economy being marginalized. The move towards South-East Asia proved to be a strategy of trade reorientation, with the objective of precluding the risk of major markets—in particular West Europe and North America—closing their doors to India. In the eyes of Indian decision-makers, a special trade relationship with ASEAN looked like a lifeline.

But the ASEAN itself appeared to be engaged in an increasingly extensive economic integration. The 1967 Bangkok Declaration, which organized the Association, had already emphasized economic cooperation. But not much progress had been made, since handling political and security issues had so far been predominant. Since the 1980s, however, ASEAN devoted greater efforts to economic cooperation. Thus, in 1992, the Association's six Heads of State took the initiative to complete the transition towards a Free Trade Area by 2008. In September 1994, ASEAN's Economy Ministers decided to accelerate the process by advancing the cut-off date to 2003. This measure was a major move forward towards the integration of the region's economies, and a worrying development for New Delhi. Indeed, the ASEAN Free Trade Area (AFTA) provided for a common preferential tariff and aimed at dismantling the barriers that had continued to stand in the way of intra-regional trade. With the formation of a regional market, companies operating locally would benefit from economies of scale, whereas for intra-regional trade, external tariff barriers would be much higher than the common preferential tariffs. Thus, India feared that the growth of its exports to this region—among the most dynamic in the world—would be gravely affected. That is why Indian decision-makers had been asking for the establishment of special links between India and AFTA, notably for conducting trade facilitation programmes.[68] New Delhi was all the more interested in increasing economic cooperation with South-East Asia as it could envisage the further expansion of the Association and its potential market with the entry of Vietnam and the inclusion of the remaining South-East Asian economies—Cambodia, Laos and Myanmar.

BIMST-EC AND THE KUNMING INITIATIVE: THE MODEL OF THE EAST ASIAN GROWTH TRIANGLES

In addition to enhancing its links with South-East Asia, India also started to get involved in a sub-regional project, the BIMST-EC, and in a mega-group, the IOR-ARC, formed on the APEC model. While these two regional groupings represented two extremes in the spectrum of regionalization, they nonetheless had points in common. They were both formed around a maritime area and were striving to reproduce the Asia-Pacific's modes of economic integration. The IOR-ARC was originally launched in 1997 by fourteen countries spanning over Africa, the Middle East, South and South-East Asia and Oceania, with the objective of promoting economic cooperation around the Indian Ocean Rim. However, this initiative never really took off, as its members failed to show any substantial commitment to the project.

Organized around the Bay of Bengal, BIST-EC was set-up at the inaugural Bangkok Ministerial Conference on 6 June 1997 and initially brought together Bangladesh, India, Sri Lanka and Thailand. The event took place in the midst of euphoria, to the point of being described as a landmark in the history of sub-regional cooperation. Myanmar became a member in December 1997 and the group's acronym was changed to BIMST-EC. Thailand was the originator of the sub-regional project, in accordance with its Look West policy launched in the 1990s. In fact, it was the Vice-Minister for Foreign Affairs, Surin Pitsuwan, who brought up the idea of a growth triangle between India, Sri Lanka and Thailand in the Andaman Sea, for the first time in October 1994.[69] The birth of BIMST-EC in 1997 came to give concrete shape to Bangkok's initiatives to ensure an opening to markets in the Indian sub-continent and, by extension, in Africa.[70] Indeed, there was keen competition among the South-East Asian countries, concerned about finding new outlets towards the Indian Ocean. Hence, BIMST-EC was a means for Bangkok to position itself on the chessboard of regional memberships.

The setting up of a regional forum in the Bay of Bengal was also motivated by the potential for economic cooperation among member-countries.[71] Bangkok intended to promote a growth area that could provide a bridge between ASEAN and SAARC, as each member-state initially belonged to one or the other organization. The official declaration announcing the setting up of BIMST-EC took note of its trans-regional character and specified that the organization did not intend replacing any bilateral, regional or multilateral cooperation agreement to which the member-states were already committed, but rather complement it.[72] Hence, BIMST-EC was consistent with other Indian regional projects. It bolstered New Delhi's partnership with ASEAN and, more generally, fit in well with India's Look East policy. Indeed, Ranjit Gupta, India's Ambassador to Thailand, stated, 'The mood in Bangkok is upbeat on India. The launch of the Bangladesh-India-Sri-Lanka-Thailand Economic Cooperation (BIST-EC) should provide further impetus to this interaction.'

The objective of BIMST-EC was to 'create an enabling environment for rapid economic development, through the identification and implementation of specific projects in the sectors of trade, investment and industry, technology, human resource development, tourism, agriculture, energy, infrastructure and transportation'.[73] Among the numerous priorities so identified, BIMST-EC members underlined that the development of transportation and communications represented a foundation that was necessary for future cooperation irrespective of the fields envisaged. The medium term objective of BIMST-EC was to create multiform communication nodes between international road transportation, internal sea routes, regional air networks and port installations. The project was quite ambitious in view of the reality of the area concerned. It aimed at no less than the formation of sea-land or air-land networks, based on the model on which East Asian economic integration was built.

Sub-regional cooperation in the Bay of Bengal aimed at intensifying economic interactions between areas in India and South-East Asia that were geographically close, so as to create a sub-regional growth pole. Although the project was meant to be of a trans-national nature, it was fully promoted by the states themselves. Furthermore, the governments were the ones who implemented the project, since BIMST-EC's protagonists were the Foreign Affairs Ministers from New Delhi, Bangkok and other participating countries. The issue before the group's thinkers was that, in a context of liberalization, inter-governmental cooperation made it possible to optimize the growing interaction between the region's economies. Moreover, the second BIMST-EC Ministerial Conference reaffirmed that political will was crucial to sustain the project's momentum. As in the case of the partnership between India and ASEAN, state agencies intended to win over the support of civil society for the project, in particular, the business community and academic circles. Indeed, they went as far as to talk about the advent of the 'BIMST-EC community'.[74]

The creation of BIMST-EC reflected widespread enthusiasm for sub-regional cooperation in East Asia. Whether they were called triangles, polygons or simply growth areas, there was a substantial surge in new sub-regional cooperation projects, especially since the early 1990s. These new schemes could be seen as extensions of previous experiences with regard to export promotion areas, technology and industrial parks, and other forms of sub-national cooperation. For the ASEAN countries, it was also a flexible way of encouraging intra-regional cooperation, without going through formal agreements calling for the approval and participation of all the Association's members. As was clearly noted by BIMST-EC's Concept Paper, sub-regional cooperation in economic areas undoubtedly helped in making growth in the Asia-Pacific region more dynamic. In fact, it made it possible 'to increase economies of scale and complementarities in the production base as well as increase the size of markets and facilitate the spill-over of growth across national borders, in response to economic forces'.[75] Consequently, BIMST-EC deliberately drew inspiration from sub-regional cooperation experiences in East Asia. On this account, it constituted a further vehicle of integration in the East Asian economic region for the concerned South Asian countries, or at least, for some parts of their territories.

Although they stood out as trans-national economic areas, growth triangles were often promoted by the states themselves. The South China Sea growth triangle, bringing together Hong Kong, Taipei and the South Chinese provinces, proved an exception in this regard. The spontaneous economic development that took place was the outcome of the People's Republic of China's economic openness and the promotion of special economic areas since 1978. In most other cases, growth triangles stemmed from the public sector's voluntarism. The same held true for the Greater Mekong area, including Cambodia, Laos, Myanmar, Thailand, Vietnam and the Chinese province of Yunnan. In 1991, the six Mekong states gave an impetus to the process by establishing a working committee on sub-regional trade, entrusted with the task of studying their potential for cooperation. In the case of SIJORI (Singapore-Johor-Riau), which brought Singapore together with the southern part of the Malaysian province of Johor and the Indonesian island of Riau, the three governments formalized specific arrangements and created an umbrella for the private sector, which made it possible to coordinate activities within the triangle.[76] BIMST-EC was inspired by similar state voluntarism in which governments tried to provide basic infrastructure and establish policies that would facilitate its inception, in the hope that the functioning of the market forces within the area defined would follow. Beyond that first phase, BIMST-EC, like any other sub-regional economic cooperation area, would have to essentially draw from private sector initiatives and activities.

Growth triangles were often based on the theory of comparative costs and advantages. Thus, they brought together neighbouring areas, either for delocalizing certain production lines, as in the case of SIJORI, or for optimizing the use of natural resources and developing the infrastructure at the sub-regional level, like the triangle established in 1993 between South Thailand, the four northern Malaysian provinces and northern Sumatra in Indonesia. More often than not, sub-regional cooperation activities dealt with issues that went beyond free trade. In this, they stood apart from traditional regional arrangements such as APEC, AFTA and SAARC. Sub-regional economic areas were not so much concerned with trade in goods and services as with transnational movements of capital, work, technologies and information, and, above all, the promotion of infrastructure linking the territories they covered.[77] Consequently, sub-regional cooperation worked towards the expansion of resources in the region and the growth of future production, rather than on making immediate profits on the static yield of existing resources. For instance, one of BIMST-EC's primary objectives was to develop transport infrastructure, which itself translated the dynamism of such cooperation project. Indeed, such sub-regional forums were outward looking and truly in tune with the theoretical principle of open regionalism. There was no issue of discrimination. Sub-regional cooperation could even be seen as a transitory step towards much more thorough and inclusive regional integration. It was particularly appropriate for countries completing their transition from a formally centralized and planned system towards a market economy, with export-based growth strategies. China understood this well and was involved in several growth areas. India, which became greatly concerned about its export performance, started following in its footsteps, thanks to the setting up of BIMST-EC.

Sub-regional cooperation activities also distinguished themselves from traditional regional arrangements in that they did not necessarily cover the entire territory of the concerned countries. Often, in the case of at least one of the participating countries, only a part of the national territory could be engaged in the sub-regional forum. In the case of India's participation in BIMST-EC for instance, it was essentially the states along its eastern coast and in the North-East that would be involved in cooperation projects. In fact, Indian sites proposed for different studies were mostly located along the eastern coast, in Kolkata, Chennai and Visakhapatnam. These were some of India's territories that were most involved in the Look East policy and, therefore, also those involved in BIMST-EC.[78] All in all, New Delhi seemed to be encouraging the states on the eastern coast to spearhead its policy of economic integration to the East Asian region. At the same time, Indian authorities were exploring the prospects of integrating some of their most landlocked territories in the North-East in a trans-national cooperation programme. Thus, Ambassador Ranjit Gupta asserted: A particularly important feature from the Indian point of view is the BIMST-EC, which should help greatly in the economic development of the North-Eastern states of India, which are geographically remote from the rest of India and have lagged behind in development despite considerable richness of resources.[79]

The concern for disadvantaged national territories was a characteristic of several other Asian sub-regional cooperation projects. The growth triangle between Indonesia, Malaysia and Thailand (IMT-GT) and the greater Mekong sub-regional economic cooperation project (GMS) also aimed at paying greater attention to the most disadvantaged sub-regional territories.

Despite the initial enthusiasm, BIMST-EC struggled to gather momentum. This was partly due to the economic crisis that seriously affected Thailand in August 1997. In addition, as in the case of IOR-ARC, BIMST-EC suffered from a lack of commitment on the part of governments. The stagnation of the process was all the more regrettable since the project had a fairly decisive scope from the viewpoint of India's regional insertion in East Asia. In the first place, BIMST-EC represented the extension of Asian modalities for regional integration to the economies of the Indian subcontinent, or at least, certain parts of these economies. It also promoted the ambitious long-term vision of a Bay of Bengal growth pole, extending to the Malaysian and Singaporean shores. A potential ocean-based grouping that could be structured from the port of Chittagong in Bangladesh to that of Haldia in West Bengal was even considered by JICA's Japanese consultants.[80] But the reality failed to live up to hopes about the region's potential. Although it was quite promising, BIMST-EC—like IOR-ARC—appeared to be suffering from teething problems. In addition, the regional sub-group seemed to be moving further from the growth triangles' model, as the Ministers of Economy and Commerce of the member-states decided, in April 2000, to reflect on ways in which preferential trade arrangements could be implemented so as to lead to a BIMST-EC free trade area.[81]

In the same spirit of sub-regional cooperation as BIMST-EC, was another initiative, the so-called Kunming Initiative, named after the capital city of the Chinese province of Yunnan. This project, still in its embryonic stages, wished to initiate an economic integration process between south-western China, India's eastern and North-Eastern states, Myanmar and Bangladesh. In fact, the province of Yunnan, which experienced rapid economic growth, was increasingly keen to open to its southern and western neighbours. In this matter, its aim was no less than to become the bridge between the Indian subcontinent and South-East Asia, and it would seem that it had Beijing's full support in that respect. Yunnan even discussed major projects for the revitalization of ancient trade routes between China and South Asia, all the way to Central Asia. The reconstruction of 'the Old Burma Road', which linked the province of Yunnan to Myanmar, had already begun and could, in time, revive the Stillwell Route (or Ledo Route), which provided a link between Myitkyina, in northern Myanmar, and Ledo, in Assam, during the Second World War.[82]

On the Indian side, contacts were established with the authorities in the Chinese province, especially at the instigation of Brajesh Mishra, Prime Minister A.B. Vajpayee's Principal Secretary and National Security Adviser. Thus, a conference took place in Kunming in August 1999, with the participation of Indian, Bangladeshi and Burmese academics. The event was organized by the Yunnan Academy of Social Sciences, one of the main promoters of the regional cooperation project between the four states.[83] The conference enthusiastically recommended the development of rail, air and road links between the concerned regions, in order to intensify their trade and tourist flows. The states of Bengal and Assam showed an interest in this initiative, which remained essentially of a Track II nature. In any case, the developments around BIMST-EC and the Kunming Initiative finally demonstrated that at the top of the Indian state, political leaders started to consider sub-regionalism to be an important vehicle for development. They therefore encouraged regional cooperation projects that were sometimes limited to a part of the national territory. For New Delhi, this amounted to accepting the fact that some states would develop faster than others—a development that seemed to be inevitable in the new context of economic liberalization.

NOTES

1. Isher Judge Ahluwalia, 'L'Ouverture de l'Inde aux Echanges et aux Investissements', in I.J. Ahluwalia, R. Mohan and O. Goswami, under the supervision of Charles Oman, *Reformes des Politiques en Inde*, Paris: OECD, 1996, p. 19.
2. P.V.N. Rao, 'Indo-Korea Economic Interaction', speech at the luncheon hosted by presidents of Apex Economic Organizations of Republic of Korea, Seoul, 10 September 1993, *Selected Speeches*, New Delhi: Ministry of External Affairs, 1997, p. 402.
3. J.N. Dixit, *My South Block Years: Memoirs of a Foreign Secretary*, New Delhi: UBSPD, 1996, p. 47.
4. *The Times of India*, 13 April 1995, quoted in Christophe Jaffrelot, 'L'Inde et l'Asiatisme', 1997, p. 237.
5. Manmohan Singh, 'The Economy: An Unsatisfactory Record', *The Times of India*, 1 August 1997.
6. *The Asian Age*, 24 September 1995, quoted in Jaffrelot Christophe, 'L'Inde et l'Asiatisme', p. 237.
7. Quoted in Christophe Jaffrelot, 'L'Inde et l'Asiatisme', p. 237.
8. *India Today*, 'Learning from Asian Tigers', 31 October 1993, p. 66.
9. *The Times of India*, 8 March 1997.
10. K.S. Rana, 'Restructuring the MEA', Foreign Service Institute, *Indian Foreign Policy, Agenda for the 21st Century*, vol. 1, New Delhi, Foreign Service Institute: Konark Publishers, 1997, pp. 230–1.
11. Statement by External Affairs Minister of India, I.K. Gujral on the occasion of the Post-Ministerial Conferences of ASEAN (PMC – 7 + 10), 24 July 1996, Jakarta.
12. World Bank, *The East Asian Miracle: Economic Growth and Public Policy*, Oxford: Oxford University Press, 1993.
13. A.N. Ram, 'Challenges to Economic Diplomacy', in N. Jetley, ed., *Indian Foreign Policy, Challenges and Prospects*, New Delhi: Vikas Publishing House, 1999, p. 117.
14. Ajan Roy, 'A MITI in the Making?', *Business India*, 16–29 December 1996.
15. Interview with Muchkund Dubey, New Delhi, 18 November 1997.

16. For the institution of the economic policy in India, refer to Rana, 'Restructuring the MEA', p. 231; Dixit, *My South Block Years*, pp. 58–9; P.M.S. Malik, 'The Changing Face of India's Economic Diplomacy: The role of Ministry of External Affairs', Foreign Service Institute, *Indian Foreign Policy*, pp. 238–9; Ministry of External Affairs, *Annual Report 1993–4*; New Delhi, MEA, XP Division, 1994, pp. 105–8.
17. Dixit, *My South Block Years*, pp. 58–9, 390–8.
18. R. Thakur, *The Politics and Economics of India's Foreign Policy*, New York: St. Martin Press, 1994, pp. 12–13.
19. Dixit, *My South Block Years*, p. 266.
20. *India Today*, 'Indo-ASEAN Relations: Time for a Rethink', 15 October 1995, p. 60.
21. The Joint Commissions are bilateral bodies set-up with the objective of promoting cooperation in different sectors, from science and technology to culture, including political and economic relations. Often managed by the Ministry of Foreign Affairs, representatives of the Economic Ministry and the business sectors of both countries also participate in the meetings of these institutions.
22. Dixit, *My South Block Years*, p. 254.
23. E. Sridharan, 'The Problem', in *Wooing Japan*, Seminar, no. 397, September 1992, p. 16.
24. B.M. Oza, Former Indian Ambassador to the Republic of Korea, 'Observations on Indo-Korean Relations: Past, Present and Future', R.R. Krishnan, ed., *The Fifth India-Korea Conference*, 22 December 1994, New Delhi: India International Centre, 1995, pp. 101–2.
25. Meeting with Sanjay Baru, Senior Consultant, RIS, New Delhi, 17 April 1998.
26. Ministry of External Affairs, *Annual Report 1992–3*, p. 101.
27. Centre for Policy Research, *Report of the CPR Delegation to Taiwan*, September 1994.
28. Ministry of External Affairs, *Annual Report 1994–5*, MEA: New Delhi, XP Division, 1995, pp. 17–18.
29. Ministry of External Affairs, *Annual Report 1995–6*, MEA: New Delhi, XP Division, 1996, p. 22.
30. Jean-Luc Domenach, *L'Asie en Danger*, Paris: Fayard, 1998, p. 184.
31. V.P. Dutt, *India's Foreign Policy in a Changing World*, New Delhi: Vikas Publishing, 1999, p. 321.
32. Asrani, 'India-Japan Relations', pp. 347–8.
33. Rajesh Mehta, 'The Role of ODA', Japan Foundation, ed., *Dimensions of India-Japan Relations*, New Delhi: Japan Foundation, New Delhi Office, 1997, pp. 105–25; FICCI, Report on the 27th Joint Meeting

of the India-Japan Business Cooperation Committees, New Delhi, 13 November 1996.

34. Apart from aid and loans, official Japanese aid could also take place through the Japanese Technical Cooperation Programme, which offers training programmes, deputes Japanese experts overseas and provides technical services for certain types of projects.
35. CII, CEOs Mission to Japan, A Report, 30 May–2 June 1994.
36. Satu P. Limaye, 'The Japan-India Encounter', *RGICS Paper*, no. 38, 1997, p. 9.
37. CII, CEOs Mission to Japan, A Report, 8–11 June 1997.
38. Oza, 'Observations on Indo-Korean Relations', p. 104.
39. Meeting at the Embassy of Thailand in India, New Delhi, 21 April 1998; Thammasat University and Information Department, Ministry of Foreign Affairs, *Seminar on Thai-Indian relations in the Present Decade and Prospects for Cooperation in the Future*, 1 August 1997, Bangkok, 1997, pp. 23, 275, 283–5, 328.
40. Dutt, *India's Foreign Policy in a Changing World*, p. 252.
41. MVIRDC, *India and ASEAN: Partners in Progress*, Bombay: MVIRDC, World Trade Centre, 1993, p. 29.
42. M.G. Asher and R.S. Rajan, 'Singapore-India Economic Relations: Exploring Synergies for Mutual Benefit', in Y.M. Cheong, V.V.B. Rao, eds., *Singapore–India Relations: A Primer*, Singapore: Centre for Advanced Studies, Singapore University Press, 1995, p. 166.
43. Keynote Address by Brigadier-General (NS) Lee Hsien Loong, Deputy Prime Minister, 'Integrating the Indian Economy into the World: A Singapore Perspective', in SICCI, *Global Indian Entrepreneurs Conference—India: The Uncaged Tiger, Summary of Proceedings*, Singapore: SICCI, 1996, Annex. B; Joseph L.H. Tan, 'Singapore's Foreign Direct Investment in Indo-China and Myanmar: Opportunities and challenges', *RIS Occasional Paper*, no. 50, 1997, pp. 29–32.
44. Kripa Sridharan, 'The evolution and Growth of India-Singapore Relations', Y.M. Cheong, V.V.B. Rao, eds., *Singapore–India Relations: A Primer*, pp. 33–4.
45. Ministry of External Affairs, *Annual Report 1993–4*, p. 13; Faizal Yahya, 'Singapore-India: A Confluence of National Interests', *Asian Studies Review*, vol. 19, no. 2, pp. 28–9.
46. Ministry of External Affairs, *Annual Report 1994–5*, pp. 16–17.
47. Meeting, CII Overseas Office, Singapore, June 1998.
48. Meeting, CII, Research Division, New Delhi, February 1998.
49. CII, 'Moving to the Market: Sustaining Reforms in India and Asia', *CII Communiqué*, March 1997, no. 9.
50. CII, 'Proceedings of the Partnership Summit. CII Centenary 1895–1995', Calcutta, 4–6 January 1995.
51. B. Bhattacharyya, 'India's Foreign Economic Policy: Evolving Context

and Tasks', Foreign Service Institute, *Indian Foreign Policy: Agenda for the 21st Century*, vol. 1, p. 210. Muchkund Dubey, interview, New Delhi, 18 November 1997. Satinder Palaha and H.L. Sharma, 'Towards Economic Integration through Regional Trade Blocs', *Occasional Paper*, no. 4, Indian Institute of Foreign Trade, 1996, pp. 1–34.

52. Quoted in Sanjib Pohit and Rajesh Chadha, 'Should India Join a Free Trading Bloc?', *Foreign Trade Review*, vol. 31, no. 4, January–March 1997, p. 41.
53. Taranath P. Bhat, 'Trade Blocs and Global Trade Prospects', *Foreign Trade Review*, vol. 31, no. 4, January–March 1997, p. 72.
54. The twelve countries that participated in the first APEC summit in Canberra were Australia, Canada, Japan, New Zealand, South Korea, the United States and the ASEAN members (Brunei, Indonesia, Malaysia, Philippines, Singapore and Thailand). At the Seoul Summit in 1991, it was the turn of Hong Kong, Taiwan and China to be admitted. Mexico and Papua New Guinea became part of APEC at the Seattle Summit in 1993, and Chile became a member at the Bogor Summit in 1994.
55. The concept of open regionalism was defined in the APEC Eminent Persons group report, in 1994.
56. Pelkmans and Fukasaku, 'Evolving Trade Links between Europe and Asia: Towards an "Open Continentalism"?', Kiichiro Fukasaku, ed., *Regional Co-operation and Integration in Asia*, Paris: OECD, 1996, p. 94.
57. During an UNCTAD seminar on regional integration, in January 1996, the participants of developing countries outside the Asia-Pacific region stated their concerns faced with APEC's growth (quoted in Ippei Yamazawa, 'APEC's New Development and its Implications for Nonmember Developing Countries', *The Developing Economies*, vol. 34, no. 2, June 1996, pp. 114, 132–4.
58. In this case, the United States were especially concerned with not leaving the European Union in an advantageous position of a 'free-rider'. They affirmed that they were ready to offer Europe the benefits of APEC's liberalization if the former was to reciprocate with equivalent measures on the basis of the most favoured nation.
59. Asian Development Bank, *Asian Development Outlook 1996–7*, Hong-Kong: ADB and Oxford University Press, 1996, p. 181; Ming Tang, 'Asian Economic Co-operation: Opportunities and Challenges', in K. Fukasaku, ed., *Regional Co-operation and Integration in Asia,* p. 214.
60. Muchkund Dubey, 'APEC and Open Regionalism', in B. Ghoshal, ed., *ASEAN and South Asia*, New Delhi: Sterling Publishers, 1998, p. 235.
61. ANZCER: Australia-New-Zealand Closer Economic Relations Agreement.
62. Mukul Asher, 'India & APEC', *The Hindu*, 21 June 1997.
63. Jagdish Bhagwati, 'Regionalism and Multilateralism: an Overview', in

Jaime de Melo and Arvind Panagariya, ed., *New Dimensions in Regional Integration*, Cambridge: Cambridge University Press, 1995, pp. 9, 22–51.

64. J. Coussy, 'L'Inde face à la Régionalisation de l'Economie Mondiale', *Les Etudes du CERI*, no. 23, February 1997, p. 5.
65. Bath, 'Trade Blocs and Global Trade Prospects', *Foreign Trade Review*, vol. 31, no. 4, January–March 1997, pp. 53–74.
66. R. Behl and L.D. Mago, *India-ASEAN Trade Cooperation and Investment Opportunities*, New Delhi: Indian Institute of Foreign Trade, 1996, p. 35.
67. P.L. Sanjeev Reddy, 'Prospects of India-ASEAN Trade', in RGIS, *India, Southeast Asia and the United States: New Opportunities and Prospects for Cooperation*, Bangalore Conference Papers, 9–10, 1995, RGIS Project no. 16, 1996, p. 115.
68. Statement by External Affairs Minister of India, I.K. Gujral, on the Occasion of the Post Ministerial Conference of ASEAN (PMC-7+1), 24 July 1996, Jakarta, § 17. In fact, during its first meeting, on 25 and 26 May 1998, the Indo-ASEAN Working Group on Trade and Investment recommended that a study should be conducted on the possible establishment of India-AFTA relations.
69. Ganganath Jha, 'ASEAN and India: Dawning of a New Partnership', *The Indonesian Quarterly*, vol. 25, no. 2, p. 162.
70. Interview, Commercial Division, Embassy of Thailand in New Delhi, April 1998.
71. Concept Paper, Bangladesh-India-Sri Lanka-Thailand Economic Cooperation (BIST-EC), 5 June 1997, § 1.5.
72. Declaration on the Establishment of the Bangladesh-India-Sri Lanka-Thailand Economic Cooperation (BIST-EC), Bangkok, 6 June 1997, § 3.a.
73. Declaration on the Establishment of the Bangladesh-India-Sri Lanka-Thailand Economic Cooperation (BIST-EC), Bangkok, 6 June 1997.
74. Report of the Special BIMST-EC Ministerial Meeting, Bangkok, 22 December 1997, Agenda Item 5, p. 2.
75. Concept Paper, Bangladesh-India-Sri Lanka-Thailand Economic Cooperation, Introduction, § 1.1, 5 June 1997.
76. Tang, 'Asian Economic Co-operation', in K. Fukasaku, ed., pp. 195, 203.
77. ADB, *Asian Development Outlook 1996–7*, p. 179.
78. The southern states of Tamil Nadu, Andhra Pradesh and Karnataka promoted their own Look East policy, especially as they were anxious to attract FDI from South-East Asia. West Bengal also tried to open up to East Asia, but it was not as consistent as the southern states in its efforts to woo its neighbours.
79. Ranjit Gupta, Ambassador of India to Thailand, 'Indo-Thai Relations',

in Thammasat University and Information Department, Ministry of Foreign Affairs, *Seminar on Thai-Indian Relations in the Present Decade and Prospects for Cooperation in the Future*, 1 August 1997, p. 24.

80. *The Times of India*, 26 April 1997.
81. Rajesh Mehta, 'Establishment of Free-Trade Arrangement among BIMST-EC Countries', *RIS Discussion Papers*, no. 2, 2002, p. 21.
82. P. Stobdan, 'Myanmar: Breaking out of Isolation', *Strategic Analysis*, February 1995, p. 1345. See part III, Chap. 6, § 6.2 for details concerning strategic concerns aroused by the construction of this route.
83. 'The Kunming Initiative for a Growth Quadrangle between China, India, Myanmar and Bangladesh', 14–17 August 1999, *China Report*, 36: 3, 2000, pp. 417–24.

CHAPTER 2

Evolution of Trade and Investment Flows

2.1 Trade and Investment Flows between India and North-East Asia

In the context of the Look East policy, the classical model of the 'flying geese' came to have a certain seductive effect.[1] This model of economic integration through the relocation of the industrial activities of Japanese companies placed India theoretically in the advantageous position of a 'designated receiver' of East Asian capital. Although it was considered controversial elsewhere in Asia, for India, the 'flying geese' metaphor had the advantage of validating its desire for enhanced economic ties with East Asia. To recall, the 'flying geese' model started with the relocation of Japan's labour-intensive activities to Singapore, Hong Kong, Taiwan and South Korea. As these economies entered the category of Newly Industrialized Countries (NICs), they lost their comparative advantage and Japanese investments reoriented themselves toward Thailand, Malaysia and Indonesia. In the process, South Korea, Taiwan and Singapore also started investing in those ASEAN economies. But, the increase in manpower costs in South-East Asian countries slowed down investment growth, particularly in the manufacturing industry of Thailand and Malaysia. Japan and the NICs then started considering China and Vietnam as more attractive destinations as they were lower-wage countries. The ASEAN investors, in turn, started relocating their own production units elsewhere in Asia. Hence, India was positioned as the last link in the relocation process. Applying the dynamics of the 'flying geese' model, India hoped that its abundant and low-cost manpower would attract investments not only from Japan, but also from the Asian NICs as well as other South-East Asian countries.

SCEPTICAL JAPANESE INVESTORS

It is widely acknowledged that Japan played a central role in the Asian regionalization process. Indeed, the investment and production strategies of Japanese businesses established functional ties between Japan, the NICs, the ASEAN countries and China. Japan started investing massively in East Asia in the mid-1980s. It moved from a vertical division of labour where it imported raw materials in return for finished products to a horizontal division, where it also imported Asian manufactured goods.[2] Thus, in the early 1990s, East Asia became a production base for Japan and a springboard for re-exportation to other regions of the world. Because of its economic liberalization, India expected to receive Japanese investments, as was the case for most East Asian countries, the most recent example at the time being that of China. Besides, Japan was historically one of the primary suppliers of economic aid to India. Analyses of Asian regionalization tended to show that Japanese government aid was linked to the commercial concerns of its enterprises and that it was preparing the right environment—notably in terms of infrastructure—for the influx of private investments. The triangular structural links between Tokyo's aid policies, the direction taken by the investments of Japanese multinationals and the export strategies of its manufacturers that had units in the NICs and in ASEAN countries were, therefore, at the roots of the inter-penetration of Asian economies.[3] Japanese aid to India did not, until then, lead to large-scale trade interactions. But, with the liberalization of its economy, India certainely hoped to benefit from an influx of Japanese private capital.

The surveys undertaken by the Indian Institute of Public Opinion clearly revealed the expectations regarding Japan. In 1994 for instance, the archipelago topped the list of countries with which it was important to have 'very good relations'.[4] Indeed, 78 per cent of respondents felt that it was important to have 'very good relations' with Japan. Besides, relations with the archipelago were considered 'very good' by 43 per cent of the respondents and 'rather good' by 50 per cent of them. The 1996–7 survey confirmed that Japan continued to be seen as an important country in Indian external relations.[5] For 72 per cent of those questioned, it was 'very important' to cultivate good relations with the archipelago, while 20 per cent believed that it was 'fairly important'. As compared to the United States, 62 per cent of the respondents said that it was 'very important' and 30 per cent said that it was 'fairly important'. Furthermore, 40 per cent of the Indians polled believed they had the best relations with Japan, against 35 per cent for the United States. Japan was also identified as the country with which India had the highest trade (27 per cent), before Russia (25 per cent), the United States (24 per cent) and Great Britain (7 per cent). Finally, Japan was seen as the best source for the 'type of technological development that India needed'. Japan therefore carried 34.5 per cent of the votes polled, before the United States (26 per cent), Russia (13 per cent) and Germany (9 per cent).

Moreover, by the early 1990s, the Indian business sector became very interested in Japanese work culture.[6] Some of India's biggest industrial groups started experimenting with Japanese management techniques, as they were considered an essential factor in the economic success of that country. For instance, the Godrej conglomerate was overtly inspired by the *Kaizen* techniques to sensitize its workers to improve productivity.[7] The Godrej Soap factory in Bombay attributed annual savings of nearly Rs. 2 million to its *Kaizen* cell. Godrej held a *Kaizen* Day twice a year, during which the CEO shook hand with each staff member. In the agricultural machinery sector, Mahindra and Mahindra boasted of having reduced costs by Rs.,1.5 million in just a few years, thanks to the adoption of Japanese management systems. With a 4,000-strong work force, the Mukand Group established a Total Quality Management (TQM) secretariat. The manager, Neeraj Bajaj, affirmed that the *Juran,*[8] Quality Circles, training and education, and ISO-9000 standards were the company's 'four pillars'. Manufacturing electric products, the Onida Group also adopted TQM in 1993 and formed workers' committees to ensure compliance with maintenance standards. Finally, in the textile industry, the Mafatlal Group introduced the *Juran* concept and educated its 11,000 employees about its new interpretation of quality. The creed adopted by the company was no longer that of complying with the given specifications, but that of responding to the consumer's wishes. The introduction of the Japanese management techniques could be seen as an important step in the process of establishing a base of high quality Indian suppliers for the Japanese industry. Indeed, many Japanese companies based themselves on the concept of *keiretsu*, a chain of suppliers and manufacturers that acted as an entry barrier for competition, while guaranteeing high quality levels. If Indian industrial circles adopted Japanese management systems, it would indeed be much easier to forge joint ventures and establish commercial ties with the archipelago, as Japanese investors preferred to move into markets with which they were familiar.

With Japan being targeted as a major source of foreign investments, Indian Chambers of Commerce increased their efforts to woo that country. The private sectors of the two countries already had co-operation mechanisms in place for several years. FICCI's Joint Business Council was, in fact, instituted with Japan in 1975. Another important forum of interaction for the private sector was the Indo-Japanese Commercial Cooperation Committee (IJCCC), which had been created in 1966. The committee intensified its activities in the early 1990s, particularly with the setting up of a special cell for the development of industrial infrastructure. It also organized seminars on foreign investments in India, sponsored by the World Bank. The first seminars took place in Tokyo and Osaka, in 1995.[9] As for CII, in 1992, it identified Japan as an 'A+ priority zone' and opened its ninth international office in Osaka in June 1996. This decision clearly reflected the importance CII gave to the East Asian region, in particular the Far East. The office was also to cover South Korea. The Confederation increased the number of initiatives aimed at Japanese business communities, who seemed rather motivated at the time. Delegations followed close on each other's heels, at the rate of several per year. Japan was also the partner country for the Twelfth Indian Engineering Trade Fair, in February 1997. This biennial event was in fact the most important trade fair in India, and Japan came to be the first Asian country to be a partner in a CII Industrial Trade Fair. Almost 150 Japanese companies came to participate in the event, constituting the largest representation ever achieved until then by a partner country. Moreover, the Twelfth Trade Fair reflected the strengthening of relations between India and East Asia: of the thirty-five countries participating, fourteen were Asian, with South Korea, Singapore, Thailand and Vietnam at their head.[10] Japan's successful participation in the trade show raised hopes about a fresh start in bilateral economic relations.

In spite of all these initiatives, India's hopes with regard to the influx of Japanese capital were, on the whole, thwarted. Although they did increase after the opening up of India's economy, Japanese investments remained at a fairly low level. In 1996, India still accounted for just under one per cent of Japan's overall investments in the world. This figure was more or less the same as the one in the early 1960s, when the archipelago made very few foreign investments.[11] While Japanese foreign investments increased considerably during the following decades, India's share did not change.[12] However, the Japanese government was very interested in the opening up of the Indian economy and endeavoured to promote opportunities for increasing bilateral relations. India's economic liberalization did not leave business circles indifferent either. As a corollary to official Japanese visits, India welcomed several delegations composed of Japanese private sector leaders, notably the *Keidanren*, the Federation of Economic Organizations of Japan. The country even seemed to have improved its image in the eyes of Japanese investors during the second half of the 1990s. According to a survey conducted by Japan's EXIM Bank in 1995, Japanese investors classified India seventh among the most promising countries, before the Philippines, Singapore and the United Kingdom, in the middle term. In a long-term perspective, India rose to the third place. A new survey carried out by the same institution in 1997 placed India second in the long-term, but it maintained its seventh position in the middle-term perspective.

Because of its new economic policy, India benefited from a fresh influx of Japanese capital, but of a limited volume. After the start of the reforms, Japanese investments increased from Rs. 2,574 million in 1993 to about Rs. 15,142 million invested in 1995, reaching Rs. 19,063 million in 1997. However, in comparison with other foreign investors, this increase proved to be disappointing. Whereas in 1991, Japan was the second-largest investor in India, in 1997, it fell to the seventh position. In other words, Japanese investments did not increase as rapidly as investments by other countries, particularly the United States and the United Kingdom, and occasionally South Korea and some South-East Asian countries. However, it must be noted that unlike South Korea and the South-East Asian countries, Japanese invest-ment flows were regular and maintained their levels from one year to the next.

According to experts from Batliboi and Co. and Ernst and Young, over 40 per cent of approved Japanese investments were translated into actual investments. The rate fell to 10 per cent in the case of the United States. It is true that the gap between the two countries narrowed when considering their respective actual investments. Nevertheless, from 1994 to 1998, Japan accounted for just 4 to 5 per cent of FDI

TABLE 2.1: APPROVED FDI INFLOWS FROM THE UNITED STATES AND JAPAN BETWEEN 1991 AND 1997

(*Rs. in million*)

		1991	1992	1993	1994	1995	1996	1997	Total 1991–7
Total FDI in India		5,341	38,875	88,595	141,872	320,717	361,468	548,913	1,505,780
USA	–Amount	1,858	12,315	34,618	34,881	70,543	100,558	135,698	390,474
	–Share in total FDI in India (%)	(34.7)	(31.6)	(39.0)	(24.5)	(21.9)	(27.8)	(24.7)	(25.9)
	–Rank	1	1	1	1	1	1	1	1
Japan	–Amount	527	6,102	2,574	4,009	15,142	14,882	19,063	62,301
	–Share in total FDI in India (%)	(9.8)	(15.6)	(2.9)	(2.8)	(4.7)	(4.1)	(3.4)	(4.1)
	–Rank	2	3	6	5	6	7	7	4

Note: Calculated on the basis of the monthly newsletters of the Secretariat for Industrial Approval from 1991 to 1997.

TABLE 2.2: ACTUAL FDI INFLOWS FROM JAPAN AND THE UNITED STATES IN INDIA FROM 1994 TO 1999

(*Rs. in million*)

	1994–5	1995–6	1996–7	1997–8
USA	6,339	6,509	8,576	25,540
Japan	2,981	2,038	3,433	6,080

Note: Calculated from the Reserve Bank of India's annual reports from 1994–5 to 1997–8.

in India, both from the viewpoint of approved and actual investments.

Most Japanese investors that established themselves in India did so in association with a local partner. Indeed, joint ventures offered easier access to market information and enabled them to use the Indian partner's plant and network. Moreover, half the Indo-Japanese enterprises were established during the economic liberalization era. Of a base of 364 Indo-Japanese companies in 1996, the consultants, S.R. Batliboi and Co. and Ernst and Young, estimated that 52 per cent were established during the period 1991–6, 26 per cent between 1980 and 1990 and 21 per cent before 1980. The most successful joint ventures were in the sectors of passenger vehicles, two-wheelers, spare parts, chemicals and dry cell batteries. The best-known example was that of the Maruti-Suzuki joint venture which, until 1995, monopolized 80 per cent of the Indian automobile market. Following the extraordinary success of the company, several other Japanese companies associated with Indian partners in the sector of motor parts. Maruti itself set-up five joint ventures that it used as suppliers.

Moreover, the survey conducted in 1996 by S.R. Batliboi and Co. and Ernst and Young revealed that the main pull factor for Japanese investors was the immense potential of the Indian market. So, 90 per cent of the investors questioned answered that the primary reason for their presence in India was the domestic Indian market while 47 per cent of them did so because of both low operational costs and an established legal system. Thirty-three per cent of the entrepreneurs questioned spoke of the availability of qualified manpower and 30 per cent of political stability. The poll thus showed that the Japanese investors were likely to be let down in their expectations. In the first place, the Japanese confessed that they did not intend to use India as a re-exportation base since they were relying on the emergence of the

Indian market. However, the myth of the Indian middle class' spending power barely met its promise in the mid-1990s. In the consumer durables sector, for example, the strategy of Japanese investors in India was long based on forecasts of an enormous domestic market, before they came to understand how low the consumption levels of the so-called middle class remained. Sony paid for its bad assessment. Its Indian branch, which started producing television sets in 1996, saw its sales fall well below forecasts and its inventory rise. The number of people who could afford to buy foreign brands proved to be limited to far less than the 150 million initially forecast.[13] For the same reason, another Japanese giant in current consumption electric goods, Hitachi, first limited itself to distributing its products in India rather than setting up a production base there.[14] As for the argument concerning political stability put forward by Japanese investors, it was likely to prove untrue given the uncertainties emerging in 1996. Clearly, the governmental instability witnessed from 1996 to 1998 affected the general investment climate. But it seemed that Japan was far more vulnerable to it than other foreign investors. The optimist mindset prevailing in the West, but also in South Korea, was not so much affected by the political upheaval taking place in India.

In the end, India played only a marginal role in the strategies of Japanese investors during the 1990s. When New Delhi launched its liberalization policy in the early 1990s, the Japanese economy was suffering from a recession that hit real estate and foreign exchange markets badly. Japan's total foreign direct investments suffered a sharp decline. The reduction in capital exports had a knock-on effect on Europe and North America, in particular. However, Japanese investments remained high in the NICs and in the ASEAN economies, and increased considerably in China. When Japanese investments bounced back in 1993, it was again essentially to the benefit of East Asia. One year after opening up, the Indian economy, for its part, received no more than 0.6 per cent of Japanese investments in Asia, falling very far behind China (26 per cent), Hong Kong (18 per cent), Indonesia (12 per cent), Malaysia (12 per cent), Singapore (9 per cent) and Thailand (8 per cent). Between 1991 and 1994, Japan's yearly investments in Asia witnessed a remarkable growth of over 63 per cent, rising from USD 5,936 million to USD 9,565 million. But India did not even receive 1 per cent of this amount in the same period.

While the Japanese actively increased their investments in East

Asia during the 1990s, it was notably because of the appreciation of the Yen in relation to the Dollar, which led to a rise in domestic costs and posed the danger of falling competitiveness. The Japanese strategy was therefore redirected toward cost reduction through the transfer of production bases abroad and intra-industrial trade. But Japanese enterprises did not include India as a production base in this process. Besides, India and Japan followed a rather divergent logic. The main goal of Japanese companies was to produce and sell within the market of the country in which they were established. India's primary goal in inviting foreign capital was to increase exports and infrastructural investments. However, for infrastructure investments, the Japanese proved less competitive than the Americans or the Europeans. Infrastructure was a marginal sector for Japan's overall investments.

SOUTH KOREA: AN ENTHUSIASTIC 'NEWCOMER'

More than Japan, it was South Korea that tended to include the Indian economy in the Asian region, on the basis of the 'flying geese' model. To a certain extent, India and South Korea had a complementary industrial and commercial base.[15] In the beginning of the 1990s, the Korean economy was in a transitional phase: wage increases, notably those of qualified manpower, high interest rates and a strong national currency; all these factors affected export competitiveness. The automobile and electrical consumer goods sectors were facing difficulties. Korean conglomerates—the *chaebols*—therefore tried to redirect some of their activities toward low manpower-cost countries. At the time, wages in India were seven times lower than in South Korea and the country was looking for investments that came with middle-level technologies. Korean business communities were therefore interested in the Indian market for several reasons: to relocate their factories, to establish re-exportation bases, or to develop their computer software industries.[16] Another imperative for businesses such as Daewoo and Hyundai was that they had to compensate for the increase in development and manufacturing costs through greater production volumes abroad. Japan had undergone a similar transitional phase when, at the end of the 1970s, it went from low-capital and highly labour-intensive production to hi-tech, high value-added industries. At the time, the Indian economy was not open enough to benefit from Japanese investment flows. But by the mid-1990s, India was able to offer policies and infrastructure that attracted South Korea's investments and technical resources.[17]

TABLE 2.3: APPROVED FDI INFLOWS FROM JAPAN AND SOUTH KOREA BETWEEN 1991 AND 1997

(Rs. in million)

		1991	1992	1993	1994	1995	1996	1997	Total 1991–7
Total FDI in India		5,341	38,875	88,595	141,872	320,717	361,468	548,913	1,505,780
Japan	–Amount	527	6,102	2,574	4,009	15,142	14,882	19,063	62,301
	–Share in total FDI in India (%)	(9.8)	(15.6)	(2.9)	(2.8)	(4.7)	(4.1)	(3.4)	(4.1)
	–Rank	2	3	6	5	6	7	7	4
South Korea	–Amount	61	394	293	1,068	3,142	32,209	19,559	56,728
	–Share in total FDI in India (%)	(1.1)	(1.0)	(0.3)	(0.7)	(0.9)	(8.9)	(3.5)	(3.7)
	–Rank	13	13	19	11	18	2	6	5

Note: Calculated on the basis of the monthly newsletters of the Secretariat for Industrial Approval from 1991 to 1997.

TABLE 2.4: ACTUAL FDI INFLOWS FROM JAPAN AND SOUTH KOREA IN INDIA BETWEEN 1994 AND 1998

(*Rs. in million*)

	1994–5	1995–6	1996–7	1997–8
Japan	2,981	2,038	3,433	6,080
South Korea	376	799	222	12,380

Note: Calculated on the basis of the Reserve Bank of India's annual reports from 1994–5 to 1997–8.

Prior to 1991, Korean investments in India were at a very low level. It was only with the liberalization that they began to grow. In January 1994, for example, there were 178 Indo-Korean enterprises, of which 98 had been established after 1991. Indian partners received Korean technology in 111 cases.[18] In fact, Korean capital flows increased considerably in 1996, rising to Rs. 32,209 million, i.e. an increase of more than 900 per cent in relation to the previous year. Hence, South Korea became the second-largest foreign investor in India after the United States, far above Japan. In 1996, the *Korea Economic Weekly* devoted a special report to India and affirmed that the country was one of the most promising markets for Korean industry.[19] But in 1997, Korean investments fell again to Rs. 19,560 million. The country then came down to be the sixth-largest foreign investor in India, just above its neighbour, Japan.

In terms of actual investments, the fluctuation proved fairly high. Actual South Korean investment flows were fairly modest between 1994–7. The marked increase in investments approved in 1996 was translated into real terms between 1997–8. South Korea then rose to the third position after Mauritius and the United States. Korean actual investments were then twice as high as Japanese investments.

The increase in Korean capital flows partly resulted from the interest of the *chaebols* in India's economic liberalization. The biggest *chaebols* set-up plants or offices in the country, whether it was Hyundai or Daewoo, Samsung or the Lucky Goldstar (LG) group. Most were in the automobile or electrical products industries, although they also tried to penetrate the infrastructure, chemicals and plastic industries sectors. In the wake of Daewoo and Hyundai, which set-up their automobile manufacturing units in India, several Korean manufacturers specializing in motor parts tried to set-up joint ventures with Indian partners, with the goal of becoming suppliers of the Indian subsidiaries of Daewoo and Hyundai. In other words, the establishment of these big Korean parent companies in India also attracted enterprises that subcontracted their activities.[20] Moreover, the main *chaebols* came to India with the aim of using their branches as export bases. Contrary to the Japanese, the potential of the immense Indian market was not necessarily the Koreans' main investment motive.

The example of Hyundai provides a good illustration of the enthusiasm of the *chaebols* with regard to India in the 1990s. Initially, the car manufacturer wanted to enter India through a joint venture. Unable to find a satisfactory partner, the Koreans finally decided to set-up a wholly-owned company. The decision to come in on their own was also partly because they feared being late in the race to capture the country's potential market. The proposed investments initially stood at USD 700 million, with total planned investments of USD 1.3 million. The car manufacturing unit was located in Chennai (Tamil Nadu), in order to be able to export to the Middle East and South-East Asia. Indeed, Hyundai did not intend to sell on the Indian domestic market alone, as it was aware of its limitations. The factory's production capacity was 100,000 cars per annum, which far surpassed the demand on the Indian market and would make it possible to export cars from Chennai. Another *chaebol*, Samsung, set-up office in India in 1995 to sell colour televisions, in particular.[21] To be able to export its products to South-East Asian countries, such as Malaysia and Indonesia, the *chaebol* decided to install a second production unit in Chennai.[22] Having announced a USD 629 million project, the company did not hide the fact that the Indian market was one of its priorities. In 1997, Samsung Electronics identified India as one of its four most strategic markets.[23] But for all that, the conglomerate did not intend to invest in hi-tech semiconductor technologies. Only middle-level technologies were to be transferred from South Korea, a decision which corresponded fairly well with the 'flying geese' development model.

As for Daewoo, the second-largest Korean *chaebol*, it set-up several branches in India. Daewoo India had already finalized two power plants, in Madhya Pradesh and Himachal Pradesh. In the second half of the 1990s, Daewoo Anchor Electronics undertook the construction of two factories, in Pune (Maharashtra) and Greater Noida (close to Delhi), to manufacture electrical goods. Once again, the medium term project was for the development of production units to provide international standard components for Daewoo.[24] As for

Daewoo Motor, it was the first automobile manufacturer to set-up shop in India during the economic liberalization period. The *chaebol* entered India in 1993 to produce light trucks, and took over from the Japanese Toyota company, which withdrew from the joint venture signed with DMC. Daewoo had just launched its globalization strategy. Since its investment plans had been stalled due to several corruption cases in China, the Korean group immediately redistributed its funds to India. The *chaebol* began the sale and production of its vehicles in 1995. Its manufacturing unit was established close to Delhi and was one of the largest foreign investments ever made in the Indian automobile sector, at Rs. 36,000 million.[25] Hence, in the first half of the 1990s, at a time when Korean actual investments stood at just USD 63.5 million, the biggest investor was DMC-Daewoo, with a paid-up capital of USD 37.8 million. Moreover, Daewoo Motors planned to invest USD 905 million in 1997 to set-up six joint ventures specializing in the manufacture of motor parts.[26] At the time, the *chaebol* had high expectations for the export of its small car model manufactured in India. In addition, Daewoo Motors India exported its vehicles to the parent company in Korea, and the Delhi subsidiary was thinking of strategic alliances with Daewoo suppliers in the world. The company already had an agreement to provide components to the Chinese and Ukrainian subsidiaries. It also got in touch with the *chaebol's* subsidiaries in Indonesia, Vietnam and Uzbekistan. Daewoo's establishment in India could, therefore, lead to the generation of intra-industrial flows with other Asian economies.

On the whole, Korean investors seemed less demanding than their Japanese counterparts with regard to the unforeseeable nature of the Indian environment. Japanese investors traditionally harboured a rather cautious attitude and took a lot of time to study a country before investing in it. The Japanese thus sent a large number of delegations to India during the initial phase of its reforms, so as to gather enough information to decide whether to invest or not. Such delays took place in the case of China too, where Japanese investments peaked only fifteen years after the reforms began. In comparison with the wait-and-see policy of its Japanese neighbours, the Korean decision-making system proved faster and was driven by a more optimistic mindset. Besides, the Koreans felt that the Japanese cautiousness presented them with a good opportunity to gain a foothold in India.[27] Thereafter, they proved to be very aggressive in marketing and pricing. Whether in the field of automobiles or household appliances, Korean manufacturers were, indeed, in the most competitive sectors, all the more so as they were relatively new on the Indian market and did not benefit from the reputation of quality that was attached to Japanese products.

The optimism of the Koreans could also have been a result of their lack of experience in the Indian market. The Japanese, who, on the contrary, had been trying to invest in the country for a decade, had lost their enthusiasm. In fact, very few of the Indo-Japanese joint ventures of the mid-1980s proved successful and Japanese investors came to the lasting conclusion that the subcontinent's market generated very few returns. In the end, the total approved investments of Japan and South Korea between January 1991 and December 1997 were quite close. With Rs. 62,301 million, Japan was the fourth-largest foreign investor in India. South Korea, which invested Rs. 56,728 million, was in fifth place. While the two amounts were close, the difference lay in the fact that India had banked a great deal on Japan, putting the archipelago's investment capacity on an equal footing with that of the West. However, the total amount of American investments (Rs. 390,474 million) was more than six times higher than Japanese investments between 1991 and 1997. From that point of view, the opening up of India led more to the globalization of its economy than to an integration into the East Asian region.

LIMITED TRADE LEVELS WITH JAPAN AND SOUTH KOREA

Initially small in volume, Indo-Korean trade witnessed strong growth, and rose from about Rs. 15,300 million in 1992–3, to Rs. 49,700 million in 1996–7. Hence, it more than tripled in just four years. However, South Korea accounted for just two per cent of Indian imports and hardly more than one per cent of its exports. India essentially exported raw materials (cotton, oil cake, natural gas, organic chemicals and agricultural products) while importing organic chemicals, iron and steel, non-electric machines and electronic products from South Korea.[28] As for the volume of Indo-Japanese trade, it stood at Rs. 82,960 million in 1992–3 and rose to Rs. 148,862 million in 1996–7. Until 1996–7, Japan was India's second largest trade partner. But India was an inconsequential trade partner for the archipelago. Japan was the source for 6–7 per cent of Indian imports and provided especially chemicals (12 per cent), steel goods (9 per cent), electric generators (7.3 per cent) and textile machinery (4 per cent). On the whole, Japan accounted for over 7 per cent of India's total exports. It was the second most important export destination, after the United States. Most Indian exports were divided between precious stones and jewels (29.2 per cent), seafood (19 per cent) and iron ore (15 per cent). This fairly small export basket reflected the insufficiency of Japanese investments in bilateral trade. In other words, India did not re-export to Japan the manufactured or semi-manufactured goods that it would have manufactured in production units built with Japanese investments.

Thanks to the dismantling of Indian trade barriers, Japan's exports to India rose by 20 per cent annually between 1992 and 1996. In the same period, Indian exports rose by 10 per cent due to the competitiveness of certain products such as shrimp and textiles. However, trade between Japan and other Asian countries quadrupled in the previous ten years whereas Indo-Japanese trade only doubled. From the Indian point of view, trade with Japan did not grow at as high a rate as India's overall trade. Japan's share in Indian imports declined from 7 per cent in 1991–2 to 5.5 per cent in 1996–7. In the same way, Japan's share in Indian exports fell from 9.2 per cent in 1991–2 to 6 per cent in 1996–7. In fact, Indo-Japanese trade was relatively inelastic and limited in the variety of products. For it to increase, a larger volume of Japanese investments had to be made to gradually turn India into a manufacturing centre, as had been the case for South-East Asian economies.

2.2 The Economic Interactions between India and South-East Asia

According to the 'flying geese' model of regional integration, South-East Asian economies were to reproduce the logic of relocation of their manufacturing activities to the benefit of their South Asian neighbours. Theoretically, Indian reforms were a good omen for economic relations with Malaysia and Singapore, where major structural changes were taking place. Indeed, these two economies, which were fast losing their comparative advantages in labour-intensive industries, had to relocate their production units.[29] To give an impetus to the economic interaction, the Chambers of Commerce and Industry in India and South-East Asia organized fora, seminars,

TABLE 2.5: TRENDS IN INDIAN EXPORTS TO JAPAN AND SOUTH KOREA BETWEEN 1991 AND 1997

(Rs. in million)

		1991–2	1992–3	1993–4	1994–5	1995–6	1996–7
Total Indian exports		440,418.1	536,882.5	697,513.9	826,741.1	1,063,533.4	1,188.170.8
Japan	–Amount	40,711.1	41,604.3	54,605.3	63,631.3	74,111.8	71,208.5
	–Rate of growth (%)	/	(2.2)	(31.2)	(16.5)	(16.4)	(-3.9)
	–Share in Indian exports (%)	(9.2)	(7.7)	(7.8)	(7.7)	(7.0)	(6.0)
Korea	–Amount	5,883.3	5,064.8	6,474.7	10.438.3	14,994.2	18,405.8
	–Rate of growth (%)	/	(-14)	(27.8)	(61.2)	(43.6)	(22.7)
	–Share in Indian exports (%)	(1.3)	(0.9)	(0.9)	(1.2)	(1.4)	(1.5)

TABLE 2.6: TRENDS IN INDIAN IMPORTS FROM JAPAN AND SOUTH KOREA BETWEEN 1991 AND 1997

(*Rs. in million*)

		1991–2	1992–3	1993–4	1994–5	1995–6	1996–7
Total Indian exports		478,505.4	633,745.2	731,010.1	899,706.6	1,226,781.4	1,389.196.8
Japan	–Amount	33,754.6	41,356.2	47,742.8	64,050.6	82,539.9	77,654.1
	–Rate of growth (%)	/	(22.5)	(15.5)	(34.1)	(28.8)	(-5.9)
	–Share in Indian imports (%)	(7.0)	(6.5)	(6.5)	(7.1)	(6.7)	(5.5)
Korea	–Amount	7,872.1	10,285.7	17,705.5	19.765.7	27,590.8	31,367.5
	–Rate of growth (%)	/	(30.6)	(72.1)	(11.6)	(39.5)	(13.6)
	–Share in Indian imports (%)	(1.6)	(1.6)	(2.4)	(2.1)	(2.2)	(2.2)

Source: RBI, *Handbook of Statistics on Indian Economy*, 8 January 2002.

trade shows, aimed at promoting information flow between Indian and South-East Asian business communities. Indeed, the first essential stages of the economic rapprochement between India and the ASEAN had to consist in helping their business communities to know each other.

HOW TO HELP THE BUSINESS COMMUNITIES OF INDIA AND ASEAN KNOW EACH OTHER?

On a bilateral level, FICCI and ASSOCHAM began to develop their initial contacts with South-East Asia during the 1980s, thanks to the shared mechanism of the Joint Business Council (JBC). These institutions aimed at being catalysts for the promotion of economic interaction between India and a given country. JBCs were established with China in 1984, Malaysia in 1986 and Singapore in 1988. Two new JBCs were created in 1990, with Thailand and Indonesia. The activities of JBCs with East Asian countries intensified in the early 1990s, as a reflection of the increasing interest of the Indian private sector in its eastern neighbourhood.[30] But as these mechanisms were fairly recent, they had yet to become more effective. The Indian and South-East Asian private sectors were still at a stage where they had to get to know each other. While CII had a mechanism similar to JBCs—called country committees[31]—its work was directed more toward the promotion of India's potential abroad. Besides the convening of major international trade shows, CII tried to integrate with the networks of East Asian economic institutions. In Singapore, CII signed agreements with various bodies, such as the Productivity Standards Board and the Regional Institute for Technology. The most important of these agreements was the one reached with the Singapore Confederation of Industries in September 1994, which enabled it to open its representative office within the premises of the Singaporean institution. The primary mission of the office was to act as an information agency for India and encourage the formation of joint ventures with ASEAN countries. Thanks to its physical presence, CII acquired a certain visibility in Singapore. CII also tried to join the networks of other South-East Asian economic institutions and, to this end, signed agreements with the Industrial Development Authority of Malaysia and the Federation of Industries of Thailand.

At the multilateral level, an ASEAN-India Business Council (AIBC) was set-up in 1993, after New Delhi was granted the status of sectoral partner in the Association. The objective of this institution, representing the private sectors of India and the ASEAN, was to strengthen the means available for intensifying economic relations between the two sides. To this effect, it endeavoured to promote the exchange of delegations and trade information. For instance, the Indian part of the AIBC published the first index, identifying 700 Indian enterprises that already had, or wished to have, trade relations with South-East Asia.[32] This database was put on the website of the Global Indian Business network of the Singapore Indian Chamber of Commerce and Industry.

The AIBC met for the first time on 14–15 November 1996, in New Delhi. The plans of action drawn up showed that the primary objective of the private sector of India and the ASEAN was to integrate the Indian economy with the intra-regional networks structuring East Asia.[33] In the motor parts sector, for example, the AIBC tried to find complementarities to intensify intra-industrial flows between India and South-East Asia. In fact, it was anticipated that the establishment of major Japanese and Korean automobile manufacturers in the subcontinent would lay good foundations for the creation of trade flows between their Indian and South-East Asian subsidiaries, notably with Thailand and Malaysia. The AIBC also intended to promote partnerships between small and medium-scale enterprises (SMEs) in India and the ASEAN. The initiative was very important, because SMEs predominated in both the Indian as well as the ASEAN economies. South-East Asian SMEs had begun to expand their operations to the entire Asian region, to set-up operations as a corollary to the activities of multinationals. The promotion of joint ventures between Indian and South-East Asian SMEs was, therefore, aimed at integrating the Indian production system in the networks already established in the region. Indeed, the expertise acquired by the ASEAN SMEs could help increase the added value of Indian exports and give them better access to Asian distribution networks. To give an example, South-East Asian companies could improve the quality and design of Indian textile products, while in the horticulture and food processing sectors, they could bring in new production technologies. Inversely, India had more advanced technological expertise in some sectors than South-East Asia, notably in the computer software or medical education sectors.[34] On the whole, India offered opportunities of technology transfer at less elevated costs than those practised by the West and Japan. Thus, during a period when Malaysia and Singapore were involved in an industrial restructuring process, India appeared to be a major source of engineering and technical expertise.[35]

CROSS-INVESTMENT FLOWS BETWEEN INDIA AND SOUTH-EAST ASIA

Indian companies had been investing in South-East Asia since the end of the 1960s. With the creation of these first joint ventures, India acquired a certain visibility in specific sectors such as the palm oil sector in Malaysia, the textile, steel and hotel industries in Indonesia, and the pharmaceutical and synthetic textile industries in Thailand. More recently, Indian companies specializing in computer software and information technologies entered in the services sector in South-East Asia. Nonetheless, India's share in the total investments made in ASEAN countries was negligible in the 1990s. In terms of aggregated data, East Asia[36]—or South-East Asia more precisely—was the region of the world that, in 1995, accounted for the highest number of operational joint ventures with India. The ASEAN concentrated fifty-six operational joint ventures of which twenty were in Malaysia, fourteen in Singapore, eleven in Indonesia and ten in Thailand. All these operations in South-East Asia drained funds from India amounting to Rs. 599 million. However, it must be noted that while the African continent only had twenty-eight operational joint ventures, the Indian funds invested there were higher, with Rs. 683 million. If the joint ventures being set-up were also taken into account, it would once again be the ASEAN that, with 121 operations, would head the list, followed by the European Community and its eighty-two Indian joint ventures. But if, in addition to operational joint ventures and those being set-up, wholly-owned subsidiaries were taken into account, Indians would be doing far more business in the EC than in the ASEAN.

In Malaysia, several Indian joint ventures that were set-up in the 1970s failed. There were several reasons for that, ranging from poor planning and management, to inadequate partners, and stern restrictions imposed on capital imports from India or even the recession in the local market. Nonetheless, in 1995, Malaysia was once again the country with the highest number of Indian joint operational ventures (twenty). It was also placed second in the list of countries that received the most Indian investments, for operational joint ventures (Rs. 238 million), after Kenya (Rs. 418 million).[37] A considerable volume of Indian investments in Malaysia was concentrated in the manufacturing, textile and food industry sectors.[38] Major Indian groups were among the best established Indian companies, such as Tata Engineering and Locomotive Co., JG Glass Industries, Kirloskar Engineering and Hindustan Safety Glass. In Thailand, India was ranked, on an average, as the fourteenth largest foreign investor in the 1990s. The foremost Indian investor in the country was the Aditya Birla Group, which headed three joint ventures specializing in the manufacture of rayon, acrylic and black carbon. One of the biggest units in north-east Thailand was a paper manufacturing unit that belonged to the Thapar Group. Major Indian companies such as Ansal, Unitech, Som Dutt also established ties with Thai partners in the construction sector.[39] In Indonesia, the biggest Indian companies were Ispat Indo and Essar in steel, besides Indo-Rama in textiles. Indian business was essentially in the steel, textile and rubber sectors.

A number of major Indian public or private corporations operated in the entire South-East Asian region. The public sector company IRCON, for example, subcontracted a railway project in Indonesia and signed a contract in 1994 with Thailand for the rental and maintenance of diesel locomotives manufactured in India. In the same fashion, some major industrial groups of the Indian private sector were already very well established in South-East Asia in the 1990s. While it operated on all continents, the pharmaceutical multinational Ranbaxy was especially present in the region, with its business in China, Hong Kong, Malaysia and Thailand, in addition to its new projects in Myanmar and Vietnam. Specializing in chemicals and textiles, the Aditya Birla Group was active in Indonesia, Philippines, Thailand and Malaysia. The manufacturer of steel office furniture, Godrej and Boyce was another of the large Indian industrial groups that successfully established itself in Malaysia, Indonesia and Singapore. However, the presence of these major Indian groups in various ASEAN economies did not necessarily create major intra-industrial flows. Nonetheless, it must be noted that the Indian groups that invested in South-East Asia were inclined to associate with a South-East Asian partner to operate back in India. Usha Martin Telecom, which had a cable manufacturing unit in Thailand, set-up a successful venture with Telekom Malaysia in cellular telephone services in Calcutta. Unitech, a major Indian construction company, had some projects in Thailand and associated with the Singapore Consortium[40] to build offices in Gurgaon. Godrej and Boyce joined with Singapore's Intraco and Hong Kong's Double Kingdom for a telecommunications equipment manufacturing project.

TABLE 2.7: ACTUAL FDI INFLOWS FROM SINGAPORE, JAPAN AND SOUTH KOREA IN INDIA BETWEEN 1994 AND 1998

(*Rs. in million*)

	1994–5	1995–6	1996–7	1997–8
Japan	2,981	2,038	3,433	6,080
Singapore	768	2,011	2,684	/
South Korea	376	799	222	12,380

Note: Calculated from the annual reports of the Reserve Bank of India between 1994–5 and 1997–8.

As for the investments of South-East Asian countries in India, the economic opening undoubtedly led to an influx of funds. Before the liberalization era, South-East Asian investments in India were almost non-existent. Between 1991 and 1997, the total amount of approved direct investments from the ASEAN region accounted for about seven per cent of the total foreign investments approved by the Indian government.[41] In particular, Singapore's investments started becoming substantial in 1995, with declared investments of Rs. 9,910 million. After 1994, Singapore ranked between eighth and thirteenth among foreign investors in India.[42] Moreover, it appeared that for Singapore, the transformation rate of investment authorizations into actual investments was fairly high. In this respect, the city-state established itself as a primary investor, at least between 1994 and 1998.[43]

The city-state was especially interested in the infrastructure and services sectors in India. Besides the much publicized Bangalore information technology park, Singapore invested in the tourism, electronics, hospital and management sectors, and in the development of real estate and consultancy services. A considerable part of the investments from the city-state went through Mauritius, which is one reason for the modest official figures.[44] From a geographical viewpoint, Singapore's investors showed a preference for Chennai and Mumbai, India's two main trading ports. However, aggressive marketing by Karnataka and Andhra Pradesh succeeded in attracting a large volume of investments.

Whether in India or Malaysia, the number of Indo-Malaysian ventures increased dramatically after August 1991. In 1995, there was an influx of private investments from Malaysia. Investment authorizations rose then to Rs. 13,861 million and made Malaysia the sixth largest foreign investor in India. In 1997, Malaysia was the fifth highest foreign investor in India, behind the United States, Mauritius, the United Kingdom and Germany. With investments worth Rs. 21,046 million, the country even stood ahead of South Korea and Japan.[45] Malaysia invested in the telecommunications, electric equipment and engineering sectors, as well as in aquaculture and in the agro-food, palm oil and natural rubber sectors. Malaysian companies also showed great interest in the infrastructure sector, particularly in the development of port facilities in Tamil Nadu and Andhra Pradesh, and in various highway projects in different parts of India. A dozen Malaysian businesses responded to bids for highway projects in Haryana, Gujarat, Maharashtra and Andhra Pradesh. The Malaysian giant, Renong, became an important player, very determined to win a piece of the Delhi-Bombay highway. Generally speaking, Malaysian investors showed a clear preference for south India, in particular with regard to the setting up of joint ventures. Of the sixty-six joint ventures (financial or technical) approved by the Indian government between August 1991 and early 1998, half of the Indian partners were from one of the three south Indian states of Karnataka, Tamil Nadu or Andhra Pradesh. Thus, Tamil Nadu was the state that hosted the highest number of Indo-Malaysian joint ventures (nineteen), followed by Andhra Pradesh (eleven), New Delhi (fourteen), Maharashtra (five), Karnataka (three), Goa (three) and West Bengal (two).[46] Geographical proximity therefore played an important role in attracting Malaysian capital.

There were two peak periods in Thai investments in India. The first occurred in 1993, with close to Rs. 3,700 million invested. The second wave of investments took place in 1995. With Rs. 19,681 million announced, Thailand rose that year to the rank of third largest investor in India, behind the United States and Israel. Most Thai funds were initially aimed at the fisheries, aquaculture and animal fodder sectors, reflecting the pre-eminence of the largest Thai investor in India—the CP agro-industrial group. Fisheries and aquaculture had actually been identified as important cooperation sectors by the Indian and Thai Prime Ministers during P.V. Narasimha Rao's visit to Bangkok in April 1993. Following the visit, two rounds of discussions on cooperation in fisheries were held. After 1994, Thai investments diversified, and included the polyester and automotive parts industries, as well as the hotel sector. In 1995, Thai telecommunications companies invested more than Rs. 11 million in India. In terms of actual investments, Thai funds rose in 1994 to

TABLE 2.8: APPROVED FDI INFLOWS FROM MALAYSIA, SINGAPORE AND THAILAND BETWEEN 1991 AND 1997

(*Rs. in million*)

		1991	1992	1993	1994	1995	1996	1997	Total 1991–7
Total FDI in India		5,341	38,875	88,595	141,872	320,717	361,468	548,913	1,505,780
Mal.	–Amount	1.8	744	85	252	13,861	423	21,046	36,413
	–Share in total FDI in India (%)	/	(1.9)	(0)	(0.1)	(4.3)	(0.1)	(3.8)	(2.4)
	–Rank	/	8	/	/	6	/	5	8
Sing.	–Amount	13	602	667	2,655	9,910	3,197	8,619	25,665
	–Share in total FDI in India (%)	(0.2)	(1.5)	(0.7)	(1.8)	(3.0)	(0.8)	(1.5)	(1.7)
	–Rank	/	10	16	8	11	13	11	13
Thail.	–Amount	0	25	3,684	100	19,681	765	259	24,514
	–Share in total FDI in India (%)	/	(0)	(4.1)	(0)	(6.1)	(0.2)	(0)	(1.6)
	–Rank	/	/	6	/	3	/	/	14

Note: Calculated from the monthly newsletters of the Secretariat for Industrial Approval between 1991 and 1997.

Rs. 118 million and Thailand to the fifteenth rank. In 1995, they rose further to Rs. 144 million while Thailand was ranked at the eighteenth place.[47] Geographically, Thai investors were especially interested in the state of Orissa. At the end of 1997, while Thailand was in the throes of a financial crisis, the Amata Group conducted an important survey project for the construction of a petro-city in Orissa.

If all the authorizations for investment granted from January 1991 to December 1997 are taken together, Malaysia would be the eighth largest foreign investor in India, Singapore would come thirteenth and Thailand fourteenth. India's leaders had clearly indicated that they hoped to attract investments from South-East Asia in the energy, telecommunications, road and harbour infrastructure sectors. The projects proposed by Singapore, Malaysia and Thailand showed that the private sector was following behind institutional strategies, to a certain extent. With regard to Indonesia, it made only minor investments in India, in the traditional sectors of paper-making plants. However, these projects had the advantage of generating intra-industrial trade, as intermediate products were imported from Indonesia and the end products re-exported. This held true for the Indonesian conglomerate, Sinar Mas, which set-up a paper-making plant in India. Raw materials and semi-finished goods were imported from Indonesia while the finished products were meant for the domestic and international markets.

INDO-ASEAN TRADE

With regard to trade, a major obstacle resulted from the fact that India and the ASEAN economies were competing against each other and were not complementary. India essentially exported primary products that had little added value and barely succeeded in selling its best export products or non-traditional products, because it then entered into competition with the other Asian countries. The ASEAN countries imported precious stones and jewels, textile and agricultural products, chemicals, machines and pharmaceutical products from India. India's imports from ASEAN included vegetable oil, oil products, electronic components, textile products, telecommunications equipment and certain specific chemicals.[48] Since essentially primary products were being traded, there was very little intra-industry and intra-business trade between India and the ASEAN economies. However, trade of this kind was essential as, it had been the engine of growth in world trade for several years.

In spite of these difficulties, trade between India and the ASEAN increased substantially during the reforms period. It rose from Rs. 71,500 million in 1992–3 to close to Rs. 204,000 million in 1996–7; hence, it almost tripled. In 1992–3, the ASEAN accounted for 6 per cent of India's foreign trade. This figure rose to eight per cent in 1996–7. However, from the point of view of the ASEAN economies, trade with India remained insignificant—about one per cent of their total external trade in the 1990s. Consequently, there was an asymmetry in the importance of this trade for the respective parties. In the Indian perspective, the ASEAN became increasingly important, both as a source of imports and as an export market. The ASEAN economies accounted for 5.6 per cent of Indian imports in 1992–3 and 7.4 per cent in 1996–7. Inversely, the ASEAN received only 6.7 per cent of Indian exports in 1992–3. The figure rose to 8.5 per cent in 1996–7. According to a survey by Rajesh Mehta, the increase in India's overall exports in the 1990s was the result of their re-direction towards Asian markets.[49] Indian exports to Asia's main markets would therefore have risen by more than 20 per cent per year between 1990–1 and 1995–6. A marked growth took place notably in exports to Indonesia (50 per cent), Hong Kong (26 per cent), Malaysia (22 per cent) and South Korea (22 per cent).

Within the ASEAN, Singapore remained India's primary trade partner. In 1994–5, the city-state attracted almost 40 per cent of Indian exports, followed by Thailand (22 per cent), Malaysia and Indonesia, each accounting for around 15 per cent. Singapore also accounted for 46 per cent of Indian imports from the ASEAN, ahead of Malaysia (26 per cent), Indonesia (17 per cent) and Thailand (9 per cent).[50] However, the impact of India's opening on trade with the city-state must be put in perspective. In fact, the importance of Singapore in India's overall trade actually declined, from 2.6 per cent in 1980 to 1.7 per cent in 1992, after reaching a peak of 3.3 per cent in 1984 and 1989.[51] The reduction of Singapore's share in the volume of trade between India and the ASEAN took place to the benefit of Malaysia, Indonesia and Thailand.

SINGAPORE AS A SPRINGBOARD TO THE ASIA-PACIFIC?

Rather than being one of the primary foreign investors in India, Singapore aimed to play the role of 'catalyst' with regard to India's economic opportunities. In other words, the city-state wanted to serve

TABLE 2.9: TRENDS IN INDIA'S EXPORTS TO ASEAN COUNTRIES FROM 1991 TO 1997

(*Rs. in million*)

		1991–2	1992–3	1993–4	1994–5	1995–6	1996–7
Total FDI in India		440,418.1	536,882.5	697,513.9	826,741.1	1,063,533.4	1,188,170.8
ASEAN	–Amount	25,103.8	35,971.1	52,313,5	59,525.3	89,339.8	100,994.5
	–Growth rate (%)	/	(43.2)	(45.4)	(13.7)	(50.0)	(13.0)
	–Share in Indian exports (%)	(5.7)	(6.7)	(7.5)	(7.2)	(8.4)	(8.5)
Indo.	–Amount	3,617.1	4,011.2	7,368.9	8,719.1	22,157.5	21,010.2
	–Growth rate (%)	/	(10.9)	(83.6)	(18.3)	(154.1)	(-5.1)
	–Share in Indian exports (%)	(0.8)	(0.8)	(1.1)	(1.1)	(2.1)	(1.8)
Mal.	–Amount	4,989.8	5,498.1	7,757.2	8,997.3	13,151.1	18,855.3
	–Growth rate (%)	/	(10.2)	(41.0)	(16.0)	(37.4)	(46.1)
	–Share in Indian exports (%)	(1.10)	(1.0)	(1.1)	(1.1)	(1.2)	(1.6)
Sing.	–Amount	9,584.9	17,045.6	23,586.5	24,186.1	30,159.4	34,700.1
	–Growth rate (%)	/	(77.8)	(38.3)	(2.6)	(24.6)	(15.5)
	–Share in Indian exports (%)	(2.2)	(3.2)	(3.4)	(2.9)	(2.8)	(2.9)
Thail.	–Amount	4,896.2	7,346.0	11,205.6	12,205.6	15,819.2	15,871.2
	–Growth rate (%)	/	(50.0)	(52.5)	(13.9)	(23.9)	(0.3)
	–Share in Indian exports (%)	(1.1)	(1.4)	(1.6)	(1.5)	(1.5)	(1.3)

TABLE 2.10: TRENDS IN INDIA'S IMPORTS FROM ASEAN COUNTRIES FROM 1991 TO 1997

(*Rs. in million*)

		1991–2	1992–3	1993–4	1994–5	1995–6	1996–7
Total Indian exports		478,508.4	633,745.2	731,010.1	899,706.6	1,226,781.4	1,389,196.8
ASEAN	–Amount	31,103.0	35,489.7	34,357.4	61,180.0	89,555.0	102,800.5
	–Growth rate (%)	/	(14.1)	(-3.1)	(78.0)	(46.3)	(14.7)
	–Share in Indian imports (%)	(6.5)	(5.6)	(4.7)	(6.8)	(7.3)	(7.4)
Indo.	–Amount	1,649.5	1,736.7	3,753.0	10,083.0	15.425.0	21,252.3
	–Growth rate (%)	/	(5.2)	(116.1)	(168.6)	(52.9)	(37.7)
	–Share in Indian imports (%)	(0.3)	(0.2)	(0.5)	(1.1)	(1.2)	(1.5)
Mal.	–Amount	9,720.6	11,754.8	7,837.6	15,387.8	30,196.3	39,317.1
	–Growth rate (%)	/	(20.9)	(-33.3)	(96.3)	(96.2)	(30.2)
	–Share in Indian imports (%)	(2.0)	(1.9)	(1.1)	(1.7)	(2.5)	(2.7)
Sing.	–Amount	17,125.1	18,307.1	19,664.4	28,249.3	36,523.9	37,747.5
	–Growth rate (%)	/	(6.9)	(7.4)	(43.6)	(29.6)	(3.5)
	–Share in Indian imports (%)	(3.5)	(2.8)	(2.7)	(3.1)	(2.9)	(2.7)
Thail.	–Amount	1,195.5	1,688.9	1,794.4	5,388.5	5,675.3	7,000.3
	–Growth rate (%)	/	(41.2)	(6.2)	(200.3)	(5.3)	(23.3)
	–Share in Indian imports (%)	(0.2)	(0.2)	(0.2)	(0.5)	(0.4)	(0.5)

Source: RBI, *Handbook of Statistics on Indian Economy*, 8 January 2002.

as a mediator for all companies interested in the Indian market, whether they were of Indian origin, from Singapore or elsewhere. In fact, the notion of being a catalyst went back to the concept of 'strategic alliances' formed by the city-state's authorities and was a corollary of its regionalization programme. Aware of its experience and know-how in collaborating with multinationals, Singapore proposed to these global firms that 'strategic alliances' be forged, by investing jointly in the region's developing economies. To carry through its regionalization programme, Singapore undertook to develop expertise on the region's economies, with the help, among others, of the Institute of South-East Asian Studies (ISEAS). While South-East Asia remained the core interest of its research, ISEAS also intended to cover East Asia and the Indian Ocean. The city-state's authorities also asked Singapore National University to set-up a study group on India. This research group, which held conferences and seminars, acted as a platform for interaction between Singapore's academic, business and governmental circles. In the private sector, Drew and Napier, one of Singapore's oldest consultants, established a department specializing on India in 1994. The target customers covered Singaporean companies or multinationals based in the city-state.

A number of multinationals covered India from their regional office in Singapore (some others handled the subcontinent from the Middle East or directly from the metropolis). In the case of some multinationals, the initial strategy for penetrating the Indian market was indeed launched from Singapore. Thereafter, if business in India justified it, an office was opened there. Based in Great Britain, Holiday Hospitality, owner of the Holiday Inn hotel chain, established its reservation centre for the Asia-Pacific region in Singapore and developed a promotional strategy for the Indian market from the city-state.[52] Another example was Reuters, which established its subsidiary in India with Reuters Singapore handling the operation. The same was true for British Gas, Motorola Singapore or Forit Investment. In the last case, the company was based in Britain and set-up an office in Bombay. But, it was the Singapore subsidiary that managed all investments in the energy sector in India.

In the financial sector, Singapore's role *vis-à-vis* India was even more important. In fact, banks adopted strategies of approaching the Indian market from Singapore itself. For instance, toward the end of the 1990s, the Credit Investment Bank of Canada (CIBC) covered India from its regional office for the Asia-Pacific, based in the city-state. Since CIBC business in India was fairly limited, it was more advantageous for it to centralize its resources in Singapore rather that set-up an office in India.[53] Other big banks like Golm and Sax or Merril Lynch adopted the same approach strategy, before setting up a company with an Indian partner. Moreover, the numerous international banks based in Singapore were interested in the opportunity of financing various projects in India, notably in the infrastructure field. Crédit Lyonnais and Singapore's Citybank thus set-up a fund for India. Furthermore, thanks to funding from Singaporean banks, Indian companies were able to establish ties with third countries in the region. For example, in April 1997, India's Nagarjuna Group established a sugar factory in Vietnam's Mekong delta, with funding from Singaporean investors. Nagarjuna Holdings Vietnam was, therefore, a company registered in Singapore, taking the guise of a joint venture between the Nagarjuna industrial group and Singapore's Keppel financial group, which invested in it through its Vietnam fund.[54] Singapore was very pleased with this project, as it had indeed proposed to finance Indian initiatives in third countries such as Vietnam several times. In this matter however, it must be recognized that Singapore had to face competition from London and Hong Kong, particularly as the banks in these major financial centres had many ties with Indian business.

For Singapore, playing the role of 'catalyst' also meant being the regional base for all Indian companies desirous of gaining a foothold in the vast Asia-Pacific market. Thus, Singapore conducted a vigorous campaign to be a mediator, providing transportation and other services necessary to India's globalization drive. In order to encourage big Indian corporations to set-up office in the city-state, the Singapore Trade and Development Council (STDB) granted three of them—ITC Global, Swiss Am Singapore and Bloomsbury Trading—the envied status of 'Approved International Trade'.[55] In the late 1990s, more than sixty Indian companies had established branches or sales agencies in the city-state.[56] Most of these companies chose Singapore as a base to develop their commercial and financial operations in South-East Asia.[57] For example, the Greaves group, based in Bombay, set-up a subsidiary in Singapore so that it could take charge of its exports to third countries as well as its investment operations in South-East Asia. As for Ranbaxy's office, it served as a link between India and South-East Asia. It was also a showcase for the Indian parent company's international technologies and practices. In East Asia, besides

Singapore, Indian multinationals could set-up their sales agencies in Hong Kong.

Concerning trade flows, the STDB estimated that a quarter of Singapore imports from India would be for re-export, essentially to Malaysia, Indonesia, Vietnam, Hong Kong and South Africa. Inversely, in 1991, 41 per cent of Indian imports from Singapore actually came from a third country. The figure stood at 52 per cent in 1993. The percentages for re-export to India were higher than Singapore's total average re-exports, which were around 35 to 39 per cent.[58] Hence, Singapore played an important role as a trade warehouse for India's business in the region. However, as New Delhi developed bilateral ties with other South-East Asian countries, a larger proportion of trade took place directly, without transiting through Singapore. Singapore's re-exports therefore were likely to be affected. In the same way, while a large part of India's trade with China and South Africa passed through Singapore, New Delhi gradually moved toward more direct ties with these two countries. Finally, Singapore faced competition from other export centres, such as Dubai, Hong Kong and Mauritius. All these factors accounted for the decline of Indian imports from Singapore, which fell from 3.2 per cent in 1980 to 2.7 per cent on average between 1980 and 1992 and 1.5 per cent in 1992. It also appeared that Singapore did not compare well with Hong Kong as far as Indian exports were concerned. Hong Kong attracted 4.1 per cent of Indian exports in the world in 1992–3 and its market share continued to rise, reaching 5.7 per cent in 1995–6. In the same period, Singapore's share fell from 3.1 per cent to 2.8 per cent.[59] Hong Kong was therefore a much more important distribution centre for Indian exports in Asia than Singapore and its position further strengthened with the opening up of India's economy. Singapore's position, on the other hand, was better from the viewpoint of Indian imports, in spite of the decline mentioned above. Hong Kong accounted for barely one per cent of Indian imports in the world.

2.3 People-to-People Networks between India and East Asia

Three perspectives were selected to assess the density of human networks between India and East Asia during the 1990s: the linkages with the diaspora, tourist flows and air-traffic and, finally, the mobility of human resources. All these people-to-people contacts had strong economic dimensions, with 'the human integration' of India in Asia often being a corollary of its economic integration. Thus, states attempted to make use of or mobilize these human networks as they endeavoured to accelerate the dynamics of regional integration. At the same time, the fact that a number of people-to-people networks existed even before India's Look East policy must be borne in mind. They generally tended to strengthen along with the opening up of India's economy.

THE INDIAN DIASPORA IN SOUTH-EAST ASIA—A SPEARHEAD OF THE LOOK EAST POLICY?

It was not possible to identify and list all NRI networks as the diaspora organized itself according to different schemes, based on a variety of objectives. In some cases, there were worldwide networks operating as pressure groups or furthering the Indian government's reforms. For instance, in India, a few individuals took the initiative to organize the diaspora as a whole. Thus, there emerged a Non-Resident Indian Welfare Society of India whose task was to strengthen the 'emotional ties' between India and the non-residents. But with the opening up of the economy, the association also encouraged NRIs to invest in India.[60] According to the Society's officials, the moderate level of NRI investments was due to bureaucratic red-tape and India's complex laws. Thus, the Society set-up pressure groups to influence the Indian government and defend the rights of NRIs, particularly concerning investments. At the same time, several political figures were members of its Board Committee.[61] Among other activities linked to East Asia, the Society organized conventions in Singapore and Bangkok and, in May 1997, it published the first directory of NRIs living in East Asia.[62] There was also another diaspora network, promoted by the World Organization of Persons of Indian Origin. Founded in 1989 in New York, the association's objective was to establish ties on the one hand between all NRIs and, on the other, between the diaspora and India. Like the NRI Welfare Society, the World Organization of Persons of Indian Origin served as lobby in New Delhi so that NRIs could gain greater rights in India.

Like government agencies, the Indian business community too hoped that the diaspora in East Asia would respond to the opening up of India's economy and offer the country special business opportunities.

However, the Indian diaspora in Asia did not appear to play the role of a natural conveyor of the Look East policy. In Singapore, for instance, the Indian community was most heterogeneous and the different groups it was composed of had very few interactions among them.[63] Their overall socio-economic profile was not very high. A large part of the diaspora here originated from south India, having left it three generations earlier. A second wave of emigration to Singapore occurred toward the end of the 1950s. Essentially from north India—Delhi, Punjab, Gujarat and Sindh—a large number of these emigrants became traders. But generally speaking, India's expectations were far beyond what the Indians of Singapore could offer.[64] The latter did not have any great capital sources, so few investments could be hoped for. Since they did not have any real industrial activities either, India could hardly count on any transfers of technology. The Singapore Indian Chamber of Commerce and Industry (SICCI) essentially consisted of traders and very few industrialists. Small in size and with very limited means, its members did not seem to show any specific preference for India, *a priori*. In 1998, SICCI's activities in relation to India accounted for less than 10 per cent of all its activities taken together.[65]

However, the SICCI secretariat played a fairly important role as an intermediary for institutional cooperation. It hosted most Indian delegations in Singapore and was also responsible for the ASEAN-India Business Council and the Singapore-India Joint Business Council. SICCI also promoted India's liberalization in Singapore. For instance, it published a brochure entitled, 'Doing Business with India' in 1994 and held several conferences on the subject of the Indian market. In particular, SICCI set-up Parameswara Holdings Ltd in 1993, a public corporation for spearheading the investments of Singaporean NRIs in India. However, the company proved to have limited means. Most of the time, it was a part of consortiums of Singaporean companies that invested in real estate development (Technology Parks in Bangalore and Gurgaon or New Bombay's Industrial Park).[66] SICCI also appeared to have strong links with the Government of Singapore and its regionalization programme. In accordance with its objectives of opening up to the region, the Singapore government encouraged its various ethnic communities to maintain economic ties with their country of origin. The Deputy Prime Minister, Lee Hsien Loong, once affirmed, 'We have turned our ethnic diversity to advantage. Chinese Singaporeans have a natural edge operating in China, Indian Singaporeans in India, and Malay Singaporeans in South-East Asia.'[67] In this regard, SICCI emerged as the Government of Singapore's arm specializing on India. The paradox was not trivial: while the transnational logic between India and South-East Asia had to develop, it would essentially be with the impetus of the government.

The presence of a few prominent individuals of Indian origin in Singapore also helped to mobilize the networks of some of the city-state's major economic agencies in favour of India, especially those that were not of Indian origin. Thus, the India Business Group (IBG) was born in August 1993 to act as an informal platform for businessmen interested in the Indian market.[68] Its Director, Davinder Singh, was a member of the Singaporean Parliament. Initially, the IBG had just seventeen members. In 1998, they were over 200. The IBG differed from the SICCI in that it was specifically India-oriented. Indeed, these two bodies constituted two different channels for the promotion of bilateral ties, each with its own network of relations. However, many of their members of Indian origin were the same. But contrary to the SICCI, there were many entrepreneurs of Chinese or Malaysian origin in the IBG. Furthermore, governmental or semi-governmental companies were omnipresent in the group. Hence, the IBG was able to mobilize a far higher investment potential than SICCI. This was hardly surprising, as this economic group was set-up by the government. Its secretariat was actually in the premises of the STDB and included members of Singapore's Economic Development Board (EDB) and Ministry of Foreign Affairs. The IBG's activities consisted of carrying forward the dialogue with India's political leaders and industrial associations. It closely monitored developments in India's economic reform process and held talks with the Government of Singapore on the initiatives and directions to be taken to reinforce commercial and industrial relations with India. In the 1990s, there was no similar body in the city-state to promote economic interactions with any other country.

On a larger scale, it was not easy to assess the degree of commitment of the Indian diaspora in South-East Asia *vis-à-vis* the economic opening up of the motherpand. Quantitative data was not available in most cases. The only possibility was a qualitative approach, based either on specific examples, or on overlaps between various interviews. A difference also had to be made between, on the one hand, ethnic networks that generated micro-economic relations between India and South-East Asia, and projects with investments of a larger scale, managed by major industrial groups of Indian origin. Concerning ethnic networks, south India maintained close ties with Singapore and Malaysia. Trade flows—sometimes clandestine—and a number of small enterprises linked south India to South-East Asia, often through the networks of the Tamil diaspora. These activities, of a modest scope, were difficult to assess, as they did not fall into the ambit of cooperation institutions at the central level. Thus, the commercial section of Singapore's High Commission in India acknowledged that it only centralized 50 per cent of the information related to the investments of its nationals in India, since most flows of funds to south India were taking place without its knowledge. The same held true for the Joint Business Council mechanism promoted by FICCI and ASSOCHAM. These fora were far more sought after when they operated with North-East Asian countries.[69] The lack of familiarity and the language barrier were the factors that drove businessmen to go through Chambers of Commerce. In the case of South-East Asia on the other hand, it was possible to do without the services and activities of the JBC. Some companies already had contacts there thanks to the diaspora's networks. Unlike the Far East, the ASEAN countries were not unknown territory. Hence, a large number of companies ignored the institutional mechanisms for cooperation and ventured forth on their own. Thus, the strategies adopted by private players were scattered and difficult to identify.

The NRIs in Singapore, with a high socio-economic status, were not natural intermediaries for taking forward India's economic liberalization. Some of them were even fairly sceptical with regard to their country of origin. If the following quotes were to be believed, the feeling of loyalty of businessmen of Indian origin for their native land was far from evident—at least, with regard to the economic sphere. George Abraham, the SICCI Secretary, made his view of India clear: 'There is one perception which I find strange in India . . . among the bureaucrats and the government. They think that if you are an NRI it is your duty to come and invest in India. This is nonsense (. . .) But there is no earthly reason why I would want to run to India to invest just because my grandfather and father were Indians. At the end of the day it is dollars and cents.'[70]

The IBG Director further explained that for Singapore's Indians, the decision to invest in the country would be based on purely rational economic calculations that took into account their specific assets, in this case their familiarity with the language and culture. As for Shabbir

H. Hassanbhai, the Director of Parameswara Holdings, he affirmed with great pragmatism that although cultural and ethnic ties helped in business, it was profit, more than feelings, that was the decisive criterion for Indian businessmen. Therefore, it was economic interest that seemed to override cultural solidarities in the choice of investments for most NRIs. In other words, if the Indian economy faced any problems, it was very likely that Singapore's NRIs would turn away from it like any other economic actors.

Nevertheless, some very prosperous Singaporean NRIs invested in India, including Thakral, the Agio Group, Windmill International, Scott Holdings, the Kewalram-Chanrai Group and Dadi Balsara. They sometimes got together in a consortium and turned essentially to the real estate and infrastructure development sectors. Thus, Thakral associated with Windmill and PHL to develop an industrial park in the vicinity of Mumbai. The same group, Thakral, this time with Sat Pal Khattar and PHL, undertook the construction of office buildings and a technological park in Gurgaon (Haryana). However, it must be noted that these activities in India could in no way be compared with the Thakral strategy in China. The group, which was already a very important player on the Chinese electronics market, set-up three new joint ventures in China and Hong Kong, in August 1997.[71] Another large group, Agio Counter Trade, specialized in petroleum development in Russia, created an Indian subsidiary to build a reservoir for oil products at the Paradeep port terminal (Orissa). Some groups, such as Dadi Balsara's, a Singaporean multimillionaire, initially had ambitious plans with regard to India. But they soon had to lower their ambitions. In this regard, NRI projects were apparently no less affected by the problems that most other foreign investors in India faced.

Like Singapore, Malaysia encouraged its Indian community to forge commercial ties with India. The influential Minister of Indian origin, Samy Vellu, played an active role in intensifying Indo-Malaysian economic relations during the 1990s. In fact, there was a Federation of Chambers of Trade and Industry of Malaysian Indians, which was quite interested in the Indian market.[72] Furthermore, the Malaysian or Chinese companies that invested in India tended to hire people of Indian origin, either employing them directly, or using them as intermediaries. According to the Malaysian High Commission in New Delhi, NRIs played an important role in the influx of funds to India and some headed some of Malaysia's biggest investment projects.[73] For instance, Measat (MBNS), a big company specializing in satellite transmission, increased its projects multi-fold to expand its distribution network in India. The company was already operating in the Philippines, Vietnam, Indonesia, Taiwan and Australia. None other than Ananda Krishnan owned it—one of Malaysia's richest Indians. NRI companies also took up various power plant projects in south India.

As for Hong Kong's Indian community, it had a special profile in East Asia. With approximately 27,000 persons, this community was fairly prosperous, which partly helped explain the sometimes high investment and trade figures with India. A certain number of Indians were highly-reputed diamond cutters. And precious stones constituted a major part of the bilateral trade between India and Hong Kong. As for the multimillionaire, Umesh Saraf, and one of the biggest families of Hong Kong, the Harilelas, they announced various large-scale investment projects. In Indonesia too, there were a few big NRI fortunes ready to invest in India. The Lohias, owners of Indorama, headed the third biggest Indonesian industrial group and a large network of companies in South-East Asia. Based in Indonesia, Indorama Synthetics established itself in Thailand and Sri Lanka. The multinational had a sales agency in Singapore and undertook to set-up two enterprises in India.[74] The Lohias had in fact themselves shown interest in India since 1986, when Rajiv Gandhi initiated liberalization measures. The 1991 reforms led them to make greater investments. Texmaco was another Indonesian multinational that was very close to the centre of power in Suharto's time. Its founder belonged to the south-Indian community living in northern Sumatra. The group made two major acquisitions in India through its company, Polynsido.

However, the role of the Indian diaspora in South-East Asia could not be compared to that of the overseas Chinese in the growth of China's economy. In the guide 'Business Opportunities in India' published for the Singapore business community, the authors evoked the marginal role of Singaporean and South-East Asian NRIs: 'The Indian business community in South-East Asia may have played a catalytic role in building business linkages, and dispelling negative perceptions. But, unfortunately, and for a variety of reasons (. . .), their contributions and, hence, influence in the communities in which they live, including India, have been marginal.'[75]

Finally, it must be noted that instead of making massive direct investments in India, Singapore's NRIs were a growing source of deposits. The United Arab Emirates, Saudi Arabia, the United States, Great Britain and Oman were traditionally the main sources of NRI remittances to India. But, between 1992–3 and 1996–7, funds from Singapore rose by 685 per cent. In 1996–7, Singapore rose to the sixth rank among the countries from which remittances of this kind originated.[76]

DEVELOPMENTS IN AIR TRANSPORT AND TOURIST FLOWS

Decision-makers at the political level considered human flows as a key factor in the rapprochement between India and the ASEAN. The promotion of tourism and intensification of air-traffic were therefore important sectors of institutional cooperation, especially since they were closely linked to the economic activities binding India to East Asia. Concerning aerial links between India and East Asia, there was a marked increase after the early 1990s. An agreement on civil aviation was signed in March 1992, enabling Korean Airlines to fly to Bombay and Delhi, and Air India to fly to Seoul and Pusan. An air traffic agreement concluded in May 1993 with Vietnam allowed direct services between the two countries. In 1995, Royal Brunei Airlines established regular flights between its capital and Kolkata. Finally, after a twenty-two-year break, air-traffic between Kolkata and Rangoon was restored in early 1996. The same year, air links between India and the Far East were simplified thanks to the concessions made by Beijing. In fact, the Chinese government granted air passage to Air India, enabling it thenceforth to start direct flights to Japan.[77] On the Japanese side, the airline companies resumed their flights between India and Japan in 1996. All Nippon Airways (ANA), Japan's first passenger airline, operated a Delhi-Tokyo flight via Bangkok. Japan Airlines (JAL) started direct flights between Tokyo and New Delhi and Tokyo and Mumbai after a four-year break.[78] Air India operated five flights per week.

As for the air-traffic between India and South-East Asia, it was traditionally fairly dense. In addition to Air India's flights, India's domestic airline, Indian Airlines, was also flying to South-East Asia, linking Chennai-Kuala Lumpur, Bangkok-Kolkata, Delhi-Bangkok and Singapore-Kolkata.[79] On its part, Singapore Airlines increased its capacities on the Chennai and Delhi routes in September 1997, apart from its daily link with Mumbai and Chennai. In 1997, Malaysian Airlines requested authorization to cover more Indian destinations, as well as to increase its flights to Mumbai and Chennai. It must be added that the intensification of intra-Asian travel also attracted India's major hotel chains to the region. The Oberoi group, owner of two hotels in Indonesia and several franchises in Singapore generally considered South-East Asia a priority area. In fact, in accordance with its 'girdling strategy', it was supposed to have a presence in regions where business travel was most frequent. It was a way of increasing its visibility and making businessmen their regular customers when they travelled to India. Particularly since the number of customers from East Asia visiting India's business hotels rose in the 1990s.[80]

Tourism was identified as a high potential sector for cooperation between India and the ASEAN. This multilateral approach was backed by Singapore's initiatives, the latter being very determined to develop tourist ties with India on a bilateral basis. Thus, the Singapore Tourism Promotion Board (STPB) set-up an office in Mumbai, in 1993. Its aim was to promote the city-state both as a leisure destination for well-off Indian families and as a luxury destination for Indian businessmen. The STPB's campaigns first targeted Mumbai and Chennai. Then, during the visit of Goh Chok Tong in India, in 25 January 1994, Singapore and New Delhi signed a five-year pact aimed at intensifying bilateral tourist ties. At the same time, the city-state proposed nine tourism-related investment projects in India. The interest in the tourism sector could be explained by the fact that it too was incorporated in the city-state's economic regionalization programme. The aim was to ensure that tourists visiting Singapore would also be encouraged to go to neighbouring countries. India therefore became a partner country in Singapore's economic regionalization programme, just like Vietnam, Myanmar, China, Australia, Indonesia and Malaysia. Promoting tourism in its partner countries meant developing a market in which the city-state's airlines and hoteliers would be the first to gain a foothold. Accordingly, HPL, a Singaporean hotel chain, established a base in India quite early.[81]

Traditionally, East Asia was the region that attracted the largest number of Indian tourists. With close to 700,000 Indian visitors arriving in 1996, East Asia's market share stood at 39 per cent.[82] With the exception of Singapore, these destinations were indeed less costly than Europe and North America. However, the appeal of East Asia decreased in the 1990s. This region, which attracted 44 per cent of the world's Indian tourists in 1987, saw its market share fall to

37 per cent in 1994 and 1995. Among the Asian countries, it was Singapore that Indian tourists visited the most. The city-state hosted about 30 per cent of Asia's Indian tourists in 1996. But Singapore's market share in the Asian region, which stood at 45 per cent in 1987, was also on the decline. Thailand's share also fell from 22 per cent in 1987 to 18 per cent in 1996. On the other hand, Indian tourists increasingly headed toward Hong Kong, China and South Korea. For Hong Kong, the percentage of Indian tourists in Asia rose from 14 per cent in 1987 to 15 per cent in 1996. For China, the increase was even more marked: 1.7 per cent in 1987 to 8 per cent in 1996. As for South Korea, it attracted 1 per cent of the region's Indian tourists in 1987. In 1996, its market share rose to 5 per cent.

From the viewpoint of the South-East Asian countries, the flows of Indian tourists had to be seen in the right perspective. In 1996, for example, Indian tourists in Thailand accounted for barely 2 per cent of all tourists in the country.[83] However, Indians stayed the longest in Thailand, with an average of eighteen days in 1996. Singapore witnessed a relative decline in the number of Indian tourists between 1991 and 1993. India, from where 5.8 per cent of the tourists to Singapore came in 1980 accounted for barely 3 per cent of all tourists in 1996. In spite of this relative decline, Indian tourism was important enough for Singapore not to disregard it. With an average length of stay of seven days, Indian tourists remained in the city-state much longer than the 3.7 days average for all other visitors. Further-more, taking all nationalities into consideration, Indian tourists were among those who spent the most, with an average of S$ 894 per head. In 1996, Indian tourism brought S$ 277 million to the city-state. In the tourism sector, India was Singapore's third highest source of revenue, after the whole of ASEAN (S$ 2,102) and Japan (S$ 643).[84] The city-state's success with Indians resulted from what it stood for, along with Dubai: the biggest shopping centre in the region. Singapore cultivated a cosmopolitan and sophisticated image that attracted the wealthiest sections of the Indian population. The city-state may also have benefited from Malaysia's restrictive policies with regard to Indian tourists. Since visas were very difficult to obtain, there was a substantial decline in the number of Indian tourists in the country, from 47,000 in 1992 to 15,000 in 1993. The same year, the number of Indian tourists visiting Singapore stood at 180,000. The Malaysian visa problem was due to the restrictive immigration policies adopted by Kuala Lumpur. Most clandestine workers came from Indonesia and Bangladesh, but Indians were being increasingly monitored. So Malaysia's Consulate in Chennai followed particularly restrictive policies, as Tamil Nadu was the main potential source of Indian emigration to South-East Asia.[85]

The number of Indian visitors to East Asian countries exceeded by far the number of East Asian visitors to India. At the same time, in absolute numbers, there were an increasing number of Asian tourists visiting India.[86] In 1996–7, close to 100,000 Japanese visited the country, as well as 56,300 Malaysian nationals, 48,400 Singaporeans and 17,000 Thais. In the case of Singapore and Malaysia, a large part of the tourists were, in fact, people of Indian origin. But in terms of relative values, the percentage of Asian tourists in relation to the total number of tourists in India showed a different countrywise trend. The share of the Japanese tourists in India increased slightly, from 3 per cent in 1990–1 to 4 per cent in 1996–7. The same was true for Malaysia, though to a lesser degree. In 1990–1, the percentage of Malaysian tourists in India was 2 per cent, rising to 2.4 per cent in 1996–7. For Singapore, the relative number of tourists in India remained at 2 per cent. For Thailand, a decline was observed in a percentage that was already small: 0.7 per cent in 1990–1, falling to 0.4 per cent in 1996–7. The European Union and North American nationals accounted for close to half the tourists visiting India.

NETWORKS OF EXPERTISE

In some fields, India offered an expertise that was of great interest to East Asian countries, hence the number of projects for cooperation in the human resources sector, involving qualified staff in particular. The importance of state initiatives in the promotion of these human resource flows must once again be underlined, even though multinationals were playing an increasingly important role, along with the public agencies. In the first place, technical and scientific cooperation had been a traditional element of the relations between India and South-East Asian countries, both at bilateral and multilateral levels. Through its International Technical and Economic Cooperation programmes (ITEC), the Indian government provided aid to developing countries in its fields of expertise. ITEC was the active realization of the great ideals of South-South cooperation. The projects fell under the purview of the Ministry of External Affairs and were carried out on a bilateral basis. For the year 1996 alone, for example, training courses were imparted to around seventy civil trainees from South-East Asia.[87]

In the specific framework of the partnership between India and the ASEAN, the first institutional dialogue, in January 1994, added science and technology as a new sector of cooperation. The research themes chosen were sophisticated materials, information technologies and biotechnology. In fact, the ASEAN was very keen to take advantage of India's know-how in these fields. There were already some programmes of cooperation between India and Malaysia, as well as Singapore and the Philippines, in the fields of health and education. Prestigious medical institutes, like the All India Institute of Medical Sciences or the Maulana Azad Medical College, were used to hosting Malaysian students.[88] In another example, the Chief Minister of the province of Malacca signed an agreement with the medical college of Manipal to set-up a similar establishment in its territory. In 1997, Malaysian clinics and private hospitals were allowed to recruit Indian nurses. Most of them were trained in institutes in south India, in particular in Kerala. Kuala Lumpur even considered allowing Indian doctors and professors of medicine to work in the country, as it suffered from a shortage of qualified staff in the medical sector.

In the IT field, India enjoyed a comparative advantage that was extensively used in the framework of its exchanges with South-East Asian countries. During his visit to Malaysia in August 1995, Prime Minister Rao concluded an agreement on the setting up of a computer software training institute in Kuala Lumpur. The centre was to train about 25,000 people in South-East Asia, over a five-year period. But India's private sector had already gone further. An Indian organization of international stature specializing in computer training, NIIT, had already opened a centre in Singapore in January 1994.[89] The establishment offered advanced training for high-level professional programmers, coming from the entire region. In early 1997, NIIT signed an agreement with the Indonesians of the YPLP Trust to offer its IT training services. Besides, a number of Singaporean companies associated with Indian IT firms. For example, HL Technology (HLT), the IT branch of the Hong Leong conglomerate, entered into a partnership with Kale Consulting, based in Mumbai. The Indian company therefore sent its technical staff to HLT's Singapore offices, to do programming work. In another example, Singapore International Airlines (SIA) delegated its computer data programming work to the Indian company, Damatics. The joint venture involved setting up a computer development centre on the premises of Damatics in Mumbai. Generally speaking, Indian software experts were highly in demand, traditionally in the West, but also, and increasingly, in East Asia. Singapore and Malaysia were the most active in attracting them. Indian computer programmers accounted for almost 60 per cent of the staff used in the Super Multimedia Corridor close to Kuala Lumpur.[90] An increasing number of Indian computer specialists emigrated to China, South Korea and Japan.

The establishment of Asian multinationals in India was the best pledge for the intensification of human flows between India and its eastern neighbourhood. Indeed, most of the time, Indian staff received training in the parent company. Moreover, some companies, such as Samsung, invested at the university level. Thus, Samsung's Indian subsidiary instituted a system of research allowances for students of Delhi's Indian Institute of Technology and Bangalore's Indian Institute of Science.[91] Besides the financing they were offered, IT students did a summer training programme in South Korea. In short, Samsung's initiative was aimed at investing in the human resources in India while offering more opportunities to Indian students and its own staff. Other Korean multinationals such as Daewoo or LG incorporated the establishment of research centres in their Indian subsidiaries within their investment projects. Multinationals set-up by NRIs also generated human resource flows. For instance, in the Indonesian firm, Indorama, most members of the technical and engineering staff were of Indian nationality. According to the management, it would be impossible to find qualified staff in Indonesia, which justified the expatriation of Indian staff. Thus, about 300 expatriate Indians worked in Indorama's different units in South-East Asia.[92] While Indorama was legally an Indonesian firm, in practice, it had a strong Indian spirit. As for the Polynsido group, the other Indonesian multinational of Indian origin, it too employed over 500 Indian expatriates and the highest echelons of the management communicated just as much in Bahasa Indonesia as in Tamil.[93] Finally, Indian companies of international stature also participated in human resource flows. India's major hotel groups recognized South-East Asia's expertise quite early on. Since 1982, the Taj Group had been holding training programmes, no longer just in Europe but also in South-East Asia. Oberoi followed the same logic and held training programmes for its own staff in Singapore, in Kuala Lumpur and Hong Kong, in 1997.

Lastly, a little more needs to be said about Singapore, insofar as it became an increasingly attractive pole for Indian expatriates. Whether they were of Indian origin or other nationalities, often Anglo-Saxon, they were numerous in the banking and financial sectors, in IT and engineering, as well as in the academia and journalism. Outside the academic environment, the presence of an expatriate Indian community was related to the large number of multinationals based in Singapore. The success of these Indians resulted from their mastery of English and their familiarity with the multinational work culture. They therefore conveyed the image of a cosmopolitan, highly qualified and competitive India, thereby contributing to a positive change in Singapore's perceptions with regard to India. Moreover, Singapore had adopted a deliberate policy of attracting the most qualified Indian experts, in order to sustain its economic regionalization efforts. The city-state's companies, which had both capital and expertise, lacked qualified manpower to develop their activities abroad. In this perspective, India represented a valuable and inexhaustible source of talent.[94]

At the Nonaligned Summit in Jakarta in 1992, Prime Minister Goh Chok Tong had offered Prime Minister Rao to recruit qualified Indians for working in either Singapore, or the offices of Singaporean companies abroad. The Economic Development Board of Singapore (EDB) had already organized several recruiting campaigns in India. In 1993, the EDB offered employment authorizations to 3,000 engineers, of whom 400 received a permanent resident status. The EDB conducted a fresh campaign in 1994 to recruit almost 240 Indian professionals for various multinationals based in Singapore. This desire to attract foreign talent was reaffirmed by Prime Minister Goh Chok Tong in his speech to the nation in August 1997. Singapore also intended to attract the region's most brilliant students. Indeed, Lee Kuan Yew called upon the city-state's most prestigious educational establishments to attract students from Hong Kong, Indonesia and India.[95] Besides, Singapore International Airlines and Neptune Orient Line offered scholarships for Indian students wanting to study in Singapore's universities. About fifty Indian students were selected each year. The scholarship often came with the condition of a three or six year stay in Singapore. There were also quite a large number of Indian students at the doctoral level, notably in engineering specializations. However, it must be noted that all Indian expatriates in Singapore were not necessarily qualified, a number of them worked as employees of service companies or as construction workers.

NOTES

1. During an AIBC meeting in 1997, Deepak Banker, the IAECC Chairman, asserted that India was developing on the basis of intra-regional complementarities as defined by the ' "flying geese" paradigm' (*ASEAN-India Business Council Meeting*, 14 October 1997, Singapore). In 1996, addressing India's new ASEAN partners, the Minister of External Affairs, I.K. Gujral, asserted, 'In terms of intra-industrial collaborations and production mobility, we hope to take part in the formation of flying geese in the Far East and South-East Asia' (I.K. Gujral, 7+10).
2. François Gipouloux, 'L'Asie Orientale: Un Nouvel Atelier Nippon?', in Gemdev, *L'intégration Régionale dans le Monde*, Paris: Karthala, pp. 45–62.
3. Glenn Hook, 'Japan and the Construction of Asia-Pacific', in A. Gamble and A. Payne, eds., *Regionalism and World Order*, London: Macmillan, 1996, p. 183.
4. *Monthly Public Opinion Surveys*, vol. XL, no. 10, July 1995.
5. *Blue Supplement of the Monthly Opinion Surveys of the Indian Institute of Public Opinion*, vol. XLII, nos. 5–6, February–March 1997.
6. The Indian industrial sector had actually got interested in Japanese management techniques in the early 1980s. However, the experience of the early 1980s often proved far from conclusive and India's interest in Japanese methods died quickly. The best-known example of the successful import of Japanese techniques is that of the company, Maruti Udyog Limited (MUL), which entered into a partnership with the car manufacturer, Suzuki, in 1984, to produce motor vehicles. See, ASSOCHAM, FICCI, *A Report on Nineteenth Joint Meeting of the India-Japan Standing Committees*, 18 April 1996, Hakone, Japan.
7. B.K. Karanjia, *Godrej: A Hundred Years 1897–1997*, vol. 2, New Delhi: Viking Penguin India, 1997. *Kaizen* is a process for the continuous improvement of production by each individual.
8. Quality improvement through management participation.
9. ASSOCHAM & FICCI, *A Report on Nineteenth Joint Meeting of the India–Japan Standing Committees*, 18 April 1996, Hakone, Japan.
10. CII, *Twelfth Indian Engineering Trade Fair in Retrospect*, 9–15 February 1997, New Delhi.
11. S.R. Batliboi & Co. and Ernst & Young Pvt. Ltd., *Pattern of Japanese Investment in India*, November 1996.
12. However, it must be pointed out that in the first half of the 1980s, a wave of Japanese investments swept into India, thanks to several collaborations in the automobile sector. In 1981, the public sector company, Maruti Udyog, entered into a partnership with Suzuki Motors, in accordance with the government's plan to develop a 'national car'.

Although the joint venture was immensely successful, enthusiasm waned in the second half of the 1980s. The liberalization measures launched in 1985 failed to attract Japanese investors, who had become sceptical due to the mediocre results achieved by the joint ventures established in the sector of light commercial vehicles.

13. *The Asian Wall Street Journal*, 18 March 1997.
14. *The Economic Times*, 16 April 1998.
15. CII, *Seminar on India-Korea Economic Cooperation, Proceedings*, New Delhi, 18 July 1995.
16. CII, *Workshop on 'Asia Vision 2000'*, Seoul, 15–26 May 1995.
17. World Trade Centre, *A Report on South Korea*, Bombay, July 1993.
18. R.R. Krishnan, *The Fifth India-Korea Conference*, 22 December 1994, New Delhi: India International Centre, p. 67.
19. Embassy of India in Seoul, *Monthly Round-up on Indo-Korean Economic Relations*, January 1996.
20. P.V. Satyanarayana, 'The Korean Invasion', *Business World*, 7 October 1997.
21. *Business India*, 1–14 June 1998.
22. Ibid., 22 September–5 October 1997.
23. *The Asian Age*, 24 November 1997.
24. *The Hindu*, 13 June 1997.
25. Ibid., 23 June 1999.
26. *The Economic Times*, 6 April 1998.
27. Meeting with Hyundai, Bombay, March 1998; Far Eastern Economic Review, 2 November 1995.
28. CMIE, *Foreign Trade and Balance of Payments,* July 1999, p. 326.
29. M. Ariff, 'Anatomy of Economic Reform Process: Regional Perspectives, Opportunities and Strategies', RGIS Project no. 16, 1996, *India, South East Asia and the USA: New Opportunities and Prospects for Cooperation,* Bangalore Conference Papers, 9–10 August 1995.
30. Interview, FICCI, New Delhi, April 1998.
31. The 'Country Committees' are groups of businessmen interested in a particular country, i.e. businessmen who have, or want to have, trade relations with the country concerned. Headed by a Chairman, they meet two to three times a year to discuss specific issues.
32. *India-ASEAN Commercial Directory*, compiled and published by Amarjit Singh, MBE, Advisor, the ASSOCHAM for the IAECC, 1st edn., New Delhi, 1996.
33. ASEAN-CCI, *Report of the Proceedings of the ASEAN-India Business Council*, 14–15 November 1996, New Delhi.
34. George Abraham, *Report on the Proceedings of the ASEAN-India Business Council-ASEAN Section Meeting*, 9 April 1996, Jakarta, Indonesia, Annex 5.

35. Ariff, 'Anatomy of Economic Reform Process'.
36. Indian Investment Centre (IIC), *Summary of Joint Ventures Abroad Approved up to 31 December 1995*. According to IIC's grouping, East Asia is composed of China, Hong Kong, Indonesia, South Korea, Malaysia, Mongolia, Philippines, Singapore, Thailand and Vietnam.
37. IIC, *Summary of Joint Ventures Abroad*, p. 1. If the joint ventures being set-up are also taken into account, Malaysia received Rs. 872,100 million until December 1995.
38. FICCI & ASSOCHAM, *Fourth Meeting of India-Malaysia Joint Business Cooperation Committees: A Report*, 10 April 1995, Kuala Lumpur.
39. World Trade Centre, *India and ASEAN*.
40. The Singapore Consortium is partly composed of NRIs: Thakral Invt. Holding, First Capital Corp., Khattar Hldg, Parameswara Hldg.
41. This figure does not truly reflect the exact nature of investment flows from ASEAN for two reasons. In the first place, Indian statistics do not provide a country-wise break-up of investments made by non-residents. But a considerable diaspora lives in South-East Asia, which may invest in India. These investment flows are classified under the heading NRI, rather than with reference to their country of origin. In the second place, the double taxation cancellation treaty between Mauritius and India makes it very advantageous to make investments via the island. That is why Mauritius continues to figure among India's highest foreign investors. Some Asian countries, such as Singapore, use the island as a base, thereby distorting the data. Moreover, 35 per cent of the investments that go through Mauritius apparently come from NRIs (*The Times of India*, 26 March 1998). One may therefore suppose that investments by NRIs from Singapore, Hong Kong and Malaysia take place in the name of the island. As for the United States, and United Kingdom, their investments would amount to seventeen per cent and fifteen per cent respectively, of Mauritius FDI in India. Mauritius also has extensive expertise with regard to India's complex regulations concerning FDI and investments by non-residents. That is also the reason why many investors choose to go through the island. In spite of these contingencies, Indian statistics give a fairly accurate idea of the evaluation of South-East Asian investment flows in India.
42. For purposes of comparison only, it may be pointed out that Hong Kong's investments in India were higher than those of Singapore in some years. In 1996 for example, they rose to Rs. 5,079 million against Rs. 3,198 million for Singapore. But Singapore proved to be more aggressive than Hong Kong overall: between 1991 and December 1997, the city-state was the thirteenth highest investor in India, while Hong Kong placed only nineteenth.
43. Actual investment flows from Hong Kong were sometimes higher than

those from Singapore. In 1995–6 for example, Hong Kong's actual investments stood at Rs. 3,346 million.

44. The best example was that of Parameswara Hldg, a company for investments in India run by Singapore Indians, which established a subsidiary in Mauritius. Conversely, an overestimating of the investments recorded on account of Singapore is possible, because these may have been made by the regional offices of multinationals based in the city-state.
45. For Malaysia, no data is available on actual investments.
46. High Commission of India in Malaysia, *Malaysian Joint Venture in India*, March 1998.
47. CMIE, *Monthly Review of Investment Projects*, May 1997.
48. CMIE, *Foreign Trade and Balance of Payments*, pp. 386–9.
49. Rajesh Mehta, 'Trade Policy Reforms, 1991–2 to 1995–6: Their Impact on External Trade', *Economic and Political Weekly*, 12 April 1997.
50. Behl and Mago, *India-ASEAN Trade Cooperation and Investment Opportunities*, p. 22.
51. Asher and Rajan, 'Singapore-India Economic Relations', p. 127.
52. *The Hindu*, 25 March 1998.
53. Interview, Canadian Imperial Bank of Commerce, June 1998.
54. *The Hindu*, 7 October 1997. As there is no stock exchange in Vietnam, most companies that are set-up there are registered in Singapore.
55. ITC Global's corporate office is in Singapore, Swiss Am Singapore is a branch of the Birla Group and Bloomsbury is held by Phoenix Overseas, a company based in New Delhi. Thanks to this award, the income tax rate imposed on these companies is just ten per cent, whereas the normal rate is twenty-seven per cent for international trade. Asher and Rajan 'Singapore-India Economic Relations', p. 162.
56. The public sector companies present there are the State Trading Corporation, MMTC and Shipping Corporation of India, among others. In the private sector, the major Indian industrial groups such as Godrej or Tatas already have offices in Singapore, as do ITC, Peerless Group, Kirloskars, Greaves, Ispat Alloys, Vedika Investment Services, Mastek, Sumeet, etc.
57. Behl and Mago, *India-ASEAN Trade Cooperation and Investment Opportunities*, p. 98.
58. Ibid., pp. 98, 132.
59. CMIE, *Foreign Trade and Balance of Payments*, p. 111.
60. NRIs Welfare Society of India, information brochure.
61. Among others, it had several members of Parliament with the Congress (I) leanings, a former Home Minister, Buta Singh, and Prof. S.S. Ahluwalia. The Board Committee also had journalists and lawyers among its members.

62. Deepak Singh, ed., *NRIs Directory, Hong-Kong, Japan, Singapore, Malaysia, Thailand, Philippines, Taiwan,* New Delhi: NRI Welfare Society of India, 1997.
63. These are persons of Indian origin but of Singaporean nationality, not the Indian expatriate community mentioned in the following point.
64. Interview, Salil Tripathi, *Far Eastern Economic Review*, Regional Economics Correspondent, Singapore, 10 June 1998.
65. Interview, SICCI, Singapore, 17 June 1998.
66. Parameshwara Holdings Ltd., *Report on Investments in India (to the Shareholders)*, 10 July 1997.
67. Keynote Address by Brigadier-General (NS) Lee Hsien Loong, Deputy Prime Minister, 'Integrating the Indian Economy into the World: A Singapore Perspective', in SICCI, *Global Indian Entrepreneurs Conference-India: The Uncaged Tiger, Summary of Proceedings*, Singapore, SICCI, 1996, Annex. B; Tan, 'Singapore's Foreign Direct Investment', *RIS Occasional Paper*, pp. 29–32.
68. Interview, *India Business Group*, Singapore, June 1998.
69. Interview, FICCI, New Delhi, 3 April 1998. The JBC with China, for instance, seemed to be very active because Indian businessmen were wary of venturing alone in this market.
70. *The Hindu*, 20 January 1998.
71. *Singapore Trade News Issue,* April 1997.
72. Interview, Malaysian Indian Chamber of Commerce, Kuala Lumpur, 3 June 1998.
73. Interview, Indian High Commission in Malaysia, Commercial Section, Kuala Lumpur, June 1998.
74. There were two other independent companies, including Indorama Synthetics held by the elder brother, O.P. Lohai, and based in India, and Indorama Chemicals, based in Thailand.
75. T.T. Meng, L.A. Meng, J.J. Williams, R. Zutshi, *Business Opportunities in India*, Nanyang Business Report Series, Singapore: Prentice Hall, 1997, p. 5.
76. *The Economic Times*, 10 July 1999. Almost 90 per cent of such deposits are received unclassified, of amounts under Rs. 10,000, from tourist expenditure or capital receipts. NRI transfers for family members or for repatriating savings, personal gifts or donations, constitute just 4 to 6 per cent of the total.
77. *Indian Recorder*, 26 August–1 September 1996.
78. ASSOCHAM, *FICCI Report on the 27th Joint Meeting of the India-Japan Business Cooperation Committees*, New Delhi, 13 November 1996.
79. *Indian Recorder*, 13–19 August 1994. The company planned to cover Vietnam, Hong Kong and South Korea.

80. Interview, Oberoi, Bombay, March 1998. To give an example, Oberoi's occupancy, according to the various nationalities, were as follows in 1997: 27 per cent of the clients were North American, 39 per cent were European, 13 per cent were South-East Asian and 9 per cent were from the Far East.
81. Interview, Singapore Tourism Promotion Board, official representative, Mumbai, 3 March 1998, Assistant Manager, Regional Tourism (South Asia & Oceania), 26 June 1998.
82. World Tourism Organization, *India—Top Destinations*, 1998, p. 80. In 1996, the market shares for the other regions, in descending order, were as follows: South Asia: 16 per cent, Middle East: 14 per cent, Europe (EU + East Europe): 14 per cent, North America: 12 per cent, Africa: 3 per cent.
83. Tourism Authority of Thailand, 'International Tourist Arrivals to Thailand by Nationality', in *Thailand Tourism Statistics*, 1997.
84. Singapore Tourist Promotion Board, *Tourism in Brief*, June 1997.
85. Interview, Indian High Commission in Kuala Lumpur, June 1998.
86. CMIE, 'Tourist Arrivals by Major Countries', in *Foreign Trade and Balance of Payments*, July 1999, pp. 454–5.
87. The breakdown was as follows: Indonesia: 15, Laos: 11, Malaysia: 4, Phil.: 2; Thailand: 8, Vietnam: 31.
88. Apparently, following a recent decision of the Supreme Court concerning admissions in vocational schools, it will be more difficult for Malaysian students to pursue their studies in India than in the past.
89. Asher and Rajan, 'Singapore-India Economic Relations', pp. 144-5.
90. B. Ghoshal, 'Indian Diaspora in South-East Asia and the Emerging Relations between India and ASEAN: An Economic Perspective', Working Paper for the Workshop co-organized by Centre for Study of National Security Policy, JNU (New Delhi), Centre de Sciences Humaines (New Delhi), in collaboration with Institute of Southeast Asian Studies (Singapore), *India-ASEAN Economic Relations*, New Delhi, 17–18 March 2001.
91. *The Times of India*, 5 March 1997.
92. Interview, Indorama, New Delhi, June 1999.
93. *Business India*, 6–19 October 1997, pp. 82–3.
94. G. Shantakumar, 'Human Resources Complementarities between Singapore and India: Formulating Strategy for a Win-win Situation', Y.M. Cheong and B.V.V. Rao, *Singapore-India Relations*, pp. 246–69.
95. *The Hindu*, 20 October 1997.

CHAPTER 3

Challenges to the Look East Policy

3.1 The Limitations of India's Economic Opening

Although it had begun well, the integration of India's economy with East Asia stood as a long-term process by the late 1990s. From the Indian side itself, and in spite of the determined efforts made by the nation's top echelons, serious organizational obstacles hampered the effective implementation of the Look East policy. Internal rivalries between different state departments came to the fore and the policies launched by the government, whether economic liberalization or economic diplomacy, were not as streamlined as the rhetoric would suggest. More so, these government plans did not carry along all the stakeholders to be involved in the process, especially the private sector. Asian investors did not fail to notice these multiple contradictions and found it difficult to remain optimistic, when faced with the uncertainties created by the Indian government's instability.

LACK OF COORDINATION

Cooperation between the different ministries did not occur as naturally as required for an efficient economic diplomacy policy. The Ministry of Foreign Affairs found it very difficult to integrate with the government's economic activities, and the Ministries of Commerce and Finance did not recognize its legitimacy in this matter.[1] Some Indian diplomats also regretted the fact that foreign postings were still under-utilized, whereas they ought to have been the backbone of economic diplomacy. The diplomatic corps also found itself handicapped by a shortage of staff, both at the intermediary and higher levels. To cite an example, the Indian High Commission in Singapore had to devote an increasing share of its manpower and time to play host to the various dignitaries visiting the city-state: central and state ministers, legislators, and even presidents of political parties. It reached such an extent that middle-level diplomats were obliged to neglect their normal work, including essential work related to trade and investment.[2] Indian diplomats still appeared to suffer from a lack of expertise in economic affairs. Yet, the Ministry of Foreign Affairs did attempt to depute its personnel to other ministries, in order to acquire additional skills. But the move was resisted both due to the reluctance of its personnel, who were little inclined to interchange postings in different departments, and the bureaucratic clan mentality, which made it difficult to share skills.

Within the business world, bitter rivalries put the three apex chambers of commerce and industry at loggerheads, with the youngest and the more dynamic CII on one side and the older and more traditional FICCI and ASSOCHAM on the other. Competition did not spare the new ASEAN-India Economic Cooperation Committee.[3] When, in 1993, Indian and ASEAN officials were laying the foundations of the sectoral partnership, they believed that it was necessary to integrate the private sector in the new dialogue. From the ASEAN side, an institution representing the business world had already been established: the ASEAN Chamber of Commerce. But the organization representing the Indian side proved fraught with problems. Far from collaborating to form a single representative body, the three chambers of the Union, on the contrary, unleashed intense competition along with hectic lobbying to obtain the status of the sole representative of the Indian private sector. Added to this rivalry was the divergent views held by the officials of the Ministry of Foreign Affairs, each one trying to promote the candidature of one of the three chambers of commerce.[4] These disagreements undoubtedly slowed down the execution of the whole cooperation machinery. As the deadline for the Indo-ASEAN dialogue compelled a solution, FICCI was designated to represent the Indian private sector at the Bali summit, in January 1994.

The mechanism finally decided upon was more of a compromise solution, in which the secretariat of the institution would be held by rotation on an annual basis by FICCI, ASSOCHAM and CII. The solution at least made it possible for all three chambers to be involved in the process. Though not an effective system, it did received the support of all the players concerned. But, the establishment of a rotating secretariat did not seem to prevent the rivalry between the chambers, which continued to trouble the institutional dialogue. Such lack of cooperation between the three chambers of commerce did not facilitate interaction between the government bodies and the business world, in the context of the Look East policy.[5] As some of the representatives of the three chambers confessed, the rotating secretariat system posed the problem of continuity of work in relationship with ASEAN.[6] It must be clarified that the recent character of the ASEAN-India Economic Cooperation Committee did not in itself suffice to explain the difficulties in coordination within the Indian private sector. A much older institution, the Japan-India Economic Cooperation Committee, also suffered from the incapability of the business world to ensure a coherent representation, with the Indian side hopelessly divided against itself. Its representative character was at times doubtful, especially when the Japanese partners met different business groups in succession, with each one claiming to represent the national interest.[7]

Apart from the organizational problems between the apex chambers, the Indian private sector still appeared to be very little involved in the institutional and the political process of cooperation. The Look East policy gave the impression of being a confidential initiative, of which the business world seemed to be quite ill informed.[8] Whereas they were aware of the policy, the private sector's representatives were quite often sceptical about it. To them, the Look East policy seemed to have all the hallmarks of a government policy, with a plethora of advertisements and displays of grand intentions. The officials' fascination for a rapprochement with Asia was thus qualified as a rhetorical exercise. To cite an example, they found fault with the initiatives of the joint commissions, accusing them of being highly ineffective. Admittedly, these intergovernmental institutions did create a policy framework that would eventually involve the private sector. But very often, the decisions taken did not go beyond lip service. Such was the case with the ambitious policy unfurled by the Indian government to build hospitals in Malaysia or the grand official plans to establish an Indian commercial office in one of the ASEAN countries. Moreover, the government's desire for a rapprochement with East Asia was entrusted to diplomats and, therefore, suspected of ensuing from political and security concerns rather than purely commercial reasons. Thus, there was a certain sense of disconnection, for the business community followed its own logic, which was essentially profit-driven. This underlying mismatch between the government's ambitions and the business world's attitude reflected a more general truth, i.e. the ill repute of the political leadership's elite. The private sector thus displayed a certain defiance *vis-à-vis* the government's resolve, as according to them, they were very tired of parliamentary instability and political intrigues.

The perception of the NRIs or Persons of Indian Origin living in Singapore was very specific in nature, with regard to the Look East policy, insofar as these individuals were well informed about New Delhi's policy towards this region. For most of them, this laudable initiative was unfortunately not pursued diligently enough by the Indian government. Apart from the discourse, the opening up to Asia was not based on a well-profiled or integrated strategy. The implementation of the avowed objectives was selective and did not concern itself with mobilizing the different stakeholders involved in Indo-Singaporean relations. Another recurrent theme was that the rapprochement with Asia came admittedly as a good initiative, but constituted just one of the cogs in the larger policy of globalization. And above all, there was no question of turning India's back to the West.

While it was true that Indian entrepreneurs evinced a growing interest in South-East Asia, it was probably due to the region's strong economic growth in the first place. Some businessmen ironically asserted that in the matter of 'Looking East', many of them were ahead of the decision-makers. From the point of view of some representatives of the private sector, the increase in trade flows between India and the East Asian economies was more the result of a natural phenomenon of profit-seeking and market forces rather than an aggressive and integrated policy.[9] The Look East policy thus appeared to be a general trend, bringing together different stakeholders, with each one following a different strategy. At the most, the business community was willing to grant that the government action had succeeded in creating a certain state of mind—a favourable climate for East Asia. However, the private sector did not necessarily consider this region a priority zone. Western markets still continued to attract them strongly. Besides, many Indian entrepreneurs believed that Japan dominated South-East Asian markets and that made competition very difficult in the region.[10] In 1999, a FICCI report observed that in India, there was a typical tendency to consider industrialized nations as more promising markets and to concentrate most of their energies to penetrate them. Analysts of the chamber of commerce regretted that Indian exporters had still not realized the importance of South-East Asian markets.[11]

All said and done, the link between the official Indo-ASEAN dialogue and the reality of trade flows seemed tenuous. Often, the private sector had little notion of the institutional cooperation processes taking place not only at government level but also between the chambers of commerce. It must perhaps be added that the relative indifference of the business world was due to the fact that their representative institution, the ASEAN-India Economic Cooperation Committee, was mainly composed of entrepreneurs who already had a foot in the South-East Asian door. This institution seems to have failed to create the dynamics of welcoming newcomers for reinforcing economic ties with ASEAN. It had, at best, bettered existing ties. Thus, at the committee's meeting in August 1997, the government delegation and representatives of the business world reckoned that, on the economic front, India had not gained sufficiently from its partnership with ASEAN.[12] They also indicated that on an individual basis, many Indian businesses had a profitable economic relationship with South-East Asia and they would be welcome to pass on their experience and success to the whole business community. In other words, the sentiment that emerged was that there was a disconnection between the institutional process and the realities of economic cooperation.

THE UNCERTAINTIES OF THE ECONOMIC REFORMS

The vagaries of Indian political life rendered the liberalization agenda rather unpredictable, and this could hardly please foreign investors. In fact, the country suffered from chronic governmental instability, largely due to the structural decline of the Congress party, which began in 1984. When the party came back to power in 1991, it headed a minority government. And while Prime Minister Rao's team headed towards reforms, it had to face considerable opposition from within the party. The Finance Minister, Manmohan Singh, managed to kick-start the liberalization regime in foreign trade and direct foreign investment, but vested interests that benefited from the days of the *licence raj* were ranged against him. These were industrialists from previously protected sectors and the authorities who granted licences, often through politicians, for purely electoral gains.[13] Rao's Congress (I) party finally lost the general elections in April 1996, leaving the economic reform process incomplete. Government regulations on FDI were still quite restrictive and needed to be improved. Manmohan Singh did, indeed, replace quantitative restrictions by tariffs whose levels he reduced gradually. But, in 1996, Indian tariff protection was still among the highest in the world. Lastly, the Finance Minister was unable to overcome the very strong opposition to his plan of dismantling the license regime on consumer goods. Thus, the Congress' defeat in 1996 put a question mark on the future of the reforms, for certain old parties coming to power could alter the process. To the right of the political spectrum, the BJP had never ceased to flay the Rao government's globalization policy, whereas most of the left formations maintained a rather confused position, traditionally imbued with anti-imperialist ideology, thus always likely to challenge the economic liberalization policy.

India's political instability and its repercussions on the future of the reforms were a continuous concern for East Asian investors. In contrast to the West, many in Asia believed that a strong and permanent political power was the hallmark of an efficient economy. As a keen observer of relations between New Delhi and Tokyo, expert Satu Limaye said, 'India's much celebrated democracy does not have the same resonance for Japanese as it does for most Westerners. Many Japanese privately agree with Singapore's Senior Minister Lee Kwan Yew that democracy impedes rather than facilitates economic growth.'[14] East Asian political and economic leaders would have nothing less than a stable and strong government in New Delhi, fully determined to accelerate the pace of liberalization. However, in 1996, the fractured political scene could only result in the formation of a coalition government. Such a formation, which normally last for barely over two years, would make the reform process all the more difficult.[15] Not surprisingly then, H.D. Deve Gowda's United Front government, which came to power in July 1996, was supported by a disparate coalition of thirteen parties. Though essentially a left of centre government, it chose the reformist P. Chidambaram as its Finance Minister and continued with economic liberalization. But, in early November 1997, the Congress party withdrew its support to the government during a vote of confidence in parliament. The United Front government fell in just a year and a half after taking over the helm of affairs. Consequently, certain projects with East Asian investments were deeply affected by these changes. During the post-ministerial conference at Kuala Lumpur in July 1997, Malaysian officials could no longer withhold their exasperation: 'What has shocked us is that even projects that were informally cleared by an Indian Prime Minister get frozen when a new team takes office. Is there no continuity in policy in Delhi?.'[16] And to cite an example, the Malaysian highway project that was cleared by the Congress government was shown the red light when Deve Gowda's Janata Dal took over the reins.

The fall of the United Front government in November 1997 seemed to reinforce the feeling that the liberalization process was flagging. The team in power, under the leadership of I.K. Gujral, found itself paralysed till the elections, which were to be held in March 1998. Not only could no decision be taken on reforms till that date, but furthermore, the electoral campaign did not indicate that any of the major parties would be capable of proposing a coherent economic policy. The discussions were no longer about a reversal of the reform process, as would have been the case during the 1996 election, but about what direction it should be given. The editorial of the daily, *The Hindu*, revealed its concern, 'More than six years after the reform process began, there is a distinct uneasiness across the political spectrum with aspects of economic liberalization.'[17] Every coalition had reservations about certain elements of the past and future liberalization programmes. The confusion was basically due to the fact that while it was unthinkable to return to the era of a controlled economy, at the same time, there was also a reluctance to embark upon the second phase of reforms, which should logically have followed the programme launched in 1991. Therefore, political formations adopted an economic agenda that was increasingly dictated by vested interests. The BJP was quite adept at this game and became the spokesperson for the most protectionist business interests. The Indian companies that felt threatened by the opening up of the Indian economy gladly took refuge in the concept of *swadeshi*. In the BJP rhetoric, this concept meant 'a preference for national products'.[18] In other words, while the BJP was in favour of the liberalization of the domestic market, it opposed the globalization of the Indian economy, especially the massive and indiscriminate inflow of foreign capital.

South-East Asian countries were particularly sensitive to the lack of transparency in the Indian decision-making system. Economic and political leaders discussed the dimensions of factional power games without being able to disentangle the skeins of their influence. They were mainly concerned by the rapport between the BJP and the business world, and wondered whether the big industrial families supported or not the opening up of India's economy. Most of Singapore's economic experts felt that without a return to political stability, they would not be able to achieve their investment plans. Thus, they preferred to adopt a wait and watch policy during pre-electoral periods, especially during the March 1998 elections. Indeed from the city-state's viewpoint, BJP's *swadeshi* rhetoric was far from reassuring.[19] Malaysia and Thailand found themselves in the same uncertain situation.[20] During the CII's Partnership Summit in January 1998, Thailand's Vice Prime Minister, Dr Panitchpakdi, did not hide his irritation *vis-à-vis* the Indian reform process: 'We are watching the Indian economic reforms with awe and apprehension. Reforms need consensus, but in India there is no consensus—I am being blunt.'[21]

Thus, when the March 1998 elections brought the BJP to power, the morale of East Asian investors was down as was their general perception about relations with India. First and foremost, the Hindu Nationalist Party headed a heterogeneous coalition, which clouded any predictions about the reform process. In addition, the BJP election manifesto had proclaimed that it would continue the liberalization policy on the *swadeshi* platform, so that Indians would be the first beneficiaries of change.[22] In this scheme of things, the national industry had to be protected from any excessively abrupt opening up to international competition and foreign investments were limited to play a minor role in the economy. They would, however, be permitted in the crucial infrastructure sectors (ports, energy and roads) and for promoting high-end technology exports. In the consumer goods sector, media and insurance, the inflow of foreign capital was likely to be restricted. Theoretically, the BJP did not foresee the opening of Indian economy to the rest of the world before ten years. In Singapore, a study conducted by the Singapore Trade and Development Board (STDB) in June 1998, forecasted that the 1998–9 BJP budget was likely to affect exports from the city-state, due to additional taxes of four per cent imposed on imported goods. While Singaporean investors still bore India's potential in mind, they at that point no longer wanted to commit themselves. The uncertainty surrounding the BJP government thus perpetuated the wait and watch attitude. Those who already had a foot in the door in India continued their projects, while those who intended to invest preferred to wait.

Another major hurdle for foreign investors was the conservative spirit of the Indian administrative machinery. The bureaucracy that had for a long time prospered under the controlled economy found it difficult to accept the loss of power brought about by the economic liberalization process. Thus, the implementation of policies was slow, opaque and chaotic. Like most foreign investors in India, East Asians complained about the maze of the administrative system, whose functioning was devoid of transparency, and deplored its rigidity. Many Japanese investors regretted that the deregulation mindset had not yet percolated to the lower levels of the administration, nor had it been really imposed at the level of the states.[23] They were also angered by the delay their companies suffered during the process of awarding investment projects. Similarly, at the post-ministerial summit of July 1997, ASEAN officials aired their concerns about the slow authorization procedures for various projects.[24] Singapore's representatives complained especially about the particularly long and complicated registration process for foreign companies.[25] These investors coming from a country known for the efficiency of its administrative machinery could not but be baffled by the complexity of India's bureaucratic practices. The same was the case with other East Asian countries who, due to their economic growth, strove hard, in those days to present a model of good governance, i.e. an efficient management of public affairs. George Yeo, Singapore's Minister of Information and Arts, thus qualified India's bureaucracy as 'suffocating' and, drawing a comparison between the Indian and Chinese business environment, said, 'While in China, the problem is a lack of institutionalization, in India, the problem is perhaps one of too much institutionalization. The bureaucracy in India can be suffocating.'[26] In the same vein, former Prime Minister Lee Kuan Yew believed that in China, it was sometimes enough to contact the mayor or the party secretary to remove an obstacle, whereas in India, the legal system and bureaucratic rigidity could boomerang negatively on the foreign investor.[27]

Lastly, problems of corruption were often associated with bureaucratic hurdles and political intrigues. The phenomenon even seemed to take on a new dimension in the new context of the economic reforms.[28] In fact, it was the credibility of the liberalization process that seemed to be tainted by many corruption cases that emerged on a daily basis. East Asian investors undoubtedly played up their indignation at this practice—at least, until the 1997–8 financial crash that revealed their own failings. However, in the case of Singapore, investors sensed a real vulnerability in the Indian context, as most of the heads of governmental agencies were very attached to the ideals of public service and were at a loss when they had to pay off Indian politicians. From this perspective, Singaporeans did not have the endurance of Western companies, which were prepared to lose ten years to get into the Indian market. However, the same Singaporean investors admitted that similar problem of under-the-table payments existed in China and Vietnam. But in India, they confessed to being particularly lost due to the vagaries of the bureaucracy, which created unheard-of situations, such as the cancellation of signed contracts and contradictory judgements given by different administrative tribunals.

The failure of the Tata-SIA (Singapore International Airlines) investment project illustrated a good number of the pitfalls of the reform policy. Most of the Singaporeans involved in this affair still remember the misadventure of this attempt at a joint venture.[29] High profile media coverage blew the matter out of proportion and symbolized, for the city-state, the various stumbling blocks in the Indian market. The initial project planned to create a domestic aviation company that seemed promising, for it was a joint venture with Tata, the first family of Indian industry, and SIA, one of the most viable airlines in the world.[30] The Tata Group and SIA were to hold a forty per cent stake each in the future company, while Indian institutional investors were to hold the remaining twenty per cent. But, the multiple turnarounds that plagued the project's licensing process between 1995 and 1998 highlighted the lack of coordination between the different arms of the Indian administration in the absence of a clearly defined policy, as well as the changes of mind due to changes in government (no less than four) and the influence of protectionist groups on the final decision. The Foreign Investment Promotion Council (FIPC), the tribunal attached to the Ministry of Industry that was authorized to permit investment projects, actually granted permission to the Tata group and its Singapore partner twice (in February 1995 and December 1996). But each time, the Ministry of Civil Aviation put a spoke in the wheel by coming up with a new regulation at the last minute, driving Tata and SIA to modify their application for permission. To make it worse, the affair rapidly became enmeshed in political stakes and the Tata-SIA project became a veritable battle in the trenches within the Deve Gowda coalition government, between the supporters of liberalization (Ministries of Finance, Industry and Foreign Affairs) the protectionists or nationalists (Ministry of Civil Aviation and, in this instance, the Prime Minister himself). The lobbying against Tata also regrouped CEOs of domestic airlines, parliamentarians, former civil aviation ministers and many trade union federations. The Tata-SIA partnership was indeed suspected of being a Trojan horse for international companies in the domestic aviation sector. Under the BJP government, the Civil Aviation Minister would oppose the FIPB granting permission no less than four times after examining the file. On 1 September 1998, the group's managing director eventually announced that the project of setting up a domestic airline was abandoned. Weary of waiting for authorizations for three years, he blamed the government's and bureaucracy's doggedness in this matter.[31] The failure of this major project clearly revealed the influence of protectionist groups both in the political class and the business world.

3.2 East Asias' Misgivings about India

In East Asia, perceptions inherited from the past had a long-lasting impact and could not be easily wished away by the latest charm offensive launched by New Delhi. The enthusiasm of the business circles for India started faltering in 1997. Their cold-shouldering was evident, independently of the financial crisis of July in the same year. It was due to the Indian context itself and, especially, the multiple difficulties encountered by Asian investors whose many projects came to be blocked or aborted. Therefore, the initial distrust that the East Asian private sector entertained about the Indian market continued to prevail. Also, material obstacles such as inadequate infrastructure in transportation marginalized India in the Asian regionalization process.

A Disappointing Economic Opening Up

In Singapore, the optimism of the first half of the 1990s came to be replaced by a more circumspect attitude, mixed with a feeling of disappointment. In 1997 and 1998, according to a STDB official, the priority accorded to India would be about 'intermediary', whereas it topped the list from 1993 to 1995.[32] Contextual parameters partly explained this slowdown. Although Singapore considered that it was spared, relatively speaking, the financial crisis that shook South-East Asia instilled a climate of uncertainty that was not very conducive for investments. But, above all, it was the developments of the Tata-

SIA affair that dampered the investors' morale. SIA was, in fact, an important economic player of the city-state and its perceptions influenced the business community as a whole. In this connection, a certain exasperation about the malfunctioning of Indian bureaucracy cropped up within the company. Apart from the failed project with Tata, SIA was worried about its future activities in India and, above all, feared the cancellation of contracts that had already been signed, on the granting of air routes. Some of the officers admitted to feeling powerless when confronted with the lack of transparency in India's decision-making system. They did not even know which tribunal to appeal to in case of a problem of interpretation of contracts. They also added that, sometimes, there was a situation of conflict whose nature and causes they were unable to understand.[33] Thus, for SIA, the most disarming part was the absence—interpreted as a refusal—of any communication from Indian authorities. Therefore, the company's managers felt they were working blindfolded, with the additional frustration that apart from the reversals, which they could endure, there was no learning process here either. Lastly, SIA's problems were not a unique case: in addition to the bogging down of the Bangalore International Airport case, there were several others, such as the uncertainties surrounding the 'Chennai corridor',[34] the Hotel Radisson mishaps in Delhi[35] and disappointments in cooperation in the tourism sector.[36] The recurrent misadventures of these Singaporean projects, theoretically large-scale ones, were extensively covered by the media and convinced a large number of the city-state's investors that the Indian environment was unfavourable. Conversely, Indo-Singaporean *success stories* that could counteract the distressing visibility of these problematic cases in the city-state were very rare. Only the opinion of the investors involved in bilateral relations and the dissemination of information on the success of particular projects could determine the investors' state of mind *vis-à-vis* a market.

Malaysian investors also approached India with grand plans for the highway sector. But the dithering by Indian authorities put an end to their illusions. The Renong group started its first negotiation for various projects in 1993. In 1995, the Malaysians offered to invest forty million dollars to make a detailed study of Indian National Highways. But the Indian Ministry of Transport later changed its orientations, and nothing concrete happened afterwards.[37] Malaysian investors finally had to content themselves with segments of highways. Moreover, numerous delays in project finalization and in awarding contracts made the credibility of the process suspect and escalated costs for the Malaysian group.[38] Thai pioneers in India, such as the multinationals CP and Gerondine, had similar discouraging experiences. These groups encountered such problems in entering the Indian market that other potential investors preferred to remain on their guard.[39] The CP group's experience would have also contributed to spread the message that it was easier to invest in China. It therefore looked like the Thai Look West policy basically ensued from the desire of political decision-makers in Bangkok. Like India's Look East policy—but on an even larger scale—the business world hardly followed the government's policies. Thailand's investments in India occurred somewhat by default, the favourite destinations being South-East Asia, Europe, Japan and the United States.

From 1997 onwards, South-East Asian officials communicated the dissatisfaction of their business communities. At the post-ministerial conference of July 1997, ASEAN officials displayed their unhappiness and warned India that it was likely to miss ASEAN's 'business bus'.[40] One of the Association's representatives declared, 'Today, the cool reception given to our business proposals is resulting in a downswing in the interest ASEAN countries showed towards India during 1991–6'. The negative attitude was further defined in Dato Ajit Singh's speech at the CII summit in 1998. The ASEAN's Secretary General regretted that despite all the efforts put on both sides, the investment and trade turnover still remained much lower than what it ought to be.[41] The India-ASEAN partnership was recognized as having an immense potential for cooperation, but South-East Asian officials believed that it was very difficult to make it rise to its real heights. For some of them, especially those posted in India, India's Look East policy and good intentions were nothing but a rhetorical exercise and rarely implemented expression of intent.[42]

Perhaps the disappointment felt by South-East Asian investors was also a result of their high demands and their excessive impatience. As Jean Coussy correctly observed, what East Asian countries expected from India was 'a liberalism higher than they themselves had shown during the initial years' of their own opening onto the world market.[43] The Japanese private sector, for example, could not stop deploring the fact that India's reform process continued to trail behind that of South-East Asia. Thus, Japanese investors gave the impression of wanting to right away find conditions similar to those offered by the dragons. As early as in 1993, the former Japanese

Ambassador to India in New Delhi, Eijora Noda, explained: 'Success stories of ASEAN countries welcoming Japanese investment with adequate infrastructure are already known in India but it may be useful if further studies of Japanese joint-ventures in ASEAN countries be made by Indian business circles.'[44] The report given by the consultants Batliboi and Ernst and Young in 1996 did not show any changes in the perceptions of Japanese companies. Their standards still remained in the South-East Asian economies and they wanted to see Indian conditions that were at least as favourable. The study concluded with the following report: 'The Japanese companies felt that the Indian Government should follow the example of other South-East Asian countries in providing an appropriate environment and adequate range of industrial support facilities and technical support services to enable industry to function effectively.'[45]

Consequently, India's hesitations regarding its reform policy were little understood by Japanese investors. In 1992, Tokyo had even taken the initiative to indicate the methods to follow to make the country more attractive. During this first official Japanese mission, twenty-one demands were made, aimed at improving the environment for Japanese investors. New Delhi gave a favourable reply to most of them, except two points perceived as essential by the Japanese: the liberalization of the labour market[46] and permission for hundred per cent direct foreign investment for equity participation. During the second official mission in 1994, the Japanese delegation was put on the defensive *vis-à-vis* its Indian counterparts' overt irritation. New Delhi refused in no uncertain terms any concessions on the two points the Japanese were insisting on: the exit policy and hundred per cent foreign investment. Thus, a climate of mistrust and misunderstanding surrounded the dialogue between the two countries. The Indians were dissatisfied with the limited capital flow coming from Japan. They felt the Japanese wanted to avoid taking any risks and expected to enjoy special treatment.[47] But the notion of special treatment was not often accepted in India, even though the Finance Minister, P. Chidambaram, had announced during his visit to Tokyo, in November 1996, that a special cell would be set-up in the FIPB to attend to Japanese investments. But no formal appointments were made, which confirmed the doubts of the Japanese investors with respect to India's promises.[48] The other bone of contention between India and Japan was on capital account convertibility. In fact, Japanese businessmen complained that they could not repatriate their capital as easily as from other countries, and that they did not have faith in Indian insurance companies. The government's insistence on a high level of indigenization, in spite of lacunae in the local sub-contracting industry, was also another point of friction.[49]

ASEAN business circles had also requested that the Indian programme of reforms be accelerated. Right from the first ASEAN-India Economic Cooperation Committee meeting in February 1995, they also demanded a nodal agency that would look after investments originating from their member states.[50] But this type of demand for special treatment met with the same rigidity as the Japanese experienced. India replied that the best solution for South-East Asian investors would be to enter into a joint venture with a local partner, in order to obtain authorizations quickly, without getting lost in the maze of administrative procedures. Another ASEAN hobbyhorse was a more liberal aviation policy. But it proved difficult to obtain concessions in this matter too. In general, ASEAN representatives pointed out that India should 'instil greater confidence in the minds of ASEAN investors'. In other words, only new liberalization measures, implemented at a rapid pace, could step up economic relations with South-East Asia.

But faced with these demands, India's representatives continued to emphasize the constraints of its democratic machinery and advised foreign investors to be patient and understanding with India's own pace of reforms. Far from being satisfied, South-East Asians sometimes came to doubt the non-discriminatory nature of selection procedures for foreign investment projects. At the post-ministerial summit in July 1997, some ASEAN officials complained informally of being at the receiving end of tacit discrimination in India.[51] Some of them had the feeling that their companies were not dealt with on the same terms as those applied to European or North American counterparts. Malaysia, particularly, could hardly appreciate questions raised on an informal agreement for one of its television channels to beam its programmes to India. An official said: 'We hear that the new (post-Congress) government is against the Malaysian company (which incidentally has very close links to the ruling UMNO party) beaming services to India because of cultural pollution. Are Asian programmes considered polluting? What about shared cultural values?' And they did not fail to underline that Western companies had the monopoly over the television market in the foreign sector.

In Singapore's case, it should be added that investors failed to understand why it was so difficult to transplant their standards in

Indian conditions. Some, therefore, put up too high a price tag, not realizing that India preferred less expensive options. In this sense, the city-state experienced more difficulties than Malaysian or Thai investors. For Singapore, the disappointment was much greater than for others, as their businessmen initially believed that they could make a fast buck in India.[52] In spite of the many contacts between the two countries, it appeared that there was a mismatch in the Indian and the Singaporean approach to the issue of investments. Quite often, Singapore—and, in general, all the ASEAN countries—took a short-term interest in India. Therefore they did not hesitate to show their impatience *vis-à-vis* a country that always held a long-term vision. In comparison, China and Vietnam offered quicker profits, which could partly explain how these two countries succeeded in mobilizing much more capital originating from South-East Asia than India.

MAJOR PSYCHOLOGICAL BARRIERS

Whether they were from Japan, Thailand, Malaysia or Singapore, all major business representatives underlined the fact that there was insufficient information about the opportunities on offer in India throughout the 1990s. The lack of knowledge was as serious as their perceptions, which were influenced by the often negative experience of the past. Thus, a joint venture between the Anand and Toshiba groups left a scar of scepticism in the minds of Japanese investors with respect to India. Formed in the early 1970s to manufacture dry batteries, the company encountered management problems, an inability to procure raw material and a bad distribution network, all at the same time. It had to suspend its operations in September 1991, at a time when India was launching its open economic policy. And since it was one of the first collaborative ventures between India and Japan, the Anand and Toshiba groups' story was taken as a case study—unfortunately—by investors eyeing the Indian market. All through the 1990s, it turned out that Japanese industrialists were not fully aware of the economic reforms implemented by New Delhi. They believed that the country was not a growth market, especially compared to South-East Asia or China, and that it was not capable of absorbing many of their industrial products and consumer goods.[53] India certainly enjoyed a greater visibility in the Japanese media, but the image retained was that of a mysterious and mystic country, subject to numerous epidemics.

Even in Singapore, the South-East Asian country that was most interested in the Look East policy, India remained a distant country. The authors of the *Business Opportunities in India* guidebook, which was meant for Singapore business community declared, 'India still remains an enigma'. And they also underlined that the lack of knowledge propagated a 'fear of the unknown'[54] in business circles. India still suffered from a negative image and extensive efforts in information and promotion remained to be accomplished. Furthermore, India was considered a vast country, with a galloping population and endemic poverty. Singapore's business circles were not yet aware of the level of development reached by the Indian private sector. Everywhere else in South-East Asia, information on Indian liberalization remained limited during the 1990s. In January 1998, the ASEAN Secretary-General, Dato Ajit Singh, was worried that even businessmen from the Indian diaspora had very little knowledge about the reforms.[55] How, then, could it be different for others who did not have specific ties with India? Consequently, stereotypes persisted and spread the image of an underdeveloped country turned in on itself. Very few East Asians knew about the technological progress achieved by India and the technological and scientific expertise available in the country. For them, India appeared unfit to offer anything that they could not procure elsewhere. Unfavourable comparisons were made between Indian and Japanese or NIC products, overlooking the difference in import costs. This contempt was also related to the presence of underprivileged communities of Indian origin in these countries, which reinforced the clichés of a poor India. New Delhi had thus to step up its promotional effort with respect to the East Asian business communities, through systematic participation in International Fairs, and a greater dissemination of information. In other words, India had a long way to go before building up a reputation of being a favourable destination for foreign investors. This conclusion highlighted the inadequacies of the Look East policy, especially as it was described at first as a public relations exercise.

Added to the lack of updated information on India's economy was the incomprehension that could arise out of differences in business culture.[56] A section of the Indian business community had certainly failed to take note of the specific practices of their counterparts. In its relations with Japan, this gap was particularly evident. From the Indian point of view, the Japanese built in too many precautions in their investment policy. They acted with excessive circumspection and elaborated painfully detailed plans. Negotiations with the Japanese were thus considered tortuous and slow-moving. This incomprehension was largely due to different decision-making systems in either country. In India, the government made decisions and instructions were followed down to the lowest structure of the organization. In Japan, decision-making was a consensus building measure, thus slower. In a collaborative framework, the cult of excessive secrecy and the Japanese clan mentality was deplored. The reserved nature of the Japanese was not much appreciated and they were often reproached for barely willing to share their experience with their Indian counterparts. These prejudices were partly formed during the trial of strength that opposed the two partners of the Maruti-Suzuki company. Though often cited as a model of success, the management of the joint venture company was often beset with tensions after 1993. The Indian government especially reproached the Japanese for not transferring the latest technology and delaying the spare parts indigenization programme. The company officials blamed the management style practised by Suzuki, describing it as 'very authoritarian'.[57] These divergences revealed that India knew very little about Japanese business practices and culture.

Conversely, the Japanese side felt the same lack of familiarity. Thus, the Batliboi and Ernst and Young study showed that for forty-four per cent of Japanese entrepreneurs interviewed, the different business mindset and culture constituted major obstacles for trade. Identifying suitable partners was a difficult exercise in the Indian context. To cite an example, Japanese companies claimed that they followed a longer-term perspective than their Indian counterparts. The importance the Japanese attached to personal and lasting bonds made them feel closer to the Chinese business culture and created a gap with Indian practices, seen as closer to the Westerners.[58] Stereotypes were long-lived in Japan, where Indians had the reputation of being talkative, little inclined to listen and given to debate when it was required to find a consensus. The loquacious nature of Indians was, therefore, interpreted as a lack of credibility. It was true that the fluency of Indian businessmen in English put their Japanese interlocutors at a disadvantage during negotiations, and could be interpreted as arrogance.[59] Apart from this, Japanese businessmen considered the Indian business community to be intelligent on the whole, albeit loud-mouthed and disorganized, with very few ethical values.

There were also significant misunderstandings between the Indian and Singaporean business circles. These remarks by the authors of the *Business Opportunities in India* were revealing: 'Ask a Singapore businessman who has dealings with India and he is more likely to say that Indians are complicated.'[60] Therefore, 'understanding Indians' perhaps constitutes 'the major hurdle to cross while investing in India'. And to underline this, they gave the example of the different connotations attached to the term 'trust': 'To the Indians, the word "trust" corresponds exactly with that contained in the *Oxford English Dictionary*, namely "a firm belief in the reliability or truth or strength of a person or thing". To the Chinese, however, the word "trust" had a deeper meaning as it also embodies the concept of timeliness including punctuality at meetings and in meeting deadlines and payments.'[61]

The guide concluded on a tolerant note: 'It is important when doing business in India not to impose conditions that one is familiar with in Singapore. Allowing for leeway and flexibility is essential when investing in India.' Most Singaporean investors however talked about a sense of frustration with regard to Indian proposals, which, according to them, remained pending. Therefore, they concluded that their Indian interlocutors were undoubtedly gifted for public relations, but they regretted that beyond the rhetoric and the enthusiasm flaunted, few projects were achievable and few promises made were implemented.

In most other East Asian countries, the Indian business community suffered from a certain lack of credibility.[62] Indian companies were often suspected of following a short-term strategy, aiming to make quick profits, rather than establishing a long-term economic relationship. In Thailand and the Philippines, the Indian business world inspired little trust.[63] This perception was influenced by the presence of a diaspora in these two countries that indulged at a certain time in usury. Everywhere, it was the lack of Indian reliability that was condemned. South-East Asian business communities also complained about delays in delivery schedules, the absence of after sales services and products of a mediocre quality. Even the Koreans warned their potential investors in India. In one of their recommendatory guides, the Korean government agency for the promotion of trade and investment underlined the laxity of their Indian counterparts, who were often devoid of any sense of responsibility. And the guidebook added that if there were complications in an agreement, the hierarchical superiors were inclined to disown any responsibility, maintaining that the subordinates had acted independently of the management. It was, therefore, better to approach the Managing Director right at the beginning.[64]

Finally, North-East Asian investors were exercised over the inertia of the Indian corporate culture. At a time when Japanese management had become popular in India, Japanese or Korean investors, on their part, highlighted the disparities. The Korean managers of Hyundai stressed, above all, on the lethargy of the Indian corporate culture, as compared to their country.[65] The staff found it difficult to adapt to the standards imposed by their Korean partners, especially where working hours and punctuality were concerned. But they added that while adaptation levels were slow, it did take place. According to North-East Asian managers, the laxity and fatalist attitude of factory workers hampered the pace of development, as well as the process of quality improvement and innovation. Some Japanese added how difficult it was to manage factory hands, who were undisciplined and heterogeneous.[66] Coordination and teamwork were difficult to achieve in a stratified society. Low worker productivity and frequent friction in industrial relations were discouraging factors for the Japanese. Thus, in terms of productivity the value added per worker in the Indian manufacturing sector was just one-tenth of what it was in Japan, and one-fourth that of Singapore. Interestingly, India drew attention to the fact that it had the second largest pool of manpower in the world, at low cost. But if more critical parameters were included, such as productivity, quality and competence, India's manpower was not a strong enough point to attract investors. The country lacked skilled workers in developing sectors and the lack of education made it difficult for them to adapt to new technologies. In other words, the myth of Indian manpower was fading.[67]

Lastly, differences in the standard of living were added to the differences in business practices and corporate culture. Living conditions in India were often described as difficult. Most of the expatriate Asians based in the country found the environment not very favourable and declared that they experienced problems in adapting to it. For sixty per cent of the Japanese companies interviewed by Batliboi and Ernst and Young, difficult living conditions in India were a real hurdle. Residential and hotel accommodation were deemed insufficient and overpriced. Lastly, the Japanese community in India frequently cited the impossibility of finding Japanese cuisine as a major disadvantage. More specifically, regulations and restrictions imposed on the import of Japanese food, especially rice, made life difficult. For many expatriates from Singapore, staying in India was an unpleasant thought. Many investment firms were exercised over the difficulty of finding employees willing to expatriate themselves for a long period, in India as well as in China and Vietnam. The comforting, planned and orderly world of the city-state stood, in fact, in stark contrast with the changing, unpredictable and uncontrollable Indian environment.

GEOGRAPHICAL DISTANCES AND LACK OF COMMUNICATION NETWORKS

The geographical distance separating India from Japan constituted a major stumbling block for high capital inflows. For 89 per cent of the Japanese businessmen surveyed by Batliboi and Ernst and Young, distance was the main reason for the low level of Japanese investments in India. Japanese business houses traditionally preferred to invest in neighbouring countries due to their geographical proximity. Therefore, they had until then targeted South-East Asia and China. Of late, Vietnam was becoming a popular destination. The preference for proximity could be explained by the general structure of Japanese production processes, wherein manufacturers depended heavily on a vast supplier network. The lack of good quality local suppliers in developing countries constrained them to fall back on domestic suppliers. Therefore, it was imperative that they remained close to Japan. This reasoning was all the more evident in the case of SMEs. The latter represented approximately 1 per cent of Japan's direct investment in India. Access to the subcontinent seemed to be more difficult compared to most other East Asian countries, and even compared with Western Europe or North America.

While distances are not so great between India and South-East Asia, major obstacles to cross-regional flows nonetheless remained. Regionalization through the movement of people was still in its infancy. South-East Asian business communities complained about inadequate air links between India and the region and felt that there were not enough direct flights to various ASEAN capitals. They also complained about the difficulty of finding seats on domestic flights and the lack of hotel infrastructure.[68] In addition, there was a demand for the development of the flow of goods by air (cargo). Kolkata was a good example, as it could occupy the position of a central hub for the trade in goods between India and South-East Asia. But the services and equipment at the airport were not equal to the ambition of the West Bengal government. The warehouses reserved for goods to be exported lacked cruelly in space and suffered from a chaotic management. Delays in the delivery of goods were a recurrent feature and the frequency of international flights was insufficient.[69] As for maritime transport, inadequate equipment at the Indian ports put the brakes on the regionalization potential of the east coast. Indian companies did not have enough warehouses at their disposal in Singapore's port to gain from its position as a hub and reexport to other Asian countries.[70] Similarly, cooperation between the Malaysian ports of Penang and Klang and the ports of Vishakhapatnam and Chennai was not very well developed.[71] India's cargo capacity was inadequate, especially for maritime trade between the export promotion zones on the east coast and South-East Asia.

Lastly, the prevailing surface transport did not link India and South-East Asia very effectively. Bangladesh, the north-east Indian states and Myanmar formed an enclosed and under-developed area, especially with regard to communication infrastructure. Not easily accessible, this space represented a veritable obstacle to efficient land connections between India and South-East Asia. An ambitious plan for a South Asian rail corridor linking Myanmar, Bangladesh, India, Pakistan and Iran was much thought of, but it appeared to be difficult to implement.[72] In the meanwhile, there were no direct rail link between India and Myanmar. As for the road network, it begged to be developed. The main link between India and Myanmar connected the two frontier towns of Tamu, in Myannar, and Moreh, in Manipur. But, serious tension prevailed in these areas, as they were prey to different insurrectionist movements. Moreover, smuggling was rampant in this region. In November 1997 for example, the Rangoon government decided to close the frontier post for a month, in reprisal for the agitation launched by the Samata party that was protesting against drug smuggling.

In spite of these difficulties, the ambitious Asian highway plan was still alive. According to the ESCAP regional bureau officials, based in Bangkok, the section linking Singapore to Malaysia and Thailand had already been completed. In late 1997, a bridge linking Thailand and Myanmar was opened to traffic. But, the section linking South and South-East Asia was weighed down with various problems that delayed the implementation of the project. Myanmar insisted that the highway entry point, at Tamu in its territory, should originate from north-east India, i.e. the Indian town of Imphal, and not from South-East Bangladesh. Thus, the Imphal-Tamu sector was agreed upon, but the Bangladesh link still continued to pose problems. Thailand was financing the construction of the highway in the eastern part of Myanmar, whereas India was helping out with the western section. During the 1990s, Indian authorities indeed realized the great importance of investing in the communication network linking the north-east of the country to South-East Asia, via Myanmar. In 2001, India finally inaugurated the frontier road linking the town of Moreh, in Manipur, to Tamu on the other side of the frontier, up to Kalenmyo, the first nodal point in Myanmar's road network. Major projects have been under consideration since the end of 2001 to extend this route to Thailand in order to create a 'transport corridor' between India and Thailand.

3.3 The Look East Policy Challenged by the Asian Crisis

To the difficulties slowing down India's integration with East Asia, whether institutional, political or psychological, were added three important events that were *a priori* not favourable to a rapprochement: the Asian crisis that was triggered in mid-1997, the coming to power of the BJP-led government in March 1998, followed by the latter's decision to hold nuclear tests in May of the same year. In the following points, there will be a greater focus on the effects of the 1997 Asian crisis on the process of India's integration with the region. Moreover, in the context of the crisis, the BJP government's attitude towards the weakened economies will be analysed. Finally, the ties between India and relatively unharmed Asian economies like Singapore will be dwelt upon.

A Weakening of Trade Ties

The Asian economic recession occurred against all expectations. The first ominous signs appeared in June 1997, when Thailand saw its currency, the Baht, cave in. Within a few weeks, the crisis spread to the entire region, and strongly affected Indonesia, Malaysia and the Philippines. South Korea also bore the brunt of the crisis. Among the factors leading to the crash, the most determining ones were the debt overload of the region's economies, the corruption of the leadership's elite and the archaic regulation mechanism of capital markets. Multilateral Financial institutions descended upon the region in full force and dealt with each country separately. The IMF interceded in a big way in Indonesia, Thailand and South Korea. Malaysia, which was less affected, decided to find its own way out. India was not directly affected by the bankruptcy of its neighbouring economies. The Rupee remained comparatively stable and financial markets fended off the storm. But the good showing of the Indian currency also revealed that India's integration with Asia's capital network, both in terms of investment and trade, had remained modest.

The major investors in India came from the countries that were the most affected by the crisis. The repercussions of the South Korean crisis were felt clearly in the FDI inflow for the year 1998. South Korea was the sixth largest investor in 1997; it slid down to the fourteenth place in 1998, investing only one-sixth of the previous year's amount. The Japanese fared better, although there was a slight dip. Surprisingly, in 1999, South Korea re-emerged as the second-largest investor in India, just behind Mauritius, but ahead of the United States.[73] That year, South Korea's investments accounted for more than twelve per cent of foreign investment in India. As for Japan, it came in in the sixth place. But the years 2000 and 2001 witnessed the collapse of South Korean investments in India. Japanese investments also diminished, but in a less dramatic fashion. The reduction of FDI in India was a general trend during these two years and Japan became the third largest investor in India in 2000, and fifth in 2001. In spite of these fluctuations, Japan and South Korea respectively maintained the fourth and fifth positions in the total approved investments between 1991 and 2001.

As for actual FDI inflow from South Korea, there was a sharp rise in 1997–8. Thus, the country became the third-largest investor in India, after Mauritius and the United States, but ahead of Japan, accounting for 10 per cent of the actual total capital inflow in India. This peak indicated the materialization of numerous investment undertakings signed in preceding years. But, the actual investments from South Korea declined sharply from 1998–9 onwards, and this setback continued in the following years. Actual Japanese investments generally followed a steady progress. In 1998–9, Japan was the third largest supplier of actual FDI to India, after Mauritius and the United States.

TABLE 3.1: FDI INFLOWS FROM JAPAN AND SOUTH KOREA BETWEEN 1997 AND 2001

(*Rs. in million*)

		1997	1998	1999	2000	2001	Total 1991–2001
Total FDI In India		548,913	308.135	283,665	370,394	268,746	2,736,721
Japan	–Amount	19,063	12,828	15,947	8,275	7,352	106,704
	–Share in total FDI in India (%)	(3.4)	(4.1)	(5.6)	(2.2)	(2.7)	(3.9)
	–Rank	7	8	6	3	5	4
South Korea	–Amount	19,560	3,683	36,489	410	667	97,979
	–Share in total FDI in India (%)	(3.5)	(1.1)	(12.8)	(0.1)	(0.2)	(3.6)
	–Rank	6	14	2	18	18	5

Note: Based on the Newsletters of the Secretariat for Industrial Approvals between 1997 and 2001.

TABLE 3.2: ACTUAL FDI INFLOWS FROM JAPAN AND SOUTH KOREA BETWEEN 1997–8 AND 2000–1

(*Rs. in million*)

	1997–8	1998–9	1999–2000	2000–1
Japan	6,080	9,890	6,152	7,156
South Korea	12,380	3,590	346	1,096

Note: Based on the annual report of the Reserve Bank of India between 1997–8 and 2000–1.

Korean investment fluctuations in India were partly due to the difficulties faced by many *chaebols*. The latter were, in fact, badly hit by the economic crisis.[74] Most of them, however, made an effort to maintain their presence in India, although early in 1998, many Korean bank operations in India were paralysed and major commercial institutions like the Commercial Bank of South Korea and Hanil Bank had to wind up their activities. However, to display its will to maintain relations with India, South Korea was the partner country for the Indian Engineering Trade Fair organized by CII, in February 1999.[75] The fair received the visit of the Korean Prime Minister Kim Jong Pil, who did share his optimism on the growth of bilateral ties in the future.[76] About 150 Korean companies participated and more than 1,000 Korean delegates visited the fair, thus making the event a successful one. South Korea's participation established its expertise in the automobile, electrical consumer goods and in the telecommunications' equipment sectors. In spite of the unfavourable economic conditions, the fair was also attended by delegations from China, Japan, Malaysia, Singapore and Taiwan.

In point of fact, the activities of the *chaebols* set-up in India during the Asian crisis underwent several changes. Generally, they continued with their investment plans for the year 1998, but had to resort to financial contractions in 1999, especially in the electrical household appliances sector. Most of them, however, maintained their plan of a long-term integration of the Indian market to intra-industrial flows. Thus, in May 1998, the Indian subsidiary, Samsung India Electronics (SIEL), launched four electrical household appliances products at the same time, with a plan to re-export them to other countries the following year. However, in March 1999, the *chaebol* realized that its investment for the following year would be reduced to a minimum.[77] Though shattered by the economic crisis, SIEL finally managed to stabilize its situation. Heartened by the positive response to its products in India, the company announced investment projects worth USD 215 million in 2001 for the next four years. Samsung intended to proceed with an increase of its production capacity for televisions and household electrical equipment as well as with an upgrading of the equipment in R&D and software centres.[78] LG, which also came with ambitious plans, completed its plant in Greater Noida, near Delhi, in April 1998. In 1999, the company announced that a considerable investment (289 million dollars) would be earmarked for its Indian operations for the next six years. LG foresaw exports of no less than USD100 million worth of electrical appliances from its Indian unit in the next ten years.[79] In the same perspective, Daewoo Anchor Electronics established itself in India with the intention of manufacturing and re-exporting electrical consumer products. But the *chaebol* was forced to slow down its Indian investment programme.

In the automobile sector, Korean firms launched their products at a time when the Indian market seemed somewhat obsolescent. This clever strategy was accompanied by a veritable price war between Hyundai's Santro and Daewoo's Matiz models, launched in October and November 1998 respectively. Hyundai's Indian factory came to be the largest investment by the company abroad.[80] In spite of its financial problems, Hyundai continued its programme of integrating its Indian subsidiaries into intra-industrial flows. In 1998, Hyundai Motor India (HMI) began to export its components and spare parts (engine and transmission parts) to its Korean parent company, to the tune of USD one million. In the assembled cars' segment, HMI's priority remained the domestic market, without losing sight of its re-exportation goals to foreign markets. With the launch of the Santro in September 1998, the Korean company succeeded in less than a year to capture a ten per cent share of the passenger car segment.[81] The setting up of the Hyundai factory in India proved to be a real success and, within a few months, the *chaebol* became the second largest car manufacturer in the country after Maruti-Suzuki. In contrast, Daewoo's experience was a failure. In June 1999, the Indian unit had to undertake a large scale reconstruction, due to heavy losses. Daewoo did not adopt suitable strategies for its Indian unit, which was initially created for manufacturing heavy duty engines. Then, with the Asian crisis, the *chaebol* had to reorient itself to market demands, i.e. to the small car segment. The company realized too late that it ought to have launched a small model—even in India—to sell viable volumes. Moreover, Matiz was launched in October 1998, with a low level of indigenization—only 25 per cent. This resulted in a price tag that proved to be too high for the Indian market. Lastly, the parent company's bankruptcy at the end of 2000 seriously affected the operations of the Indian subsidiary, to such an extent that the production units of Daewoo Motors India had to be shut down. Unable to manage the growing debt overload, Daewoo Motors India was finally put up for sale at the end of 2002.

The Asian crisis also affected FDI inflow from South-East Asia. In 1998, despite a slight reduction in its FDI in India, Malaysia emerged as the largest Asian investor, ahead of Japan. But in 1999, Malaysian investments collapsed and the country dropped to the eighteenth position, whereas it was in the sixth position in 1998. FDI figure became even worse in 2000 and remained at a very low level in 2001. Projects as important as the setting up of the Proton automobile factory in Andhra Pradesh were not finalized due to the economic crisis. Capital inflow from Singapore remained more or less stable in 1998 and 1999, before showing a clear downswing in 2000 and 2001. As for Thailand, its investments in India had become negligible after 1996. As far as total investments approved between 1991 and 2001 were concerned, Malaysia ranked tenth, Singapore eleventh and Thailand eighteenth.

The collapse of Asian currencies also translated into a great imbalance in the Indian balance of trade. National currencies depreciated around 50 per cent in Malaysia and the Philippines, 75 per cent in South Korea and Thailand and about 299 per cent in Indonesia. Indian exporters working with South-East Asia found themselves in difficulties. The crisis naturally brought about a shrinking of East Asian markets, along with import compression. Indian exports to ASEAN economies decreased by 10 per cent for 1997–8, 25 per cent for 1998–9, before showing a growth of 38 per cent in 1999–2000. Generally, ASEAN represented 8.5 per cent of international Indian exports in 1996–7. Its share was reduced to 7 per cent in 1997–8 and hovered around 5 per cent between 1998 and 2001. The depreciation of the South-East Asian currencies eroded the competitiveness of Indian products not only in Asia, but also in the Third World market. Indian exports were all the more affected as they were quite similar to exports from Thailand or Indonesia. The most affected sectors were cooking oil, cotton, precious stones, machines, iron ore and semi-finished iron and steel products.

As for imports from South-East Asia, there was a marked rise of

TABLE 3.3: APPROVED FDI INFLOWS FROM MALAYSIA, SINGAPORE AND THAILAND BETWEEN 1997 AND 2001

(*Rs. in million*)

		1997	1998	1999	2000	2001	Total 1991–2001
Total FDI In India		548,913	308,135	283,665	370,394	268,746	2,736,721
Malaysia	Amount	21,046	18,031	1,161	158	1,057	56,822
	–Share in total FDI in India (%)	(3.8)	(5.8)	(0.4)	/	(0.4)	(2.0)
	–Rank	6	6	18	24	14	10
Singapore	–Amount	8,619	7,673	8,260	3,232	3,798	48,628
	–Share in total FDI in India (%)	(1.5)	(2.5)	(2.9)	(0.8)	(1.4)	(1.7)
	–Rank	9	10	9	7	8	11
Thailand	–Amount	260	3	70	4	12	24,604
	–Share in total FDI in India (%)	/	(0)	(0)	(0)	(0)	(0.9)
	–Rank	/	/	/	/	/	18

Note: Based on the Newsletters of the Secretariat of Industrial Approval between 1997 and 2001.

TABLE 3.4: TRENDS IN INDIAN EXPORTS TO ASEAN COUNTRIES BETWEEN 1997 AND 2001

(*Rs. in million*)

		1997–8	1998–9	1999–2000	2000–1
Total Indian exports		1,301,006.4	1,397,531.4	1,595,613.9	2,035,710.1
ASEAN	–Amount	89,898	66,940	92,377.2	101,785.5
	–Rate of growth (%)	(-10.9)	(-25.5)	(37.9)	(10.1)
	–Share in Indian exports (%)	(7)	(4.7)	(5.8)	(5)
Indonesia	–Amount	16,251.1	7,794.3	14,108.1	18,262.4
	–Rate of growth (%)	(-22.6)	(-52.0)	(81.1)	(29.4)
	–Share in Indian exports (%)	(1.3)	(0.6)	(0.9)	(0.9)
Malaysia	–Amount	18,208.8	13,533.6	19,373.4	27,783.1
	–Rate of growth (%)	(-3.4)	(-26.6)	(43.1)	(43.4)
	–Share in Indian exports (%)	(1.4)	(0.9)	(1.2)	(1.3)
Singapore	–Amount	28,978.5	21,772.7	29,150.3	40,070.4
	–Rate of growth (%)	(-16.4)	(-24.8)	(33.8)	(37.4)
	–Share in Indian exports (%)	(2.2)	(1.5)	(1.8)	(1.9)
Thailand	–Amount	12,784.3	12,504.5	19,481.7	24,218.4
	–Rate of growth (%)	(-2.7)	(-2.1)	(55.7)	(24.3)
	–Share in Indian exports (%)	(1.0)	(0.9)	(1.2)	(1.1)

Source: RBI, *Handbook of Statistics on Indian Economy*, 8 January 2002.

22 per cent in 1997–8, 36 per cent in 1998–9 and 32 per cent in 1999–2000. ASEAN economies thus continued to increase their share in Indian imports. From 7.4 per cent in 1996–7, they reached 10.5 per cent in 1999–2000, before falling back to 7.7 per cent in 2000–1. Faced with the risk of an importation boom descending on the Indian market, a section of the political class and business world even attempted to pressurize the government, to obtain either a depreciation of the Rupee to maintain the competitiveness of India's exports, or a temporary tariff protection to safeguard the domestic market.

The Asian crisis had a less dramatic effect on India's trade with Japan and South Korea, even while it generated certain fluctuations. Indian exports to Japan decreased in a small way. Japan's share in total exports from India had, in effect, gone down from 6 per cent in 1996–7, to 5.4 per cent in 1997–8 and hovered around 4 per cent between 1998 and 2001. Conversely, there was a sharp rise in Indian imports from Japan, especially in 1998–9, when there was an increase of nearly 30 per cent compared to the previous year. The share of Japanese importation in India's total imports, however, remained quite stable, around 5 per cent between 1997 and 2000, but fell to 3.6 per cent in 2000–1. Trade and commerce with South Korea were subject to much greater fluctuations. Indian exports declined sharply between 1997 and 1999. The share of South Korea in India's total exports continued to diminish and hovered around 1 per cent between 1997 and 2001. As for imports from South Korea, they increased by 18 per cent in 1997–8 and 57 per cent in 1998–9. Their share in India's total imports fluctuated between 2 to 3 per cent between 1997 and 2000, before falling to 1.7 per cent in 2000–1.

LOOKING EAST DESPITE THE ASIAN CRISIS

In India, the press, major economic institutions and the political class kept a close watch on the unfurling of the Asian crisis. Generally, India refrained from gloating and, in spite of their difficulties, the East Asian countries continued to arouse its admiration. In the beginning of 1998, the Finance Minister, P. Chidambaram, underlined the continuing validity of the Asian development model, much maligned in other parts of the world. He asserted: 'It has become increasingly fashionable to denigrate the achievements of the East Asian Miracle. Such criticism is largely misplaced. During the period of the Miracle,

TABLE 3.5: TRENDS IN INDIAN IMPORTS FROM ASEAN COUNTRIES BETWEEN 1997 AND 2001

(*Rs. in million*)

		1997–8	1998–9	1999–2000	2000–1
Total Indian imports		1,541,763.0	1,783,318.5	2,152,364.7	2,308,727.6
ASEAN	–Amount	125,550.0	171,026.0	225,998.2	177,772.0
	–Rate of growth (%)	(22.1)	(36.2)	(32.1)	(-21.3)
	–Share in Indian imports (%)	(8)	(9.7)	(10.5)	(7.7)
Indonesia	–Amount	27,190.9	34,880.9	41,547.1	41,583.9
	–Rate of growth (%)	(27.9)	(28.8)	(19.1)	(0.0)
	–Share in Indian imports (%)	(1.7)	(1.9)	(1.9)	(1.8)
Malaysia	–Amount	43,813.2	67,664.8	87,706.6	53,761.4
	–Rate of growth (%)	(11.4)	(54.4)	(29.6)	(-38.7)
	–Share in Indian imports (%)	(2.8)	(3.8)	(4.0)	(2.3)
Singapore	–Amount	44,519.0	58,232.6	66,490.1	66,878.0
	–Rate of growth (%)	(17.9)	(-30.8)	(14.1)	(0.5)
	–Share in Indian imports (%)	(2.8)	(3.2)	(3.0)	(2.8)
Thailand	–Amount	8,671.2	11,490.0	14,203.0	15,437.9
	–Rate of growth (%)	(23.8)	(32.5)	(23.6)	(8.6)
	–Share in Indian imports (%)	(0.5)	(0.6)	(0.6)	(0.6)

Source: RBI, *Handbook of Statistics on Indian Economy*, 8 January 2002.

TABLE 3.6: TRENDS IN INDIAN EXPORTS TO JAPAN AND SOUTH KOREA BETWEEN 1997 AND 2001

(*Rs. in million*)

		1997–8	1998–9	1999–2000	2000–1
Total Indian exports		1,301,006.4	1,397,531.4	1,595,613.9	2,035,710.1
Japan	–Amount	70,556.9	69,501.3	73,031.7	81,979.9
	–Rate of growth (%)	(-0.9)	(-1.4)	(5.0)	(12.2)
	–Share in Indian exports (%)	(5.4)	(4.9)	(4.7)	(4.0)
South Korea	–Amount	17,376.6	12,953.5	20,650.6	20,593.5
	–Rate of growth (%)	(-5.6)	(-25.4)	(59.4)	(-0.2)
	–Share in Indian exports (%)	(1.3)	(0.9)	(1.2)	(1.0)

Source: RBI, *Handbook of Statistics on Indian Economy*, 8 January 2002.

TABLE 3.7: TRENDS IN INDIAN IMPORTS FROM JAPAN AND SOUTH KOREA BETWEEN 1997 AND 2001

(*Rs. in million*)

		1997–8	1998–9	1999–2000	2000–1
Total Indian imports		1,541,763.0	1,783,318.5	2,152,364.7	2,308,727.6
Japan	–Amount	79,714.7	103,734.4	109,883.0	84,159.1
	–Rate of growth (%)	(2.6)	(30.1)	(5.9)	(-23.4)
	–Share in Indian imports (%)	(5.1)	(5.8)	(5.1)	(3.6)
Korea	–Amount	37,230.8	58,664.3	55,177.4	40,830.9
	–Rate of growth (%)	(18.6)	(57.5)	(-5.9)	(-26.0)
	–Share in Indian imports (%)	(2.4)	(3.2)	(2.5)	(1.7)

Source: RBI, *Handbook of Statistics on Indian Economy*, 8 January 2002.

these countries had achieved an average economic growth of 7 per cent, a feat unparalleled in world economic history, raised the living standards of their people, eradicated abject poverty and improved the quality of life indices.'[82]

The Minister added that India could never feel at an advantage because of the Asian crisis: 'East Asia has also demonstrated the critical importance of universal and good quality primary education and health care—areas in which India has fallen behind.' These comments echoed in numerous editorials that continued to compare India's achievements with those of East Asia. The general sentiment could be summarized thus: if India was spared by the crisis, this nonetheless did not place it in an advantageous position. The country's economy continued to lag behind the economies of East Asia even in times of crisis.[83] Most of the time, India's attitude *vis-à-vis* the economic difficulties of the Asian countries consisted of drawing a lesson for its own open economic policy. The bankruptcy of the neighbouring economies sustained the debate on the reforms to be undertaken and, especially, the reforms to be avoided, in order not to be vulnerable to such economic reversals. Generally, the thinking confined itself to the liberalization of the financial sector. For many observers, the lesson to be learnt was one of prudence. India had to proceed with measured financial liberalization, especially in the field of capital account convertibility, and this had to be done despite the pressure exerted by the international financial community.[84] Another lesson was that economic liberalization had to be accompanied by protective measures and counterweights to the activities of the private sector.

As for the BJP coalition government, in power since 1998, it endeavoured to work out mechanisms to maintain trade links with South-East Asia. With a moderate Prime Minister, Atal Behari Vajpayee, at the helm, the party displayed a pragmatism that its *swadeshi* rhetoric would have never led one to believe. One reason for this line of action was that India, whose budget deficit stood at six per cent of the GDP, was in dire need of external financing and could ill-afford to follow a policy of restriction on investments. The new government could not, therefore, ignore the ASEAN's economic difficulties, as this region represented nearly seven per cent of the foreign capital inflow to India and eight per cent of its total exports in normal times. In April 1998, during the second ASEAN-India Economic Cooperation Committee meeting, the Secretary of Economic Relations in the

Ministry of Foreign Affairs, S.S. Devare, underlined that New Delhi remained steadfast in the pursuit of the Look East policy. In point of fact, a special mention was made about the ASEAN in the new government's National Agenda, formulated in April 1998, at the very moment when the crisis was in full swing in Asia. As a consequence, S.S. Devare explained that India's role had to be one of 'understanding and solidarity' *vis-à-vis* its 'ASEAN brothers, in these difficult times'.[85] New Delhi's cooperative and helpful position was reiterated officially during the ASEAN Post-Ministerial Conference in Manila, in July 1998.[86] In addition, in April 1998, the Indian Ministry of External Affairs proposed seven lines of actions along which trade and commerce could be maintained between India and South-East Asia. The proposals mentioned were many: government to government credit, EXIM Bank credit to finance trade and commerce or to help inflow of investments, barter trade, EXIM Bank financing for feasibility studies on infrastructure projects, guarantees and counter-guarantees for financing trade and commerce and reinforcement of Indian technical and economic cooperation programmes with ASEAN.

Some of these proposals took shape in the following months and clearly showed that India was concerned not to let the Asian crisis ruin the gains made by its Look East policy. For example, in May 1998, New Delhi offered South-East Asian countries long-term credits for the purchase of equipment, especially in the engineering, machinery, automobile and iron and steel work sectors, hoping that in this way, it could supply South-East Asia with products that were previously bought from developed countries.[87] As its equipment cost less, India considered itself in an advantageous position to sell its products to these impoverished countries. India also promoted a barter system with South-East Asia, as this would allow trade to continue while preserving precious reserves of strong currencies. In September 1998, the Commerce Secretary, M.P.P. Prabhu, visited Malaysia, Thailand and the Philippines, to try and maintain India's export levels to these countries. He offered to extend lines of credit from the EXIM Bank to importers from each of these countries.[88] The proposals were reiterated to encourage bilateral trade, either in Rupees or in local currency. However it appeared that the line of credit proposed by New Delhi did not motivate South-East Asia countries much.[89] Nevertheless, the barter system came to be successful in the case of Indo-Malaysian relations.[90] In June 1999, the Indian government announced that it had obtained a contract for the construction of a railway line in Malaysia for the government undertaking, IRCON International. The Malaysian contractor was the public undertaking KTM Berhad, which would pay for the work in palm oil, through an international trading company that was also a public undertaking—the MMTC. The latter committed itself to supplying 200,000 tonnes of palm oil over a period of two and a half years. The money accrued from the sale of palm oil would be credited to IRCON. Once again, it was the political leaders who stepped up efforts to maintain the dynamics of rapprochement between India and the ASEAN. The institutional process continued in spite of the crisis and a working group on trade and investment held its first meeting in May 1998, in New Delhi. However, within the Indian chambers of commerce, activities in relation to South-East Asia took place in slow motion.[91]

All said and done, New Delhi made the most of the stability of its economy in those circumstances where the tigers and the dragons were on a weak wicket. After having been roundly criticized for its slow pace and hesitations, the Indian method of liberalization seemed to have earned more plaudits. For instance, the 1998 edition of the India Economic Summit, jointly organized by CII and the World Economic Forum, emphasized that India would be one of the rare countries along with China to register positive growth during that financial year.[92] Through failing to measure up to the wishes of foreign investors, the pace of reforms had permitted India to escape the turmoil of its Asian neighbours, which were cited as models previously. The fact that the Rupee had not been made entirely convertible had proved to be the trump card. Indian decision-makers did not fail to underline the 'solid fundamentals' of their economy, which did not suffer from certain weaknesses that had swept away their East Asian neighbours.

Heartened by this new-found credibility, the Indian diplomacy invited its ASEAN interlocutors to reconsider the importance of the country and the opportunities on offer. The Secretary for Economic Relations in the Ministry of Foreign Affairs, S. Devare, underlined, for instance, that the interdependence of East Asian economies had spread the contagion of the crash. As a result, he was of the view that the ASEAN members should reorient their trade relations to extra-regional markets, as a measure of prudence. With a growth rate of six to seven per cent in 1997–8, India could become the driving force of regional and international growth.[93] Echoing Devare's views, the

Indian representative to the Post-Ministerial Conference of July 1998, Jaswant Singh, asserted, 'It would always be useful for ASEAN to find invigoration from extra East Asian neighbouring countries like India.'[94] India took advantage of its economic well-being to reiterate its strong desire for a rapprochement with East Asian regional bodies. S. Devare emphasized that 'This might be the right moment to consider the complementarities between AFTA and India and the value addition AFTA-India linkages would bring to both economies.'[95] Consequently, the creation of a regional trade and investment zone between India and ASEAN was adopted as a medium to long-term objective. India also sought to place itself in an advantageous position in the framework of the Initiatives for ASEAN Integration (IAI), which the Association had launched to reduce the gap between its members, more particularly the new entrants—Cambodia, Laos, Myanmar and Vietnam. New Delhi offered its help in sectors in which it was particularly competitive, notably in information technology, human resources and space technology, which came to be widely welcomed by ASEAN. All in all, the Asian crisis had both negative and positive results on India's Look East policy. On the negative side, it certainly dampened down the dynamics of the economic rapprochement between India and East Asia, especially in terms of trade and investment flows. But on a more ideational level, it somewhat put India in a more advantageous position, as a large and fairly stable economy, eager to help out its partners in crisis. There is no doubt that since the economic crisis of the late 1990s, many in East Asia have started to consider the Indian market in a more positive way.

THE SINGAPORE EXCEPTION

Because it was relatively spared by the financial crisis, Singapore constituted a special case and remained India's major partner in East Asia. Bilateral relations enjoyed a sort of 'convergence of interests' in a climate changed by the bankruptcy of most of the other regional economies. In fact, in 1998, the Singapore government informed its companies, especially its SMEs, that it would guarantee access to new markets, in order to compensate for the decline in regional demand.[96] And India figured among the top stable markets outside the South-East Asian zone. Besides, the new BJP government proved to continue with the reform process, which reassured the Singaporeans to a great extent. The Indian budget presented in June 1998 contained various measures pertaining to infrastructure, information technology and telecommunications sectors. The government also went ahead with dismantling quantitative restrictions, by withdrawing 340 products from the trade restriction list. In August 1998, the Commerce Minister, Ramakrishna Hegde, undertook a trip to Singapore, during which he hastened to reassure the business community about India's liberalization process.[97] The STDB Director, Stephen Lee, admitted on this occasion that the East Asian economic crisis had ironically placed India in a good position to present a positive image and attract investors from Singapore. India, on its part, depended more specifically on the central location of Singapore to maintain its bilateral trade with other South-East Asian economies. The city-state had vast experience in the field of barter trade and India wished to gain from this.

More importantly, Singapore endeavoured to adopt strategies more suitable to the Indian context. After the SIA debacle that was widely covered by the media, Singapore's business circles opted for a low-key approach. Henceforth, they would follow a planned and deliberate strategy to avoid the media glare, more so as the freedom of the press in India stood out as a destabilizing factor for them. For instance, the Ports Authority of Singapore (PSA) worked to maintain a low profile throughout its campaign for developing India's port infrastructure. After its proposal for the Jawaharlal Nehru Port of Mumbai was rejected, PSA decided to get involved in a joint venture in Chennai, in order to better apprehend the sector's state-wise evolution. In fact, the Singaporeans came to be awarded two contracts for the supply of equipments to two ports—Tuticorin (Tamil Nadu) and Pipavav (Gujarat). But they were careful not to attract publicity, especially because it was at these very sites that the city-state's entrepreneurs were exploring the possibility of erecting thermal power plants.[98] What's more, far from making the headlines, these SMEs were to meet with a resounding success and prop up an important part of Indo-Singaporean relations, particularly in the electronics, computers and trading sectors.[99] For a majority of SME joint ventures, authorizations were processed at state level, whereas infrastructure programmes and other mega projects were dealt with by the federal authorities. Consequently, Singapore's SMEs concentrated on the Indian states that were the most favourable to foreign investments.

Singapore also came to terms with the fact that in India, it was necessary to adopt a medium to long-term strategy. This could be seen in the speech of George Yeo, Minister for Information and Arts and second Minister of Commerce and Industry: 'India is opening up in her own way and according to her own timetable. Those who are committed to India and work with the internal logic of India's transformation will be richly rewarded.' Adopting a long-term perspective was also one of the STDB's recommendations to potential investors in India.[100] This organization proposed various strategies to overcome the inherent difficulties in the Indian context. For instance, to offset the many unknown factors of the local market, a joint venture with a local partner seemed to be the best way to enter the country. A partner with good contacts in political and bureaucratic circles could avoid a number of unexpected contingencies. However, as it was not always possible for Singaporean investors to identify trustworthy partners, it was recommended that they approach public sector undertakings and major industrial groups. Finally, the STDB drew their attention to the diversity of opportunities available statewise. This enabled Singapore's business circles to understand India's diversity in a more sophisticated fashion. The STDB thus recommended that India be seen as 'diverse economic centres'. This approach conformed to the classic strategy of the city-state, which consisted of balancing the risks by spreading investments geographically. To be more precise, the STDB's strategy was to direct trade and financial inflows to states viewed as having a greater growth potential. The first list of priority states included Maharashtra (Mumbai-Pune-Nashik), Tamil Nadu (Chennai-Coimbatore), Karnataka (Bangalore-Mysore), Delhi and Haryana (Delhi-Gurgaon-Faridabad). Then, a second list of recommended states had Andhra Pradesh (Vizag-Hyderabad), West Bengal (Kolkata), Kerala (Cochin) and Gujarat (Ahmedabad-Vapi).

Despite the various setbacks they suffered, Singapore's investors also showed great endurance *vis-à-vis* the Indian market. Thus SIA remained determined to invest in India. In fact, the Indian case was not exceptional. The company had encountered similar problems in Cambodia, from where it finally withdrew, and in China, where its projects suffered considerable delays due to domestic political compulsions. In contrast, in India, SIA enjoyed a profitable partnership with the Taj Group of hotels in Chennai, and in a Taj subsidiary, Airline Software Development Consultancy.[101] Moreover, the company, which began its operations in India in 1986, had seen steady growth in its passenger traffic. India indeed offered great potential for international airline companies. It was a country that was still greatly under-serviced, whereas most other international destinations were overloaded.[102] Besides, India occupied an unavoidable strategic position: because of its link to Europe and Africa, SIA aircraft had to take air route over-flying the subcontinent. For example, in 1998–9, no less than thirty-seven countries were in the fray to get permission to increase their air services to India.[103] Among them were Hong Kong, South Korea and Thailand. In 1998, Singapore, along with Malaysia, was one of the few countries to which the Union Government granted rights for additional flights. Malaysian Airlines was permitted to increase its operations from six to seven flights a week. In return, Air India introduced a new link between Bangalore and Kuala Lumpur in 1999.[104]

As for SIA, it got Trivandrum (Kerala) as an additional destination and higher passenger capacity on its direct flights to Mumbai, Delhi and Chennai. In return, Air India, that had started a Hyderabad-Singapore flight, could transit via the city-state to service destinations in South-East Asia and Oceania. SIA began its operations to Trivandrum in June 1999, with two weekly flights. The STPB thus hoped to attract visitors from Kerala and, in the middle term, promote this state as a tourist destination serviced from Singapore, in accordance with its tourism regionalization programme. The air link also testified to the increased human traffic between south India and Singapore. Singapore was aware that the dynamic of personal trips between India and South-East Asia was quite high and intended to be the first to gain from this. Besides, the importance of the Indian market for Singapore's tourism industry was further strengthened. In 1998 for example, the share of Indian tourists increased by eight per cent, whereas the total tourist arrival declined by thirteen per cent.[105] Indian Airlines, on its part, undertook various measures to intensify traffic between India and Singapore. The airline that had just one weekly flight in 1987, soon started ten flights a week.

Not surprisingly then, Singapore leaders were soon to send strong political signals of their renewed interest in the Indian market. Prime Minister, Goh Chok Tong, visited India at the end of January 2000. For his third visit to India since the launch of the reforms in 1991, his itinerary included Delhi and the three most dynamic southern states of Andhra Pradesh, Karnataka and Tamil Nadu. This choice confirmed the strong ties that continued to grow between south India and

South-East Asia. It also displayed Singapore's predilection to deal directly with state governments rather than with the central government's bureaucracy. As for Prime Minister Vajpayee, he visited Singapore in April 2002, mainly with an economic agenda. During his visit, the decision to form a working group on the feasibility of a Comprehensive Economic Cooperation Agreement (CECA) between the two nations was taken.[106] This project, which was far more ambitious than a simple Free Trade Agreement, showed that the city-state desired to remain a privileged partner of India. The decision to work towards CECA with India also reflected a more general trend in Singapore's trade strategies: indeed since the Asian crisis, the city-state has become increasingly eager to conclude bilateral trade agreement with major partners in the world, rather than just pursuing multilateral efforts towards regional integration.

After 2001, Singapore once again headed numerous investments projects, including some large-scale ones.[107] The Indian market looked promising in contrast to the wobbly economic climate in South-East Asia. The interest of Singaporean investors concentrated in two sectors—infrastructure and information technology. It must be noted that the advances made by India in IT started changing its image in East Asia, especially in Singapore, where a growing number of articles in the press devoted to the country's performance in this field. Moreover, Indian engineers were increasingly sought after in the region. During his 2000 visit, Goh Chok Tong signed an agreement to create a special committee in the IT sector. Furthermore, after some difficult beginnings between 1997 and 1999, the Bangalore Information Technology Park—one of Singapore's major investment projects in India—finally met with success.[108] It was essential that this flag-project, which was launched in 1994 with strong political support from both the Singaporean and Indian governments, be successful for future ties between India and the city-state. The political implications attached to the technology park were once again clearly visible when Goh Chok Tong himself inaugurated the IT Park in January 2000, during his visit to India. Then it was George Yeo, Minister of Industry and Commerce, who launched the second phase of the work, in November 2000, during an important diplomatic and trade tour of the country. Still in the IT sector, SingTel and the Indian conglomerate, Bharti Enterprises, signed an agreement worth USD 650 million in October 2001, to lay an 11,800 km long undersea cable. This optical fibre network, described as one of the largest in the world in terms of capacity, would link Singapore to Chennai and Mumbai.[109] The Singapore-Chennai link was inaugurated in April 2002.

It must also be noted that after 2001, Malaysia and Thailand evinced a spurt in interest in their Indian neighbour. Thailand's Prime Minister, Thaksin Shinawatra, visited India in November 2001 to boost the country's Look West policy, and was especially interested in state-of-the-art technology. A study to look into a free trade zone between the two countries was commissioned. Prime Minister Vajpayee, on his part, visited Malaysia in May 2001, leading one of the most important business delegations that had ever accompanied a head of the Indian state abroad. Several agreements were signed between companies in the two countries. But the visit took place in an atmosphere of tension, because of India's decision to increase customs duties on palm oil imports a few months earlier. To maintain its export level to India—its largest foreign market—Malaysia awarded the Indian public sector company, IRCON, a huge railway electrification project. This contract, valued at USD1.8 million, would be paid in palm oil. Barter trade thus continued to sustain a large share of trade between India and Malaysia. More generally speaking, it eventually became apparent that the two economies had managed to establish positive synergies, with Malaysia bringing large-scale investments to Indian highway projects, while the Indian presence could be very much felt in the railroad sector in Malaysia.

In October 2002, it was Prime Minister Mahathir who visited both Delhi and Hyderabad, to attend the first India-ASEAN Business Summit in the company of Prime Minister Vajpayee. The event, jointly organized by FICCI and the Ministries of Foreign Affairs, Commerce and Industry, concentrated on possible cooperation in infrastructure, energy, investment, trade, finance and tourism, as well as biotechnology and information technology. Above all, this Summit was an occasion to visualize prospects of an economic partnership agreement between India and ASEAN. This project reflected the latest developments impacting regional economic cooperation in post-crisis Asia.[110] Indeed, towards the end of the 1990s, ASEAN showed a growing desire for a rapprochement with Japan, China and South Korea. A new mechanism of regional cooperation, 'ASEAN+3' thus took shape, originally to try and protect the region against further economic turmoil. As part of this new trend, in November 2001, ASEAN decided to enter into consultations with China to establish a free trade zone in the following ten years. India, for its part, became anxious not to be marginalized by the new wave of regional integration in East Asia. As a result, New Delhi signed a framework agreement for the setting up of a free trade area with ASEAN in ten years, in late 2003. The bilateral free trade agreement with Thailand was finalized in 2004. This Indian urge to conclude free trade agreements—whether bilateral (with Thailand and Singapore) or multilateral (with the ASEAN)—should be interpreted as India's desire to catch up with the new dynamics of regional integration underway in post-crisis East Asia. Indeed, apart from weakening the emerging economic interaction between India and East Asia, the economic crisis proved instrumental in prompting ASEAN to commit itself to the ASEAN+3 mechanism, which left India somewhat lagging behind.

NOTES

1. J.N. Dixit, *My South Block Years*, p. 396; P.M.S. Malik, 'The Changing Face of India's Economic Diplomacy', FSI, *Indian Foreign Policy*, vol. 1, p. 239.
2. *Frontline*, 'Special Feature: Singapore', 8 August 1997.
3. Dixit, *My South Block Years*, p. 268.
4. At the highest level of the Ministry of Foreign Affairs, Minister Dinesh Singh had for a long time advocated the creation of a new body specifically for relations with the ASEAN, the 'Indian Chamber of Commerce for South-East Asian countries', with the industrialist R.P. Goenka, president of FICCI, at the helm. However, P.M.S. Malik, Joint Secretary in the Ministry of Foreign Affairs, promoted the candidature of CII, underlining the fact that the Confederation had already established contacts with South-East Asia.
5. Interview, Ministry of External Affairs, New Delhi, March 1998.
6. Meetings, ASSOCHAM, New Delhi, February 1998; FICCI, New Delhi, February 1998.
7. P.A.N. Murty, *India-Japan: Dimensions of their Relations: Historical and Political*, New Delhi: JNU, ABC Publishing House, 1986, p. 410.
8. The observations made in this paragraph are mainly based on interviews conducted in 1998 with representatives of Indian business houses that already had business or financial relations with East Asia, including: Consulting Engineering Services (India) Ltd., New Delhi, Birla-Yamaha Motor Corporation, New Delhi, Taj Group, Mumbai, Lloyds Group, Mumbai, Ranbaxy, New Delhi, Godrej, Mumbai.

9. Interviews, CII, FICCI, ASSOCHAM, New Delhi, 1998 and 1999.
10. CII, *The Partnership Summit, 1998: Networking Global Partnerships. A Retrospective.*
11. FICCI, *India-ASEAN Trade Relations*, New Delhi, 1999.
12. India-ASEAN Economic Cooperation Committee Meeting, 8 August 1997, New Delhi.
13. M.D. Chaudhuri, 'Liberalisation without Reform', *Seminar*, no. 437, January 1996, p. 32.
14. Limaye, 'The Japan-India Encounter', p. 10.
15. E. Sridharan, 'Coalition Politics', *Seminar*, no. 437, January 1996, pp. 53–6.
16. *The Times of India*, 27 July 1997.
17. *The Hindu*, 7 December 1997.
18. C. Jaffrelot, 'Inde: La Politique Introuvable', *Societal*, no. 19, May 1998, p. 33; C. Jaffrelot, *The Hindu Nationalist Movement in India*, New York: Columbia University Press, 1996, pp. 491, 537.
19. Interview, Singapore High Commission in India, Commercial Service Division, New Delhi, April 1998.
20. Interview, Malaysian High Commission in India, Commercial Service Division, New Delhi, April 1998.
21. CII, *The Partnership Summit*, 1998, p. 5.
22. Bharatiya Janata Party, *Election Manifesto '98*, New Delhi: BJP, 1998.
23. S.R. Batliboi & Co. and Ernst & Young Pvt. Ltd., *Pattern of Japanese Investment in India.*
24. *The Times of India*, 27 July 1997.
25. ASSOCHAM, FICCI, *Third Meeting of India-Singapore Joint Business Council, a Report*, 7 September 1998, Chennai.
26. BG (NS) George Yeo, Minister for Information and the Arts and Second Minister of Commerce and Industry, 'Good Long-Term Climate for Economic Reform in India', 1997.
27. Opinions were actually divided on the advantages offered by the Indian market compared to that of China. Prime Minister Goh Chok Tong, for example, underlined that it was easier to invest in India, due to a relatively impartial judicial system, knowledge of English and, unlike former communist countries, the existence of a mixed economy.
28. Hilton L. Root, 'A Liberal India: The Triumph of Hope over Experience', *Asian Survey*, vol. 38, no. 5, May 1999, p. 533.
29. Interviews, Singapore, June 1998.
30. SIA is Singapore's national airline, in which the government held a 52 per cent stake.
31. Tata Group, *Tata Airline Facts*, Mumbai 1998. Document given by the Tata group.
32. Interview, STDB, Singapore, June 1998.

33. Interview, Singapore Airlines, Singapore, June 1998.
34. The concept was first formulated in 1988. Despite Tamil Nadu's enthusiasm for putting it back on the agenda in the early 1990s, nothing has come out of it yet.
35. The project was launched by a consortium of investors from the United States and Singapore, in which the city-state had a twenty per cent stake. Just when the hotel was to be opened, the Indian administration went back on certain points regarding the acquisition of the land on which the hotel was built. The promoters were forced to begin a new phase of negotiations with the Airports Authority of India and the Delhi Development Authority, two bodies that were themselves at loggerheads on their respective capacities to resolve the issue. Meanwhile, the hotel remained shut and the investors were very anxious about its falling into disrepair.
36. Indian officials had actively promoted the tourism sector in Singapore. They had even signed an agreement in 1994 to encourage cooperation, and Singaporean investors were very optimistic. But according to STPB officials, nothing, or nearly nothing, was undertaken afterwards. India did not even figure in the list of priority zones for investment. Singapore's distrust can be better understood due to the fact that the tourism department comes under the Ministry of Civil Aviation.
37. Interview, Malaysian High Commission in India, New Delhi, April 1998.
38. *The Hindu*, 20 December 1996.
39. Interview, Embassy of Thailand in India, New Delhi, April 1998.
40. *The Times of India*, 27 July 1997.
41. Dato Ajit Singh, § 7. Copy of speech made at the CII Partnership Summit of 1998. Document obtained from CII, 1998.
42. Interviews, Singapore High Commission in India, New Delhi, April 1998; Malaysian High Commission in India, April 1998; Embassy of Thailand in India, New Delhi, April 1998.
43. Jean Coussy, 'L'Inde Face à la Régionalisation del l'Economic Mondiale', p. 35.
44. Eijora Noda, 'A Common Cultural Heritage', *India International Centre Quarterly*, Spring–Summer 1993, vol. 20, nos. 1–2, p. 76.
45. S.R. Batliboi and Co. and Ernst and Young Pvt. Ltd., *Pattern of Japanese Investment in India*, p. 37.
46. This concerned the exit policy, in other words, pruning surplus manpower in privatized government undertakings. This issue is particularly sensitive as it is very difficult to lay off salaried employees in India.
47. Satu Limaye, 'Sushi and Samosas: Indo-Japanese Relations after the Cold War', in S. Gordon, *India Looks East*, p. 171 and 'The Japan-India Encounter', p. 12.
48. FICCI, *20th Joint Meeting of the India-Japan Standing Committee*, 8 May 1997, Nagoya, Japan.

49. H.S. Prabhakar, 'North-East Asia and India', *World Focus*, vol. 18, no. 6, June 1997, p. 16.
50. AIBC, *Report of the ASEAN-India Business Council (AIBC)*, 16 February 1995, New Delhi.
51. *The Times of India*, 27 July 1997.
52. T.T. Meng et al., *Business Opportunities in India*, p. 7.
53. *The Times of India*, 6 April 1997.
54. T.T. Meng et al., *Business Opportunities in India*, p. 5.
55. CII, *The Partnership Summit*, Chennai, §8. Dato Ajit Singh referred mainly to his remarks made at The International Conference of Indian Entrepreneurs *The Uncaged Tiger*, held at Singapore, in June 1996.
56. Rajaram Panda, 'India and Japan: Perceptions and Misperceptions', *India-Japan Relations*, New Delhi: The Japan Foundation, 1997, p. 47. Panda outlined three distinct major trends in the business world. First, the Western culture, described as offensive and not very sensitive to different social and religious practices. Then, Japanese business culture, extending to North-East Asia (South Korea and China) was reserved, prudent and based on a long-term perspective. As for the Indians, they first sought to make a fast buck to the detriment of a long-term strategy.
57. *The Times of India*, 23 September 1997.
58. Limaye, 'The Japan-India Encounter', p. 10.
59. S.N. Mishra, 'Indo-Japan Intellectual Cooperation', *The Japan Foundation Bulletin*, New Delhi Office, March 1997, no. 12, p. 5.
60. Nanyang Business Report Series, *Business Opportunities in India*, p. 5.
61. Ibid., p. 32.
62. B. Ghoshal, 'East Asian Miracle and India', *World Focus*, vol. 18, no. 6, June 1997, p. 12.
63. Faculty of Political Sciences, Thammasat University & Information Department, Ministry of Foreign Affairs, *Thai-Indian Relations Over the Past 50 Years (1947–97)*, 30 July 1997, Bangkok, p. 143.
64. *The Asian Age*, 23 October 1997.
65. Interview, Hyundai, Mumbai, March 1998; Samsung, Mumbai, March 1998.
66. Limaye, 'The Japan-India Encounter', p. 10; N. Murthy, *India-Japan. Dimensions of their Relations–Economic and Cultural*, p. 77.
67. *India Today*, 15 November 1995, p. 66.
68. AIBC, *Report of the ASEAN-India Business Council*, 16 February 1995.
69. *The Times of India*, 11 October 1997.
70. ASSOCHAM, FICCI, *Third Meeting of India-Singapore Joint Business Council*, 7 September 1998, Chennai.
71. *Financial Express*, 6 December 1995.

72. *Business Standard*, 26 February 1999.
73. The decline of US FDI in India was linked to the sanctions imposed after the Indian nuclear tests of May 1998 (from Rs. 135,698 million in 1997, they fell to Rs. 35,620 million in 1998). This was equally true for Japan, in addition to the economic crisis that plagued the country.
74. F. Godement, *Dragons de Feu, Dragon de Papier*, Paris: Flammarion, 1998; Domenach, *L'Asie en Danger*.
75. CII, *Trade Fair Times*, no. 1, April 1999.
76. Cited in CII, *IETF'99 In Retrospect*, 12–17 February 1999, New Delhi.
77. *The Hindu*, 4 January 1999.
78. Ibid., 22 May 2001.
79. *The Economic Times*, 29 April 1999.
80. *The Hindu*, 8 October 1998.
81. Ibid., 18 July 1999.
82. CII, *The Partnership Summit 1998*, pp. 5–6.
83. N.S. Siddharthan, 'Lessons from the East Asian turmoil', *The Hindu*, 27 January 1998; Swaminathan S.A. Aiyar, 'Lessons from the Asian Currency Crisis', *The Times of India*, 8 February 1997.
84. Nagesh Kumar, 'East Asian Economic Crisis and South Asian Growth Prospects: A Note', *RIS Digest, Special Issue on East Asian Economic Crisis*, September 1998; FICCI, *South-East Asian Crisis: Lessons for India*, New Delhi, 1998.
85. Statement by H.E. Shri Sudhir Devare, Secretary of Economic Relations, India, on the occasion of the Second ASEAN-India JCC, Singapore, 28 April 1998, §6.
86. Statement by Deputy Chairman Planning Commission of India, Jaswant Singh, on the occasion of the ASEAN 31st Post-Ministerial Conferences (PMC 9+1), 29 July 1998, Manila.
87. *The Times of India*, 5 May 1998.
88. *The Hindu*, 9 September 1998.
89. Interviews, Singapore, June 1998.
90. *The Economic Times*, 23 June 1999.
91. Interviews, FICCI, New Delhi, 10 December 1998 and 9 July 1999.
92. *The Economic Times*, 24 November 1998.
93. Statement by H.E. Shri Sudhir Devare, § 4.
94. Statement by Deputy Chairman Planning Commission of India, Jaswant Singh, on the occasion of the ASEAN 31st Post-Ministerial Conference, (PMC 9+10), 30 July 1998, Manila § 12.
95. Statement by H.E. Shri Sudhir Devare, § 11.
96. Goh Chok Tong, *Asian Economic Crisis: Singapore's Response*, Keynote Address by Mr Goh Chok Tong, Prime Minister of Singapore, at the Official Opening Dinner of World Economic Forum's 1998 East Asia Economic Summit, 12 October in Singapore.

97. *The Hindu*, 21 August 1998.
98. Ibid., 13 October 1998.
99. *Financial Express*, 6 July 1998.
100. STDB, *India: New Opportunities*, Singapore, STDB, 1998.
101. *Business India*, 24 February–9 March 1997, p. 157.
102. Interview, Singapore Airlines, Singapore, June 1998.
103. *The Economic Times*, 29 March 1999.
104. *The Hindu*, 6 June 1999. While the demand for the new Bangalore-Kuala Lumpur flight was not high, it remained viable due to the huge success of the Chennai-Kuala Lumpur link. The company also considered connecting Bangalore to Bangkok, via Chennai.
105. *The Asian Age*, 22 June 1999.
106. *The Hindu*, 16 May 2002.
107. *FEER*, 25 January 2001, pp. 49–52.
108. The Bangalore IT park was launched in January 1994, as a flagship project and with the active involvement of goverment authorities from India and Singapore. This project required extensive visibility and was supposed to help in the fruitful development of future bilateral relations. In spite of the strong political support it was offered, the IT park did encounter several problems in the initial phase of its development.
109. SingTel also acquired twenty-seven per cent of the Bharti Group's shares for a sum of 400 million dollars. These two operations constituted the largest investment made until then by Singapore in India and the third largest made by SingTel in the world, behind its investments in Belgium and Thailand.
110. R. Stubbs, 'ASEAN+3: Emerging East Asian Regionalism', *Asian Survey*, vol. 17, no. 3, May–June 2002, pp. 440–55.

CHAPTER 4

Ideological Underpinnings

4.1 Back to the 1930s and 1940s: India's pan-Asian Dreams

Due to its economic growth, East Asia acquired an unprecedented visibility on the international scene. The phenomenon reached such an extent during the 1990s that, sometimes, Asia and East Asia came to be spoken of as the same conceptual entities. In the process, India found itself relegated to the periphery of the region and an 'imaginary' dividing line appeared to confine it to the fringes of the 'East Asia Miracle'. This perceptual schism reflected the economic and political dynamics of the 1990s, as an East Asian region was in midst of structuring itself under the impact of the flows of capital, goods and people, as well as through the efforts made by Heads of States for more concerted action, both in the strategic and political arenas. The regionalization process also involved searching for a definition of the idea of Asia. This quest for a regional identity engendered the notion of 'Asianism' in the early 1990s, i.e. 'a cultural vision of an Asia with a specific value system and which cannot be reduced to a Western or 'universal' vision'.[1] Those who put forth such arguments, especially the leaders of Malaysia and Singapore, created a discourse based on 'Asian values', that showered praise on the natural qualities of 'Asian' societies—in other words, social order and the individual's devotion to the community and economic development. But the Asianist argument also reposed on a neo-Confucianism that was supposed to incarnate the foundation of Asian spirituality and culture. Those in South-East Asia who sought to unravel the common characteristics of Asian societies tended to do so while disregarding the civilization and culture of India and confining themselves to China and Japan. In other words, the definition of the 'New' Asia was monopolized by one part of the continent alone, while excluding India—a country that nevertheless contributed the most in terms of culture and intellect to forge the notion of Asia. Indeed, simply going back fifty years in time would show that India was the beacon of the continent's emancipation. Since the end of the nineteenth century, Indian intellectuals were those who, along with their Japanese counterparts, had contributed the most to shaping the concept of 'Asia'.

THE PRE-1947 ASIAN DREAM

While Indian nationalist intellectuals started to be aware of an Asian entity towards the end of the nineteenth century, the idea had by that time to be appropriated and reinterpreted, for the notion imported from the West was not very gratifying.[2] Indian and Japanese intellectuals then set upon the quest for 'Asianness'. First and foremost, it was the contention of Asia's spiritual wealth that would gild Asia's escutcheon anew. Even before the official formation of the Indian National Congress in 1885, Keshab Chandra Sen, one of the leaders of the Brahmo Samaj, formulated one of the first discourses on Asian unity. In 1883, he gave a lecture entitled, 'Asia's Message to Europe'[3] and recalled the humiliating conditions to which his continent had been reduced. In an era when European supremacy was commonly accepted, Sen worked to give its people their pride back, by proclaiming that Christianity was born in Asia. To show that the origins of Christianity—the majority religion of the West—were to be found in Asia, provided further proof to the argument that the East was essentially spiritual. Consequently, the East could boast of having a moral mission *vis-à-vis* the West, which was seen as materialist. This dichotomy between the East and West appeared as a constant feature of pre-independence Asianism. It was, in effect, an intellectual mechanism that made it possible to raise the entire continent's self-esteem, in the face of European hegemony. In other words, it provided a metaphor, thanks to which Asia could assert its superiority over Europe.

The emergence of an Asian consciousness among early Indian nationalists was also spurred by the Japanese model. The archipelago's successful modernization created a feeling of pride in many Asian intellectuals. Swami Vivekananda, an ardent Bengali nationalist, set sail for Japan in 1893, and returned highly impressed. For him, the archipelago's development was the forerunner of Asia's awakening and a model that should be replicated elsewhere in the continent. Vivekananda's close friendship with the Japanese artist,

Okakura Kakuzo, also led him to promote the idea of Asia's spiritual unity. Given the moral superiority of the continent's peoples, he asserted that the Asian ethos should conquer the world and convert the West. The relationship of domination between the East and the West was once again inverted. In the arena of international politics, Indian nationalists celebrated the Anglo-Japanese alliance signed in 1902. By signing such an alliance with Japan, England was seen as treating an Asian power on an equal footing for the first time in modern history. A few years later, Japan's victory over Russia provoked a great wave of enthusiasm in India. The Russo-Japanese war of 1905 came, in a way, to incarnate the East-West confrontation. And an Asian power's triumph symbolized the end of Western hegemony,[4] as well as Asia's awakening. Thanks to its new status, Japan became a major source of inspiration for Indian nationalists.

Among the early Indian nationalists, Rabindranath Tagore came into his own as the great poet-philosopher of Asia. In 1881, he expressed his solidarity with China and denounced the opium smuggling indulged in by Europeans and the consequent economic deterioration of the country. The declaration of the First World War aggravated his bitterness against western civilization. Tagore had long believed that Europe would be the backbone of Civilization and Progress. But his hopes were dashed, and he developed a highly critical attitude towards Europe, which in his judgement had lost all moral underpinnings in the name of efficiency.[5] The old continent's materialism, its obsession with scientific organization, had become a Pandora's Box for humanity and, in the final analysis, proved the East's moral superiority. According to Tagore, the East-West dichotomy was reflected in their respective perceptions of and approaches to the universe. The West saw the world as essentially confrontational in nature and sought to subjugate it through conquest. The taste for war and the energy spent on raising forces reflected the ultimate desire to control and master nature. On the contrary, the Eastern attitude—imbued with contemplation and adoration—adhered to the desire of an intimate understanding of and harmony with the universe. Seeking the inner truth, along with spiritual well-being, the sense of personal sacrifice and acceptance of duties that structure human societies were the specific characteristics of the Asian ethos, as opposed to the selfish individualism and belligerence of the West. Tagore thus demonstrated that the sources for renewal were to be found in his native continent, Asia. Having predicted the inevitable decline of the West that was then engulfed by the First World War, the poet anticipated Asia's renaissance. And the portent of such an awakening was Japan. Until the 1920s, Tagore was full of admiration for the archipelago, for in his view, it had been able to preserve the Asian ethos while assimilating Western scientific techniques. Japan had not aped the West—it had appropriated its technological advances, while respecting its own original traditions.

More to the point, the idea of renaissance was based on ancient history. For those who put forth the argument of Asia's paralysis and passivity, Tagore responded by saying that civilization blossomed first in Asia. He recalled a mythical era when 'the whole of eastern Asia from Burma to Japan was united with India in the closest tie of friendship, the only natural tie which can exist between nations'.[6] Asia was then organically united: 'There was a living communication of hearts, a nervous system evolved through which messages ran between us about the deepest needs of humanity.' Asia's mythical past was opposed in every way to the European political system that was founded on nation-states geared to compete with each other. Tagore's ideal was to revive this Asia, united in its burgeoning cultures and spiritual traditions. Wearing the halo of the first Asian recipient of the Nobel Prize, the poet set to work on his pan-Asianist ideals, by travelling extensively in the continent. Bowing to the logic of cultural diplomacy, he reinforced friendly relations between India, China, South-East Asian countries and Japan, which he visited many a time during the 1920s. His trip to China culminated in the creation of an Asian Association in Shanghai, the first concrete success of his ideal of a united Asian culture. A few years later, he established Shantiniketan, a university for higher studies on Asia.

The intellectual effervescence around the idea of Asia soon gave rise to a grand design of political mobilization at continental level. During the 1920s, militants of the Indian National Congress participated in various pan-Asian conferences: the Baku Conference in 1920, the First Pan-Asian Conference at Nagasaki in 1926 and the Pan-Asian Conference at Shanghai.[7] The Congress of Oppressed Nations, held in Brussels in 1927, assumed special importance. This assembly aimed at consolidating various liberation movements and struggles against imperialism. The first direct contact between Asian nationalist militants was established and Nehru felt that most Asian countries evinced a strong desire for closer ties.[8] In the 1930s, the nationalists of the Indian Congress took the initiative to organize various pan-Asian summits, such as the Asian Conference on Education at Benares in December 1930, the Asian Conference on Women in Lahore in January 1931, and the Pan-Asian Labour Conference in Colombo in May 1934. At the same time, Nehru took unofficial diplomatic trips to Myanmar and Malaysia in 1937, and to Sri Lanka and China in 1939. Nehru's visit to Beijing forged the Indian ideal of close cooperation with its Chinese neighbour. It also underlined India's solidarity with China against the Japanese aggressor. India's sympathy for China had, in fact, strengthened with the increasing disappointment with Japan's expansionism. Japan's attack on Korea in 1910–11 and the twenty-one ultimatums delivered to China altered to a great extent the admiration for Japan prevailing among a section of the Indian intelligentsia. The archipelago, which till 1920 was a role model in the eyes of a section of Indian nationalists, was accused of having succumbed to imperialist temptations imbibed from the West.

Soon after the First World War, the ideal of Asian solidarity evolved into plans for regional integration. The idea of an Asian Federation then became very much in vogue among the Indian intelligentsia. In 1928, the Congress got ready to organize the first session of the Pan-Asian Federation, to be held in 1930. However the Civil Disobedience movement launched by the Congress made it impossible to organize such a conference. Nevertheless, the enthusiasm of Indian nationalists for the idea of an Asian Federation did not die down, more so as it fitted in logically with the liberation of the nations of the continent. Indeed, it was felt that if the Asian countries stood united, independence would come faster. However, the concept of an Asian Federation fluctuated greatly. In August 1940, Nehru invoked a potential Eastern Federation, bringing together China, India, Myanmar, Sri Lanka and Afghanistan.[9] A few months later, he enlarged this regional plan to include Nepal, Thailand, Malaysia and Iran, as well as any other interested Asian nations.[10] Whatever the scenario, the Federation was not to be seen as a block or an alliance based on any logic of alignment. Nehru, who remained faithful to the thinking of Tagore and Vivekananda, conceived this plan as a quest for the renaissance of the spirit of Asian civilizations. The Asian Federation, in its substance, was the expression of an ideal model of international relations.

Thus, even before formally achieving independence, the interim Indian Government organized an Asian Relations Conference in March–April 1947. On the occasion of this event, Delhi played host to 250 delegates coming from both extremities of Asia, from Turkey and Egypt to Australia and New Zealand. Organized by a non-official and a non-political institution—the Indian Council for World Affairs—the conference was meant, in a way, to be the first phase in the formation of the Eastern Federation, and the principal objective was to discuss the common problems confronted by Asian countries in the post-war era. The discussions revealed the will of these nations to eradicate imperialism, colonialism and all forms of discrimination. Similarly, the participants pledged their solidarity with all liberation movements.[11] But above all, the conference established that Asia existed and was capable of making its voice heard in the international arena. In short, the Asian Relations Conference was seen as the first concrete statement of Asia's awakening. Jawaharlal Nehru wrote, at the time, 'an amazing success from every point of view. I think we can definitely call it the beginnings of a new era in Asian history. (. . .) We are all Asia-conscious at present.'[12]

As he clearly stated in his inaugural address, Nehru had the distinct feeling of living a historical moment. He was aware of the past grandeur of Asian civilizations and, thus, was convinced that the colonial era represented just an eclipse in their long history. Though it was an inevitable trend, the Asian Renaissance would become a reality only when all the nations of the continent would have gained their freedom. It appeared that the Congress party's pan-Asianism—especially Nehru's—was borne on the wings of its nationalism. Asian unity was founded on the shared experience of European domination and on the general aspiration for freedom in the continent. From this, Indian nationalists deduced a functional link between India's freedom struggle and other freedom movements in Asia. If India, which constituted the foundation of the British colonial empire, obtained its independence, the whole European imperial edifice would be shattered. The other argument put forth by Indian Congressmen was that when the nations of Asia attained independence, a natural cooperation would be established between them. Then, Asia would be able to play its due role in the world—the role of a peacemaker, which was characterized by the spirit of harmony. Thus, Asian cooperation was the first stage leading to the ideal new world order. Based on this chain of assumptions, the elites among India's Congressmen were imbued with a sense of responsibility for Asia's future and committed themselves to lead the movement for the decolonization of the whole continent.

In this perspective, the Indonesian issue was an occasion for India to take on the mantle of the defender of Asia's freedom. From July 1947, following Holland's repression in Indonesia, New Delhi referred the matter to the United Nations' Security Council and participated in its deliberations. Then, one of the first and most important acts of independent India in international affairs was to hold a Conference on Indonesia, which took place from 20 to 23 January 1949. The main objective of this gathering was to support the Indonesian Nationalist Movement and to put more pressure on the Dutch government. In the process, New Delhi played host to fifteen Asian countries, and the Conference on Indonesia, which was presided by Nehru, appeared to be the Second Asian Relations Conference.[13] There had been plans to hold a second conference in China. However, they did not materialize. The Indonesian issue thus gave India the opportunity to remain the backbone of pan-Asianism. Besides, Nehru recalled his commitment to the Eastern Federation plan in his speech to the assembly, and asked whether it was not 'natural' for independent Asian countries to begin thinking of a 'more permanent arrangement' than the conference, so that they could ensure 'effective mutual consultations and take counsel together to pursue (our) common goals'.

INDIA IN ASIA: A CONTROVERSIAL ROLE

The various conferences organized in the 1930s and 1940s clearly reflected India's ambition to be the leader of the Asian nations. Indeed, very soon after the formation of the Congress in 1885, Indian nationalists developed their vision of India's foreign policy, based on certain determining factors. According to them, India was destined to play a major role in Asia due to its geographical position, both in the Indian Ocean and within the Asian continental landmass, where it adjoined South-East Asia, as well as the Far East and the Middle East. This argument was also corroborated by the fact of India being the cornerstone of the British Empire. Another underlying factor of India's pre-eminent position in Asia was the many cultural strands that it had woven over many a thousand years with other Asian countries. Such an assumption however implied a fairly sensitive point: the Indian civilization's influence on the rest of Asia—glorified by the rediscovery of Greater India's cultural sphere. It is indeed of importance to note that, in India, the discovery of Asia took place in the context of the nationalist awakening. Thus, India's perception of Asia was fashioned by the need to forge a sense of pride so necessary for nationalism. In the process, certain Indian intellectuals endeavoured to show that the civilization of the sub-continent had radiated over the whole of Asia.

It was Kalidas Nag, an intellectual close to Tagore, who sponsored research on the Indian civilization's influence on Asia. After several voyages accompanying the Nobel Laureate to East Asia, he started the Greater India Society in 1926.[14] This movement of intellectuals based in Calcutta then began to publish regular bulletins called the *Journal of the Greater India Society*. The contributors—both Indians and Europeans—revealed and analysed the expansion of ancient Indian civilization in South-East Asia, China, Tibet and Central Asia. The articles were based on the vestiges of Buddhist expansion—sculptures, paintings, temples and inscriptions—and some Brahmanical remnants in these areas.[15] They advanced the theory that Buddhist expansion started as early as in the third and second centuries before Christ, through a land route linking China, Central Asia and India. Maritime routes linking the Indian Ocean and the South China Sea would have been established since the beginning of the first century of our era and would have allowed for the export of elements of Indian civilization to a great part of South-East Asia until the thirteenth century.

However, rather than speaking about the export of certain characteristics of Indian culture, the intellectual proclivity of the Greater India Society was to emphasize an actual process of Indianization. When the Greater India Society's scholars used the term 'Indianization', they meant not only that the language, literature and religion, but also the political and social institutions of South-East Asia were derived from Indian civilization. For instance, Majumdar's work, entitled *Ancient Indian Colonies in the Far East*,[16] was one of the Society's first publications. In this study, the author established that India launched the process of colonization in South-East Asia through commercial relations, as early as in the second century of our era and spoke about a forgotten Indian 'colonial Empire'.[17] In the process, he seemed to draw a parallel with a more recent period, the period of European colonization that his country was then experiencing. The experience of the British colonization of the subcontinent thus made the authors of the Greater India Society draw a parallel with the ancient Indianization of South-East Asia that they soon turned into a civilizing mission.[18] However, the Indianization process differed from European colonization in a fundamental way.

As Kalidas Nag explained, the Indian expansion very rarely turned into economic exploitation or political domination, as it was inspired by Emperor Ashoka's legacy: 'But there was no sordid chapter of continued economic exploitation or political domination in the development of Greater India which, coming as a legacy from Emperor Ashoka of the 3rd century BC, continued for over 1,000 years to foster the fundamental principle of *maitri* (fellowship) and *kalyana* (universal well-being) which form the bed-rocks of Hindu-Buddhist idealism.'[19]

Nag thus asserted that India was 'the heart of Asian Humanism'.[20] In other words, Indian colonial expansion was not driven by material interests and it was more of a cultural and religious order. Published between 1934 and 1959, the *Journal of the Greater India Society* conveyed the idea that India was the cradle of Asian civilization. This intellectual current thus nurtured a tendency in India to consider South-East Asia as an extension of the subcontinent rather than an area of convergence where Indian cultural elements were progressively blended with Polynesian and Malayan cultures, as well as the Chinese influence. Moreover, these works hardly spoke about the strands that Islam had woven between India and South-East Asia during a subsequent era. But, it was precisely because the reasoning of the Greater India theory promoted the argument of cultural expansion that it confined itself to the Hindu-Buddhist influx. These two religious currents were indeed born in India and had radiated from there, which enabled the authors to attribute to their country the status of a cultural and spiritual matrix of Asia. Islam, on the other hand, brought to mind the memories of India's own 'invasion'. In other words, the Greater India theory defended the idea of India's sphere of cultural influence in Asia.

While India displayed a somewhat patronizing attitude *vis-à-vis* South-East Asia, it considered China as its alter ego. The intellectuals of the Greater India society saw China as the second great source of civilizational influence in Asia and, therefore, professed a great admiration for the country. Furthermore, it was widely thought that the two neighbours had enjoyed excellent relations for millennia.[21] In this perspective, the proponents of the Greater India theory highlighted the role of Buddhist missionaries in establishing close ties between the two countries. The figure of Fa-Hien, a Chinese Buddhist pilgrim (399–414), who braved the Gobi desert to receive the teachings of the Buddha in Patna, was often cited as symbolizing the mutual enrichment that united India and China. However, it must be stressed that the tendency to recall ancient Sino-Indian relations was based upon the Buddhist connection. It showed that India was the one that extended its influence to China, and not the opposite. Once more, it was the argument of India's influence on Asia that was emphasized. Nevertheless, the members of the Greater India Society dreamt of resuscitating this ancient relationship and always worked toward Sino-Indian cooperation in the cultural and scientific fields.

According to the Greater India theory, the spread of Buddhism from India to Central and East Asia was at the origin of the spiritual homogeneity and cultural unity of the continent. Moreover, Buddhism being derived from the Hindu philosophical matrix, there were close affinities between the Hindu majority in India and the Buddhist countries of East Asia. Without exaggerating the influence of the Greater India theory on nationalist leaders, it seemed to have established an intellectual environment that was fairly loaded with underlying meanings. For instance, the Greater India theory was faithfully exploited by the Hindu nationalist group. Within the splinter group the Hindu Mahasabha,[22] certain militants had, for example, planned to organize a federation of all the nations that followed the Hindu or Buddhist religions. They dreamt of forming a pan-Buddhist block comprised of Japan, India, Tibet, Thailand, Sri Lanka, Cambodia, Java, China and Myanmar.[23] The Hindu Buddhist solidarity cultivated by these organizations was never so apparent as in their sympathy for Japanese imperialism. While the majority of Indians condemned Japan for its aggressive policy toward China, the Secretary General of the Hindu Mahasabha implored the Japanese Prime Minister and its people to believe that Hindu India did not support the Congress' condemnation. The members of the Congress' extremist cells also maintained some friendship with the archipelago. With the slogan 'Asia for Asians', certain nationalists like Subhas Chandra Bose, were swept away by the promise to liberate Asia from the yoke of the European colonial powers.

The Greater India concept never figured as an official reference in the Indian National Congress. Nevertheless, its influence remained significant.[24] Nehru himself was influenced by the works of the Greater India Society, since he made a reference to it in his book *The Discovery of India*. In fact, he spoke about 'the rich civilization they built up in their colonies and settlements and which endured for over thousand years'[25] and declared that the peoples of South-East Asia still nurtured a 'feeling of respect and friendship, for old memories endure and people have not forgotten that there was a time when India was a mother country to these and nourished them with rich fare from her own treasure-house'.[26] Nehru took up some of the arguments about India's cultural sphere of influence and the intrinsic ties between Buddhism and Hinduism. Like many other Indian nationalists, he believed that there was a great intimacy between the majority Hindu community of his country and its South, South-East and North-East Asian neighbours. This vision of India as the mother of all Asian civilizations probably explained the responsibility felt by certain members of the academic and diplomatic circles of that era for South-East Asia. K.M. Panikkar for instance, a historian and career diplomat who was close to Nehru, said that in the post-war context, India was necessarily the pivot of South-East Asia's economic development, political emancipation and strategic stability. He recalled that from the first century to the middle of the fifteenth century, the whole region (except Myanmar) was politically within the Indian sphere. Even when the Arabs arrived in the fifteenth century, followed by the Portuguese, in the sixteenth century, India continued to be the basis of the various political systems in South East Asia. This historical perspective led Panikkar to the following argument: India, which had seen South-East Asia develop within its orbit for nearly 2,000 years, was more than ever invested with a predominant role for this region at a time when European imperialism was crumbling.[27] In other words, Panikkar reckoned that India's independence and the creation of a stable and autonomous government were all the more urgent as the country had to fulfil its 'obligations' *vis-à-vis* South-East Asia's liberation.

But, this paternalism came to be too apparent during the Asian Relations Conference of 1947. The speeches delivered by the Indian representatives made many references to India's influence on the whole of Asia, and more generally, the Indian delegation did not hide the fact that it considered itself as the driving force of the continent's future. During his inaugural address, Nehru himself declared that India was 'the natural centre and focal point of the many forces at work in Asia'.[28] Furthermore, it was the founder of the Greater India Society, Kalidas Nag, who was appointed to write the preliminary documents on the discussion of the theme on Asia's 'Cultural Problems'. As a corollary to the conference, an architectural exhibition was held with the open aim of demonstrating the 'predominantly central position' that India occupied in Asia, both from the point of view of lines of communication and cultural flows. Regarding South-

East Asia, the exhibition displayed Hindu and Buddhist relics that bore witness to the influence of the Indian civilization on these lands. In many respects, the conference appeared to be the political translation of the Greater India theory, and this gave rise to undisguised opposition.

Indeed, the discussions during the conference revealed that the other Asian nations were not willing to acknowledge India's leading role. Small nations like Sri Lanka, Myanmar, Malaysia and Indonesia expressed in no uncertain terms their fear of an 'aggression, not necessarily political but economic and demographic, by their big brothers like China and India'.[29] Therefore, the idea of a regional Asian organization seemed, to them, to be filled with danger—that of becoming the subjects of one of the Big Brothers. The South-East Asian opposition to their huge neighbours also ensued from the problematic presence of Indian and Chinese diasporas. Since the 1920s, the fear of being drowned by an Indian demographic wave had nurtured anti-Indian movements in Myanmar, Malaysia and Sri Lanka. Finally, the tendancy of certain Indian intellectuals, like Kalidas Nag, to assert that the Indian diaspora was the contemporary incarnation of the Modern Greater India, could not but aggravate South-East Asian fears.[30] The Chinese delegation, for its part, adopted a prudent attitude, and was reluctant to see India being recognized as the leader of the Asian cultural pack. In fact, China did not have a very flattering opinion about India, and rivalry between the two was already apparent, in spite of Nehru's goodwill. Thus, at the Asian Relations Conference, the two neighbours did not seem to be particularly fond of each other and Beijing insisted that India should not become the permanent host of pan-Asian conferences.[31]

THE FAILURE OF INDIA'S ASIANISM IN THE POST-COLONIAL ERA

The Asian Relations Conference constituted both the zenith of Asian solidarity and the beginning of its decline.[32] Despite an apparent success, the conference pointed toward future conflicts between the countries of the continent. The leading role that Indian Congressmen wanted to be awarded with received the consent of very few nations. Nehru then lost his enthusiasm for the Asian Federation plan and, in 1950, accepted for the first time that Asia was not a political entity and the pan-Asian conferences were of little use.[33] His vision of Asia after this became much more realistic. It was no longer based on the idealistic ambition of creating an Asian Federation, and more on preserving some independence for the newly-born nations, faced with the creation of two rival blocks. Thus, Nehru endeavoured to hedge between the growing polarization of the Cold War, more so as India and China were also drifting towards opposite poles—liberal democracy on one side, and communism on the other. Besides, Nehru was worried about the growth of the communist movements in Indonesia, Malaysia, Myanmar, and even India. Not only did Nehru strongly condemn South-East Asia's communist movements, he also supported the repressions against the communist rebellions that erupted in Indonesia and Malaysia. As for Myanmar, he promised military and financial aid to U Nu to stifle the communist insurrection there. In this context, the Eastern Federation plan seemed more utopic then ever. Thus, Nehru shifted to the idea of non-alignment, which was more suitable in a context of growing regional and international rivalries.[34]

Moreover, the non-alignment option had the advantage of offering some breathing space so as to attempt establishing cordial relations with China. At that time, Beijing was very critical of India, accusing Nehru of being a vassal of the imperialist block. Nevertheless, Nehru continued to mollify the communist regime in Beijing. India was one of the first countries to recognize the Popular Republic of China, proclaimed by Mao Zedong on 1 October 1949. Nehru was truly delighted at the birth of a united and powerful China. In his view, the liberation of the largest oppressed nation in Asia marked a critical step in the process of emancipation of the continent. Thus, Nehru remained convinced that the two nations would continue maintaining the friendly relations they had cultivated through thousands of years.

At the same time, India, which had established itself as the spokesperson for Asia in the United Nations during the 1950s,[35] acted as a mediator between the western block and China, in periods of crisis. Indian diplomacy actually devoted its energy to breaking the diplomatic isolation of China. It strongly supported China's entry into the Security Council throughout the negotiations on the Korean War, between 1950 and 1953.[36] It also strove to find a solution to the Korean civil war thanks to a formula for the exchange of POWs with an Indian Protection Force assuming charge of the delicate task of repatriating prisoners. While Asia still remained a priority, India's initiatives arose more from the desire to avoid the extension of the

Cold War to Asian soil, rather than pan-Asian concerns. The same desire of international appeasement guided the Indian position *vis-à-vis* the Indo-Chinese conflict. India abstained from supporting the Vietnamese communist movement until 1954. But when the conflict entered Cold War logic and the risk of massive American intervention was imminent, Nehru decided to get involved and appealed for an immediate ceasefire. He participated in the forum of the five Asian powers at the Colombo Conference,[37] on 10 April 1954, and drew up a six-point agreement, which was later presented by Krishna Menon in Geneva. However, all these Indian initiatives were not totally altruistic; they actually proved that New Delhi still very much aspired to play the role of Asian spokesperson and, henceforth, of Africa too. And while the series of events in 1954 and 1955 appeared to mark the zenith of India's prestige, they were also the forerunners of its marginalization in Asia.

Nehru's extensive efforts to establish a healthy relationship with China culminated in his meeting with Chou En-lai, in April 1954. Their joint communiqué instituted the 'Panchsheel', i.e. the five principles of peaceful coexistence—mutual respect for the integrity and sovereignty of each other, non-aggression, non-interference in each other's internal matters, equality and mutual assistance, and peaceful coexistence. For Nehru, the principles seemed all the more promising as they stemmed from the common cultural source of the *Panchasheel*, i.e. the five Buddhist virtues. India also emphasized its close ties with Beijing when the United States launched the South-East Asian Treaty Organization,[38] on 8 September 1954. Nehru condemned non-communist East Asian Nations, most of which had, by 1954, entered into a pact with the American alliance system. From the Indian viewpoint, these nations, which had barely freed themselves of the colonial yoke, had immediately become vassals in a system that was nothing else but a new version of a protectorate.

As for the Bandung conference, from 18–24 April 1955, it was supposed to extend the spirit of *Panchsheel* to all the nations of Asia and Africa. At this event, Nehru endeavoured to ensure that China be recognized as a legitimate power in Asia. It is paradoxical that the very success of his initiative was of more benefit to China than India. Chou En-lai managed to convince a large number of South-East Asian nations that peaceful coexistence was possible. And while the initial contacts between China and the other Asian countries appeared reassuring, tensions cropped up between Nehru and the five powers of the Colombo conference. In a way, Bandung marked the end of India's ambitions for the continent and further diluted India's Pan-Asianism in the larger global issues of the Third World, South-South Cooperation and, especially, Non-Alignment. From 1955 onwards, India's foreign policy became increasingly indifferent to the political and military developments in its eastern neighbourhood. Then, China's invasion of Tibet in 1959 and the border war with India in 1962 came as bruising experience, and the Sino-Indian conflict put an end, once and for all, to Nehru's dreams of Asia.[39] The trauma was all the more painful since India believed in an idealized vision of Sino-Indian history. As a result, a strong sense of betrayal was to linger, which would make the renewal of ties a difficult task. The 1962 humiliation considerably tarnished India's aura and its foreign policy orientations would remain affected for a long time. The erstwhile global ambitions nurtured by India were henceforth to be confined to its South Asian neighbours.

While India's diplomacy retreated into its shell and increasingly neglected its South-East Asian neighbours, one political current in India continued to demand a special focus on this region. It came from the Hindu nationalist party, the Jana Sangh. Based on its defiance to communist China, the party called for India to make common cause with South-East Asia, on the basis of its commonality of interests. Thus, the Jana Sangh revived several elements of the Greater India theory. For instance, its ideologue, Balraj Madhok, declared that the East Asian countries belonged to the same cultural family as their 'elder sister' India did, and they expected her to play the 'natural role of a friend and guide'.[40] Therefore, according to him, New Delhi should have taken the initiative to revive cultural and religious ties within the Indo-Buddhist family. In the same perspective, M.L. Sondhi, another Jana Sangh member, asserted that India could well build a Buddhism-inspired consensus with countries like Thailand, Cambodia, Laos and Myanmar. In brief, the Jana Sangh recommended that the government turn more towards East Asia rather than the West, asserting that this zone represented India's natural sphere of influence.[41]

In spite of the Jana Sangh's insistence, the rift between India and East Asia continued to widen throughout the Cold War. During the 1960s and 1970s, India's relations with South-East Asia became the by-product of its contentious relations with Pakistan and China. To counter what it perceived as a Sino-American rapprochement, New

Delhi started leaning increasingly on the USSR and finally signed an Indo-Soviet Friendship Treaty, in 1971. This decision was diametrically opposed to its interests in South-East Asia, where most nations supported the West. China, which had moved considerably closer to the United States after President Nixon's visit to Beijing, was henceforth welcomed as a legitimate power in the international arena. Its acceptance by South-East Asia, which began at the Bandung Conference, was legitimized in 1974, when, for the first time, an ASEAN country—Malaysia—established diplomatic relations with Beijing. On the contrary, relations between India and ASEAN deteriorated, especially due to their divergent viewpoints on the issue of the Indo-Chinese peninsula. In 1980, the Indian Foreign Minister—none other than P.V. Narasimha Rao—declined Malaysia's invitation to participate in the ASEAN Foreign Ministers meeting. New Delhi was indeed on the verge of recognizing the pro-Vietnamese regime of Heng Samrin in Cambodia. This decision, which was partly aimed at strengthening Vietnam against China, was seen as a veritable slap in ASEAN's face, whose priority was, precisely, to ostracize the Samrin regime. The fact was that India's perspective was based on politico-strategic concerns, to the detriment of economic aspects, and it considered its relations with ASEAN as secondary.

4.2 India's Asianism in the 1990s: Catching up with the 'New Asia'

During the 1970s and 1980s, the Cold War continued to aggravate ideological differences between India and most East Asian states. But it was perhaps economic performances that widened the rift even more blatantly. Thanks to their successful development, the ASEAN nations joined the stream of high growth economies, led by Japan and South Korea. That was when the Pacific metaphor emerged, in reference to this part of Asia that enjoyed exceptional growth rates. The dividing line became clearly visible between India, with its autarkic economic system, and its eastern neighbours, integrated within the prosperous and highly publicized Pacific sphere. However, the much-talked about prediction about the 'Pacific Century' could not leave India indifferent. Not surprinsingly, the first reorientation of Indian foreign policy took place under Rajiv Gandhi. The young Prime Minister made several official visits abroad where he gave a dynamic image of his country. Between 1986 and 1989, he conceived a new policy for South-East Asia, and aimed at developing economic relations with the countries of this region, with Singapore and Thailand heading the list. At the same time, there was a spurt in economic relations with Japan. Finally, Rajiv's visit to Beijing, in December 1988, opened a new era of detente between the two neighbours. In the late 1980s, the situation was thus favourable for a greater interest in East Asia. But, it was especially in the post-Cold War period that New Delhi worked to assume a role in Asia's renaissance. Needless to say, the diplomatic approach to East Asia was markedly different from the Nehruvian era. New Delhi did not, however, renounce in totality its heritage from the pre-independence era and redefined certain elements of its pan-Asianism of the 1930s and 1940s. But its discourse proved more modest in its ambitions: the priority was to sensitize its East Asian interlocutors to the opening of the Indian economy.

KEEPING A LOW PROFILE AND RESPECTING EAST ASIAN DIPLOMATIC SENSITIVITIES

In the early 1990s, India woke up to South-East Asia's economic success and felt it was lagging behind. This underlying malaise was well described by analyst Gurcharan Das: 'Some in India (. . .) suffer from such envy that they can't bear the thought that the East Asian countries, which were poor like us in the fifties, have gone ahead by a generation.'[42] Economic preoccupations predominated in the new open policy towards East Asia. As it has already been mentioned, the main aim of the Look East policy was to incorporate the Indian economy in the Asian economic regionalization. But New Delhi also wanted to become a member of the different institutions that were giving shape to the East Asian region. ASEAN was the number one target, as the association was considered to be at the heart of Asian regionalism. New Delhi thus found itself knocking on ASEAN's doors, some ten years after having ignored their invitation to a post-ministerial conference. In so doing, India came to realize that its South-East Asian policy had to be reformulated. Nehruvian paternalism was no longer valid. On the contrary, pragmatism and humility were the order of the day. At the same time, to attract investors and integrate with regional institutions, India had to emphasize its geographical, cultural and historical closeness with East Asia. India thus attempted to participate in the creation of an 'Asian consciousness' and, to this effect, lay emphasis on the 'rediscovery of a shared past'.[43] But the return to history was based on selective criteria and was driven by very present-day concerns. In brief, the Indian diplomacy adapted itself to the prevailing sensibilities and norms of East Asia.

The first imperative to be complied with was not to ruffle its partner's feathers. In this regard, the commemoration of the Asian Relations Conference, in October 1987, already portended the new Indian approach: that of wearing its modesty on its sleeve. Organized by the New Delhi-based India International Centre, it was an unofficial event and primarily brought together intellectuals.[44] The euphoria of the first edition was transformed into a sober assessment of the past forty years. A modest approach to the possibilities of future cooperation was examined, while recognizing that sub-regional entities such as ASEAN or SAARC, were more effective than pan-Asian initiatives. The participants noted, above all, that Asian countries had remained strangers to one another. This moderate posture came to be the driving force behind the Look East policy of the 1990s. Thenceforth, Indian diplomats strove to formulate as consensual as possible a picture of ancient ties. Most of the speeches made on East Asia did refer to the intense religious and cultural exchanges India had with the region, in the early centuries of our era. But invoking ancient relations between India and East Asia—in particular South-East Asia—was a delicate diplomatic exercise that was likely to bring back memories of the Greater India theories. References to this period of history were far from appreciated by these countries, even in the 1940s and 1950s. They would be even less welcome in the 1990s, as the thesis of Indian cultural expansion had been largely transformed in South-East Asia.

The invalidation of the Greater India theories was first the work of Western historians, who brought into focus the richness of pre-existing local cultures.[45] To cite an example, as early as in 1959, Jean Filliozat accused the Greater India scholars of exaggerating the importance of Indian elements in South-East Asian civilizations, to the detriment of the syncretism promoted by local cultures.[46] Criticism of such intellectual tradition gradually developed within some circles of Indian historians. Romila Thapar did not hesitate to classify the works of the Greater India Society as part of the pan-Hindu movement.[47] D.P. Chattopadhyaya considered that the views of Indian historians specializing in Ancient India continued to create problems, especially in South-East Asia, where Indian historiography on this period was accused of suffering from a colonial and paternalistic mindset.[48] In

Indonesia, for example, Dutch historians and archaeologists adopted the opposite view of the theory of Indian colonization.[49] The latter set forth the hypothesis that the South-East Asian monarchs invited the Brahmins at their own initiative. Thus, India did not impose its culture. Rather, the peoples of South-East Asia assimilated certain elements of Indian culture on their own initiative. Therefore, the argument of ancient India's contribution to the civilization of the region was very likely to be misunderstood and to aggravate the feeling of cultural oppression. Taking into consideration the different interpretations of ancient history, Arun Dasgupta, recommended that Indian diplomatic circles avoid the Greater India theory in its classical form and warned: 'We have to be very cautious about raising this subject of ancient India's contribution to Indonesian culture. If we are not careful we are likely to be misunderstood. Clearly the Greater India concept cannot be of much use today in its older form. It was born out of a nationalist fervour and inevitably produces a nationalist reaction in South-East Asia.'[50]

This new intellectual approach was somewhat more respectful of the vision that South-East had of itself. For instance, Chan Heng Chee, former director of ISEAS, recalled, at one of Prime Minister P.V. Narasimha Rao's conferences, that South-East Asia was, above all, like a crossroads of influences: 'South-East Asia is a region which lies between the two oceans, the Indian and the Pacific, between two giants, India and China. Historically and culturally, it has been enriched by the settlement and by the heritage of these two civilizations interacting with the indigenous peoples and cultures. India, through trade and missionaries, left a strong imprint of Hindu culture on many ancient South-East Asian empires.'[51]

In this portrayal of South-East Asia, Chan Heng Chee first underlined the importance of local cultures. He then observed that the Chinese pole had marked South-East Asia as much—if not more than—the Indian one. China had, in fact, influenced a great part of this region for several centuries, as it enjoyed deep cultural and commercial ties with its South-East Asian neighbours, between the eighth and fifteenth centuries. Trade between the ports of China and the Malayan Sultanates flourished, until the advent of the West put an end to this prosperous period. From this perspective, any debate on the pre-eminence of India's influence seemed very much misplaced.

Therefore, New Delhi strove to adopt a consensual diplomatic approach. Its new diplomatic discourse revolved, thenceforth, around the dilution of the idea of South-East Asia's Indianization and focused on the theme of syncretism. India and South-East Asia were presumed to have enjoyed symbiotic relations, which gave rise to a veritable process of interpenetration of their civilizations. The speech by the Indian Foreign Minister, I.K. Gujral, at the ASEAN post-ministerial conference[52] in July 1996, was a good example of the desire not to hurt South-East Asian pride: 'Where else have entire civilizations grown up in such a proximity and symbiosis, sustaining, re-inventing and enriching each other over the vicissitudes of centuries?'[53] On the occasion of India's first participation in a post-ministerial conference, I.K. Gujral went to the extent of reversing the theory of Indianization and declared that 'the footprints of South-East Asia are to be seen in every aspect of India's ethos'.[54] In other words, New Delhi sought to draw an ideal portrait of the ancestral closeness between India and South-East Asia. Gujral then gave special consideration to vague temporal clichés of a distant past, as if exchanges between the two zones went back to the dawn of time: 'We have been neighbours and friends in time, space and existence for as long back as we can remember'.[55] In the same fashion, the Indian ambassador to Thailand, Ranjit Gupta, made a speech at Thammasat University that was just as accommodating. Far from the complacency of yore, he displayed a rather grateful attitude to the Thai people, asserting that they had known how to adopt and preserve important aspects of the sub-continent's civilization.[56] Above all, Ranjit Gupta stressed the active role played by South-East Asian countries in importing Indian culture. In no way was it imposed on them. Furthermore, he clearly stated that these cultural elements were first adopted in Indonesia and Cambodia, before Thailand imported them 'of its own accord'.

In the 1990s, India took good care not to talk about any process of Indianization, and not to boast about being the mother of all Asian civilizations. This diplomatic stand, which was taken in order not to hurt South-East Asian sensibilities, marked a change in India's foreign policy practices. For a long time indeed, New Delhi thought that it was destined to exert a dominating influence over Asia and in the international arena, due to the grandeur of its ancient past. But by the 1990s, it appeared that some members of the diplomatic corps had realized that this assumption was obsolete. In a critical analysis of India's foreign policy for the past fifty years, J.N. Dixit, a former Foreign Secretary, concluded that India suffered from an exaggerated opinion of its role in international affairs. He added that, with its high moral grounds and references to its civilization, New Delhi had alienated a good number of its interlocutors. But if Dixit was to be believed, India would be more conscious of the sensibilities of its South-East Asian counterparts in the future: 'It is obvious that if we tell our neighbours in the ASEAN that their culture and their language and their history are all the exclusive result of Indian civilizational forces, they would resent this superciliousness. They have their own sense of identity and their national pride.'[57]

Another diplomat, Professor S.D. Muni, shared the same critical view of the diplomatic style inherited from Nehru. He recalled that many Asian leaders found him too moralizing and paternalistic[58] and were never inclined to share his vision of India's natural destiny to play a pivotal role between a flourishing Asia and Western superpowers. S.D. Muni's criticism attacked the very foundation of Nehru's foreign policy. In his view, economic and military components, which constituted the core of a state's might, were downplayed in favour of a moral and spiritual conception of international relations. As a result, in matters of foreign policy, Nehru concentrated his energies on resolving crises, in keeping with his quest for international peace. On the other hand, very little effort was made in the External Affairs Ministry to develop bilateral relations, particularly with South-East Asian countries. Sharing this view, Arjun Asrani, a former Ambassador to Thailand and Japan, regretted that India had ignored opportunities for economic cooperation with Japan during the 1950s, when Tokyo had proposed to support the Asian Development Fund. South-East and North-East Asian countries, on the contrary, swept the painful memories of Japanese imperialism under the carpet and cooperated with the archipelago, in keeping with their pragmatic approach to foreign policy. The former diplomat concluded most pragmatically: 'Today, it is we who are knocking at the door of APEC for admission. (. . .) we should have shown better understanding of the pragmatism of the neighbours to our East instead of treating them as American surrogates.'[59]

The low profile taken by the Indian diplomacy was therefore aimed at demonstrating that the country did no longer claim to be Asia's leader because of the grandeur of its ancient civilization. New Delhi would only attempt to attract the goodwill and cooperation of its eastern neighbours from then on. This measured approach was all the more in tune with reality as India had neglected its relations with South-East Asia for a long time and considered it a non-priority region.[60] Moreover, in the early to mid-1990s, ASEAN did not have a very flattering opinion about India. The Association had not forgotten that New Delhi had been a close ally of the USSR and a firm friend of Vietnam, at a time when communism was their biggest threat. These misgivings were compounded by concerns about the ambitions of the Indian navy in the Bay of Bengal in the late 1980s. Thus, India was fully aware of the suspicions and discomfort that any invocation of its past glory was likely to provoke. As a result, New Delhi preferred to play a prudent game and talk about priorities more suited to the times—pragmatism, consensus, equal partnership—precisely the cardinal points of ASEAN's diplomatic functioning. The keynote of India's policy with regard to the ASEAN was 'quiet diplomacy', i.e. a modest and discrete diplomacy. New Delhi and the Association also agreed that their partnership should commence in an incremental manner. The first time it participated in a post-ministerial conference, India spelt out, through its representative, I.K. Gujral, the new tenets of its foreign policy in South-East Asia: 'We (. . .) will handle the partnership with pragmatism and consensus orientation, taking a leaf out of the ASEAN book.'[61] The days of Indian arrogance were over, with the country officially promising to toe the line of the region's diplomatic practices and principles. Therefore, during the ASEAN post-ministerial conferences, Indian diplomats maintained a low profile, and endeavoured, above all, to listen and take note of the views of ASEAN's member countries. In its speeches as well as in practice, Indian diplomacy displayed a commendable effort to appear as a credible partner, along with a willingness to adapt itself to the ASEAN way.

INSTRUMENTALISING THE SHARED VALUES WITH EAST ASIA

It appears that Indian diplomacy adapted itself to the norms set by its South-East Asian interlocutors by proceeding to a selective recycling of the pan-Asianism of the 1930s and 1940s. Thanks to this pragmatic approach, it was able to emphasize the notion of Asian values to achieve its objective of economic and institutional integration in the Asian region. More precisely, the reference to a shared past—devoid of its polemic dimensions—allowed India to propose a definition of an Asian identity that enhanced the contribution of its civilization. We have indeed seen that, as a first step, Indian diplomacy focused extensively on recalling how close the Indian and South-East Asian civilizations were. On the basis of that cultural syncretism, it then proceeded to define an Asian ethos that expressed itself through a profound sense of symbiosis and harmony. This, according to Prime Minister P.V. Narasimha Rao, could be seen in the proclivity to seek consensus and avoid conflict that characterized India and most other Asian societies.[62] This sense of harmony was raised to an abstract level that emphasized the capacity to embrace both the 'individual' and the 'collective' at the same time. Referred to extensively in Prime Minister P.V. Narasimha Rao's speeches in East Asia, these issues conveyed the vision of holistic and organic societies, which put a premium on compassion and sharing. In his 1994 Singapore Lecture, the Indian Prime Minister evoked 'the essentially Asian ethos of compassion, harmony and a sense of sharing, where the individual and the collective entities are beautifully blended to make life a consistent whole'.[63] Other common virtues of India and East Asia were their deference for the past and the respect for family ties.[64] In brief, Asian societies stood out as they preserved their traditional values. In many respects, the Indian diplomatic discourse defined the idea of Asia as opposed to a West that was traditionally considered as modern, individualistic and materialistic.

In so doing, New Delhi based its approach on a very classical line of argument that consisted in founding the unity of Asia on the importance given, throughout the region, to spirituality. Referring to Tagore and Okakura, Rao reiterated in Japan that 'Asia is one, the essence of that oneness being spirituality'.[65] And he added that this aspiration towards the immaterial explained the richness of its philosophies and religious systems. At the same time, this definition helped Prime Minister Rao highlight the contribution of his country to the Asian ethos by invoking 'the great religions of Buddhism and Hinduism that spread across this vast continent'.[66] Thus, Indian diplomacy of the 1990s gladly recalled the trajectories of Buddhist expansion from India to East Asia. These ancient contacts constituted an ever-enduring religious affiliation between India and Buddhist nations like Thailand, Japan or South Korea. 'Buddhism came to Korea from India via China, and forms an enduring common link between us', declared Prime Minister Rao during his visit to Seoul.[67] New Delhi then put forth the argument that, given their common religious heritage, the peoples of India and East Asia shared a legacy of peaceful traditions, friendship and tolerance, and were infused with a deep sense of comradeship.

But when Rao highlighted the shared values between India and East Asia, it was in reference to Indian concepts that he so often rediscovered in other cultures. To illustrate his point, in a speech in Thailand, he spoke about 'the indefinable and untranslatable sense of what is called *rita* in Sanskrit—something ingrained as an instinct of sight in our societies'.[68] In brief, invoking Buddhist links led to the definition of an Asian identity that fully acknowledged the importance of the Indian civilization. The paradox was that Buddhism was almost extinct on Indian soil and, to be more precise, had been driven away by Hinduism. Islam, which, on the other hand, was an important rallying point between the subcontinent and a number of South-East Asian nations, was rarely referred to.[69] It was true that emphasizing the Indian origins of Buddhism enhanced the prestige of India, which was then seen as a latecomer *vis-à-vis* the success of the tigers and dragons.[70] Moreover, Buddhism had left behind an incomparable spiritual and artistic heritage in East Asia. This was testified, in the field of architecture, by the Angkor monuments in Cambodia, Ayutthaya in Thailand or Borobudur on the island of Java, sites that were also a source of national pride. Moreover, whether it was Theravada or Mahayana, Buddhism had often spread Hindu tradition and art. Thanks to these recurrent references to ancient history, Indian diplomacy could present its country as a natural—if not inalienable—member of the New Asia. In this regard, the semantics of community or family were very much evident in diplomatic speeches describing the ties between India and its neighbours in East Asia. Thus, Rao declared in his Singapore Lecture that Indian and East Asian civilizations were 'organically linked'.[71] In Thailand, he spoke of 'a kindred nation',[72] given the common Buddhist heritage. Similarly, most of his addresses asserted, recurrently, that Asian countries were 'brethren'. As for I.K. Gujral, he used the strong metaphor of the 'mother continent of Asia'. This formula appeared to be patterned on 'Mother India', the highly emotionally-charged nomenclature that Indians attributed to their motherland.

More importantly, the definition of an Asian identity, with India as one of the civilizational mainstays, was meant to uphold the aims of the Look East policy. By highlighting the values shared with East Asia, India hoped to facilitate economic relations, as well as its admission in regional institutions. In fact, the Indian discourse asserted that, given its cultural affinity with South-East Asia, New Delhi was a natural partner of ASEAN. In other words, India was convinced of being able to adapt itself easily to the ASEAN way. This, in any case, was Foreign Minister I.K. Gujral's argument: 'We are confident that with our common traditions of *Ahimsa*, *Panchsheela* and *Samanvaya*, of tolerance and gentleness, we can slip into the ASEAN culture easily'.[73] The notions of shared values and common historical experiences were also used to stress the fact that India was different from the other partners of the South-East Asian Association and aspired to enjoy a privileged relationship.[74] Indian diplomacy therefore proceeded to use culture and history consciously so as to spur on the new Indo-ASEAN partnership. Foreign Minister I.K. Gujral did not hide this fact and asserted that the age-old ties between India and South-East Asia ought to be the 'emotive driving force' for a significant development of Indo-ASEAN relations.

An identical logic was followed in bilateral relations with each East Asian state. In Thailand's case, for example, the alleged proximity with the Indian value systems was expected to ensure prosperous relations, in any field. Thus, Prime Minister Rao declared confidently, 'Whether it is a political dialogue or commercial relations, cultural affinities or scientific and technological exchanges, academic interaction or religious links—every area of India-Thailand cooperative action is imbued with a sense of shared values that reinforces our ties.'[75] Seen from this perspective, Indian foreign policy had not rid itself completely of the culturalist vision of Asian cooperation that most nationalists had held at the time of independence. It continued to establish an intrinsic link between cultural affinities and political relations. The same presupposition still existed, according to which political or economic cooperation was self-evident due to a so-called common cultural base. However much Indian diplomacy may have founded its hopes on the notion of a shared past, it was not a premise that could be taken for granted, especially with the pragmatic nations of South-East Asia.

But, it was still at the level of the states of the Indian Federation that the exploitation of cultural ties was the most evident. For a state like Bihar—whose landlocked position and economic dynamism could not be used as an asset for South-East Asia—only its historical heritage remained. In 1995, Chief Minister Laloo Prasad Yadav went to promote—not without aplomb—the potential of one of India's poorest states to investors in Thailand and Singapore. It was not by accident that the Chief Minister chose to visit South-East Asia for his first foreign tour. Indeed, to buttress his claims, Yadav exhumed the

Buddhist past of his state, deliberately reminding his audience that Bihar was the land of King Ashoka, who had sent Buddha's message to distant East Asian countries.[76] Lacking in economic potential, Bihar, thus posed as a historic and religious centre and, on this basis, called for the attention of Buddhist nations.

But Indian political leaders did not just play the card of common values to awaken East Asia's interest. They also re-appropriated the 'Asian Century' discourse. In the early 1990s, this cliché was very much in vogue in all of East Asia, as well as in the West. In this connection, New Delhi hastened to remind everyone that the early Indian nationalists were among the most fervent harbingers of the continent's awakening. Once again, Indian diplomacy relied on the sort of legitimacy bestowed by history to become a part of contemporary and future regional developments. In this light, Indian leaders very often referred to the early thinkers about Asia's renaissance. In the Singapore conference, one of Rao's most important speeches aimed at launching the Look East policy, Rabindranath Tagore was quoted extensively, for the Indian poet had predicted Asia's renaissance right at the beginning of the twentieth century. Indian diplomacy also initiated a lexical recycling of Nehru's speeches. Thus, the generic title always used to refer to Indo-ASEAN relations was 'Friends and Neighbours',[77] which had already been used by Nehru in his inaugural address at the Asian Relations Conference. Similarly, India obtaining the status of ASEAN's dialogue partner marked, according to I.K. Gujral, 'a second phase of Asian resurgence',[78] the first being Nehru's attempts to unify the continent's various nations. Asian audiences were also reminded systematically that India's initiative was instrumental in the organization of the first Asian Relations Conference, in 1947.

Indian diplomacy did not stop at emphasizing the contributions of its national elite in the formulation of the Asian Century. It also recalled Nehru's fervour for Asian solidarity, as for him, India's independence was intrinsically linked with the political freedom of the continent's other nations. Thus, I.K. Gujral declared, 'After half a century's struggle for freedom, virtually the first political act of independent India was a reaffirmation of Asian solidarity.'[79] This reminder was obviously construed as an invitation to the North-East and South-East Asian countries to evince a similar spirit of mutual consideration at a time when India was opening up its economy. In this sense, the logic of India's diplomatic discourse remained faithful to Nehru's vision: Asia could only progress collectively. In other words, Asia was seen as an entity whose different parts should evolve in the same direction. Perhaps this was the meaning that should be attributed to Gujral's declaration that 'The vision of Asia for the next millennium must have its roots in the long centuries of past history which we share and which indeed created our identity.'[80] Moreover, the idea of a common destiny was very much present in the speech. The title of I.K. Gujral's address in 1996 bears testimony to this fact: 'India and the ASEAN: A Shared Destiny'. But the repeated invocation of Asia's common history, in the final analysis, had but a single objective: to convince the world that India was a stakeholder in Asia's resurgence.

However, history does not support the argument on Asian unity. In the twentieth century, the continent was the victim of several wars. As for New Delhi, it had evinced little interest in East Asia since the 1960s. But to preserve its internal cohesion, India's diplomatic discourse declared that Asian countries had torn at each other or ignored each other solely because of the Cold War.[81] The Indian discourse thus succeeded in explaining that despite their natural inclination for cohabitation and cooperation, India and East Asian nations had spent a major part of their history ignoring each other's existence. The era of colonization followed by the Cold War rifts had kept them apart, in spite of their ancient relations based on syncretism.[82] Flowing from this, the discourse remained silent about the ties that could have been forged during the colonial era. For instance, a large chunk of the Indian diaspora reached South-East Asia under the British Empire as plantation labourers. Moreover, British colonization had left behind a legacy that was common to both India and South-East Asia, especially the legal system. In Singapore, the then Minister of Information and Arts, George Yeo, did not fail to mention this shared legacy to promote India's potential.[83] But New Delhi's official version continued to state that, twice—during the colonial era and the Cold War—Asia had suffered a veritable 'alienation' under the Western stranglehold. As a counterpoint, this alienation thesis proved that Asian renaissance could emanate only from the rediscovery of its identity and unity.

Indian leaders had not missed their mark. While their discourse sometimes retained certain Nehruvian messianic inflections, they, however, knew that henceforth they had to play for essentially commercial and financial stakes. In this perspective, the major concern of India's diplomacy was to constantly recall that India meant to play its part in Asia's *economic* resurgence. Underlying the commitment to return to the 'mother continent of Asia' was the necessity to attract Asia's investments. Thus, it is not surprising that a substantial part of this diplomatic discourse dwelt extensively on promoting India's economic potential, though never forgetting to mention the notion of shared history, in the past and in the future. Propelled by the principles of economic diplomacy, India's diplomats attempted to convince investors on the basis of Asian solidarity and the collective destiny of the continent's nations. Thus, Rao declared, 'My present endeavour is to draw, as much as possible, investment and co-operation from the Asia-Pacific countries, in consonance with our common concept and solidarity and my faith in our common destiny.'[84] Investing in India therefore meant completing the process of Asia's resurgence. In fact, the opening up of India's economy had to be seen as the awakening of an indispensable actor in the continent's evolution. Rao thus reassured that 'The countries of the Asia-Pacific will find in India a reliable partner, a vast market, the process of whose development will simultaneously involve the renaissance of a great and noble civilization which we all share in some measure.'[85]

In brief, India's diplomatic discourse in the 1990s was structured, above all, around its economic concerns and referred to historical and cultural affinities in order to sensitize foreign investors. The concept of shared values was primarily aimed at reassuring Asia's business communities for whom India was often either an unknown factor or a country plagued by various tensions. By guaranteeing that India obeyed a value system akin to theirs, diplomats attempted to provide a sense of familiarity and convince investors that it would be easy to set-up projects in India. The sense of closeness to a culture or a country was often a favourable parameter for investment flows, especially from Japan and Singapore. Thus, before a Japanese audience, Prime Minister Rao strove to prove that consensus was a long-standing tradition that continued to drive a number of aspects of day-to-day life in India.[86] In so doing, he sought to downplay one of the main fears of the Japanese with regard to the chaotic, undisciplined and even conflict-ridden character of the Indian society.

4.3 The Hindu Nationalist Approach

Given the intellectual connection between the Greater India theory and the Hindu nationalist movement, the coming to power of a coalition government led by the Bharatiya Janata Party in March

1998 could have resulted in a divergence in India's diplomatic discourse with regard to East Asia. Moreover, when the party took up the reins of the government, the 1997 financial crisis had seriously tarnished the image of the tigers and the dragons. It must therefore be seen how the BJP handled India's cultural past *vis-à-vis* a politically and economically weakened region. Further, a clear distinction must be made between the BJP, the political party in power, and its ideological political base, the RSS (Rashtriya Swayamsevak Sangh or National Volunteers' Association).[87]

EAST ASIA IN THE SANGH PARIVAR'S PERSPECTIVES

The diplomatic discourse of the BJP-led government on South-East Asia proved more along the moderate lines followed by its predecessors in power rather than the tenets of the Greater India theoreticians. The Planning Commission's Deputy Chairman, Jaswant Singh's speech at the ASEAN post-Ministerial Conference in July 1998, reflected the continuity of the discrete approach adopted by New Delhi. There were no references to the cultural past of Greater India, as the speaker preferred to underline values that were traditionally considered as Asian. Thus, the problems caused by the region's economic crisis turned into an opportunity to make much of the endurance of Asian people and their sense of collective good.[88] The shared values between India and ASEAN were also emphasized, as was done in the times of P.V. Narasimha Rao and I.K. Gujral. Following the footsteps of his predecessors, Jaswant Singh pointed out that the absence of conflicts between India and the states of the region was proof enough, not only of their secular and fraternal bond, but above all, of a common culture founded on pacifism and consensus.[89] Similarly, the Asian mind was endowed with a unique sense of 'symbiosis',[90] again put in explicit terms as a 'creative fusion'.[91] Furthermore, the promise of the Asian Century remained alive, despite the transient economic difficulties faced by the region. As for the speeches made at the 1999 post-ministerial conferences, they were, above all, technical and pragmatic.[92] The usual references to ancient times were henceforth replaced by specific proposition centred on scientific and technical cooperation.

But the cultural organizations that spawned the BJP continued to promote the Greater India tradition. Since its foundation in 1925, the most important amongst them, the RSS, had upheld its aim to forge a Hindu Nation through a vast psycho-social reform movement.[93] One of the RSS' earliest ideologues was Golwalkar, who became its president in 1940. Interestingly, this Hindu nationalist precursor drew his inspiration from the Greater India theories when he described the territory that constituted the concept of Bharat, the original motherland. His 'expansionist' conception of ancient India can be seen clearly in the following metaphor: 'It was this picture of our motherland with the Himalayas dipping its arms in the two seas, at Aryan (Iran) in the West and at Sringapur (Singapore) in the East, with Sri Lanka (Ceylon) as a lotus petal offered at her sacred feet by the Southern Ocean, that was constantly kept radiant in people's mind for so many thousands of years.'[94]

Golwalkar supported his claims with evidence from ancient texts like the epic poems or *Puranas*, in which *Bharat* spilled over to the East as well as the West. Thus, *Bharat's* Western expansion encompassed Iran and Afghanistan, *Aryan* and *Upaganasthan* respectively. To the east, Myanmar was shown as the old *Brahmadesha* and Tibet appeared under the name of *Trivishtap*, the land of Gods and *Kailas*, abode of *Parameshwara*, the Supreme God.

The Greater India theory also inspired Golwalkar when he invoked the spiritual empire of ancient India (in this case, Hindu India): 'Our powerful political empire too spread over these south-east areas and continued for 1,400 years, the Shailendra empire alone flourishing for over 700 years—standing as a powerful bulwark against Chinese expansion.'[95] Of course, this colonization could in no way be compared to that of the West, for it was not driven by material gain. Furthermore, the indigenous peoples 'adored' the Hindu nation. Never did any insurrections or revolutions take place, for the colonists never indulged in a policy of domination or exploitation. Thus, Hinduism took strong root in these lands and, even today, the daily way of life of the people was Hindu. Golwalkar advanced the theory that most individuals had a Hindu name, many had the physical traits of Hindus and were proud of their Hindu heritage, even though many had converted to Islam. The ideologue then dwelt on a specific example—that of Indonesia, where he was pleased to see that the majority Muslim population drew on Hindu culture for its national heritage and values.[96] Apart from the glorification of India's influence, this tendentious vision of the Indonesian archipelago echoed, above all, domestic concerns. In fact, this example, taken from a foreign country, aimed to prove to Indian Muslims that they could incorporate themselves in the Hindu matrix since their Indonesian brothers had done the same, and of their own will.

Even today, *Organiser*, one of the RSS' main journals, has a predilection to write about expressions of Hinduism in East Asia.[97] Ancient India's influence is glorified and the authors have no hesitation in asserting, for example, that Malaysia has 'a glorious Hindu past' and that 'several centuries ago, it was part of the Hindu Empire'.[98] Golwalkar's writings also inspired school texts written by Vidya Bharati, the Sangh Parivar's organization in charge of education.[99] In these books, which were distributed in about 6,000 schools run by Vidya Bharati, in the late 1990s, the Indian map comprised of Pakistan, Bangladesh and the Himalayan kingdoms (Bhutan, Nepal, Tibet), and encroached upon Myanmar. The texts described the oceans surrounding the sub-continent based on Hindu cosmogony. The Indian Ocean was designated as *Hindu Mahasagar*, the Arabian Sea became *Sindhu Sagar* and the Bay of Bengal was renamed *Ganga Sagar*. They also affirmed that China owed its culture to Indian influence. In brief, Hindu India's influence was very much described in the Greater India tradition.

THE ASSIMILATION OF BUDDHISM INTO THE HINDUTVA MOULD

Clearly, RSS thinkers always considered Hindu India as the major source of influence of the various Asian civilizations. This hypothesis was so obvious to them that they fully reabsorbed Buddhism into the Hindu fold. Whereas India's diplomatic discourse in the 1990s confined itself to the idea that Buddhism was born in India, the RSS, on its part, asserted that Buddhism was just a tributary of Hinduism. This kind of appropriation was already present in Golwalkar's writings and was defined in two stages. At first, the ideologue stated that the degeneration of the Buddhist sect led its members to betray Hindu society and the 'mother religion', i.e. Hinduism or, more specifically, Brahmanism. Thus, because its disciples worked only to destroy Hindu traditions and culture, the sect was eliminated and disappeared from the native soil. But, Buddha was preserved as the incarnation of the god Vishnu.[100] In other words, Buddhism as a heterodox movement that contested the Hindu society was annihilated, while Buddha was salvaged by Hinduism and included in its pantheon.

But experts such as Cynthia Keppley Mahmood have given a very different account of the historic relationship between Buddhism and Hinduism in the Indian context.[101] According to her, Buddhism, like

Jainism or Sikhism, could be conceptualized as counter-cultures evolving against the predominant or majority culture, incarnated by Brahmanism. Indeed, the first Buddhist texts came as a reaction to Brahmanism. For example, the very ancient *Majjhima Nikaya* was composed of a series of opposing views between Buddha and his Brahmin interlocutor, and the existence of the four *varnas* was repudiated in it. Besides, the *vaishyas* and the *shudras* were the first to convert to Buddhism and were very soon qualified as heterodox by Brahmin tradition. Then, Buddhist sub-culture developed beyond the subcontinent and steadily liberated itself from Brahmin thought, against which it was originally created. As Buddhism began to gain autonomy, it developed into a threat to the intellectual and social order of Brahminism. As a result, most Brahmin apostates came to be persecuted, even though such an assertion has very few takers in contemporary India. Keppley Mahmood therefore considered that one of the fundamental characteristics of Brahminism could be found in its continuous penchant for intellectual hegemony. Its tradition was driven by the dynamics of inclusion of all heterodox elements, which absorbed Buddha as Vishnu's *avatar*, and Sikhs as a caste or sect of Hinduism. Even today, Hindu nationalists typically appear to incarnate the assimilating propensity of the Brahminical tradition.

Thanks to the two-pronged movement of neutralization and absorption of Buddhism, the RSS was further vindicated in asserting that India was the spiritual seat of Asia. This vision was clearly enunciated, for example, during the inaugural ceremony for the construction of an Indo-Japanese cultural centre in 1998.[102] The Indian delegation was led by the RSS's Sarsanghchalak,[103] Professor Rajendra Singh, and Ashok Singhal, president of the Vishwa Hindu Parishad.[104] The latter started by underlining the fact that 'Buddhism and Hinduism are two bodies with one soul'. It must be noted that this project was the culmination of a private initiative sponsored by the Modi Foundation, named after the Indian industrialist, who worked for 'reinforcing the intrinsic unity among the peoples of Vedic and Buddhist beliefs throughout the world'. But, according to the Hindu nationalist logic, to proclaim the kinship between the two religious currents implied asserting the claim of the paternity of Hinduism with regard to Buddhism. Thus, for them, it was Hindu India that had bequeathed an immeasurable spiritual legacy to East Asia, through Buddhism. That is why Singhal declared, in all confidence, that India was bound to rediscover its role as the cultural and spiritual mother of Asia, and even the world—'For a few centuries, India could not offer its message of *dharma* and culture to the world. The day has come to take up the torch again.' The *Organiser*, for its part, commented in no uncertain terms that the Indo-Japanese complex would, in fact, be 'a centre for spreading Hindu culture in the Far East'.

Unsurprisingly, this appropriation of Buddhism has not always gone down well with its followers. In the mid-1990s for instance, a controversy arose at Bodh Gaya, the high seat of Buddhism in India, regarding the management of temples by Hindu priests. The RSS branch in the state of Bihar then countered critics by asserting its traditional ideology of assimilation. They said the dispute was misplaced, since the Buddha was a part of the Hindu pantheon and was as much revered as other Hindu gods. Furthermore, Brahmins originally worshipped the three sacred elements at Bodh Gaya—the temple, the tank and Buddha's statue.[105] The re-appropriation strategy of the origins of Buddhism once again testified to the Hindu priests' propensity to absorb all religious streams that asserted a distinct identity from their religious thought. In brief, Buddhists could exist as long as they accepted Hinduism as the mother religion. But this was distasteful to certain Buddhist monks, who wished to preserve their autonomy, and be independent of the Hindu mainstream.

The RSS' strategies for assimilating Buddhism began to be reflected at the political level when, in September–October 1998, the BJP government's Minister for Tourism launched an initiative of great significance, the Bauddha Mahotsav (Grand Buddha Festival). Created *ex nihilo*, this new religious festival was supposed to be held annually, from the end of October to the beginning of November, in the main Buddhist holy places of Uttar Pradesh and Bihar. Officially described as 'a humble attempt on the part of India to facilitate cultural, intellectual and spiritual exchange among the students, disciples and followers of Buddhism', Bauddha Mahotsav was also to play an important role in the promotion of religious tourism in India. To be more precise, the organization of this event fulfilled two complementary objectives. In a pragmatic and economic perspective, its main aim was to attract tourists from Buddhist countries. Thus, the Minister for Parliamentary Affairs and Tourism, Madanlal Khurana, took great pains to promote the festival in North-East and South-East Asian countries. Some monks even sent their emissaries to several Buddhist countries to spread the message of the new festival. Political leaders too did not take a back seat, since Madanlal Khurana himself went with a parliamentary delegation to Malaysia, Indonesia, Thailand and Singapore, to promote the event.[106]

From an ideological point of view, the Bauddha Mahotsav aimed to make a place for north India in the world map of holy places. The organizers aspired to no less than making Bodh Gaya the 'Holy Land' of Buddhism, in the model of Semitic religions. Madanlal Khurana was quite open about it when he declared that 'If the Vatican and Mecca can draw millions of visitors from all over the world every year, why should we not develop our sites and attract tourists from the predominantly Buddhist South-East Asian countries?'.[107] The Sangh Parivar being an expert in matters of politico-religious manipulation, the 1998 Bauddha Mahotsav took place in the presence of government representatives. In particular, Union Home Minister, L.K. Advani, a Hindutva hardliner, was allowed to make controversial comments. Advani indeed stated that Lord Buddha did not found any new religion and that he only reiterated, with a new emphasis, the ideals of the Indo-Aryan civilization. Advani also called for greater socio-cultural interactions between the people of India and the Buddhist countries of East Asia, in a way reminiscent of the Greater India tradition. These comments offended many Buddhist monks, while some Indian observers spoke about an attempt 'to saffronize Buddhism'. Others commented that the organizers were more concerned about the facilities provided for the political invitees and were not particularly sensitive towards the rites of the followers of the Theravada sect.[108] Finally, it was a rather peculiar version of the Look East policy that could be seen here. The Sangh Parivar's objective consisted not so much in looking eastwards and more in leading the Buddhist people of East Asia back into the Hindu fold.

HINDU NATIONALISM AND THE DIASPORA IN SOUTH-EAST ASIA

The BJP has displayed a much stronger desire than most other Indian political parties to strengthen links with the diaspora. Traditionally and ideologically, the BJP has been more inclined to grant special privileges to Non-Resident Indians (NRI). In its 1998 election manifesto, the party clearly enunciated the resolve to abandon the traditional policies enforced thus far. 'We will depart from the current policy of disinterest and disregard for Non-Resident Indians and actively pursue a policy that will nourish the umbilical link between all people of Indian origin, wherever they may be, with their motherland.'[109] This organic metaphor revealed the sentimental rapport evidenced by the Sangh Parivar for the diaspora. The BJP thus drew up a multidimensional policy that intended to 'strengthen the economic, social, cultural, emotional and spiritual links between Mother India and her children abroad'.[110] With regard to the Indian diaspora in South-East Asia and the Gulf countries, the BJP promised to 'play an active role in ensuring job and social security for Non-Resident Indians working in the Gulf and South-East Asian countries, with special emphasis on preventing exploitation and providing legal assistance'.[111] Lastly, the manifesto promised to re-examine the difficulties encountered in giving dual citizenship. The request for this privilege, long called for by the NRI community, had never received any positive feedback in India so far.

When the BJP came to power, it did not procrastinate to take concrete steps. During his 1998–9 budget speech, the Union Minister for Finance, Yashwant Sinha, announced the launching of the People of Indian Origin (PIO) Card. With this initiative, PIOs would enjoy special benefits in the economic, cultural, financial and educational fields. Possessing the card exempted them from applying for visas to visit India. Sinha clearly stated what he expected from the diaspora, in return for the benefits given: 'I am looking for a situation where the involvement of NRIs in India will be comparable to the overseas Chinese in China.'[112] The BJP government reiterated its political commitment to the diaspora during the second International Conference of Indian Entrepreneurs. The event took place in New Delhi on 12–13 November 1998. While FICCI and the Indian Investment Centre organized the event, the government showed a strong presence and the Prime Minister, A.B. Vajpayee, inaugurated the event himself. The latter used the forum to announce the formation of a committee to study the issue of dual citizenship.[113]

The Union Minister for Home Affairs, L.K. Advani, officially launched the PIO card in early April 1999.[114] Advani pointed that this document was likely to benefit fifteen million Indians and that through it, holders would be strengthening their emotional ties with India, while at the same time contributing to the socio-economic and cultural development of their motherland. Thus, this decision constituted an important step towards the granting of dual citizenship, which the majority of the diaspora had long wanted.[115] These measures, along with the speeches delivered on the occasion, primarily aimed at strengthening ties between the BJP and the Indian diaspora in the West, as the latter offered enormous support by financing the party's and its affiliates' activities. With regard to the financial side, Indians living in the West were a more fortunate lot and, thus, the most important potential investors. But, the BJP's initiative could also be of consequence to the Indians in South-East Asia. Many of the Indians living in this region belonged to third or fourth generation migrants. They could thus be eligible for PIO Cards.

At the same time, the inter-ethnic harmony in these countries was rather sensitive to the links that each community maintained with its country of origin, especially when it concerned India or China. In this perspective, the issue of dual citizenship appeared even more problematic. Mostly demanded by the Indian diaspora in the West, it could be damaging to Indian communities living in South-East Asia, if it were awarded. In countries with strong feelings of nationalism and where relations between ethnic groups were subject to tensions, the idea of dual citizenship was likely to create problems.[116] Indian minorities were always suspected of maintaining stronger ties with their country of origin and their lot was often linked to the vagaries of events occurring in India. For instance, the 1969 inter-communal violence in Malaysia resulted in the voluntary departure of nearly 60,000 Indians. Fully aware of the delicate situation, most Indian leaders visiting South-East Asia had always advised members of the diaspora to integrate fully in their country of adoption. In 1993, Prime Minister Narasimha Rao had taken great care, during his visit to Thailand, to make it clear that the issue of dual citizenship posed 'insurmountable difficulties'. The steps taken by the BJP in this field could thus create a sense of unease in South-East Asia.

As for the RSS, it undertook the task of giving a structure and unity to the Hindu diaspora, thus duplicating the psycho-social work it had done on the Hindu community in India. This project, which followed the movement's homogenizing logic, consisted of gathering and organizing Hindus in India as well as abroad. RSS organizations were especially active in Europe and North America. But they were also germinating in East Asia.[117] *Organiser* compiled a list of fifty-one *upa-shakhas* in Myanmar, three in Hong Kong, and one in Thailand. The rest of South-East Asia had nineteen.[118] The Hindus of the diaspora also grouped themselves under the banner of the Vishwa Hindu Mahasangh, which held its fifth international meeting in February 1994. The approximately 505 participants that met at the Banaras Hindu University[119] discussed means to strengthen the unity and welfare of the Hindu community scattered over the five continents. But, the organization also intended to take up proselytizing work. In fact, the Mahasangh's Secretary-General, Dr Jogendra Jha, stressed upon the need for an organized effort to propagate Hinduism in the world. With regard to the diaspora in South-East Asia, representatives from Indonesia and Malaysia attended the meeting. Besides, the Mahasangh's Vice-President was none other than an Indonesian, Oak Punyatamaja.[120]

The ideology that the RSS systemized for the diaspora was, in fact, based on the notion of race. This was the only way possible to unite all the members of the Hindu community in the world. In the eyes of the RSS, religion could not be a binding factor for the Hindus of the diaspora by itself, for they may or may not follow Hindu rituals. As for citizenship, it was but a superficial element of identity as members of the same family could be citizens of different countries. Their common identity had, therefore, to be based on the Hindu race.[121] In so doing, the RSS ideologues ascribed to the expatriate Hindu community the characteristics of the more prosperous and more structured diasporas. Whether it was the Chinese, Japanese, Jews or even Anglo-Americans, these diasporas were united because, from the RSS viewpoint, they were imbued with a strong sense of identity fostered by the idea of a common race. The RSS thus aimed to make the Hindus the world-over realize that they shared the same blood, in order to establish greater cohesion between them. Thanks to this ethnic approach, the RSS promised the ascendancy of the Hindu diaspora. It was in this perspective that it expressed its pleasure at the success of a number of Hindus in the Ministry of Foreign Affairs in Singapore or Malaysia.[122] However such a discourse could have turned against the Hindu communities in South-East Asia. It was an approach fraught with danger.

The RSS also expressed deep concern for the fate of the members of the diaspora. Hence, it was incensed with the condition of certain Hindus in Malaysia and even went to the extent of suggesting interventionist measures. In 1998 for instance, *Organiser* described the violence perpetrated against the Hindu community, following the construction of a temple in the state of Penang.[123] The authors reported that the Muslim clergy instigated communal violence against the Hindus. It is true that Malaysia being a country with a Muslim majority, it was easy to reactivate the sense of vulnerability experienced by the Hindus to Islam. In this way, the RSS replicated in an external context the leitmotif from which Hindu nationalism was developed.[124] It was also quite probable that this external detour was driven by domestic imperatives, to validate the discourse on the need to defend and restructure the Hindu nation in India. However, the RSS exercise went further, since the organization advocated certain measures with regard to the situation in Malaysia, and this was in total opposition to the traditional policy of the Indian government. Thus, the *Organiser* declared: 'In any case, the BJP government ought to take note of the plight of the Hindus and Hindu shrines abroad' and, in the meanwhile, the 'Vishwa Hindu Parishad and other Hindu organizations may well inquire from the Malaysian government what exactly is happening to the Hindus and Hindu temples in Malaysia'.

However, it should be remembered that the fanaticism of the RSS definitely constituted a danger for the diaspora in the Muslim countries of South-East Asia. The events of 1992 stood testimony to this fact. In Malaysia for example, the destruction of the Ayodhya mosque provoked Islamist groups into attacking Hindu temples in the state of Perak. But the community's reaction was moderate by far, contrary to the violent attitude claimed by the RSS. Because Malaysian Hindus felt vulnerable, they avoided any violent reaction when confronted with the aggressiveness of certain radical Muslim groups. Their response was mostly directed inwards, as members of the community strove to strengthen and protect their religious institutions in a peaceful manner.[125] As for the Malaysian Indian Congress (MIC), the political party representing the Indian community in the coalition government, Barisan National, it also maintained a very moderate position. The MIC's members accordingly decided not to articulate Indian interests in too obvious a manner, fearing the backlash of certain Malaysian communities or the more radical factions of United Malays National Organization (UMNO).[126] Mahathir had also driven home the point to MIC leaders that they had everything to gain by formulating their demands in a discrete and conciliatory manner. Therefore, following the demolition of Hindu temples in the state of Perak, in 1992, the MIC president declared that only a political solution could calm down the situation and hastened to appeal to the more motivated sections of the Hindu community to remain calm and refrain from any strong reaction. In such a context, where Malaysian Indians had to keep a low profile to uphold their assimilation, the recent initiatives of Prime Minister A.B. Vajpayee, would have appeared particularly ill-timed. During his visit to Malaysia in May 2001, Prime Minister A.B. Vajpayee actually referred to the murder of four Persons of Indian Origin in a suburb of Kuala Lumpur. This attitude was, by any logic, far from appreciated by his Malaysian counterparts.[127]

NOTES

1. François Godement, *Dragons de Feu, Dragons de Papier*, Paris: Flammarion, 1998, p. 173.
2. Birendra Prasad, *Indian Nationalism and Asia*, New Delhi: B.R. Publishing Corporation, 1979.
3. Keshab Chandra Sen, 'Asia's Message to Europe', in Kalidas Nag, *Greater India*, Calcutta: Brahmo Mission Press, 1960, p. 737.
4. Bimla Prasad, *The Origins of Indian Foreign Policy—The Indian National Congress and World Affairs: 1885–1947*, Calcutta: Bookland Pvt. Ltd., 1960, pp. 41–5.
5. Rabindranath Tagore, *Nationalism*, London: MacMillan & Co. Ltd., 1917, reprint London: Paper Mac, 1991, p. 33.
6. Ibid., p. 58.
7. T.A. Keenleyside, 'Diplomatic Apprenticeship: Pre-Independence Origins of Indian Diplomacy and its Relevance for the Post-Independence Foreign Policy', in Verinder Grover, ed., *Introduction to International Relations and India's Foreign Policy*, New Delhi: Deep and Deep Publications, 1992.
8. Report submitted by Nehru to the All India Congress Committee on the International Congress against Imperialism held at Brussels in February 1927, in Prasad, *Indian Nationalism and Asia*, Appendix I, p. 303.
9. Jawaharlal Nehru, *An Autobiography*, Bombay: Allied Publishers, 1962, p. 608; Tan Chung, 'Nehru's dreams of an Eastern Federation', in Surjit Mansingh, ed., *Nehru's Foreign Policy: Fifty Years On*, New Delhi: Mosaic Books, 1998, p. 100.
10. Jawaharlal Nehru, *The Unity of India: Collected Writings, 1937–40*, London: Lindsay Drummond, 1941, p. 327
11. K.P. Karunakaran, *India in World Affairs*, New Delhi: Oxford University Press, 1952, p. 84.
12. Letter to Asaf Ali, 7 April 1947, in Sarvepalli Gopal, *Jawaharlal Nehru: A Biography*, vol. I: *1889–1947*, New Delhi: Oxford University Press, 1975, p. 345.
13. The governments represented at this conference were Afghanistan, Australia, Myanmar, Sri Lanka, Egypt, Ethiopia, Iran, Iraq, Lebanon, Pakistan, the Philippines, Saudi Arabia, Syria and Yemen.
14. Kalidas Nag, *The Discovery of Asia*, Calcutta: The Institute of Asian African Relations, 1957, p. 259.
15. U.N. Ghoshal, 'Progress of Greater Indian Research during the Last Twenty Years (1917–42)', *The Journal of Greater India Society*, vol. 9, no. 2, July 1942. Republished in 1987 by U.N. Goshal, ed.
16. R.C. Majumdar, *Ancient Indian Colonies in the Far East, Champa*, vol. I, Lahore: The Punjab Sanskrit Book Depot, 1927, *Ancient Indian*

Colonies in the Far East, Suvarnadvipa, vol. II, Calcutta: Modern Publishing Syndicate, 1938 (new edn., *Hindu Colonies in the Far East*, Calcutta: Firma K.L. Mukhopadhyaya, 1944, 1966).

17. R.C. Majumdar, *Ancient Indian Colonies in the Far East*, vol. I, p. xxiv.
18. Majumdar, *Hindu Colonies in the Far East*, 1966, pp. 27–8. The 1944 and 1966 editions are in fact shorter and watered down versions of two original works published in 1927 and 1938, which are more imbued with the idea of India's civilizing mission in Asia. For example, Majumdar asserted in the first volume that it was the Indian colonizers 'mission' to bring civilization to that 'mass of barbarians' pp. xxiv, 201.
19. Nag, *The Discovery of Asia*, p. 569.
20. Ibid., p. 135.
21. Ibid., p. 204.
22. Created in 1915, the *Hindu Mahasabha* was a confederation of *Hindu Sabhas* (Hindu forums), which worked to defend and reform Hinduism.
23. Prasad, *Indian Nationalism and Asia*, p. 178.
24. T.A. Keenleyside, 'Nationalist Indian Attitudes Towards Asia: A Troublesome Legacy for Post-Independence Indian Foreign Policy', *Pacific Affairs*, vol. 55, no. 2, Summer 1982, p. 210.
25. Jawaharlal Nehru, *The Discovery of India*, New Delhi: Jawaharlal Nehru Memorial Fund and Oxford University Press, 1991, p. 201.
26. Ibid., p. 210.
27. K.M. Panikkar, *The Future of South-East Asia*, London: MacMillan Company, 1943.
28. Asian Relations, *Report of the Proceedings*, p. 20.
29. Ibid., pp. 74, 103.
30. Nag, 'Indians Abroad', *The Modern Review*, April 1930, re-published in the volume, *Greater India*, 1960.
31. Gyaneshwar Chaturvedi, *India-China Relations: 1947 to Present Day*, Agra: M.G. Publishers, 1991, p. 7.
32. Warner Levi, *The Challenge of World Politics*, London: Prentice-Hall, 1968, p. 49.
33. *The Statesman*, 17 June 1950, quoted in Keenleyside, p. 225.
34. Chung, 'Nehru's Dreams', p. 106. The idea of non-alignment was, however, announced as early as in 1946, in the speech, 'Future Taking Shape', 7 September 1946, in Grover, ed., *Introduction to International Relation*, p. 321.
35. India happened to be the largest Asian country in the organization because the PRC did not have any representation, while Japan would become a member only in 1956. R. Venkataraman, 'India's Foreign Policy', Grover, ed., *Introduction to International Relations*, p. 469. The author was India's representative at the United Nations General Assembly between 1953 and 1961 and the President of the Indian Union.

36. Chaturvedi, *India-China Relations*, p.14.
37. The Colombo conference brought together Sri Lanka, Myanmar, Indonesia, Pakistan and India.
38. This defence treaty comprised of Australia, the United States, France, Great Britain, New Zealand, Pakistan, the Philippines and Thailand. But the treaty zone also included Cambodia, Laos and South Vietnam. New Delhi's opposition to SEATO was all the more vehement as it included India's fraternal enemy, Pakistan.
39. Among the South-East Asian countries, only Malaysia supported New Delhi during the 1962 conflict with China.
40. Balraj Madhok, 'India's Foreign Policy—the Jana Sangh View', in Grover, ed., *Introduction to International Relations*, p. 165. Madhok was a former member of parliament and president of the Bhartiya Jana Sangh.
41. Mohammed Ali Kishore, *Jana Sangh and India's Foreign Policy*, New Delhi: Associated Publishing House, 1969, p.105.
42. Gurcharan Das, 'East Asian Boom Slows Down', *World Focus*, vol. 18, no. 6, 1997.
43. D. Camroux, 'Des Nations Imaginées à la Région Rêvée', D. Camroux and J.L. Domenach, *L'Asie Retrouvée*, Paris: Seuil, p. 56.
44. E. Gonsalves, ed., *Asian Relations Conference*, New Delhi: Lancer International, 1988.
45. O.W. Wolters, *History, Culture and Religion in South-East Asian Perspectives*, Singapore: Institute of South-East Asian Studies, 1982.
46. Jean Filliozat, 'Inaugural address at the session on 'Studies on Greater India', All India Conference.
47. Romila Thapar, *Ancient Indian Social History—Some Interpretations*, New Delhi: Sangam Books Ltd, 1984, p. 15.
48. D.P. Chattopadhyaya, 'Lifeworld, Science and Technology: An Indian perspective', in N.N. Vohra and J.N. Dixit, eds., *Religion, Politics and Society in South and South-East Asia*, New Delhi: Konark Publishers and India International Centre, 1998.
49. Please refer to J.V. Van Leur, *Indonesian Trade and Society*, The Hague, W. Van Hoeve, 1955.
50. Arun Dasgupta, 'Intellectual and Academic Cooperation between India and South-East Asia', in Baladas Ghoshal, ed., *India and Southeast Asia: Challenges and Opportunities*, New Delhi: Konark Publishers, 1996, p. 83. Arun Dasgupta is a professor in History of South-East Asia, at the Calcutta University.
51. Chan Heng Chee, 'Closing Remarks', in P.V.N. Rao, 'India and the Asia-Pacific: Forging a New Relationship', *Singapore Lecture Series*, ISEAS, 1994, p. 35.
52. Post-ministerial conferences follow ASEAN summits, and it is primarily the ASEAN dialogue partners that gather together: Japan, South Korea, China, The United States, Canada, Australia, New Zealand, the European Union, and Russia. These conferences take place annually.

53. Statement by the External Affairs Minister of India, I.K. Gujral, on the occasion of ASEAN's post-ministerial conferences (PMC -7+10).
54. Statement by the External Affairs Minister of India, I.K. Gujral, on the occasion of the ASEAN's post-ministerial conferences (PMC -7+1), 24 July 1996, Jakarta, §3.
55. Ibid., §3.
56. Thammasat University & Information Department, Ministry of Foreign Affairs of Thailand, *Thai-Indian Relations in the Present Decade and Prospects for Cooperation in the Future*, Seminar Papers, 30 July–1 August 1997, Bangkok: Ministry of Foreign Affairs of Thailand, pp. 142–3.
57. J.N. Dixit, *Across Borders, Fifty Years of India's Foreign Policy*, New Delhi: Picus Books, 1998, p. 311.
58. S.D. Muni, 'Nehru's India in Asia: Anatomy of a Blurred Vision', in S. Mansingh, ed., *Nehru's Foreign Policy*, p. 109.
59. Asrani, 'India-Japan Relations', pp. 350–1.
60. Kripa Sridharan, *The ASEAN Region in India's Foreign Policy*, Aldershot: Dartmouth Pub. Co., 1996.
61. Statement by the External Affairs Minister of India, I.K. Gujral, on the occasion of the ASEAN's post-ministerial conferences (PMC -7+10), 24 July 1996, Jakarta.
62. P.V. Narasimha Rao, 'India and Japan', Speech at the banquet hosted by Prime Minister Miyazawa of Japan, Tokyo, 23 June 1992, *Selected Speeches*, p. 391.
63. P.V. Narasimha Rao, 'India and the Asia-Pacific: Forging a New Relationship'. 1994, p. 17.
64. P.V. Narasimha Rao, 'India and Japan', Address to the Japan Institute of International Affairs, on the occasion of the fortieth anniversary of the establishment of diplomatic relations between India and Japan, Tokyo, 23 June 1992, *Selected Speeches*, p. 367.
65. P.V. Narasimha Rao, 'Shared Democratic Values', Address to the Japan Institute of International Affairs, Japan, 24 June 1992, *Selected Speeches*, pp. 367–96.
66. P.V. Narasimha Rao, 'India and the Asia-Pacific: Forging a New Relationship', p. 9.
67. P.V. Narasimha Rao, 'Indo-Korean Relations', Speech at the banquet hosted by the Korean President, Seoul, 10 September 1993, *Selected Speeches*, p. 401.
68. P.V. Narasimha Rao, 'Centre of Indo-Thailand Interaction', Speech while accepting an Honorary Degree in Liberal Arts Conferred by Thammasat University, Bangkok, 8 April 1993, *Selected Speeches*, p. 455. The concept of *rita* came from Vedic philosophy and described the natural order of things.
69. It is accepted nowadays that India played an important part in the Islamization of the Indonesian archipelago.

70. Jaffrelot, 'L'Inde et l'asiatisme', pp. 229–51.
71. P.V. Narasimha Rao, 'India and the Asia-Pacific: Forging a New Relationship', p. 9.
72. P.V. Narasimha Rao, 'India and Thailand', Speech at the banquet hosted by Thailand's Premier, Chuan Leekpai, Bangkok, 7 April 1993, *Selected Speeches*, p. 451.
73. Statement by the External Affairs Minister of India, I.K. Gujral, on the occasion of the ASEAN's post-ministerial conference (PMC -7+1), § 9.
74. Statement by the External Affairs Minister of India, I.K. Gujral, on the occasion of the ASEAN's post-ministerial conferences (PMC -7+10), § 3.
75. P.V. Narasimha Rao, 'India and Thailand', p. 453.
76. *India Today*, 31 August 1995, p. 23. Ashoka Maurya, who lived between 268 and 239 BC is considered in the Buddhist tradition as the ideal sovereign. His reign is considered to mark the golden age of Buddhism in India.
77. Inaugural speech at the Asian Relations Conference, New Delhi, 23 March 1947, in *Jawaharlal Nehru's Speeches*—September 1946–May 1949, vol. 1, Publication Division, Ministry of Information and Broadcasting, Government of India.
78. I.K. Gujral (PMC-7+10), § 18.
79. Ibid., 'Areas of Common Concern in the Asian Region', Asian Media Convention, 24 February 1997, in I.K. Gujral, *A Foreign Policy for India*, New Delhi: Ministry of External Affairs, 1998, p. 183.
80. Ibid., p. 183.
81. I.K. Gujral (PMC -7+10), § 18.
82. Ibid., § 4.
83. George Yeo, 'Good Long-Term Climate for Economic Reform in India', *A Bimonthly Selection of Ministries Speeches*, March–April 1997, Ministry of Information and the Art, Singapore, 7 March 1997, p. 72.
84. P.V. Narasimha Rao, 'India and the Asia-Pacific: Forging a New Relationship', op. cit., p. 13.
85. Ibid., p. 17.
86. P.V. Narasimha Rao, 'India and Japan', p. 391.
87. To learn about the history of these two formations, refer to Christophe Jaffrelot, *Les Nationalistes Hindous*, Paris: Presses de la Fondation Nationale des Sciences Politiques, 1993.
88. Jaswant Singh, (PMC 9+10), § 4.
89. Ibid. (PMC 9+1), § 4.
90. Ibid. (PMC 9+10), § 13.
91. Ibid. (PMC 9+1), § 11.
92. Statement by the Minister of External Affairs, Jaswant Singh, at the ASEAN's 32nd Post-Ministerial Conference (PMC 10+10) Plenary Session, Singapore, 27 July 1999; Statement by the Minister of External

Affairs, Jaswant Singh, at the ASEAN's 32nd Post-Ministerial Conference (PMC 10+1) Session with India, Singapore, 28 July 1999.

93. The RSS was founded in Nagpur, within the Hindu Mahasabha movement. It became a separate entity in 1939–40.
94. M.S. Golwalkar, *Bunch of Thoughts*, p. 111.
95. Ibid., p. 10.
96. Ibid., p. 209.
97. The *Organiser*, 'Thaipusam: The Hindu festival of Singapore', 2 March 1997; 'Myanmar observes Hindu Festivals', 1 December 1996; 'Varsha Pratipada in Indonesia', 21 May 1995; 'Bharat in China', 6 November 1994; 'Lord Ganesha Blesses Indonesia Currency', 20 September 1998.
98. The *Organiser*, 'Hindus in Malaysia', vol. XLVII, no. 18, 3 December 1995.
99. *The Pioneer*, 'RSS Propagating Hindutva through Textbooks', 25 October 1998.
100. M.S. Golwalkar, *Bunch of Thoughts*, p. 94.
101. Cynthia Keppley Mahmood, 'Rethinking Indian Communalism: Culture and Counter-Culture', *Asian Survey*, vol. XXXIII, no. 7, July 1993.
102. The *Organiser*, 26 April 1998, vol. XIIX, no. 39, pp. 10–11; p. 20.
103. The *Sarsanghchalak* is the RSS' supreme leader.
104. The Vishwa Hindu Parishad (Universal Hindu Association) was founded in the early 1960s with the mission to promote the unity of the Hindu religion. Christophe Jaffrelot observed that from the beginning, the VHP sought to strengthen the ties between the Hindu pantheon and the Buddhist world (Jaffrelot, 'L'Inde et l'Asiatisme', p. 245).
105. The *Organiser*, 16 July 1995, vol. XLVI, no. 50.
106. MEA, *Annual Report*, 1998–9, p. 25.
107. 'Bauddha *Mahotsav* takes off . . . but flounders', *Rediff on the Net*, 12 November 1998.
108. Monks from Burma complained that no arrangements had been made for their lunch before noon, in conformity with their rites.
109. BJP, *Election Manifesto'98*, p. 37.
110. Ibid., p. 37, § 2.
111. Ibid., p. 37, § 7.
112. *Business India*, 15–28 June 1998.
113. *The Economic Times*, November 1998.
114. Ibid., 1 April 1999.
115. For all its claims, the PIO Card does not confer voting rights. Those eligible for PIO Cards are any former holders of an Indian passport, or any person whose grandparents or great grandparents were born

and had been permanent residents of India, or else, either the wife of an Indian citizen or one of the individuals mentioned above.

116. V. Suryanarayan, 'Overseas Chinese in South-East Asia: A Comparative Study', *Strategic Analysis*, December 1995, pp. 1207–23.
117. The *Organiser*, 'RSS Abroad', 28 January 1996, vol. XLVII, no. 26, p. 33.
118. The *shakha* (branch) is the base unit of the RSS. It is the local or ward branch in which the members, called swayamsevaks, gather for their daily routine of physical training.
119. The *Organiser*, 6 February 1994, vol. XLV, no. 27.
120. Ibid. Faithful to the Hindu Nationalist vision of India's influence in the region, Punyatamaja asserted that the 'Indonesian civilization is entirely founded by Hinduism'.
121. Ibid., 'Coming of the Hindu Age', 23 October 1994, p. 5.
122. Ibid., 3 December 1995, vol. XLVII, no. 18, p. 17. The Labour Minister, Sami Vellu, and two other Deputy Ministers, one for agriculture and the other for commerce, were Indians.
123. Ibid., 'Hindu Temples Evoke Muslim Fury', 7 June 1998, vol. XLIX, no. 45, p. 17.
124. Jaffrelot, *Les Nationalistes Hindous*, pp. 33–41, 405–12.
125. K. Ramanathan, 'Hinduism in a Muslim State: The Case of Malaysia', *Asian Journal of Political Science*, vol. 4, no. 2, December 1996, pp. 42–62.
126. Ibid., p. 55. S. Samy Vellu was very unequivocal in his condemnation of the NPE and the fate suffered by the Indian community. But this attitude only provoked the anger of the second rung of the UMNO party, which demanded his resignation from the cabinet.
127. *The Hindu*, 18 May 2001.

CHAPTER 5

Institutional Integration

5.1 Some Successful Forays in South-East Asia

The preceding chapter has shown that distinct changes were made in India's discourse with regard to East Asia in order to improve the country's image and further the objective of insertion in regional institutions. What remains to be seen is whether the new diplomatic approach achieved the anticipated results. New Delhi met with some success as far as South-East Asia was concerned. The states of the region first formulated a collective response at the ASEAN level, by agreeing to engage in an institutional dialogue with New Delhi. They also responded bilaterally, as shown by Thailand's initiative in setting up the BIMSTEC project and the Mekong-Ganga cooperation programme.

A FRUITFUL DIALOGUE WITH THE ASEAN

Since the inception of the Look East policy, New Delhi has focused its diplomatic efforts on the ASEAN. Indeed, the Association appeared to be at the heart of new cooperation dynamics in East Asia. In addition, the ASEAN states initiated a dialogue with the major powers outside the region in the 1970s. Hence, the European Community became a dialogue partner in 1972, Australia in 1974 and New Zealand in 1975. Japan, Canada and the United States began a dialogue with the ASEAN in 1977. South Korea was made a new dialogue partner in 1991. However, it was only in 1977 that a special institutional mechanism was put in place, to regularize consultations with different partners. Consequently, the dialogue assumed a concrete shape in the form of Post-Ministerial Conferences, which followed the Association's annual ministerial meetings. At the summit meeting held in Singapore on 27–8 January 1992, the ASEAN decided to confer upon India the status of a Sectoral Dialogue Partner. Thus, barely a year after launching its Look East policy, New Delhi took its first step towards a full partnership. From ASEAN's viewpoint, the decision coincided with an important moment in its evolution. Indeed, 1992 marked a new phase in the Association's history.[1] Twenty-five years after it was born, ASEAN held its first post-Cold War summit meeting in end January 1992. The Association was of the view that it had given final shape to its construction and then intended to enter an era of maturity. Henceforth more confident, the member-states wished to give a fresh impetus to their organization and undertook different activities to consolidate regional cooperation.

J.N. Dixit, India's Foreign Secretary at the time, who was directly involved in the launching of the partnership, reported that ASEAN intended to associate itself with New Delhi essentially on an experimental basis. Indeed, ASEAN's new interest in India was mainly due to the latter's economic reforms. But since it was difficult to predict the way liberalization would evolve, ASEAN did not wish to overcommit itself. On the other hand, the Association had a well-known habit of retaining sufficient room for manoeuvre in order to be able to find the right tempo in developing partnerships with its individual interlocutors. Besides, it would seem that the United States and Japan encouraged ASEAN to grant India the status of a sectoral partner. In fact, such a tie was expected to give India an additional incentive to pursue its liberalization process.[2] Even within the Association, a state like Singapore came down in favour of India's candidature. As it happened, the city-state was the host of the 1992 summit meeting. Therefore it was Singapore that drew up the agenda and submitted it to its partners. Obviously, New Delhi benefited greatly from Singapore's influence. As a matter of fact, the latter was entrusted with the task of coordinating the sectoral dialogue with India. The sectors of cooperation identified concerned trade, investment and tourism.

At its fifth summit meeting in Bangkok, on 14–15 December 1995, ASEAN decided to raise India to the status of a Full Dialogue Partner. New Delhi could therefore participate in the Post-Ministerial Conferences and thereby, also became a member of the ARF, the ASEAN's security forum. Thus, it did not take very long for India's efforts to bear fruit as New Delhi came to be associated with ASEAN just five years after launching its Look East policy. This proved a major success for the Look East policy. In South-East Asia, Singapore was the most active state in defending the Indian candidature. For instance, as early as in January 1995, Goh Chok Tong, Singapore's Prime Minister, said that his country would support New Delhi's elevation to the status of a Dialogue Partner.[3] The city-state's influential Senior Minister, Lee Kuan Yew, also greatly encouraged ASEAN to reconsider India's position. Moreover, Singapore continued to be the dialogue coordinator with India. Among the other states that were in favour of India's candidature were Thailand and the Philippines. India also greatly benefited from Vietnam's admission, since the latter was one of its closest allies in South-East Asia. Interestingly, New Delhi became a Dialogue Partner at the same time as China and Russia. Thus, ASEAN appeared to be confident enough to engage a dialogue simultaneously with three major Asian powers.

The decision to raise India's status demonstrated that ASEAN was well disposed to maintaining multi-dimensional interactions with its big neighbour. While the sectoral partnership only dealt with limited and purely functional fields of cooperation, the status of Full Dialogue Partner paved the way for interactions in the political and strategic fields. Hence, the Look East policy of the years 1992–5 succeeded in convincing the South-East Asian nations about India's credibility. Indeed, the Singaporean Foreign Affairs Minister, Professor Jayakumar, recognized that while it had started on an experimental basis, the sectoral partnership proved to be quite fruitful: 'It has therefore been a matter of great satisfaction to both sides that this cautious first step has led to a rapid growth in our relations.'[4] Thanks to this conclusive probationary period, ASEAN felt sufficiently at ease with its Indian interlocutors to deal with a broader range of themes. The Full Dialogue Partner status was also the outcome of the intense economic diplomacy that New Delhi had engaged in South-East Asia. Several bilateral meetings took place between 1992 and 1995, especially at the Foreign Affairs Ministers' level, which made it possible to strengthen ties in a host of fields. Finally, it was India's successful economic diplomacy that made an appreciable political rapprochement possible. By putting forward the consensual theme of mutual economic gains, Indian and South-East Asian decision-makers got used to conferring with each other and exchanging views on a wide variety of subjects.

By virtue of its dialogue partnership, India had to learn the 'ASEAN way'. According to Amitav Acharya, a specialist in the subject: 'The "ASEAN way" consists of a code of conduct for inter-state behaviour as well as a decision-making process based on consultations and consensus.'[5] In other words, it was not so much the content as the manner in which talks were held that mattered. The approach called for a high degree of discretion, flexibility, and pragmatism. All confrontations had to be avoided, thereby ensuring that more efforts were devoted to reaching a consensual solution. The informal nature of the meetings was supposed to help in putting participants at ease and to give a greater room for manoeuvre for more flexible decision-making, allowing for different countries' negotiating positions to evolve. Often, the dialogue process had no proper structure and the agenda was not clearly defined. Issues were debated on an *ad hoc* basis, whenever the need arose. There was undoubtedly a certain amount of institutionalization within the ASEAN, but in the context of regular and flexible inter-state coordination. Above all, the ASEAN sought to avoid the European model, which favoured a bureaucratic style of functioning, where the decision-making authority was seemingly very centralized and powerful. In this way, the member-states saved themselves the risk of delegating their sovereignty, and the ASEAN remained, above all, at the service of national governments. Given these characteristics, India was all the more inclined towards such a partnership, as this mechanism safeguarded a country's sovereignty. Indeed, the 'Asian way' was akin to a socialization process where national sensibilities were carefully dealt with. As was summed up by Sophie Boisseau du Rocher, the states had all the advantages of cooperating in this scheme of things: 'The cost is minimum, the risk is nil, and the potentialities, on the other hand, are enormous.'[6]

Besides, the ASEAN intended to instil its consultation practices in its Indian partner. Thus, additional meetings between Indian and ASEAN's High Officials were gradually included in the agenda, apart from the initial cooperation institutions. The purpose behind such exchanges was to ensure 'a platform for discussing sensitive issues'.[7] The ASEAN premises were based on the fact that increasing the opportunities for meetings with Indian officials would 'build up confidence and comfort levels and nurture habits of co-operation'.[8] With the ASEAN, India experienced the empirical approach of cooperation, where practice preceded all theoretical construction. In fact, the watchword for the partnership was pragmatism. Participants followed a 'step-by-step' strategy that ensured definite progress. Singapore's Foreign Minister, Prof. Jayakumar described the method followed by the Association in the following terms: 'The process has been a tested one and a step by step approach is prudent. The challenge is to build on the foundation that we have laid.'[9] He also recommended that an inordinately ambitious approach should be eschewed and deliberately modest objectives should be adopted for quick and tangible results.[10] Indeed, a learning process was to take place in the course of cooperation, which would improve interactions as each partner learned about the other's concerns. For the South-East Asian states, the method also helped in putting New Delhi to the test, by ensuring that the country maintained a low profile and bid its traditional claims to pan-Asian leadership goodbye.

As for New Delhi's rather formalistic tradition, it apparently adapted itself adequately enough to the style practised in South-East Asia. In 1998, Professor Jayakumar officially recognized that the Indo-ASEAN dialogue proved to be progressing 'at a faster and more constructive pace than some of our other dialogues'.[11] The success was largely attributed 'to the generous spirit of accommodation of the Government of India, which is working hard and in good faith to find fresh ways and means to add more value to the process'. India appeared to have discerned the specificity of ASEAN's diplomatic practices and endeavoured to comply with them.[12] There was frequent, regular and friendly interaction between the bureaucracies. A certain amount of closeness did develop, through regular consultation practices in particular.[13] At the same time, it would seem that the 'ASEAN way' sometimes came up against the institutional and formal traditions of Indian diplomacy. After all, the propensity of Indian speakers to make grand speeches as well as their attraction for pomp and ceremony could not disappear in just a few years![14] Consequently, in their speeches, officials sometimes accumulated project proposals and tended to set-up a multiplicity of institutions. In short, from the point of view of the ASEAN pragmatic nations, Indians wished to go too far too fast. Therefore, they often had to moderate the overflowing enthusiasm of their interlocutors from New Delhi. ASEAN's strategy remained the same—a gradual implementation of cooperation programmes, while consolidating consultation practices.

The major hurdle in the Indo-ASEAN dialogue proved to be India's political instability. As it happened, a major part of intra-ASEAN cooperation was built on individual relationships between leaders who had remained in power for a fairly long time, rather than on the solidity of institutions. Prime Minister Rao seemed to have understood the regional propensity for interpersonal networks well. During his five years in power, he set out to weave quite close relationships with several influential leaders in South-East Asia. A fairly important and revealing event in this regard was his participation in the prestigious series of Singapore Lectures, in 1994. This lecture series, inaugurated by the Institute of South-East Asian Studies (ISEAS), invited eminent personalities to come and speak before a panel of the city-state's elite. Furthermore, it was significant that Rao's intervention was presided over by the charismatic and influential Lee Kuan Yew, Senior Minister in the Singapore Prime Minister's office. Apart from the ISEAS, Rao established contacts with many other think-tanks close to the South-East Asian governments. I.K. Gujral followed Rao's example by attempting to forge close relations with South-East Asian decision-makers. He too did not fail to visit the ISEAS, in his capacity as Minister of Foreign Affairs in August 1996. But, from 1996 till 1998, given the fragility of the governments in New Delhi, it proved to be more difficult to establish personal and informal relations, and even more so, networks between decision-makers. To compensate for the frequent changes in government, Singapore tried to maintain contacts with India's main political parties, even when they were in the opposition.[15]

Another way to deal with governmental instability was to set-up networks of influential personalities. Thus, the Indian government offered to initiate a series of Indo-ASEAN meetings during the July 1996 Post-Ministerial Conference. In this regard, New Delhi undertook to invite twelve personalities from ASEAN and send twelve Indian personalities to South-East Asia. The organizer of these exchanges was the Ministry of Foreign Affairs, in collaboration with the New Delhi-based institute of Research and Information System (RIS) for the Non-Aligned and other Developing Countries. The speakers could be politicians, intellectuals or even entrepreneurs. The organization of this lecture series was clearly related to the creation of a network of decision-makers. By increasing the number of interactions between Indian and Asian leaders, it aimed at changing the *a priori* negatives, enhancing knowledge about each other and more generally, stepping up flows of ideas between India and ASEAN.[16] The themes covered in the lecture series ranged from a comparison of development choices in India and ASEAN, to the potential for economic cooperation, including prospects for political strategies, globalization and multilateralism, as well as socio-cultural ties.

The Indo-ASEAN lecture series enabled well-known South-East Asian personalities to voice their views. The first speaker was none other than Mahathir Mohammad, in December 1996. The choice of the Malaysian Prime Minister was the result of diplomatic calculations. Not only was he a key player in South-East Asia, but his visit to India made it possible to restore the balance with Singapore, given the numerous invitations offered to the city-state's decision-makers. In 1997, it was the Filipino economist Villegas who took the floor. Between May and August 1998, no less than five lectures were organized, successively inviting Thaksin Shinawatra, at that time the former Thai Vice-Prime Minister, Kavi Chongkittavorn, the senior editor of the Thai daily *The Nation*, J. Soedrajdad Djiwandono, the former governor of the Indonesian Central Bank, Dr. Juwono Sudarsono, Indonesia's Minister of Education and Culture and finally, Professor Tommy Koh, Ambassador in the Singapore Ministry of Foreign Affairs. The Director of the Malaysian Institute of Economic Research, Mohammed Ariff, gave a lecture on 10 May 1999, as well as Datuk Seri Syed Hamid Albar, Malaysia's Foreign Affairs Minister, a few months later. In January 2001, the ASEAN Secretary General, Rodolfo C. Severino, delivered the eleventh lecture in the series. On the Indian side, Professor U.R. Rao, a space research specialist, gave a lecture in Malaysia and Dr R.A. Mashelkar, the CSIR Director-General, visited Thailand. Dr C. Rangarajan, the former Governor of the Reserve Bank of India, was invited by the ASEAN Secretariat to present a lecture in Jakarta, on 26 February 2000.

Consequently, from 1991 onwards, a corpus was gradually constituted on the development of new relations between India and South-East Asia. The topic was steadily formalized as a research and policy theme and, thereby, acquired a certain visibility in academic and policy-making circles. By increasing their interactions, public and private actors in India and ASEAN took part in a second track process, which is often at the basis of cooperation mechanisms in Asia. Such consultations between researchers, think-tanks and policy-making bodies on both sides helped in integrating India in the mental maps of East Asian decision-makers. Thus, in the 1997 ASEAN Post-Ministerial Conferences, the Finance Minister P. Chidambaram offered to use the Indo-ASEAN fund to commission a study for the creation of Indian research centres in South-East Asia and, vice-versa.[17] Jaswant Singh, the Indian representative at the 1999 Conferences, revived the idea of forging long-term academic ties. He offered to set-up a network of ASEAN-Indian think-tanks in order to 'expand political interactions', both in the field of economic cooperation as well as in the global issues of disarmament, security and capital flows.[18]

Furthermore, a number of institutions were set-up within the India-ASEAN dialogue framework for working towards a rapprochement between the administrations.[19] The meetings organized by these cooperation bodies were opportunities for consultations and, on this account, note must be made of the regularity of meetings since 1993, which probably lay behind the improved understanding between bureaucracies. The ASEAN-India Joint Cooperation Committee was a key institutional mechanism for instigating the dialogue.[20] It essentially dealt with functional and economic cooperation issues. Its purpose was to further Indo-ASEAN cooperation in the seven sectors identified: trade and investments, science and technology, tourism, infrastructure, human resource development and human resource mobility. While it was mainly under the responsibility of the Foreign Affairs Ministry, the institution also gathered together representatives from all the other concerned ministries and held its general meeting every two years.

The dialogue partnership also succeeded due to the rapid establishment of different working groups specializing in specific Indo-ASEAN sectors of cooperation. The Indo-ASEAN Working Group on Trade and Investment was the institutionalized form of the Trade and Investment Expert Group set-up in 1992. Its exploratory nature enabled a better understanding of each other's interests and concerns. On the Indian side, it was the Ministry of Commerce, with participation from the Ministry of External Affairs, which looked after coordination. There was also an ASEAN-India Working Group on Science and Technology, which identified three fields of cooperation: IT, biotechnology and advanced equipment and machinery. The science and technology sector proved to be one of the fastest progressing sectors of cooperation. Indeed, the ASEAN understood well that it could greatly benefit from Indian expertise in advanced technologies. As for the ASEAN-India Working Group, it aimed at enabling the two parties to identify viable projects, clarifying problems inherent in project approval procedures and formulating new ideas. Meetings were held twice a year and aimed at enhancing transparency and rapidity in project implementation. There was also an ASEAN Committee in New Delhi, which brought together the foreign missions of the association's member-countries for monthly meetings. Set-up in March 1993, following the sectoral partnership, this mechanism enabled a better coordination of exchanges between India and South-East Asian countries.[21]

Moreover, a 'Meeting of High Officials' was institutionalized to expand and strengthen the dialogue between India and the ASEAN.[22] This mechanism was a discussion platform to deal with policy and security issues, at the level of the Secretaries of Foreign Affairs. The inaugural meeting took place on 9 February 1998, in New Delhi and was the first political dialogue between India and the ASEAN's high officials. From an institutional point of view, these meetings took place in addition to the Post-Ministerial Conferences and ARF meetings. They made it possible to identify guidelines for the cooperation mechanisms of other Indo-ASEAN working groups. Discussions included political, cultural and functional aspects of Indo-ASEAN relations. Regional issues were raised, relating to the economic and financial situation in Asia, ARF's progress, political developments in South Asia and the China Sea. Finally, participants also discussed international issues, including disarmament and trade.

Thanks to its status as a dialogue partner, India took part in the multilateral institutions set-up by the ASEAN. The Post-Ministerial Conferences, the highest-level meetings in the dialogue process, can be divided into two types of consultations. To begin with, a meeting takes place between each partner country and all the ASEAN members (10+1). A second type of meeting gathers all the ASEAN members with all their partners (10+10). This (10+10) meetings offered India an opportunity to speak in front of an international audience and once again to place the Look East policy within the general framework of its foreign policy. Indeed, ASEAN had major Asian and Western powers as its partners and on this account, the Post-Ministerial Conferences (10+10) had an international reach that went beyond the sole framework of regional cooperation. Overall, thanks to its dialogue with the ASEAN, New Delhi made the most of the additional channel of communication to make its voice heard in the international arena. Further, on the fringes of these conferences, Indian representatives conducted ministerial-level bilateral consultations with each ASEAN member, as well as with the other ASEAN dialogue partners. At the level of bureaucracies, dialogues were conducted at the same time among different ASEAN Director Generals and the Indian MEA's Economic Affairs Secretary, with a more functional approach.

The generally high-ranking Indian delegations testified to the importance New Delhi has given to ASEAN Post-Ministerial Conferences. For its first meeting, on 28 and 29 July 1996, the country was represented by its Foreign Affairs Minister, I.K. Gujral, who had extensive experience in international relations.[23] The following year, in July 1997, it was the Finance Minister P. Chidambaram who headed the Indian delegation, which also included the Minister of State for External Affairs, Saleem Shervani. A member of various governments since 1991, Chidambaram emerged as a 'pillar' of India's reform policy. By the same token, New Delhi gave an essentially economic aspect to its representation at the 1997 Post-Ministerial Conferences. For its third participation, on 27–9 July 1998, in Manila, India was represented by Jaswant Singh, Vice-Chairman of the Planning Commission, who had become the main interlocutor of the international community, in the delicate context that followed the May 1998 nuclear tests. The same Jaswant Singh headed the Indian delegation again, though this time in the capacity of the External Affairs Minister, for ASEAN's Post-Ministerial Conferences in 1999 and 2000. In 2001, it was K.C. Pant, the Planning Commission Vice-Chairman at the time, who led the Indian delegation.

Overall, the dialogue partnership clearly stepped up interactions between India and ASEAN at the political, economic and academic levels. It further led to the creation of several institutional mechanisms for cooperation, in a very short span of time. The paradox was that New Delhi strengthened the institutional dialogue in 1998, at a time when the ASEAN was going through both an economic and political crisis. Despite the unfavourable general context, ASEAN's spokespersons seemed satisfied with the way the process had developed. In July 2000, one of the main coordinators of Indo-ASEAN relations, S. Jayakumar, Singapore's Minister of Foreign Affairs, affirmed that 'Although the dialogue is the newest amongst the ten Dialogue Partners, the partnership that has built up between ASEAN and India has been extraordinary. Progress has been steady and substantive.'[24]

As a proof of their satisfaction, the ASEAN member-states gave their agreement, in November 2001, for the establishment of a specific ASEAN-India summit, on the model of the summits that the Association held with China, South Korea and Japan. The new Summit Meeting, which is convened annually, enables India and the ASEAN to consult each other at the highest level—that of Heads of Government—and no longer that of ministers, as was the case in the dialogue partnership. The first ASEAN-India Summit was held in November 2002, in Phnom Penh, in the presence of Prime Minister A.B. Vajpayee. At the end of the meeting, the two parties decided to launch cooperation programmes to fight terrorism and work towards the establishment of a free trade area in the following ten years. The 2002 Summit

Meeting, which was essentially devoted to ways in which economic cooperation between India and the ASEAN could be stepped up, was a testimony to the two parties' desire to upgrade ties. The Summit Meetings have since been an annual feature and have greatly reinforced the partnership between India and the ASEAN.

BIMSTEC AND THE MEKONG-GANGA COOPERATION: AT THE CROSSROADS BETWEEN SOUTH AND SOUTH-EAST ASIA

BIMSTEC and the Ganga-Mekong Cooperation Programme, as well as the Kunming Initiative, which was dealt with earlier, have certain points in common. Recently set-up, they promote new geographical units spanning South and South-East Asia. Apart from the fact that they are developing at the sub-regional level, these different projects testify to the success of the Look East policy. Indeed, New Delhi has not simply sought to reinforce its ties with already existing regional groupings in Asia, it has also promoted the setting up of new organizations in which it is a founding member. Furthermore, it must be noted that these different projects highlight the pivotal position of Myanmar in the context of the revival of ties between India and East Asia.

In terms of regional identity, BIMSTEC blurs the distinct borders between South-East Asia and South Asia and, by extension, between East Asia and the Indian subcontinent. This observation is all the more significant as BIMSTEC is originally a Thai project. Moreover, one of the underlying hypotheses for the creation of this grouping is that in an increasingly interdependent world, the best way of guaranteeing economic prosperity is through 'meaningful cooperation among countries of the same sub-region, already bound together by ties of history and culture'.[25] From this point of view, BIMSTEC indeed brings together countries that are greatly influenced by Buddhism. Apart from Bangladesh, Sri Lanka, Myanmar and Thailand are centres of *Theravada* (the little vehicle) Buddhism. Indeed, this philosophical trend spread from south India to Myanmar and Thailand, via Sri Lanka. In any case, the birth of BIMSTEC reflects East Asia's opening onto its western neighbour. Interestingly, only a specific part of South Asia takes part in BIMSTEC. There is Bangladesh to begin with, which appears increasingly sensitive to its eastern neighbourhood,[26] and Sri Lanka, which had long wanted to become a member of the

ASEAN. As for India, it is precisely the Indian states on the east coast that are the most concerned in the project. In other words, it is maritime India—historically the area turned towards South-East Asia—that has been acknowledged here. Pakistan has been excluded from the group, as if dismissed to Islamic Asia—or at least, the Near-East. Nepal has only managed to obtain an observer status.[27] It has even been argued that the development of BIMSTEC could in time favour the concept of a Bay of Bengal community extending to the whole of South-East Asia.[28]

As an extension of BIMSTEC, the Mekong-Ganga Cooperation, better known as MGC, was launched in 2000, in an effort to link up India to five riparian ASEAN countries on the Mekong River, i.e. Thailand, Myanmar, Vietnam, Laos and Cambodia. Thus, India has come out of its South Asian environment—no other SAARC country is part of the project—to associate itself with peninsular South-East Asian states, in a project that is essentially based on the idea of common cultural links. As in the case of BIMSTEC, Thailand played a dynamic role and undertook to work with its neighbours to promote cultural tourism, especially for the purpose of highlighting their Buddhist heritage. An initiative was thus established, called 'Suwannaphoum', with Myanmar, Cambodia, Laos and Vietnam.[29] India then offered to join the project, with the Minister of External Affairs, Jaswant Singh, seemingly taking a personal interest in it.[30] The Mekong-Ganga Cooperation was formally launched in July 2000, during the ASEAN Post-Ministerial Conferences, with the priority objectives of promoting the tourism, cultural and educational sectors. India's participation in this South-East Asian project is partly based on its Buddhist heritage. As in the case of BIMSTEC, the postulate is that cultural proximity between member-countries enables the formation of a natural region, which would further facilitate their interactions and cooperation. Irrespective of the concrete shape it finally assumes, the MGC programme shows that some South-East Asian countries are ready to include India in their sub-regional cooperation projects, on the basis of their common cultural and historical heritage.

Currently, the development of the MGC falls essentially within the purview of the ASEAN. MGC meetings are held just after the ASEAN Post-Ministerial conferences. In fact, ASEAN has given a favourable response to the new regional project. It is true that the MGC's objectives could complement those of the ASEAN, whose main current concern is to work towards the accelerated development of the CLMV

(Cambodia, Laos, Myanmar, Vietnam), which have recently been admitted and which suffer from considerable economic backwardness as compared to the founding members. ASEAN could only be delighted at the thought that India might take charge of a part of the programme known as Initiatives for ASEAN Integration. In July 2001, the MGC members adopted the Hanoi Action Programme, which proposed various measures for cooperation for the coming six years (2001–7). Unfortunately, the MGC project has very few financial means at its disposal. One of the organization's first steps has been to ask for support from international institutions such as the Asian Development Bank or the World Bank, especially with regard to funding the road and rail link projects between India and the Mekong countries. In any case, the new regional concept, which is quite original, would require time before it carries any weight.

Finally, it must be added that in its enthusiasm to promote regional cooperation, Bangkok undertook to organize the Asian Cooperation Dialogue, in the spirit of the 1947 Asian Relations Conference. The event, held in June 2002 in Thailand, gathered together ministers from about seventeen countries, i.e. the ten ASEAN states (with the exception of Myanmar), along with China, Japan, India, South Korea, Bangladesh, Pakistan, Bahrain and Qatar. From Bangkok's point of view, especially Prime Minister Thaksin Shinawatra's, the Asian Cooperation Dialogue is intended to formulate an agenda of priorities common to South-East, North-East and South Asia. The first session, held in an informal atmosphere, seemed to have been limited merely to a discussion on preliminary and general issues, with prospective fields of cooperation ranging from poverty alleviation to the promotion of Asian culture and tourism, including energy security and infrastructure development.[31] The fact remains that the ACD initiative seems to further confirm Thailand's propensity to transcend the sub-regional borders separating the Indian sub-continent from South-East Asia. ACD sessions have since been convened annually in various Asian countries.

5.2 India's Exclusion from the Core of East Asian Regionalism

Originally, New Delhi considered its dialogue partner status with the ASEAN as a springboard for its gradual participation in APEC and the Asia-Europe Meeting (ASEM). Indeed, the ASEAN played a key role in these organizations and New Delhi hoped to make the most of its support. But the South-East Asian states proved not very inclined to meet India's expectations. For they were much too preoccupied by making the most of APEC and ASEM to promote a specific East Asian group, the EAEC (East Asian Economic Caucus), to which India was not invited. As a result, India found itself excluded from the most important identity-building project in the region, overriding APEC, ASEM and EAEC, in the new incarnation of ASEAN+3.

KNOCKING ON APEC'S DOORS

Since September 1991, on the eve of the Seoul ministerial meeting, New Delhi had been expressing its desire to join APEC.[32] Not only was its application rejected, but the following ministerial summit held in Seattle, in 1993, imposed a three-year moratorium on the admission of any new members. However, a promise was made to formulate new admission criteria in 1995. Obviously, New Delhi lacked any significant political support within the organization, despite pressures on South-East Asia. An appraisal of the positions of some influential East Asian personalities within APEC would show that, in 1994, India's integration was far from being backed unanimously.[33] For instance, Yusuf Wanandi, an important intellectual figure on the Asian scene, did not favour India's integration. According to the Director of the Jakarta Centre for Strategic and International Studies, India did not fulfil two main criteria for admission: belonging geographically to the Asia-Pacific on the one hand, and having close economic ties with the region on the other hand. Its chances for integration were therefore 'limited', even if they would increase with time. According to Wanandi, the determining parameter would remain the compatibility between the Indian economy and APEC economies. The former Malaysian Finance Minister, Tun Daim Zainuddin, or the spokesperson of the Thai Prime Minister's Office, Abhisit Vejjajiva, also advocated caution: India had to prove itself as far as economic efficiency was concerned before it could be accepted. The North-East Asian leaders were likely to be even less favourable to India's candidature, not because they were opposed to New Delhi *per se*, but because they were concerned about safeguarding the effectiveness of APEC's mechanisms from too systematic an expansion. Tokyo was rather well disposed toward South Asian countries. But its benevolence was not reflected in any concrete support, especially since Japan preferred its protégés—Mongolia and Peru. Finally, Seoul believed it preferable to consolidate the APEC process rather than expand to include new members.

Noordin Sopiee, Director General of Kuala Lumpur's Institute of Strategic and International Studies and member of the APEC's Eminent Persons Group had a more positive attitude: 'I think it's logical that India should be considered for APEC; certainly that it should be integrated into Asia-Pacific dynamism (. . .) Why? It's a major player. Of course, India's part of Asia. Where else can it be?' India's economic potential formed the basis for Sopiee's analysis. As a matter of fact, Singapore's and Malaysia's Heads of State were also very encouraging with regard to India's candidature. During his visit to New Delhi in 1994, Malaysia's Prime Minister Mahathir Mohammad affirmed that he would personally have been happy to welcome India into the APEC, had there not been strong opposition to such a decision.[34] Likewise, in the fringes of his Singapore Lecture in September 1994, the Indian Prime Minister, P.V. Narasimha Rao, speaking about a fresh application for India's integration in APEC, said, 'I don't want to knock on closed doors'. But Singapore's Prime Minister Gok Chok Tong seemed keen to qualify this scepticism by responding, 'the doors may be closed but are not locked'.[35] Finally, the city-state's Foreign Affairs Minister, S. Jayakumar, asserted in 1996, 'It would be hard to imagine an Asia-Pacific century without India's participation.'[36]

In fact, New Delhi reiterated its desire to be associated with APEC in July 1996, during the ASEAN Post-Ministerial Conference. The question was also raised with each APEC member during the bilateral meetings accompanying the ASEAN'S conferences, but in vain. The APEC Economic Leaders Meeting, which took place in the Philippines in November 1996, did not admit any new member. The decision was taken to define membership criteria for the next summit, to be held in 1997 in Vancouver. So New Delhi continued to campaign for its candidature. Indian diplomats underlined the country's geographical position, the intensity of its trade and financial flows with the APEC economies and the potential of economic cooperation with the Asia-Pacific region. At the same time, New Delhi asked for the right to take part in three APEC working groups, generally open to non-member countries. At least, it managed to get an invitation to the group on regional cooperation in energy. New Delhi also tried to gain acceptance in the other APEC working groups, on science, industrial technologies and trade promotion.

In anticipation of the Vancouver APEC summit in end November 1997, India increased diplomatic and personal pressures on friendly countries for support for its candidature. Vice-President Krishan Kant made the most of his visit to Kuala Lumpur during the G-15 summit, to raise the issue with member-states such as Malaysia and Indonesia.[37] The External Affairs Minister, I.K. Gujral, went on an official visit to Canada, the summit's host country, just a few weeks before the event. His discussions with Prime Minister Jean Chrétien and the Foreign Affairs Minister Lloyd Axworthy ensured him Canada's support, Canada being an important APEC member.[38] But the United States and Australia expressed their opposition in advance against India's incorporation. No less than eleven countries had applied for APEC membership, including Mongolia, Peru, Russia, Panama, Colombia, Vietnam and Ecuador. Most South Asian countries too had put in their application, whether it was India, Sri Lanka, Bangladesh or Pakistan. At the Vancouver summit, the APEC members admitted Russia, Peru and Vietnam, before imposing a ten-year moratorium on new memberships. A consensus was reached on not admitting India on the grounds that its economy was not sufficiently open. And yet, once again, it was apparently the lack of political weight and the absence of significant support within the APEC that cost New Delhi its entry into the forum.[39] Given the situation, the regional or specific interests of members made it easy to understand the choice of the three countries admitted. Henceforth a member of G-8, Russia had become a priority for the United States. Vietnam, since it was an ASEAN member, naturally received the support of the Association, while Peru obtained the favour of the Latin American countries. Vietnam and Peru's applications were strongly supported by Malaysia and Japan. In fact, India had been hopeful of the support of precisely these two states.

The APEC decision to reject India's application was partly based on valid economic grounds. In fact, India was an enormous geographical mass whose integration could prove risky for the future of the group itself. Furthermore, the pace of its liberalization remained slow. At the same time, New Delhi had backed its application with strictly economic criteria that it considered solid.[40] Indian diplomats believed that their country fulfilled five prerequisites in support of their application to the APEC, i.e.: (1) the applicant economy should be located in the Asia-Pacific region; (2) it should enjoy substantial economic ties with the APEC members, and APEC's share in its international trade should be quite high; (3) it must pursue an outward-looking economic and free trade policy; (4) it should accept the various objectives as enunciated in the APEC statements; and (5) it should produce an individual plan of action for fulfilling these objectives and start taking part in collective plans of action, through APEC's programmes of work. With regard to the last condition, the Secretary for Economic Relations, A.N. Ram announced in 1997 that his government had already prepared an individual plan of action, in tune with those formulated by the APEC members, for achieving these objectives.[41] New Delhi also promised to remove all trade barriers by 2010, in order to meet APEC's membership criteria. This initiative proved that India had accepted APEC's objectives, although it had not yet been incorporated in the group. As for the third criterion concerning the extent of economic flows with APEC, the economist, Mukul Asher, presented the following facts. Merchandise trade between India and the Asia-Pacific region had risen from 38.6 per cent of its overall trade in 1993–4 to 39.4 per cent in 1995–6. India's GNP was increasingly closer to the rest of the Asia-Pacific region. Between 1991 and May 1996, the APEC economies accounted for 56.8 per cent of the entire amount of foreign direct investment approved by the Indian government (not including NRI investments). India was also an important beneficiary of portfolio investments from APEC countries, with the United States and Hong Kong heading the list. In 1994, it would have received 4.7 billion dollars, i.e. more than any developing economy within APEC.

From India's point of view, APEC could not be complete without the inclusion of the second largest Asian country. Indeed, Finance Minister P. Chidambaram went as far as affirming that APEC without India would be like Hamlet without the Prince of Denmark. Above all, New Delhi's inability to become a member of the organization was a handicap for its globalization policy. Given the uncertainty that hung over the development of open regionalism, it would have been much more comfortable as a member of APEC. Moreover, the problem of India's marginalization with regard to major regional blocks had not yet been sorted out. APEC was a significant consultative forum in the field of economic policy that enabled bilateral diplomacy within a multilateral framework.[42] Not being a part of it was a handicap for India's economic diplomacy. Finally, until 1997, APEC had been giving concrete shape to a prosperous economic zone in which India hoped to find a place. For its Look East policy, India's exclusion from the forum was a major failure, apart from the fact that it highlighted the shortcomings in its economic liberalization policy.

While successive Indian governments earnestly sought APEC membership, their approach seemed to suffer from a lack of expertise on the institution itself. These gaps were partly related to the fact that Indian think-tanks did not have access to international research networks on APEC. As a result, Indian academic circles did not have the means to develop any proper study programme on this institution, nor did they have the opportunity to participate in international academic conference on APEC. The subsidies for the organization of, or participation in such conferences came from the network of the various APEC research centres that prepared the work for ministerial meetings. So the funding choices made by these centres reflected the priorities established by the decision-makers of the member countries. Since India did not figure in the APEC's academic agenda, Indian specialists were marginalized from APEC's Track II process. Consequently, India's policy with regard to this regional organization was not based on an adequate knowledge of its institutional mechanisms. This was especially harmful as the APEC research corpus became increasingly vast and technical. Besides, India could at times have given the impression that it wished to be included in APEC without truly knowing why, or just because it did not want to be excluded from it.[43]

AN EXCLUSIVE REGIONAL PROJECT: THE EAST ASIAN ECONOMIC CAUCUS

Not only did India remain outside APEC but it was not even co-opted by the East Asian states that were seeking to redefine the concept of their region, within the forum. Indeed, in December 1990, Malaysian Prime Minister Mahathir proposed to set-up an East Asian Economic Group (EAEG). Much more restrictive than APEC, the project would only bring together South-East and North-East Asian states, so that they would have their own economic group, faced with the European Union or the NAFTA. But, the EAEG proposal essentially aimed at undermining the construction of APEC, which, according to Malaysia, was nothing but a tool at the service of American interests. More precisely, Mahathir believed that, since its performance was not up to par economically, the United States would tag along behind the East Asian high-growth economies, through APEC. With its anti-Western connotations, the proposal inevitably raised a fair amount of controversy. The United States and Australia opposed it, while the Washington allies, Japan and South Korea, gave a cautious response. The debate culminated in 1993, when Mahathir refused to attend the first APEC summit in Seattle.

However, by 1992, the Malaysian Prime Minister had redefined his project to find a compromise solution. Thus, EAEG became the East Asian Economic Caucus (EAEC), a consultative forum that would make it possible to maintain a minimal dialogue between the various countries involved. The idea of a region corresponding to East Asia and forming a distinct and exclusive institutional arrangement thus remained. Moreover, the EAEC saw the emergence of a regional consciousness among East Asian decision-makers. As affirmed by Richard Higgott, 'The EAEC is a politico-ideological construct—'imagination'—of the region, rivalling APEC.'[44] Consequently, its importance did not lie so much in its institutional success as in its symbolic reach. Conceptually, Mahathir's project challenged the metaphor of the Asia-Pacific region as it excluded the Anglo-Saxon countries of Oceania and ignored the weight of the United States as well as the economies of the American Pacific coast.[45] The EAEC also went beyond the South-East Asia metaphor, precisely the one that had included South Asia in the 1950s. The latter was henceforth left on the periphery. Finally, what was striking was that, apart from its 'anti-Western dimension', the EAEC matched Japan's sphere of co-prosperity.[46]

By becoming a sub-group of APEC in 1992, the EAEC worked for the development of an East Asian vision through the search for common stands. Thus, APEC's Asian members succeeded in imposing their preferences on their Anglo-Saxon partners. Eschewing institutional complexities, formal negotiations and restrictive decisions and developing consultative habits ensuring that all the participants were at ease were some of the typically Asian norms to which the Anglo-Saxon countries had to submit.[47] The East Asian states also ensured that APEC only laid down broad principles, thereby leaving some flexibility as far as their implementation was concerned. Above all, the East Asian countries were able to stand together, thereby moderating the ultra-liberal agenda of the United States. Consequently, in 1994, in Bogor, the Americans found a tough opposition, in getting East Asian countries to commit themselves to open their markets by 2010 or 2020, depending on their level of development. In 1995, in Osaka, East Asian countries showed even greater reticence and formed the beginnings of a block within APEC. As noted by Jean Marie Bouissou, 'we could see collective interest in action, which well and truly transformed Asia into a meaningful space'.[48] It must be noted that the EAEC also gained substance outside APEC. In June 1996 for instance, an East Asia Ministerial Meeting was held in Kuala Lumpur for support and assistance to the Mekong region. Although devoid of any decisive importance, the event gave East Asian ministers an additional opportunity to meet and prepare cooperation programmes.[49] The meeting—on a limited but precise subject—reflected the pragmatism of the East Asian approach to regional cooperation.

INDIA'S EXCLUSION FROM ASEM

Set-up in 1996, the ASEM (Asia-Europe Meeting) was conceptualized as a forum that would bring together the European Union and East Asia. In some way, it was to constitute the third angle, tying together the most powerful regions of the world—North America, Europe and Asia. The ASEM started off as an ASEAN initiative to which the European Union responded favourably. The two states that took the greatest interest in the project were France on the European side, and Singapore on the Asian side.[50] In fact, the broad outline of the forum was prepared in 1994, at the conclusion of Singapore's Prime Minister Goh Chok Tong's visit to Paris. The city-state then organized a 'Europe-East Asia' summit the following year. Singapore was then seeking an international diplomatic role, which the partnership with Europe could well offer. Moreover, the city-state was undoubtedly one of the Asian members that was the most favourable to APEC. However, this did not prevent Singapore from promoting the ASEM concept in the whole East Asian region, by stressing the fact that such an organization would help balance relations with the United States. In fact, on the Asian side, the advantage of a forum with Europe was to counterbalance the APEC process.

As far as the EU was concerned, there was renewed interest in Asia. Indeed, Europe was becoming aware of the economic success achieved by East Asia and the fact that it was barely engaged in the region. In July 1994, the European Commission proposed a 'New Asian Strategy', which received the green light from the Heads of Governments (the European Council) at the Essen summit in December 1994. The decision gave a significant political signal: relations with Asia would henceforth be among the items of priority on the EU's otherwise heavy agenda. It was true that the Europeans were concerned with APEC's rising power. Not being associated with it, they strongly feared that they would be economically penalized by the US strategy in the Asia-Pacific region. So the Bangkok summit in March 1996 marked the official birth of a partnership between Europe and Asia. The participants made a political commitment to reinforce the third angle of the Asia-Europe-North America triad. This informal and rather unstructured summit, in the so-called Asian style, was described as successful. Above all, Europe recognized the existence of a 'homogeneous and autonomous' Asia that it agreed to treat as an equal. But the Asia thus recognized only included ASEAN, China, Japan and South Korea. India was excluded from it, as also the US and Oceania.

Logically, economic relations constituted the most important—if not the most essential—field of cooperation, as both Europe and Asia were interested in enhancing trade and financial flows. The ASEM members decided to base their partnership on common commitments to a market economy, an open multilateral trade system, non-discriminatory liberalization and open regionalism. They also intended to strengthen their cooperation in the sectors of education, professional training and science and technology. However, the new Asia strategy adopted by the European Union did not deal with trade policies alone. The Europeans also insisted on expanding the agenda, though with rather uneven support from their East Asian partners. Some of the commitments made during the first ASEM meeting dealt with the strengthening of the political and strategic dialogue between the two regions.[51] The promotion of an effective reform of the United Nations and the pursuit of systematic efforts to reduce nuclear arms at the international level were also included in the fields identified for cooperation.

As for India, it tried to join the ASEM process even before the 1996 Bangkok inaugural summit. In addition, Indian representatives extensively participated at the Venice Euro-Asian forum, which was organized by the Italian chairmanship of the EU on 18–19 January 1996, in preparation for the Bangkok forum.[52] In the absence of official membership, India also participated in ASEM's Track II process. In fact, at the Bangkok summit, the participants set out to create non-official cooperation mechanisms—for instance, the Council for Asia-Europe Cooperation (CAEC), bringing together Asian and European research institutes to discuss a wide range of issues and thus prepare the future agenda for a Europe-Asia partnership. Above all, the CAEC included the viewpoints of Asian countries outside the ASEM. Consequently, for the first CAEC plenary meeting, held in Paris in November 1996, Indian researchers were also invited.[53]

But as far as the institutional process was concerned, India did not find sufficient support among the East Asian states. Nonetheless, India's membership would not have changed ASEM's functioning to any great extent. Indeed, ASEM cooperation process should be considered as an array of relationships between different states, on a variety of themes. Thus, ASEM was defined as a flexible partnership, in which different states worked together on specific issues.[54] In other words, all members did not need to cooperate on all issues. ASEM's purpose was not to forge an agreement that would unite all its twenty-six members on a specific policy issue. Rather, it sought to initiate a series of closer and more varied Euro-Asian relationships. In this respect, India's exclusion seemed to have more to do with political rather than institutional considerations. All the more so since the Europeans were in favour of India's admission. For instance, in 1996, the Italian Foreign Affairs Minister, who also headed the European troika, asserted that the Union would be 'very happy if India were to be invited'.[55] In January 1998, in his inaugural speech to the Europe-Asia Foundation, Jacques Santer, the European Commission President, noted that it would be logical if in its first expansion, the ASEM first included the main aspirants in Asia. Indeed, there was a numerical imbalance between European members, numbering fifteen, and the Asian participants, who were only ten. For the second ASEM summit, which was to take place in April 1998, India, Pakistan, New Zealand and Australia therefore appeared to be natural candidates to the forum. But this meant disregarding the prevailing internal dissensions with regard to such an expansion. In fact, certain ASEAN members, Malaysia among them, insisted on admitting Myanmar, which had just joined the ASEAN, on a priority basis. But the EU violently opposed this, so much so that states such as Malaysia preferred to block any expansion process. The upshot was that during its second summit, ASEM members decided not to admit any new member. It must be added, however, that as far as Japan was concerned, it was in favour of the entry of Australia and New Zealand.[56] Once again, it seemed that South Asian countries had very little support from their East Asian neighbours.

Nonetheless, New Delhi continued to receive support from the Europeans. The United Kingdom indicated that it would strongly defend the applications of India and Pakistan—as well as those of Australia and New Zealand—before the 2000 ASEM summit, in South Korea. On 12 March 1999, the European Parliament adopted a non-binding resolution by which it called for the strengthening of relations between India and the Union. The forum also recommended the European Union to support India's participation in the ASEM process.[57] But the East Asian members were the ones who refused to include the countries of the Indian subcontinent. Further proof was offered during Mahathir's visit to New Delhi in December 1996, when he ignored India's requests concerning its participation in ASEM.[58] The Malaysian delegation put forward the view that the process would need to be consolidated before it was expanded. The fact was that the ASEAN wished to remain at the centre of the ASEM process and was, therefore, concerned about its over-expansion. However, the real basis for the East Asian position was, above all, symbolic. A fact that should not be overlooked was that ASEM had originated with Singapore's Prime Minister, Goh Chok Tong. Not too far back, the city-state's decision-makers apparently made a clear distinction between the fast-growing economies of South-East and North-East Asia and the slower and less advanced South Asian countries. In the 1990s, the East Asian countries had acquired a new international aura, thanks to their development. And from the viewpoint of most of the region's decision-makers, ASEM was legitimately only concerned with this part of Asia, which had managed to raise itself up to the level of Western powers.

Following the APEC and EAEC controversies, ASEM pursued the process of building an East Asian regional identity. Indeed, it must be understood that the organization of Asia's representation in the forum was under the responsibility of the East Asian states themselves. Thus, the first ASEM summit was held in Thailand. As the host country, Bangkok was responsible for organizing Asia's participation. Thereafter, the Asian members decided that one ASEAN country and one non-ASEAN Asian country would take care of the coordination of future summits, when they were to be held in Europe. In this instance, for the 1998 London summit, it was Singapore and Japan that managed all the activities.[59] More importantly, these two countries were the ones who decided to exclude India. By opposing the admission of South Asia and White Asia, ASEAN was indirectly promoting the EAEC project through its partnership with Europe. Thus, ASEM contributed to consolidating Mahathir's initiative, for although the process was in its infancy, one of its first successes was of enabling East Asian states to function as a 'coherent group'.[60] This was especially so since the officials of the participating Asian states consulted each other before presenting a joint stand. Finally, ASEM cast a true light on the relations between India and East Asia. ASEM was indeed an identity-building process that demarcated an economically prosperous Asia—and, therefore, part of the 'big league', along with the United States and the EU—while the economically less flamboyant Asia remained on the periphery. This Asia, defined by just the eastern part of the continent, was given more or less due recognition by a part of Europe. Only Japan seemed anxious to temper India's exclusion. Prime Minister Ryutaro Hashimoto deputed a special envoy to India to inform the officials about the deliberations during the Asia-Europe summit held in London in early April 1998.[61] As for Japan's Ambassador to India, he recognized that during the ASEM summit in London, 'the absence of South Asia in this bi-continental dialogue was indeed noticeable'.[62] He added that his Prime Minister Hashimoto had insisted that the issue of admitting the four candidates be considered more favourably during the High Officials' meeting as well as at the Foreign Ministers' summit meetings.

New Delhi's institutional failures with regard to ASEM, APEC and EAEC showed that the East Asian capitals wished to limit their region to Myanmar's western border. This perception led to impatience and frustration on the part of India, since it considered itself to be a natural part of the region. But, in the case of ASEM (as in that of APEC), India came to be in competition with states that were already part of a regional organization. That was the case with Vietnam, for instance, which received support for its entry into APEC because it was already part of the ASEAN, while Malaysia did not hesitate to block ASEM's expansion process on the issue of Myanmar. There appeared to be a vicious circle of marginalization at play here, to the extent that a country like India, which did not belong to a regional organization, found it even more difficult to join new mega-regional arrangements. Another difficulty faced by New Delhi was that it did not enjoy strong and constant support, but only at best selective favourable recommendations. For example, Thailand was in favour of India's application, both in the case of ASEM as well as APEC.[63]

But, it had to bow down to the principle of consensus. Finally, from a political point of view, India's exclusion from ASEM was much more harmful than its exclusion from APEC. Contrary to APEC, which essentially resembled a gathering of Asia-Pacific economies, ASEM was a more structured process, with a greater political dimension. In addition, after all the controversy it had faced, European unity was increasingly becoming a point of reference in Asia. On this account, ASEM assumed greater symbolic importance in the constitution of an 'Asia' region in the late 1990s. In other words, ASEM promoted the original EAEC project, which was to be greatly reinforced with the Asian economic crisis.

ASEAN + 3 *VERSUS* THE ASEAN + INDIA SUMMIT

The definition of Asia that was originally proposed by Mahathir re-emerged during the 1997 economic crisis and took concrete shape in a mechanism that associated ASEAN with China, South Korea and Japan, i.e. the 'ASEAN+3'. The new formula for regional cooperation came as a solution for ASEAN, which was going through difficult times due to the financial hardship faced by its member-states and its expansion to slow-developing countries in the Indo-Chinese peninsula. Strengthening cooperation with China, Japan and South Korea also made it possible to stand together to gain influence in the overall management of financial flows and sway decisions taken by the West. Thus, in December 1997, China, South Korea and Japan took part in an informal summit held in Kuala Lumpur, for the first time. The organization of this event enabled ASEAN's Heads of State and Government to meet their Chinese, Japanese and Korean counterparts as part of an exclusive club. These meetings were held again in Hanoi, for the sixth ASEAN summit in December 1998. Deemed useful, the 'ASEAN+3' process was henceforth renewed every year. The mechanism was also extended to financial affairs, as shown by the ASEAN+3 Finance Ministers' meeting in end April 1999, and the Japanese proposal for creating an Asian Monetary Fund. In fact, it was in the financial sector that progress was the most substantial: the thirteen East Asian states tried to set-up a collective surveillance system for the regional economy and established a network of monetary agreements to help each other in the event of new financial hardships. The beginnings of institutionalization were underway, in particular with Japan suggesting the creation of 'ASEAN+3 High Officials

Meetings' and South Korea the formation of an East Asian Vision Group,[64] a forum that would seek to identify various means to accelerate and deepen the ASEAN+3 process.

Consequently, East Asian decision-makers were gradually trying to build a collective vision of their region.[65] But the consultation process was taking place without the participation of India. Nevertheless, New Delhi understood fairly clearly that it was being marginalized with regard to recent developments. It thus called for a strengthening of cooperation mechanisms with the ASEAN in November 2000, through its integration in the 'ASEAN+3' meetings. Singapore's Prime Minister, Goh Chok Tong, relayed the request during the fourth ASEAN Informal Summit in end November 2000. But the ASEAN's leaders refused to invite India for the 'ASEAN+3' meetings, on the grounds that the newly-constituted forum had yet to be consolidated.[66] In fact, ASEAN's Heads of Government essentially sought to expedite the ASEAN+3 process and not expand it. Thus, in agreement with their counterparts in South Korea, China and Japan, they decided to promote new initiatives in favour of closer cooperation within East Asia, during the fourth informal summit.

Alternately, New Delhi also suggested setting up 'summit meetings' specifically between India and the ASEAN, based on the 'ASEAN+3' model. Once again, the association deemed the request a bit premature, though India's traditional friends—Singapore, Vietnam, Cambodia and Laos—supported the idea of an ASEAN+1 summit. Apart from historical connections, the support of the Indo-Chinese countries could be understood in the light of the recent Mekong Ganga Cooperation, which had been launched in 2000. Singapore, on its part, remained very involved in its objective of building multi-dimensional cooperation with India. The strongest opposition came from Malaysia, which was all the more harmful since it had become the dialogue coordinator for the India-ASEAN partnership in 2000. The reticence on Kuala Lumpur's part was largely political, as it was closely associated with the difficult relations between India and the Islamic world: whether it was related to its own Muslim minority, to the deepening of its conflict with its Pakistani neighbour or to the Kashmir issue, India appeared at odds with Islamic sensitivities. Moreover, one could not exclude the possibility that Kuala Lumpur wished to oppose Singapore's stand, with whom it had somewhat confrontational relations at times. Consequently, in May 2001, Prime Minister A.B. Vajpayee once again proposed the idea of an Indo-ASEAN summit, during a visit to Kuala Lumpur, only to meet with a public and official refusal.

At the Hanoi ministerial meeting, held in the end of July 2001, the ten ASEAN Foreign Ministers once again discussed the hypothesis of an India-ASEAN summit. The Secretary-General, Rudolfo C. Severino, came out more or less in favour of the idea, while Bangkok joined the growing consensus for a separate summit with India. Faced with this situation, Malaysia decided to consult its Prime Minister. The decision to establish a separate ASEAN-India summit was finally taken in November 2001.[67] Mahathir ended up by going along with the idea of an ASEAN-India summit, while clarifying that in any case, the mechanism would remain distinct from ASEAN+3, which only concerned East Asia.[68] The birth of an ASEAN-India summit thus appeared to be a muted success. While it marked a step forward for the Look East policy, it did not give India access to ASEAN+3, which was henceforth at the heart of East Asia's regionalism. On the one hand, ASEAN showed that it was determined to strengthen its ties with India. But, on the other hand, it continued to ensure that India was kept away from the construction of the East Asian regional group.

Various observations could be derived from the India-ASEAN Summit episode. Firstly, the refusal to include India in 'ASEAN+3' showed that the country remained somewhat distant from the South-East Asian horizon. Secondly, the consolidation of EAEC in the form of ASEAN+3 helps conceptualize the gradual development of regionalism in the Asia-Pacific. In this framework, an amorphous grouping of states belonging to the same region tries to graft themselves on to a smaller group of states that constitutes a more united whole. Indeed, it appears that a hard core, bringing together East Asian states, has emerged through the EAEC/ASEAN+3 project. In this perspective, the relations between Australia and the EAEC help understand the Indian case *vis-à-vis* ASEAN+3.[69] Indeed, the states that aspire to join the hard core of Asian regionalism, such as Australia, enjoy the status of associate members, but do not have access to decision-making mechanisms, which are reserved for members of the core circle. Certainly, Australia has highlighted its geographical position, which is partly steeped in East Asia and even its strong economic ties with this area. But these arguments could not hold water against the cultural definition that certain East Asian leaders wish to give the region. While excluding from their region any states considered culturally different, these leaders have nonetheless ensured that they retain functional ties with them in the economic and security fields. So the 'first-tier' or hard-core states have negotiated as a block with each aspiring state, taken individually. In this way, states that are excluded but useful have been associated with 'first-tier' states, without challenging the political project or the internal cohesion of the core group. Thus, the dialogue partnership system, along with the Post-Ministerial Conference mechanisms can be interpreted as an example of gradual regionalism, as can the establishment of specific summits of the ASEAN-India type, on the periphery of ASEAN+3 summits. India and Australia enjoy the status of 'second-tier' members, despite their aspirations to become part of the hard core, as represented by the EAEC in the early 1990s or the ASEAN+3 in the late 1990s. And yet, just like Australia in the case of the EAEC, New Delhi's application to the ASEAN+3 appeared to hit a snag over the cultural definition of Asia. Thus, the question of whether India stands a chance of being incorporated in the region, defined in cultural terms, beyond economic and geographical criteria, should be raised.

NOTES

1. Sophie Boisseau du Rocher, *L'ASEAN et la Construction Régionale en Asie du Sud-Est*, Paris: L'Harmattan, 1998, p. 127.
2. J.N. Dixit, *My South Block Years*, New Delhi: UBSPD, 1996, p. 265.
3. *The Straits Times*, 4 January 1995.
4. Opening Statement by Prof. S. Jayakumar, Minister for Foreign Affairs of the Republic of Singapore, at the ASEAN Post-Ministerial Conference, Kuala Lumpur, 1997, § 3 & 4.
5. Amitav Acharya, 'Ideas, Identity, and Institution-building: From the 'ASEAN way to the Asia-Pacific way?', *The Pacific Review*, vol. 10, no. 3, 1997, p. 328.
6. Boisseau du Rocher, *L'ASEAN et la Construction Régionale en Asie du Sud-Est*, p. 243.
7. Opening Statement at the second ASEAN-India Joint Co-operation Committee Meeting in Singapore by the Minister for Foreign Affairs, Prof. S. Jayakumar on Tuesday, 28 April 1998, p. 2.
8. Ibid., p. 2.
9. Opening Statement by His Excellency, Prof. S. Jayakumar, Minister for Foreign Affairs of the Republic of Singapore, at the ASEAN Post-Ministerial Conference, Kuala Lumpur, 1997, § 7.

10. Opening Statement by His Excellency, Prof. S. Jayakumar, Minister for Foreign Affairs of the Republic of Singapore, at the ASEAN Post-Ministerial Conference, Manila, 29 July 1998.
11. Opening Statement at the Second ASEAN-India Joint Co-operation Committee Meeting in Singapore by the Minister for Foreign Affairs, Prof. S. Jayakumar on Tuesday, 28 April 1998.
12. Interviews, Ministry of External Affairs, New Delhi, March and April 1998; Interview, High Commission of Malaysia in New Delhi, May 1998.
13. Interview, official from the High Commission of India in Singapore, June 1998; Singapore Ministry of Foreign Affairs, official, Singapore, June 1998.
14. Interview, Singapore Indian Chamber of Commerce and with an official in the Singapore Ministry of Foreign Affairs, June 1998.
15. Interview, official from the Singapore Ministry of Foreign Affairs, Singapore, 20 June 1998.
16. Interview, Sanjaya Baru, Senior Consultant, RIS, New Delhi, 17 April 1998; *India-ASEAN Lecture Series, Concept Paper*, document presented by Sanjaya Baru, RIS.
17. Statement of P. Chidambaram, Finance Minister of India, on the occasion of the Post-Ministerial Conferences of ASEAN (9+1) Session, Kuala Lumpur, 29 July 1997, § 22.
18. Statement of Jaswant Singh, Foreign Minister of India, on the occasion of the Post-Ministerial Conferences of ASEAN (10+1) Session, 1999, p. 1.
19. Joint Press Release, *The First ASEAN-India Joint Cooperation Committee Meeting*, New Delhi, 14–16 November 1996, (http://www.asean.or.id); Opening Statement at the Second ASEAN-India Joint Co-operation Committee Meeting in Singapore by the Minister for Foreign Affairs of Singapore, S. Jayakumar, on Tuesday, 28 April 1998; Opening statement by S. Jayakumar, at the 1998 PMC (9+1) Session with India, 29 July 1998, Manila.
20. The AIJCC took over from the ASEAN-India Sectoral Cooperation Committee, which had met twice—in January 1994 in Bali and in February 1995 in New Delhi.
21. Interview, official from the High Commission of Malaysia in New Delhi, May 1998.
22. Opening statement by S. Jayakumar, Minister for Foreign Affairs of Singapore, at the 1998 PMC (9+1) Session with India, 29 July 1998, Manila, § 3.
23. I.K. Gujral was notably India's Ambassador to the USSR from 1976 to 1980, and later External Affairs Minister from 1989 to 1990. He then became Prime Minister for ten months between 1999 and 1998.
24. Opening Statement by S. Jayakumar, Minister for Foreign Affairs,

Singapore, at the PMC (10+1) Session with India, 29 July 2000, Bangkok, Thailand.

25. Declaration on the Establishment of Bangladesh-India-Sri Lanka-Thailand Economic Cooperation (BIST-EC), Bangkok, 6 June 1997.
26. A.F. Salahuddin Ahmed, 'Bangladesh—A Bridge between South Asia and South-East Asia: Utopian Dream or Present-Day Imperative?', in N.N. Vohra and J.N. Dixit, *Religion, Politics and Society in South and South-East Asia*, New Delhi: India International Center, Konark Publishers, 1998, pp. 71–86.
27. MEA, *Annual Report, 1998–99*, p. 96. Nepal and Buthan were made full members of BIMSTEC in 2004.
28. V. Suryanarayan, 'India and South-East Asia: Shared Destiny', N. Jetley, *India's Foreign Policy, Challenges and Prospects*, p. 199.
29. 'Suwannaphoum' is a Thai variant of the Sanskrit word 'Swarna Bhumi', which means 'land of gold'. But when ministerial delegations of the concerned countries met in Vientiane, on 10 November 2000, the project was simply renamed Mekong-Ganga Cooperation (MGC), with Laos asking that the term 'Suwannaphoum' be deleted (Ganga-Mekong Swarnabhoomi project: http://www.indiagov.org).
30. Jaswant Singh's personal interest in India's north-east region, which is potentially at the heart of the MGC, would be due to the fact that he served in the 1962 Sino-Indian war in Arunachal Pradesh. He later took up the post of the BJP coordinator for the north-eastern region of India.
31. *Frontline*, 6–19 July 2002.
32. MEA, *Annual Report, 1994–95*, p. 109.
33. Hamish McDonald, 'Joining Up: India Looks to Strengthen Ties with Asia', *FEER*, 22 September 1994.
34. *The Pioneer*, 19 December 1996.
35. *Indian Recorder*, 8–14 October 1994.
36. *The Times of India*, 21 August 1996.
37. *The Hindu*, 17 July 1997.
38. *Indian Recorder*, 12–18 February 1997; *Foreign Affairs Record*, 1–7 January 1998, p. 3344.
39. V. Jayanth, 'India to Keep Alive Its Bid for APEC Membership', *The Hindu*, 26 November 1997.
40. Mukul G. Asher, 'India and APEC', *The Hindu*, 26 June 1997.
41. *The Hindu*, 26 November 1997.
42. Ibid., 'India and APEC', *The Hindu*, 26 June 1997.
43. Quoted in Marika Vicziany, 'Regionalism, Sub-regionalism and APEC: The Case of India', John Ingleson, ed., *Regionalism, Subregionalism and APEC*, Clayton, Victoria: Monash Asia Institute, 1997, p. 205.
44. Richard Higgott, 'Libre-échange et Régionalisme Asiatique', D. Camroux and J.L. Domenach, *L'Asie Retrouvée*, Paris: Seuil, 1997, p. 85.

45. Khoronen, *Japan and Asia Pacific Integration.*
46. Karoline Postel-Vinay, *Le Japon et la Nouvelle Asie*, p. 80. The greater East Asia co-prosperity sphere was coined by the Japanese military during the Second World War and covered North-East and South-East Asian countries under Japanese domination.
47. Ibid., p. 84.
48. J.M. Bouissou, 'Le Japon Peut-il Donner sens à l'Asie?', Z. Laidi, ed., *Géopolitique du Sens*, p. 271.
49. P. Korhonen, *Japan and Asia Pacific Integration*, p. 194.
50. Hanns Maull, Gerald Segal and Jusuf Wanandi, eds., *Europe and the Asia Pacific*, London: Routledge, 1998.
51. Yeo Lay Hwee, 'The Bangkok ASEM and the Future of Asia-Europe Relations', *Southeast Asian Affairs*, 1997, pp. 37–8.
52. David Camroux and Christian Lechervy, 'Close Encounter of a Third Kind? The Inaugural Asia-Europe Meeting of March 1996', *The Pacific Review*, vol. 9, no. 3, 1996, p. 451.
53. Conseil pour la Cooperation Europe-Asie, 'Europe-Asie: renforcer le dialogue informel', *Les Cahiers de l'IFRI*, no. 19, 1997.
54. Ibid., p. xiv.
55. *Indian Recorder*, 8–14 April 1996.
56. *The Hindu*, 3 March 1998.
57. http://india.indiaorg/foreign Relations-India-European Union Relations.
58. *Business Standard*, 16 December 1996.
59. Maull, Segal and Wanandi, ed., *Europe and the Asia Pacific*, pp. 79–80.
60. Ibid., p. xi.
61. *The Hindu*, 7 April 1998.
62. Hiroshi Hirabayashi, 'South Asia and Its Eastern Neighbours', 19 April 1998 (http://www.japan-emb.org.in/lectures).
63. Interview, Embassy of Thailand in India, New Delhi, 21 April 1998; Thammasat University and Information Department, Ministry of Foreign Affairs of Thailand, Seminar on 'Thai-Indian Relations in the Present Decade', p. 26.
64. Jürgen Rüland, 'ASEAN and the Asian Crisis: Theoretical Implications and Practical Consequences for South-East Asian Regionalism', *The Pacific Review*, vol. 13, no. 3, 2000, pp. 432–3.
65. Stephen Leong, 'The East Asian Economic Caucus (EAEC): "Formalized" Regionalism Being Denied', B. Hettne, A. Inotai and G. Sunkel, eds., *The New Regionalism*, vol. 3, *National Perspective on the New Regionalism in the South*, The New Regionalism Series, London: Macmillan, 2000, pp. 57–103.
66. *The Hindu*, 25 November 2000.
67. Ibid., 19 November 2001.
68. Ibid., 6 November 2001.
69. Michael Wesley, 'The Politics of Exclusion: Australia, Turkey and Definitions of Regionalism', *The Pacific Review*, vol. 10, no. 4, 1997.

CHAPTER 6

Cultural and Religious Links

6.1 The Indian Civilization on the Periphery of the 'New Asia'

In terms of their symbolic implications, BIMSTEC and ASEAN+3 suggest contrary interpretations, with the opening of East Asia onto India in the first case and its exclusion in the second. But in the prevailing situation, the scope of the ASEAN+3 process is much greater than that of BIMSTEC. These institutional ambiguities partly reflect the vague feeling of proximity that East Asians may have with regard to the Indian civilization. Indeed, there often is a nebulous attitude with regard to India's cultural influence in Asia. Without being excluded or overlooked, the Indian heritage has not been fully recognized either. So the subcontinent has so far remained confined to the periphery of the 'New Asia'.

A DISTANT SPIRITUAL SOURCE

In the context of the Look East policy, Indian diplomatic circles have readily orchestrated their spiritual ties with East Asia, especially those pertaining to Buddhism. What remains to be seen is the response this has elicited from East Asia. In other words, what has been the reaction of East Asian countries, faced with an India that proclaims to be the birthplace of Buddhism? In more general terms, it has to be seen whether any of these ancient ties has survived to the extend that it could give added weight to India's contemporary position and nurture a feeling of cultural proximity. On this account, it is necessary to dwell on current religious and spiritual flows between India and the Buddhist or Hindu communities living in East Asia. In fact, the networks of Buddhist organizations have created a number of ties between the subcontinent and various East Asian nations. In Japan, most of India's admirers can be found in Buddhist religious circles.

The older generations retain the image of a country that is Buddha's birthplace.[1] They therefore nurse a certain degree of respect for it, reinforced by memories of the war. On the Indian side, various private organizations are intent on maintaining contacts with Buddhist communities in East Asia. For instance, in November 1997, the Asia Society conferred the Tagore Peace Prize on a Japanese, Daisaku Ikeda, Chairman of Soka Gakkai International, a Buddhist peace organization.[2] The same month, the Modi Foundation, along with the World Buddhism Foundation, jointly organized a seminar in Meerut on the theme of 'Great Religions of Asia'. The event allowed for a dialogue between Hindu *swamis* and Buddhist or Shinto monks from Japan.[3] In addition, a number of Buddhist organizations in the archipelago have funded the construction of temples in India. Thus, there are temples following the Japanese Buddhist cult in Leh (Ladakh), New Delhi or Bodh Gaya. In the latter, considered the most important Buddhist pilgrimage site in the world, most countries with a large Buddhist population have built a temple or a monastery. Specifically, there are a Burmese *vihara*, a Thai temple, and a Japanese monastery, visited by a large number of Japanese tourists.

In South Korea, Buddhist groups also show a special interest in maintaining ties with India. Similarly, in Thailand, some monks stress their spiritual debt to India. Thus, the Bikkhu Buddhadasa, an influential reformer of Buddhism in Thailand,[4] affirmed that the Thai civilization was essentially built on Indian foundations: 'The truth is that what we term our culture, originated from and was based on Indian culture and religions.'[5] In addition, Buddhadasa did not hesitate to speak about the consanguinity of the Indian and Thai peoples and the deep bonds between their religious systems: 'There is a combination of Indian flesh and blood in ours. We unconsciously have Hinduism as our mother and Buddhism, our father.' In fact, the only time that the monk went abroad was to visit north India.

At the same time, a re-appropriation of the Theravada Buddhist legacy in India has taken place. In the state of Maharashtra for example, the Vipassana Research Institute has initiated a major project consisting of transcribing and publishing all Buddha's teachings (*Dhamma Vacana*).[6] Thus, Buddhist canons have been transcribed in the Devanagari script, based on a Burmese script, and later transferred to CD-ROMs. In addition, the centre has developed a computer programme that should make it possible to easily convert the Devanagari versions of Pali texts into the Burmese script. The programme has also included transcriptions in the Sinhalese, as well as Roman and Thai scripts. More than 232 volumes are to be published by the Institute, which has received aid from Burmese experts. In so doing, India has tried to bring back the Buddhist canons, as the *Dhamma Vaccana* had practically disappeared from its soil. But this project is also proof of the desire to enrich the world Buddhist corpus. In fact, Buddha's words have been preserved in Myanmar, Sri Lanka, Thailand and Cambodia, but always in different scripts—or even versions. Therefore, the purpose of the Vipassana Research Institute has been to put all these transcriptions in relation to each other, on the basis of an Indian version. Furthermore, this project is of significant historical interest. Buddha's teachings are not just a testimony of the spiritual and philosophical life of ancient India, but also provide information about its political, cultural and economic systems. Hence, the Vipassana Research Institute project is truly global, consisting as it does of highlighting all the different aspects of India's Buddhist past.

Hinduism has also nourished various flows between the subcontinent and the Indian diaspora settled in South-East Asia. For instance, the Malaysian Hinduism reform and revitalization movement, underway since the 1980s, has led to new religious ties with India.[7] The phenomenon has entailed an increase in requests for recordings of Hindu hymns and texts that originate in the subcontinent. In this context, the teachings of Gurus Trimuruga Kirubanada Variar and Pulavar Keeran have become quite popular, as they provide access to knowledge about Hinduism to a large number of people. Finally, as there are very few Brahmins in Malaysia, temple managements have employed Brahmin priests from Tamil Nadu on a contract basis. The Chettiars are the most skilled in obtaining such services because of their extensive sponsorship networks in Tamil Nadu. Otherwise, Malaysian Hindus could have decided to become priests themselves and go to India to learn prayer rituals.

These historical and religious ties have traditionally been cultivated at the official level. For instance, decision-makers in countries with large Buddhist populations tend to recognize India as a sacred land. During his visit to New Delhi, the Korean President, Kim Young Sam, saluted the Indian civilization's contribution to Asia's religious heritage: 'India is the spiritual home of all Asians. Buddhism and Hinduism spread from India to greatly influence the cultures and lives of people in most Asian countries.'[8] But the Korean President did not confine himself to ancient religious flows. He also underlined the exemplary figure of Mahatma Gandhi, who was 'a great Indian leader of the modern age, who immensely influenced the thought and mind of the Korean people'.[9] Indeed, it was the Mahatma's non-violence campaign that inspired Koreans to free themselves from the yoke of Japanese imperialism. Kim Young Sam added that he, himself, had drawn great inspiration from the Gandhian experience in the recent struggle for democracy. Thus, in Kim Young Sam's vision, India stood out as a model of emancipation through the ages.

Moreover, Buddhist links have frequently been considered as symbols of the cordial relations between India and Buddhist nations. This has been the case with Laos, for instance. On an official visit in 1995, the Indian External Affairs Minister did not miss the opportunity to plant a young shoot of the Bodhi Tree from Bodh Gaya in a temple in Vientiane.[10] The same has also been true for relations between India and Thailand. Throughout 1996, a festival of India was organized in honour of the fiftieth anniversary of the accession to the throne of the Thai King Bhumibol. Sponsored by the Indian Council for Cultural Relations,[11] 'the festival's theme highlighted the Buddhist message of tolerance and peaceful coexistence'. The event was marked in particular, by a play on the life of King Ashoka. The festival ended with an exhibition of Buddha's sacred relics in Puthamonthon.[12] The following year, the royal government of Thailand provided a pavilion to house these relics, during the celebrations of the fiftieth anniversary of its independence.[13] At the same time, a reciprocal Festival of Thailand was held in India. That the Indian government granted so much attention to the celebrations of the Thai King Bhumibol's accession to the throne in 1996 was in no way fortuitous. In fact, the Hindu tradition contributed extensively to shaping the conception of power in a large part of South-East Asia.[14] But, it is in Bangkok that this influence is the most visible today. Indeed, Thailand's royalty presents certain typically Hindu characteristics. For instance, Brahmanic ceremonies are associated only with the royal institution. The Indian theory of royalty has deeply inspired Thai sovereigns, especially the idea that they are *avatars* of Lord Vishnu. Thus, Vajiravudh, the sixth king of the Bangkok era decided to take the name of Rama VI and to posthumously name the five preceding kings Rama I to Rama V. Bhumibol, the current heir to the throne, is Rama IX. The official language and, more specifically, the royal vocabulary, are very close to Sanskrit. Finally, the legitimacy of the Thai sovereign continues to be founded on a combination of Buddhist and Hindu beliefs, which impose obeisance to the ten *Rajadharma*, i.e. the ten virtues according to Buddhist writings.

As far as Japan is concerned, it has been anxious to preserve India's Buddhist legacy. The archipelago is aware of the fact that some of its distant origins could be found in the subcontinent. Consequently, the Japanese Ambassador to New Delhi, Hiroshi Hirabayashi, once said, 'Buddhism is India's greatest export to Japan'.[15] In fact, in ancient Japan, India was known by the name of *Tenjiku*, a place located high in the sky above. The country that was Buddha's birthplace (*Hotokesama*), was mentioned as a mythical land, unlike China, which was quite real in the Japanese universe. Certain gods of the Hindu pantheon, such as Saraswati or Lakshmi, have been integrated in Japanese Buddhism and they have become guardian deities, known by the names of Taishakuten and Benten respectively.[16] In fact, Tokyo has offered considerable assistance for the restoration and preservation of Buddhist archaeological sites. The UNESCO Aid Fund and the Japan Trust Fund have particularly enabled the protection of the Buddhist monuments in Sanchi and Satdhara. Tokyo has also financed archaeological excavation work on ancient Buddhist sites, through its ODA programme. Hence, in February 1994, several remains—notably of stupas dating back to the second century BC—were excavated around Bhopal.[17] The ICCR, on its part, has played on Japan's interest in India's spiritual heritage. For instance, it organized an exhibition entitled 'King Ashoka, Mahatma Gandhi and Nehru—The Healing Touch' in Japan, from October to December 1994. This event, which marked the 125th anniversary of Mahatma Gandhi, aimed at promoting the philosophies of pacifism and non-violence.[18] By the same token, India was able to reinforce its image of an intellectual and philosophical centre, radiating its influence up to the furthest confines of Asia.

India and the South-East Asian countries have also conducted several cultural cooperation initiatives to commemorate ancient ties, both Buddhist and Hindu. The organization of these events shows that these countries are willing to give due recognition to their Indian heritage, perhaps even to give it greater visibility in their entire populations—not just communities of Indian origin. Indonesia, for instance, has been quite willing to celebrate its Indian legacy. Of course, such attitudes have been facilitated by the living influence of the Hindu civilization in the island of Bali, one of the main tourist sites in the country. Thus, in 1992, a Ramayana festival was celebrated in the island, with the participation of a delegation of Indian artists. In early 1993, India and Indonesia organized a major cultural event, 'Bali Yatra'. A sailing expedition connected Orissa to the Indonesian archipelago, to commemorate ancient seafaring ties between the two lands. At the same time, a festival was held in Bali, accompanied by seminars on cultural relations between the two countries.[19] In more general terms, Hindu symbols are still quite visible, even at national level, since it is Lord Ganesha whose image can be seen on Indonesian banknotes, while the national airline is called Garuda.

The Indian government has also tried to help preserve sites of Hindu origin in South-East Asia, to the extent possible. In accordance with an agreement concluded with Cambodia in 1986, India conducted a programme for the restoration of certain temples in the Angkor Vat complex. The project, spreading over seven years, was managed by the Archaeological Survey of India and concluded in May 1993.[20] In fact, in April 2002, New Delhi signed a new agreement with Cambodia to restore a temple near Angkor Vat.[21] New Delhi also signed a Cultural Exchange Programme with Vietnam, to cover, among others, research projects on ancient historical contacts. As for Singapore, it has been keen to highlight ancestral cultural links with India by organizing several exclusive exhibitions. Thus, the city-state managed to get a set of rare sculptures on loan from the Kolkata museum, which left India's shores for the first time. The collaboration led to the organization of an exhibition called 'The Path of the Buddha'.[22] The Singapore National Museum then hosted the exhibition, 'Alamkara, Five Thousand Years of India'. This cultural event, of considerable stature, was held from July 1994 to January 1995 and allowed the city-state's inhabitants to discover the richness of ancient India. In April 1997, the first wing of Singapore's Asian Civilizations Museum opened its doors to the public. While the permanent collection pertained to the Chinese cultural heritage, a temporary inaugural exhibition was organized around the epic, *Ramayana*. Subsequently, the museum set out to devote a section to South Asia.[23] The collection highlights south India in particular, for the direct benefit of Singapore's Indian communities. In fact, the collection intends to reflect the cultural affinities that Singapore's South Asian communities have with their parent culture. The main objects displayed testify to the influence of Indo-Buddhist art in South-East Asia, especially in Thailand and Indonesia. However, there should be no misunderstandings regarding the rationale behind Singapore's cultural policy. The initiatives of the city-state are less of a bilateral nature and more of a national nature. Above all, they seek to limit the impact of Westernization, by trying to highlight the original cultures of its various ethnic communities.

Cultural cooperation between India and East Asian countries has not just sought to cultivate the memory of historical ties. There has often been a convergence of interests between Indian and East Asian countries with regard to the use of cultural ties for economic ends. For instance, Indian states harbouring Buddhist relics have realized that their religious legacy could attract many pilgrims, if properly developed. Thus, they have undertaken to build up their tourist potential among countries with large Buddhist populations. The most active have been the states of Bihar and Orissa, the first because of Bodh Gaya, and the second because of Dholagari. Gujarat and Uttar Pradesh have also been in the running. In so doing, Indian states have been greatly encouraged by the Central Government, which has been concerned about developing 'Buddhist Trails' in the entire territory.[24] Interactions for the promotion of 'Buddhist tourism' have thus taken place at different levels: representatives from the Central Government as well as state governments have cooperated with Thai, Korean and Japanese national tourist organizations and travel agencies.

On their part, the Japanese have been quite keen to invest in India's Buddhist past for purposes of tourism. In 1997, a Japanese delegation consisting of representatives from the tourism industry and investment agencies was invited for promotional Buddhist tours in Uttar Pradesh and Bihar. Tokyo had already released funds for the state of Maharashtra. Through its development aid agency, it contributed to the construction of a museum, which is replicating the frescoes in the Ajanta caves through computer simulation.[25] Similarly, the state of Bihar managed to arouse the interest of its Thai neighbours. During his visit to Thailand in August 1995, Laloo Prasad signed agreements with the Shivnath Investment Company and the Usha Siam Company. These two companies, based in Bangkok, were engaged in developing the state's Buddhist sites, especially by modernizing its airport and building a meditation centre.[26] Finally, the promotion of Buddhist tours was one of the motivations behind India's participation in BIMSTEC. One of the organization's primary objectives was to promote a regional airline to increase tourist and trade interactions among member-states. To launch the cooperation programme, the Indian delegate, Saleem Iqbal Shervani, Minister of State for External Affairs, did suggest that the focus should be on Buddhist tours for tourists in each member-state. A similar reasoning lay behind the Mekong-Ganga Cooperation. In fact, the November 2000 Vientiane declaration required the six participating countries to conduct 'strategic studies' for the promotion of tourism and the facilitation of communication links. The document suggested, in particular, the launch of a 'Ganga-Mekong' tourist guide and the organization of excursions to major Buddhist pilgrimage sites in the region.[27]

As far as Singapore is concerned, it has displayed great expertise in making the most of its cultural heritage for commercial purposes. It has successfully applied its strategy at two levels: first, on behalf of the national tourist industry, and second, within the framework of external economic relations. Thus, the city-state has emphasized its Indian heritage to bolster its image as a colourful and multi-ethnic destination, ideal for holidays. The Singapore Tourism Promotion Board (STPB) brochures do not fail to highlight the Indian district of Serangoon, where you can find the main Hindu temples and meeting areas. Moreover, in Singapore, as also in Malaysia, the Indian community celebrates many Indian festivals, the main ones being Deepavali, Thaipusam, Pongal and Vaisakhi. The STPB has thus chosen Deepavali[28] as being representative of the city's multiculturalism.

The city-state has also been well aware of the fact that cultural ties could constitute a useful resource for strengthening economic relations with India. In fact, New Delhi has grasped this premise well. Very soon in their rapprochement policy—beginning on 5 May 1993—the governments of both states signed an agreement on Art, Heritage and the Archives.[29] This official document, which gave due recognition to the historical and cultural contacts between India and Singapore, was, in fact, in line with very contemporary economic and political concerns. Firstly, it formed part of the city-state's cultural regionalization programme, as it made it possible to host various troupes of Indian artists. While these shows were generally organized for the Indian community, they also helped in furthering Singapore's ambition to become a major centre of the arts in Asia. But the main thrust of the agreement lay in the article pertaining to the organization of several exhibitions on India. As regard these exhibitions, the signatories were targeting the entire population of Singapore in order to create awareness about Indian culture. Contrary to shows organized by Indian artists, the target audience would include all ethnic communities, not just the diaspora. The aim was thus to initiate a process familiarizing Singapore's citizens—considered as potential investors—with the Indian world. In fact, it had already been noted that India was an unknown land for a significant part of Singapore's business circles. It so happens that the business community tends to think that it is preferable to learn about a country's culture first, before venturing into its market. In fact, the economic underpinnings of the agreement could be seen in its asymmetry. While bilateral exchanges were mentioned officially, in practice, cultural flows were to be essentially unilateral. Different aspects of Indian culture were to be presented to the people of Singapore without any reciprocal movement. This economic logic also suited the promoters of the Look East policy, whose main objective consisted of mobilizing East Asian capital. All in all, Indian and Singaporean leaders signed an agreement in the cultural field with the purpose of promoting relations between business communities.

A COUNTRY ON THE FRINGES OF CONTEMPORARY CULTURAL REPRESENTATIONS

When they have been used for commercial purposes, ancient ties have helped enhance economic cooperation. But quite often, their influence on contemporary perceptions has remained fairly limited in East Asia. And while New Delhi has applied itself to practising a certain cultural diplomacy, it has not been enough to nurture a feeling of proximity. Consequently, in cultural terms, the Indian sub-continent has so far not been very integrated in the 'New Asia'. The Indian heritage has often been diluted in national cultures or else it has been forgotten. For instance, Indian leaders have played a lot on Buddhist ties, hoping to arouse a feeling of proximity. But, very often, Buddhism is just one religious affiliation among others. As observed by François Godement, 'Buddhism's sphere of influence is evidently immense, but often very limited in intensity'.[30] There has been a superimposition of different religious currents within the same population: Buddhism with a Hindu influence, has combined with multiple versions of Confucianism, as well as Islam and Christianity. Thus, *Mahayana* (Great Vehicle) Buddhism often proves a 'minority' trend, whether in China, South Korea, Japan or again in Vietnam. It prospered in China till the sixth century BC, but was later overtaken by Confucianism. Besides, the Chinese introduced Buddhism in South Korea, and later in Japan, in around the sixth century. But in Japan, Buddhism faced competition from neo-Confucianism and Shintoism from the nineteenth century onwards. Similarly, in Singapore, the practice of Buddhism in the Chinese community has blended with Taoism and Confucianism. On the other hand, *Theravada* (Little Vehicle) Buddhism, which travelled to Sri Lanka from India, and later to the Indo-Chinese peninsula, has retained considerable influence in modern society. But then, Buddhism has often been a source of national identity, at the expense of its universalistic dimension.[31] It is here that the *Theravada* current distinguishes itself from *Mahayana* Buddhism, which rather favours the idea of a South-East Asian community.

Among the general public, the Indian past has often been either forgotten or has remained unknown. According to the former Ambassador of India in Vietnam, J.C. Sharma, very few people know that the temples in the centre and south of the country have a Hindu legacy dating back to the kingdom of *Champa*, from the second to sixteenth centuries. He added, 'Every time I spoke about Hindu temples in Vietnam, people used to look at me with surprise.'[32] Indeed, a phenomenon of extensive appropriation has occurred in areas formerly under Indian influence. While, for instance, the *Ramayana* and *Mahabharata* have greatly inspired the Thai and Indonesian traditions, the latter have also acquired a certain originality of their own. In fact, certain episodes of the *Ramayana* have inspired a national dance in Thailand and have re-emerged in the form of poems, puppet plays or shadow plays in several South-East Asian countries. But, in Thailand for instance, Indian epics are so well integrated and adapted to the local culture that only very few people suspect the Hindu origin of these traditions.[33] Thus, the *Ramakien* cannot be considered merely as a translation of the *Ramayana*. These versions of the *Ramayana*, which were composed by several Thai kings—the most complete version was written by King Rama I of Bangkok in the eighteenth century—constitute a unique text, based on the themes of the Indian epic.[34] The characters have become typically Thai and Buddhism has replaced Hinduism.

Even those who understand the extent of Hinduism's influence in Thailand hardly feel close to India. An intellectual reversal has taken place, in which Thailand is not so much indebted to India as it is the sanctuary of India's most precious cultural elements. From the Thai point of view, the subcontinent lost the richness of its original civilization under the effect of British colonization. Thailand, on the contrary, which has never been colonized, has retained the essence of Indian culture. Thai scholars thus feel that their beliefs and rituals are more faithful to the pure form of Buddhism than those of the Buddhist currents surviving in India. In a way, Thailand has been able to preserve the ancient Buddhist culture that India has forgotten. Moreover, Hindu and Buddhist religious systems are considered quite different from each other. From the point of view of many Thais, their beliefs are not comparable with those of the Hindus, in the same way that their rites and teachings and—by extension—their way of life and thinking are different. Finally, beyond the controversy over the ties between the two civilizations, Thailand has developed much more rapidly than its bigger neighbour. Especially until the 1997 financial crisis, the Thais believed they were much more modern and developed and, consequently, they didn't feel close to a country whose overriding image was that of poverty.[35] This complex of superiority, based on economic success, also held true for the rest of South-East Asia. Even in Singapore, the Asian country that knows India best, India's image has not always been positive. In fact, the city-state's perception about India is largely influenced by the presence of a diaspora that originates from the south of the peninsula. Thus, it tends to confine itself to the Dravidian culture. Moreover, since the south Indian community is overall not quite so prosperous, the cliché of an under-developed India is sometimes reinforced.

The feeling of proximity that many Indians feel towards South-East Asia is not readily reciprocated. The gap in perceptions is clearly visible in diplomatic interactions. Many Indian diplomats have a feeling of familiarity when they travel to South-East Asia. Whether it was Cambodia, Thailand, Indonesia or Malaysia, an Indian official from the ASEAN division confessed to a 'feeling of déjà vu'.[36] Likewise, Ranjit Gupta, India's Ambassador to Thailand once said that when Indians visited the country, they did not see any significant difference: 'We are all aware of the extensive commonalities of religion, language and culture between our two civilizations. The overall cultural milieu and environment is so familiar that for an Indian, being in Thailand is like being at home. This naturally makes interaction and mutual understanding that much easier.[37]

However, the perceptions of East Asian diplomats with regard to the Indian context prove different. In fact, assertions such as those of

Ranjit Gupta are not understood in South-East Asia, or even quite unappreciated. A diplomat from the Embassy of Thailand in New Delhi once criticized the pretensions of the Indians and their inability to appreciate the cultural specificity of their neighbours: 'They think that they brought in the culture, the way of life and do not acknowledge the people of the country.'[38] A similar response was given by an official in the High Commission of Malaysia, who believed that the Indians 'are very proud of their culture'.[39] And yet, he added, their society remained very traditional and conservative, and had hardly evolved as compared to the level of modernization achieved by Malaysia.

At least until the late 1990s, most decision-makers in East Asia continued to establish a clear 'line of demarcation' between their region and the subcontinent, thereby indicating that the two belonged to distinct cultural spheres. In 1994, Lee Kuan Yew recalled that India had followed a historical trajectory that was quite different from that of East Asia: 'India has always been oriented towards the West. All the major invasions, including the British, came from India's west. South-East Asia and East Asia barely figured in India's consciousness.'[40] The Senior Minister also stressed that New Delhi's Look East policy was fairly recent, as if to mark the distance separating the Indian experience from that of East Asian nations: 'New Prime Minister Rao has got India to look East, towards the dynamism of the Asia-Pacific. History will record that he is the Indian leader to look both East and West.' The feeling of closeness has just been as lacking in nations that are nearer, such as Thailand. Kavi Chongkittavorn, the Senior Editor of the daily *The Nation*, noted in 1997 that 'India remains at the periphery of Thai diplomacy'. Bilateral relations 'somehow still lack the kind of warmth and intensity so essential to mutually beneficial interaction'.[41]

But, perhaps, it is with Tokyo that the feeling of distance is the greatest. In Japan, the fact that India's ancient influence is given due recognition plays no role in creating the conviction that it is a natural member of the 'New Asia'. India's Buddhist past does not enhance its contemporary image. Perhaps, it just furthers its exotic and mystical dimension. Also, a fair amount of ignorance persists, leading Rajaram Panda to conclude, 'Despite the perceived clean historical past and talk of Buddhism that originated in India and then travelled to Japan and other countries, India-Japan relations are always a hostage to many misperceptions that have hindered in developing a mutually satisfying relationship.'[42] Most Japanese have little knowledge about the subcontinent's society, history and culture. Indeed, the most ignorant in this respect are the post-industrial Japanese generations.[43] Although India is generally known for being the birthplace of Buddhism, it attracts few tourists from the archipelago.[44]

The difference in perception between Indians and Japanese on the notion of Asia is, in fact, quite revealing.[45] The area that Indians call 'East Asia' corresponds to what the Japanese simply refer to as 'Asia'. In India, the Far East is essentially associated with the Japanese archipelago and the Korean peninsula while, from the point of view of Japan, the Far East starts north of the Philippines and covers both South Korea and Taiwan. These differences in conception are reflected in the perception each country has of its own geographical location within the continent. India believes that it is located between the East and the West. But, Japan dismisses India to beyond its neighbourhood, which comprises China and the ASEAN countries. So the Arakan and Himalayan mountain passes appear to constitute both a significant natural and imaginary border in the Japanese collective perception. Moreover, it should not be forgotten that Japan's perception of Asia was long reduced to the region under Chinese influence. Indeed, China and South Korea have been, 'the central reference point in the Asian heritage of the Japanese'.[46] Thus, in speeches by Japanese diplomats, India belongs to a region defined as 'West Asia'.[47] The geographical area referred to as South Asia by the West (Bangladesh, Bhutan, India, Maldives, Nepal, Pakistan and Sri Lanka) becomes 'South-West Asia' in Japanese diplomacy and constitutes a distinct division within the Bureau of Asian Affairs in the Foreign Ministry. Japanese officials often refer to 'South-West Asia' as a separate sub-system within Asia, to which it is difficult to draw the attention of decision-makers.[48] Popular and diplomatic perceptions are more or less the same in South Korea. Indeed, during his 1996 visit to New Delhi, the Korean President, Kim Young Sam affirmed that India was located in West Asia.[49]

However, Japan is one of the nations with which independent India has had the oldest official cultural exchanges. A cultural agreement between Tokyo and New Delhi was signed as early as in 1956 and a Joint Indo-Japan Cultural Commission was set-up at the same time.[50] More recently, in 1990, Prime Minister Toshiki Kaifu set-up a South-West Asia Forum, following his visit to the region. Members of this group of intellectuals took part in an important cultural mission that was sent to South Asia in 1993 and stressed the importance of cooperation with India. At the same time, a Japan House was opened in Shantiniketan, in February 1994. This was the first cultural and academic institution for Japanese studies in India. Nonetheless, Indian social sciences lag behind in knowledge about contemporary Japan as compared to many South-East Asian countries.[51] As far as Japan is concerned, it seems to devote its academic interest to ancient India. In fact, Japan is the foreign country where Sanskrit is the most studied. Unfortunately, the same does not hold true for studies on contemporary India. As a result, academic exchanges are not very intense. In May 1997, there were only 181 Indian students in Japan. In 1998, only 3863 Indian students learned Japanese. From this perspective, India does not seem to share in the passion for Japanese studies that has developed elsewhere in Asia.

In South-East Asia, academic circles have showed renewed interest in Indian studies, which were not very extensively developed otherwise. In particular, the beginnings of academic cooperation have been noted with Thailand.[52] In April 1993, a Centre for Indian Studies was opened in the Thammasat University in Bangkok, with the support of the Indian community in Thailand. The Centre has organized regular lectures on themes pertaining to contemporary India. In July 1997, for instance, it jointly organized an important seminar on Indo-Thai relations along with the Ministry of External Affairs. The event commemorated the fiftieth Anniversary of India's independence as well as the institution of diplomatic relations between the two states. Thammasat University has also begun offering courses in Hindi in its study programmes. In this regard, an agreement was signed with the Banaras Hindu University (BHU) for academic cooperation. Another agreement was signed in September 1994 between ICCR and the Thai Centre for International Studies, thanks to which a first Indo-Thai symposium could be organized in March 1996. Lastly, ICCR regularly sends an associate professor to the Centre of Sanskrit Studies in the University of Silpakorn. Finally, in Singapore, the city-state's National University instituted a new programme specially intended for South Asian studies, in 1999.[53]

The fact remains that official cultural flows between India and East Asia are not a priority. The only official body representing Indian culture in East Asia is the Jawaharlal Nehru Indian Cultural Centre (JNICC) that was set-up in Jakarta in 1989. The complex organizes a host of events to give greater visibility to Indian culture in the country. Of the twelve Indian cultural centres in the world, Europe has three, one each in Moscow, Berlin and London. There are two just for South Africa, in Johannesburg and Durban, and two in central Asia—in Tashkent in Uzbekistan and Almaty in Kazakhstan. As for ICCR, its activities are limited due to the lack of resources, which is further aggravated, according to certain diplomats, by muddled policies.[54] Conversely, Japan appears to be the only country from East Asia that organizes regular activities in New Delhi. In fact, the Japan Foundation opened an office in the Indian capital in 1993. Its activities consist of organizing seminars, concerts, exhibitions and film festivals. The foundation's activities are supplemented by those of the Japanese Information and Cultural Centre, attached to the embassy. This cell offers courses in Japanese and holds movie shows every week. But the other major cultural organizations are for the most part Western, with the most active being the British Council, the French Alliance Française and the German Max Müeller Foundation. In any case, these institutions only concern a tiny minority of the capital's population. Generally speaking, Indian society is much more exposed to Western culture than to the culture of East Asian countries. Professor Varun Sahni feels quite rightly that, 'For at least three centuries, India's links have been almost exclusively with the Atlantic world; east of Burma is still *terra incognita* for most Indians.'[55] The fact is that India's middle classes are essentially turned towards the West. There are considerable academic ties, and all families among the political or economic elite generally have at least one member living in the West. In 1990–1, there were 840,000 Indians in Great Britain, 500,000 in Canada, 800,000 in the USA, i.e. a total of 2,140,000 Persons of Indian Origin just in these countries, as compared to 1,400,000 in South-East Asia.[56]

At the level of the public in general, the distribution of films is equally revealing about the Indians' attraction to American culture. Most cinema halls offer either national productions or Hollywood films. It is rare to see Asian films—from Hong Kong or Japan—on Indian screens. Popular music from Japan, China or South-East Asian countries has very few listeners in India. The music channel MTV India essentially broadcasts Indian or Western songs. Major Japanese store chains that line most avenues in South-East Asian cities cannot be seen in India. Fashion remains either traditional, or draws inspiration from or is imported from the West. Japanese ready-to-wear clothes are practically non-existent, contrary to the case in South-East Asia. Even the canons of Indian beauty are closer to those of the West or the Middle East. In the advertising world, the models that are most appreciated are those with a Caucasian face. Models from the north-eastern states of India, whose features are reminiscent of Sinic populations, hardly meet with any success and have to emigrate to East Asia. In general terms, India has not yet experienced any phenomenon pertaining to the regionalization of popular culture as seen between North-East Asia and South-East Asia.[57]

However, it is of interest to note that some Indian cultural trends have successfully found their ways to East Asia. While the Indian government institutions have been striving hard to highlight 'high culture' abroad, it is popular Indian culture that meets with the greatest success with regard to exports.[58] Perhaps India has tended to dwell too much on historical ties and its high culture, at the expense of modern and popular cultural flows that have brought various East Asian nations closer together. More easily accessible than the art forms of high tradition, Hindi pop songs, movies from Bollywood and Tamil Nadu, Indian cuisine are all important cultural vehicles, especially in Singapore and Malaysia. Indian movie stars are also quite popular everywhere in South-East Asia. Hindi and Tamil films usually account for more than a quarter of all movies shown on the city-state's screens.[59] Even the youth in Tokyo have seemed to evince a certain enthusiasm for Tamil films.[60] According to M. Verma, Programming Director of the MTV Asia network, based in Singapore, the Indian diaspora is a natural niche for promoters of the arts. The influence of Hindi pop first spread through the Indian community and later to the entire society. In addition, since 1996, the TV channel Sun TV, broadcasting from Chennai, has been received in Malaysia. It is intended essentially for the about 3.5 million Tamilians living in the country.[61] Finally, in Singapore, Indian 'haute couture' has acquired a certain visibility, while jewellery and even contemporary art are well on the way to becoming popular. Indeed, India's cultural niche in South-East Asia could perhaps be found less in its high culture—a product of ancient civilization—and more in its popular and mainstream culture—very alive and, moreover, very export-worthy.

6.2 India as a Minor Source of Inspiration for Asianism

On the whole, despite its many cultural ties, India has seemed to remain on the fringes of regional identity-building in East Asia. This peripheral position came to be reflected in the debate on Asian values.

Asianism, which essentially developed before the 1997 economic crisis, was not a system of thought in the strict sense of the term. Deprived of any true internal cohesiveness, the concept acquired substance thanks to different essays published by East Asian polemicists. To deal with this intellectual current, the views of the authors constituting it shall be presented, selecting the most explicit analysis for each theme broached. But first, note must be taken of the fact that the validity of Asianist assertions mattered less than their political force. And it was because Asianism assumed an important identity-related dimension that its relation with India constitutes the basis of the present analysis. In fact, the series of discourses did not really take India into consideration. It is true that the Asianist wave was at its peak in 1992–3 and India had then just begun to open up. At times, however, Asianists could not cut corners by undermining the importance of the Indian civilization in the development of the continent. Thus, India sometimes appeared on the fringes of the discourse on Asian values.

THE ASIANIST RHETORICS

Asianism's promoters were top political leaders, based essentially in Singapore and Malaysia, whether it was former Prime Minister Lee Kuan Yew and his successor, Goh Chok Tong, or Prime Minister Mahathir Mohamad and his Vice-Prime Minister and Minister of Finances, Anwar Ibrahim. Several high officials in the city-state took up their leaders' line of argument, such as the Permanent Foreign Secretary Kishore Mahbubani, Minister of Information and Arts George Yeo, the retired diplomat and henceforth Director of the Institute of Policy Studies Tommy Koh or, finally, Bilahari Kausikan, permanent representative of Singapore at the United Nations. Academics who were very close to government circles drew on this intellectual trend, such as Chan Heng Chee, the Director of ISEAS, and John Quah, Professor at the National University of Singapore, or Nordin Sopiee, Director General of the Kuala Lumpur Institute of Strategic and International Studies. In Japan, certain eminent voices were raised in defence of Asianism, including that of Yoishi Funabashi, the journalist, Ogura Kazuo, the diplomat, Yotaro Kobayashi, the industrialist and the philosopher, Takeshi Umehara.

Most of these personalities shared the same assessment, that of the decline of the West. Thus, using a moralizing tone, Lee Kuan Yew talked of the 'break down of civil society' in the United States, eroded by violence, drugs and the lack of civic responsibility.[62] As for Europe, it was characterized by a fortress-like attitude, through which it believed it could ignore the problems on its borders, particularly in North Africa. Public deficits, which were corrupting the economies of the old continent, only revealed the inability of the welfare state to reform itself. Very often, the vision of North America and Europe's decline was tantamount to a scathing criticism of the value systems upon which Western societies were based. As a counterpoint, the authors of these views engaged in applauding Asia's growth, which they found in the virtues of their societies. The values upheld did vary here and there, but they always placed considerable importance on the Asian social order, discipline and collective traditions in which the family represented a vital unit. Asianists used parameters that were related to their societies, culture, and political and economic organization, all at the same time. Mainly, however, Asian values were defined in opposition to what was commonly seen as 'Western liberalism', which was supposedly characterized by excessive individualism and a propensity to open political disputes and conflict, among other things.[63]

Asianism was a discourse driven by a certain underlying culturalism. Thus, the intellectual construction of the Singapore school was founded on neo-Confucianism. When Lee Kuan Yew spoke about values common to East Asia, he explained that from his point of view, the region included South Korea, Japan, China, Vietnam and Singapore.[64] The rest of South-East Asia was a distinct whole since it had been both 'Indianized' and 'Sinicized'. Consequently, the Singapore Senior Minister defined a homogeneous regional area corresponding to the Sinic sphere of influence and differentiated it from a more hybrid Asia. Singapore's Asianism claimed a Confucian heritage, which made China the cultural matrix of Asia. It was true that the Chinese community accounted for 77 per cent of the city-state's population. However, such a discourse said nothing about the Indian community, which accounted for more than 7 per cent of the population. Even Kishore Mahbubani, who was himself of Hindu origin, considered Confucius a major referent since, as early as in the sixth century BC, he had expounded 'one clear vision of a well-ordered society'.[65] In the case of Singapore's Asianism, China's sphere of influence appeared to largely eclipse the Indian heritage. In fact, China had often received support from the city-state's intellectuals.

In Malaysia, the construction of Asian values proved to be less consistent. Neo-Confucianism was initially tempting. The Malaysian Look East policy, whose intention was to trigger a cultural revolution, had, in fact, taken the Confucian countries of North-East Asia as a model of development.[66] Apart from taking up the culturalist analysis according to which Confucianism was one of the major factors of economic growth, Malaysian Asianism originally proved very pro-Japanese.[67] Mahathir's craze for Japan was also aimed at gaining Tokyo's approval for his EAEC project. But, the arguments of a Japanese regional leadership far from convinced the Japanese themselves, not to speak of most other Asian nations. Furthermore, from the domestic perspective, it was difficult for Malaysian leaders to remain silent about the importance of Islam. Thus, Mahathir ended up defending the notion of 'Asian civilization'. More neutral, the concept of Asia made it possible to eschew the Confucianist argument, which, by applauding Chinese culture, was viewed as a provocation for Malaysian and Indian communities. But, while oscillating between the values of Islam and those of neo-Confucianism, Malaysian Asianism hardly expressed any interest in the Indian heritage.

For the most part, Asianism was a homogenizing discourse. It took shape deliberately by dint of rapid simplifications in order to create cultural entities that would be based on a shared neo-Confucianism.[68] As a result, such a line of reasoning largely excluded the Indian civilization from its definition of Asian values. But this sort of intellectual construction was less concerned with scientific validity than with political effectiveness. It was most often a defensive strategy that also shed considerable light on the difficulties faced by the states in the region. In fact, Asianism made it possible to justify the authoritarian regimes in South-East Asia and their opposition to any contentions of the civil society. It helped support the incorporation of Myanmar and Vietnam in the ASEAN, as well as the stands taken by China. On the other hand, Asianism did not promote any truly political project. Indeed, if there was any concrete manifestation, it was to be found in the EAEG project, despite its inconsistencies. But several contradictions came to the fore: for instance, how could a Buddhist country like Thailand or a Christian one like the Philippines accept the argument of neo-Confucianism? One way out would be by making Asian values sufficiently vague to be able to include a vast and diversified whole.[69] Thus, George Yeo foresaw the emergence of a distinct Asian civilization that would carry forth traditions that were not just Confucianist but also Taoist and Mahayana Buddhist.

In fact, if the Asianists could lay claim to any regional specificity, it was that of their accelerated economic development. As Bilahari Kausikan explained, the growth rates of the countries in the region were a vital common denominator, which could form the basis of culturalist analyses, or even of feelings of identity: 'Economic success has engendered a greater cultural self-confidence. Whatever their differences, East and South-East Asian countries are increasingly conscious of their own civilizations, and have (like some Western scholars) tended to locate the sources of their success in what is regarded as distinctive about their own traditions and institutions.'[70]

It was the growth rates that finally revealed the closeness of their value systems to Asian nations. Thus, J.L. Domenach believed that Asianism actually explained the success achieved by the tigers and dragons economies by values that were supposedly intrinsic to Asian societies. This was an 'ethico-economic moment, i.e. a meeting between moral values and economic impetus'. The logical consequence was that India, which was still lagging behind, could hardly be part of this sort of discourse. Furthermore, another Asianist of Indian origin, Bilahari Kausikan, made a clear distinction between East Asian countries and those of South Asia. The former became powers that equalled the West, while the states of the Indian subcontinent remained minor players, in the same category as those in South America and Africa. There was therefore a wide gap between the Indian diplomatic discourse, which strove to underscore shared values, and the pragmatism of Asianist polemicists. While New Delhi relied on religious history and heritage to revive a feeling of closeness, the Asianists essentially based themselves on present and future economic performance. But the 1997 economic crisis seriously disturbed this discourse, and rubbed out its most triumphant accents. The collapse of the tigers and dragons economies indeed brought to light their structural weaknesses and undermined certain pivotal Asianist arguments.

ASIANISTS' REFERENCES TO INDIA

Asianism was often a changing and inclusive discourse, juggling with the notions of Asia and East Asia by sometimes blending them together and sometimes keeping them apart. Consequently, some of its variants did take India into consideration. This happened with Noordin Sopiee, Mahathir's adviser, who headed the 'Commission for a New Asia'.

The report, published in 1994, was to be 'a reasonable Asianism charter', according to the formulation used by Jean-Luc Domenach. As it happened, Indian representatives took part in the Commission, as well as delegations from Australia, Bangladesh and Russia. In addition, India occasionally appeared in Asianist writings, in particular when it came to announcing the rise of Asia as an economic power and its future supremacy over the West. Thus, issues such as the opening up of the Indian economy and projections concerning the vastness of its own market were mentioned.[71] Kishore Mahbubani explained, for instance, that the Asian workforce was considered as a threat to the American system: 'But in a world that is changing rapidly, especially with the emergence of billions of workers from China, India, Indonesia, and elsewhere, ready to compete with American workers on the level playing field of a global marketplace, the failure of the American political system to engineer change through short-term sacrifices could lead to catastrophic consequences later.'[72]

Thus, India was taken into consideration to try to tilt the balance in favour of Asia in the economic power relationship while comparing it to the West. In other words, it was the results expected from the economic reforms that drew the attention of Asianists and not India's contributions to the Asian cultural heritage.

In terms of values, references to the Indian civilization depended on the objectives of the line of reasoning adopted. Sometimes described as being a 'close' neighbour, India could also be presented in a retrograde light, if necessary. When Tommy Koh strove to mitigate his stand by recognizing that there were Asian values that had to be condemned, his first example was the caste system practised in Hinduism.[73] India was therefore included in talks on Asian values, but to better preserve what comprised their core, i.e. supposedly Confucian virtues. Much more scathing than Tommy Koh in his criticism of the West, Kishore Mahbubani used the same rhetorical strategy. When he described the state of stagnation into which the United States had fallen and the dangers it ran, he made a comparison with the fossilization of Hindu society under colonial rule. A prisoner of its beliefs and taboos at the time, the subcontinent's civilization had fallen into a state of 'mental ossification'. It seemed much easier, when talking about colonization, to take the example of a country that was on the fringes of the 'new Asia', rather than one within it. In fact, Mahbubani believed that Indian intellectuals were not yet fully freed from the dominance of Western thinking. In the two examples above, the Indian civilization was included in the Asianist line of reasoning, but as a foil for values that were deemed specific to East Asia.

On the other hand, faced with the individualistic values of the West, Asianists liked to speak on behalf of Asia as a whole, rather than just East Asia. According to them, it was Asia as a whole that was built on the strength of the institution of the family. So this line of reasoning, based on the cohesiveness of Asian societies, included the subcontinent's civilization. Thus, Kishore Mahbubani asserted, 'Among Asians who have become widely dispersed across continents, be they Chinese, Korean, or Sindhi, the extended family remains a strong source of support and comfort. The net effect of this is simple: few Asian individuals ever feel that they are on their own.'[74] Mahbubani explained that in India, as in East Asian countries, close social ties existed between family solidarity networks. They also often imposed heavy obligations on each other. But, in doing so, individuals helped each other and ensured their survival. Traditional societal structures in South Asia and East Asia were therefore recognized as being very close. Even Lee Kuan Yew admitted that the Indian society's values were not too far from those of Confucianism: 'When I say East Asians, I mean Korea, Japan, China, Vietnam, as distinct from South-East Asia, which is a mix between the Sinic and the Indian, though Indian culture also emphasizes similar values.'[75] In a way, Singapore's Senior Minister demarcated a hard core of Asian values, essentially based on Confucianism. But, Indian culture was not excluded and was part of the amorphous grouping of Asian values. From the perspective of domestic policy, this was perhaps a nuance that was aimed at not alienating Singapore's Indian minorities. The fact remained that in the fundamental distinction between Western individualism and Asian collective values, the Asianist clan included India.

Certain Asianists sometimes tried their hand at a very open vision of Asia. India's civilizational heritage was thus recognized and highlighted. In a fairly surprising analysis, Brigadier-General George Yeo, then Singapore's Minister of Information and Arts, broke down the attempt at homogenization through Lee Kuan Yew's neo-Confucianism. The metaphor of East Asia was itself questioned to the benefit of the Indian heritage. Indeed, Yeo asserted, 'There is, for example, the influence of Indian civilization which has given to South-East Asian Society a certain gentleness which characterizes the region and makes it so different from North-East Asia.' Thus, Yeo suggested that there was as much compatibility between South-East Asia and the Indian subcontinent as the Far East, if not more. The Minister added that over their long history, the similarity of values between South and South-East Asia was evident and that it still prevailed in current relations: 'Because of rapid economic development in the Western Pacific, we are much more inclined today in South-East Asia to identify ourselves with East Asia than with South Asia. From a historical perspective, this is a temporary mood. . . . It is the Indian influence on Javanese, Malay and Indo-Chinese cultures which underlies the ASEAN magic for *musyawarah dan mufakat*.'[76]

This observation assumed a very important dimension, as *mukafat* and *musyawarah* were considered as the founding principles of the 'ASEAN way'. Furthermore, these were concepts that ASEAN's leaders offered as being specific to their mode of functioning and that were often contrasted with Western consultation methods. In other words, in the distinction between Western and Oriental diplomatic practices, George Yeo not only placed India in the Asianist 'camp', but also acknowledged the Indian origin of practices specific to the ASEAN way. Above all, it appeared that certain ASEAN officials followed a line of argument similar to that of the Indian diplomats who upheld the Look East policy: contemporary relations between India and the ASEAN were nourished by their shared past and common values. Consequently, Mahathir also officially recognized that the great closeness of the Indian and ASEAN civilizations formed the basis for their dialogue partnership: 'The historical and cultural linkages and the existing traditional ties form the basis or foundation on which strong ASEAN-India relations can be built. Being Asians, both our regions share many similarities which include eastern values and culture.'[77]

Finally, Kishore Mahbubani fully involved India in the process of Asian renaissance, defined as the rediscovery of the immense cultural heritage of the continent's civilizations. Till some time ago, he recalled, only Westerners studied and preserved the treasures of Asian civilizations. But, now, Asians had become aware of the richness of their history and culture. This re-appropriation had given them a sense of pride and allowed them to move forward more surely on the path of modernity. And yet, the author did not limit this phenomenon of revival solely to East Asia. To uphold his line of reasoning, he took examples from the whole of the continent: 'For the first time in centuries, an Asian renaissance is underway. Visitors to Asian cities—from Teheran to Calcutta, from Bombay to Shanghai, from Singapore to Hong Kong—now see both a newfound confidence as well as an interest in traditional language and culture.'[78] The Asia referred to here, corresponded to the broader sense of the concept, i.e. from Iran to South-East Asia, deriving from the first Asian Relations Conference. The intellectual posture of the Indians was also cited as an example of the modesty that was typical of Asians, especially when Mahbubani invited the Americans to go through a process of self-criticism with regard to their own model of society: 'This is one fundamental lesson that Americans can learn from Asians: to move ahead, one has to shake off the debris of history. (. . .) No Chinese or Indian intellectual labours under the illusion that his society has achieved the best possible social arrangements, valid for all time.'

Thus, Mahbubani did not limit the Asian renaissance to the economic take-off of the tigers and dragons economies alone. He described the phenomenon of revival in a broader cultural and philosophical perspective, which included the entire continent.

The perspective was almost the same as the one presented by the Japanese journalist, Yoichi Funabashi.[79] His vision of the evolution of Asia also included India fully. The polemicist was delighted at the birth of the Asian awareness, which had essentially taken place thanks to the spread of management models. And to illustrate this, he cited as an example the Maruti-Suzuki joint venture in India. Funabashi also mentioned the flow of ideas among the Asian middle classes, thanks to the development of communication technologies. He cited the example of the Star TV television channel, which broadcasts in China, Thailand as well as India. Likewise, the Indian government channel was successfully broadcasting the Japanese television serial 'Oshin'. In fact, Funabashi was one of the rare Asianists who ever mentioned India's Look East policy in his comments.

In the case of Japan, J.M. Bouissou even believed that an 'identification process' was taking place with India.[80] Japanese intellectuals who believed in 'going beyond modernity' sought a connection between Asian and Western values, and increasingly referred to Rabindranath Tagore and Mahatma Gandhi. Indeed, there was an astonishing return to the origins of Indian Asianism. The Japanese line of thought was largely based on the concept of 'symbiosis', i.e. a harmony of differences. This metaphor, which was quite in vogue, also made it possible to feed the collective imagination and rethink

Japan's relationship with Asia. It was based on the idea of the mutual enriching of different Asian civilizations. Thus, in contrast with the unifying 'wild geese' model, the logic of symbiosis suggested that various Asian nations were progressing in accordance with an internal logic and in harmony. This was equally true of the relationship with the West. Rather than seeking confrontation, this approach favoured reconciliation and syncretism. Much less confrontational and provocative than the Asian values rhetoric, the concept of symbiosis was quite close to the Indian discourse. In addition, the images of the Silk Road aroused great passion in Japan. The phenomenon manifested itself in the popularity of televised serials such as *Silk Road* and *Asian Highway*, which highlighted ancient Asian civilizations. The last version of the serial *Asian Highway* referred to South Asia as well as Central Asia, formerly Soviet Asia. Indeed, historically speaking, the Silk Road made it possible to export Buddhism from India to China, via Central Asia. Accordingly, the emphasis on the Indian subcontinent's heritage made it possible to put China's omnipresence into perspective, both geographically and culturally. From the Japanese point of view, the Asian horizon therefore began to spread beyond the Chinese continental mass, thereby including India. All in all, the Silk Road led to the emergence of a metaphor of Asia that was much more open and vast than the contemporary vision that was limited to East Asia.

NOTES

1. Panda, 'India and Japan: Perceptions and Misperceptions', pp. 45, 49.
2. *The Hindu*, 24 October 1997.
3. *The Asian Age*, 25 November 1997.
4. His interpretations of *dhamma* found a large audience among the urban elite. His death, on 8 July 1993, was followed by a state funeral. Donald K. Swearer, 'Centre and Periphery: Buddhism and Politics in Modern Thailand', in Ian Harris, ed., *Buddhism and Politics in Twentieth-century Asia*, London: Pinter, 1999, pp. 216–18.
5. Karuna Kusalaya, 'Thailand's Cultural Links with India', Thammasat University and Information Department, Ministry of Foreign Affairs of Thailand, seminar on 'Thai-Indian Relations in the Present Decade and Prospects for Cooperation in the Future', 30 July 1997, pp. 257–61.
6. *Indian Recorder*, 17–23 December 1995.

7. K. Ramanathan, 'Hinduism in a Muslim State: The case of Malaysia', *Asian Journal of Political Sciences*, vol. 4, no. 2, 1996.
8. Address by Președent Kim Young Sam at a Luncheon Hosted by Three Economic Organizations of India, 26 February 1996, in *New Partners for Common Prosperity, President Kim Young Sam's Visits to India and Singapore and Participation in the Asia-Europe Meeting, 24 February–4 March 1996*, Korean Overseas Information Service, Seoul, The Republic of Korea, March 1996, p. 13.
9. Remarks by President Kim Young Sam at a Dinner Hosted by President Shankar Dayal Sharma of the Republic of India, 24 February 1996 in *New Partners for Common Prosperity, President Kim Young Sam's Visits to India and Singapore*, p. 10.
10. MEA, *Annual Report 1995–6*, p. 25.
11. The ICCR is an autonomous body, funded by the Ministry of External Affairs, which deals with official cultural exchanges. The Foreign Secretary is the *ex-officio* Vice-President.
12. Thammasat University and Information Department, Ministry of Foreign Affairs of Thailand, seminar on 'Thai-Indian Relations in the Present Decade and Prospects for Cooperation in the Future', 30 July 1997.
13. *The Times of India*, 10 October 1997.
14. Lucian Pye, *Asian Power and Politics: The Cultural Dimensions of Authqrity*, Cambridge, Mass: Harvard University Press, 1985, p. 414.
15. *Cityscan*, June 1999.
16. Noda, 'A Common Cultural Heritage', p. 73.
17. *Indian Recorder*, 5–11 March 1994.
18. MEA, *Annual Report 1994–5*, p. 27.
19. http://india.indiagov.org / india-indonesia relations.
20. MEA, *Annual Report 1993–4*, p. 15.
21. *The Hindu*, 10 April 2002.
22. Chakravati Ram Prasad, 'Culture and Complementarities: Implications of the Singapore-India MOU on Culture, Heritage and the Archives', in Y.M. Cheong and V.V. Bhanoji Rao, *Singapore-India Relations: A Primer*, pp. 40–51.
23. The Singapore Asian Civilizations Museum has four sections that correspond to a division of the continent into four cultural areas: South-East Asia, East Asia (i.e. North-East Asia and more specifically China), West and Islamic Asia, and South Asia.
24. Interview, Indian Ministry of Tourism, New Delhi, April 1998. The places that should not be missed on these tours include Sarnath, near Varanasi, where Buddha gave his first sermons, Kushinagar where he breathed his last and, Bodh Gaya where he attained Enlightenment.
25. *Indian Recorder*, 25 June–1 July 1997.
26. *India Today*, 31 August 1995, p. 23.

27. Amit Baruah, 'Looking East', *Frontline*, vol. 17, no. 24, 25 November–8 December 2000.
28. Deepavali, the festival of lights, is celebrated all over India towards the end of the year.
29. 'Culture and Complementarities', pp. 40–51.
30. Francois Godement, *La Renaissance de l'Asie*, Paris: Edition Odile Jacob, 1996, pp. 32–3.
31. Ducan Mac Cargo, 'Bouddhisme et Identité Asiatique: de Nouveaux Mandalas pour la Puissance Régionale Thaïlandaise', in D. Camroux and J.L. Domenach, *L'Asie Retrouvée*, pp. 187–205.
32. *The Hindu*, 12 December 1997.
33. Satya Vrat Shastri, 'Hindu Culture in Thailand', in Vohra and Dixit, eds., *Religion, Politics and Society in South and South-East Asia*, pp. 57–8.
34. http://www.indiaemb.or.th/html/indo-thai-relations.html: Srisurang Poolthupya, 'Cultural Affinity Between Thailand and India', November 1997, p. 6.
35. Interview, Embassy of Thailand in India, New Delhi, April 1998; Thammasat University and Information Department, Ministry of Foreign Affairs of Thailand, seminar on 'Thai-Indian Relations in the Present Decade and Prospects for Cooperation in the Future', 30 July 1997, pp. 142–3.
36. Interview, Ministry of External Affairs, New Delhi, March 1998.
37. Ambassador of India to Thailand, Ranjit Gupta, 'Indo-Thai Relations', Thammasat University and Information Department, Ministry of Foreign Affairs of Thailand, seminar on 'Thai-Indian Relations in the Present Decade and Prospects for Cooperation in the Future', p. 18.
38. Interview, Embassy of Thailand in India, New Delhi, April 1998.
39. Interview, High Commission of Malaysia in India, New Delhi, May 1998.
40. Lee Kuan Yew, 'Opening Address', P.V. Narasimha Rao, 'India and the Asia-Pacific', p. 2.
41. *The Nation*, 1 August 1997, p. 297.
42. Panda, 'Introduction', *India-Japan Relations*, p. 5.
43. Asrani, 'India-Japan Relations', p. 356.
44. In 1995, it only received 0.5 per cent of the eleven million Japanese who travelled abroad, especially to the United States and Europe.
45. Panda, 'Perceptions and Misperceptions', pp. 50–1.
46. Postel-Vinay, *Le Japon et la Nouvelle Asie*, p. 12.
47. http://www.japan-emb.org.in/lectures/Embassy of Japan in India, Speeches by Hiroshi Hirabayashi, Ambassador of Japan to India, January 2000.
48. Satu Limaye, 'Sushi and Samosas', in S. Gordon and S. Henningham, eds., *India Looks East*, pp. 179–80.

49. South Korean President Interviewed, *World Focus*, 16 February 1996, p. 16.
50. This inter-governmental forum is supposed to enable an exchange of very broad views on cultural cooperation.
51. Kazuo Ando, 'Preface', *Dimension of India-Japan Relations*, New Delhi: The Japan Foundation, New Delhi Office, 1997, p. li (Kazuo Ando was the director of the Japan Foundation in New Delhi).
52. http://india.indiagov.org/foreign relations-Thailand. Srisurang Poolthupya, 'Cultural Affinity Between Thailand and India', November 1997, p. 6.
53. MEA, *Annual Report 1999–2000*, p. 17.
54. J.N. Dixit, 'Culture as an Instrument of Diplomacy', Foreign Service Institute, *Indian Foreign Policy*, vol. 1, pp. 418–28.
55. Varun Sahni, 'India as a Global Power: Capacity, Opportunity and Strategy', Foreign Service Institute, *Indian Foreign Policy*, vol. 1, p. 33.
56. Ramesh Thakur, 'Between East and West, from South to North', in S. Gordon and S. Henningham, eds., *India Looks East*, p. 18.
57. J.M. Bouissou, 'Penser l'Autre en se Pensant Soi-même: le Japon face à l'Asie', D. Camroux and J.L. Domenach, *L'Asie Retrouvee*, pp. 301–26.
58. Sahni, 'India as a Global Power', p. 29.
59. Assessment based on the list of some 875 films authorized by the Singapore Department of Films and Publications (http://sg.gov//culture & entertainement//movies: FPD, 'titles reviewed and approved').
60. Brij Tankha, 'India-Japan and the Coming Century', *Seminar*, no. 472, December 1998, p. 42.
61. Quoted in Jaffrelot 'L'Inde et l'Asiatisme', note 30, p. 250.
62. Fareed Zakaria, 'Culture is Destiny: A Conversation with Lee Kuan Yew', *Foreign Affairs*, vol. 73, no. 2, March–April 1994, p. 111.
63. In a fairly accurate listing, Tommy Koh identified ten values that were typical of East Asia. Firstly, Asian societies did not function on the basis of an extreme form of individualism, as the interests of the individual were offset by those of the family and society (1). Asian families were quite close-knit and thus led to true social solidarity (2). East Asian people respected education much more than people in the West (3). They practised the virtues of economy and frugality (4), as well as those of hard work (5). In the political field, there was a national consensus between the government, business circles and unions (6). There was an Asian version of a social contract. The government provided for law and order and met the basic needs of citizens as far as work, housing, health and education were concerned. In return, the latter submitted to authority and to the law (7). In certain Asian countries such as Singapore, the government sought to make each citizen a stakeholder of the country's future in order to build a community-based society (8). East Asian societies expected that their government would maintain a

morally healthy environment in order for them to be able to bring up their children properly (9). The governments in East Asia were in favour of a free press but, contrary to the West, they did not feel that such freedom was an absolute right (10). For Tommy Koh, as for most Asianists, these values explained the economic success and social harmony that reigned among the East Asian countries (Tommy Koh, 'Does East Asia Stand for Any Positive Values?', in *The Quest for World Order*, Singapore: The Institute of Policy Studies, and Times Academic Press, 1998, pp. 349–51).

64. Zakaria, 'Culture is Destiny', p. 113.
65. Kishore Mahbubani, 'Go East, Young Man', *The Washington Quarterly*, Spring 1994, p. 20.
66. D. Camroux, 'Malaisie: Retour vers un Futur Oriental', D. Camroux and J.L. Domenach, *L'Asie Retrouvée*, pp. 125–45.
67. Besides, in collaboration with the conservative Ishihara Shintaro, Mahathir wrote a project entitled 'The Asia that can say no'. The two authors urged Tokyo to endorse its role as the leader of Asia, so that the region could stand up to the West.
68. Alan Dupont, 'Is there an "Asian Way"?', *Survival*, vol. 38, no. 2, pp. 13–33.
69. Yoichi Funabashi, 'The Asianization of Asia', *Foreign Affairs*, vol. 72, no. 5, p. 78.
70. Bilahari Kausikan, 'East and Southeast Asia and the Post-Cold War: International Politics of Human Rights', *Studies in Conflict and Terrorism*, vol. 16, pp. 248–9.
71. Kishore Mahbubani, 'The Pacific Impulse', *Survival*, vol. 37, no. 2, Spring 1995, p. 113.
72. Mahbubani, 'Go East, Young Man', p. 16.
73. Koh, 'Does East Asia Stand for Any Positive Values?', *The Quest for World Order*, p. 357.
74. Mahbubani, 'Go East, Young Man', p. 12.
75. Zakaria, 'Culture is Destiny', p. 113.
76. *The Arts* (Singapore), November–December 1995, p. 4 (cited in K. Sridharan, 'Indian and ASEAN: The Long Road to Dialogue', *The Round Table*, no. 340, 1996, pp. 473–4).
77. Speech by the Prime Minister of Malaysia the Honourable Dato Seri Dr. Mahatir Bin Mohamad at the ASEAN-India Lecture Series in New Delhi on 21 December 1996, § 3.
78. Kishore Mahbubani, *Can Asians Think?*, Singapore: Times Books International, 1998, p. 25.
79. Funabashi, 'The Asianization of Asia', *Foreign Affairs*, vol. 72, no. 5.
80. Bouissou, 'Penser l'Autre en se Pensant Soi-même: Le Japon Face à l'Asie', p. 317.

CHAPTER 7

Harmonizing the Strategic Environment

7.1 Changes in the ASEAN's Perceptions

Perceptions about India's potential strategic role in Asia improved considerably in the early 1990s. Major states in the region began to postulate that New Delhi could well contribute positively to regional stability. This came as a new development for India had not always been considered as a benign power. In the 1980s, relations between India and the ASEAN were at their lowest, due in particular to the Indo-Chinese imbroglio. In addition, New Delhi went in for a modernization programme of its military, without taking the pains to offer any explanations. Its image suffered because of this, especially since the ASEAN states found themselves strategically quite fragile. However, in the space of a few years, the perception of India's role underwent a change within ASEAN. The end of the bipolar logic naturally contributed to a reassessment of India, especially since New Delhi took great care to transform its image. The development of the Indian Navy which had become a major focus point that fed the fears of the South-East Asian states at the end of the 1980s, convinced them a few years later of India's benevolence, before leading to initial contacts in the field of defence. Looking back at the decade preceding the launch of the Look East policy enables a better appreciation of the progress achieved in Indo-ASEAN relations during the 1990s. Indeed, India's main achievement was that from the early 1990s onwards, it started to enjoy good, trustworthy relations with the South-East Asian states, thus preparing its admission to the ARF.

New Delhi's Ambiguous Intentions in the Indian Ocean

The end of the Cold War aroused much uncertainty among East Asian states. This region, which had so far been structured by bipolar alignments, feared becoming a strategically fluid, if not unpredictable, area.[1] Above all, it was the prospects of American disengagement that generated fears of a 'strategic vacuum' in the region, within the ASEAN. While the Association's members had never articulated a common strategic perspective as a basis for cooperation in defence matters, they jointly supported the premise according to which sustained American military deployment generated a stabilizing effect on the entire region. More precisely, the small South-East Asian states feared that their region would bear the brunt of any rivalry between the bigger Asian powers, in the event of a withdrawal by the United States. As it happened, China, and Japan were among the powers that were suspected of wanting to enhance their influence in South-East Asia, but so was India.[2] Already in February 1990, Singapore's Vice-Prime Minister Goh Chok Tong had included New Delhi in the 'club' of suspect powers. In fact, he had anticipated that the dismantling of American bases in the Philippines would lead to competition between India, China and Japan for occupying the void left in South-East Asia.[3] Indeed, Singapore and the United States signed an agreement in November 1990, which authorized America's naval and air defence forces to make greater use of the city-state's military facilities. This agreement, which aimed at offsetting the possibility of an American disengagement from South-East Asia, was further reinforced in January 1992, after Washington's announcement of an imminent withdrawal from the Philippines, in November 1991. Other agreements were signed in South-East Asia, which gave the American forces limited access to Malaysian and Indonesian ports. But these few initiatives could not replace the system that Washington had established in the Philippines during the Cold War. In fact, the United States withdrew from the archipelago in September 1992, thereby closing the largest overseas base they had ever had. They also moved all their tactical nuclear weapons from the Korean peninsula. Both in South Korea as well as in Japan, they came under a great deal of pressure to reduce their military presence.

More than ever attentive to the redistribution of power in their region, the ASEAN members closely followed the military developments taking place in their three largest neighbours. Although India by itself appeared less threatening than China and Japan, it was considered an ambitious peripheral power and suspected quite early of having designs on its South-East Asian neighbourhood. The possibility of India's ascendancy was far from reassuring for the ASEAN. At the end of the Cold War, New Delhi continued to grumble about the scale of America's presence in South-East Asia and did not conceal its concerns when Singapore decided to grant American military forces access to several of its facilities. Thus, in May 1990, the annual Ministry of Defence report noted: 'Singapore's offer of base facilities to USA could bring international strategic rivalries close to our shores. . . .'[4] This analysis reflected India's traditional reservations with regard to any American military presence in any nearby area. In fact, New Delhi continued to perceive the ASEAN as a component of the US alliance system, especially because of the military ties binding the Philippines and Thailand with Washington. In other words, the Indian foreign policy of the early 1990s still suffered from 'vague anti-ASEAN prejudices'.[5]

Until the start of the 1990s, the ASEAN states were concerned with the expansion of the Indian Navy and suspected New Delhi of wanting to become a significant naval power in the north-eastern waters of the Indian Ocean. The fears of the ASEAN were all the more acute since in those days, India was still considered as being very close to the Soviet block. In the logic of alignment prevailing at the end of the 1980s, India's close ties with the USSR and Vietnam led the ASEAN to believe that the three powers could well support each other in the hypothesis of increased regional tensions. Faced with this implicit axis, the ASEAN adopted a stand very similar to that of China, which condemned Vietnam's presence in Cambodia. Were Sino-Soviet rivalry to deteriorate, it could have led to India and Vietnam's engagement, which would have been disastrous for the rest of South-East Asia.[6] Indeed, not much more was needed by certain Asian experts to conclude that India represented a potential threat. It is true that India's defence expenditure had begun to rise substantially since 1982–3. The World Watch Institute classified India among the leading arms importing countries over the 1988–92 period. The country purchased arms worth about 12.2 billion dollars, followed by Japan, whose purchases amounted to 9.2 billion dollars.[7] The most worrying aspect was that New Delhi was investing in the modernization and expansion of its forces with a view to projecting its military might and power.

If India were seeking the status of a regional power in the Indian Ocean, its naval forces would be the best pointer, as they would serve as an instrument *par excellence* for projecting power. As it happened, three main acquisitions in the 1980s transformed the Indian Navy into one of the most powerful in the region. In 1987, the country bought a second aircraft carrier, the *INS Viraat*, formerly the British Navy's *Hermes*. The following year, New Delhi signed a three-year lease for a Soviet nuclear-propelled submarine, the *INS Chakra*. In 1989, it acquired a German license to produce conventional submarines. No less than twenty-nine warships and eight kilo-class Soviet submarines were added to its naval forces between April 1986 and April 1991. Thus, New Delhi seemed determined to obtain the requisite means to become a regional power in the Indian Ocean. In concrete terms, this meant that India would try to acquire 'a capability for exercising independent action anywhere in the Indian Ocean region sufficient to affect outcomes in the way New Delhi would like'.[8] Seen from the South-East Asian perspective, these developments gave the impression that the Indian Navy was on the verge of becoming an offensive combat force, likely to dominate not only the immediate vicinity, but perhaps also the north of the Indian Ocean as a whole. To that could be added the untimely statements made by certain Indian officers. For instance, when Major General Afsir Karim AVMS (Retd) asserted in the *USI Journal*: 'Our strategic boundaries obviously extend far beyond our geopolitical boundaries to the whole Indian Ocean region.'[9] Finally, alarmist reports by the American Department for Defence advanced the theory that India would be capable of maintaining a permanent submarine force base in the Malacca Strait as early as 1995[10] and that by the end of the decade, it could even have a group of aircraft carriers to fight a war anywhere in the Indian Ocean and its vicinity.

It was indeed India's acquisition of aircraft carriers that impressed itself the most on South-East Asia's perceptions. For these are the most visible and most prestigious instruments of any naval force for projecting its might. As it happened, the ASEAN, which till then was essentially focused on China and the Indo-Chinese peninsula, realized that the Indian fleet owned two aircraft carriers and that it planned to commission a third by 1997. In comparison, even a power as formidable as China had by then not acquired even a single aircraft carrier. Suddenly, the Indian Navy's might appeared disproportionate in the Asian context. And these developments took place at a time when the South-East Asian states were weighing up the strategic and economic importance of their new maritime territory. In fact, the 1982 UN Conference on the Law of the Sea had expanded the Exclusive Economic Zone (EEZ) by 200 nautical miles. In doing so, states such as Malaysia and Indonesia inherited extremely valuable EEZs, which included oil resources and natural gas deposits in the South China Sea. Therefore, the expansion of the Indian Navy did not fail to draw the attention of these countries. In addition, New Delhi set-up facilities on the Andaman and Nicobar Islands in 1985 in order to establish a military base in Port Blair. This decision sparked off panic reactions in South-East Asia and Australia, especially since the nature of the equipment based there remained unknown for a long time. Were these facilities meant for long-range strike and maritime reconnaissance aircraft or merely for surveillance in India's maritime area?[11] Since New Delhi's intentions remained equivocal, several experts in the region speculated that the base could augment India's maritime strike range in the Malacca Strait as well as the extent of its maritime reconnaissance in the South China Sea.[12]

India was all the less reassuring since it did not have a very positive image abroad. Most international strategic experts credited it with pretensions of wanting to become a dominant power, if not in Asia, at least in the region closest to it. In fact, initiatives taken at the end of the 1980s gave the impression that New Delhi was pursuing a policy of regional hegemony. In accordance with a controversial agreement signed between Prime Minister Rajiv Gandhi and Sri Lankan President Jayewardene, India dispatched its peacekeeping forces to the island in 1987. As many as 60,000 Indian troops gathered in northern Sri Lanka between 1987 and 1990, with their presence becoming increasingly suspect. Although, the Premadasa government did ask for their withdrawal, New Delhi turned a deaf ear. In 1988, New Delhi deployed its troops in the Maldives to save the ruling regime from an armed *coup d'état*. India also stood out for a rigid posture, which brought it into conflict with its Nepalese neighbour in 1989. These events no doubt besmirched India's image. In fact, the entire subcontinent was in the grip of several kinds of tensions and New Delhi did not seem to be doing anything to ease the situation. As for the Indo-Pakistan relations, they had emerged as a focus of major tensions in Asia. For the record, the discord aggravated dangerously in 1987 during the Indian 'Brass Tacks' exercises. Then, in 1990, the two states spiralled into an imminent conflict over Kashmir. The last few months of 1991 saw relations go downhill again in the entire subcontinent.

As a result, India emerged as a destabilizing factor in South Asia, but also potentially in South-East Asia, because of its naval forces. During a visit to New Delhi in June 1989, the Indonesian Naval Chief, Admiral Rakefendo, officially expressed the concerns of the region's governments and requested a clarification about the Indian Navy's long-term expansion plans.[13] Suspicions about India's militarization programmes persisted, even though radical changes had begun to alter the strategic order in the Asian region. In the early 1990s, when the Cold War was going through its final spasms, the ASEAN continued to regard India as aspiring to project its might in South-East Asia. This was testified by Tommy Koh, a former Singaporean diplomat and Director of the Institute of Policy Studies, who referred to his suspicions in 1992: 'Are we prepared to allow the vacuum created by the US withdrawal to be filled by Japan, China or India, or a consortium of the three?'[14] But far from the hypothesis of a consortium, the ASEAN rather feared that New Delhi's intentions would exacerbate its underlying rivalry with China, which could have repercussions on South-East Asia or the Indian Ocean.

East Asian prejudices with regard to the Indian military's modernization programme degenerated further with New Delhi's inability to explain its intentions. Traditionally, there was a lack of consistency in the pursuit of clearly defined objectives in India's strategic thinking.[15] Whence the number of qualms India's military build-up aroused in the neighbourhood. A propensity for excessive secrecy and lop-sided coordination, devoid of any centralized forum, handicapped the formulation and explanation of India's strategic approach. In many respects, there was no government institution that fulfilled the mission of planning military strategies. A National Security Council was proposed in 1990, during the V.P. Singh government. But by mid-1992, the institution had still not been set-up. Decisions in defence matters were often taken on an ad hoc and short-term basis, while the long-term national vision remained shrouded in uncertainties.[16] Indeed, the Indian defence policy had become so ambiguous essentially because the country had no true security doctrine. Besides, New Delhi did not publish any White Paper on its defence policy, an initiative that would have largely contributed to easing vague feelings of insecurity in the case of the ASEAN.

India's political leaders contented themselves with responding to the ASEAN's concerns by declaring that an increase in military forces did not necessarily imply a change in plans or intentions. But ASEAN's decision-makers kept raising questions, faced as they were with interlocutors who experienced such difficulties in explaining their naval expansion projects and their arms acquisition programmes, especially for missiles. They even found it easy to believe that Indian authorities applied themselves to obscuring their long-term projects. The irony was that New Delhi was unable to proffer any credible explanations, essentially because it had not taken the trouble to integrate its new arms into a consciously developed strategic programme. Consequently, Indian Admirals did not believe that there was any need to provide additional justifications, other than asserting that India's very size called for a strong navy. Furthermore, India's decision-makers seemed to feel once again that history constituted the best proof of their assertions. Thus, officials averred that never had the country demonstrated any needless aggression; when it had gone beyond its national borders, it was only to subsequently move back. They also recalled that the subcontinent had been colonized by the Europeans because of their supremacy over the seas. But rather than such general statements, the ASEAN wanted explanations based on India's defence policy, especially at a time where major international upheavals were taking place. There was, therefore, significant discrepancy between New Delhi and the ASEAN capitals in the early 1990s. India failed to understand that its South-East Asian neighbours harboured suspicions in this regard, since it had claimed peaceful intentions. But the fact remained that it did very little to communicate its real ambitions in clear and open terms.

But it could be equally possible that New Delhi neglected its public relations policy because it was convinced that the accusations made by the ASEAN states enabled them to justify their own militarization programmes. This hypothesis could be confirmed by the statements made by some South-East Asian military officers, which put ASEAN's concerns about India into perspective. Indonesia's Lieutenant General A. Hasnan Habib acknowledged that with the exception of a few individual statements, the expansion of the Indian Navy did not seem to draw a lot of attention in South-East Asia. In any event, the concerns expressed about India were not comparable with the strong reaction Japan's expansion programme of its maritime role had provoked a few years earlier.[17] India's militarization did not even appear to have figured on the agenda of ASEAN's high officials meetings, nor did it seem to be the subject of discussion during the ASEAN Foreign Ministers' annual meetings. General Hasnan Habib further added that, in the early 1990s, the ASEAN states were essentially concerned with their internal security problems.

WANING STRATEGIC DIVERGENCES

During the Cold War, interactions between India and the ASEAN fell within the purview of the paradigm of derived relationships, which Kripa Sridharan defined in the following terms: 'Derived relationship is a product of interactions arising out of a state's secondary interests. Secondary interests differ from primary interests in terms of their intensity and urgency.'[18] In a derived relationship, the attention remains fixed on crucial interests, while action is directed to the area of secondary interests. During the Cold War, India's policy concerning the ASEAN was derived from its general foreign policy, i.e. it depended on its relationship with the big powers—the United States and the USSR, and with regional powers—China and the Indo-Chinese part of the South-East Asian region. As it happened, relations with each of these principal partners came to change—in fact, there was general peace all around, thanks to the post-bipolar order. More precisely, India's relations with the USSR and Vietnam had begun to disintegrate gradually, so much so that the paradigm of derived relationships seemed to become obsolete.

The sudden disintegration of the USSR in December 1991 left New Delhi quite isolated strategically. Although its friendship treaty with Moscow had never been an alliance, India considered that Soviet nuclear forces protected it from the Chinese and American powers. Military cooperation was such that, in the mid 1980s, the Soviet block supplied almost seventy per cent of the main Indian arms systems.[19] As it happened, the collapse of the Eastern Block entailed a dismemberment of the production lines that left India in disarray as far as the maintenance of its military equipment was concerned. In the strategic and political fields, ties with the USSR were so close that New Delhi initially refused to recognize the reality of the changes introduced by President Mikhail Gorbachev and endeavoured to preserve its relationship as it had been in the past. And yet, in the years following the collapse of the Soviet Union, the close ties New Delhi had enjoyed with Moscow began to wane. Russian Foreign Minister Andrei Kozyrev set new principles for Russia's foreign policy in January 1993: of the list of ten priorities stated, India only came in the seventh position.[20] In other words, India could hardly count on its former complicity with Moscow. More than ever, it had to find fresh strategic support in Asia. The Look East policy fell well within the purview of this delicate situation.

In this perspective, the pacification of tensions in the Indo-Chinese peninsula was quite welcome as it could portend an improvement in Indo-ASEAN ties. The support that New Delhi had unfailingly offered the Vietnamese regime during the Cold War was one of the main bones of contention in its relationship with the ASEAN. Till 1989, before the USSR had began calling into question its support to Hanoi, Vietnam had the leading military forces in the South-East Asian region and was perceived as a significant threat by the ASEAN. Consequently, at the end of the 1980s and again in the early 1990s, Indo-Vietnamese ties were a matter for concern for the Association. To make matters worse, in January 1989, Secretary-General Nguen Van Linh visited India to sign an agreement by which New Delhi agreed to defer the redemption date for Vietnam's debts to June 1991. The Vietnamese leader also expressed his pleasure at obtaining the promise of a Rs. 100 million credit, apart from another credit for the same amount, for the purchase of Indian production equipment. Quite often, the Indo-Vietnamese friendship seemed to be on the verge of dealing with fields that were more sensitive. For instance, New Delhi had more than once offered to send its specialists to Vietnam for cooperation in the civil nuclear energy sector. A few months after the announcement of the Soviet withdrawal from the Cam Ranh Bay base, Indo-Vietnamese ties paradoxically seemed to threaten the stability of South-East Asia even more. In 1990, an *Asian Defence Journal* article went as far as claiming that New Delhi and Hanoi had engaged in preliminary discussions for the use of the Cam Ranh Bay base by Indian warships.[21]

At the same time, New Delhi's discrete participation in Cambodia's peace process testified to its loss of influence in Indo-China. In fact, despite its presence at the Paris and Tokyo conferences, respectively in 1991 and 1992, India's activities in Cambodia proved to be increasingly limited.[22] Not much more was required to reassure the ASEAN about the role and intentions of its huge neighbour. Let us recall that several initiatives launched by New Delhi during the 1970s and 1980s had only ended up exasperating the members of the Association. And while Indonesia had been ready to agree to New Delhi playing a role in the International Control Commission at the end of the 1980s, it had no intention of granting it a political role in the resolution of the Cambodian conflict. From the point of view of Jakarta and other ASEAN capitals, India remained a peripheral player that belonged to South Asia and not South-East Asia. But during its participation in the process for the resolution of the Cambodian conflict in the early 1990s, New Delhi appeared to be a fairly innocuous negotiator, ready to let the ASEAN states run events in the peninsula. Its low profile could not fail to please the Association's members. As for Vietnam, rid of its status of a pariah state since it had withdrawn from Cambodia in 1989, it undertook to quickly reshape its external relations with the ASEAN members. Thus, Vietnam was no longer a source for tension between New Delhi and the ASEAN. On the contrary, the normalization of ties between the ASEAN and this traditional ally of India provided a trump card to the latter's Look East policy. The epilogue to the history of Indo-ASEAN dissension in the Indo-Chinese peninsula took place in 1992 when, during its fourth summit, held in Singapore that year, the ASEAN took the decision to allow Vietnam to accede to the 1976 Amity and Cooperation Treaty. It must be added that the resolution of conflicts in Indo-China also benefited Indo-Thai relations. In fact, the Sino-Vietnamese confrontation in Cambodia had fuelled a significant level of cooperation between China and Thailand, and from the Indian viewpoint, this nurtured the fear of Beijing trying to play an active role in the Indian Ocean. Following the Cambodian imbroglio, New Delhi saw a slight loosening of strategic Sino-Thai ties, to the advantage of its own relationship with Bangkok.

Further, the end of the Cold War paved the way for an improvement in relations between India and the major powers of the region—the United States, Japan and China. First of all, the feeling of insecurity that followed the collapse of the Soviet block led New Delhi to try to improve its ties with the United States. The latter, on their part, proved to be quite willing to raise the level of their strategic exchanges with India. America's goodwill partly followed its logic of 'burden sharing', i.e. the sharing of the financial burden posed by international peace-keeping efforts. Because it was increasingly costly to take on the role of the world's policeman, Washington gave increasing credit to the idea of global collective security based on regional collective responsibilities. In other words, the United States had the intention of structuring a new world order in which they would retain their leadership, but without having to bear its entire cost. Thus, they set out to establish regional alliance networks, such as the one they forged with the ASEAN. In the Indian Ocean, maintaining security meant engaging in cooperation with India—or at least, obtaining its neutrality—to the extent that it was a significant maritime power in the region.

Inviting India to be a *status quo* power was all the more necessary since this maritime space was vital for security in the Persian Gulf and international oil flows. Among the institutions that contributed to the reappraisal of India's strategic role in the Indian Ocean, the US Pacific Command in Hawaii seemed to have played a significant role. From 1989 onwards, the Hawaii base's Chief of Staff began to formally invite New Delhi to conduct joint maritime exercises. The United States reiterated their offer in 1991 through General Kick-leighter, who proposed to consolidate bilateral cooperation in matters of defence.[23] Thus, the first joint naval exercises between India and the United States took place in May 1992. And 'Malabar 1995'—the second stint of these bilateral exercises—was the most important naval exercise in which the Indian Navy had ever participated.[24] American decision-makers increasingly began to refer to India as an important emerging power. The softening of America's strategic approach was also the outcome of a growing business lobby officiating in Washington. All in all, the Indo-American rapprochement in the early 1990s took place thanks to a convergence in bilateral trade interests and perceptions of regional stability.

The considerable improvement in relations with the United States had a positive impact on ties between India and Japan. Although the Soviet threat had receded, Washington remained Japan's primary military ally. In January 1992, President George Bush and Prime Minister Kiichi Miyazawa held a summit during which they stressed the importance of their alliance in the uncertain post-Cold War context. Thanks to the 1960 pact, renewed in 1996, Japan continued to benefit from the American nuclear umbrella and assistance in the event of aggression. Thus, the United States played a pivotal role in the relations between India and Japan, because Tokyo tended at that time to model its foreign policy on that of Washington. The removal of the divergences between India and Japan resulted less from their bilateral policies and more from the indirect effects of changes that were affecting their respective foreign policies, as well as the international environment in general.[25] In addition, Tokyo fully supported the American position on the NPT and the Missile Technology Control Regime.[26] Japan believed that despite its flaws, the NPT provided a guarantee against nuclear proliferation and for that reason, it did not stop urging all the states to sign the treaty. Thus, when he visited Tokyo in June 1992, Prime Minister Rao reached an understanding with his Japanese counterpart Kiichi Miyazawa for conducting official talks on non-proliferation and nuclear issues. These consultations, which actually took place in New Delhi in March 1993 and continued in 1994 and 1995, at least allowed both parties to better appreciate their respective positions.[27] Finally, an informal dialogue on security was also established with the Japanese Self Defence Force (JSDF). It even seemed as if the JSDF officials were much keener to meet Indian military officers than were the representatives of Japan's Foreign Affairs Ministry.[28]

The protection of maritime routes was an essential concern for Japan, which imported almost 70 per cent of its crude oil from the Gulf countries in the early 1990s. This energy dependence had made Tokyo very sensitive to the security of the straits that provided a passage between the Indian and Pacific Oceans, especially the Malacca Strait. But for all that, Japan did not truly perceive India as a potential guarantor of the security of international maritime traffic, and Japan left entirely this task in the hands of the United States. In this regard, naval cooperation between India and the United States was hailed for improving Japan's perception of India's strategic role. In fact, it must be recalled that until 1990, Japan's White Paper on defence noted the preoccupations expressed in South-East Asia with regard to a possible Indian military threat. It is true that the archipelago's security was closely linked to that of South-East Asia, insofar as any major upheaval in the region could have repercussions on some of its vital interests, especially as far as the protection of sea lanes was concerned. In more general terms, Indo-American naval cooperation was a positive development for several countries in East Asia. In fact, Washington headed the alliance network throughout the Asian region, with Japan, Taiwan and South Korea in North-East Asia, and the Philippines, Singapore and Thailand in South-East Asia, apart from Australia in the South-West Pacific. Thus, the rapprochement with the United States helped India improve its relations with all its partners in East Asia. Consequently, it appeared that initially, New Delhi's new approach with regard to East Asia continued to depend on its relationships with the sole remaining superpower, besides its relationship with China, the emerging new power in the region.

Since the beginning of the 1980s, India and China had been seeking a *modus vivendi* that would enable them to pursue broader strategic objectives. Prime Minister Rajiv Gandhi's visit to Beijing in 1988 initiated a warm-up that extended to the early 1990s. In December 1991, the Chinese Prime Minister, Li Peng, went on a six-day visit to

New Delhi. No Chinese Prime Minister had visited India in thirty-one years. In fact, the most important initiative for restarting negotiations on border disputes came from him during his meetings with Prime Minister Rao. An agreement was signed that once again authorized the flow of trade on certain border points between India and the autonomous region of Tibet. Between 1991 and 1994, New Delhi and Beijing took a host of measures to try to resolve their border conflicts. In November 1992, the Joint Working Group initiated a series of security and confidence-building measures aimed at reducing the number of troops on either side of the border and at demarcating the border line. After three rounds of negotiations, India and China managed to conclude an agreement to 'maintain peace and tranquillity' along the line of actual control in their Himalayan territories. The agreement was finalized and signed during Prime Minister Rao's visit to Beijing in September 1993. Since the resolution of the border dispute proved to be quite difficult, the two sides decided to put the issue on the backburner. By virtue of the 1993 agreement, the two neighbours undertook to respect the existing line of control, i.e. they would stand by the *status quo* by reducing their military forces along the border on the basis of the principle of 'equal and mutual security'. The signing of this agreement established a certain amount of normality in the relations between the two giants, and economic, technological and cultural exchanges experienced an increase as of 1991.[29] Direct contacts began to develop between the top military hierarchies of the two countries. In December 1993 for instance, the Vice-Chief of Staff of the Chinese army, Lt. General Xu Hui-Zi, went on a friendly visit to India.[30] In return, the Indian Minister of Defence visited China. Beijing was also ready to go as far as to support India's candidature for a non-permanent seat in the Security Council. Another unexpected proof of the Sino-Indian warm-up was China's supply of enriched uranium to the Indian atomic power station in Tarapur, near Mumbai, in January 1995.[31]

INDIA'S NAVAL DIPLOMACY

The end of the Cold War gave New Delhi the opportunity to make a better impression on its East Asian neighbours. In this connection, India's political and military leadership took note of the symbolic and concrete importance of 'naval diplomacy'.[32] Indeed, a modern fleet could carry out a host of activities apart from its traditional role as defender of national maritime borders. In India's case, it made it possible to promote friendly diplomatic ties with riparian nations in the Indian Ocean. Friendly visits by warships from different national fleets were also a significant indication of benevolent military relationships. India's naval forces essentially undertook to participate in confidence and security-building measures, both through joint naval exercises and cooperation with other combat fleets to protect shipping lanes, and conduct counter-piracy as well as search and rescue operations. To the positive effects of the Indo-American naval exercises may be added the Indian Navy's own initiatives towards South-East Asia. For New Delhi, getting in touch with South-East Asian capitals directly, in order to establish contacts in defence matters, meant that it had cut itself off from the paradigm of derived relationships. The improvement in relations with South-East Asia was not just considered as an upshot of the rapprochement with Washington. It thenceforth became a strategic objective in its own right, one that New Delhi intended to follow actively. Thus, at the end of 1991, in a major about-turn, the Indian government agreed to revive high-level interaction with foreign navies. This long-awaited decision by India's naval officers put an end to some twenty-five years of isolation.[33] From the end of 1991 onwards, India participated in several naval exercises with Indonesia. Later, it was the turn of Singapore in early 1993. These exercises made it possible to build greater cooperation, institute better transparency in operations, and thus establish trustworthy relations with the various South-East Asian states.

The Indian Navy also took the initiative to increase the frequency of its visits to the ports of the Indian Ocean's riparian countries, especially those that had expressed concerns about the nature and extent of its expansion. In 1990–1, two Indian battleships visited Penang and took part in the international fleet review that marked the fiftieth anniversary of the Malaysian Royal Navy.[34] Between 1991 and 1994, the Indian Navy visited some twenty-two countries and about twenty-five naval bases. Indian warships even went to China for the first time in 1995. Conversely, Indian naval dockyards received an increasing number of foreign visitors, especially from Indonesia and Malaysia, but also from Australia, Russia, the United States and Great Britain. In November 1993, the first Chinese battleship—a training ship equivalent to a destroyer—visited the Bombay naval base. Finally, to put an end to all suspicions, New Delhi invited military attachés from South-East Asia to visit its Great Nicobar facilities in the Andaman Sea. The latter therefore learnt that there were neither any Jaguar strike aircraft nor any long-range Bear maritime reconnaissance craft in the Port Blair base, although the crafts available could be equipped with such instruments. The base's facilities therefore fulfilled the functions of maritime reconnaissance, while also targeting poaching and smuggling. The military facilities in Port Blair were also meant to prevent fishermen of South-East Asian or Chinese origin to permanently settle down in the 500 or so islets in the vicinity.[35] After 1991, ships from Australia, France, Indonesia, Malaysia and Singapore all paid a visit to Port Blair. Even with Thailand, a country that was traditionally very suspicious of India's motives, perceptions started improving. On 27 October 1993, an agreement was signed for demarcating offshore borders between India, Myanmar and Thailand, at the tri-junctional point 7 in the Andaman Sea.

In their official speeches, Indian diplomatic and military officials took great care to state their peaceful intentions clearly. In a fairly uncommon act of repentance, the former Indian Army Chief of Staff, General K. Sundarji, acknowledged before the 1992 Asia Pacific Defence Conference that India's military intentions had been the subject of speculation for the past several years and that, indeed, 'the Government had not helped matters by not setting out a clear line on its doctrinal view'.[36] On 16 February 1994, the Chief of Staff, Admiral V.S. Shekhawat excluded any major expansion of India's naval forces in the near future. He added that India was pursuing a policy of 'good neighbourliness' with the aim of promoting peace and development in the Asian region.[37] In the diplomatic field, the Indian Prime Minister also set out to put an end to any concerns about his country's maritime ambitions. On this account, P.V. Narasimha Rao's political style probably worked in favour of the new Indian approach. The lack of charisma for which he was often ridiculed in India was highly appreciated in South-East Asia. Less concerned about his international image than the direct interests of his country, the Prime Minister managed to credibly embody the new discreet and pragmatic Indian approach. Less burdened with ancient ideological orientations, Narasimha Rao represented what South-East Asia could expect from India.[38] During the 1994 September Singapore Conference, he set out to dispel ASEAN's concerns about India's naval ambitions. Refuting any eventuality of an Indian intervention in South-East Asian maritime affairs, he asserted that his country had only 'a keen analytical interest' with regard to security issues in the region, such as the territorial disputes in the South China Sea. Narasimha Rao also clarified that India's role in regional security would be limited to United Nations peacekeeping operations. Finally, his comments on the risk of rivalry between Asian powers were unequivocal: 'There is no cause whatsoever for the alarmist views propounded about India's alleged expansionist designs, or its blue water Navy.'[39]

Indian experts such as Rahul Roy-Chaudhury further explained that New Delhi had no aspirations to gaining the status of a great maritime power.[40] The acquisition of aircraft carriers, destroyers and frigates, the construction of additional combat ships and the proposed acquisition of a new aircraft carrier all seemed like an attempt to acquire regional 'sea-control', rather than the 'sea denial' capacity worthy of a great power. In other words, in the hypothesis of an armed conflict, the Indian Navy intended to ensure that it had control over the use of the sea against regional adversaries, but not against global powers. Moreover, India's maritime economic interests in themselves justified the expansion of its naval force. Otherwise, how else would it defend its 7600 km-long coastal border and an EEZ of 220 million sq km, with major oil exploration programmes? How would it protect maritime routes that provided passage to almost ninety per cent of its foreign trade? If these issues were borne in mind, it was easy to see that India's naval expansion fulfilled peaceful economic imperatives and not expansionist designs. Besides, with the statements made by Narasimha Rao and Indian military officers, the message about India's benevolence seemed to have got through to East Asian interlocutors. Consequently, during his January 1994 visit, Singapore's Prime Minister, Goh Chok Tong, acknowledged that India had a legitimate interest in possessing a large navy to defend its coasts.[41]

From a South-East Asian point of view, the most tangible proof of Indian goodwill pertained to the way the defence budget evolved. The 1991 payment crises and ensuing economic reforms demanded that government expenses be brought down, which led to substantial cuts in defence allocations and, more specifically, a slowdown in the naval force modernization programme. While accounting for 4 per cent of the GNP in 1986–7, military expenditure began to decline in 1988–9, amounting to 3.6 per cent of the GNP. After 1990, defence expenses remained below 3 per cent of the GNP, at around 2.5 per cent,[42] without taking into consideration the 1992 devaluation.

The decline in real terms was even higher, given the substantial drop in the value of the Rupee *vis-à-vis* the Dollar after 1990.[43] In constant Rupee values at the 1980–1 rates, it transpired that military expenses had practically stagnated between 1986–7 and 1995–6, showing a rather downward trend over ten years. Another indicator was the share of defence expenditure in the government's overall expenses, which was down from 11 per cent in 1987–8 to 8 per cent in 1993–4.[44] However, these figures came to be the subject of controversy. Several international experts suggested that the official defence budget concealed other military expenses and was the subject of selective exclusions. After 1983–4, defence pensions were no longer included in military expenses, as also the manufacture of equipment in defence-related companies. Nuclear and space programme activities were not included in the defence budget, while they potentially had military applications.[45] Thus, the defence budget share in the GNP did not decline as much as the Indian government had been claiming. Between 1986 and 1992, military expenses remained at about 4 per cent of the GNP. However, in real terms, defence expenses had gone down in recent years, but there too, not as much as India claimed.

Of the three Indian forces, it was the Navy that suffered the most from the effects of the reduction in the military budget. While naval expenses went up between 1987–8 and 1989–90, they subsequently dropped by about 25 per cent in constant terms over a short period of four years.[46] Naval modernization and expansion prog-rammes became secondary issues in India's defence agenda. In the early 1990s, the Indian Navy entered a critical phase, to the extent that only half of its vessels were operational, the other half remaining docked.[47] According to the United Nations' Register of Conventional Arms, India did not acquire even a single warship from a foreign source between 1992 and 1995. Fundamental long-term acquisition programmes were halted due to the lack of resources. As for the ambitious objectives of the Indian fleet's self-reliance, they came up against the slow indigenization of shipbuilding and the limited available capacity in shipyards. The Indian Navy was also hit very hard by the consequences of the collapse of the USSR. During the 1990–2 period, the dismemberment of Soviet production networks disturbed the supply of spare parts and sophisticated weaponry. The severity of the crisis can be appreciated in the light of India's dependence on Soviet equipment. In early 1995, twenty-five of India's forty main surface combat ships—i.e. almost two-thirds—were of

Soviet origin, as also fifteen conventional submarines.[48] In fact, the lack of maintenance and preparation was felt quite severely at the start of the decade.[49] The engine room in the aircraft carrier *INS Viraat* took water and had to be docked for six additional months. In May 1994, the other naval aircraft carrier, the *INS Vikrant*, was damaged by a fire aboard. In 1992, a light frigate of Soviet manufacture was damaged at sea off the Andaman Islands, during routine exercises.

The state of the Indian armed forces finally showed that the country placed greater emphasis on land defence rather than the capability of projecting its might through the navy.[50] Contrary to the wishes of the former Naval Chief, Admiral Ramdas, who defended the concept of a fighting fleet, India chose to allocate its resources to coast guard units for controlling smuggling and poaching. Thus, the government opted for the construction of low tonnage vessels for the surveillance of near shore waters. The new Chief of Naval Staff, Admiral Shekhawat, continued to follow this policy in 1993. India's maritime capacities revealed that the country's major concern was to protect the waters surrounding the Indian peninsula. Existing facilities in the Andaman and Nicobar Islands continued to be focused on the surveillance and maintenance of maritime security. In more general terms, the deployment of India's military forces showed that the country never ceased to be a continental nation. The army always received the best deal in the military budget. Naval expenses never rose beyond 14 per cent of the overall defence expenditure, while the army received about 60 per cent. Chronic regional instability led to an arms race between India and Pakistan in the 1980s, but their defence systems remained subcontinental in nature, concentrating on the defence of land frontiers and internal law and order, at the expense of the acquisition of forces with a significant strategic range. Further, the Indian armed forces were essentially posted in the north of the country, on the west coast near Mumbai and in the Himalayan regions. At the most, certain Indian strategic experts saw in the Indian Ocean a third front, after Pakistan and China. But the fact was that at the start of the 1990s, the country did not identify any real maritime threat. Besides, in the more specific case of the deployment of its naval forces, it was more the west coast of India that became a strategic issue. Indeed, oil supply lines from the Persian Gulf pass clear off the coast of Pakistan.

In the early 1990s, the army was subject to fewer budgetary

restrictions than the Navy, due to the turbulent internal situation that was rife in India. The challenges within the country—along its borders for instance—were such that New Delhi was hardly in the position to engage itself in any undertaking aimed at projecting its might. On the contrary, it was working on organizing its military resources and forces to manage its immediate environment, which was quite unstable. Thus, strategically, India had withdrawn into itself. Its security vision refocused on the South Asian environment, and Indian decision-makers were convinced that existing threats were essentially internal in nature, in the short as well as the medium term. This development meant that as long as India's immediate environment remained unstable, New Delhi was hardly likely to devote itself to playing the role of a regional power, even if it so wished. The two national fleets were straightaway considered as being sufficiently significant not to have any rival in the Indian Ocean. Any addition was henceforth considered futile.[51]

INDIA'S ROLE IN ASIA'S SECURITY ARCHITECTURE

With the end of the Cold War, the definition of security became contingent upon the economic interdependencies that emerged between the countries of Asia. Therefore, economic interests appeared to have overtaken purely security-related issues and India did not escape this fundamental trend. In fact, economic liberalization played a part in modifying the definitions of security. A new perception of power came to light, embracing both military forces as well as economic success—in fact, any form of influence such as 'soft power', a complex set of cultural, diplomatic and economic factors. All in all, power had to be multi-dimensional in nature. Above all, New Delhi increasingly acknowledged the intrinsic relationship between trade and security. In East Asia, the stature that China and Japan had acquired in the international arena was essentially because of their economic power. The attraction of the Chinese market and the unequalled competitiveness of the Japanese economy granted these two states significant political and strategic leverage in their relationships with other major world powers. Japan's experience particularly struck Indian minds since it proved that it was not necessary to be a military power to raise oneself to the rank of a world power. This phenomenon, explained with the help of the concept of fungibility, revealed that in the contemporary international system, one specific type of resource could be converted to another type. And financial means were unquestionably the most fungible of all a power's resources. Thus, the Indian expert Varun Sahni concluded: 'The lesson for India is a stark one. The inability to compete economically in the capitalist world system cannot be compensated by any other power resource. India will not be able to carve out an advantageous niche for itself in the world system if it does not overcome its lack of economic competitiveness in the coming decades.'[52]

New Delhi finally realized that it had not been able to establish the kind of beneficial interdependencies that characterized the prosperous economies of East Asia, between a flexible foreign policy, a dynamic international trade and significant foreign investments, and access to the most sophisticated technologies and information. This awareness raised a paradoxical situation for Indian decision-makers: the traditional concept of true independence could no longer be maintained without a better access to the world economy. The status of India's regional might was also henceforth dependent on its capacity to improve its performances in the fields of high technologies, which also required a strong link between the Indian economy and the world market. Indeed, it seemed that disappointing performances in certain R&D fields were linked to the fact that India had been isolated from the world economy. Changes in the concept of security and definition of power and, above all, new interdependencies between the economy and defence led to a review of and a correction in India's oceanic ambitions. Consequently, India's naval modernization programmes had to remain modest until such time that the country became a leading commercial power.[53] Only then would New Delhi have both the need as well as the resources to build a veritable naval force of international significance. All in all, it was by becoming a commercial power that its interests in maritime affairs would increase and be taken into consideration.

As for most East Asian states, they appeared to have understood the multi-dimensional nature of security a long time ago. For instance, without ever becoming a military alliance, the ASEAN had managed to function as a security alliance.[54] In general terms, increasingly closer political and economic ties between East Asian nations had considerably raised their interest in maintaining peace and tranquillity in the region. Thus, economic factors played a decisive role in the way the general structure of security in East Asia came to evolve. In the early 1990s, the predominant postulate in the region was that economic interdependency fostered friendly political and military ties. From this perspective, Indian experts acknowledged that rising economic flows with East Asia would also make it possible to enhance India's strategic role and prestige in the region, as the example of China's regional integration had shown. In the meantime, India did not enjoy the multi-dimensional influence that China did in Asia—far from it. But it had at least begun to adopt a conception of security that was fairly close to the one pursued by the countries of East Asia.

In any event, it seemed that, by placing their economic interests in the forefront, India and the ASEAN were able to deal with more strategic issues without any delay. The decision to attribute the status of a sectoral dialogue partner to India in 1992 was essentially the outcome of economic arguments. It was the ASEAN Ministers of Economic Affairs who upheld India's candidature while the Foreign Affairs Ministers remained more reticent, due in particular to the Indo-Pakistan conflict.[55] Consequently, the ASEAN revived its dialogue with India, giving priority to economic interests and relegating strategic issues to the background. And yet, strategic considerations remained in the forefront in the minds of ASEAN's decision-makers. In fact, they initiated India's integration in the dialogue mechanism at the same time as they undertook to reinforce the political and security-related role of the post-ministerial conferences. Indeed, since the early 1990s, the ASEAN states had been concerned about finding a security mechanism capable of handling the post-Cold War context. Until then, the region's strategic order was primarily based on a network of bilateral treaties linking the two superpowers to different Asian states. The United States had secured the collaboration of Japan, South Korea, Philippines and Australia, while the Soviet Union had forged a close relationship with North Korea and Vietnam. Taking note of the end of the bipolar logic, ASEAN's decision-makers undertook to redefine regional security from a multilateral perspective.

The Fourth ASEAN Heads of Government Summit, held in Singapore in January 1992, took the important decision to openly tackle cooperation in security matters with its dialogue partners within the framework of the Post-Ministerial Conferences.[56] Until then, the formal procedures of ASEAN's Post-Ministerial Conferences were limited to issues of economic cooperation, although discussions had sometimes informally dealt with political and strategic problems. Post-Ministerial Conferences seemed to constitute the most adequate institutional mechanism for a security dialogue as they already involved twelve countries of the Asia-Pacific region (the six ASEAN states, the United States, Japan, Canada, Australia, New Zealand and South Korea), apart from the European Community. The People's Republic of China and Russia had been enjoying the status of invitees since 1991. Laos and Vietnam were observers since 1992. Above all, the ASEAN project now had Washington's stamp of approval. Since it had been functioning until then on a network of bilateral ties, the United States did not much favour the idea of strengthening the Post-Ministerial Conferences in order to promote consultations on regional security. But at the start of the 1990s, the Clinton administration recognized that a multilateral security dialogue had to take over from the old bilateral mechanisms whose effectiveness was being called into question by the new regional context. The ASEAN was also concerned about stabilising ties between Washington and Tokyo. In fact, most Asian capitals wanted to ensure that Japan would never be able to exercise any military power without the American guarantee. But, even though the Japanese-American alliance was considered a pillar of regional stability, it suffered many political tensions since the end of the Soviet threat, apart from an increase in frictions of a commercial nature. In this regard, Washington's approval for participation in the Post-Ministerial Conferences was crucial. On its part, Japan fully supported the process since it intended to be a stakeholder in the future structure of cooperation in the field of regional security. The ASEAN Regional Forum (ARF) stemmed from summit discussions held in January 1992 and appeared as an institutional extension of Post-Ministerial Conference structures. In fact, the ARF concept received general support at the June 1993 Post-Ministerial Conference in Singapore. Despite obtaining the status of a sectoral dialogue partner, New Delhi remained on the periphery of the process that gave birth to this institutional forum for regional security.

But, beyond economic interdependencies and pious discourses on multilateral security mechanisms, military power remained an essential concern for several states in the region. In fact, the 1990s corresponded to a period of military modernization in the whole of East Asia. Increases in budgetary allocations to defence often made it possible to focus on the quality of equipment, not just its quantity. Above all, the states of the region sought to acquire arms made with increasingly sophisticated technologies and of an offensive rather than a defensive character, so as to reinforce their means of projecting power. They also engaged in the national development of the R&D

sector and their defence industries. This trend was radically in contrast with the decline in arms expenditure in the other regions of the world: in North America, Europe and the Middle East. Furthermore, in East Asia, military modernization benefited the naval and air forces first and foremost, which was hardly surprising insofar as most regional tension points were associated with disputes pertaining to maritime borders or claims on territories close to the coast.[57] In this respect, East Asia still suffered from a series of disputes, to say the least. In the short-term, the three most sensitive tension zones were the Korean peninsula, the impasse between China and Taiwan and various conflicts in the South China Sea. The differences between China, Taiwan, the Philippines, Malaysia, Brunei and Vietnam around the Spratly and Paracels Islands in the South China Sea were particularly disturbing. In fact, control over these islands would confer an important strategic advantage since the sea lanes crossing this area were among the busiest in the world. While latent disputes did exist between ASEAN member states, it was Beijing, above all, which appeared to be the most destabilizing factor in Asia, especially in the South China Sea.

Since conflicts in East Asia were primarily maritime in nature, an overview of the major navies involved could help in determining the strategic issues at stake. The various Asian fleets could be classified in three categories, in terms of size: large, medium and small.[58] The first category consisted of the Chinese Navy, the Japanese maritime defence force and the Indian Navy. The fleets of Australia, Taiwan, South Korea, Indonesia and Thailand were in the category of medium naval forces. Finally, North Korea, Malaysia, Singapore and Vietnam belonged to the last category. Given the limitations of the South-East Asian naval deterrent force and the signs of America's disengagement from the region in the early 1990s, many questions were raised about the future role of the navies of major Asian powers, especially with respect to the Chinese Navy, which constituted the third largest in terms of personnel assigned, after the United States and Russia. In fact, since the mid-1980s, Beijing had embarked upon a major renovation, expansion and modernization programme of all its armed forces. To such an extent that in the early 1990s, China's naval expansion largely eclipsed any concerns that Indian manoeuvres could have provoked. It was actually one of the fastest-growing navies in Asia, thanks to its Russian connection, in particular. Although the Chinese Navy was one of the biggest in the world in terms of personnel and ships allocated, its capacity for transporting combat forces remained limited. It remained a coastal patrol force, despite its programmes for the modernization of surface combatants and submarines. Therefore, its ability to operate with impunity in the waters of the Pacific Ocean—and more so in the Indian Ocean—should not be exaggerated. In comparison, the Japanese Navy was modern, but defensive in nature. It did not have the means to project its power and it was quite unlikely that it would become a significant offensive force in the near future. Japan considered its security relationship with the United States and the presence of American troops on its territory as essential to its security. However, the archipelago was no less concerned about China's rising power, especially since Tokyo had maritime differences with Beijing with regard to the Senkaku Island. In 1995, for the first time, Japan aired its concerns over the increase in China's military might and its aggressive attitude on the issue of the Spratly and Paracels Islands.[59]

As for the Indian Navy, it had embarked upon a massive self-reliance programme in the early 1980s, undertaking to build a variety of ships autonomously. Meanwhile, one of its main characteristics was the use of equipment of different origins—of Soviet, Western and Indian manufacture. With a fairly modern conventional submarine force, consisting of German HDW and Soviet kilo-class submarines, the Indian Navy was by then the only one in Asia to own medium-sized aircraft carriers. Moreover, it could pride itself on the considerable operational experience of its ships. But, mainly, India was a power in South Asia and not in the greater Indian Ocean. Further, its naval forces continued to suffer as the result of a relative absence of strategic thinking. The Chiefs of Naval Staff stressed on the size and profile of the type of Navy that India wished to have, but without coordinating with the other two armed services or proceeding to a realistic assessment of the financial resources available. Moreover, these projects had not been drawn up within the framework of a general policy expounded by the central political power. All in all, India wished to be a pre-eminent power in the vast Indian Ocean, but it lacked the strategies and resources necessary to build and implement the policy.[60] With respect to South-East Asia, the Indian Navy was able to carry out surveillance in the region, thanks to its long-range maritime reconnaissance aircraft, the TU-142m (8,000 km). However, since its independence, its maritime operations had been confined to its South Asian neighbourhood, whether it was in the 1971 Indo-Pakistan war or the dispatch of peacekeeping forces to Sri Lanka and intervention in the Maldives toward the end of the 1980s. Moreover, the Indian Navy suffered many limitations as far as its capacity to project its might beyond its immediate surroundings was concerned. Contrary to a number of assertions, the Andaman and Nicobar Islands base did not allow New Delhi to keep the Malacca Strait under surveillance, even less to close it off. On the other hand, the archipelago offered alternative maritime routes to access the Indian Ocean. All in all, it was difficult to imagine any intervention by India in the event of a conflict in the South China Sea. New Delhi had no major interest in South-East Asia, although widespread political upheavals could have repercussions on its security. While it was unlikely that the Indian Navy would assume an active role in South-East Asia, it could, however, be a useful ally for many navies in South-East Asia, in the hypothesis of a conflict.

Among the three largest Asian navies, China finally found itself in an advantageous position in the South China Sea. The South-East Asian fleets were limited and they did not have the means to counter a large external power. The Indian and Japanese navies could hardly play any effective role unless tensions worsened in the South China Sea. In the aftermath of the Cold War, China forged diplomatic ties with its formerly quite distrustful neighbours—Indonesia, Singapore and South Korea—while also beginning to air its maritime claims in the South China Sea quite openly. In February 1992 for instance, the Chinese authorities adopted a law that resulted in the incorporation of the entire contentious area it claimed in Chinese territory. The short and medium-term developments in China therefore became a fundamental concern for strategic analyses in South-East Asia. For its part, India began to involve itself in East Asian affairs in the context of China's predominance. Its image markedly improved in the early 1990s. From a rather unpredictable—if not destabilizing—factor, it became a benign *status quo* power.

7.2 An Indian Counterweight to China's Might?

With the end of the Cold War, China's strategic position was greatly improved. The collapse of the USSR, its primary military rival, relieved it of the biggest threat weighing heavily on its territory. Beijing, which no longer had much to be concerned about the security of its northern front, could now devote itself to its eastern front. This reorientation drew on the rise in China's strategic power in Asia. Whether it was the ASEAN, Japan or India, most states in the neighbourhood now had to find new ways of handling China's predominance in the post-Cold War context. The ASEAN took the lead initiative to support China's peaceful return to Asia. India's policy *vis-à-vis* Beijing was more ambiguous: it appeared as a mix of confidence-building measures, permanent suspicions and a growing feeling of rivalry. Triangular interactions between India, China and the ASEAN were therefore very complex and were primarily characterized by their asymmetry. Since Indo-ASEAN ties were less developed, they became quite dependent on Sino-Indian relations on the one hand, and Sino-ASEAN relations on the other. Consequently, China emerged as a pivotal element, which partly determined the nature of Indo-ASEAN strategic relations. Thus, although driven by the same fears *vis-à-vis* China, India and the ASEAN tackled this common problem very prudently. It even appeared that at first, the ASEAN refused to acknowledge the existence of these shared fears. However, there was one subject on which there was a convergence of views between India and the ASEAN: the growing involvement of China in Myanmar. Indeed, Myanmar found itself at the crossroads of Indian, Chinese and ASEAN strategic preoccupations.

CHINA'S ASCENDANCY: A COMMON SOURCE OF CONCERN FOR INDIA AND THE ASEAN

Thanks to its sharp economic growth, China continued its military modernization, a development that became a constant source of concern for its neighbours. While defence expenditure remained quite low in the 1980s, it began to rise rapidly as of 1988 for the restructuring of all China's military forces. In addition, major shifts took place in the military doctrine of the People's Liberation Army. By virtue of the new generic concepts of 'limited war under high-tech conditions' and 'active defence', the Chinese army became increasingly professional and modern under Deng Xiaopeng. Beijing chose to concentrate on rapid modernization in a few critical fields: tactical arms, communication and logistics, nuclear weapons and ballistic missiles, shipbuilding, aerospace and a certain number of other fields with dual-use technologies. Thus, it appeared that China was equipping itself with the necessary means to rapidly project its might. In this respect, the country largely benefited from the opportunities offered by the former Soviet Union's arms market. In the summer of 1990, during the Russian President Boris Yeltsin's visit to Beijing, the two states signed a document on strategic cooperation. The high level of military cooperation that was established considerably helped the modernization of all the Chinese armed forces.[61]

The Chinese arms purchases from Russia were so sizeable that they could easily affect the balance of power in Asia. Chinese decision-makers proved to be particularly fond of the Sukhoi 27, a long-range strike combat aircraft.[62] China's military expenses were difficult to assess and estimates differed. The publication of official figures was only indicative, since in all likelihood, large segments of expenses were not taken into account, although they were directly associated with defence. According to India's main think-tank, the Institute for Defence Studies and Analysis (IDSA), China's defence expenditure in 1991 was estimated at 21.21 billion dollars against the 6.42 billion declared. In 1996, IDSA's estimates were of 30.27 billion dollars, i.e. 242.15 billion Yuans, against the official Chinese figure of 70.23 billion Yuans.[63] Thus, IDSA estimated that the official Chinese defence expenditure only accounted for one-fifth of its actual expenditure. Indeed, the Chinese official budget only seemed to include the budget for human resources and possibly a few operational costs. Capital expenditure for the acquisition of military equipment and expenditure in the R&D sector did not seem to have been included. In 1992, China probably became Asia's prime military power, ahead of the USSR. More importantly, IDSA's speculations showed to what degree Indian experts were suspicious of their neighbour's military developments.

Indeed, the improvement in relations undertaken by the two Asian giants since 1988 did not succeed in wiping out India's mistrust. Overall, both the military and academic circles supported the government's efforts to revive relations with Beijing.[64] The officials of the Ministry of External Affairs were the most confident and hopeful of a gradual improvement in bilateral ties, thanks, in particular, to economic and cultural exchanges. And yet, the vast majority of India's political decision-makers and observers were no less fearful of China's expansionist ambitions and kept a close watch on all developments along the Himalayan border, the military establishment being one of the most suspicious in this regard. To the credit of military experts, it was true that the trajectories of Indian and Chinese arms expenditures showed an increasingly marked gap. According to an IDSA study,

India accounted for 5.2 per cent of the overall defence expenditure in Asia in 1988. This figure had fallen to 3.1 per cent in 1994, before rising to 3.5 per cent in 1995 and 3.6 per cent in 1996. As for Chinese expenses, they rose constantly, which explained the growing gap with Indian figures. China accounted for 10.5 per cent of Asia's overall military expenses in 1988, i.e. almost double the Indian percentage. But in 1994, Chinese defence expenditure accounted for 12.2 per cent of Asian expenses, i.e. four times that of India. The gap was almost the same in 1996, with Chinese expenses estimated at 13 per cent of Asia's total military expenses. While there was a total reduction of 23.5 per cent in Indian expenses between 1988 and 1996, Chinese expenses seemed to have increased by 125 per cent over the same period.[65] At the start of the 1990s, the Indian armed forces had to face a difficult period of budgetary restrictions. On this account, it even seemed that one of the main advantages of the 1993 Sino-Indian agreement was that it helped resolve certain dilemmas in India's defence management, since the reduction in military troops along the Tibetan border helped in bringing in the reinforcements that were deemed necessary for the defence of the border against Pakistan.

India's mistrust of China was largely based on the fact that Beijing had maintained its military cooperation with Pakistan. Allies during the Cold War, Beijing and Islamabad continued to enjoy close ties in the new international context. India was especially unhappy with this situation as relations with Pakistan had remained very tense. In concrete terms, China was accused of continuing to transfer its technological know-how to Pakistan for the development of short-range ballistic missiles.[66] To that may be added revelations about the potential delivery of 5000 Chinese magnetic rings for Pakistan's nuclear programme in 1996. While it engaged India in a dialogue, China did not stop pursuing its special relationship with Pakistan. To the irritation of the Indians, it continued to adroitly balance the visits of its top dignitaries between New Delhi and Islamabad. For instance, the New Delhi visit of China's Foreign Minister Qian Qichen in July 1994 coincided with that of its Defence Minister Chi Haotian to Islamabad. Furthermore, Beijing's 'levelling-out' policy was not limited to Pakistan and sometimes involved India's other neighbours in South Asia. In the same month of July 1994, Beijing's diplomatic agenda called for the visit of an important military delegation to Myanmar.[67] Besides, Sino-Indian relations seemed to have once again reached a deadlock after 1993. Although Joint Working Groups continued to work on the implementation of the 1991 bilateral agreement, no real notable progress was achieved. In its 1994–5 annual report, the Defence Ministry stressed the positive effects of the Joint Working Group's deliberations and political and military interactions, but underlined that the arming of Pakistan by China was 'cause for concern', just as were Beijing's activities in Myanmar.[68]

Above all, China refused to establish any links between its atomic programme and that of India. In the eyes of Indian authorities, this refusal was an excuse for it to continue to develop its nuclear arms programme. Since the explosion of its first atomic bomb in Lop Nor in 1964, China had never shown any willingness to stop its nuclear test programmes. The fact that it signed the NPT in 1992, after having ignored this document for twenty-two years, was not, from New Delhi's point of view, reassuring in itself. In fact, Indian observers remained sceptical as far as the extent to which China's central and local authorities respected the treaty. Further, the United States Information Services assured the world that the country continued to participate actively in nuclear proliferation, especially as far as Pakistan was concerned. Lastly, Beijing might have unilaterally declared its commitment to 'no first use' and ensured that it would not use atomic arms against non-nuclear-weapon states (NNWS), but it was not clear whether this commitment concerned all NNWS or just those that were part of the NPT. In the second hypothesis, India would be under real threat, since it was not a signatory of the treaty. For all these different reasons, New Delhi harboured strong doubts as far as China's nuclear intentions were concerned—doubts that, moreover, allowed it to justify its own position as a non-declared nuclear state. In fact, New Delhi maintained an ambiguous policy that essentially consisted of keeping the nuclear arm option open. For its part, Beijing had been claiming inflexibly that its atomic programme was directed towards the world's major nuclear powers and not India. Because of this, it did not envisage even the tiniest concessions in its relationship with South Asia. Thus, China could well support the nuclear free zone project in South Asia, although it had already excluded any reduction or inspection of its own nuclear arsenal.[69] China clearly manifested that it was not ready for any compromise when, during the Indian President's visit in June 1992, it proceeded with a nuclear explosion.

In many respects, China's intransigence validated the Indian line of argument concerning the implacable domino effect governing the nuclearization and proliferation processes. While Pakistan viewed its nuclear programme as a means of dissuading India, the latter intended to maintain its nuclear forces for dissuading China, which, in turn, fitted its nuclear strategy within an international framework, especially with regard to the United States and Russia. Thus, Indian decision-makers did not hesitate to stress the extent to which bilateral, regional and international responsibilities were intermingled. Above all, this line of argument showed that New Delhi's nuclear strategy was part of a wider Asian framework, because it was essentially linked to China. However, at this point, Beijing was concerned about not giving New Delhi the least opportunity of deploying a stand—even less a doctrine—on an Asian scale. In this regard, it applied itself to first keep its Indian neighbour within its South Asian sphere by inflaming its dispute with Pakistan. In the second instance, Chinese decision-makers refused to hold any consultations on the nuclear issue with Indian interlocutors, on the pretext that India was not recognized as a nuclear-weapon state.[70] Serious dissensions between India and China on the nuclear issue showed quite early that the two powers nurtured competitive aspirations in Asia. More precisely, New Delhi aspired to expand its strategic vision towards East Asia, while China intended containing India within a purely South Asian context.

To this was added the ambiguous attitude of the United States towards China and Pakistan. During his visit to China in October 1994, the Defence Secretary, William Perry, seemed to seek cooperation with Beijing in order to tackle the nuclear issue in South Asia. This approach exasperated India, which saw Washington seeking the support of a country that was seen as one of the main causes of the nuclear problem in the subcontinent.[71] Subsequently, and in order to avoid too strong a reaction from India, Perry clarified that non-proliferation in South Asia also involved China. Beyond this episode, New Delhi also accused Washington of maintaining it in a position of weakness, by refusing to recognize its just place in the world. What was worse, by placing India and Pakistan on the same level, the United States continued to favour Islamabad, as far as India was concerned.[72] And yet, the American Congress had voted an amendment preventing military and economic assistance to any undeclared nuclear powers in 1988. In a serious violation of the Pressler Amendment, Pakistan was granted an American arms sales package worth USD 23 million in 1991.[73] Thus, the disappearance of the Cold War alignments far from favoured India in the strategic scenario of the early 1990s.

New Delhi lost its special relationship with the Soviet block and found itself quite isolated, while Islamabad continued to benefit from the benevolence of its former American and Chinese allies.

In more general terms, a substantial part of the dispute between China and India pertained to their competitive aspirations for international status. Contemporary heirs of the most ancient civilizations in the world, the two nations saw each other as major natural powers. Thus, the Director of IDSA, Jasjit Singh, affirmed: 'China is the primary strategic challenge for India; and China itself will need to reassess its views regarding India's future role.'[74] To deal with this latent rivalry, the Indian expert proposed to conduct further consultations so that Beijing could be brought gradually to consider India on an equal footing and not in the South Asian context. But while its relationship with China greatly occupied the Indian mind, the opposite was not borne out in any way. Consequently, there was a clear asymmetry of perceptions between the two neighbours. China occupied an essential place in India's diplomatic agendas and strategic analyses, while Beijing for its part, attached little importance to its neighbour. From the Chinese perspective, it was irrelevant to be compared to a power so inferior. Indeed, Chinese leaders considered their country a future superpower, rather comparable to the United States.

Most ASEAN states too were perturbed by China's conduct. Indeed, the latter did not show much willingness to look for compromises on various disputes with its neighbours in the South China Sea.[75] In May 1996 for instance, China ratified the United Nations Convention on the Law of the Sea (UNCLOS) while requesting that its maritime jurisdiction be recognized over not just 370,000—but 3,000,000 sq km. This demand took Chinese claims to the heart of the South China Sea. Irrespective of how closely concerned it was, ASEAN was careful not to give too constrictive an aspect to its security initiatives. The rule was to look for a compromise with the Chinese authorities while trying not to offend them. Thus, with the ARF, the ASEAN put in place a specific institutional instrument to 'contain' China's ascendancy. In fact, this forum was a response to the objective of 'creating a space for discussion where disputes are dealt with before they become a crisis'.[76] Chinese decision-makers were thus invited for greater sociability, without fearing that their country would be designated as 'Enemy no. 1'. Indeed, the ARF approach was more of a gradual, step-by-step approach, since it sought, above all, to gain China's confidence. Thus, the ASEAN took note of Beijing's opposition to a multilateral forum dealing with its bilateral disputes. This requirement reduced the ARF's room for manoeuvre, but its acceptance enabled China's participation in the dialogue, which was ASEAN's primary objective. As for Beijing, it joined the ARF, though not without some apprehension. Not participating in the only multilateral forum in the region would have entailed political costs that the Chinese authorities wished to eschew.[77] This choice proved that the ASEAN exercised, to say the least, a certain power to incite and persuade its giant neighbour. Beijing even initiated a bilateral dialogue on its territorial disputes in the South China Sea. But it refused unwaveringly to discuss issues of sovereignty and continued to express its preferences for a bilateral rather than a multilateral dialogue. Thus, the July 1994 ARF session in Bangkok failed to reach a consensus on the Spratly issue, because of Beijing's opposition. Similarly, China opposed Taiwan's participation in the ARF.

The practice of engaging China deployed by the ASEAN was thus the subject of controversies and there were many speculations flying around about its short and medium term effectiveness. Whether they were official representatives at ARF meetings or non-governmental participants at the meetings of the Council for Security Cooperation in the Asia-Pacific, several Asian experts justified their approach in the name of a so-called 'comprehensive' or cooperative security. The concept embraced everything at the same time— economic prosperity, social stability and military power. In other words, the ASEAN states were hopeful that their growing economic ties with China would guarantee a degree of benevolence. The boldest among the ASEAN experts even discerned an Asian culture for regional security. Not content with the reign of peace in Asia, Kishore Mahbubani stated that it was highly improbable that disputes would break out in the region.[78] Asians had everything to gain from peace. Why would they endanger their prosperity and their formidable growth by engaging in armed conflicts? According to him, Asia was developing a collective culture for regional security, which reconciled western concepts such as national sovereignty with more Asian traditions. Apart from the well-established tradition of non-interference in the internal affairs of a state, the Asian way of tackling difficult relations was based on the desire to not humiliate anyone. Ensuring that one's interlocutor was able to 'save face' automatically implied that the risks of slipping into an armed conflict would be considerably reduced. Asian security practices also accepted the concept of hierarchy, thereby eschewing direct confrontation, and rather than setting up formal institutions to tackle security issues based on the Atlantic model, they opted for setting up networks. However, from the viewpoint of several Western observers, the concept of 'comprehensive security' seemed to have very little substance, even less any chance of ever being implemented. Its essential usefulness was to justify practices that were so-called specific to Asian security. Thus, Gerald Segal affirmed that the ASEAN preferred to deceive itself as far as the imminence of China's might was concerned, as well as it capacity to deal with it: 'East Asians may simply be suffering from a lack of will, or to put it more generously, from a prudent desire to avoid a problem that is too big for them to tackle.'[79] He also observed, and quite rightly so, that East Asia had not yet implemented any arms control programmes, or had done so extremely informally.

Faced with the rising ascendancy of China and the ASEAN concerns, several Indian political and military leaders saw an opportunity to give greater weightage to their country in the strategic equation in Asia. Thus, the hypothesis of an Indian counterweight to China began to surface. Wasn't India the only nation in Asia with the size, power and population of China?[80] In some respects, it was possible to postulate that the ASEAN was also thinking about the theory of an Indian counterweight when it began to engage in a dialogue with New Delhi in 1993. Extremely sensitive to any military development in the region, the ASEAN states could not ignore that India still intended to become 'a prominent regional power'.[81] With economic liberalization, it was also reasonable to foresee that a higher growth rate would not take too long to enable an increase in military expenditure, as elsewhere in Asia. Furthermore, India's technological choices at the time when it obtained the status of a sectoral dialogue partner were quite revealing as far as its ambitions were concerned. Whether its budget accorded priority to fundamental research, heavy industry or infrastructural development, all these choices were aimed at upholding the emergence of a regional military power along the Indian Ocean coast and in the hinterland.

But ASEAN's priority was to engage China, not contain it. The Association and its security arm, the ARF, only promoted dynamics of cooperation and evaded the balance of power logic. From the ASEAN's point of view, any improvement in the relations between New Delhi and Beijing was not only welcome, but also necessary for any rapprochement with India. In other words, New Delhi could hardly depend on the ASEAN to play an overt role to counterbalance China. Such a posture would be far from reasonable for regional security, especially since the ASEAN nations did not intend to place Beijing and New Delhi on an equal footing. Although India had superior conventional arms, the South-East Asian states considered China as Asia's emerging superpower, particularly because of its economic growth. Thus, it would be absurd to be caught up in antagonism with this future giant. Furthermore, there were very few certainties about the kind of power that China would become. Giving China the benefit of the doubt, there was a distinct hope that disputes would be resolved peacefully and progressively and that China would become increasingly conscious of its international conduct. In any event, the ASEAN had no interest in taking measures that would upset China. To develop an extremely close strategic relationship with India would be the kind of premature initiative that could appear as an anti-Chinese entente. In the meantime, a *status quo* situation prevailed. The ASEAN knew full well that Beijing had nothing to gain by precipitating tensions in the South China Sea, because its military ability was inadequate for the time being, in the hypothesis of a conflict being triggered. But, it was clear that with economic growth, time would favour China, its programme of military modernization and its rise as a political power.

Even in India, there was no true consensus on the stand to be adopted *vis-à-vis* China. Some experts like Kanti Bajpai clearly asserted that India did not have to adopt a 'counterbalance' position. Bajpai was among the Indian analysts who believed that China had a *status quo* position *vis-à-vis* India.[82] He strongly opposed the idea—nonetheless pre-eminent in his country—that China constituted the greatest threat to India. Looked at closely, India had nothing to fear from its neighbour, according to him. On the border issue, Beijing had already got the bulk of what it wanted by managing to get the Xinjiang route to Tibet secured and, therefore, there was very little chance of a fresh confrontation with India. As for the hypothesis concerning the rivalry of influence between India and China in South-East Asia, it was fantastical and overestimated India's status in the region. The fact remained that India was not a credible rival of China in South-East Asia. Apart from its diaspora networks and its economic weight, Beijing had reinforced its presence through its capacity to project its military might. India just did not have any similar assets. According to Bajpai, the argument of the Chinese threat was prevalent in India because it served several objectives on the international chessboard. First and foremost, it helped justify the Indian nuclear option. Some also used it to enhance India's strategic interest in the speculations the West made—especially the United States—when they worried about China's rising power. Finally, others used the argument of the Chinese threat to draw the attention of East Asian countries—Japan and the ASEAN members—that were also trying to deal with Beijing's behaviour.

Besides, the argument of India as a counterbalance to China was no more likely to seduce Japan than the ASEAN. China was a threatening factor both in the Indian as well as the Japanese strategic outlook and, in fact, both countries had a fairly comparable approach favouring constructive engagement. Prudent cooperation would therefore surely continue to guide Tokyo and New Delhi's approach with regard to Beijing.[83] But succumbing sometimes to the temptation of seeing Japan emerge as a counterbalance to China on its eastern side, several Indian analysts evoked the possibility that in the near future, New Delhi and Tokyo could come together to contain China. It was quite true that for the Indians, who were somewhat short on strategic partners, such a scenario looked quite exciting—though hardly likely. To keep China at bay, Tokyo was much more likely to leave it up to its security alliance with the United States, rather than rely on its own military forces and those of its partners in South-East Asia. An alliance with India would be a last resort solution. The Indian hypothesis of an entente with Japan to contain China would above all alienate the South-East Asian states. Furthermore, such a suggestion showed that the subcontinent had not shared the region's experience of Japanese militarism. Indians did not have the same prejudices as most East Asian nations with regard to any military role played by Japan. Thus, they interpreted Japan's role in the region in a macro-strategic way—that of a regional safeguard to China, while Tokyo was careful not to publicly endorse such a posture.[84] Indeed, it would mean direct confrontation with China, while at the same time hurting the sensibilities of South-East Asia. Consequently, Tokyo applied itself to maintaining a good neighbourly relationship with Beijing.

Since they were still novices in the complex stakes involved in East Asia, Indian diplomats made a few *faux pas*, especially in the early 1990s.[85] Among other things, Indian officials sometimes showed too much fervour and enthusiasm, which gave the impression that

New Delhi considered its admission to regional forums as obvious, as something that was inevitable. This position was all the more misplaced from the ASEAN's point of view, since the subcontinent still remained limited to a perspective that was quite distant from the imminent issues raised by the development of Japan and China. Thus, India's credibility found itself tarnished by its premature initiatives.[86] During preparatory negotiations for the setting up of the ARF, a part of India's academic and political circles suggested that New Delhi should put in a request to take part in the forum. But, in the preliminary meetings with diplomats of the major ASEAN states, Indian officials were requested not to raise the issue of their membership. In other words, the ASEAN officials recommended that New Delhi follow a rule that was important in South-East Asia: that of self-restraint. Indeed, nothing could have been more counter-productive for India and its Look East policy than to give the impression that it was exerting pressure on the ASEAN. From the perspective of South-East Asian diplomats, so long as India had not consolidated its economic power nor eased its tensions with Pakistan, its participation in a security association could not be envisaged.

As it happened, India failed to follow these recommendations. When the ARF was constituted in July 1994, New Delhi seemed to have once again let it be known informally that it wished to be a member.[87] Since this move did not elicit any response, India once again raised the hypothesis of its membership in the ARF in end 1994-beginning 1995, a suggestion that was officially rejected by the ASEAN, this time round. This development harmed India's image by placing the ASEAN's categorical refusal on the debit side. According to the diplomat J.N. Dixit, this diplomatic error was not even the outcome of political stubbornness in the eagerness to become an ARF member, but the ill-advised result of a communication gap between different levels of India's diplomatic hierarchy. Informed about the opinion of the ASEAN's decision-makers, Prime Minister Rao had in fact advocated that India refrain from evoking its candidature to the ARF in any way whatsoever during the January 1994 sectoral dialogues. Thus, while the higher-ups in the Indian decision-making process had intended to submit to the ASEAN's diplomatic requirements, there seems to have been a lack of coordination with their diplomats, who, on their part, had prepared a request for membership to the ARF.[88] Despite these errors, New Delhi gradually learned to maintain a certain distance, which was basically what the ASEAN expected from it. The argument of a counterbalance to China was not put forward—at least at the official level. The mistrust cultivated by the Indian political and military leadership *vis-à-vis* Beijing finally led them to believe that it would be better to continue to engage their neighbour rather than aspire to contain it. It was also in the interests of its bilateral relationship with China that New Delhi did not play the counterweight card too ostensibly. This seemed an even wiser choice as it was closer to the approach adopted by the ASEAN and even allowed a rapprochement with the Association. It explains why New Delhi adopted a discrete diplomatic mode and kept a low profile in South-East Asia. Thus, ASEAN and India seemed quite determined not to give the impression of forming a coalition against China.[89]

AN INDO-ASEAN RAPPROCHEMENT IN REACTION TO THE SINO-BURMESE COMPLICITY

Located in the tri-junction of the Indian subcontinent, China and South-East Asia, it would be an understatement to say that Myanmar assumed crucial strategic importance.[90] In India's strategic memory, Burma's invasion by a hostile power meant that an imminent threat weighed over national security. When Japan invaded Myanmar in 1942, India understood that this aggressor was capable of attacking its land frontiers, carrying out air raids on its strategic and military centres, and affecting navigation in the Bay of Bengal. As far back as in 1944, a diplomat, K.M. Panikkar, had drawn attention to Myanmar's strategic importance: 'The defence of Myanmar in fact is the defence of India and it is India's primary concern no less than Burma's to see that its frontiers remain inviolate. In fact, no responsibility can be considered too heavy for India when it comes to the question of defending Burma.'[91]

In India's traditional worldview, Myanmar was considered an immediate neighbour, part of the first concentric circle. Most analyses conducted by the Indian diplomacy and the Ministry of External Affairs' annual reports testify to this fact, because in all these, relations with Myanmar were considered on the same footing as those with other neighbouring countries of South Asia, like Bhutan, Nepal, Bangladesh, Sri Lanka, the Maldives and Pakistan. Thus, ties with Rangoon were included in the South Asian diplomatic sphere rather than being discussed in the chapter on South-East Asia.

Prior to the 1990s, New Delhi had strongly supported the Burmese pro-democracy movement, which had put it on a bad footing with Rangoon's military junta.[92] Between 1988 and 1991, India more than once denounced, with great virulence, the measures of repression enforced by the Burmese state. The then Minister of External Affairs, P.V. Narasimha Rao, even defended an open policy of welcoming Burmese refugees and of permitting several groups of pro-democracy students to establish themselves in India. The All India Radio had, moreover, experienced great popularity in Myanmar for its on the field reporting and for its proclaimed sympathy for the democratic movement.[93] But the criticism that it had indulged in, had greatly irritated the junta in power. The regime had counter-attacked through its controlled press by denouncing the stain brought on by the Indians on Burmese culture and history.[94] From the end of 1991 onwards, New Delhi became aware that it could not afford to alienate itself from Rangoon's military regime and as a consequence, strove for more pragmatism. In August 1992, Myanmar's Vice-Minister of External Affairs visited Delhi, on the Indian government's invitation. In 1993, India engaged in a 'constructive dialogue' with the government in power, without completely turning its back on the pro-democracy dissidents. An Indian trade delegation comprising government officials and businessmen visited the country.[95] In his capacity as Permanent Secretary of External Affairs, J.N. Dixit travelled to Rangoon to revive diplomatic and trade relations, in March–April 1993. Then in 1994, the Home Secretaries of both countries started to hold regular consultations. In February 1995, the Commerce Minister, P. Chidambaram, inaugurated the first Indian trade show in Myanmar. When this trade show was held for the second time in the Burmese capital in November 1997, India offered the government in Rangoon a credit line of USD 10 million to promote economic cooperation and bilateral trade. From an economic approach, India later moved over to decisions of a political nature. In late 1997, the Indian government disallowed the pro-democratic party of the national coalition government of the Burmese Union,[96] led by Aung Suu Kyi, from opening an office in Delhi.

An important factor in New Delhi's new posture was that the internal situation in Myanmar had direct repercussions on India's security. Indeed, quite often, insurgent movements that troubled the Indian north-eastern states had their rearguard in Myanmar. Rebel groups on both sides of the border were ethnically very close to each other and helped each other in their respective struggles against the Indian and Burmese states. Thus, different Naga rebel groups infiltrated into Myanmar. Indian intelligence agencies even claimed that, since 1986, the United Liberation Front of Assam had been sending its cadres for training to the headquarters of the National Socialist Council of Nagaland (Khaplang), which were based in Myanmar. All things considered, it seemed that a confrontation took place between New Delhi and Rangoon for a certain period, through their insurrectionist groups. For several years, New Delhi suspected the Junta of giving refuge to rebel group camps on its territory, in retaliation for the support that it provided Burmese democratic factions.[97] On its part, India offered help to the Kachin Liberation Army, which was fighting Rangoon from the north of the country. In compensation for this support, the Kachins began to train and equip the Kuki and Chin tribes in the jungles of Manipur, so that they could fight Naga rebels and other insurrectionary groups opposed to New Delhi. India also supported the Chin people, who were also fighting for their independence against Rangoon. The SLORC (State Law and Order Restoration Council) counter-attacked by increasing its aid to insurgents such as the Nagaland National Socialist Council and the Manipur Liberation Army.[98]

The vulnerability of India's north-eastern states was aggravated by the fact that this region was becoming a hub for illegal trade in narcotics and arms. It would be an understatement to say that the Burmese border was porous and led to drug trafficking as well as the proliferation of small arms. Once again, New Delhi suspected the SLORC of having stricken deals with rebel groups to allow drug trafficking through its north-eastern territories. On this account, India feared that narcotic flows would get redirected to its frontiers from the golden triangle.[99] Manipur had apparently already noted an increasing number of heroine-dependency cases. The unchecked movement of refugees to the states of Nagaland and Arunachal Pradesh caused further difficulties in these tense areas. Finally, in the early 1990s, Indo-Burmese relations worsened due to the ties that Pakistan was supposed to maintain with the SLORC. Although this was not confirmed, several reports spoke of the military aid Pakistan had provided. In any event, an exchange of military missions had definitely taken place.

While the situation in the north-east took on the scale of a national security issue in the early 1990s, New Delhi undertook to establish a collaborative relationship with the Burmese Junta as far as law and order was concerned. In March 1993, the two states signed a cooperation agreement to fight against drug trafficking. On its part, the SLORC seemed to have reduced its assistance to the Nagas in the north of its territory. The two states signed a cooperation agreement on 21 January 1994 on the surveillance of transborder flows. The objective of this collaboration was to suppress drug trafficking and smuggling activities and, at the same time, promote trade. Negotiations for the agreement took place between the Myanmar Minister of Foreign Affairs and the Indian Ministers of External Affairs, Trade and Home Affairs.[100] The same year, Khin Nyunt, the SLORC strongman, personally visited India. In May 1994, the Indian Army Chief, General B.C. Joshi, made a highly publicized visit to Myanmar to discuss bilateral relations and security issues. A direct consequence of this visit was that authorities in Rangoon seemed to close their eyes to incursions of Indian troops into Burmese territory in pursuit of Naga rebels, a little later on in 1994.[101] In end 1994–early 1995, India and Myanmar held a strategic dialogue at the request of the SLORC itself.

India's policy of appeasement *vis-à-vis* Myanmar was also the outcome of mounting concerns in the face of Chinese infiltrations into that country. Indeed, while relations with New Delhi continued to deteriorate during the 1980s, Rangoon entered a *de facto* alliance with Beijing. In 1988, an agreement was concluded between the two states to legalize bilateral trade, which rose substantially with time. Transportation infrastructure developed on both sides of the border to facilitate traffic and Chinese consumer products invaded the Burmese market, to the detriment of those from Thailand.[102] China's interest in Myanmar can be better understood from a historical perspective. Over the centuries, Myanmar gave the south-western Chinese provinces commercial access to the Indian Ocean. Therefore, Beijing's successive regimes always wished to maintain this privilege. For south China, particularly its Yunan province, the 'Burma route' continued to offer a way of taking part in the economic regionalization of South-East Asia.[103] Consequently, a technical and economic cooperation agreement was signed in 1991, which saw China provide Myanmar with massive aid for civil infrastructural projects, bridges, roads, railway lines and port facilities. Thus, China's most immediate objectives seemed to be economic, and the investment in the development of the land route to Myanmar reflected its desire to access South Asian markets.

However, Indian observers continued to be concerned by the intensification of Sino-Burmese defence cooperation. The effects of this cooperation could be seen in the several contacts between high officials of Myanmar and China after 1989. The Chinese Minister of Foreign Affairs, Qian Qichen, himself visited Rangoon in 1993. After 1988, the year when international sanctions were imposed on the Junta, the major share of Myanmar's arms and military equipment came from China. Neither the exact value of these weapons nor any details of acquisitions were available, but these purchases were apparently negotiated at favourable terms for SLORC. According to some estimates, China supplied arms worth over USD 1.5 billion, including combat aircraft, maritime patrol vessels, heavy artillery, tanks and anti-aircraft missiles since 1990. Myanmar's armed forces ballooned from 186,000 men in 1988 to 300,000 in 1992. Chinese arms seemed to have been deployed primarily along the Indo-Burmese border, apart from the transfer of battalions initially intended to fight communist rebellion in the north-east of the country. According to the expert, P. Stobdan, the number of Burmese battalions along the Indian and Bangladeshi borders rose from five in 1988 to thirty-two in 1992.[104] From mid-1992 onward, several international defence reviews put forward the view that Rangoon seemed to have accepted a Chinese offer to build a deep water port on Hainggyi Island, at the mouth of the river Bassein, which flows into the Bay of Bengal. Different versions of the story were heard, some claiming that the port could be used to facilitate Chinese trade flows into the Indian Ocean, an objective constantly sought by successive regimes in Beijing, while other more alarmist versions cited the construction of a major naval base capable of providing fuel and maintenance equipment for Chinese naval ships. China also seemed to be involved in the construction of maritime reconnaissance facilities in the Coco Islands. Located south-west of the Burmese coastline, these islands were quite close to the Indian territories of the Andaman and Nicobar Islands and just 40 km away from the Indo-Burmese maritime border. Further, the hypothesis according to which the Chinese had built a radar station—indeed a modern, high-capacity information transmitting station—did not fail to arouse great concern within the Indian diplomatic and military circles. New Delhi feared that China would be able to keep its intermediate range ballistic missile equipment situated between Orissa and the Andaman Islands under surveillance—or perhaps its maritime routes through the Andaman Sea and the Malacca Strait. The Burmese regime was heavily indebted to China for the aid it had been provided with. Consequently, Beijing would have the means to exert massive pressure on Rangoon in the years to come.

All these assertions were not necessarily proven, but the fact that India took them so seriously gives an idea of the extent of the suspicion and fear that the Sino-Burmese rapprochement inspired. Unable to earn Rangoon's favours, New Delhi at least wanted Myanmar to serve as a buffer zone with China. The mounting influence of Beijing in this area, whose neutrality was essential, thus appeared very worrying for Indian security. Chinese and Burmese attempts at clarification failed to appease India's speculations. China may have tried to reassure New Delhi when it declared that it had no plans to set-up a naval base on the Hainggyi or Coco Islands and the SLORC may have asserted that suspicions of Chinese military bases in Myanmar were unfounded, but in vain. From the Indian perspective, China was henceforth a threat in the north as well as in the south of the territory. In other words, New Delhi, which tended to consider the Indian Ocean as its own preserve, took very seriously the prospects of a potential rivalry with China in this sphere of influence. In this regard, the Andaman and Nicobar archipelago acquired strategic importance of the first order in India's calculations. Thus, in early 1994, the government offered to set-up an aerial enclosure in the Andaman and Nicobar Islands so that the coast guard could improve its aerial surveillance.[105] Some plans also provided for the introduction of a large number of aircraft and maritime patrol vessels to prevent illegal poaching by foreign trawlers. In this connection, Indian coast guards intercepted three Chinese trawlers flying the Burmese flag in the Andaman Sea in August 1994. They were unpleasantly surprised to note that these boats had been equipped with sophisticated radio equipment.[106] This incident, which was highly commented upon in India, convinced experts that Beijing was seeking to establish a surveillance mechanism of India's naval capabilities, perhaps even to secure a presence for itself in the Indian Ocean. In December 1994, the leaders of the Military Staff Committees advised the government to take note of the increase in Chinese military activities in the Bay of Bengal, which according to them was an outcome of the closer military cooperation between China and Myanmar.[107] The Ministry of Defence's annual report for the year 1994–5 also mentioned that Beijing was building a road network linking its border towns with ports and main railway junctions in Myanmar.[108]

While Myanmar was perceived as a factor of instability in South Asia, the same was also true for South-East Asia. In this regard, a certain convergence of views took place between India and the ASEAN on the nature of the situation in Myanmar, which was considered a cause for concern. Indeed, since 1988, all Burma's neighbouring countries had had to deal with an influx of refugees at their borders. In Thailand, in India as well as in Bangladesh, Laos and China, the presence of these refugees created local pockets of tension. From a geostrategic perspective and due to its close ties with Myanmar, China was suspected of wanting to exert greater influence in South and South-East Asia, either directly or through Rangoon. After all, the People's Republic of China had three fleets—in the 'northern sea' (Yellow Sea), 'eastern sea' (East China Sea) and 'southern sea' (South China Sea) respectively. Its immense maritime front provided it an incomparable influence on East Asia. But access to the Bay of Bengal, indeed a presence in its waters, would add a definitive asset to its seafaring might. It would potentially enable it keep a tight hold over peninsular South-East Asia and gain access to the Malacca Strait. No matter how questionable, these hypotheses were of great concern to many South-East Asian states.

Among the ASEAN members, Thailand was one of the states that was the most concerned with China's growing influence in Myanmar, a country with which it shared a long border. First and foremost, China's economic predominance in Myanmar resulted in the loss of the Burmese market for the Thai industries.[109] Furthermore, Bangkok took a dim view of China's military assistance to its neighbour, which had always been viewed suspiciously. Thus, *The Defence of Thailand 1994*, the first White Paper ever published by the Thai Ministry of Defence, described Myanmar as 'strategically important', considering it on the same footing as Vietnam, i.e. with a certain degree of suspicion.[110] The document took note of China's military assistance and observed that Rangoon owned an increasing number of combat aircrafts, tanks and rocket launch vehicles, while its naval forces allowed it to operate along the Tenassarim coastline for the protection of oil and gas drilling platforms built by foreign investors. *Defence 1994* concluded that the Burmese armed forces could grow into a formidable power, with their acquisition of new arms. The document finally affirmed that uncertainty along the Thai borders could pose a crucial security problem.

Having perceived Bangkok's concerns fairly early, New Delhi seemed to have tried to play the situation to its advantage. Indeed, on his April 1993 visit to Thailand, Prime Minister Rao apparently raised the issue of China's involvement in Myanmar, thereby implying to his interlocutor, Chuan Leepkai, that India could take on a strategic, counterbalancing role—a proposal that was quite bold, in fact, given the fact that Thailand had been traditionally close to Beijing.[111] In any event, India's diplomatic attempts showed that it was totally in New Delhi's interest to highlight, if not exaggerate, China's infiltrations in Myanmar. In fact, the Indian political and military leadership greatly emphasized the risks and threats that the Myanmar situation represented, as this helped them stress the strategic importance of their country on the Asian chessboard. Thus, during his visit to Delhi in November 1993, the Thai Minister of Foreign Affairs, Prasang Soonsiri, asserted that he considered that India could play a 'balancing role' in the new Asian order, along with China, Japan and other dominant powers.[112] Besides, the two states initiated paramilitary cooperation—involving, in particular, an exchange of information with regard to the movements of criminals, terrorists, arms and drugs' traffickers—so as to re-establish law and order in the territories bordering Myanmar.

In the face of the growing infiltration into Myanmar by China, the ASEAN undertook to take Rangoon into the South-East Asian orbit, both in the economic and political fields. The Indonesian Minister of Foreign Affairs, Ali Alatas, visited Myanmar in February 1994, followed by Singapore's Prime Minister Goh Chok Tong, in April 1994. In July 1994, the ASEAN leaders indicated that they intended to extend their regional horizon to Myanmar: in a significant gesture, they invited Rangoon to attend the ASEAN Foreign Ministers' summit, as well as ARF sessions. Just before the financial crisis erupted in 1997, Singapore and Thailand had become Myanmar's primary partners, along with China. The South-East Asian economies also raised themselves to the rank of major foreign investors in the country. India, on its part, upheld Myanmar's gradual integration in the ASEAN. Indeed, New Delhi preferred to see Rangoon move closer to South-East Asia, rather than have a neighbour that was under the Chinese heel.[113] India, henceforth, tended to align itself with the ASEAN policy. Like the Association, India applied itself to engaging in relations with Myanmar's military regime, contrary to the Western position requiring the country's isolation. During its twenty-ninth ministerial summit in July 1996, the ASEAN welcomed the representative of Rangoon's military regime as an esteemed guest and a future member. India largely made the most of this event by emphasizing that, thanks to Myanmar's admission, it would henceforth share a land boundary with the ASEAN. Not content with congratulating Rangoon's for its entry into the association, Indian diplomacy concluded that such a development could only be favourable to its economic relations with South-East Asia. At the 1997 post-ministerial conferences, Finance Minister P. Chidambaram clearly reaffirmed that India intended to develop close links with Myanmar, in order to 'give a new dimension' to Indo-ASEAN relations.[114] Indeed in 1999, the government officially defined its policy with regard to Myanmar as that of 'constructive engagement', thereby modelling it on that of the ASEAN.[115]

If India supported ASEAN's policy of constructive engagement in the early 1990s, it was also because it knew that despite the improvement in its relationship with Rangoon, it would never be able to compete against Beijing's influence or that of South-East Asian capitals on the SLORC. The perceptions that the Burmese had with regard to their Indian neighbour suffered from many racial prejudices, to which were added numerous historical differences.[116] Although Myanmar was part of the British Empire and had been governed from Calcutta, relations between the two countries had never been very cordial. In the 1980s, the Junta had further tarnished India's image, in retaliation for the assistance New Delhi had been providing to pro-democracy movements. A number of articles appeared in the 'controlled' press, resurrecting the 'grime' that the Indian civilization had inflicted on the Burmese culture. The Burmese elite were heavily riddled with a general antipathy towards India, a state that had violated the fundamental principle of non-intervention in the internal affairs of another state.

No matter the degree of hostility, New Delhi had to compromise more than ever with the SLORC, since the handling of the Burmese issue was an essential link in its Look East policy. Stobdan, an expert on Myanmar working for IDSA, thus explained the regional dimension of Indo-Burmese ties: 'Relations with Myanmar cannot just be a bilateral affair—rather it should be seen as a matter of regional security and India's long-term interest in South-East Asia.'[117] The alternative scenarios could be expressed in the following words: prosperous commercial links with Rangoon would provide New Delhi and its north-eastern states with an opening to South-East Asia, an opening that would be unique and irreplaceable, since it would be by land. On the other hand, the deterioration of its ties with Rangoon could lose it the sympathetic attitude of the ASEAN states, since the Association was determined to give Myanmar a new image. New Delhi would thus find itself excluded from a regional sub-system that was increasingly defined by triangular interactions between Rangoon, the ASEAN and Beijing.

As for the ASEAN states, they had started to invest in the country ever since it opened up, in September 1988. And emulating Thailand and Singapore, New Delhi intensified its initiatives to develop trade flows with Myanmar. In late April 1998, the Home Secretary, B.P. Singh undertook a two-day visit to Rangoon, in the framework of the bilateral consultations established between the two countries since 1994. New Delhi informed its counterparts of its desire to open a second trade point at Champa-Rih, along the boundary of the Indian state of Mizoram. The first trade point had been opened at Moreh-Tamu, in 1995, in the Indian state of Manipur. A third point of entry was likewise considered from the state of Nagaland.[118] An additional factor was that New Delhi also became aware of the immense resources possessed by its neighbour, notably in oil and natural gas. The re-orientation of the Indian diplomacy therefore was also based on well-calculated economic interests.

To complete the analysis of the geostrategic stakes in Myanmar, the Burmese authorities' room for manoeuvre also needs to be considered. From the SLORC's perspective, its alliance with China would enable it to take advantage of special regional treatment, especially by states that had initially been over-critical, such as India. Despite the assistance and gestures of friendships it had received over the years, the SLORC observed China's long-term ambitions with a great deal of mistrust and suspicion. Most members of the Burmese military hierarchy had not forgotten that until 1988, Beijing had supported the Communist Party of Burma, against which they had been fighting. In addition, Burmese military leaders were quite pernickety as far as issues of sovereignty and national independence were concerned. It would therefore be quite problematic for them to allow China to establish military bases on their territory. At the same time, the SLORC's indebtedness *vis-à-vis* China was such that the provision of bases or equipment could be a means of paying it off.[119] In any event, it was rather with the ASEAN that the SLORC saw its future and it showed a fair amount of interest in the economic and political development models proposed by the Association. Therefore, it would be logical that the SLORC's long-term objective would be to have more balanced relations with its different neighbours—China, but also India and the ASEAN.

SOUTH ASIA OR SOUTHERN ASIA?

The latent rivalry between India and China in Asia in general, and in Myanmar in particular, called into question the theoretical relevance of the concept of South Asia as an analytical grid that made it possible to define the issues affecting India's security. Thus, since the early 1990s, a few eminent Indian specialists tended to place New Delhi's strategic concerns within the broader framework of Southern Asia. It must be noted straightaway that the concept did have any precise meaning. American experts often had the propensity to use the expressions 'South Asia' and 'Southern Asia' indifferently.[120] The situation was, of course, different for India. The use of the concept of Southern Asia reflected different aspects of the nation's security concerns. In particular, it revealed the growing importance of the Burmese issue on the eastern side. It was also the corollary of the discourse on India's nuclear policy, which was essentially related to China. Finally, it went along with a certain tendency New Delhi had to consider itself as China's counterweight in Asia. That South Asia was deemed too narrow and limited a geopolitical unit to take account of India's strategic problems was not a new development in itself. But this argument seemed to gain increasingly gain credit in the 1990s. Expectedly, it was the strategic experts focussed on India's maritime issues who were the first to denounce the analytical inadequacy of the concept of South Asia. Hence, Rahul Roy-Chaudhury recommended that India's strategic horizons be expanded, above all to assess the scale of the challenges that China posed to regional security. No analytical grid could be commensurate with India's security issues simply by pasting Afghanistan and Myanmar as attachments to the concept of South Asia, as some did from time to time. China definitely had to be included in the regional vision of India's security, so much so that according to Roy-Chaudhury, the Indian Ocean's north-eastern region could become a zone of maritime rivalry between India and China.

Air Commodore Jasjit Singh of the Indian Air Force also defended the concept of Southern Asia, because, as he remarked, South Asia did not take into account the existence of four of India's border states, i.e. China, Myanmar, Thailand and Indonesia.[121] Jasjit Singh provided an extensive definition of the concept of Southern Asia, which covered China, the Central Asian states, Iran, Afghanistan, the countries of South Asia, Myanmar, Thailand, Malaysia, Indonesia and Singapore, apart from the waters of the northern Indian Ocean and the Persian Gulf.[122] Southern Asia, as defined by Jasjit Singh, thus appeared to be an improbable survival of Nehru's Eastern Federation of the pre-Independence years. With the same utopian touch, Jasjit Singh further proposed that the region's states undertake a process of confidence-building measures. The principle of mutual and equal security, which was the subject of a Sino-Indian agreement, could even form the basis of a cooperative regional approach, along with the five principles of peaceful co-existence.[123] While certain Indian experts were quite enamoured of the concept of Southern Asia, the fact remained that it was quite vague. However, whatever its version, one of the obvious merits of this concept was that it covered the overlapping zones between South Asia and South-East Asia, two strategic complexes that were usually analysed separately. This loose unit also made it possible to include India in the security balance in South-East Asia, while refocusing ASEAN's strategic position between the Asia-Pacific and the Indian Ocean. But above all, the emergence of the concept of Southern Asia in the early 1990s revealed the desire of many Indians to free their nation of a strictly subcontinental context. At the same time, the process of formulating India's foreign policy had not yet completely digested the upheavals that had occurred on the international scene. Indian political and academic circles had been theoretically experimenting with the various strategic perspectives that their country could espouse. Because of this, New Delhi was still beset with certain indecisiveness as far as its potential role in Asia was concerned.[124]

NOTES

1. The Soviet presence in the Asia-Pacific region began to shrink fairly fast at the end of the 1980s. In December 1989, Moscow started to withdraw from Vietnam's Cam Ranh Bay base.
2. Chandra Jeshurun, ed., *China-India-Japan and the Security of South-East Asia*, Singapore: ISEAS, 1993.
3. *The Straits Times*, 26 February 1990 (cited in Kripa Sridharan,.*The ASEAN Region in India's Foreign Policy*, Aldershot, England: Darmonth Pub. Co., 1996, 1997, p. 176).
4. *Asian Recorder*, 21–7 May 1990 (cited in Sridharan, *The ASEAN Region* p. 174).
5. Ramesh Thakur and Carlyle A. Thayer, *Soviet Relations with India and Vietnam*, London: Macmillan, 1992, p. 256.
6. G.V.C. Naidu, 'Post-Cold War Pacific Asian Security: Indian Perceptions and Options', IDSA, *Delhi Papers*, no. 1, September 1994, p. 27.
7. *Indian Recorder*, 11–17 June 1994. The United States was the world's primary arms exporter.
8. S. Gordon S., *India's Rise to Power: In the Twentieth Century and Beyond*, New York: St Martin's Press, 1995, p. 331.
9. *USI Journal* (Delhi) 121, no. 504, April–June 1991 (cited in n. 15 of G. Tanham, 'Indian Strategic Culture', *Washington Quarterly*, Winter 1992).
10. Gregory Copley, 'South Asia: Zone of the New Great Powers', *Defence and Foreign Affairs*, 17, May–June 1989, p. 10 (cited in R. Thakur and C.A. Thayer, *Soviet Relations with India and Vietnam*, p. 91).
11. Gordon, 'Indian and South-East Asia: A Renaissance in Relations?', in S. Gordon and S. Henningham, ed., *India Looks East: An Emerging Power and its Asia-Pacific Neighbours*, p. 219.
12. But the plan to set-up a base on Great Nicobar Island was finally stopped, seemingly on financial grounds. Mohammed Ayoob, *India and South-East Asia: Indian Perceptions and Policies*, Singapore: ISEAS & Routledge, 1990, p. 43.
13. G.V.C. Naidu, 'India, ASEAN and the ARF', *Strategic Analysis*, vol. 19, no. 6, September 1996, pp. 851–62.
14. Cited in Dick Wilson, 'The Asian Security Management Challenge: A Future "Trinity" of China, Japan and India', *RGICS Paper*, no. 10, 1994.
15. Tanham went as far as to assert that India did not really have any strategic culture (G. Tanham, 'Indian Strategic Culture', pp. 129–42).
16. Gordon, *India's Rise to Power*, pp. 3, 5–8; R. Roy-Chaudhury, 'India's Security Policy', *Strategic Analysis*, May 1996, p. 183.
17. Lt. Gen. (Rtd) A. Hasnan Habib, 'Southeast Asian Perceptions of India's

Strategic Development: An Indonesian View', in Ross Babbage and Sandy Gordon, *India's Strategic Future: Regional State or Global Power?* London: Macmillan, 1992, pp. 107–22. The Japanese naval programme had been designed to protect the sea lanes in the South China Sea.

18. Sridharan, *The ASEAN Region*, pp. 6, 9.
19. Gordon, *India's Rise to Power*, p. 69. According to Gordon, seventy per cent of the main weapons of the Indian Air Force and 75 to 80 per cent of those of the Navy were of Soviet origin.
20. The country's priorities were: (1) the Commonwealth of Independent States, (2) arms control and international security, (3) economic reforms, (4) the United States, (5) Europe, (6) the Asia-Pacific region, (7) the Near East and South Asia, (8) the North-East, (9) Africa, and Latin America. Vinay Shukla, 'Russia in South Asia: A View From India', Gennady Chuffrin, ed., *Russia and Asia: The Emerging Security Agenda*, Stockholm: SIPRI, and Oxford University Press, 1999, pp. 249–51.
21. *Asian Defence Journal*, September 1990, p. 108 (cited in Thakur and Thayer, *Soviet Relations with India and Vietnam*, p. 254).
22. India was one of the eighteen nations that participated in the Paris Conference on Cambodia that ended on 23 October 1991 with the signing of a peace treaty, which was supposed to put an end to thirteen years of war. A conference on Cambodia bringing together thirty-two nations took place in Tokyo on 22 June 1992. India was chosen as the Co-Chairman of the Control Commission for this conference, to assist UNTAC in enforcing the peace agreements.
23. Chintamani Mahapatra, 'Indo-American Relations after the Cold War', *Asian Strategic Review 1995–6*, New Delhi: IDSA, 1996, p. 241.
24. Ravinder Pal Singh, ed., *Arms Procurement Decision Making*, vol. 1, Stockholm: SIPRI and Oxford University Press, 1998, p. 1325.
25. Limaye, 'The Japan-India Encounter'.
26. K.V. Kesavan, 'India and Japan', Foreign Service Institute, *Indian Foreign Policy*, pp. 327–8.
27. MEA, *Annual Report 1993–4*, p. 21.
28. Limaye, 'Sushi and Samosas' in Gordon and Henningham, eds., *India Looks East*, p. 183.
29. Thus, the volume of bilateral trade rose from 0.2 billion dollars in 1988 to 1.16 billion in 1995. C.V. Ranganathan, 'India–China Relations—Retrospect and Prospects', Foreign Service Institute, *Indian Foreign Policy, Agenda for the 21st Country*, vol. I, p. 244.
30. Jasjit Singh, 'Future of Sino-Indian Relations', *Strategic Analysis*, March 1994, p. 1517.
31. This sale had the approval of the International Atomic Energy Agency. Tarapur had not been receiving its supplies since October 1993, as India had rejected the IAEA's proposal for inspection of its nuclear equipment. *Indian Recorder*, 5–11 February 1995.

32. R. Roy-Chaudhury, 'The Role of Naval Diplomacy in India's Foreign Policy', in Foreign Service Institute, *Indian Foreign Policy*, vol. 2, pp. 194–206.
33. During this long period, the Indian Navy contented itself with conducting joint exercises with Australia and New Zealand in 1977, and with Indonesian naval warships off the coast of Surabaya in 1989. R. Roy-Chaudhury, *Sea Power and Indian Security*, London: Brassey, p. 201.
34. Roy-Chaudhury, 'The Role of Naval Diplomacy in India's Foreign Policy', *FSI*, p. 197.
35. Gordon, *India's Rise to Power*, pp. 294–5.
36. (r)MDBU-The Star(r)MDNM-, 28 February 1992 (quoted during the seminar jointly organized by CSH and ISEAS on the theme 'ASEAN-India Relations', 18–19 September 2000, Singapore.
37. *Indian Recorder*, 26 February–4 March 1994.
38. Shekhar Gupta, 'India Redefines Its Role', London: IISS/Oxford University Press, *Adelphi Paper*, no. 293, 1995, p. 63.
39. *FEER*, 22 September 1994, pp. 10, 17.
40. Roy-Chaudhury, *Sea Power and Indian Security*, pp. 124–5. George Tanham supported the opposite view.
41. Sridharan, *The ASEAN Region in India's Foreign Policy*, p. 178.
42. Roy-Chaudhury, *Sea Power and Indian Security*, pp. 145, 185–6. In 1992–3, they only accounted for 2.7 per cent of the GNP. They dropped to 2.4 per cent in 1993–4, before going up marginally to 2.5 per cent in 1994–5. SIPRI's figures on India's military expenditure were even more modest: from 3.1 per cent of the GNP in 1988, they seemed to have dropped to 2.5 per cent in 1991 and had never crossed this threshold since then. http://www.sipri.org
43. J. Singh, 'An Indian Perspective', Gordon and Henningham, eds., *India Looks East*, p. 55.
44. The total government expenditure includes government resources spent by state governments, which do not include the financial costs of defence. The defence share in the central government's expenditure is different. State government resources are not taken into account and, therefore, it is not a very precise or revealing rate. In 1987–8, the rate was seventeen per cent; in 1993–4, it was fifteen per cent.
45. Sandy Gordon, 'Indian Defence Spending: Treading Water in the Fiscal Deep', *Asian Survey*, vol. 32, no. 10, October 1992, pp. 937–9.
46. Roy-Chaudhury, 'The Indian Navy: Past, Present, and Future', *Asian Strategic Review 1995–6*, New Delhi: IDSA, 1996, p. 99.
47. G.V.C. Naidu, 'Navies of Asian Major Powers and Security of South-East Asia', *Strategic Analysis*, vol. 19, no. 12, March 1997, p. 1664.
48. Roy-Chaudhury, 'The Indian Navy: Past, Present, and Future', *Asian Strategic Review 1995–6*, New Delhi IDSA, 1996, pp. 99, 113.

49. Gupta 'India Redefines its Role', p. 38.
50. Gordon, *India's Rise to Power*, pp. 137, 224, 330.
51. Varun Sahni, 'Just Another Big Country', in George K. Tanham, K.P. Bajpai and A. Mattoo, *Securing India*, p. 162.
52. Sahni, 'India as a Global Power', *Indian Foreign Policy*, p. 34.
53. Ibid., p. 25; S. Mansingh, 'India as a Global Power: Capacity, Opportunity and Strategy', Foreign Service Institute, *Indian Foreign Policy*, pp. 48–51.
54. Boisseau du Rocher, *L'ASEAN et la Construction Régionale en Asie du Sud-Est*, p. 269.
55. Dixit, *My South Block Years*, p. 266.
56. M. Leifer, *The ASEAN Regional Forum: Extending ASEAN's Model of Reginal Security,* London: IISS Oxford Univesity Press, Adelphi Paper no. 302, July 1996, p. 21; Jusuf Wanandi, 'Asia-Pacific Security Forums: Rationale and Options from the ASEAN Perspective', in D. Ball, R.L. Grant and J. Wanandi, *Security Cooperation in the Asia-Pacific Region*, Washington, D.C.: Center for Strategic and International Studies, vol. XV, no. 5, Significant Issues Series, 1993, pp. 10–12.
57. Udai Bhanu Singh, 'Growth of Military Power in South-East Asia', *Asian Strategic Review, 1994–5*, New Delhi: IDSA, 1995, pp. 311–49.
58. G.V.C. Naidu, 'Navies of Asian Major Powers and Security of South-East Asia', *Strategic Analysis*, vol. XIX, no. 9, December 1996, pp. 1334–7.
59. Naidu, 'Navies of Asian Major Powers and Security of South-East Asia', *Strategic Analysis*, vol. XIX, no. 12, March 1997, pp. 1660–4.
60. Roy-Chaudhury, 'The Limits to Naval Expansion', in Tanham, Bajpai and Mattoo, eds., *Security India: Strategic Thought and Practice in an Emerging Power*, New Delhi: Manohar, 1996, p. 193; Tanham, 'Indian Strategic Culture', p. 134.
61. Ranganathan, 'India-China Relations—Retrospect and Prospects', *FSI*, p. 250.
62. In 1991 Beijing ordered 24 Sukhoi Su-27SK in a USD 700 million contract. In 1995, China again purchased 24 Sukhoi Su-27SK in a USD 2.2 billion contract. Finally, in 1996, according to a SIPRI estimate, Beijing seemed to have decided to equip itself with almost 200 Sukhoi Su-27SK, after obtaining a license from Russian manufacturers for assembling them. G. Chuffrin, *Russia and Asia: The Emerging Security Agenda*, Stockholm: SIPRI and Oxford University Press, 1999, pp. 506–7, < http://www.sipri.se/projects/armstrade/atmethods.html>.
63. Jasjit Singh, 'Trends in Defence Expenditure', *Asian Strategic Review*, 1995–6, New Delhi: IDSA, 1996, pp. 31, 41.
64. J. Mohan Malik, 'Sino-Indian Relations and India's Eastern Strategy', in S. Gordon and S. Henningham, ed., *India Looks East*, pp. 125–6.

65. Jasjit Singh, 'Trends in Defence Expenditure', *Asian Strategic Review* 1995–6, p. 30.
66. Thus, since 1991, Pakistan has acquired more than fifty short-range ballistic missiles M-11 of Chinese origin. It has also proceeded with the deployment of eighteen short-range ballistic missiles Hatf-1 and Hatf-11, which were of indigenous manufacture, but with Chinese technology. Roy-Chaudhury, 'India's Security Policy', *Strategic Analysis*, May 1996, p. 186.
67. J.M. Malik, 'Sino-Indian Relations and India's Eastern Strategy', in Gordon and Henningham, eds., *India Looks East*, p. 147.
68. *Indian Recorder*, 7–13 May 1995.
69. J. Singh, 'Future of Sino-Indian Relations', *Strategic Analysis*, March 1994, p. 1514.
70. Rear Admiral Raja Menon, *A Nuclear Strategy for India*, New Delhi: Sage, 2000, p. 29.
71. Mahapatra, 'Indo-American Relations after the Cold War', *Asian Strategic Review 1995–6*, p. 246.
72. George K. Tanham, 'Indian Strategic Concerns in the 1990s', *RGICS Paper*, no. 28, 1995, p. 17.
73. Roy-Chaudhury, *Sea Power and Indian Security*, p. 98.
74. Jasjit Singh, 'Future of Sino-Indian Relations', *Strategic Analysis*, March 1994, p. 1517.
75. Tensions between China and Vietnam reached a peak in July 1994 with regard to oil drilling rights in the Tu Chinh zone, in the South China Sea, an area that was precisely the subject of a dispute between the two states. In February 1995, the South-East Asian states learnt that Chinese naval forces had installed equipment on the Mischief Reef, which was unoccupied in the Spratly Islands. Such an act amounted to a provocation for Vietnam and the Philippines, which also had claims on the maritime territory. In March 1995, China did not hesitate to proceed with intimidating military manoeuvres in the Taiwan Strait, while elections were being held in the island. The United States had to deploy their naval forces to thwart Chinese presence.
76. Boisseau du Rocher, *L'ASEAN et la Construction Régionale en Asie du Sud-Est*, p. 219.
77. Acharya, 'Ideas, Identity and Institution-building', *The Pacific Review*, pp. 319–46.
78. Kishore Mahbubani, 'The Pacific Impulse', in *Can Asians Think*?, Singapore: Times Book, 1998, pp. 115–37.
79. Gerald Segal, '"Asianism" and Asian Security', *The National Interest*, Winter 1995–6, p. 62.
80. Mohan Malik, 'Sino-Indian Relations and India's Eastern Strategy', in Gordon and Henningham, ed., *India Looks East*, p. 127.
81. Gordon, *India's Rise to Power*, p. 137.

82. Kanti P. Bajpai, 'State, Society, Strategy', in G.K. Tanham, K.P. Bajpai and A. Mattoo, ed., *Securing India: Strategic Thought and Practice in an Emerging Power*, New Delhi: Manohar, 1996, pp. 143, 149–50.
83. Limaye, 'The Japan-India Encounter', *RGICS Paper*, no. 38, 1997, p. 14.
84. Thakur, *The Politics and Economics of India's Foreign Policy*, p. 231.
85. Gordon, *India's Rise to Power*, p. 225.
86. Dixit, *My South Block Years*, pp. 17, 269.
87. *A posteriori*, New Delhi denied that it had ever presented its candidature. But, the fact was that in 1994, it already considered and claimed that it could play a role in the Asia-Pacific region. Indeed, during his visit to Hanoi, Prime Minister Rao was said to have affirmed that his country intended to be able to play a more significant role in the Asia-Pacific region, in particular in the ARF. Udai Bhanu Singh, 'Evolution of the ASEAN Regional Forum', *Asian Strategic Review 1995–6*, New Delhi: IDSA, 1996, p. 142.
88. Dixit, *My South Block Years*, pp. 268–9.
89. Sridharan, 'India-ASEAN Relations: Evolution, Growth and Prospects', in C. Jeshurun, *China-India-Japan and the Security of Southeast Asia*, Singapore: ISEAS, 1993, p. 63.
90. In July 1989, the military regime adopted the official name of 'Union of Myanmar' (or *Myanmar Naingngan*, a direct transliteration of the official name in the Burmese language). In fact, the country has changed its name several times. When it acquired its independence in 1948, the official name chosen was 'Union of Burma'. In 1974, the country opted for 'Socialist Republic of the Union of Burma'. In 1988, the former name 'Union of Burma' was put back in the agenda, before the new change in 1989.
91. Quoted in V. Suryanarayan, 'India and Southeast Asia: Shared Destiny', in N. Jetley, ed., *India's Foreign Policy: Challenges and Prospects*, p. 206.
92. The economic crisis that affected the country led to the formation of a movement of revolt against the autocratic regime of Ne Win in 1988. As of August 1988, the protest movement had reached the dimension of a pro-democratic movement. But the military junta fomented a *coup d'état* in September 1988 and formed the State Law and Order Restoration Council (SLORC), while promising to hold multi-partisan elections. In May 1990, the National League for Democracy easily won the elections. But, the SLORC refused to cede power and reduced the movement to silence. Aung San Suu Kyi, its leader, resided under surveillance. Suu Kyi was awarded the Nobel Peace Prize in 1991.
93. V.P. Dutt, *India's Foreign Policy in a Changing World*, p. 228.
94. At the time of the British Raj, Myanmar had been administered from Calcutta. But India and Myanmar had never been on good terms.

95. *FEER*, 1 April 1993, p. 9.
96. Elected Members of Parliament during the 1990 general elections who had been dismissed by the military junta that has held the reins of power since 1988.
97. *Indian Recorder*, 1–7 October 1994.
98. A. Selth 'The China-Burma-India Triangle', in S. Gordon and S. Henningham, eds., *India Looks East: An Emerging Power and its Asia-Pacific Neighbours*, Canbarra: Australian National University, 1995, p. 192.
99. The golden triangle includes Laos, Myanmar and Thailand.
100. *Indian Recorder*, 29 January–4 February 1994.
101. *India Today*, 15 August 1995.
102. D.J. Steinberg 'Myanmar as Nexus: Sino-Indian Rivalries on the Frontier', *Terrorism*, vol. 16, pp. 1–8.
103. P. Stobdan, 'China's Forays into Burma: Implications for India', *Strategic Analysis*, vol. 16, no. 1, April 1993, p. 24.
104. Ibid., p. 24.
105. *Indian Recorder*, 26 February–4 March 1994.
106. Ibid., 24–30 September 1994.
107. Ibid., 29 January–4 February 1995.
108. Ibid., 7–13 May 1995.
109. Steinberg, 'Myanmar as Nexus', *Terrorism*, pp. 1–8.
110. Chaiwat Satha-Anand, 'Thailand: The Layers of a Strategic Culture', in Ken Booth and Russel Trood, eds.; *Strategic Cultures in the Asia-Pacific Region*, London: Macmillan Press, 1999, p. 151.
111. *FEER*, 22 April 1993.
112. Dutt, *India's Foreign Policy in a Changing World*, pp. 239–44, 260.
113. Gordon 'Indian and Southeast Asia: A Renaissance in Relations?', in Gordon and Henningham, eds., *India Looks East*, p. 217.
114. Statement of P. Chidambaram, Finance Minister of India on the occasion of the Post-Ministerial Conferences of ASEAN (9+1) Session, 29 July 1997, § 4.
115. MEA, *Annual Report 1999–2000*, p. 7.
116. Stobdan, 'Myanmar: Breaking out of Isolation', *Strategic Analysis*, pp. 1341–51.
117. Ibid., p. 1351.
118. *The Hindu*, 28 April 1998.
119. Selth, 'The China-Burma-India Triangle', p. 201.
120. See for example Rodney W. Jones, 'Old Quarrels and New Realities: Security in Southern Asia after the Cold War', *Washington Quarterly*, Winter 1992, pp. 105–28.
121. J. Singh, 'An Indian Perspective', in Gordon and Henningham, eds., *India Looks East*, p. 57.

122. Ibid., 'Future of Sino-Indian Relations', *Strategic Analysis*, March 1994, p. 1518.
123. Roy-Chaudhury, 'India's Security Policy', *Strategic Analysis*, May 1996, p. 185.
124. Naidu, 'Post-Cold War Pacific Asian Security: Indian Perceptions and Options', *Delhi Papers*, no. 1, p. 88.

CHAPTER 8

Integrating Defence Interests

8.1 A Growing Strategic Influence in Asia

During the decade of the 1990s, not only did India become increasingly entrenched in the East Asia region, but it did so in a rather positive way. The increased visibility of India's power was evidenced in three specific ways. Firstly, New Delhi had closer cooperation with various nations of East Asia in defence matters. Besides, India was one of the Asian countries that had a highly developed defence industry and above all, as of the 1990s, it acquired a high level of competence in dual use technology that de facto made it an important player in the future evolution of the Asian strategic balance. Finally, New Delhi undertook to ease tensions with its immediate neighbours. As tensions eased a little in South Asia, ASEAN began to see India more as a stabilizing power, and New Delhi broke itself away from the stifling shackles of South Asia. The logic of the matter is indeed quite simple: the more tensions build up in South Asia, the more India is entangled in them, thus running the risk of enclosing itself in the subcontinent's strategic limits.

ENHANCED DEFENCE COOPERATION BETWEEN INDIA AND EAST ASIA

Though the paradigm of derived relationship no longer truly reflected India's rapport with South-East Asia, ties with the great powers of the region—the United States, Japan and China—remained important for the evolution of the Look East policy. And not only was there warmth in the bilateral relations with each of these important powers, but India was also more in tune with each of them in a regional and even a global perspective. In other words, the 'big' three gradually began to accept India as a major power in the future Asian strategic order. For example, the United States, which harboured certain misgivings about China and its military build-up, started considering, from the beginning of the 1990s, India as a potential counterweight to China's growing power. Based on this theory, the Commander-in-Chief of the US Pacific Command sought to increase contacts with India. Between 1994 and 1996, the two parties sought 'a comprehensive bilateral engagement',[1] along with other initiatives, including increased interaction in defence matters and the outline of a strategic dialogue framework. During the American Defence Secretary, William Perry's visit, India and the United States signed a defence exchange agreement in January 1995. The document defined a formula in very general terms of a strategic cooperation that would ensure peace and stability in Asia. Changing American interests in the region and India's growing involvement in South-East Asian economic activities contributed in slowly reinforcing New Delhi's role in maintaining peace and security in Asia.[2] The first round of the Indo-American strategic dialogue took place at the end of October 1997 and ended on an encouraging note.[3] It was showcased as the beginning of a 'strategic dialogue', which was not restricted to military matters, but was seen as a discussion on the whole gamut of Indo-American relations. The possibility of a real dialogue remained nonetheless limited due to fundamental divergences on the nuclear as well as the Kashmir issues that the Clinton administration particularly wanted resolved. New Delhi's misgivings were also due to the close ties that the United States managed to maintain with Pakistan and to the Clinton administration's growing inclination to engage in a 'strategic alliance' with Beijing from 1995 onwards.

New Delhi and Tokyo also attempted to move towards more stable relations. During Foreign Minister, Pranab Mukherjee's visit to Tokyo, in September 1995, the two parties agreed to promote regular high level visits by either side. Another interesting element was that both the Indians and the Japanese decided to incorporate their respective approach to Asia in their diplomatic dialogue.[4] In May 1997, Prime Minister Ryutaro Hashimoto's Liberal Democratic Party (LPD) issued its first document on Japanese foreign policy. It advised the government to adopt a policy oriented more towards South Asia due the fact that: 'South Asian countries, India in particular, are now assuming increasingly major roles in the international affairs of the Asia-Pacific region.'[5] The document described India as a major power in the region and underlined its strategic position for the security of the sea lanes upon which Japan was heavily dependent. These favourable positions on both sides took on a more concrete shape when the Japanese Foreign Minister Yukihiko Ikeda visited India, in July 1997. The first visit by the head of the Japanese diplomacy in ten years marked Tokyo's growing strategic interest for the region. Japan intended henceforth to develop 'a greater strategic relation' with New Delhi and hastened to dispel the notion that bilateral relations were confined to nuclear non-proliferation, to the detriment of other issues. New Delhi and Tokyo decided to hold regular defence exchanges and an annual dialogue on security at the ministerial and Prime Ministerial levels. This dialogue was mainly inspired by Foreign Minister Ikeda's proposals: 'We should exchange our views on the security environment, not only relevant to South Asia but also to the whole of Asia and the world. We should discuss confidence-building measures and preventive diplomacy for peace and security.'[6] In other words, Tokyo began to gradually realize that New Delhi was a major power in its own right in Asia, not to say a partner of increasing importance for ensuring stability in the region. Indeed, in his meeting with the Indian press, Ikeda affirmed: 'If India goes ahead with its Look East policies, there will be increasing opportunities for us to act in concert for regional interests as well.'[7]

Japan's intentions were largely based upon its preoccupations on the energy front. Without coming out openly, Tokyo was increasingly worried about the conditions for oil and gas procurement from Central Asia and the Persian Gulf. In this perspective, Japan kept a close watch on China's interactions with Central Asian Republics and the Middle East countries. Not surprisingly, New Delhi and Tokyo decided to start a dialogue on energy issues, in order to understand their respective compulsions in the matter and thereby, formulate a joint response. Furthermore, Japanese diplomacy had a predilection for informal dialogues, as such contacts helped it to express itself more freely on fundamental strategic issues, outside the official constraints it was bound to follow.[8] The Japanese leadership thus took the initiative to start several informal dialogues with their Indian counterparts. Academic circles of both countries also intensified their interactions thanks to various non-official fora in the political and strategic domain. Thus, IDSA has been engaged in the Track II process with Japan since 1996. It is also to be noted that the Tokyo Global Forum organized the first Indo-Japanese dialogue on the security of Asia, in October 1996, in cooperation with IDSA.[9] Tokyo appeared eager to carry further these informal dialogues, as the Minister for Foreign

Affairs Ikeda suggested setting up 'a committee of wise men' in July 1997, underlining the fact that the strategic dialogue should go beyond issues of trade and investments.[10] Such dialogues constituted an important part of the security architecture of the region and it was an encouraging development that Indian diplomats and military officials were invited to participate in them.

Finally, even Beijing appeared to make some efforts to win over New Delhi. In November 1996, the President of the People's Republic of China, the Secretary-General of the Communist Party and the President of the Armed Forces Control Board, Jiang Zemin, visited Delhi for the first ever visit made by a Chinese Head of State and Chief of the Communist Party.[11] In many respects, this event seemed to point to a new phase in the policy of rapprochement between the two neighbours. Not content with asserting that neither country posed a threat to the other, President Zemin even encouraged Sino-Indian cooperation for the stability of Asia and the world. Jiang Zemin's visit revived bilateral links in several directions: it consolidated the climate of confidence the two countries were striving for gradually and it made China adopt a more moderate and less partisan public posture on the Indo-Pakistan conflict. In the wake of Zemin's visit, India and China signed several treaties, including one that undertook to promote new confidence-building and security measures along the line of actual control (LAC). Signed on 29 November 1996, this important document reinforced the 1993 treaties that undertook to maintain peace and tranquillity on the Himalayan border area. It also endorsed speeding up the process for finalizing the demarcation of the LAC, with a view to reducing the number of military personnel deployed in the geographical zones indicated in the treaty. Based on this document, the two countries pledged not to engage in military conflict against one another. In response to the Chinese military's invitation, the Indian Joint Chief of Staff, Lt General V.P. Malik, visited China in May 1997. At his reception, the Defence Minister, Chi Haotian, assured him that China desired friendly relations with India for the sake of peace and stability in Asia. High-level contacts continued till December 1997 and witnessed cordial relations, even though India remained watchful of the Sino-Pak connection and the finalization of the demarcation of the LAC. Informal Track II exchanges took over these interactions in order to strengthen the climate of cooperation.[12]

With the South-East Asian countries, New Delhi intensified joint exercises, according to the ASEAN way. When the various ASEAN countries conducted joint military exercises between them, it was always within a bilateral framework, or at the most a trilateral one. Therefore, the question of joint exercises with ASEAN as a whole did not arise. Besides, in the early 1990s, the first strategic contacts between India and South-East Asian countries took place in the maritime field. It was symbolically important that the naval forces of these countries be the backbone of the rapprochement since it was the Indian naval expansion that had led to a chill in relations with the ASEAN in the late 1980s. The misunderstanding once removed, India and the ASEAN countries rapidly expanded military contacts to other wings of the military, especially the air force. On 2 February 1993, the Indian Defence Minister, Sharad Pawar, and his Malaysian counterpart, Najib Razak, signed a treaty of military cooperation.[13] It was the first treaty to be signed between India and a member of the ASEAN in military matters. Under this agreement, the Indian military undertook to train Malaysia's Air Force pilots and its future Russian MiG-29 fleet. The agreement also covered the construction of defence infrastructure, the modernization and training of the army, regular exchanges of personnel, the supply of spare parts and even maintenance services for Russian and British equipments bought by Malaysia and finally, the joint but limited production of naval and air armament.[14] In practice, Malaysian Air Force pilots began training at Pathankot the same year, i.e. 1993. In 1994, India trained Malaysian pilots in MiG-29 fighter jets.[15] More than a hundred Malaysian Air Force personnel underwent training at that time in India. In 1995, New Delhi sent Indian Air Force flight instructors to Malaysia to supervise training on the Russian MiG-29 that Kuala Lumpur had just purchased.[16]

Military cooperation was a part of the general programme of enhanced ties between India and Singapore. In this matter, the two countries especially intensified naval cooperation. In February 1993, warships from Singapore and India took part for the first time in bilateral exercises off the Andaman Islands. For four days, the vessels conducted basic tactical exercises while the Indian Dornier aircrafts carried out aerial surveillance manoeuvres. The experiment was repeated in February 1994, for a period extended to seven days. During this exercise, Singapore sent two missile corvettes to the open sea off the Andaman and Nicobar Islands, which along with an Indian frigate, undertook combat techniques against an Indian submarine. The official objective was to promote professional interactions and to strengthen bilateral exchanges between the two fleets. These joint exercises became an annual feature and so also high-level visits of the two countries' top naval brass. In March 1994, Commodore Kwek Siew Jin, Chief of Naval Staff of the Republic of Singapore, visited India. It was the first visit in ten years made by a Chief of the Singapore Navy.[17] In September 1994, New Delhi and the city-state signed a treaty of cooperation in defence matters. Under the terms of this document, India placed at the disposal of Singapore some of its submarines for annual training exercises in anti-submarine warfare.[18] In a fresh initiative in public relations, New Delhi allowed foreign battle ships access to its Vishakhapatnam submarine base. Singaporean warships were included in the list of privileged fleets, which, for the first time, anchored at the Indian submarine base in early 1996.[19] Since Vishakhapatnam stood as a sensitive base located on the coast of the Bay of Bengal, in the state of Andhra Pradesh, it was a welcome step for the Indian Ocean riparian states like Singapore, which gained a lot from such initiatives. Also, the two countries engaged in new anti-submarine warfare exercises off the coast of Vishakhapatnam in March 1996. The Singapore Chief of Naval Staff, Vice-Admiral Kwek Siew Jin, participated in the closing ceremony of the joint exercises, making his second visit to India in just about two years.[20]

From October 1991 to December 1996, the Indian Navy conducted nearly twenty-six naval exercises, with navies of thirteen countries in the Indian Ocean.[21] Most of these modest scale exercises involved about two warships from the two countries concerned, for a day or two. Amongst the Indian Ocean riparian countries, New Delhi mostly concentrated on the Bay of Bengal countries. Thus, since 1995, navies from the Bay of Bengal riparian countries have been invited to take part in multilateral exercises, under the name code of MILAN (Meeting of the [Littorals Bay of Bengal] Andaman and Nicobar). These joint manoeuvres, promoted by India, aim to develop regional maritime cooperation. Further, MILAN is a forum that helps the navies' young officers and seamen to get to know and work with each other. This initiative is as much a military training as a creation of a social network between the members of the national fleets. Recreation activities, food festivals, cultural exchanges are a part of the training programme. For the 1997 edition, MILAN exercises were held at Port Blair, from 14 to 18 February.[22] About eleven ships, which represented the fleets of Bangladesh, Indonesia, Malaysia, Singapore, Sri Lanka, Thailand and host India, took part. By playing its hand to the fullest in the Track II process, the Indian Navy participated in the creation of a peace regime thanks to enhanced and inter-personnel cooperation, which was in tune with the strategic approach of South-East Asian nations. But even though the Indian Navy increased its joint exercises with different maritime powers, some of whom were from other regions, it did not engage in similar activities with China. New Delhi did not want to give the least toehold to Chinese presence in the Indian Ocean region, even if such exercises were important to create a climate of confidence.[23] Faced with this paradox, the Indian Government just proposed reciprocal visits of Chinese and Indian warships to their respective ports.

While strengthening military contacts with ASEAN countries, India maintained close ties with Hanoi. New Delhi had always considered Vietnam as a pre-eminent power in South-East Asia and its closest ally in the region. It had stood by the country without break since 1947. This sympathy at first was born out of the genuinely anti-colonial and nationalist principles of independent Vietnam's founding fathers.[24] Later, the Indian leaders saw a parallel between their experience and that of Vietnam in the international arena. From New Delhi and Hanoi's viewpoint, both had been forced by American and Chinese policies to turn towards the USSR, in 1971 and 1978 respectively. Yet, in the beginning, both countries had tried to avoid this process, by sticking to their non-aligned principles. Consequently, Indo-Vietnamese friendship was considerably enhanced by their strong antipathy to China. Throughout the 1990s, an uninterrupted succession of bilateral visits involving leaders at the highest level confirmed, if necessary, the premium placed by the two nations on their continued bond of closest friendship. Among the most important visits was the one made by the Secretary-General of the Communist Party of Vietnam, Do Muoi, to New Delhi, in September 1992 and Prime Minister, P.V. Narasimha Rao's visit to Hanoi in 1994, during which the two nations signed the protocol of military cooperation for the maintenance of equipment and military training.[25] These exchanges also involved the highest ranking officers of the military hierarchy. It was thus that the Deputy Minister for Defence and Chief of Staff, General Dai Dinh Luyen, visited New Delhi in May 1995 whilst one of the most important armed force officer, Chief of Indian Naval Staff, Admiral V.S. Shekhawat, visited Vietnam in May 1996. In March 1997, it was the Vietnamese Prime Minister, Vo Van Kiet, who kept up this 'diplomatic ballet' between the two capitals with a state visit to India, whilst Minister of State, Saleem Shervani, went to Hanoi in August 1997.

Furthermore, Vietnam became a member of the ASEAN, on 28 July 1995. Not only was New Delhi pleased with this development, it even believed that Vietnam's integration would help its overall relations with the Association. In fact, Hanoi continued to attach particular attention to its ties with India. A diplomat affirmed that: 'While liberalizing the economy, diversifying and multilateralizing the external economic ties, the task of strengthening and developing the traditional friendship and multisided cooperation with India always occupies a special place in the foreign policy formulation of Vietnam.'[26] An indication of the 'special place' India occupied in Vietnamese diplomacy was provided by Prime Minister Vo Van Kiet. The latter in fact was all praise for India's 'stabilizing role', during P.V. Narasimha Rao's visit, in 1994.[27] The Vietnamese leader at that time spelled out in clear terms that Hanoi had always considered India as a counter-balance to Chinese power. Despite the end of the Cold War, it seemed that certain alignments continued in the perceptions of some Asian leaders. Also, in the matter of military cooperation, New Delhi offered Vietnam the possibility of spare parts supply and maintenance service under favourable commercial terms. This initiative was born out of a certain common sense as the arsenal of both countries had a number of common equipment of Russian origin. With as much as three-fourths of the Vietnamese People's Army armament of Soviet origin, both quick repairs and a regular supply of spare parts were indispensable.[28] It should, however, be acknowledged that this proposal did not lead to anything concrete. But it could well have been the launching pad for closer military ties. As for India and Laos, on 21 January 1996, they signed a treaty to strengthen their defence ties.[29] Vientiane was especially keen on assistance in the installation of military training and maintenance equipment.

AN EMERGING POWER IN THE FIELD OF MILITARY AND PARAMILITARY TECHNOLOGY

At the end of the 1980s, India stood out as one of the largest military industry bases in Asia, and commercial prospects for the Indian defence industry in the region looked very promising. The earlier military cooperation with the USSR emerged as a trump card for large-scale trade. New Delhi was increasingly tempted by the financial godsend of arms export. Albeit a big buyer in the armament market, India had till then abstained from becoming a seller, due to its non-alignment policy and the idealistic stand taken in various international fora. This went to such an extent that at the end of the 1980s, New Delhi had prohibited its public sector undertaking Hindustan Aeronautics Limited (HAL) from delivering two squadrons of Jaguars to Thailand, citing that the latter was hostile to Vietnam, a traditional friend of India. Ideology still prevailed over pecuniary gains at that point of time. Yet, it was financial reasons that brought about the first shift in policy. From the end of the 1980s, India began to turn towards the international market. The national armament industry found itself in the doldrums due to budgetary cuts. The aeronautical company HAL was the most affected as the Indian government's orders for Jaguar, MiG-21, 23, 27 and Dornier-228 aircrafts petered out. HAL then began to bid for international maintenance contracts, a painful choice if ever there were one, for it meant the company would function more as a service agency rather than a manufacturing unit.[30] Budgetary restrictions also made defence officials think about arms export. In 1989, a special committee was created for this purpose and the Defence Minister, K.C. Pant, began establishing contact with several potential markets, like Malaysia and Vietnam, apart from Iran, Libya and Iraq, interested in buying Indian arms.[31] As part of an unprecedented promotional effort, several Indian public sector units participated in the Singapore aerospace fair, in 1990. Vietnam did evince an interest in acquiring the production line for MiG-29 aircrafts. However, negotiations did not bear fruit.

In the 1990s, India's sense of urgency to gain a foothold in the international arms market became much more apparent. In this perspective, HAL even envisaged the possibility of creating joint ventures with foreign partners,[32] and involved itself actively in marketing efforts such as the international aviation trade fair organized in Bangalore since 1993. As for arms export, India especially turned to South-East Asia. The most lucrative zone till then was the Middle East, but the countries of the region preferred to get their supplies from Pakistan. All said and done, a real armament boom was taking place in South-East Asia and New Delhi played its card of technical expertise in Russian equipment to the fullest. At a time when the market for the former USSR armament had become the focus of potential buyers,

New Delhi made the most of its expertise acquired thanks to its close military cooperation with Moscow. Besides, Indian authorities endeavoured to negotiate with their Russian counterparts further training in the know-how of production and maintenance of Russian-made arms. For instance, in May 1994, India seemed to have concluded a deal with Russia for the purchase of thirty fourth-generation MiG-29M fighter jets, after receiving assurances that the public sector undertaking HAL would be the service agency for all types of MiGs, for the whole of South and South-East Asia.[33] In other words, India appeared to try and become a big maintenance hub in Asia for Russian and former Soviet military equipment.

India also attempted to don the garb of an intermediary for trade in Russian arms. In this field, it made the most of the post-Cold War era and took advantage of the East Asian states' fancy for buying from the Russian market. This was evident in the huge arms deal signed between Russia and Malaysia, in 1994, in which the Indians were present in various levels of the transaction. Since the early 1990s, Malaysian authorities had been negotiating with their Russian counterparts for the supply of a large number of MiG-29 fighter jets. But before actually buying these jets, Kuala Lumpur asked permission to study the Indian experience in this matter. Malaysian Defence Minister Najib Razak therefore visited India in March 1992 to evaluate the MiG-29s in the Indian Air Force and to hold detailed discussions with the Defence Minister Sharad Pawar, General S.F. Rodrigues and other top defence officials. These discussions helped the Malaysians appraise the possibility of purchasing Indian equipment. On 29 June 1993, the Malaysian Defence Minister, Najib Razak, announced the purchase of eighteen Russian MiG-29 jet fighters. India, for its part, would provide logistical support for these aircraft, as provided for in the Indo-Malaysian treaty for defence cooperation that was signed in February 1993. Malaysia was already using India's services for maintaining its fleet of Alouettes, helicopters of Indian manufacture. Kuala Lumpur must have been satisfied with these services as the Royal Malaysian Air Force also evinced interest in purchasing more Alouettes helicopters and Dornier-228 aircraft.[34] As for the contract between Malaysia and Russia, it was officially signed on 7 June 1994, after two years of negotiations. In this context, it must be underlined that the Indian firm Agio helped the parties negotiate the contract terms. This Indian company, which is based in Singapore and specializes in barter trade, in fact, found a financial arrangement that brought down the sale value of MiG-29 aircrafts for Malaysia. Indeed, SIPRI figures confirmed that the eighteen MiG-29 Fulcrum-C were sold at a price of USD 600 million, with counter-trade worth 200 million (of which 150 million in the form of barter).[35] More generally, it must also be noted that Malaysia was the first non-communist country of South-East Asia to purchase Russian military equipment.

Both Russians and Indians knew only too well that giving shape to a joint strategy in the matter of sales and maintenance services of armaments would work to their advantage. During P.V. Narasimha Rao's visit to Russia in June–July 1994, the two countries inked treaties for establishing joint ventures in civil and military aviation. Of particular importance was the joint venture worth USD13.5 million, between the Indian company HAL and the Industrial Credit and Investment Company of India (ICICI) and on the Russian side, Moscow Aircraft Production Organization, Mikoyan Design Bureau and the armament export company, Rosvooruzheniye. This alliance was formed to offer its services for upgrading Russian equipment used in India and other developing countries.[36] Another large-scale project was a joint venture formed in September 1994 between the Russian MiG company and the Indian firm Agio for providing its services for fighter jets sold in Asia.[37] The fruitful cooperation in the matter of MiG sales to Malaysia seemed to have convinced the two partners of the advantages of a long-term alliance. The Russians knew only too well that there were a large number of MiG aircraft in South Asia, South-East Asia and China. Most of these countries found it difficult to buy spare parts and get their aircraft serviced for maintenance. The new Russo-Indian company was meant to fulfil this need and would first explore the possibility of barter trade to promote its services with the MiG owners. According to Raj Sayall, Director of Agio, the new joint venture company would make it possible to increase financial arrangement practice, already widely used. In 1993–4, several contacts took place with Malaysia for the prospective sale of Russian helicopters of various categories. New Delhi negotiated with Kuala Lumpur the sale of the Mi-25 Russian helicopter and kept a close watch on Malaysia's interest in the HAL-manufactured Chetak helicopters as well as the Cheeta helicopters for relief and rescue work.[38] Generally, Malaysian authorities were of the opinion that Indian aid would be welcome as it would strengthen their own military industry. In March 1994, it was the turn of a Thai military delegation to visit India and express its interest for the prospective purchase of equipment manufactured by the country.[39] Finally, though it was basically interested in armaments exports, New Delhi also purchased some equipment from East Asian market. In 1991, it obtained the license to manufacture three Samar Class coastguard cutter vessels from South Korea. In 1995, it placed an order with Singapore for three TaraBai class coastguard patrol vessels, which were delivered in 1997–8.[40]

The partnership with Russia for the sale of MiG combat jets was just one aspect of India's potential in the Asian armament market. The sensitive fields of Research and Development, especially in dual-use technologies, could also ensure a bright future for India, in terms of trade. During the 1990s, Indian investments in the dual-use technology field began to bear fruit and bestowed upon the country a *de facto* strategic importance that East Asia could no longer ignore. Some Asian leaders were quick to act. During his state visit to India, from 19 to 22 December 1996, Prime Minister Mahathir stopped by Bangalore where he made it a point to visit the defence-related high-technology facilities of Hindustan Aeronautics Limited (HAL), Indian Space Research Organization (ISRO) and Aeronautics Development Establishment (ADE).[41]

Whether it was research in nuclear energy, in ballistic missile technology or in the military use of space, India had, in all these three domains, the potential to enhance rapidly its capabilities and become a major power in Asia.[42] Besides, the Indian authorities were fully determined to pursue indigenous programmes launched in each of these sectors, regardless of the international regimes in place and of the growing external pressure. Indeed, there already existed some programmes of cooperation with some South-East Asian states in the matter of non-military nuclear use. For instance, the Bhaba Atomic Research Centre had been training scientists from Vietnam, Malaysia, Thailand and the Philippines. Thailand especially sought to establish collaboration with India to develop its nuclear energy sector.[43] Besides, India was as passionately attached to its missile programmes as to its nuclear development and refused to suspend any work despite American pressure. Similarly, budgetary constraints did not affect the military activities of the Integrated Guided Missile Development Programme (IGMPD). This military missile programme was very quickly executed towards the end of the 1980s, with the arrival of A.P.J. Abdul Kalam to the Defence Research and Development

Organization (DRDO).[44] Quick results being the order of the day, a medium-range tactical surface-to-surface missile, Prithvi, was designed. The second missile to come out of the DRDO laboratories was the Agni, a medium-range ballistic missile whose development was rather sporadic. However, it is to be noted that in the domain of the military use of missiles, India did not entertain any contact with South-East Asian states, nor with any other country.[45]

India's advances in missile technology also offered civil uses of high commercial values. In brief, Indian research in missile technology resulted both in military and civil uses and both activities were carried out simultaneously by two institutions. While the IGMPD covered the military missile programme, the ISRO confined itself to the peaceful use of missiles, i.e. satellite launch vehicles. As it happened, the sector of launch vehicles and satellite communication offered formidable financial and strategic stakes. This partly explained why the Indian leadership had been highly critical of international regimes for non-proliferation of ballistic missile. This was evidently another bone of contention with the United States that headed the project for giving a concrete shape to the Missile Technology Control Regime (MTCR).[46] For the Indians, *ad hoc* regimes such as the MTCR, the London club, and any other control over export of dual use material, technology and equipment, was nothing but denying the developing countries' access to new technologies. Therefore, the major powers had both strategic and commercial interest in setting up such regimes. From the Indian point of view, the MTCR was in consonance with the protectionist policies of the Western powers that were concerned with retaining their monopoly over the huge market of launch vehicles and satellite communication services, especially when confronted with new competitors like India.

Indeed, while the Indian space programme had just begun to take wings, it seemed to hold the promise of considerable commercial potential. After twenty years dedicated to development and experimentation, this programme became operational in the mid-1980s with specific missions. In fact, the Indian space programme reached a turning point in September 1997, with the development of a Polar Satellite Launch Vehicle (PSLV). The PSLV helps put reconnaissance satellites in orbit at an optimal altitude of 800 to 900 km. Previously, satellite launch capacity was limited to light loads and a low altitude of 300 to 450 km, which was not sufficient for the main military and commercial applications. The successor to PSLV, the Geo-synchronous

Satellite Launch Vehicle (GSLV), was to soon make it possible to launch heavy communication satellites to an altitude of 36,000 km. Only five space programmes in the world have the capacity to execute such operations: those of the United States, European Union, Russia, China and Japan.[47] The Indian space programme was thus all set to enter the exclusive club of the five international space agencies possessing geostationary capacity.[48] Some forecasts could be made in this respect.

The PSLV and the GSLV probably would have more commercial applications than military ones, since financial preoccupations had become ISRO's main concern during the 1990s. As a part of the economic liberalization policy, ISRO began to offer its services on the international space market. It even created a company named Antrix in 1992 to function as the marketing division of the Indian space agency.[49] And the second-generation satellite launch vehicles, the PSLV and GSLV, offered very competitive prices on the global market. Based on the forecast of a growing international market—especially in Asia—for communication satellites, ISRO could hope to be awarded some contracts for launching commercial satellites. It must be noted that Indonesia had already accepted an Indian proposal for installing a ground station at Biak (Kalimantan) for the continued surveillance of ISRO's Geo-synchronous Satellite Launch Vehicle. Furthermore, ISRO won a contract from Seoul in 1998 to launch a South Korean satellite with a payload of 100 kg from a PSLV-C2.[50]

Apart from its satellite-launching programmes, ISRO began to find clients for its own satellites. The INSAT (Indian National Satellites) were, for instance, an important asset for the Indian public sector television channels which wanted to use these satellites (INSAT-2C) to transmit their programmes to South-East Asia and the Middle East. The high demand for telecommunications in India and in East Asia, promised full use of the services proposed by INSAT.[51] In fact, Antrix and ISRO entered into a contract with an American firm, Eosat, for the promotion of Indian satellite data on the international market. Eosat had already signed deals with representatives of Japan, Thailand and Australia for using these data. Finally, in January 1995, India and Malaysia agreed to jointly develop two micro-satellites, with a payload of 50 kg. This development was interpreted in India as a very encouraging step, which justified the efforts taken for getting a piece of the global aerospace market—indeed, a most competitive market. That India helped in the design and manufacture of a satellite for Malaysia also contributed to the strengthening of bilateral ties. Finally, in March 1996, the polar satellite launch vehicle (PSLV) put a 930-kg satellite in orbit from the Sriharikota base. This IRS (Indian Remote Sensing) satellite possessed quite a high precision resolution, which allowed it to become one of the leaders in the commercial satellite imaging market in a few years.[52]

The advances made by India in the civil uses of satellite technology raised the question of its strategic implications. In fact, launch vehicles can be used for both civilian and military purposes. That was the reason why the transition from PSLV to GSVL was delayed; Washington prevented any transfer of cryogenic engine technology to India. There were a number of speculations concerning the capacity of the GSLV to endow the country with intercontinental ballistic missiles (ICBM). In its defence, New Delhi gave assurances that the PSLV and GSLV were not military rockets but satellite launch rockets. On the other hand, if it wanted to, it could try and arm the PSLV with a 1.2-ton warhead for a striking range of 15,000 km. Thus, the Indian space programme did have important military applications. Moreover, it had already manufactured a nuclear warhead cruise missile, the Agni, which was capable of hitting targets in some parts of China.[53]

It would also seem that communications and remote sensing satellites launched for commercial purposes could have military uses.[54] Whether they are for civil or military use, communication satellites use more or less the same technology. To be more precise, the high resolution of commercial satellites blurs the difference between satellites for civil and military purposes.[55] Thus, the advances made by India would probably be quite sufficient, in the near future, for projecting its might and leverage its objectives, thanks to its satellite reconnaissance, intelligence and communication functions.[56] Even if it was still limited, India hoped that its know-how in the domain of satellite reconnaissance and communication could be considerably improved in a short span of time to cater to a military use. The new doctrine of the Indian Air Force had already begun to integrate its spatial advantage for surveillance and combat management. Military authorities would have actually resorted to using the IRS satellite images for the surveillance of ballistic missiles at the country's borders in 1996. India's satellite recon-naissance capacity was even then expected to help counter conventional Chinese threats in the short-term. IRS satellites specifically designed for military purposes could, in fact, bestow Indian armed forces with an early warning system of any movement of the Chinese army towards the Tibetan frontier. Such a system would facilitate rapid deployment of conventional forces on the Indian side, early enough to counter Chinese troops. As they were backed by a growing satellite reconnaissance and communication capacity, conventional Indian forces *de facto* represented an increasingly credible counter-balance to China. The advances made in the Indian space programme thus had important implications for deterrence and stability in Asia and they could in the near future alter the balance of power in both the Indian Ocean and the Asia-Pacific region.

EASING OF TENSIONS IN SOUTH ASIA

It would be a fallacy to think that India was turning to East Asia to overcome its problems in South Asia. It was quite evident that the ASEAN nations continued to have their own reservations *vis-à-vis* India, the moment tensions increased in its South Asian neighbourhood. An improvement in the climate of cooperation in South Asia became therefore a necessary condition for furthering the Look East policy. In this respect, the Indo-Pakistan antagonism frightened the ASEAN and was considered a major obstacle for India's inclusion in the strategic mechanisms of the region. This conflict tended to monopolize South-East Asian opinion to the detriment of other much more positive elements for determining India's status. An incident during P.V. Narasimha Rao's lecture in Singapore aptly demonstrated this phenomenon. During the question-answer session, which followed the Indian Prime Minister's speech, there was a spat with the Pakistan High Commissioner, who insisted on raising the bilateral issue of Kashmir. In his capacity as the President of the session, Lee Kuan Yew hastened to end the debate with a firm request to the Pakistani speaker to put an end to his speech. Nevertheless, this incident made headlines in the regional press; and to a certain extent, it diverted the attention from the content of Rao's speech.[57]

Besides, Indian diplomats became aware that their dissensions with Pakistan adversely affected their external relations on the whole. In 1994, Foreign Secretary, J.N. Dixit, saw a very understandable reason from the ASEAN viewpoint not to confer the status of a full dialogue partner to India: 'If they take us as fully fledged partners on politics and security, Pakistan will automatically want the same.'[58] And he further added in a speech that bordered on everything except political cant: 'Once both of us are in, it becomes a circus', as the Kashmir issue would inevitably be raised and create a scene that would paralyse all other discussions. J.N. Dixit also talked about the fact that there was lack of understanding with regard to the Indo-Pak conflict: 'The South-East Asians sometimes ask: "You are such big countries, fighting over such small pieces of territory. Why can't you rise above these things".' The confidence-building process initiated between India and China was also often cited as an example for arriving at a possible solution. But such reasoning showed that South-East Asian observers were not seized of the complexity of the Indo-Pak conflict. They especially failed to perceive that the confrontation between the two brothers turned foes was due to issues of identity and was intrinsically linked to the nation-building of both states.

Besides, there was a basic element in the Indian cultural strategy that the South-East Asian political and military communities failed to grasp: it was the deep-rooted vision that saw the subcontinent as a single geographic and cultural unit. While India's priority was the stability and security of the country, it was inseparable from the rest of the subcontinent.[59] India tended to think of itself as the peacekeeping force of the entire subcontinent, capable of establishing a *Pax Indica*, as there was a *Pax Britannica* in the olden days. In this respect, New Delhi believed that no other country should undertake any action in foreign policy or in defence matters that could be considered a threat to its security. India saw itself as a non-belligerent and benevolent nation, a peaceful and friendly policeman, who sought peace and stability for the whole region. Devoid of any claims of hegemony or territory, it asked to be recognized as the regional policeman by the major powers as well as its smaller neighbours. In this matter, it was more readily seen as a regional dictator by the outside world. It was thus that the Indonesian general Hasnan Habib observed: 'India's propensity for high-handedness in settling its differences with its smaller neighbours and its occasional big power attitude have not particularly endeared it in the region.'[60]

Such analyses, which were quite prevalent in South-East Asia, stemmed largely from the region's own history. The previously tense relations among the ASEAN countries had significantly improved especially through the good offices of the local 'big brother', Indonesia. Before Vietnam's integration, the archipelago accounted for two-thirds of the ASEAN population and territory.[61] But, it so happened that Jakarta endeavoured to be accepted by the neighbouring countries and took charge of regional order, in consonance with the premise *primus inter pares*. In other words, Indonesia placed itself on an equal footing with its partners in the interest of regional order, even if it meant restraining itself politically. In this perspective, the Indian strategic culture was out of step with that of the ASEAN and more specifically with that of Indonesia. Based on their recent historical experience, the ASEAN countries expected India to adopt in South Asia a profile similar to that of Indonesia in maritime South-East Asia. In other words, they would have liked Delhi to denounce its regional 'big brotherly' behaviour in the name of its territorial, demographic and military superiority. However, Hasnan Habib's point of view was that: 'Unlike Indonesia and other ASEAN countries, which are striving for increasingly close cooperation among themselves and are trying to widen the geographical area of cooperation eventually to include the whole of South-East Asia, India's approach to the South Asian region has tended to emphasize the potential for tensions within the region. This has had a destabilizing effect in the region.'[62]

And he concluded that New Delhi should finally accept that no developing nation could ensure on its own its national security, or the security of the region in which it finds itself. India would be better off by gaining the confidence of its neighbours, in order to promote closer South Asian cooperation.

It was quite evident that tensions in South Asia did a disservice to India's image with the ASEAN. In its capacity as a regional power, New Delhi was held responsible for the adverse condition prevailing in the region. Due to its size, India was more easily suspected of having hegemonic ambitions, or at least, it seemed natural that it makes the first overtures of peace. From the South-East Asian point of view, New Delhi did not represent a threat, but it was a destabilizing factor in its immediate neighbourhood, which limited plans for cooperation. It was also more in India's interest to work towards bettering its relations with its neighbour Pakistan as the latter was attempting to create a breakthrough with the Islamic nations of South-East Asia. In early August 1997 for instance, the Pakistani Prime Minister, Nawaz Sharif, undertook a four-day visit to Malaysia to strengthen bilateral ties, in both economic and defence matters.[63]

Indo-Pakistan tensions even had an adverse impact on relations with Tokyo. India indeed had an avowed policy: it was steadfast in refusing to discuss its differences with Pakistan except on a bilateral basis. Therefore, it took a dim view of Japan's attempt at mediation on the Kashmir issue. Between 1991 and 1994, Tokyo evinced a certain desire to play a role in Indo-Pakistan relations and in resolving the Kashmir conflict. This was sufficient for Indian leaders to accuse Japan of being manipulated by the United States. However, whereas Washington hardly hid its predilection for Islamabad, Tokyo endeavoured to follow a more neutral approach. The fact was that India did not want to be put on an equal footing with Pakistan.[64] Tokyo and Delhi could therefore hardly arrive at a compromise. South Asian instability thus continued to tarnish India's image in Japanese perceptions. In 1997, during an important visit to New Delhi, the Japanese Minister for Foreign Affairs asserted that Indo-Pakistan tensions over Kashmir and their missile race were hindering better relations with Japan.[65]

During the 1990s, the continuance of the Look East policy ran into a snag: a closer cooperation with South-East Asia required good relations with India's South Asian neighbours. It so happened that New Delhi took a first important step in this direction with its Nepalese neighbour. On 12 February 1996, bilateral relations received a great push forward when P.V. Narasimha Rao signed the Mahakali River basin treaty. But, above all, it was from mid-1996 onwards that the period of better intra-South Asian relations seemed to commence, impelled by the Gujral doctrine. This academic trained in international affairs became the Minister for Foreign Affairs in the United Front government led by H.D. Deve Gowda, in June 1996. He later became Prime Minister in April 1997. In this context, it was to be noted that the Gujral doctrine was put into practice only after the ASEAN had decided to admit India into the Asian Regional Forum (ARF).[66] It is nonetheless interesting to analyse this doctrine for its positive impact on the Look East policy. In theory, there were two versions of this document: One was the official version, expounded by I.K. Gujral himself, and the second one was more of an interpretation, given by his close advisor, Bhabani Sen Gupta. The second version was considered all the more important as Sen Gupta was believed to be the real author of the doctrine.

According to I.K. Gujral, the five official principles of the doctrine were as follows.[67] (1) India would expect nothing in return from its neighbours Bangladesh, Bhutan, Maldives, Nepal and Sri Lanka, but would give what it could in good faith. (2) No South Asian country should allow its territory to be used against another country of the region. (3) No country shall interfere in the internal affairs of the other. (4) All South Asian countries should respect the territorial integrity and sovereignty of other countries. (5) They should resolve their disputes through peaceful bilateral negotiations. All these principles aimed at reviving South Asian relations on the foundations of friendship and cooperation. This new approach was primarily founded on the principle of non-interference in the internal affairs of neighbouring countries and respect for their sovereignty. Above all, the stature and size of India were henceforth seen in a more positive way, its geographic and military superiority justifying that it adopt a series of measures to generate more confidence among its partners. In this context, it appeared as if New Delhi drew inspiration from certain aspects of the Indonesian policy in South-East Asia. This hypothesis was confirmed by the more explicit interpretation of the Gujral doctrine given by Bhabani Sen Gupta.[68] In fact, the latter affirmed that the five principles were laid down to put an end to speculations about India's hegemonic posturing. To be more precise, the doctrine's first principle was in line with the following reasoning: taking cognisance of its disproportionate position in South Asia, India would no longer apply the logic of reciprocity *vis-à-vis* its smaller neighbours, including Pakistan. It however hoped that its neighbours would respond in the same manner. The doctrine's second principle in the Sen Gupta version postulated that treaties should be drawn up between equal partners with an equal share of benefits, perhaps with some concessions for smaller neighbours, in the hope of favourable results in the future. The second principle stemmed basically from the will to take into account the sensibilities of smaller neighbours as was seen within the ASEAN. According to the third principle, India should free itself from any perception of threat from its neighbours, except in the case of Pakistan whose resources and capacity could inflict irreparable damage. Similarly, India should forget and outgrow the idea that its neighbours want to gang up against it, possibly with the help of a major power. The first three principles as explained by Sen Gupta were diametrically opposed to India's paternalistic tradition in South Asia and rather recalled the South-East Asian experience.

Bhabani Sen Gupta' interpretation of the last two principles of the Gujral doctrine was highly interesting with respect to the Look East policy. Distancing himself from I.K. Gujral's official line, Sen Gupta asserted in the fourth point that India should shake off its obsession with Pakistan, an obsession that 'chained' it to its neighbour and prevented it from pursuing legitimate and more important tasks in international affairs. Finally, the fifth and the last point spoke for itself: 'India should break out of the claustrophobic confines of South Asia, a region with no strategic resources, overburdened with poverty and population.'[69] Thus, Sen Gupta asserted that: 'India must go East in search of an Asia-Pacific identity and of larger areas of collaboration with the tigers and dragons, and with China and Japan.'[70] Though he had concentrated on formulating a policy on South Asia, this close advisor to Gujral had in fact always recommended a reorientation towards India's eastern neighbourhood.[71] Therefore, he did not content himself with presenting the Gujral doctrine and the Look East policy as complementary strategies. He suggested that one of the aims of the Gujral doctrine was to promote more actively the Look East policy, and peace in South Asia was a necessary condition for integration in the wider Asian region. This type of reasoning was not an isolated case: a growing section of the diplomatic and strategic community in New Delhi acknowledged that the aspiration to play a larger role in the international arena was not possible if India were to remain bogged down in unending sub-regional conflicts.[72]

In practice, the Gujral doctrine met with resounding success and experience showed that it was beneficial to the Look East policy. The best example was that of Indo-Bangladeshi relations. On 14 December 1996, Prime Minister Sheikh Hasina and I.K. Gujral, then the Minister for Foreign Affairs, signed the Ganges Water Sharing Treaty, which allowed Bangladesh to build irrigation canals in areas prone to annual drought. Contrary to previous Congress governments, I.K. Gujral did not ask for any road and rail links between Bangladesh and the north-eastern states of India in return for these concessions. On the other hand, by ironing out a serious point of contention with Bangladesh, the Gujral doctrine helped reopen the process that led to the creation of BIMST-EC. New Delhi had till then put the brakes on the Thailand initiative, especially due to its tense relations with Dhaka. All in all, the Gujral doctrine created a climate of cooperation in South Asia, which enhanced India's international image. By easing tensions in its immediate surroundings, New Delhi convinced the ASEAN of its benevolence and capacity to assume regional responsibility. Gujral knew this well and during his first speech in front of the ASEAN partners, he underlined the efforts made by his government to strengthen SAARC and the South Asian Preferential Trading Arrangement (SAPTA). In fact, the Minister for Foreign Affairs emphasized that the 'Look East' policy did not imply that India wished to detach itself from its 'own sub-region'.[73] In Gujral's vision, South Asia and SAARC represented the immediate neighbourhood and thus became the priority zone for India's foreign policy. Beyond the immediate neighbourhood, Gujral worked in terms of 'external circles'.[74] Central Asia and the ASEAN that were considered a part of the 'extended neighbourhood' were brought within the first circle, before the rest of the world. Thus, the ASEAN was considered a very important region for India, and was defined as the 'prosperous circle'. The great merit of Gujral and his doctrine was therefore to give clarity to India's external relations. Working to conceptualize New Delhi's vision of the world and modelling a foreign policy, I.K. Gujral greatly contributed to clearing ASEAN's perceptions. This initiative represented a great step forward for a country that had always suffered from opacity in its diplomatic and strategic choices. Sen Gupta explained it very aptly when he declared: 'Though Gujral has not spoken directly about a foreign policy "doctrine", his thoughts and actions lend themselves to a conceptualized and methodical attempt to place India centre stage in the Asia-Pacific region, and hence in global affairs.'[75]

In this sense, it appeared that I.K. Gujral extended and strengthened P.V. Narasimha Rao's Look East policy.[76] The latter did not stop with officially reassuring the ASEAN, above all he tried to lend credibility to India's declarations on South-East Asia. To be more precise, the Gujral doctrine completed the various confidence-building measures taken by New Delhi with respect to East Asia since the beginning of the 1990s. Especially in South-East Asia, Gujral declared much more firmly than P.V. Narasimha Rao ever did that his country did not have maritime ambitions. P.V. Narasimha Rao had in fact promoted relations between India and the ASEAN by always prioritizing trade and financial cooperation. Security issues were treated as a corollary to economic diplomacy, which could let some doubts linger on in South-East Asia.[77] While P.V. Narasimha Rao directed his foreign policy with an economic logic alone, Gujral once again lent more political and strategic dimensions to Indian initiatives. In this sense, his great contribution was to have officially given a clear picture of security issues, declaring India's peaceful intentions at all regional levels, in Asia. In a climate that continued to improve, Gujral was able to articulate a good policy towards the ASEAN, by establishing greater confidence.

8.2 India's Integration in the ARF

At first glance, it seemed as if India's admission in the ARF had come about quite quickly and naturally, just five years after the first bilateral strategic contacts had been established. But on a closer look, it appeared quite astonishing and raised several paradoxes. The forum was still in its embryonic stage and inexperienced when it decided to welcome India in 1996. It was still not a well-oiled machine, which made it all the more difficult to explain this decision of enlargement. The most salient feature was that India's admission to the ARF stemmed from a specific decision taken by the ASEAN—a deliberate and almost obstinate decision to invite New Delhi. It so happened that this decision was not endorsed by all the ARF members. Indeed, the ASEAN made its choice in India's favour at a time when the country's international position was not at its best. Due to its inflexibility on the nuclear issue, India was slapped with sanctions by a large part of the international community, and especially by the main partners of the ASEAN. In any case, India's involvement in the ARF mechanism remained very modest during the first two years, in 1996 and in 1997.

A Controversial Decision

The ASEAN decided to establish the ARF in response to growing uncertainties concerning the region's strategic evolution. In fact, the Association was anxious to maintain the region's stability and peace that was so necessary for its economic prosperity. The ARF first edition was launched in Bangkok, on 25 July 1994, as a 'forum for dialogue' within which members were invited to exchange ideas on Asia in particular, and international policy and defence, in general.[78] At the time, the ARF had eighteen members: six ASEAN states (Brunei, Indonesia, Malaysia, Singapore, Thailand and Philippines), seven dialogue partners (Australia, New Zealand, Canada, South Korea, Japan, United States and the European Union), three observers (Papua New Guinea, Laos and Vietnam) and two consulting partners (China and Russia). The second ARF meeting was held in Brunei, in 1995. Some concrete proposals were put forth in a concept paper, the first document that explicitly defined the ARF approach, in the face of security problems in the region. More than a mere forum for dialogue, the ARF progressed in a slightly more formal sense, with inter-session activities and the formation of three expert sub-groups, one on confidence measures, the other on peacekeeping operations and the third on maritime search and rescue missions.

For all that, the Brunei meeting did not go as far as accepting more binding activities such as military transparency, non-proliferation and preventive diplomacy. Indeed, the concept paper that the ASEAN circulated in 1995 proposed a three-phased approach. The first phase consisted of promoting confidence-building measures, the second preventive diplomacy practices and finally, the third aimed at creating conflict resolution mechanisms. To be more precise, the forum laid stress on confidence-building measures and preventive diplomacy. Conflict resolution mechanisms remained a more distant goal, which could be envisaged only when the ARF would have acquired some experience. The ARF thus assigned itself a modest role and evolved in a gradual fashion, which was essentially based on specific ASEAN experience in political and strategic cooperation. By and large, the ARF based itself on the same principles as the ASEAN. Personal interactions were the order of the day, as well as a certain predilection for backdoor diplomacy, and an informal style of functioning. Besides, the ASEAN did not wish to institutionalize the ARF, or even set-up a secretariat for it. Decisions were taken by consensus after detailed and cautious consultations between the member states. Finally, the forum wished to move forward at a 'pace that was comfortable for everyone', by refraining to impose solutions on its members. This approach was meant to be non-legalistic, as opposed to the Western approach.

Indeed, the ARF was the brainchild of a group of small states, which were pleased that their more powerful interlocutors had accepted their creation. The ARF primary objective was, in fact, to promote stable relations between major powers, in the general interest of the region. In so doing, the ARF also became the only valid multilateral option, at least in the current state of affairs. In any event, its objective was limited in scope: the climate of regional relations were sought to be improved in the hope that bilateral and multilateral issues become more manageable. In this context, the United States continued to play a very important role and its presence next to China and Japan was considered indispensable for the new security structure. The power of the ARF model was principally due to its collective commitment to dialogue. Its more obvious weakness was that the members were primarily worried about the institution's viability even before taking up concrete issues on regional security.[79]

To some extent, this handicap could be neutralized by the Track II process that complemented the ARF: a Council for Security Co-operation in Asia-Pacific (CSCAP) was in fact established in June 1993, in order to promote parallel discussions in a more informal way. This allowed it to take up issues that were thornier than the ones on the ARF agenda. Discussions on preventive diplomacy and non-proliferation were thus shunted to the Track II level and only confidence-building measures and search and rescue missions were taken up in the intersession activities.[80] The Asia-Pacific strategic community took the first step towards India quite early, thanks to these informal discussion mechanisms. The Indian government think-tank on strategic issues, IDSA, became an associate member of CSCAP as early as December 1994. A year later, the ASEAN officially enrolled New Delhi in the ARF's intergovernmental mechanism. But the important point to be noted here is that: when India became a member of the ARF in 1996, the forum did not represent much in substance. It was still an 'empty shell'.[81] The 1995 session basically sought to find an agreement on the norms and procedures that could give the ARF an embryonic institutional identity. The few inter-session activities that took place were only concerned with instilling confidence and never actually dealt with the real issues of conflict. Also, the decision to invite India seemed to be more of an experiment, in accordance with the ARF's global approach.

However, the United States, Australia and Japan would have preferred to delay New Delhi's admission to the ARF. Their reticence stemmed from India's intractable attitude in the CTBT negotiations, which were then taking place. More specifically, whereas the United States hoped that the CTBT would be adopted at the end of June 1996, the deliberations at the Disarmament Conference had to be postponed, mainly due to New Delhi's opposition. Washington's irritation became even more evident when Clinton came to power. His administration kept up the pressure on India on the nuclear issue, but in vain. Japanese reluctance to India's candidature was also due to bilateral differences with regard to the non-proliferation and the nuclear test ban regimes. The dialogue initiated by these two states in the early 1990s did not produce any significant result.[82] In fact, Indian leaders suspected their Japanese interlocutors of being manipulated by the United States. However, Japan endeavoured to adopt a more measured approach than that of the United States and rather than admonishing New Delhi and Islamabad on the non-proliferation issue, it confined itself to recommending to the two nations to sign the NPT, with in fact very little hope of success. Tokyo also feared that if New Delhi refused to sign the CTBT and the FMCT, this decision was likely to give China a good reason to follow suit. Japan's focus on the issue of non-proliferation was in fact China and not India. Thus, New Delhi and Tokyo found themselves at loggerheads on the nuclear issue. From the Indian viewpoint, Tokyo was acting more out of a concern for its image at the international level especially when it presented itself as a power involved in the prevention of nuclear proliferation. South Asia could thus be a low risk 'testing ground' for the Japanese anti-nuclear diplomacy, as it would have very little to lose, contrary to what would transpire if the subject were to be raised with China.[83]

Dissensions between the ASEAN states and their external partners left the question of New Delhi's participation in the ARF meetings hanging in the balance for a period of time.[84] Indeed, the fifth ASEAN Heads of States and Governments Summit decided to elevate India to the status of a Full Dialogue Partner from December 1995 onwards and the decision was formally announced at the end of the ASEAN's Permanent Committee meeting in January 1996. By virtue of its new status as a dialogue partner, India was also supposed to participate in the ARF. In fact, the 1995 concept paper clearly stated that 'the ARF participants will consist of ASEAN member states, observers and consultative and dialogue partners'. But in practice, India's membership was not automatic. As New Delhi experienced it, its official participation was only confirmed a little before the July 1996 sessions. This delay was due to the irritation shown by the United States, which hardly appreciated India's candidature being processed and accepted exclusively by the ASEAN. Washington, followed by Tokyo in the matter, had many reservations about India's admission, arguing that the forum ought to define eligibility criteria before taking in new members. After parleys with Indian officials, Washington finally accepted to withdraw its objection and Japan followed suit.[85] Eventually, the ASEAN external partners had to accept the decisions taken on integrating India and Myanmar. On 10 May 1996, the ASEAN secretariat officially announced that New Delhi would be a member of the ARF.

The third ARF summit, in 1996, thus saw new members joining the assembly: India and Myanmar. China and Russia, who had already participated in their capacity as observers, also became members. In addition, the institution decided to establish a series of criteria for any subsequent membership, so that it could first consolidate before expanding further.[86] The general criteria for a state to become a member of the ARF were based on its importance for regional security and its political commitment. In practice, this amounted to a moratorium for all new candidatures, with the exception of North Korea. India therefore seemed to have entered *in extremis*, whereas a number of other nations were still knocking at the forum's door: Mongolia, North Korea, Pakistan, Kazakhstan, and Kirghizstan and even European countries such as Great Britain or France. The ASEAN options *vis-à-vis* all these candidatures turned out to be quite problematic. As Michael Leiffer observed and justly so, 'membership is a defining issue in any multilateral undertaking because it influences the content of agendas'.[87] In this context, India's admission was not a good omen from the viewpoint of North-East Asian states as it gave the impression that the ARF centre of gravity had moved away from the strategic stakes of the region. Apart from outstanding issues in the South China Sea, the highest risks of conflicts existed, in fact, in North-East Asia. It so happened that both parties to these potential conflicts were not even represented at the ARF. Taiwan was kept away as was North Korea. This serious lacuna became more complicated when the ASEAN decided to invite New Delhi to the post-ministerial conferences. From the perspective of the North-East Asian states, India's arrival would logically have the effect of diluting the objectives set forth by the ARF.

Even within the ASEAN, it was not easy to obtain a consensus with regard to India's membership. Brunei, Malaysia and Indonesia, three countries with a majority Muslim population, did not hide their reluctance with respect to India's admission and even played the Pakistani card.[88] The strongest support for New Delhi came from Singapore, Vietnam, the Philippines and Thailand. Hanoi's support was nothing but natural, given its old ties with Delhi. As for Bangkok, it had just become aware that collaboration with Indian authorities would help in managing the sub-region around Myanmar as well as the maritime zone of the Bay of Bengal. But it was Singapore, which once again, played an important role in taking the final decision.

The city-state's influence on diplomatic perceptions and the decision-making process within the ASEAN and ARF was well known.[89] And New Delhi's entry into the ARF in particular, and in the Asia-Pacific security order in general, was among the general aims of Singapore's foreign policy in the post-Cold War scenario. In fact, Singapore had started adopting a more active role on the regional and international scene, and *vis-à-vis* America, China, Japan, Russia and India. The city-state had thus outgrown from its traditional preoccupations *vis-à-vis* Malaysia and Indonesia to articulate a flexible multilateral policy that would ensure its survival as a tiny nation. Singapore promoted henceforward the 'vision of a largely tripolar Asia-Pacific security order based on co-operative engagement between the US, China and Japan, while pushing for regional accommodative structures (such as the ASEAN Regional Forum) for emerging or secondary "heavy-weights" such as Indonesia, Australia, India and Russia.'[90] It was in this perspective that Singapore supported India's candidature.

Other factors, from the South-East Asian viewpoint, also played a part in favouring India's entry into the ARF. In matters of maritime cooperation for example, India was important because of its extensive presence in the Indian Ocean, near the Malacca Straits. Furthermore, the Indian Navy was quite powerful and independent in nature. Delimitation of maritime frontiers between India and the South-East Asian nations, Thailand, Indonesia and Myanmar, were already established and posed no problems. As for peacekeeping missions, New Delhi was experienced and could impart training for the forces of the region for such missions. On its part, New Delhi promised not to raise its outstanding issues with Pakistan at the ARF and especially not raise its claims on Kashmir.[91] In fact, some of the ASEAN members feared that the Indo-Pakistani antagonism might interfere with their dialogue mechanism, more so as Islamabad had become the ASEAN sectoral dialogue partner in 1992. But according to the IDSA Director, Jasjit Singh, this fear stemmed from a lack of understanding of the Indian position. India strongly believed that contentious issues with Islamabad had to be dealt with on a bilateral basis, and never in a multilateral forum. The risk of New Delhi raising the Kashmir issue at the ARF was thus far-fetched.[92] It was Pakistan, which strove to internationalize the Kashmir conflict in the first place.

Finally and above all, ASEAN insisted on the autonomy and pre-eminence of its choices. It even appeared that the differences that emerged with respect to India's candidature only ended up strengthening the Association further in its resolve. Thus, at the ASEAN ministers press conference, Ali Alatas, the Indonesian Minister for Foreign Affairs, reaffirmed that it was up to the ASEAN to decide who would be their dialogue partner or an ARF member. A feeling of irritation was noticeable, when he declared: 'The forum was initiated by us and we would like to keep it an ASEAN institution. We would not like to ask others for approval.'[93] The ASEAN, which expected to be the moving force of regional decision-making mechanism, desired to maintain its control over the growth of the ARF, an institution it believed was its creation. But faced with the ASEAN desire to retain a central role in the ARF, several North-East Asian and Pacific states were left with a feeling of frustration. Thus, it was a delicate exercise to manage the ARF, as the aim was to set-up an alternative security mechanism that would not be dependant on the patronage of the major powers, but at the same time, that should be comprehensive enough to ensure the necessary balance of power. In other words, it was a matter of getting the region's major powers to subscribe to the rationale of the ARF, while ensuring that it remained ASEAN's prerogative. The decision to admit India could, in fact, betray certain inherent weaknesses of the ARF. Such a mechanism appeared to be able to function only in the context of a balance of power, but it could not create it by itself. The condition necessary for the ARF's success was thus the pre-existence of a stable balance of power.[94] Aware of this parameter, several ASEAN states probably believed that their security interests would be all the more protected when a large number of players participated in the regional order, the aim being to avoid the domination of a single power, whether regional or extra regional. In this perspective, India appeared to be a relatively important element in the distribution of power in Asia and its place was thus recognized within the ARF. India's admission to the ARF in 1996, at the same time as China and Russia, validated these hypotheses.

Finally, it should be noted that the ARF took in India, China and Myanmar, by the same gesture. Perhaps, the somewhat unexpected admission of New Delhi should also be seen in the framework of the ASEAN policy on the Sino-Burmese issue. Managing Myanmar appeared to be a thorny problem for the Association, for it was at stake both at the regional level, in a latent power struggle with China, and at the international level, owing to the growing divergences with the West, primarily with the European Union. Even while the EU was urging it to follow a policy of economic sanctions, the ASEAN believed that such a radical move would only end up pushing Myanmar further into the arms of the Chinese, a phenomenon that it feared more than anything else.[95] Differences between the ASEAN and the European Union on the policy to be adopted *vis-à-vis* the SLORC grew quite heated at the 1996 post-ministerial conferences in Jakarta, exactly when Myanmar was admitted to the ARF. In the face of the annoyance shown by its European interlocutors, the ASEAN clearly stated that it did not approve of the sanctions regime decreed against the Burmese military junta and it wanted to further engage the country. However, it was probable that the ASEAN felt isolated and caught in a dilemma: the necessity to limit Chinese infiltrations into Myanmar on the one hand and strong pressure exerted by the West not to have any dealings with the SLORC on the other.

Confronted with this impasse, the ASEAN representatives seemed to have sought New Delhi's support. The Association could clearly see that India, while trying to win over the military junta since the beginning of the 1990s, would have preferred to have Myanmar enter the South-East Asian orbit rather than the Chinese. New Delhi thus appeared as an additional player, who could intercede favourably in this game of intermingled pressure being exerted on Myanmar. More specifically, in conformity with their tradition, the ASEAN states assumed that a policy of cooperation and friendship on part of India, coupled with its size, would result in persuading and act as an incentive for Rangoon. Moreover, in ASEAN's judgement, the common participation of both India and China in the ARF could provide them with the opportunity of more frequent and closer interaction, especially to discuss Myanmar. India was thus supposed to support the regional policy of engaging the SLORC in order to relieve the international pressure that was weighing upon the ASEAN. In this respect, it was to be feared that ASEAN overestimated New Delhi's influence and its room for manoeuvre with regard to both Myanmar and China. Especially since New Delhi, on its part, would rather put the ball in the ASEAN court to deal with the collusion between Beijing and Rangoon. In any case, these speculations showed that China was a decisive factor in the ASEAN's decision to admit India to the ARF.

THE PARADOXICAL ADMISSION OF A NUCLEAR 'THRESHOLD' STATE

For a long time, New Delhi had maintained its line of argument on the peaceful use of nuclear energy. But, in reality, it was an undeclared (until May 1998) nuclear state. This ambiguous position was put to a severe test during the first half of the 1990s, when there was a strong revival of international initiatives for enforcing the non-proliferation regime. From the end of 1991, India was under immense international pressure to sign the Non-Proliferation Treaty (NPT). During its five years in power, the Rao government remained paralysed over this issue, which made its position even more ambivalent. It was at that time too weak a government, either to conduct a series of nuclear tests, or to commit itself to sign the treaty.[96] A small group of ministers and high officials seemed to have pressed the Prime Minister to authorise new tests, and face the fallout. But on the diplomatic front, the Indians strove to maintain an ambiguous policy and their stand essentially consisted of eschewing confrontation, while refusing to give in when national interests were at stake over the nuclear issue. But the diplomatic and technological pressure mounted even further in view of the international conference for the indefinite extension of the NPT, which was to be held in mid-1995. Signed in 1968, this treaty was the linchpin of the non-proliferation regime. India had refused to sign it in 1968, on the grounds that it stood for 'nuclear apartheid'. From the Indian point of view, the indefinite and unconditional extension of the NPT demonstrated that the five nuclear powers were not really serious about negotiating true disarmament. India refused to join the non-proliferation regime insisting on the nobler ethical principle of global disarmament, a much more radical alternative that also allowed it to justify its intransigence *vis-à-vis* international negotiations.

In fact, the government regularly announced that it would show no consideration for the NPT. For example, on 3 May 1994, Prime Minister Rao set to rest all rumours that India would be willing to amend its position on the nuclear issue. It was then politically important for the Indian leadership to show that they did not give any quarter to Western pressure on limiting its missile programme or signing the NPT.[97] In the Indian parliament, Rao affirmed that India would participate in the NPT conference only in the event that the contents of the treaty were radically modified. If, on the other hand, the content of the NPT remained unchanged, he reaffirmed that India would not sign it. Therefore, New Delhi remained outside the scope of the negotiations and as expected refused to sign NPT's extension on 11 and 12 May 1995. In this regard, it must be mentioned that New Delhi's decision was not to have any major impact on its Look East policy since the ASEAN decided to elevate it to the status of a dialogue partner only seven months later, at the Bangkok summit of 14 and 15 December 1995.

India's increasingly dissenting and isolated position *vis-à-vis* the international nuclear regime did not prevent its admission to the ARF either. The chronology of the negotiations on the Comprehensive Test Ban Treaty (CTBT) proved this paradox in a more obvious manner. During 1995, the Indian position *vis-à-vis* the CTBT was as dissenting as towards the NPT. However, in the beginning, for nearly two years, New Delhi had supported this plan along with the United States. But in 1995, when the Western nuclear powers showed their eagerness to arrive at a decision at the earliest, New Delhi began to change its tenor and its position on the CTBT's acceptability and became increasingly equivocal. Public opinion in India was totally opposed to the treaty to such an extent that it was clear no government would dare sign it. On its part, the government continued to pontificate against the CTBT, declaring that the country would not accede to the treaty without a commitment to total disarmament by the five nuclear powers.[98] In other words, India would only sign the CTBT on the condition that nuclear powers undertake to eliminate their arsenal within a limited time span.[99]

From an almost defensive approach in the early 1990s, New Delhi gradually moved towards a more assertive attitude and was on the threshold of conducting nuclear tests at the end of 1995.[100] This could have certainly been a warning of a certain magnitude that had the potential of dampening the ASEAN spirit. However, nothing of the sort happened. On the contrary, the ASEAN decided to elevate India's status at the time Washington suspected it of being ready to conduct nuclear tests. Furthermore, the Indian turnaround on the nuclear test issue was clearly evident during the CTBT negotiations in autumn 1995.[101] Thus, the ASEAN had to be aware of the rift that would pit New Delhi against its Western partners in the event it accepted to admit India in the ARF. As it happened, in January 1996, Narasimha Rao officially announced that India would not abandon its nuclear option.[102] And yet, the ASEAN states would not only maintain their decision taken in India's favour but they even went the extra mile to convince their most reluctant partners, the United States and Japan, to accept New Delhi's membership. In other words, the ASEAN states decided to admit New Delhi in the ARF fully aware that the country would not sign the CTBT and that it would be reduced to the status of a pariah state. The ASEAN's decision was all the more paradoxical as its members were strongly antinuclear. Not only had they voted in favour of the CTBT, but in fact, they had also exerted pressure on the Indian authorities to sign the treaty, by underscoring that this was the last opportunity to ban nuclear tests. But India turned a deaf ear to the ASEAN arguments. To tell the truth, the Indian delegation had even attempted to stop the CTBT from being concluded in the name of global disarmament, in the hope that this argument might sway the non-aligned countries. New Delhi, which traditionally considered itself as the leader of NAM, might thus have sought to confirm its leadership over the movement. But in this matter, it suffered a diplomatic setback since most of the non-aligned countries subscribed to the CTBT. In any case, the CTBT was signed after two and a half years of difficult negotiations. The treaty imposed a blanket ban on nuclear tests on all nations in all environments and forever. It ensured that the ban was effective and verifiable and offered a new basis to attain the aims set forth in the Review and Extension of NPT in 1995.

In many respects, the ASEAN states empathized with the Indian nuclear policy. For example, during the negotiations for the NPT's extension, differences in perceptions were sharply in focus between the major nuclear powers, led by the United States, and the non-aligned countries. While the nuclear powers wanted a permanent and unconditional extension of the NPT, most non-aligned nations were in favour of an extension for a limited period. Malaysia, Indonesia, Thailand and Myanmar thus set forth a more moderate option than the one proposed by the West. These nations were part of a group of eleven countries, which proposed on 5 May 1995 that the treaty be extended for renewable periods of twenty-five years.[103] But this option, which did not seem very coherent, had no impact on the negotiation process. Apart from this initiative, Indonesia was constantly seen as one of the countries overtly opposed to an indefinite extension.[104] Along with the Philippine diplomats, the Indonesians publicly protested several times at the United Nations against the deliberate disregard of nuclear powers for Article VI, which required the establishment of a nuclear disarmament timetable. Despite their opposition, these states finally agreed to sign the NPT.[105] Even Japan was not very convinced about the turn taken by the negotiations on the NPT. In May 1995, Japan's Ambassador at the Disarmament Conference, Yoshitomo Tanaka, did not hide the fact that his country had mixed feelings about its decision to support the indefinite extension of the treaty.[106] Japan had even attempted to take up as its own the Indian initiative for total nuclear disarmament. Indian representatives had, in fact, proposed such a resolution at the United Nations, but had finally buckled down under American pressure. And yet, once New Delhi had withdrawn its resolution in April 1995, Tokyo introduced a resolution on similar lines.

On a closer look, it appeared that the NPT conference took place in an atmosphere of considerable pressure for obtaining an indefinite extension. Thus, countries that were undecided at the beginning or inclined towards an alternative solution felt frustrated. They could do nothing against the diplomatic roadroller driven by the nuclear powers to obtain 90 votes required for a decision in their favour. Thus, many observers believed the results marked a major success for the nuclear powers. The adoption of an indefinite extension on 11 May 1995 implied the undeniable enshrining of the status of nuclear-weapon states, for they were recognized as such by the treaty. At the end of the conference, many leaders of delegation among the non-aligned countries did not hide their bitterness. This was, for instance, the case of the Malaysian representative, Hasmy Bin Agam, who observed that the nuclear club members had obtained a free hand and their arsenal was *de facto* legalized.[107] At the same time, the five nuclear powers refused to commit themselves to a definite disarmament timetable, contrary to the recommendations of Article VI of the NPT.

As regards the CTBT, the anti-nuclear East Asian states also had reasons to be dissatisfied. The CTBT negotiations proved, if it were necessary, the pre-eminence of Nuclear-Weapon States (NWS) over other states. The treaty did not prevent non-explosive tests, which meant that the five NWS could continue to qualitatively improve their nuclear arsenal without any hurdles, thanks to the simulation techniques. As in the case of the NPT, the negotiations took place amid considerable diplomatic pressure. The Disarmament Conference had thus accepted an amendment, which made the treaty operative only when the three threshold states—India, Pakistan and Israel—

agreed to participate. The purpose behind this legal manoeuvre was to make the Indian delegation give in and accept the project. India, on the contrary, only became more inflexible and categorically refused to sign the treaty. From the Indian point of view, this amendment went against all international laws, for it forced the country to be a signatory to a treaty that it did not want to accept by making it operative only after it affixed its signature.[108] Several countries were convinced, like India, that this formula concerning the implementation of the treaty was unacceptable. Several nations would have also liked to strengthen clauses pertaining to the objectives of the treaty, as well as references to nuclear disarmament. On 20 August 1996, New Delhi decided to cast its veto against the adoption of the treaty even while voting was being carried out by consensus. The Indian delegation had declared in no uncertain terms that it would allow the treaty to be adopted by abstaining to vote, provided the amendment pertaining to its signature was withdrawn. But as this proposal found no response, India finally used its veto. The draft resolution of the treaty was subsequently presented at the United Nations General Assembly where the debate on it ended on 10 September 1996 with an Australian resolution adopting the CTBT and calling for a signature conference as early as possible. About 158 members voted in favour of the Australian resolution that was seconded by 126 countries. However, it must be noted that several non-aligned countries abstained from supporting the resolution, including Indonesia and Malaysia, apart from Sri Lanka, Egypt, Nigeria, Zimbabwe and Mexico.[109] The Malaysian delegation, in particular, strongly criticized the incomplete and ineffective nature of the treaty at the General Assembly. Yet, it voted in favour of the CTBT because it considered it as a step in the right direction.[110]

The 51st session of the United Nations General Assembly was held on 30 September 1996, i.e. a few days after the CTBT was signed at the Disarmament Conference. On this occasion, the Indonesian Minister for Foreign Affairs, Ali Alatas, stressed on the shortcomings of the CTBT and the necessity to pursue total nuclear disarmament.[111] Consequently, he asked the Disarmament Conference to set-up a special committee to undertake negotiations on a programme of final elimination of nuclear weapons within a limited time span. He reminded those present that the treaty was far from fulfilling the aims of the CTBT the way the international community had originally conceived them, in addition to the fact that it still permitted the most sophisticated tests possible through simulation and that it was not truly comprehensive in nature. It just made it more difficult for a nation to develop and improve its nuclear arsenal. If Indonesia had signed the treaty, it was in order to make its contribution to total denuclearization. But the Indonesian representative affirmed in no uncertain terms that the final objective had to be total nuclear disarmament. It was, in fact, the same Ali Alatas, who explained, in the *Jakarta Post* dated 22 March 1996, how the ASEAN perceived India's nuclear position within the ARF. Inasmuch as India had been accepted as a dialogue partner, he spelled out, the ARF's entrance door was open to it, even though it was an undeclared nuclear power and had not signed the NPT. He further added that India's nuclear stand was secondary to the issues and debates in the ARF, as the forum had postponed to a distant future all debates on non-proliferation. On the other hand, Alatas pointed out that above all the ARF was anxious to ensure regional representation, and India, regardless of its nuclear arsenal, had a 'natural' place within the forum as an important player of the region.

The 1996 annual ASEAN meetings took place at the same time as when India was involved in a trial of strength with the NWS at the Disarmament Conference. To be more precise, the Post-Ministerial Conference with New Delhi took place on 24 July 1996, that is five days before the sixty-one members of the Disarmament Conference were to meet once again at Geneva, on 29 July, to discuss the final proposals of the CTBT.[112] Despite the Indian presence, neither the CTBT, nor nuclear issues dominated the July 1996 ASEAN con-ference. The Annual Meeting of the Foreign Ministers (AMM) and the ARF Post-Ministerial Conferences focused their attention on Myanmar and the rising economic concerns of the ASEAN.[113] This agenda was characteristic of the ASEAN style as well as of its desire to focus the conference agenda according to its priorities and concerns. Besides, New Delhi enjoyed the benefits of the rule of non-interference in the internal affairs of partner countries that was so dear to the ASEAN. It also benefited from the inherent limitations of the ARF, as the forum was not in a position to discuss nuclear non-proliferation.

At the press conference at the end of the ASEAN Ministerial Conference, Ali Alatas referred, once again, to the Indian position with regard to the CTBT. His quite moderate speech endeavoured to make the Indian leadership come to a compromise, urging them to modify their stand, while taking care not to sound too peremptory.

While respecting India's stand on CTBT and the ideal of total nuclear disarmament, the Indonesian minister advised the country not to waste the opportunity represented by the treaty and gave the assurance that his country was wholly in favour of the fight for the elimination of nuclear weapons and promised to fight side by side with India.[114] From a 'strategic' and 'technical' point of view however, he requested India to accept the CTBT for the time being in order to continue the fight against nuclear disarmament. To refuse the CTBT was to play into the hands of the nuclear powers, by letting the 1997 deadline go by. Alatas thus attempted to mobilize Indian diplomacy against the NWS clan. He concluded nonetheless by conceding that India had the sovereign right to adopt the stand that suited it the best. The latter responded to its interlocutors, but stuck to its stand: unless there was a substantial change in the content of the CTBT, it would not be in a position to sign the treaty.[115]

All said and done, it was international nuclear discrimination rather than India's nuclearization that irked the ASEAN. During the Bangkok summit in December 1995, the seven ASEAN heads, as well as those of Laos, Cambodia and Myanmar signed the South-East Asia Nuclear Weapons Free Zone (SEANWFZ) treaty. The terms of the treaty prohibited the production, storage and testing of nuclear weapons, while giving the signatories the individual right to grant access to the NWS maritime vessels and aircrafts. Apart from the adherence of all the regional governments present at Bangkok, the ASEAN also aspired to obtain the support of all permanent members of the Security Council. Hard pressed to see the treaty come into effect as early as possible, the ASEAN hoped that all the nuclear powers would approve of the treaty and accede to its protocol. But it soon became apparent that the ASEAN would not be able to mobilize the support of two of the major external powers, the United States and China.[116] Washington underlined that the SEANWFZ was likely to impede the free movement of its military apparatus and naval vessels. China believed that this initiative was an attempt to undermine its claim of sovereignty over some areas of the South China Sea. Consequently, at the July 1996 ARF summit, the ASEAN member states restated their position on nuclear non-proliferation in stronger terms. Following India's model, they called for a 'total and effective' implementation of the non-proliferation treaty.[117]

For New Delhi, the ARF meeting and the Post-Ministerial Conferences of July 1996 helped it conduct several bilateral dialogues of primary importance. The Indian head of delegation, I.K. Gujral, had a private meeting with the American Secretary of State Warren Christopher, the Russian Minister for Foreign Affairs A. Primakov, the Japanese Minister for Foreign Affairs Y. Ikeda, as well as his Australian and Canadian counterparts. The ARF thus helped Indian diplomacy to present a better view of its nuclear policy to the powers most opposed to it. The forum emerged as the best 'diplomatic platform' at the very moment when India needed to speak out in clear terms on the international arena and when it was on the verge of becoming a 'pariah' state. According to I.K. Gujral, the nuclear issue was also raised during multilateral meetings and revealed that other participants shared New Delhi's anxiety. This was not the least of the paradoxes: there was an emerging feeling that the Indian diplomacy left the 1996 ARF conference reassured and comforted as far as its decision was concerned. Thus, when discussions on the CTBT resumed during the Disarmament Conference, on 29 July 1996, I.K. Gujral was confident and asserted that the Indian stand was appreciated by many countries who wished to reinforce the provisions pertaining to the objectives of the treaty as well as references to nuclear disarmament.[118] The most candid in this matter was once again Ali Alatas, who in his capacity as the president of the Post-Ministerial Sessions would have 'appreciated India's principled stand, both about the goal of achieving a nuclear weapon-free world as well as the need to ensure that the CTBT bring an end to vertical proliferation'.[119] S.D. Muni confirmed Gujral's assertions and observed *a posteriori*: 'Many of the ASEAN members have shown considerable understanding and sympathy for India's stand of not signing the CTBT, notwithstanding the fact that these countries themselves have signed the CTBT. This was evident during India's maiden participation in the ARF meeting in July at Jakarta.'[120]

After all is said and done, India's admission to the ARF offered two possible interpretations.[121] The more sober and objective explanation would be that the ASEAN accepted to continue having a functional relation with New Delhi, despite the open disagreement over the nuclear issue. In fact, this was what the ASEAN leadership officially gave to understand when it said the nuclear issue was secondary in the ARF perception. According to a second analysis, of a more speculative nature, the ASEAN felt that its interest would be well served, if it welcomed in its strategic forum an undeclared nuclear state, which was moreover situated on China's western flank. Perhaps

India's implicit nuclear capability was considered an additional means—as a last resort—of exerting pressure over China. It was understandable that the official declaration did not show such reasoning. On the other hand, it was clear that the ASEAN members were shocked by China's arrogance during the negotiations on the nuclear issue. In fact, Beijing had continued with fresh underground nuclear tests a little after the NPT had been extended indefinitely, in May 1995. The 45th Chinese nuclear tests took place on 29 July 1996, at the same time that negotiations on the CTBT were striving to find a compromise to play down Beijing's objections regarding inspection and verification procedures. Japan was also hit hard by the Chinese attitude. Consequently, New Delhi certainly touched a sensitive chord in East Asia when it justified its nuclear programme citing the Chinese arsenal.

INDIA'S LOW-KEY PARTICIPATION

When it first attended the ARF, in July 1996, New Delhi was on the defensive. It was under international opprobrium at that time for its refusal to sign the CTBT. The Indian delegation thus adopted a low profile, while maintaining its stand on the nuclear options. In addition, Indian diplomats endeavoured to convince their interlocutors that their country would be a stabilizing factor in the region. I.K. Gujral asserted to his ASEAN partners: 'India can thus complement and supplement ASEAN's own quest for establishing a stable, predictable and balanced political security order in the Asia-Pacific region. Being of the region, and yet with no history of direct involvement in the conflicts of the region, we can be and we have every intention of being a constructive and stabilizing factor for peace.'[122]

I.K. Gujral also asserted that he shared the ASEAN way for creating a peaceful order: 'We share the ASEAN conviction that only a graduated, consensual and peaceful approach can help in resolving differences on sensitive, political and security issues.'[123] The speech thus appeared to hold promise. New Delhi appeared willing to play the role of a responsible and stabilizing power.

But for the ASEAN diplomats, India's assertions were soon to be seen as formal declarations. The Association was, in fact, quite disappointed by a certain lack of involvement on the part of New Delhi. During the first Post-Ministerial Conference with Indian representatives in 1996, the Singapore Minister for Foreign Affairs,

S. Jayakumar, expressed ASEAN's expectations with regard to India's participation: 'India, given its size and strategic location in the Indian Ocean, can play a constructive and positive role in contributing to the stability of the region.'[124] Faced with the certainty of China's growth, India saw itself bestowed with quite a reassuring role for the ASEAN. Objectively speaking, the country was in fact a strategic heavyweight in the region. In 1997, the Indian army was the largest in its genre in the subcontinent and second in Asia.[125] Because of the size of its population and military, the ASEAN expected India to exert some informal influence within the ARF, thereby consolidating the nascent multilateral dialogue in the Asia-Pacific region.

Furthermore, in 1998, the ASEAN decided to extend its strategic partnership with New Delhi by establishing a new consultative institution, bringing together top Indian and ASEAN officials. The aim of these meetings was to upgrade the dialogue in strategic matters and facilitate the setting up of a 'pluralistic security order' in the region.[126] Once again, it was Singapore, which from the ASEAN side, donned the mantle of India's interlocutor. The first meeting took place on 15 February 1998, between the Foreign Secretary, M. Raghunath, and his Singapore counterpart, Kishore Mahbubani. But this inaugural meeting was essentially an opportunity for the ASEAN representatives to express their frustration at India's retiring attitude in the ARF. They regretted that New Delhi was behaving as a reticent player with little confidence in the regional institution. There seemed to be an apparent gap between the ASEAN's expectations and India's perceptions. Indian diplomacy generally seemed to be floundering on the direction it should give to its participation in the ARF, whereas ASEAN had sought its admission so that it actively participate in building a multilateral security order in the region. In fact, it was for the first time that India engaged in multilateral security talks, outside the confines of the United Nations. This certainly enabled it to have better access to information and dialogue with its counterparts, both at the official and unofficial levels. At the same time, Indian diplomacy had never before discussed its security problems in multilateral fora. Therefore, it was probable that it was somewhat on its guard and hesitated to commit itself, unable to see the implications of these multilateral interactions.

Consequently, the Indian agenda for the region continued to be more economic than political. Besides, it was the Indian Finance Minister, P. Chidambaram, who led the Indian delegation to the 1997

Post-Ministerial Conferences and ARF meetings. Membership of the ARF thus did not much change the Indian approach, which continued to follow the trade diplomacy of yore, despite the innovations introduced by the 'Gujral doctrine' in 1996. This observation held no good for both multilateral and bilateral strategic relations. Thus, the defence cooperation treaty that New Delhi signed with Kuala Lumpur in 1993 seemed to have borne the brunt of an essentially commercial approach. This agreement that was very promising and ought to have covered a large spectrum of projects remained, in the final analysis, only limited to training of Malaysian Air Force personnel in India. Differences appeared at first on the issue of Indian flying instructors working in Malaysia. Then, the Malaysian party accused the Indians of wanting to find a market for their military industry rather than collaborate in the joint development of defence equipment.[127]

Many experts regretted India's essentially commercial approach, for it reduced its importance in the region. By limiting its role to economic imperatives, New Delhi failed to adopt a policy that would have a real impact on the peace and security of the region.[128] After becoming a member of the ARF, India did not take pains to fine tune its position in the forum, just as it did not contribute any specific ideas on the institution's evolution. These failures revealed that New Delhi had still not formulated a clear policy on the region. Obtaining the status of a dialogue partner and ARF membership constituted a big step forward for the Look East policy and an important leverage for Indian foreign policy. Yet, these events did not receive the attention they deserved in the Indian political circles. Apart from lobbying for admission to the different Asian institutions, the Indian leadership did not seem to have taken the necessary care to evolve a general vision on India's place in Asia. This was clearly apparent in the case of the ARF.

It must also be noted that there was an organizational aspect to this issue. Rather than being handled by the South-East Asian Division, the ARF dealings were entrusted to the Disarmament Section of the External Affairs Ministry. This department was mainly concerned with problems of international security and specifically those that pertained to the nuclear issues. To say the least, the Disarmament Section was overburdened with work. And logically, it essentially devoted itself to nuclear issues, especially from 1995 onwards when it had to manage the Indian stand at Washington and Geneva.

Handling the ARF with such a busy agenda was thus of secondary importance.[129] But the organizational problems were also more general in nature and concerned the Indian security policy as a whole. Whereas structural reforms had been undertaken in matters of economic diplomacy, the strategic aspects of the foreign policy continued to display serious deficiencies. There was no consistency in the way the various mechanisms constituting the state machinery for national security—Ministries of External Affairs and Defence, armed forces and intelligence agencies—functioned, or in their efficiency.[130] It ensued that New Delhi was unable to formulate a general vision that would integrate both its external relations and defence priorities.

Another major problem was also related to the fact that India's diplomatic and defence policies depended upon political figures in power, without there being specialized institutions to support them effectively. As an example, I.K. Gujral was originally expected to go in person to Kuala Lumpur for the ARF sessions in 1997. Symbolically, this visit would have been significant, as he also occupied the post of Prime Minister at the time. But it was precisely the joint charge of being both the Prime Minister and External Affairs Minister that prevented him from attending this important meeting.[131] This monopolization of diplomatic functions by the head of state was a frequent phenomenon since at least 1991. It often had the disadvantage of stunting the functioning of the Ministry of External Affairs, starting with foreign policy. Thus, despite the fact that I.K. Gujral took care to stay in regular contact with the Ministry of External Affairs, he remained not only preoccupied with general Prime Ministerial responsibilities, but also by the day-to-day management of internal differences within the coalition government. In this set-up in which a Prime Minister was hardly available to deal with international affairs and thereby, in which he limited his foreign ministry's room for manoeuvre, Indian foreign policy as a whole lost its dynamism.[132] Even at the level of the Track II process, Indian participation did not really come up to Asian expectations. The IDSA only sporadically participated at the Council for Security Cooperation in Asia-Pacific (CSCAP) meetings, as the institute was unable to coordinate with the Ministry of External Affairs to finance its participation at CSCAP. As for the Indian bureaucracy, it practiced informal diplomacy rather grudgingly, despite some initial steps taken in this direction. The Indians found it difficult to believe that unofficial dialogues could be an important process for furthering their security interests in Asia. Thus, India's involvement remained rather limited in the strategic community networks of the Asia-Pacific region.

Finally, if New Delhi did not fulfil the ASEAN expectations within the framework of ARF and CSCAP, it was also because it was very preoccupied with its international agenda. During 1996, for instance, Indian diplomats were essentially counting on obtaining a non-permanent seat at the Security Council. The country at that time faced competition from Japan for obtaining the seat left vacant by Indonesia. The decision to present its candidature had been taken as early as 1994, under Rao's Congress government. The United Front government, with I.K. Gujral as the External Affairs Minister, stood by that decision. New Delhi had even refused the compromise proposed by Japan for sharing the seat for a year each.[133] Furthermore, the Foreign Affairs Ministry officials were divided on the soundness of competing with Japan, a country from which India expected a lot on the economic front. In addition, after its refusal to sign the CTBT in 1996, India's chances were certainly not very bright. The vote on 31 December 1996 for a non-permanent seat in the Security Council ended in an humiliation for India: 142 states voted in favour of Japan whereas India was able to obtain only forty votes, that is one-fifth of the United Nations members.[134] Most non-aligned countries voted against New Delhi, as did the large majority of the members of the Organization of the Islamic Conference. And even the votes India did obtain were essentially by default like for instance Beijing's vote, as it wanted above all to oppose Japan's candidature.

This failure led to a major disappointment for India. The country, which believed that it had strong ties with the United Nations, suddenly found itself on a weak wicket and greatly isolated. While the decision not to sign the CTBT had given rise to euphoria, giving the impression that India was recognized as a major independent power on the international scene, the loss of the non-permanent seat in the Security Council to Japan demonstrated that India's global aspirations were far from being recognized by its peers. This incident also brought about a major debate on the disorganized nature of the External Affairs Ministry and the dysfunctioning of the decision-making process as far as foreign policy was concerned. While Indian diplomacy's shortcomings in the Asia-Pacific region remained confidential, its deficiency with respect to the United Nations did not pass unobserved. Indian commentators pointed out the lack of perceptiveness as far as the international balance of power was concerned and the lacunae in political orientation. Nevertheless, this debacle was the outcome of a misjudgement on the part of I.K. Gujral.

However, it is to be noted that these developments did not affect Indo-Japanese relations.[135] First and foremost, the issue of the candidature for a non-permanent seat had a greater impact in India than in Japan. Further, Indian observers essentially placed the thinkers of Indian diplomacy in the dock, and exhorted them to consider the Japanese approach as a lesson in pragmatism and economic diplomacy from which they had a great deal to learn. In what way did they expect to compete with a state, whose financial contribution to the United Nations was second only to the United States? Japan on its part did not crow about its victory, which could have added to India's humiliation, as it was more preoccupied with gaining a permanent seat in the Security Council. But this longer-term ambition was also in competition with that of New Delhi, which had also been fighting for obtaining the status of a permanent member in the Security Council. Indeed, neither Japan, nor India had publicly expressed their common, not to say rival, desire to become a permanent member of the United Nations Security Council. However, as of February 1995, New Delhi and Tokyo began preliminary consultations on the issue of restructuring the United Nations. And yet, in May 1996, India openly opposed the proposal of giving the status of permanent members of the Security Council to both Germany and Japan, by putting forward the argument that both these countries belonged to the group of industrialized nations and a more equitable representation entailed a membership for a country from the South. In other words, it was its own candidature that New Delhi was defending.

Relations with Japan revealed India's ambitions. New Delhi did not hesitate to vie with Tokyo, although it was an important partner in its Look East policy, to assert its claim as a major power on the international scene. India, in fact, postulated that it ought to be a permanent member of the Security Council, believing it to be a clear symbol of a major power. To tell the truth, from the time they obtained their independence, Indians had always believed their country was destined to be a major international player.[136] But, with the sustained growth of the 1990s, the nation gained in confidence and became more assertive in its aspirations for an appropriate role in international affairs. These new ambitions were an important factor that shaped India's relations with the United States and the countries of East Asia.

NOTES

1. C. Raja Mohan, 'India's Security Challenges', in N. Jetley, ed., *India's Foreign Policy*, p. 53.
2. Chintamani Mahapatra, 'Indo-American Relations after the Cold War', *Asian Strategic Review 1995–6*, p. 243.
3. Shubha Singh, 'Strategic Turn in Indo-US', *Pioneer*, 23 October 1997.
4. MEA, *Annual Report 1995–6*, p. 28.
5. *The Financial Express*, 5 May 1997.
6. *Times of India*, 28 July 1997.
7. K.K. Katyal, 'Dealing with Japan', *The Hindu*, 28 July 1997.
8. Among the 'constraints' that restrain the official stand on strategic matters, the defensive nature of the Japanese army as defined by the country's constitution, the importance of Japanese-American security relations, the choice of a strong anti-nuclear policy and the necessity to maintain good neighbourly relations with China must be noted in particular.
9. Asrani, 'India-Japan Relations', in FSI, *Indian Foreign Policy*, p. 352.
10. *Times of India*, 28 July 1997.
11. Dutt, *India's Foreign Policy in a Changing World*, p. 385.
12. Ranganathan, 'India-China Relations—Retrospect and Prospects', FSI, *Indian Foreign Policy*, p. 240. For example a seminar on Sino-Indian relations took place in Beijing on 27 and 28 August 1996. Chinese scholars and diplomats participated whilst from the Indian side it was the think-tank, Rajiv Gandhi Foundation and its affiliated body, Institute for Contemporary Studies, which took part in the event.
13. Naidu, 'India and ASEAN', *Strategic Analysis*, April 1996, p. 71.
14. Dutt, *India's Foreign Policy in a Changing World*, p. 251.
15. MEA, *Annual Report, 1994–5*, p. 20.
16. *Indian Recorder*, 2–8 July 1995.
17. Ibid., 19–25 March 1994.
18. Naidu, 'Navies of Asian Major Powers', *Strategic Analysis*, December 1996, pp. 1339–40.
19. Roy-Chaudhury, 'The Role of Naval Diplomacy in India's Foreign Policy', FSI, *Indian Foreign Policy*, p. 197.
20. MEA, *Annual Report, 1996–7*, p. 21.
21. Roy-Chaudhury, 'The Role of Naval Diplomacy in India's Foreign Policy', FSI, *Indian Foreign Policy*, pp. 201–2.
22. V. Shalini Menon, 'Milan 97—An Eyewitness Report', *Strategic Digest*, vol. 27, no. 6, June 1997, p. 793.
23. Roy-Chaudhury, 'The Limits to Naval Expansion', in Tanham, Bajpai and Mattoo, *Securing India*, p. 199.
24. Ayoob, *India and South-East Asia: Indian Perceptions and Policies*, pp. 35–6, 77.

25. Dutt, *India's Foreign Policy in a Changing World*, pp. 258–60.
26. L.K. Tran, 'Vietnam-India Multifaceted Cooperation for Development and Prosperity', Vietnam, 2 September 1945–2 September 1995 (Embassy of the Socialist Republic of Vietnam, New Delhi, 1995), p. 18 (referred in G. Jha, 'India's Vietnam Policy in Regional Perspective', *Strategic Analysis*, January 1996, p. 1431).
27. *FEER*, 22 September 1994, p. 17.
28. Chuffrin (ed.), *Russia and Asia: The Emerging Security Agenda*, p. 423.
29. *Indian Recorder*, 26 February–3 March 1996.
30. Gupta 'India Redefines Its Role', *Adelphi Paper*, p. 42.
31. Chris Smith, *India's Ad Hoc Arsenal: Direction or Drift in Defence Policy?*, Stockholm: SIPRI, and Oxford University Press, 1994, p. 141.
32. Gupta, 'India Redefines Its Role', *Adelphi Paper*, pp. 47–8. It had even discussed proposals for a joint venture with China for civil transport vehicles.
33. The contract appeared to have been signed during General B.C. Joshi' visit to Moscow in March 1993. But Yeltsin and Rao had already signed treaties on military cooperation on 28 January 1993, in New Delhi, especially the one on sale and production of Russian arms and for supply of Russian spare parts. Shannon Kile, 'Appendix 2, Chronology of Principal Defence and Security-related Agreements' in Chuffrin, ed., *Russia and Asia*, pp. 500–5; *India Recorder*, 14–20 May 1994.
34. Dornier-228 is a medium-range maritime patrol aircraft. Of Russian design, it was manufactured in India under license.
35. Appendix 3, 'Transfers of Major Conventional Weapons by Russia to Asian countries, 1992–1998', in Chuffrin, ed., *Russia and Asia*, pp. 506–12.
36. Gupta, 'India Redefines Its Role', *Adelphi Paper*, p. 61.
37. *Indian Recorder*, 15–21 October 1994.
38. *India Recorder*, 14–20 May 1994; Naidu, 'India and ASEAN', *Strategic Analysis*, April 1996, p. 71.
39. Naidu, 'Post-Cold War Pacific Asian Security: Indian Perceptions and Options', *Delhi Papers*, p. 81.
40. SIPRI, 'Military Spending and Armament, 1998', *SIPRI Yearbook 1999, Armaments, Disarmament and International Security*, Stockholm: SIPRI and Oxford University Press, 1999, pp. 471–2.
41. MEA, *Annual Report 1996–7*, p. 21.
42. Gordon, *India's Rise to Power*, p. 350.
43. *Times of India*, 4 April 1993 (referred in Sridharan, *The ASEAN Region in India's Foreign Policy*, p. 178).
44. Menon, *A Nuclear Strategy for India*, p. 209. A.P.J. Kalam was the Programme Director, before taking over the reins of DRDO and being appointed as the Scientific Advisor in the Defence Ministry.

45. It is interesting to note that Singapore had already made use of the facilities at the Chandipur missile test centre, for test firing its own cannons and missiles. Naidu, 'India and ASEAN', *Strategic Analysis*, p. 71.
46. Ravinderpal Singh, 'Indian Ballistic Missile Developments: Possibilities and Potentialities', *Strategic Analysis*, January 1991, vol. 13, no. 10, p. 1150.
47. Dinshaw Mistry, 'India's Emerging Space Programme', *Pacific Affairs*, vol. 71, no. 2, Summer 1998, p. 151.
48. After two test flights in 2001 and 2003, India successfully operated its first GSLV rocket in September 2004.
49. Mistry, 'India's Emerging Space Program', *Pacific Affairs*, p. 162.
50. Ibid., pp. 172–3.
51. Ibid., pp. 171–3.
52. Menon, *A Nuclear Strategy for India*, p. 112. In 1996, the IISS remarked that the IRS-1C satellite launched in December 1995 sent black and white images with a resolution of 6 metres that were among the most accurate in the commercial market (International Institute for Strategic Studies, *The Military Balance 1995/96*, London: Oxford University Press for IISS, p. 152).
53. Raja Menon believed, however, that even the second generation Agni II, supposed to have a range of 2,500 km, would be hardly able to strike the Chinese National Command Post in the mountainous regions of the country's west (Menon, *A Nuclear Strategy for India*, p. 114).
54. Ravinderpal Singh, 'Post-Cold War Dual-Use Technology Transfer Order: Policy Implications for India', *Strategic Analysis*, January 1992, vol. 16, no. 10, p. 1186.
55. IRS satellites of various generations were launched successively in March 1988, August 1991, September 1993, December 1995, March 1996, September 1997 and May 1999. India now has one of the most extensive IRS satellite system in the world.
56. Mistry, 'India's Emerging Space Program', *Pacific Affairs*, pp. 151, 165–7.
57. P.V.N. Rao, 'India and the Asia-Pacific', *ISEAS*, 8 September 1994, Discussion, pp. 32–3; *FEER*, 22 September 1994, p. 17.
58. Ibid.
59. Tanham, 'Indian Strategic Culture', *Washington Quarterly*, pp. 129–42.
60. Habib, 'South-East Asian Perceptions of India's Strategic Development' in Babbage and Gordon, *India's Strategic Future*, p. 108.
61. Dewi Fortuna Anwar, 'Indonesia's Role in ASEAN: An ASEAN Perspective', Baladas Ghoshal, ed., *ASEAN and South Asia: A Development Experience*, New Delhi: Sterling Publishers, 1998, pp. 99–111.

62. Habib, 'Southeast Asian Perceptions of India's Strategic Development', in Babbage and Gordon, ed., *India's Strategic Future*, p. 111.
63. *The Times of India*, 4 August 1997. Sharif signed an important treaty on defence cooperation, which in the initial phase, provided for military training of officers of either countries.
64. Limaye, 'Sushi and Samosas: Indo-Japanese Relations after the Cold War', in Gordon and Henningham, *India Looks East*, p. 176.
65. K.K. Katyal, 'Dealing with Japan', *The Hindu*, 28 July 1997.
66. The principles of the doctrine were laid down for the first time on 23 September 1996 during a speech at Chatham House in London.
67. Speech by the External Affairs Minister I.K. Gujral, 'Essential Tenets of Indian Foreign Policy' on the occasion of the Inauguration of the Indian Association for International Affairs, New Delhi, 15 January 1997, p. 6.
68. Interview, Bhabani Sen Gupta, New Delhi, 27 November 1998. Bhabani Sen Gupta, 'India in the Twenty-first Century', *International Affairs*, vol. 73, no. 2, 1997, pp. 297–314.
69. Ibid., p. 309.
70. Ibid.
71. Interview, Bhabani Sen Gupta, New Delhi, 27 November 1998.
72. Raja Mohan, 'India's Security Challenges', in Jetley, ed., *India's Foreign Policy*, p. 56.
73. Statement by External Affairs Minister of India I.K. Gujral on the occasion of the Post-Ministerial Conferences of ASEAN (PMC - 7+10), 24 July 1996, Jakarta, § 10.
74. Speech by External Affairs Minister, I.K. Gujral, 'Essential Tenets of Indian Foreign Policy', January 1997, p. 7.
75. Sen Gupta, 'India in the Twenty-first Century', *International Affairs*, p. 309.
76. Interview, S.D. Muni, School of International Studies, JNU, New Delhi, 15 November 1997; Charan Whadwa, Centre for Policy Research, New Delhi, 16 March 1998.
77. In this respect, it was necessary to remember that at the end of 1995 and in early 1996, India's image was not free of all suspicions. In an editiorial Sunanda K. Datta-Ray in early January 1996, expressed concern about the persisting propensity amidst India's neighbours to believe in the country's hegemonic intention. He observed that at a seminar in Baṇdung, the Indonesian Army Chief, General Feisal Tanjung, accused India of 'nurturing ambitions to dominate the Indian Ocean'. Similarly, Bangladesh's High Commissioner in Singapore, M.A. Malik declared that many countries suspected that the IOR–ARC process would fuel India's hegemonic interests (Sunanda K. Datta-Ray, 'An India with Hegemonic Desires?', *Pioneer*, 11 January 1996.

78. U.B. Singh, 'Evolution of the ASEAN Regional Forum', *Asian Strategic Review*, p. 138.
79. Leifer, 'The ASEAN Regional Forum', pp. 45–6. Extending ASEAN's Model of Regional Security, London: IISS/Oxford University Press, July 1996, *Adelphi Paper*, no. 302, p. 145.
80. U.B. Singh, 'Evolution of the ASEAN Regional Forum', *Asian Strategic Review*, 1995–6, p. 145; Interview, Udai Bhanu Singh, IDSA, New Delhi, 19 November 1998.
81. Boisseau du Rocher, *L'ASEAN et la Construction Régionale en Asie du Sud-Est*, p. 283.
82. Limaye, 'The Japan-India Encounter', *RGICS Paper*, p. 18.
83. Limaye, 'Sushi and Samosas', in Gordon and Henningham, eds., *India Looks East*, p. 180.
84. *Indian Recorder*, 6–12 May 1996.
85. Kesavan, 'India and Japan', FSI, *Indian Foreign Policy*, p. 329.
86. Boisseau du Rocher, *L'ASEAN et la Construction Régionale en Asie du Sud-Est*, p. 57; Leifer, 'The ASEAN Regional Forum', pp. 48–9.
87. Ibid., p. 48.
88. S. Viswam, 'India's Look East Policy', *World Focus*, vol. 18, no. 6, June 1997, p. 5.
89. Alan Chong, 'Analysing Singapore's Foreign Policy in the 1990s and Beyond: Limitations of the Small State Approach', *Asian Journal of Political Sciences*, vol. 6, no. 1, June 1998, p. 105.
90. Ibid., pp. 99–100.
91. *The Times of India News Service*, 24 July 1996.
92. Jasjit Singh, 'An Indian Perspective', in Gordon and Henningham, ed., *India Looks East*, p. 52.
93. *The Hindu*, 22 July 1996.
94. Leifer, 'The ASEAN Regional Forum', p. 57.
95. Baladas Ghoshal, 'The ASEAN Identity', *World Focus*, vol. 18, no. 6, June 1997, p. 8.
96. Menon, *A Nuclear Strategy for India*, pp. 104–5.
97. *Indian Recorder*, 28 May–3 June 1994.
98. Menon, *A Nuclear Strategy for India*, pp. 109–10.
99. *International Herald Tribune*, 9 July 1996.
100. Raja Mohan, 'India's Security Challenges', in Jetley, ed., *India's Foreign Policy*, p. 47.
101. *International Herald Tribune*, 9 July 1996.
102. Menon, *A Nuclear Strategy for India*, p. 110.
103. The eleven countries were North Korea, Malaysia, Indonesia, Jordan, Zimbabwe, Nigeria, Mali, Thailand, Myanmar, Papua New Guinea and Iran. Thérèse Delpech, 'Une victoire éclatante et fragile', *Politique Etrangère*, 'Dissuasion et non-prolifération après la conférence du TNP', vol. 60, no. 3, Autumn 1995, pp. 695–705.

104. *Indian Recorder*, 28 May–3 June 1995.
105. U.B. Singh, 'Evolution of the ASEAN Regional Forum', *Asian Strategic Review*, pp. 339–40.
106. *Indian Recorder*, 14–20 May 1995.
107. See the special edition of *Politique Etrangère*, 'Dissuasion et non-prolifération après la conférence du TNP', vol. 60, no. 3, Autumn 1995.
108. Jasjit Singh, 'Introduction', *Asian Strategic Review*, p. 7.
109. Gujral, 'Comprehensive Test Ban Treaty, Statement in Parliament', 11 September 1996, I.K. Gujral, *A Foreign Policy for India*, p. 112.
110. *Indian Recorder*, 28 October–3 November 1996.
111. http://www.dfa-deplu.go.id/english/menlu2.htm: Statement by H.E. Mr. Ali Alatas, Minister of Foreign Affairs of the Republic of Indonesia, At the 51st Session of the United Nations General Assembly, New York, 30 September 1996. Department of Foreign Affairs of the Republic of Indonesia.
112. The discussions at the Disarmament Conference were adjourned on 29 June 1996, after it had gone beyond the deadline to reach a consensus plan. The sixty-one delegations then started working individually on a new proposal before resuming deliberations at the Conference on 29 July (*Indian Recorder*, 12–18 August 1996).
113. Naidu, 'Indian, ASEAN and the ARF', *Strategic Analysis*, p. 852.
114. *The Hindu*, 22 July 1996.
115. *The Statesman*, 22 July 1996.
116. Leifer, 'The ASEAN Regional Forum', p. 49.
117. *Financial Express*, 27 July 1997.
118. Gujral, 'Comprehensive Test Ban Treaty, Statements in Parliament', 31 July 1996, I.K. Gujral, *A Foreign Policy for India*, p. 105.
119. Ibid., pp. 104–6.
120. S.D. Muni, 'The Emerging Cold War in Asia', *Strategic Analysis*, March 1997, p. 1611.
121. Deepa M. Ollapally, 'India and the New "Asian" Balance of Power', *Strategic Analysis*, July 1998, p. 523.
122. Statement by External Affairs Minister of India, I.K. Gujral, on the occasion of the Post-Ministerial Conferences of ASEAN (PMC - 7+10), § 12.
123. Ibid.
124. *The Hindu*, 25 July 1996.
125. *Strategic Digest*, vol. 27, no. 6, June 1997.
126. *Hindu*, 9 February 1998.
127. Naidu, 'India and ASEAN', *Strategic Analysis*, vol. XIX, April 1996, p. 74.
128. U.B. Singh, 'Evolution of the ASEAN Regional Forum', *Asian Strategic Review*, p. 143.

129. Naidu, 'India and ASEAN', p. 59.
130. C. Raja Mohan, 'Foreign Policy on Hold', *The Hindu*, 28 November 1997; K.K. Katyal, 'Case for Foreign Policy "Review"', *World Focus*, January 1997, p. 24.
131. K.K. Katyal, 'Take Care of the Foreign Office', *The Hindu*, 6 April 1998. By default, it was the Minister of State for External Affairs, Saleem Shervani, who was sent, mainly to assist P. Chidambaram who headed the delegation.
132. Raja Mohan, 'Foreign Policy on Hold', *The Hindu*, 28 November 1997.
133. Dutt, *India's Foreign Policy*, p. 329.
134. K. Natwar Singh, 'Foreign Policy at Sea', *World Focus*, January 1997, p. 21.
135. Limaye, 'The Japan-India Encounter', *RGICS Paper*, p. 16.
136. Georges K. Tanham, 'Indian Strategic Thought: An Interpretative Essay', in G.K. Tanham, K.P. Bajpai and A. Mattoo, eds., *Securing India: Strategic Throught and Practice in an Emerging Power*, New Delhi: Manohar, 1996, p. 82.

CHAPTER 9

India's Nuclearization and the Changed Security Dynamics

9.1 The Repercussions of India's Nuclear Tests in Asia

On 11 May 1998, India conducted three underground nuclear tests in the Pokhran region, followed by two other tests on 13 May. In response to 'the extreme provocation by India', Pakistan too proceeded with nuclear tests two weeks later. To justify its decision, New Delhi spoke of the nuclear environment in its neighbourhood. In this perspective, the tests were intended to safeguard national security. The Indian government categorically reaffirmed that it would exercise the strictest control possible on the export of sensitive technologies, especially those associated with weapons of mass destruction. It also declared that it would remain committed to a process of rapid universal disarmament towards the comprehensive and total elimination of nuclear arms. Further, it was in the name of universal disarmament that India had refused to sign an extension of the Non-Proliferation Treaty in 1995 and the CTBT in 1996—two treaties that, from its point of view, only legitimized atomic weapons and their exclusive possession by the NWS. And yet, once India refused to sign the CTBT in 1996, the trial of strength with Western diplomats further continued. Indeed, during the 1996 negotiations, it had been anticipated that if the CTBT could not be ratified by forty-four listed nations, especially India, a fresh conference of the signatories of the treaty would be organized to consider new measures. Thus, New Delhi feared that it would once again be subjected to considerable international pressure to ratify the treaty. Aware of the fact that the three-year time span for the signature of the CTBT would expire in September 1999, the new government led by the BJP took the initiative to conduct the tests as fast as possible, despite a low parliamentary majority. It was the due date for the signature of the CTBT, which partly motivated the BJP's decision.[1] On a broader level, the justification for the tests fully complied with the logic of a balance of power in Asia. However, India's nuclear tests came as a significant development, with the potential to affect all its foreign relations.

THE POKHRAN II RATIONALE

The BJP had always defended a policy of enhanced national security and, in this regard, it had always favoured an open policy as far as the acquisition of nuclear weapons was concerned.[2] The party had clearly put forward in its 1998 electoral manifesto that once in power, it would develop India's nuclear arsenal. The BJP reiterated its ambitions in its National Agenda for Governance—the general policy project prepared by its coalition government. The document, which took up most of the foreign policy themes set out in the BJP electoral manifesto, asserted that, 'to ensure the security, territorial integrity and unity of India we will take all necessary steps and exercise all available options. Towards this end we will re-evaluate the nuclear policy and exercise the option to induct nuclear weapons.'[3]

An additional factor was that the Hindu nationalists never truly believed in the Sino-Indian rapprochement that had been gradually taking place over the previous ten years. In many ways, the BJP's rise to power further aroused the deep-rooted fear of being encircled—indeed a constant feature of India's strategic culture.[4] This idiosyncrasy began building up in the 1950s, when the United States undertook to support Pakistan, and it was considerably reinforced in the 1970s. Indeed, India took a dim view of the rapprochement between President Nixon and the Chinese authorities and did not take too long in seeing a Washington-Beijing-Islamabad axis.[5] In the post-Cold War context, India remained convinced that Islamabad and Beijing were working together to gain a stranglehold over its territory. It was true that Pakistan continued to benefit from China's military assistance. China proceeded with nuclear and ballistic technology transfers in total violation of its commitments and without attracting any strong reactions from the United States. Consequently, New Delhi continued to be persuaded that China used Pakistan as a counterweight to encircle it strategically in South Asia.

This strategy of encirclement was suspected to recur again on the north-eastern border and in the Bay of Bengal. Indeed, New Delhi was increasingly concerned about China's influence in Myanmar. These infiltrations seemed to be taking place through sustained military assistance and enabled Beijing to enjoy a greater naval presence in the Bay of Bengal. China was also strongly suspected of supporting insurrectionary movements in India's north-eastern states. In fact, there seemed to be a rise in the latter's fighting spirit, despite India's policy of repression, implemented in collaboration with Myanmar authorities. New Delhi's suspicions regarding China's policy in north-east India and the Bay of Bengal built up during the 1990s and were confirmed by events that were fairly disquieting. In February 1998, Indian coastguard ships intercepted a large cargo of arms in Longoff Island in the Andamans, probably meant for military groups in the north-east.[6] Some high officials of the Indian Navy engaged in quite alarming hypotheses, fearing that from being simply a land neighbour, China was fast becoming a maritime neighbour in the Bay of Bengal, via Myanmar.[7] Finally, New Delhi noted the existence of launch pads along its Himalayan border. Indeed, there had allegedly been nuclear-tipped missiles stationed in Tibet since 1971. Originally intended for the USSR, these weapons constituted a direct threat to India in the new strategic context, insofar as they could hit several cities in its territory. Indian experts were all the more fearful since they did not have the relevant information to locate these missiles, even less identify their power or range.[8] After all, irrespective of whether it was on the western front, the Himalayan border, in the landlocked north-eastern states or along the Bay of Bengal coastline, many in India's strategic community came to see a Chinese threat in every respect. For the most suspicious experts, the objective of the Chinese activities along India's borders was to enclose the country 'in a strategic trap',[9] i.e. contain it within its immediate South Asian environment.

Not surprisingly then, relations with Beijing began to get considerably colder when the Defence Minister of the new BJP-led government's, Georges Fernandes, openly affirmed that China constituted the greatest threat to India's security.[10] In a televised interview on 3 May 1998, Fernandes explained that in fact, New Delhi had lost a lot of time in focusing on the Pakistani military threat, while it was the Chinese neighbour that represented the greatest challenge. He alleged all kinds of threats—the accumulation of nuclear weapons in Tibet, the construction of electronic listening posts on the Coco Islands and the extension of military aviation tracks to receive supersonic combat aircraft capable of attacking India in the heart of its territory. On 5 May, Beijing responded by accusing the Defence Minister of 'seriously sabotaging' the friendly relations between the two countries. The Indian government applied itself to toning down Fernandes' attacks, by stressing that it wished to maintain good neighbourly relations. The Chief of Army Staff, General V.P. Malik, discredited the Defence Minister's comments, while in the opposition, the Congress party and other left-wing parties denounced his adventurism. Fernandes nonetheless persisted with his allegations of a Chinese threat, although in his personal capacity. Despite his many detractors, the Defence Minister gave the impression of expressing out loud the hidden concerns of a large section of the Indian strategic community.

It is true that since Jiang Zemin's 'historical' visit in December 1996, little progress had taken place in finding a solution to the border dispute. The two parties had not succeeded in reaching an agreement for the implementation of clauses on the reduction of forces along the LAC, or on the exchange of military information.[11] In 1997, the tenth Joint Working Group meeting, which took place in Delhi, contented itself with ratifying the 1996 agreement on confidence-building measures, since it had been unable to implement it. The Indian authorities seemed to be losing patience with this slow-moving process. On 3 May 1998, the BJP-led government gave the green light for the launch of the second phase of work on the intermediate range ballistic missile, Agni, which was basically directed towards Chinese targets. The objective was to enhance Agni's range from 1,500 to 2,500 km.[12] The same month, the top echelon of the naval forces drafted an internal document that identified China as the greatest threat to India's security.[13] The document anticipated a growing Chinese presence in the waters of the Indian Ocean in the years to come and was concerned to see Beijing acquire a navy that included nuclear submarines, destroyers and other battleships. It added that with the leasing of various naval bases and its arms export to Southern Asia and the Middle East, China was acquiring the means to exert a growing strategic influence in the region. Consequently, the document recommended that New Delhi maintain a greater naval presence in the Indian Ocean and adopt a more structured maritime strategy.

Thus, it was in this rather altered climate that the BJP government took the decision to carry out fresh nuclear tests. Logically, New

Delhi justified itself by asserting that there were 'trends toward disequilibrium in the Asian balance of power' and designated its Chinese neighbour for the same. Further, India asserted that its nuclear capability shall be seen as a factor of stability in the Asian power equation. In an article published in the American journal *Foreign Affairs*, the nuclear diplomacy expert, Jaswant Singh, explained that the Pokhran tests could be legitimized at three different analytical levels.[14] Apart from the unacceptable international context of 'nuclear apartheid' and the immediate proximity of two nuclear-capable states, the Indian tests had to be seen in the strategic framework of the Asian region. More precisely, New Delhi decided to exercise its nuclear option as a reaction to 'trends toward an imbalance in Asia's balance of power'. Consequently, India presented itself as a power that could play a key role for the region's stability.

In the aftermath of the Cold War, an Asian balance of power is emerging with new alignments and new vacuums. India, in exercise of its supreme national interests, has acted in timely fashion to correct an imbalance and fill a potentially dangerous vacuum. It endeavours to contribute to a stable balance of power in Asia, which it holds will further the advance of democracy. A more powerful India will help balance and connect the oil-rich Gulf region and the rapidly industrializing countries of South-East Asia.[15]

Jaswant Singh dwelt on the nature of the 'vacuums' that threatened Asia's stability. The paradigm of nuclear security as built up by the NWS covered the region from Vancouver to Vladivostok. This was a club that had the four NWS as partners for peace, which used their nuclear deterrent force to assure protection to different states in the American continent and Australasia, apart from South Korea and Japan. As for China, it was a major nuclear power in a specific region—Southern Asia—that remained outside the paradigm of nuclear security. Thus, to say the least, security standards differed significantly from region to region. In other words, Jaswant Singh affirmed that Southern Asia was left to the mercy of the sole nuclear power of the region, i.e. China. It was in this sense, and following the example of other Indian experts, that he spoke about a strategic imbalance, with the Asian financial crisis of 1997 probably further reinforcing the structural instability. In other words, there was a strategic vacuum in South-East Asia insofar as the countries in this sub-region did not benefit from the paradigm of nuclear security. This analysis seemed to be even more valid in the case of the ASEAN, given that the SEANWFZ project did not get the approval of the US or of China.

The eminent strategic affairs expert, K. Subrahmanyam, proposed a complementary analysis to that of the Deputy Chairman of the Planning Commission.[16] According to him, there were Russian nuclear facilities to the north of China, and to the east, an economically powerful Japan under the American nuclear umbrella. To the West, the Central Asian Republics were under the nuclear protection of the Commonwealth of Independent States, with Russia at its head. He then observed that 'the only areas which do not have a balancing arrangement *vis-à-vis* the Chinese power and influence are South and South-East Asia'. In fact, 'China has already been exercising its power and influence on its South'. The evidence was in the proliferation towards Pakistan and perhaps even Iran, infiltrations into Burma and claims on the South China Sea. Subrahmanyam thus asserted that 'The need for a stable Asian balance of power made it imperative for India to exercise its nuclear option, and contribute to embedding China in a four-power balancing system involving Japan, the US, Russia and itself.' Only this polycentric security order would ensure maximum autonomy for the other nations in Asia. India's nuclear tests were, therefore, part of a logic that promoted a multilateral balance of power in Asia.

But beyond security perceptions proper, the nuclear tests also had to do with India's desire to establish itself as a major power in Asia, as also in the world. The issue of India's status in the world had for long been a central concern of the Hindu nationalists. Thus, the National Agenda for Governance announced: 'we will strive to secure for India a place, role and position in the global arena, consistent with our size and capability'.[17] As it happened, from the Hindu nationalist perspective, the equation between power and nuclear weapons was absolute. After all, the five permanent members of the Security Council were all NWS. In fact, following the line of argument of the Hindu nationalists, many Indians supposed that if their country had all the symbols of a major power, it would be recognized as such. Apart from nuclear weapons, long-range missiles and a major military-industrial base were considered essential elements to the status of a world power, so much so that the deliberate acquisition of these attributes was to become the only means for India of asserting itself in the world arena in the 1990s, especially with the Indians experiencing growing frustration in the face of international indifference towards their country.[18] Above all, in its quest for power, India sought to measure itself against China, a country that was similar to it in many respects, but was nonetheless universally perceived to be a major power in the world. More precisely, China was legitimately endowed with the attributes of power of which India was constantly deprived. First and foremost among them were the status as a NWS and a permanent seat at the Security Council of the United Nations. In this regard, the recourse to the nuclear option in 1998 appeared as a strong symbol, which showed that New Delhi had all the intentions of establishing itself as a power that would soon be comparable to China, even if it were at the expense of infringing upon international standards and regimes, which in any event were considered inequitable.

By asserting that it was primarily directed towards China, India's nuclear policy satisfied both purely security-related concerns as well as the power game *vis-à-vis* Beijing. In this regard, the post-Pokhran II rationale was quite revealing, since it finally aimed at elevating India to the level of China, by suggesting that there was a need for it to become a counterweight to China. Without under-estimating the reality of the Indian concerns with regard to China's strategic ambitions in Asia, it must be borne in mind that the discourse on the Chinese threat was also, to a large extent, a geopolitical construct, which stemmed from New Delhi's new ambitions. In other words, to establish the idea that India was a pole of stability in Asia, China's role as a factor—if not of instability, then at least of un-predictability—had to be magnified as a counterpoint. Moreover, it must be recalled that the perception of China as an imminent threat had become increasingly predominant in India's strategic discourse in the 1990s, even though there was a distinct improvement in bilateral relations. Thus, Vice-Admiral Raja Menon clearly explained that New Delhi did not even perceive an immediate military threat from China and that its nuclear weapons were not intended to defend its territory.[19] The Indian forces, according to him, seemed to have accepted the idea of defending the present line of actual control, as it existed on the ground. Menon added that from a historical perspective, the first generation of the Chinese nuclear arsenal was directed towards the USSR and South-East Asia, and not even towards India. And while many Indian leaders and strategic experts had accused China of adopting a targeted nuclear policy against their country over the past three decades, this was basically done to justify their own arsenal.

So, according to Menon, there was no other explanation than the following: 'The Indian arsenal exists because the Chinese arsenal exists.'[20] The absence of Indian atomic arms would indeed confine the bilateral relationship in an unequal correlation, of which New Delhi was increasingly taking a dim view.

In other words, what truly worried India's decision-makers at the end of the 1990s was their inability to make their voices heard beyond South Asia, while China had unanimously established itself as a major power in Asia. However, New Delhi refused to see China assert itself as the only power in Asia in the twenty-first century.[21] Accordingly, Pokhran II appeared to mark a 'desire to make the rivalry between the two major powers of Asia official',[22] no matter how disproportionate it might be. Indeed, the May 1998 tests broke China's nuclear monopoly in Asia.

INTERNATIONAL AND REGIONAL REACTIONS TO THE POKHRAN II NUCLEAR TESTS

The decision to conduct nuclear tests was taken in a very short span of time—less than a week—and very probably without a precise idea of the international consequences they would have, both in the short as well as in the medium term.[23] Indian diplomacy was therefore barely prepared to deal with the flood of international resentment targeted against it in the aftermath of the tests. But, after an initial phase of confusion, Indian diplomacy reorganized itself and launched a massive undertaking to explain its posture. As of 22 May, Prime Minister Vajpayee took the decision to route all major foreign policy declarations through the Ministry of External Affairs.[24] Nevertheless, it fell to the Deputy Chairman of the Planning Commission, Jaswant Singh to conduct major negotiations in relation to India's nuclear policy.

Among many others, New Delhi was subjected to reprobation by all the major Asia-Pacific powers. During the first month following the nuclear tests, the American reaction was very critical. On 15 May 1998, the United States rejected India's claim to be recognized as a Nuclear Weapon State.[25] According to international law, a NWS was one that, by definition, had exploded a nuclear weapon before 1968. This was, indeed, a determining factor, and yet New Delhi undertook a long series of bilateral meetings with the United States. At the same time, Washington seemed to be orchestrating the salvos of sanction measures to be adopted in response to these tests. To explain his decision, Prime Minister Vajpayee sent President Clinton a letter in which he explained that the Chinese nuclear arms and their proliferation towards India's western neighbour were the main reasons for his country going nuclear. This confidential document, whose contents were eventually divulged, was at the heart of China's criticism with regard to the Pokhran II tests.[26] Indeed, China reacted very strongly to the Indian tests, describing them as 'shocking'. Its condemnation, which was one of the most categorical, denounced the argument of the Chinese nuclear threat as being totally unfounded. In reality, Beijing was of the view that the tests were aimed at establishing India's hegemony in South Asia and that they complicated the normalization process along the border. Furthermore, the Chinese leadership refuted the assertion according to which they had supplied Pakistan with missiles and nuclear technology. Beijing demanded that India sign and notify the CTBT forthwith, and put an end to its nuclear programme. But from the Indian perspective, if China set itself up as a defender of the CTBT, it was not so much by real conviction, but more out of concern for preserving its superiority *vis-à-vis* India. In fact, most Indian experts did not truly take note of the Chinese reaction. They interpreted it alternately as an exercise in public relations or a panic reaction, which should subside with time. In any case, there was a substantial chill in Sino-Indian relations, due both to the nuclear tests and to the inability of the two states to understand their respective strategic perceptions.

But it was not long before events took an adverse turn for New Delhi, who saw the United States on the verge of engaging in collaboration with China for managing the nuclear conundrum in South Asia. Indeed, President Bill Clinton brought forward his planned visit to Beijing from November to July 1998, while cancelling his scheduled visits to India and Pakistan. Beijing put up a good performance as a defender of non-proliferation and, at the end of President Clinton's visit, both states came up with a common declaration on South Asia. Not content with denouncing the South Asian tests, the two countries called upon New Delhi and Islamabad not to carry out any further nuclear tests and to sign the CTBT 'immediately and unconditionally'. China and the United States also agreed to 'closely work together' in order to promote non-proliferation in South Asia and find a solution to the Indo-Pakistani conflict.[27] The two states expressed their willingness to take all necessary and immediate measures to resolve issues as complex as those of Kashmir or those concerning the risks of an arms race in South Asia. New Delhi found itself more than ever entrapped in a subcontinental context and, to its great consternation, it saw the likelihood of the Kashmir conflict becoming internationalized. The government's official reaction was quite sharp: the Sino-US declaration was described as 'hegemonic' and India declared that it 'would not take cognisance of the suggestions made for the reduction of its nuclear armament or missile development programme'. In view of India's aspirations for international recognition, especially with regard to China, the Sino-US declaration seemed far from conciliatory. New Delhi did not let up *vis-à-vis* the United States in the months to follow. In a lecture to the New York-based Asia Society on 28 September 1998, A.B. Vajpayee asserted, 'I must confess to being baffled by the unsatisfactory current state of relations between our two countries.'[28] Among the reasons he cited, the Prime Minister said, 'First and foremost, it is American reluctance to accept us as a responsible member of the international community (. . .) whether it is cooperative arrangements in the Asia-Pacific region, where we have a clearly positive, moderating and stabilizing role to play; whether it is global organizations like the UN Security Council or the discriminatory Non-Proliferation Treaty.'

New Delhi once again requested that it be recognized as a credible and responsible power in the Asian arena. As for the joint Sino-US communiqué of July 1998, it only managed to strengthen India's convictions on the existence of an entente between China, Pakistan and the United States. But American diplomacy reacted with contempt to India's declarations denouncing its understanding with Beijing. Thus, there was considerable lack of understanding in Washington with regard to India's strategic perceptions. The irony, of course, was that China had henceforth become a responsible and mature nuclear power, while India was considered the recalcitrant state. It was true that since the early 1990s, Beijing had cleverly taken several initiatives to appease the American strategic community.[29] One by one, it joined a whole lot of international security regimes and multilateral non-proliferation institutions. Consequently, China became a signatory of the NPT, the CTBT, the Chemical Weapons Convention and the Biological Weapons Convention. It also announced that it would subscribe to the principles and provisions of the MTCR. Beijing also announced a series of unilateral measures, including 'a checklist of nuclear exports' in September 1997. This initiative, which was clearly aimed at appeasing American concerns with regard to Chinese nuclear proliferation, allowed the White House to give the necessary certification for reviving the 1985 bilateral agreement on peaceful nuclear cooperation. Beijing even managed to jointly denounce the Indian tests with Moscow.[30] A month after Clinton's visit, the Russian Minister of Foreign Affairs, Yevgeny Primakov and his Chinese counterpart, Tang Jiaxuan, condemned India's and Pakistan's actions in a common declaration and invited the two countries to unconditionally accede to the NPT and CTBT. The two ministers reaffirmed their decision not to recognise them officially as Nuclear Weapons States.

Finally, in the case of Japan, the nuclear issue was a problem that was more than just sensitive. Tokyo had unconditionally accepted the extension of the NPT in 1995 and had renounced its atomic defence programme. At a time when Japanese diplomacy felt particularly weakened, the South Asian nuclear tests came as an affront, for they did symbolize the failure of Japan's international commitment for non-proliferation. The nuclear tests also showed the diplomatic limitations of economic assistance and official aid policies. Thus, Tokyo reacted very sharply to the Indian tests. A major portion of the development assistance programme was suspended, as well as loans in Yen.[31] The Ambassador of Japan in New Delhi was temporarily recalled. At the multilateral level, Japan increased its sanctions, to the great irritation of New Delhi. Not only did Tokyo support the G-8's statements of condemnation on nuclear tests, it even intended playing the host and organizer of Indo-Pakistani bilateral talks. In its capacity as a non-permanent member of the Security Council, Japan promised Pakistan to place the issue of Kashmir on the agenda immediately after the public announcement of the Indian tests. However, this offer, whose aim was to dissuade Islamabad from carrying out its own nuclear tests, did not succeed. Moreover, in early July, Japan, supposedly supported by Australia and the United States, asked for Pakistan's participation as a special observer during the ARF discussions, which were to take place at the end of the month.[32] New Delhi could not have imagined a worst-case scenario, especially since it had constantly rejected a multilateral handling of its bilateral problems with Pakistan. The Japanese initiative was conveyed by the Philippines, which was chairing the 1998 ARF sessions.[33] But Indian diplomacy managed to neutralize the Japanese offensive, with the support of some ASEAN members, such as Singapore, Vietnam and Laos.

At first, it seemed that international reactions to the Indian nuclear tests fell into two different groups—on one side, severe judgements by industrialized nations, and on the other, the less judgmental southern states. Above all, the sharpest criticism came from industrialized countries led by the United States, Japan, Germany and Australia, who all imposed sanctions. Most Scandinavian countries stopped development aid. Great Britain, France and Russia excluded any punitive action, but the European Union also condemned the tests. On 6 June 1998, it was the United Nations Security Council that condemned the nuclear tests conducted by India and Pakistan. However, in May 1998, the Durban Non-Aligned Summit approved the Indian position.[34] The Non-Aligned nations denounced the NWS for the unwarranted maintenance of their atomic arsenal in the post-Cold War era and called for a 'universal and legally binding' agreement, aimed toward the total elimination of such weapons. The NAM Foreign Ministers declared that the possession of nuclear weapons by a limited number of states created a 'highly discriminatory' situation. The final declaration did not even mention nuclear tests in South Asia.

However, the ASEAN and ARF conferences promised to be a much more difficult ordeal than the Non-Aligned Summit, especially as the main industrialized nations participated in them. Accordingly, Indian diplomacy's objective was to prevent the ASEAN from getting too influenced by its more hostile partners. In this regard, it had to convince the South-East Asian states that the Indian nuclear force made it possible to restore the balance of power in Asia. But India *a priori* suffered from a fairly serious handicap, because the ASEAN and ARF chairmanship was with the Philippines. And Manila was not content to just officially condemn India's nuclear tests. Invited to the G-8 summit in London, its delegates also participated in the action plan against India and Pakistan. The Philippine President declared his dismay with regard to India's nuclear tests and distributed his statement at the United Nations General Assembly, in the last week of June. Most South-East Asian nations officially criticized the tests, though less virulently than the Philippines.[35] For instance, Bangkok declared that in principle, it 'disagreed with any form of nuclear testing'. Furthermore, Thailand was of the view that 'India's nuclear tests were not conducive to the process of the establishment of the South-East Asia Nuclear Weapons Free Zone (SEANWFZ)'. Malaysia deplored the South Asian tests and, Indonesia adopted a critical position *vis-à-vis* India during the Non-Aligned Summit. On the other hand, Singapore issued no official statement on the issue. Even if the city-state declared itself in favour of non-proliferation, there was relative understanding of the Indian rationale within its diplomatic circle. New Delhi also obtained Vietnam's support—its traditional friend in South-East Asia.

INDIA'S NUCLEAR TESTS AT THE 1998 ARF MEETING

Soon after Pokhran II, Indian diplomacy undertook to explain its position and increase its contacts with its partners in South-East Asia. Entrusted with foreign affairs within the new BJP government, Vasundhara Raje went on a special visit to the region.[36] Her diplomatic tour began with the Philippines, which was supposed to chair the forthcoming sessions of the ASEAN and the ARF and which had adopted a very anti-Indian approach. But Vasundhara Raje assured herself of the support of India's two traditional friends, by stopping over in Vietnam and Singapore. Raje's diplomatic tour was followed up by several other visits to South-East Asia by S.T. Devare, Economic Relations Secretary within the Indian Ministry of External Affairs. This succession of visits suggested that Indian diplomacy had become more pragmatic than ever before. Far from the erstwhile arrogance with regard to the smaller South-East Asian states, New Delhi understood that it should not limit the spectrum of its interlocutors to major powers, especially with regard to the nuclear imbroglio. In any case, India's initiatives showed the importance that it henceforth accorded the ASEAN. In that sense, Raje's visits were appreciated, especially by Singapore's diplomatic circle.[37] These visits of course had a very important preparatory character, in that they tried to anticipate the conduct of debates during the ARF summit and gain the understanding of some ASEAN members.

Jaswant Singh, the Prime Minister's special envoy, led the Indian delegation that went to Manila for the ASEAN Post-Ministerial Conference. With the experience of three Indo-American series of talks behind him, Jaswant Singh had become somewhat of an expert on the Indian post-nuclear diplomacy. The Deputy Chairman of the Planning Commission expressed himself in the same terms in Manila as the ones he used with Strobe Talbott, the American Deputy Secretary of State: India's nuclear tests had to be viewed in the perspective of the overall balance of power in Asia. Jaswant Singh used both the

ARF multilateral meetings and the bilateral ones to expound on the Indian rationale. New Delhi's position in Manila essentially consisted of convincing those present that India would be a responsible and stabilizing nuclear power. Jaswant Singh once again stated that the Indian nuclear doctrine was based on minimal dissuasion and on the no-first use principle. Above all and as additional proof of restraint, Singh offered to give a legal instrument to his commitment to honour the SEANWFZ treaty. The ASEAN nations responded that the Indian offer would have to be examined further. In fact, the signature of the protocol was only open to official nuclear powers and India was not recognized as such. But, thanks to this proposal, New Delhi showed that it remained sensitive to its ASEAN partners' anti-nuclear concerns. It appeared as a much more munificent power than the United States and China, who had not yet signed the SEANWFZ protocol, to the ASEAN's disappointment.

Indian diplomacy also made the most of the 1998 Post-Ministerial Conferences to redefine its Look East policy. The core of this reshaped policy was an effort to be 'flexible and responsive to the diversity within the evolving unity of East and South-East Asia'.[38] In doing so, New Delhi sought to adapt its political and economic relations to better take into account the conditions and requirements of each South-East Asian state. These modifications also corresponded to a new-found pragmatism: 'Instead of trying to be all things to all countries', India 'will engage in sub-regional and supra regional arrangements to the extent that others value (her) contribution and participation'. The Look East policy would thus be developed only to the extent that the concerned partners were interested. There was now a desire for reciprocity. Thus, Indian diplomacy seemed to be gaining confidence in South-East Asia.

The Indian representatives finally sought to make the best use of bilateral meetings, along with multilateral conferences to explain their position.[39] Indeed, the ARF meetings marked an opportunity to revive relations, which had so far remained completely blocked with a number of states, who had been among the most hostile to New Delhi. After almost three months of strained diplomatic relations, India and Japan decided to resume their political dialogue during the ARF summit. The meeting between Jaswant Singh and the Japanese Minister of State for Foreign Affairs, Masahiko Komura, raised hopes of an easing of tensions. Jaswant Singh also informally met Keizo Obuchi, the Foreign Affairs Minister and the future Prime Minister designate. The ARF meetings also made it possible for Indian and Chinese representatives to initiate their first dialogue after the tests. Jaswant Singh held talks with the Chinese Minister of Foreign Affairs, Tang Jiaxuan, at the request of the latter. The Indian special envoy also met the American Secretary of State, Madeleine Albright, as well as the Russian and Australian Ministers of Foreign Affairs. With most ASEAN dialogue partners, the focus of discussions was on the nuclear tests. With the ASEAN members, on the other hand, bilateral meetings were more oriented towards economic cooperation, as the nuclear issues had been discussed before the conferences.

Besides, the declaration issued at the conclusion of the ASEAN ministers' conference, on 25 July 1998, proved to be more moderate than expected with regard to Pokhran II. It was in astonishing contrast to the unilateral reactions of several Asia-Pacific states, which had firmly condemned the South Asian tests. Certainly, the ASEAN nations did express their 'grave concern' and 'strongly deplored' the nuclear tests, 'which exacerbated tension in the region and raised the spectre of a nuclear arms race'.[40] The ASEAN ministers also demanded universal adherence to the NPT and CTBT in the hope of establishing a world free of nuclear weapons. Above all, the communiqué recalled that the stocks piled up by the nuclear powers sufficed to place humanity at risk. Consequently, the ASEAN ministers 'strongly urged the nuclear-weapon states to take concrete and timely measures towards the total elimination of nuclear weapons in compliance with the provisions of the NPT'. Thus, the joint communiqué of the ASEAN ministers placed India, Pakistan and the declared nuclear powers on the same footing, with regard to their obligation to create a world free of weapons of mass destruction. From a certain point of view, the communiqué ratified India's position, because it stressed that the current regime was discriminatory and that it did not meet the final objective of disarmament. The group of Anglo-Saxon states and China publicly expressed their dissatisfaction in the absence of any condemnation of India.

The moderate tone of the declaration was even more remarkable since it was a veritable disapproval of the position adopted the day before by the ASEAN session Chairman, Joseph Estrada. At the inaugural session on 24 July 1998, the Philippine representative had sharply denounced India and Pakistan for their 'irresponsible nuclear proliferation'. But the Philippine draft communiqué was later modified to subtly deplore the South Asian nuclear tests, and to avoid a blatant and public condemnation. According to the session President, it was the only way to achieve a consensus on the South Asian issue. Singapore, Indonesia and Malaysia seemed to have played a major role in mitigating the wording of the final communiqué. Logically, the collective position of the ASEAN nations was supposed to steer the direction of the deliberations within the ARF. Nonetheless, the next day, 26 July 1998, Manila resumed its anti-Indian offensive and drafted a fresh draft of the communiqué, which incorporated a condemnation of the two South Asian states. Contrary to the joint communiqué issued the day before, calling for a complete elimination of nuclear weapons, the draft declaration prepared by the Philippines focused on India and Pakistan, demanding that they sign the NPT and the CTBT 'immediately, unconditionally and unreservedly'.[41] A similar appeal addressed to official nuclear powers—a significant element of the joint communiqué on 25 July—was not included in this document.

Despite the diplomatic tenacity of the Philippines, the ARF joint communiqué expressed concern about the nuclear tests, but did not condemn them officially. Moreover, the Philippine President, Domingo Siazon, let it be clearly known that he could only 'deplore' the nuclear tests, given the divergence of opinions within the ARF. Out of respect for the desire of the other ASEAN members, his country had to 'adjust' its position, which was originally to 'condemn' the detonations. Thus, India and Pakistan were not named specifically, contrary to Siazon's initial draft. Paragraph 21, about the South Asian nuclear tests, was drafted in the following terms: 'the Foreign Ministers deplored the series of nuclear tests conducted recently in South Asia that exacerbated tension in the region and raised the spectre of a nuclear arms race'.[42] Compared with the initial fears and the general hue and cry immediately after the nuclear tests, India emerged from the ARF summit relatively spared. However, the Indian delegation dissociated itself from the final declaration.

Another gain for India was that differences of opinion between the major powers had distinctly emerged during the summit. In his closing ARF speech, Siazon did not hide the fact that paragraph 21 of the declaration had been the most controversial issue during the deliberations.[43] Two contrasting lines of thought had emerged on the South Asian issue. Australia, Canada, New Zealand and Japan were in the first group of states which demanded a more firm condemnation than the mere expression of deep concern with regard to India and Pakistan.

According to them, the nuclear detonations not only violated the non-proliferation regime, but also further threatened to revive a nuclear arms race. In this regard, they had created a very dangerous situation for South Asia, if not for the entire world, and it was therefore advisable to send a strong exemplary message to states, which might be tempted by the nuclear option. In the face of all this, a second group of states turned out to be more concerned with moderation and pragmatism. The ASEAN members, on the whole, united to prevent a condemnation of India and Pakistan.[44] Among them, Singapore, Indonesia, Malaysia, Vietnam and Laos were the most influential. Concerned with not making the involved participants (from India in this instance) uncomfortable, these states underlined the fact that the ARF should not be a forum, which allows itself to denounce its members. Finally, American diplomacy tipped the scales in favour of the moderates. In fact, the United States had not supported the anti-Indian charges of the Anglo-Saxon countries or the Philippines, but had rather opted for the middle path. This moderate position had to be attributed to the progress achieved in the separate discussions between Strobe Talbott and Jaswant Singh. After having attacked India in the P-5, G-8 and United Nations Security Council, at the ARF session, the United States deemed it was time to move ahead in a constructive dialogue.

At the end of the ARF deliberations, India's main detractors found themselves either marginalized or dissatisfied. China, which had been pushing for strong condemnation of India behind the scenes, found little support. As for the Anglo-Saxon countries, they were reduced to publicly express their dissatisfaction, in the absence of a condemnation of India. Indian diplomacy, on its part, expressed its relief. In front of the international media, Jaswant Singh affirmed that the outcome of the ARF summit was 'very satisfying' and added that 'relations with the ASEAN and ARF were extremely valuable for India'.[45] Prime Minister Vajpayee, also expressed his country's gratitude for ASEAN's moderate views in a speech before the Indian Parliament on 3 August 1998: 'While the ARF "Chairman's Statement" contained a paragraph disapproving of the recent tests in South Asia, with which we disassociated ourselves, we also found a better overall understanding on the part of ASEAN countries of the rational of our policy, as well as of the need for purposeful moves by the Nuclear Weapon States towards comprehensive, universal nuclear disarmament on a non-discriminatory basis.'[46]

It would be misleading to conclude that the efforts by most ASEAN members to prevent too firm a condemnation of New Delhi reflected certain benevolence with regard to the Indian nuclear programme. In fact, the Pokhran nuclear tests came to be discussed within the framework of a separate debate, strictly internal to the ASEAN. The divides, which emerged on the Indian question, actually reflected an internal controversy on the ASEAN's rules of functioning, especially those concerned with non-intervention in the affairs of a state and decision-making by consensus. Indeed, during the thirty-first session of the ASEAN, the Thai Minister of Foreign Affairs, Surin Pitsuwan, defended the idea of a 'flexible engagement', with the firm support of his Philippine counterpart, Domingo L. Siazon.[47] Nothing less than the golden rule of non-intervention in the internal affairs of a member-state was being challenged. Indeed, the concept of 'flexible engagement' meant that it was possible to comment and discuss the internal affairs of member-states, the moment their developments affected the interests of other partners. However, most ASEAN states continued to defend the traditional rules that governed the functioning of their organization, in particular that of non-intervention in the internal affairs of the member-states. In that sense, the possible condemnation of India—an ARF member—was part of the debate. On the whole, the ASEAN concluded that it was not in the current norms to express its disapproval of India. Thus, Siazon affirmed that in comparison with his draft communiqué—which was, in fact, quite virulent—with regard to India's nuclear tests, 'The ASEAN members were generally more reserved in their expression of judgment.' He added: 'I decided to abide by the ASEAN culture and the ASEAN tradition.'[48] India also benefited from the desire to maintain the fundamental norm of decision-making by consensus. Indeed, once again, consensus prevailed where precisely there was controversy—i.e. with regard to the condemnation of India's tests.

Some members of the ASEAN were also concerned with preserving the autonomy of the ARF. In this regard, the very active role adopted by the Philippines not only went against the conventional practices of the ASEAN, but also raised the suspicions of some of its members who suspected Manila of acting on behalf of foreign powers, such as Australia. These suspicions ran counter to the aim of insulating the conduct and control of the ARF from its dialogue partners. In other words, it was important to ensure that the ARF should continue to follow the mode of functioning, which was specific to the ASEAN.

One of the essential characteristics of the so-called 'ASEAN way' was to avoid all verbal confrontation and open criticism. Furthermore, when the framework of the ARF was established in 1995, it was primarily to encourage confidence-building measures and preventive diplomacy in the Asia-Pacific. The desire to keep a slow but steady rate of progress was also a fundamental practice of South-East Asian diplomacy. Thus, the refusal to condemn the South Asian nuclear tests should be associated with the fact that the ASEAN was keen that the ARF be kept distinct from other multilateral forums, dominated by the West. In this connection, Ali Alatas clearly explained that since the ARF was not the Security Council or the Conference for Disarmament, it would be out of place to engage in condemnatory or critical terms with regard to India.[49] In other words, the ARF was not the appropriate platform to censure New Delhi or Islamabad insofar as it defined itself as a forum of discussion, which favoured the respect due to state sovereignty. Thus, even though they disapproved of the nuclear tests, the South-East Asian members were hardly inclined to pass a severe judgement on the sovereign nature of the Indian decision.

Accordingly, despite the general hue and cry in the aftermath of the nuclear tests, New Delhi came back 'satisfied' from Manila. The July 1998 ARF conference was quite significant, because it was one of the first multilateral summits to discuss the South Asian nuclear tests in the presence of India. It was essential for New Delhi to ensure that it would not be directly condemned in such a gathering. Thanks to the moderate approach of the ASEAN, India managed to accomplish this task. New Delhi played on both the strategic as well as the economic levels to reassure its ASEAN partners and convince them that it would be a stabilizing force in Asia. In the strategic field, the unilateral commitment to respect the South-East Asia Nuclear Weapons Free Zone treaty was a testimony to the benevolent intentions of New Delhi with regard to the region. Furthermore, it was probable that some of the ASEAN members were not upset to see a nuclear power establishing itself on China's western flank. In the economic field, repeated proposals to help—even modestly—the crisis-hit economies proved India's goodwill. Interestingly, at the 1998 ARF sessions, when Jaswant Singh had a one-to-one meeting with the Foreign Affairs Ministers of Malaysia and Indonesia, nuclear tests were not the subject of discussions, officially at least. The meetings focused on modalities to maintain trade ties and the possible Indian assistance for economies in crisis. For many South-East Asian states, economic interests remained pre-eminent in their ties with India, beyond the nuclear tests episode.[50]

But, while New Delhi was able to felicitate itself for having escaped firm condemnation, it was highly criticized in Manila. With regard to the initial Look East policy project—i.e. the smooth rapprochement with East Asia—it was not certain that the nuclear tests were a very constructive development. Let us recall that when New Delhi conducted fresh nuclear tests in May 1998, there had already been considerable instability in the Asian region for the past several months. The financial crisis had upset the Asian economies since June–July 1997 and produced intense shock waves disturbing the regional balance of power.[51] In such a difficult context, India had asserted itself strongly, but would it manage to get accepted? On the economic front, the South-East Asian crisis had hurt the trade and financial relations that India had succeeded in building. From a security perspective, it was unlikely that the ASEAN would be ready to unequivocally admit India as a nuclear power, especially since Washington's strategic concerns remained a determining factor in the perceptions of the member-states. Above all, India's recalcitrant nuclear conduct overrode some of the fundamental principles of the ARF's functioning, thereby only adding to the forum's problems. In fact, the question that arose was the inability of the ARF itself to deal with the South Asian nuclear conundrum. The Pokhran tests had, in fact, destabilized the balance of power project in Asia, as envisaged by the ASEAN. First and foremost, India's nuclear policy challenged the accepted idea that in the post-Cold War world, economic interdependence, globalization and multilateral cooperation would gain the upper hand in comparison with traditional strategic concerns and military rivalries. The doubts raised were all the more disconcerting since most cooperation institutions in East Asia had been particularly weakened by the financial crisis of 1997. It was also the first time that a government in Asia denounced the Chinese threat, not hesitating to upset the fragile rapprochement built over the last ten years. Such conduct was quite unheard of in the strategic culture of which the ARF was so proud. To publicly and openly identify its adversary was hardly conceivable for the ASEAN members; even less so to admit the description of China as a threat.[52]

Further, the non-condemnation of India's nuclear tests during the 1998 ARF sessions could well have been in line with a strategy to avert the problems that such a condemnation would have raised.

Indeed, the ARF was a new and barely institutionalized forum. The founding members, who were already considerably weakened and preoccupied by the economic crisis, probably felt that dealing with the South Asian nuclear tests would be too much of a challenge for the organization. Thus, the moderation of the ARF declarations also reflected its own limitations. The fact was that no regional organization capable of dealing with the economic and political crisis that was affecting South-East Asia was in place. In 1998, the absence of effective mechanisms of multilateral cooperation, in the field of security as well as the management of financial flows, was sorely felt. Most regional players within the ARF itself felt that bilateralism was a more effective way of preserving their security interests. Thus, they still maintained strategic bilateral ties with major powers, the United States in particular. Likewise, bilateral modalities of conflict resolution between the ASEAN members prevailed over multilateral approaches.

In this context, it goes without saying that India's official nuclearization further added to the regional confusion. The May 1998 nuclear tests not only truly projected India on to the Asian strategic scene, but they also made the scenarios that could be envisaged in the medium term more complex. From then on, the Sino-Indian rivalry had the potential to slide into a situation of frictions, which would more directly involve South-East Asia. Indeed, in all likelihood Myanmar would continue to be the subject of a power play for influence between the two neighbours, even while it was an ASEAN member. The Bay of Bengal too could become another tension point, with the Andaman Islands as outposts for India and the Coco Islands for China. These complications came to the fore even when the ARF was undergoing a critical phase. The forum was already fairly overwhelmed by handling security issues in North-East Asia, with regard to Taiwan and the two Koreas. Thus, it would seem that several members were regretting their decision to have admitted India, a country that no doubt further burdened the ARF's agenda and turned its attention away from the considerable difficulties that were already undermining East Asia.

9.2 Towards a Concert of Powers in Asia?

For New Delhi, the entire focus of its post-Pokhran diplomacy consisted of ensuring that its strategic dialogues with the major powers reached a positive conclusion, especially with the United States, in order to put an end to the regime of economic sanctions and find a *modus vivendi* with international non-proliferation regimes. Moreover, India's open nuclearization brought to light the existence of two possible strategic scenarios in Asia. The first corresponded to the ARF, in which a group of weak states were taking it upon themselves to ensure a balance of powers in the region by attempting to orchestrate relationships between the major players. But, the security arrangements that seemingly prevailed in Asia were increasingly weakened and the nuclearization of the subcontinent further added to their difficulties. The second proposal put forward the idea that regional stability should be ensured at the initiative of the major powers themselves. Their rivalries as well as their attempts at readjusting their relations would be based on a concert of powers, which would eventually guarantee greater strategic stability.[53] In fact, the second strategic scenario has seemed to be well on the way to imposing itself, in view of the developments that have affected the Asian region since 2000: in addition to signs heralding the emergence of a strategic triangle between China, the United States and India, a strong American comeback has been witnessed in the unprecedented post-9/11 context.

A STRENGTHENING OF INDIA'S DEFENCE POLICY

In general, the BJP-led government proved much more sensitive than its predecessors to national security issues. Thus, it set out to streamline India's strategic policy and defence machinery. On the organizational front, a significant initiative consisted of the setting up of a National Security Council (NSC) in November 1998, a structure that was entrusted 'to define (among other things) who would be competent to press the nuclear button'. The NSC, under the chairmanship of the Prime Minister, who was assisted by a National Security Adviser with the rank of a minister, raised the hope of better coordination between foreign policy and the defence establishment. Further, the Indian defence budget for 1998–9 was presented on 1 June 1998, just after the nuclear tests.[54] There was an increase in defence allocations of almost 14 per cent in current terms, as compared to the previous year's budget estimates, which stood at 7 per cent in real terms. Later, with the 1999 September–October elections having brought it back to power, with an increased majority, the BJP-led National Democratic Alliance fully intended to improve India's nuclear arsenal. Thus, New Delhi proposed a highly ambitious nuclear draft doctrine that was to be developed on the basis of a military triad, associating air and naval forces with mobile land-based missiles.[55] No need to say, neither India nor Pakistan signed the CTBT in September 1999. As for India's military expenditures, they continued to grow—from USD 9,310 million in 1997 (at 1998 constant prices), to 9,390 in 1998, reaching 10,733 in 1999, 11,793 in 2000 and 12,879 in 2001.[56]

In general, the BJP government set out to enhance India's long-range power projection force as of the end of the 1990s. On 11 April 1999, India tested a medium-range ballistic missile (about 2,000 km), Agni II, as a logical corollary to Pokhran II. Agni II's second fire, which took place in January 2001, was supposed to give the country credible minimum nuclear deterrence. In January 2002, it was a new, shorter-range version (about 700 km) of Agni I, which was successfully tested. The new missile was supposed to be between Prithvi (with a 350 km-range) and Agni II. New Delhi also intended to enhance its capacity for projecting its might by providing its air force with the latest-generation combat aircraft. In end 2000, Russia concluded an agreement worth USD 3.3 billion to grant India a production license to manufacture 140 Sukhoi (Su-30MKI). As of September 2002, New Delhi announced the incorporation of its first squadron of ten Sukhoi-30 MKIs. In this connection, there was a possibility of India and Russia jointly producing a new version of the Sukhoi combat aircraft, the Su-30 MKI, for Malaysia.[57] Finally, it must also be mentioned that as far as advances in space technology were concerned, India finally managed to test its first Geo-Synchronous Satellite Launch Vehicle (GSLV) in May 2001. Then, in September 2002, the Indian Space Research Organization (ISRO) successfully placed a weather satellite (METSAT) in a geostationary orbit, with a Polar Satellite Launch Vehicle (PSLV).

The BJP government also gave special attention to the state of the naval forces and intended to further strengthen their role in the Indian Ocean. For instance, it was the navy that benefited the most from the 1998–9 increase in the defence budget, with an almost twenty-five per cent rise in expenditure. Furthermore, a major naval modernization programme was announced in August 1998, amounting to almost USD 2.5 billion. The BJP government seemed to be inclined to develop a strong navy, rather than giving priority to the coastal functions of its naval forces, as its predecessors had done. Besides, New Delhi intended to acquire a second aircraft carrier and had been negotiating with Russia for the purchase and renovation of the former *Admiral Gorshkov* since 1994. The negotiations finally came to a conclusion in early 2004. As part of the negotiation package, New Delhi also planned to acquire two Russian nuclear submarines, to develop its nuclear deterrence, which was supposed to be based on a triad of ground, naval and air forces.[58] Along with these plans for the acquisition of foreign equipment, the navy's indigenization programme was also underway and provided for the construction of a nuclear submarine (the Advanced Technology Vessel) and a small aircraft carrier (the Air Defence Ship). Finally, New Delhi tried to adapt some of its missiles in order to incorporate them in its naval forces. In September 2002, for instance, India successfully tested the Dhanush missile, the naval version of the Prithvi missile. Earlier, in June 2001, the country successfully tested the cruise missile, Brahmos, for the first time. Further, the commercial production of the Brahmos was supposed to begin in 2004, thanks to a joint Russo-Indian undertaking, and countries such as Malaysia had already shown some interest in this missile programme.

Another indication of India's naval ambitions was the announcement by the naval headquarters in April 1998 about the setting up of a fourth command post in Port Blair, in the Andaman Islands, which called for an increase in forces stationed there, apart from the establishment of several monitoring stations.[59] The avowed purpose of the project was to adopt a more active approach, in the face of China's increasing presence in Myanmar and in the Bay of Bengal. The enhanced maritime surveillance in the region also made it possible to monitor illegal trafficking—especially gun smuggling—and reinforce security along shipping lanes. The project, which had been in the pipeline for at least six months, was suddenly shown the green light after the interception of seventy-four smugglers in February 1998 in the Andaman Sea. In 2001, the new military base was transformed into a single command, integrating the three armed forces, with a naval officer at its head, under the direct control of the Chairman of the Chiefs of Staff Committee in the armed forces headquarters in New Delhi.[60] The strengthening of the Andaman Command was a clear reflection of India's determination to establish its military presence in the Bay of Bengal and off the Malacca Strait.

A LOOK EAST POLICY WITH AN INCREASINGLY STRATEGIC OUTLOOK

The strengthening of India's defence policy got reflected in the Look East policy, which assumed increasing strategic inflections in the late 1990s. Firstly, military contacts with South-East Asian countries were in no way affected by the 1998 nuclear tests. For instance, in August 1998, Singapore's Vice-Admiral Richard Lim visited New Delhi in order to intensify bilateral naval cooperation.[61] Then, Murli Manohar Joshi, the Minister for Human Resource Development, affirmed on his return visit from Malaysia in September 1998 that official ties had not been too damaged by India's nuclear tests. He further commented, 'many people who are very influential in Malaysia are happy about it (the Indian nuclear tests) in private conversations'.[62] At the end of 1998, India even exported 100 tons of heavy water to South Korea.[63] In addition, in September and October 1998, Indian Navy ships—two destroyers and a light frigate equipped with missiles—went on a friendly tour to South-East Asia. The stopover programme included Singapore and Vietnam. What was even more surprising was that the Indian fleet docked in Manila at the end of October and had joint exercises with the Philippine naval personnel on its agenda.[64] The fleet, which was promoting the Indian defence industry in the region, ended its tour by participating in the international fleet review in South Korea. A new promotional tour took place in May 1999. The Indian Navy then participated in a naval exhibition in Singapore and organized a conference to present its expertise and equipment.

The only country with which relations remained somewhat strained because of the nuclear tests episode was Japan. The resumption of the dialogue process proved very difficult and only began to produce concrete results in 1999. The missile test carried out by North Korea on 31 August 1998 might have sensitized Japan to India's security perceptions insofar as the hypothesis of technology transfers between Pakistan, China and North Korea was raised once again.[65] Besides, during the Pakistani Foreign Affairs Minister's visit to Tokyo in November 1998, Japanese officials refused to bring up the Kashmir question in the South Asian imbroglio, so as not to hurt India's sensibilities. In December 1998, the turnaround initiated by Japanese diplomacy became more apparent. For the first time in the last several years, the Japanese Foreign Affairs Ministry offered explanations on current events to their Indian counterparts based in Tokyo, underlining the fact that they were ready to resume high-level political contacts with India.[66] The resumption of the multi-dimensional dialogue officially took place in January 1999, with talks at the Foreign Secretary level. On the official aid front, a certain thaw was visible too. In March 1999, the Japanese government lifted the suspension of the loan programme to India and affirmed that it would be ready to resume its economic aid programme partly, if New Delhi signed and ratified the CTBT. Finally, in mid-April 1999, when India proceeded with testing the Agni missile, the Japanese government's reaction was more moderate, although it regretted this act.[67] Despite these beginnings, relations between the two countries remained cold. Japan gave very few signs of a shift in its position as far as nuclear disarmament was concerned, which was the most difficult difference of opinion to resolve with India.

While 1998 and 1999 seemed to have witnessed some shakiness in the Look East policy, with New Delhi essentially focusing on the normalization of relations with the United States, China and other Western countries, the year 2000 was to witness a distinct revival in an increasingly strategic perspective. First and foremost, New Delhi took care to consolidate its multi-dimensional ties with Vietnam and Indonesia, the two 'middle' powers in South-East Asia. The Vietnamese President Tran Duc Luong came to India on a state visit in December 1999, followed by the Indonesian President Abdurrahman Wahid, in February 2000. In return, Prime Minister Vajpayee visited Vietnam and Indonesia in January 2001. These visits were primarily an occasion for signing agreements on the enhancement of defence cooperation. It was of interest to note that Vietnam and Indonesia, the region's two largest states in military terms, were also the most wary of Beijing. In the same perspective, it must also be recalled that the Mekong-Ganga Cooperation, which brought together India and other states in peninsular South-East Asia, had been set-up in July 2000 without China's participation, although the latter was a Mekong country and was involved in other cooperation efforts in the sub-region. The Indian Foreign Affairs Minister, Jaswant Singh, certainly hastened to assure that the MGC was not directed towards China and that it did not aim to increase India's power projection in the region. China nevertheless kept a keen eye on India's involvement in the regional grouping and even asked to be associated with it in July 2001, but in vain, as the MGC members argued that it was first necessary to consolidate their cooperation project.

Furthermore, as of the 2000s, the BJP government's representatives barely missed any opportunities to underline the strategic and security dimensions of the Look East policy during their frequent travels in the region. In some respects, the rapid succession of these visits suggested that New Delhi was trying to forge an informal network with countries that might be interested in counterbalancing China.

For the record, Prime Minister Vajpayee visited Malaysia in May 2001, as well as Singapore and Cambodia in April 2002. He returned to Cambodia in November 2002 and, at the same time, visited Laos and Thailand. His Foreign Affairs Minister, Jaswant Singh, visited Singapore in June 2000 and Laos in November 2000, before going on an Asian tour in March–April 2002, which took him successively to China, South Korea, Thailand and Myanmar. In South Korea, for instance, Jaswant Singh and his counterparts announced that they had the intention of instilling a strategic dimension in their bilateral relations, which had so far been essentially economic in nature. Thus, the two states undertook to hold consultations on the fight against terrorism and to intensify military exchanges.[68] As far as Asia's decision-makers were concerned, Prime Minister Thaksin Shinawatra visited India in November 2001, followed by the Indonesian President Megawati Sukarnoputri, in early April 2002 and Mahathir Mohamad in October 2002.

But it was essentially an intensification of relations with Myanmar that brought to light the increasingly strategic designs of the Look East policy. In November 2000, a large delegation led by the regime's second key man, the SPDC (State Peace and Development Council) Vice-Chairman, General Maung Aye, visited India and seemed to have discussed possible transfers of military equipment to Myanmar. Another sign of rapprochement at the military level was the visit to Myanmar by the Chief of Army Staff, General V.P. Malik, in July 2000, followed by that of the Chief of Naval Staff, Admiral Sushil Kumar, in January 2001. The Minister of External Affairs, Jaswant Singh, later visited Myanmar in February 2001, in order to inaugurate the transborder Tamu-Kalemyo-Kalewa road, which had been built with Indian funding. Thanks to this land link, New Delhi hoped to enhance its multi-dimensional relations and, more generally its policy of engagement with Myanmar. Jaswant Singh also inaugurated a Friendship Centre for Remote Sensing and Data Processing in Rangoon, supposed to herald closer cooperation between the two countries in the field of space technologies. In July 2001, New Delhi and Rangoon agreed to renovate the Sittwe port, which enjoyed a strategic location not far from Kolkata. The same month, another Indian delegation visited Myanmar to undertake an assessment of the Kyaukphu site for building a deep-water port.[69] Finally, Jaswant Singh's second visit to Myanmar took place in April 2002 and aimed at extending the Tamu-Kalemyo-Kalewa transborder road to Thailand, if not all the way to the Indo-Chinese peninsula. New Delhi, which was determined to give itself the means to consolidate its presence and influence in South-East Asia, thus actively tried to make the most of Myanmar's pivotal position. India also had the exploitation of Myanmar's oil and natural gas fields in its line of sight. Finally, it must be added that the two states were henceforth involved in a regular institutional dialogue on transborder issues and had even announced the opening of consulates, in Mandalay and Kolkata, respectively.

India's pro-active Look East policy also succeeded in substantially improving relations with Japan. Although Tokyo was one of the capitals that had condemned the May 1998 nuclear tests the most vehemently and for a long time, New Delhi gradually managed to normalize its bilateral relations with the archipelago. Furthermore, it endeavoured to expand its bilateral cooperation agenda, essentially based on economic relations, to include issues on Asian security. This could be seen during Defence Minister George Fernandes' visit to Japan in January 2000. Later, an improvement in bilateral relations clearly transpired during Prime Minister Yoshiro Mori's official visit in August 2000. The two main subjects of bilateral differences—India's nuclear tests and Japan's economic sanctions—were set aside, to concentrate on the establishment of a 'global partnership', dealing with issues of international importance. Thus, a bilateral dialogue was institutionalized at the highest political level and an Eminent Persons' Group was set-up. Exchanges in the field of defence were marked in particular by the Chief of Army Staff, General S. Padmanabhan's visit to Japan in August 2001. In fact, it was the first visit by an Indian military official of this rank to Japan.

When he visited Japan in December 2001, Prime Minister Vajpayee confirmed the trend towards a certain strategic convergence. Following the example of the United States and in the new context of the war on terrorism, Japan lifted all the economic sanctions that it had imposed on New Delhi in the aftermath of the May 1998 nuclear tests. Above all, Vajpayee did not limit himself to directing his comments to Japanese investors; he was particularly anxious to underline the strategic dimensions of the new 'global partnership' between India and Japan. Thus, the joint declaration stemming from his talk with Prime Minister Jonichiro Koizumi affirmed that India and Japan had to work together to ensure stability and prosperity in Asia, maintain a regular exchange of views on all security-related questions, intensify military contacts and, especially, work towards the total elimination of terrorism.[70] To the satisfaction of India, neither Pakistan, nor Kashmir was mentioned. While the nuclear issue—with the signature of the CTBT topping the list—remained a bone of contention, it nonetheless seemed that Indian and Japanese leaders had finally taken cognisance of certain common concerns with regard to the future evolution of China as well as the protection of sea lanes in the Indian Ocean. Indeed, Japan, which imports a large part of its oil from the Gulf countries, had special interest in preserving security in the Indian Ocean. Thus, India's naval forces, which in Tokyo's perceptions had been a factor of discord during the Cold War, and were then seen as a parameter that was only marginal to the security of the Indian Ocean in the 1990s, slowly established themselves as a significant partner for the protection of sea lanes between the Persian Gulf and South-East Asia. In addition, the two countries became more conscious of their respective positions *vis-à-vis* China—one on its western flank and the other on the eastern flank—and started considering the strategic options that could be envisaged in the hypothesis of deterioration in the overall balance of power in Asia. Thus, it was hardly surprising to see Tokyo describe New Delhi as a 'strategic partner' in this perspective.[71]

India's diplomatic and strategic forays in East Asia enabled it to undertake active naval diplomacy with increasingly diverse partners, including Japan, Vietnam and Indonesia. In 2000, Indian coastguard ships conducted training exercises with Japanese ships in the Bay of Bengal and discussed issues related to piracy and the protection of sea lanes. Furthermore, in the autumn of 2000, Indian and Vietnamese ships conducted naval exercises in the South China Sea, which was a first for the Indian Navy. The following year, in May 2001, it was an Indian coastguard ship that took part in an international fleet review organized by Japan, as well as in joint search and rescue operations in the Tokyo Bay. On the return journey, the same ship docked in Ho Chi Minh City in June 2001 for the first friendly visit by an Indian coastguard ship to Vietnam. Moreover, New Delhi assured its assistance to Japanese self-defence naval forces, which were operating in the Indian Ocean within the framework of the international fight against terrorism. Exchanges also intensified with Indonesia: the Indonesian Chief of Naval Forces, Admiral Achmed Sutjipto, visited India in September 2000, while the Indian Chief of Naval Staff, Admiral Sushil Kumar, reciprocated the visit a few months later in

August 2001. Similarly, Indian naval ships went on a friendly visit to Jakarta in October 2000, before undertaking joint exercises with the Indonesian Navy, off the Andaman and Nicobar Islands, in September 2002. Thanks to these exercises, the Indian Navy increasingly asserted its presence in the region around the Malacca Strait. Finally, it must be added that contacts between Indian and Singaporean naval forces remained quite close and diversified, including the exchange of information, search and rescue operations, anti-mining measures, anti-terrorist fighting tactics and submarine combat exercises.

Clearly, New Delhi seemed to be increasingly determined to assert itself as a major power in the Northern Indian Ocean. To this end, the Indian authorities highlighted the need to ensure the protection of the sea lanes from the Persian Gulf to the Malacca Strait, in the face of growing transnational threats such as piracy and terrorism. In other words, a vision according to which India would be the strategic mainstay in the Indian Ocean was actively put forward. During a visit to Vietnam in April 2000, Defence Minister, George Fernandes, went as far as to say: 'Our (India's) area of interest therefore extends from the North of the Arabian sea to the South China sea.'[72] In the same fashion, high-ranking military officers showed a certain inclination to point out that India's strategic interests went beyond South-East Asia. For instance, the Chief of Army Staff, General S. Padmanabhan, affirmed that India had a 'very legitimate and intense' interest in South-East Asia, during a friendly visit to Singapore in August 2001. Then, in July 2002, the Chief of Naval Staff, Madhvendra Singh, assured that in view of the growing importance of the 'eastern maritime theatre', India would strengthen its Eastern Naval Command in the years to come.[73] But while India was concerned with extending its influence towards South-East Asia, this was essentially on a bilateral basis, i.e. through a consolidation of its strategic ties with each of the region's major states. On the other hand, New Delhi seemed to be less at ease in a multilateral framework, as shown by its participation in the ARF.

INDIA IN THE ARF: A CONTINUING OBSESSION WITH PAKISTAN AND KASHMIR

India's position in the ARF seemed to follow two logics, which had barely anything to do with the forum's outlook. Firstly, New Delhi essentially devoted itself to the imperatives of its post-nuclear diplomacy and the normalization of relations with the major powers in the Asia-Pacific. More than ever, its objective was to be a part of the 'big league'. In an interview to the daily, *The Hindu*, in 1999, Jaswant Singh clearly explained what his diplomatic priorities were that 'the centrality of India in Asia can simply not be wished away. Besides India has to conduct relations with the US, China and Russia as equals (. . .) India must engage with the great powers much more purposefully and productively than we have been until now'.[74] These comments suggested that the External Affairs Minister was reasoning according to the logic of a concert of major powers in Asia, rather than in the perspective of a balance of powers, as defended by the small ASEAN states.

In addition, Pakistan and the Kashmir issue remained the major preoccupation of Indian diplomacy, even within the ARF. What New Delhi was primarily concerned about was to keep Islamabad out of the forum and to prevent any attempt at outside interference in the resolution of the Kashmir conflict. The ASEAN members, who had originally feared that the Indo-Pakistani conflict and the Kashmir issue would get in the way of their consultation process, saw their suspicions come to life in 1999. And yet, the year 1999 seemed to have begun under a good omen: India and Pakistan had, in fact, revived a process of negotiation, which led to the Lahore Declaration on 20–1 February 1999, according to which the two states decided to engage in bilateral consultations on issues of national security, nuclear doctrine, and confidence-building measures in the field of nuclear and conventional arms. They even committed themselves to advancing mutual notifications of any ballistic missile firing tests.[75] Unfortunately, relations between India and Islamabad were soon to deteriorate again—quite seriously, in fact. Indeed, in the spring of 1999, Pakistani incursions into Indian territory led the two neighbours to a very localized armed conflict, in the border area of Kargil in Kashmir. New Delhi's restrained military rebuttal, which consisted of pushing back the Pakistani forces while respecting the line of control, earned it the favour of the international community.

However, the Kargil crisis did put Indian diplomacy in a very delicate situation as the 1999 ARF summit approached. Due to the war-like situation that prevailed at the time in this area, the Kashmir conflict was put on the multilateral agenda of discussion, to the great consternation of New Delhi. During the ARF meetings, however, the Indian delegation managed to channel the discussions in a favourable direction, because the participants—especially the United States—recognized that terrorism was a subject of concern, which had international repercussions. Thus, Jaswant Singh said that the conference had 'been an unqualified success for India'.[76] In fact, the ARF declaration reflected and supported the Indian viewpoint with regard to the Lahore process, while neither Kargil, nor Jammu and Kashmir were mentioned. At the same time, India's commitment to peace in the region was noted. India's satisfaction was essentially an outcome of the fact that its policy stance on the bilateral nature of the resolution of the conflict in Kashmir had been taken into account and respected. And yet, Pakistan had exerted a lot of pressure on some ASEAN members to make them recognize the central character of the Kashmir issue in the Kargil crisis. For the 1999 ARF summit, the Indian delegation also had another concern in relation to the signing of the CTBT. But on this issue, the formulation of the ARF declaration was careful not to be too directorial. In the same spirit of conciliation as the ARF declaration, the joint communiqué issued at the end of the thirty-second ASEAN Ministerial Meeting did not mention Jammu and Kashmir. As regards nuclear non-proliferation, it did not mention India by name, unlike the preceding year, which was interpreted by Jaswant Singh as a yardstick for the diplomatic progress achieved by New Delhi. Thus, the latter affirmed with confidence that 'India's constructive approach on non-proliferation and disarmament (issues) has been vindicated'.[77]

But Indo-Pakistani tensions once again emerged in the 2000 ARF sessions, when Islamabad increased pressure for admission in the forum. New Delhi officially opposed its admission and obtained satisfaction. The decision to refuse Islamabad's request did however raise a number of divergent views within the ASEAN, since Malaysia, Indonesia, Thailand, the Philippines and Brunei supported Pakistan's candidature. Thus, the antagonism with Pakistan remained an unfavourable parameter for the intensification of Indo-ASEAN ties, especially since the Malaysian and Indonesian leaders showed their concern for not alienating Pakistan, a member of the Organization of the Islamic Conference.[78] The state of relations between India and Pakistan continued to greatly influence the position of the Indian representatives in the 2001 ARF sessions. In this instance, the Agra summit, which had taken place a few days earlier between General Musharraf and Prime Minister Vajpayee, allowed India to make the right impression during the ARF meetings. And although the discussions between the new strong man in Pakistan, General Musharraf, and Prime Minister Vajpayee, actually ended on a rather inconclusive note, they at least allowed New Delhi to make a show of its goodwill in pursuing the conciliation process initiated at the Lahore summit.[79] Indeed, the Indian delegation at the 2001 ARF summit did not fail to raise the issue of international terrorism, with reference to the *jihadi* infiltrations that Pakistan continued to support in Kashmir.

As for the 2002 ARF sessions, they took place in the post-9/11 context and were consequently dominated by the new international priority of the war on terrorism. The 9/11 shockwave proved to be particularly violent in South Asia, where a climate of extreme tension emerged between India and Pakistan. The Indians, who were exasperated at seeing Pakistan endorsing for itself the role of a key partner in the international coalition against terrorism, started to fear that the situation in Kashmir get out of control. In fact, since military operations against Al Qaeda had chased them out of Afghanistan, Islamist movements supported by Pakistan did not take long to direct their energies towards Kashmir, which provoked a fresh upsurge of terrorist attacks in the region. Soon, it was the very heart of India that was targeted, when, on 13 December 2001, the Parliament in New Delhi was the target of a terrorist attack. In the aftermath of this incident, New Delhi chose the coercion option and proceeded with an unprecedented mobilization of its army along the line of control. The purpose behind such a move was to urge the international community to exert pressure on Islamabad so that it put a stop to all terrorist activities in Kashmir. The military face-off between India and Pakistan seemed to be on the verge of slipping into an open conflict twice—in December 2001 and in May–June 2002, i.e. a few weeks prior to the ARF sessions.

In such a context, the Indo-Pakistani conflict and the nuclear issue in South Asia were bound to be on the 2002 ARF agenda. In response to the growing tensions in Kashmir, the ASEAN ministers first appealed to the two neighbours to resume their dialogue, in a joint communiqué that was meant to be neutral and placed India and Pakistan on the same footing. However, in the ARF session, India obtained US support, with the Secretary of State Colin Powell stating that Pakistan had to stop supporting terrorist movements in Kashmir before the dialogue could be resumed. The US even felt that the Kashmir conflict had to be resolved bilaterally, thus ruling out any chances of the internationalization of the issue. The outcome of the posture adopted by the US was that the debate in the ARF plenary session was greatly influenced in favour of India. To the great satisfaction of Indian diplomacy, the ARF Chairman's declaration thus refocused its attention on Pakistan, calling for 'an immediate end to all terrorist activities in the region', so as to defuse tension between the two neighbours.[80] While the United States played a decisive role in favour of New Delhi, this was equally true for China, which abstained from opposing any criticism of Pakistan. Indeed, the US support to India and China's neutral position were not just attributable to the new post-9/11 context, in which the fight against international terrorism had become the major security concern of Asia. It was also the reflection of progress that New Delhi had achieved in its relations with the two major powers. That India could engage in 'strategic' or 'security-related dialogues' with the United States and China also suggested that it was increasingly moving towards the framework of a concert of powers in the region.

TOWARDS AN INDIA-CHINA-US TRIANGLE?

A major feature of India's post-Pokhran diplomacy is that it led to a distinct improvement in the dialogue process with Washington. In fact, the May 1998 nuclear tests placed India in the forefront of the international scene and the United States eventually had to initiate a significant shift in its strategic relations with New Delhi. Thus, the successive rounds of the non-proliferation dialogue conducted by Jaswant Singh and Strobe Talbott throughout 1998 and into early 1999, emerged as the most serious security-related exchanges ever conducted with India, apart from the fact that they made it possible to lay the foundations of a new, deeper relationship. Thanks to this dialogue, the American establishment began to understand India's concerns with respect to China's nuclear arsenal.[81] Generally, the United States slowly conceded that the Indian security horizon necessarily included China, and that it was not limited to just Pakistan or South Asia. The improvement in Indo-US relations distinctly transpired during the 1999 Kargil war, when Washington played a decisive role in persuading Pakistan to put an end to its military adventurism and encouraged it to find a peaceful solution to its conflicts with New Delhi.

Another indication that an upturn in bilateral relations was underway was when President Bill Clinton came on a tour of South

Asia—including Bangladesh, India and Pakistan—at the end of March 2000. This American presidential visit, the first to India in almost twenty years, gave an impetus to the American efforts in engaging New Delhi in a new relationship on all bilateral, regional and global issues. It showed that, despite maior disagreements, especially with regard to non-proliferation and Pakistan, the two nations strove to move their dialogue forward. Besides, Vajpayee and Bill Clinton signed a general declaration in which they asserted that close bilateral cooperation would be a factor of stability in Asia. It then seemed that the US was in the process of modifying its perceptions concerning India's role in Asia and in the world. India's satisfaction was all the greater for the fact that the very brief visit by President Clinton to Pakistan revealed a growing malaise *vis-à-vis* General Musharraf, the new key man, who had come to power after a successful *coup d'état* against the government of Nawaz Sharif. Just six months after Bill Clinton's visit, Prime Minister Vajpayee went to the United States, in September 2000. This visit confirmed the two states' willingness to bridge the gap that separated them. It was, in fact, a project that was dear to the Hindu nationalists, since they had always advocated a policy of rapprochement with Washington, which was now slowly gaining weight.

As for the team of President G.W. Bush, who came to power in January 2001, it proved to be even more favourable to a strategic rapprochement with New Delhi and soon undertook to enhance bilateral collaboration on a vast spectrum of subjects, ranging from trade and scientific cooperation to terrorism.[82] Since the new administration was less focused on the issue of non-proliferation than that of President Clinton, the Indo-US dialogue did not take long in putting the disagreement in the nuclear field on the backburner and concentrated on India's potential role in ensuring peace and stability in the Asian region. The two states took cognisance of their growing convergence of views on security in Asia, especially with respect to the protection of the Indian Ocean and the need to prevent the emergence of a hegemonic power in the region. As a proof of its renewed interest, the Bush administration designated Robert Blackwell as Ambassador to India, an expert on the issue of non-proliferation and China, who was a member of the foreign policy advisers' team during G.W. Bush' electoral campaign in 2000. In this context, which saw teams favourable to a distinct rapprochement in power in both Washington and New Delhi, the pace of visits and the level of exchanges increased considerably. A major shift in policy under the Bush administration was the promotion of exchanges between defence institutions, in particular. Indeed, the dialogue process initiated by Clinton and Vajpayee on security and non-proliferation in 2000 only concerned the Foreign Ministers, to the exclusion of defence institutions. Thus, initial contacts between defence officials took place in April 2001, when Jaswant Singh, then the Minister of Foreign Affairs and Defence, met Donald Rumsfeld, the American Defence Secretary.[83] Furthermore, New Delhi was one of the rare capitals in the world to react quite favourably to the National Missile Defence (NMD) project presented by the Bush administration in May 2001. As a result, India, along with South Korea and Japan, became one of the few countries in Asia that the White House decided to consult on the issue. The launch of an Indo-US dialogue on NMD further indicated that Washington was increasingly taking India into consideration in its general strategy for Asia.

However, the 9/11 tragedy put a temporary damper on the Indo-US partnership. Having long considered itself a victim of international terrorism, New Delhi was one of the first capitals in the world to offer its support to the United States in the fight against Al Qaeda. But India noted with great bitterness that for the military campaign in Afghanistan, Washington preferred to re-establish close ties with Pakistan, a state that India considered the hub of terrorism, both in Afghanistan and Kashmir. The new deal significantly complicated the dynamics of the Indo-US rapprochement, since New Delhi once again feared being placed on an equal footing with Pakistan. Furthermore, India could not resist denouncing America's double talk in its fight against terrorism, especially as it came to bear the brunt of a fresh upsurge of terrorist attacks in Kashmir as well as on its Parliament in New Delhi, on 13 December 2001. Nonetheless, the United States endeavoured to cooperate with India and Pakistan at the same time, assuring each that the logic of its policy was not that of a zero-sum game. Consequently, the White House first lifted the post-1998 sanctions against both India and Pakistan, which paved the way for enhanced cooperation in the military, economic and technological fields. A significant outcome of this decision was that the sale of American arms as well as the potential transfer of sensitive technologies resumed. In addition, top American military officials clearly enhanced interaction with their Indian counterparts. Two Chiefs of Army Staff visited India in less than two years, while the country had never before received such dignitaries.[84] The institutional structure for military cooperation was strengthened and the Defence Policy Group, which draws up the main lines of bilateral defence cooperation, held its first meeting in December 2001, after a gap of five years. New structures were created, in particular a Security Cooperation Group, whose role was to handle possible sales of American arms. In addition, the two states conducted consultations with regard to Afghanistan's future, shared confidential information in the war on terrorism and undertook a series of joint exercises involving their different army corps. In this instance, it was at the level of the naval forces that cooperation advanced the fastest.

Indeed, the security of the Indian Ocean proved to be at the heart of the security concerns of both India and the United States. Much before 9/11, the participation of US Navy ships in the first international fleet review organized by the Indian Navy in Mumbai in February 2001, demonstrated the renewed US interest in naval interaction with India. Later, Indo-US naval cooperation intensified in the aftermath of 9/11, with New Delhi offering logistical support for military operations in Afghanistan while American ships present in the North of the Arabian Sea enjoyed access to different Indian port facilities. Further, the first Indo-American military exercises that took place post-1998, were joint search and rescue operations organized by the navies of the two countries in December 2001. The resumption of the Malabar exercises after a gap of six years also demonstrated the US Navy's growing interest in cooperation with the Indian forces. These were held for a week in September 2002 and proved to be the largest joint exercises that the Indian and US naval forces had ever organized. Finally, from April to October 2002, the United States and India conducted joint maritime patrols in the Malacca Strait. More precisely, Indian battleships escorted American merchant ships as well as logistic support ships involved in the 'Enduring Freedom' operation in Afghanistan. The purpose behind the six-month mission was to protect these ships, which were carrying high-value cargo, against any terrorist attack and to ward off the growing phenomenon of piracy in the Malacca Strait as well as in the Bay of Bengal.

It goes without saying that from an Indian perspective, naval cooperation with the US Navy firmed up its aspirations to establish itself as a major power in the Indian Ocean. Indeed, the Indian Navy could present itself as a stabilizing and legitimate force, which, in partnership with the American superpower, assumed the responsibility of protecting the sea lanes in the region. Joint operations in the Malacca Strait allowed New Delhi to further assert its presence in this strategically sensitive zone, while strengthening the security implications of its Look East policy. Thus, it seemed that from the point of view of the United States, Indian strategic interests could, henceforth, legitimately go beyond the strict South Asian framework and spill out into the South-East Asian neighbourhood.[85] Even the influential Deputy Secretary of Defence, Paul Wolfowitz, went as far as to assert during a conference in Singapore in June 2002 that India had an 'important and positive' role to play in East Asian security.[86]

In fact, Washington considered India as a major emerging power with which it was henceforth advisable to maintain close ties. For instance, the National Security Strategy report, published in September 2002, placed India in the category of 'major potential powers', which, along with China and Russia, were meant to weigh heavily on Asia's strategic order.[87] In the reappraisal of India's might, the notion of shared values came to hold a particular place. Indeed, the American leadership liked to stress that the two largest democracies in the world were finally coming together. In the American perception, India henceforth appeared as a model of political liberalism and stability in a region that was much more familiar with authoritarian and extremist regimes. All in all, Washington tended to consider India as a stabilizing force in the Asian strategic context, especially in the face of the 'arc of instability' that run from the Gulf countries to South-East Asia, including Afghanistan and Central Asia. Thus, the United States appeared inclined to co-opt New Delhi in order to reinforce their network of partner and allied countries, willing to ensure the maintenance of peace and security in the region. It must be added that India stood out as a partner that was of even more interest from a geopolitical viewpoint, as it was one of the main military powers located between the two zones in which the United States had a strong presence—the Persian Gulf and East Asia. The rapprochement between New Delhi and Washington was thus part of the redeployment of the American power in the Asian continent, within the context of the war on terrorism.

Having said this, a major point of agreement seemed to gradually enter into the respective perception of decision-makers in New Delhi and Washington concerning India's zone of influence. Indeed, one of the main factors of misunderstanding between the two countries in the 1990s was that the United States was unable to conceive of India's strategic interests beyond South Asia, while India had considerably expanded its vision and placed its ambitions within the regional framework of Asia, in the broadest sense of the word. The American inability to transcend the concept of South Asia was partly due to the analytical framework used by the State Department and several think-tanks, which consisted of dividing Asia into sub-regions, whose strategic problematics were relatively disconnected from each other. Thus, strategic studies concerning India were most often limited to a strict South Asian framework, distinct from security issues affecting South-East Asia or East Asia on the whole. But, in this regard, it should be noted that a certain number of think-tanks in the United States began to consider India as a great power in the making, which, along with China, would be called to weigh in a decisive manner in the Asian balance of power.[88] Thus, India tended to be fully included in the analysis of the general balance of power in Asia. It was true that the fight against international terrorism, with its Islamic networks, held sway from the Persian Gulf to South-East Asia, while suspicions of the proliferation of weapons of mass destruction—between Pakistan and North Korea—probably highlighted the limitations of a compartmentalized approach. The notion of an arc of instability in Asia—from the Persian Gulf to South-East Asia—itself demonstrated the distinct shift in the American geopolitical vision. Thus, Washington started to perceive India's central position at a time when it was redeploying its forces in Asia, with a more inclusive vision of the strategic interdependencies between the different sub-regions of the continent. That a part of the American strategic community began to position India within a wider framework of regional analysis, which more or less corresponded to the geopolitical vision that the Indians had since the early 1990s, was a major structural shift for the future relations between the two countries. In other words, the United States seemed ready to support the new Indian geopolitical vision.

Overall, the 1999–2002 period of time saw India and the United States establish an increasingly closer strategic relationship in Asia, which did not fail to cause some nervousness in Beijing. In response to this rapprochement, China undertook to normalize its own relationship with India, after a period of tensions in the aftermath of the Pokhran tests. Significant initiatives were taken at the highest political level. In February 1999, Foreign Affairs officials resumed their talks and the Joint Working Group, which had completely stopped its activities in the months following Pokhran II, met again in April

1999. Minister of External Affairs, Jaswant Singh made a significant visit to Beijing in June 1999, at the end of which he decided to initiate a strategic dialogue and to once again clarify the issue of the LAC. These initiatives, which gave a new impetus to the normalization of relations, could also signify that China's perceptions *vis-à-vis* India's military capabilities were changing.[89] In other words, the Indian military arsenal could well affect China's defence course of action in the years to come. Pokhran II had indeed introduced an inevitable nuclear parameter in bilateral relations, although China's strategic planning and nuclear development priorities consisted of maintaining a credible second-strike capacity against the major nuclear powers, not of nuclearizing regional conflicts on its peripheries.[90] While Beijing did not wish for its nuclear forces to be included in the South Asian balance of power, India's growing atomic capacities could lead it to reconsider this issue in future. It would not be too long before New Delhi acquired long-range missiles equipped with nuclear warheads, capable of hitting Chinese industrial and demographic centres, located 4,000–5,000 km from its borders. With India possessing an increasingly extensive nuclear strike force, China could find itself in a position in which it would have to respond to India's nuclear challenge.

Thus, India's *de facto* nuclear policy appeared to be pushing the Chinese leadership towards a compromise. Indeed, after 1999, the two nations started intensifying their initiatives to improve bilateral relations. Beijing maintained its position of neutrality with regard to both India and Pakistan on the thorny issue of Kashmir, as demonstrated by its preference for a resolution to the conflict through bilateral negotiations during the 1999 Kargil crisis. The improvement in relations between the two neighbours was later confirmed by the Indian President K.R. Naranayan's visit to China, followed by the Foreign Minister Tang Jiaxuan's visit to India in July 2000. Later, it was the former Chinese Premier, Li Peng, who came on a nine-day visit to India in January 2001, followed by Premier Zhu Rongji, in January 2002. In addition, the two states undertook to accelerate the process for clearing disputes concerning the LAC and achieved concrete results, with an exchange of maps in order to demarcate the border along the central sector. This first important step paved the way for fresh negotiations along the western sector. But, aware of the fact that despite their respective efforts, the resolution of the border issue would be a long drawn-out process, Indian and Chinese decision-makers tried to instil fresh dynamism in their bilateral relations by playing the economic cooperation card. The new orientation appeared to indicate that Sino-Indian relations were set to enter a new phase, marked by an unprecedented diplomatic maturity and a new-found economic pragmatism. After all, prosperous trade ties were an additional insurance for stability, which could even have a positive influence on the political dialogue over the medium term. Sino-Indian relations seemed to have finally been under the influence of the Asian approach to regional security, in which intense economic interdependencies and an all-out diplomatic commitment were considered the best means of diffusing latent tensions. Thus, Premier Zhu Rongji's visit in January 2002 was a veritable exercise in economic diplomacy, as the promotion of bilateral trade ties proved to be one of the main concerns of the Chinese state dignitary. In fact, bilateral trade had already started to increase since the late 1990s, reaching USD 4.5 billion in 2002.

Over and above strict bilateral considerations, the distinct improvement in ties between China and India must also be analysed in the light of their respective relation with the American superpower. As of end 1998, Beijing had clearly seen that the United States had chosen the compromise option with New Delhi on the nuclear issue. Anxious not to bear the brunt of a possible Indo-US rapprochement, Chinese authorities were soon to reiterate the call for a multipolar world, so as to befriend India. When Jaswant Singh visited Beijing in June 1999, the Chinese authorities extensively expressed their resentment concerning the global hegemony practiced by the United States. It was true that the latter had just bombarded the Chinese Embassy in Belgrade. Thus, Jaswant Singh's hosts asserted that India and China could play a major role in creating a multipolar world order. China even began to take forward the Russian idea of a strategic triangle between Moscow, Beijing and New Delhi, as if to ward off the prospect of an Indo-American alignment. When he visited New Delhi in December 1998, Prime Minister Yevgeny Primakov had, indeed, informally mentioned the hypothesis of a 'strategic triangle' between the three major Asian states, so as to counter American domination, while promoting peace and stability in the region.[91] China, like India, had reacted with scepticism. And yet, when the former Chinese Premier, Li Peng, visited New Delhi in January 2001, he mentioned the idea of a strategic triangle with Russia. This proposal, which had at its root a desire to moderate American influence, suggested that Beijing was attracted to the idea of a multipolar world, of which

India could perhaps be a part in future. But it ran into trouble in the face of the Indo-American rapprochement, evident since Bill Clinton's visit, in March 2000.[92] Besides, New Delhi did not show much enthusiasm *vis-à-vis* China's appeals.

Beijing's suspicions only strengthened with the advent of the Republicans in the White House. During its first few months in power, the Bush administration could not hide its scepticism with regard to China, which, from its status of a 'strategic partner' under the Clinton administration was downgraded to that of a 'strategic competitor'. The distinct distrust with regard to Beijing was seemingly concomitant with the new Bush administration's infatuation with India. In many ways, the strengthening of Indo-US ties looked like a strategy aimed at containing China and different signals could validate this argument. The new American Ambassador to India, Robert Blackwell, had the reputation of belonging to a camp of hawks in the Bush administration, which, along with Defence Secretary Donald Rumsfeld and his adviser Paul Wolfowitz, advocated a policy of firmness with regard to China. As a matter of fact, Blackwell seemed to be a key player in the nascent military cooperation between New Delhi and Washington. In addition, the rather positive response that New Delhi offered to America's national missile defence plan in May 2001 was in stark contrast with the opposition of China. Finally, at the height of the Sino-American crisis over the EP3 spy aircraft, which ended up on the Hainan Island in May 2002, President Bush proved very keen to meet with Jaswant Singh, who was then on a visit to Washington.

In the post-9/11 context, relations between Washington and Beijing warmed up somewhat, without much change in the mistrust that some hawks in the Bush administration could entertain with respect to China. At the same time, military cooperation between New Delhi and Washington intensified, so much so that Beijing became vigilant with regard to developments in Indo-US relations. As for India, it kept a close eye on ties between Beijing and Islamabad. In this instance, China strove to officially maintain a neutral position in the face of the worsening of Indo-Pakistan ties after 9/11. Chinese authorities strongly condemned the terrorist attack on the Indian Parliament in December 2001 and even initiated a dialogue on the fight against terrorism with India. However, Beijing did show a penchant for Islamabad, for instance when, in June 2002, Foreign Minister Tang Jiaxuan asked the international community to adopt a more balanced attitude towards both neighbours, thereby signifying that there should not be any undue favouritism towards India. In addition, contacts between the Chinese and Pakistanis remained close and frequent.[93]

Despite a distinct rapprochement between India and China after 1999, a certain degree of distrust remained. First and foremost, China's enthusiasm for New Delhi was partly guided by the fear of an Indo-American alignment. Furthermore, the revival of India's Look East policy in an increasingly strategic perspective was not likely to please Beijing. A number of visits by Indian decision-makers since 2000 had made it possible to intensify security exchanges with various countries of East Asia, and the region could have an interest in finding a counterweight to China's ascendancy. The Indian Navy even began to establish its presence in the South China Sea, thanks to its interactions with Vietnam and Japan. Similarly, Indo-US naval cooperation in the Indian Ocean and, notably, exercises in the Malacca Strait would have surely confirmed Chinese reservations. Beijing could not be pleased to see the United States support India's aspirations in the Indian Ocean, as well as on the fringes of South-East Asia, while it aspired to enhance its influence in the region. Thus, some parts of South-East Asia and the Indian Ocean could become sensitive zones, especially those where the Indian and Chinese sphere of influence overlapped. In any event, in the early 2000s, China and India both had an interest in improving bilateral relations, since a period of peace and tranquillity would allow them to consolidate themselves—both in economic as well as military terms. In this regard, New Delhi would undoubtedly remain sensitive to any Chinese initiative—real or perceived as such—that could try to marginalize it or reduce it to the status of a sub-regional power, and would thus apply itself to enhancing its strike force. This was perhaps the implicit message that the Indian authorities were keen to convey to their Chinese neighbour when they decided to carry out a fresh test for a medium-range ballistic missile, Agni II, the day Li Peng left, on 17 January 2001.

Thus, in the early to mid-2000s, it seemed that the triangle between India, China and the United States would probably be decisive in the evolution of India's role in the Asian region. Indeed, the Indo-American dialogue remained a key element in the process of integration in the Asian strategic balance of powers. It clearly emerged through the third section that an improvement in relations between New Delhi and Washington, the sole superpower that guarantees stability in Asia, helped India in its strategic reorientation towards East Asia.

But Sino-Indian relations would also—and in fact increasingly—be a major parameter in the distribution of power in Asia. Two logics could play a role in this matter. The first concerns the growing rivalry between the two giants, in which Beijing would take a dim view of India enhancing its profile in Asia. Indeed, it emerged that in both India and China's traditional perception of their sphere of influence, there are many overlaps, in Central Asia and South-East Asia, as well as in the Himalayan region and the Indian Ocean. The second logic, on the contrary, would bring the two states closer to each other in economic terms, but also for standing up to the United States. After all, in the 1990s, the two Asian giants demonstrated a shared propensity to challenge American hegemony and promote a multipolar order in Asia, as well as the world. By the end of the decade, New Delhi seemed to play the rapprochement card with the United States, while actively engaging China. Consequently, it clearly appeared that in its strategic dimensions, India's Look East policy would increasingly depend upon its relations with China and the United States, two major powers on the Asian scene.

NOTES

1. See Raja Menon, *A Nuclear Strategy for India*, p. 113; K. Subrahmanyam, 'Nuclear India in Global Politics', *World Affairs*, July–September 1998, vol. 2, no. 3, 1998, p. 25.
2. M.L. Sondhi and Prakash Nanda, *Vajpayee's Foreign Policy: Daring the Irreversible*, New Delhi: Har-Anand, 1999, p. 28.
3. Ibid., p. 22.
4. Christophe Jaffrelot, 'Du Nationalisme Hindon au Nationalisme Nucléaire', *Etudes*, October 1998, no. 3894, p. 305.
5. G. Tanham, 'Indian Strategic Culture', *Washington Quarterly*, p. 136.
6. R. Roy-Chaudhury, 'Maritime Surveillance of the Indian EEZ', *Strategic Analysis*, vol. 12, no. 1, April 1998, p. 54. It was the Burmese authorities that seemed to have informed the Indian authorities about these arms consignments (*The Hindu*, 28 April 1998).
7. *Indian Recorder*, 21–27 May 1997.
8. Gurmeet Kanwal, 'China's Long March to World Power Status: Strategic Challenge for India', *Strategic Analysis*, February 1999, vol. 22, no. 11, p. 1724.

9. Brahma Chellaney, 'La Sécurité de l'Inde après les Essais Nucléaires', in *Politique Etrangère*, no. 3, Autumn 1998, p. 526.
10. *Indian Recorder*, 4–10 June 1998.
11. Sondhi and Nanda, *Vajpayee's Foreign Policy*, p. 106.
12. *Indian Recorder*, 4–10 June 1998.
13. Ibid.
14. Jaswant Singh, 'Against Nuclear Apartheid', *Foreign Affairs*, vol. 77, no. 5, September–October 1998, pp. 41–52.
15. Ibid., p. 48.
16. Subrahmanyam, 'Nuclear India in Global Politics', *World Affairs*, pp. 12–40.
17. Sondhi and Nanda, *Vajpayee's Foreign Policy*, p. 21.
18. Tanham, 'Indian Strategic Thought', in Tanham, Bajpai and Mattoo, ed., *Securing India*, pp. 72–82.
19. Menon, *A Nuclear Strategy for India*, p. 179.
20. Ibid., p. 182.
21. Thérèse Delpech and Arnaud d'Andurain, 'L'avenir nucléaire se joue-t-il en Asie?', in *Critique Internationale*, no. 1, Autumn 1998, pp. 8–14; J. Mohan Malik, 'India Goes Nuclear: Rationale, Benefits, Costs and Implications', *Contemporary South-East Asia*, vol. 20, no. 2, August 1998, pp. 191–212; James Manor and Gerald Segal, 'Taking India Seriously', *Survival*, IISS Quarterly, vol. 40, no. 2, Summer 1998, pp. 53–70.
22. Thérèse Delpech, 'Les Conséquences Stratégiques des Essais Indiens et Pakistanais', in *Politique Etrangère*, no 3, Autumn 1998, p. 477.
23. B. Sen Gupta, 'In Search of a Foreign Policy', *Seminar*, no. 172, December 1998.
24. *Indian Recorder*, 18–24 June 1998.
25. Ibid.
26. Swaran Singh, 'Sino-Indian Ties: Need for Bold Initiatives', *Strategic Analysis*, February 1999, vol. 22, no. 11, pp. 1729–30.
27. *Indian Recorder*, 30 July–5 August 1998.
28. Sondhi and Nanda, *Vajpayee's Foreign Policy*, pp. 75–6.
29. S. Singh, 'Sino-US Defence Ties: Whys and Hows of Their Recent Engagement', *Strategic Analysis*, April 1998, vol. 22, no. 1, pp. 76–7.
30. Vladimir Moskalenko and Tatiana Shaumian, 'Russia's Security and the Geopolitical Situation in South Asia', in G. Chuffrin, ed., *Russia and Asia: The Emerging Security Agenda*, Stockholm: SIPRI and Oxford University Press, 1999, p. 240.
31. The National Institute for Defence Studies, *East Asian Strategic Review 1998–99*, Tokyo: NIDS, 1999, pp. 55–9.
32. Islamabad, which was only a sectoral dialogue partner of the ASEAN could not participate in the ARF deliberations. Pakistan obtained this status in 1992, along with India.

33. *The Hindu*, 3 July 1998.
34. Ibid., 22 May 1998.
35. 'Chronology of Responses to Pokhran II', *Strategic Digest*, vol. XXVIII, July 1998, pp. 1091–1101.
36. *The Hindu*, 23 June 1998.
37. Interview, Ministry of Foreign Affairs, Foreign Service Officer, Singapore, 20 June 1998.
38. Statement by Deputy Chairman Planning Commission of India, Jaswant Singh on the Occasion of the ASEAN thirty-first Post-Ministerial Conferences (PMC 9+10) Plenary Session, 29 July 1998, Manila, § 6.
39. *The Hindu*, 28 July 1998.
40. Joint Communiqué of the thirty-first ASEAN Ministerial Meeting, Manila, Philippines, 24–5 July 1998, *Strategic Digest*, vol. 28, no. 10, October 1998, p. 1597.
41. *The Hindu*, 27 July 1998.
42. Statement of the Chairman of the Fifth ASEAN Regional Forum, Manila, 27 July 1998, *Strategic Digest*, vol. 28, no. 10, October 1998, p. 1589.
43. Closing Statement H.E. Domingo Siazon, Chairman, ASEAN Regional Forum, Manila, 27 July 1998.
44. *The Hindu*, 22 July 1998.
45. Ibid., 28 July 1998.
46. Suo Moto Statement by Prime Minister Shri Atal Behari Vajpayee in Lok Sabha/Rajya Sabha, *Foreign Affairs Record*, August 1998, vol. XLIV, no. 8, p. 72.
47. G.V.C. Naidu, 'The Manila ASEAN Meetings and India', *Strategic Analysis*, vol. 22, no. 8, November 1998, p. 1171.
48. *Indian Express*, 28 July 1998.
49. Ibid., 29 July 1998.
50. This order of priorities, for instance, partly guided the Embassy of South Korea's policy in New Delhi (Interview, Embassy of South Korea, Commercial Section, New Delhi, November 1998). As for the *Singapore Trade Development Board*, it organized an 'India Day' in August 1998, only three months after the tests. At that time, the Minister of Commerce, Ramakrishna Hegde, reported that India's nuclearization had not affected its political and economic ties with the South-East Asian countries.
51. Kun Young Park and Wang Hwi Lee, 'The Financial Crisis of 1997–8 and Its Impact on Security Relations in East Asia', *Asian Perspectives*, vol. 23, no. 3, 1999, p. 139; Paul Dibb, D. David Hale and Peter Prince, 'The Strategic Implications of Asia's Economic Crisis', *Survival*, vol. 40, no. 2, Summer 1998, pp. 5–26.
52. Amitav Acharya, 'Ideas, Identity and Institution-building', *The Pacific Review*, pp. 319–46.

53. Susan L. Shirk, 'Asia-Pacific Regional Security: Balance of Power or Concert of Powers?', in David A. Lake and Patrick M. Morgan, *Regional Orders: Building Security in a New World*, University Park Pa.: Pennsylvania State University Press, 1997, pp. 245–70.
54. SIPRI, *Yearbook 1999*, pp. 283–4.
55. Dinshaw Mistry, 'Diplomacy, Sanctions, and the U.S. Non-proliferation Dialogue with India and Pakistan', *Asian Survey*, vol. 39, no. 5, September–October 1999, pp. 753–71.
56. The SIPRI Military Expenditure Database [http://www.sipri.org]. Military expenditure accounted for 2.2 per cent of the GDP in 1997 and 1998, and 2.4 per cent in 1999 and 2000.
57. *The Hindu*, 21 April 2002.
58. Rahul Bedi, 'Russian Nuclear Subs High on India's Shopping List', *Asia Times Online*, 12 April 2002.
59. *Indian Recorder*, 21–7 May 1998.
60. This institution was established in October 2001 to reorganize the defence machinery at the highest level, and to strengthen planning and coordination effectiveness between the three armed forces. However, it seemed that the initiative was only partly successful at the time, with the government refusing to designate a Chief of Defence Staff.
61. *The Hindu*, 25 August 1998.
62. Ibid., 14 September 1998.
63. *The Times of India*, 28 June 1998.
64. *The Hindu*, 26 October 1998.
65. The Japanese Defence agency felt that links between Pakistan and North Korea went back to at least 1995. On several occasions, sometimes even at the Foreign Ministers' level, Japan expressed great concern to Pakistan on its ties with North Korea, especially with regard to missiles. Indeed, Islamabad seemed to have purchased North Korean technologies and equipment, to the great regret of Tokyo, who saw in these purchases a source of further funding for Korean missile and nuclear programmes. But when Tokyo warned Pakistan that it considered these transactions as a threat to its security, the latter officially denied any links with Pyongyang. The National Institute for Defense Studies, *East Asian Strategic Review 1998–99*, pp. 62–3.
66. *The Hindu*, 12 December 1998.
67. Ibid., 16 April 1999.
68. Ibid., 4 April 2002.
69. Ministry of External Affairs, *Annual Report 2001–2*.
70. *The Hindu*, 11 December 2001.
71. Ibid., 2 January 2003.
72. Ibid., 15 April 2000.
73. Ibid., 6 July 2002.

74. Ibid., 25 July 1999.
75. In fact, New Delhi tested its medium-range ballistic missile Agni 2 on 11 April 1999, and on 14 April, it was Pakistan that proceeded with the tests of its Ghauri II missiles. But, the important element was that the two sides notified each other in advance about their decisions, in the spirit of the Lahore Declaration.
76. *The Hindu*, 27 July 1999; *The Hindustan Times*, 27 July 1999.
77. Ibid.
78. Pakistan was eventually invited to join the ARF in 2004.
79. India and Pakistan could not even agree on the basis of a potential dialogue. The Indian approach consisted of holding wide-ranging and diversified consultations, putting the Kashmir conflict on the back-burner. From the Pakistani point of view, it was unacceptable to hold a dialogue without first dealing with the Kashmir issue.
80. *The Hindu*, 1 August 2002.
81. Menon, *A Nuclear Strategy for India*, p. 285.
82. Harry Harding, 'The Bush Administration's Approach to Asia: Before and after September 11', Hong Kong Asia Society, 12 November 2001 (http://www.csis.org/saprog/venu.pdf); Dennis Kux, 'India's Fine Balance', *Foreign Affairs*, May/June 2002; Satu P. Limaye, 'U.S.-India Relations: Visible to the Naked Eye', *Comparative Connections*, 4th Quarter 2001 (http://www.csis.org/pacfor/cc/0104Qoa.html); R.P. Rajagopalan, 'Indo-US Relations in the Bush White House', *Strategic Analysis*, July 2001 (http://www.idsa-india.org).
83. This had been the first meeting of the kind since 1995, when William Perry visited India.
84. The Chief of Army Staff General Henry Shelton visited India in July 2001, and his successor, Richard Myers, in February 2002. Their Indian counterpart, General S. Padmanabhan, visited the United States in April 2002.
85. It is to be noted, however, that Indonesia and Malaysia proved fairly reluctant towards the Indo-American escort operations in the Malacca Strait.
86. P. Wolfowitz P., US Deputy Secretary of Defense, 'The Gathering Storm: The Threat of Global Terror and Asia/Pacific Security', *The First IISS Asia Security Conference: 'The Shangri-La Dialogue'*, Singapore, 31 May–1 June 2002.
87. White House, *The National Security Strategy of the United States of America*, Washington, September 2002, pp. 10, 26, 27.
88. For more recent and significant studies, see in particular: National Bureau of Asian Research, *Strategic Asia 2001–2* (especially the introductory chapter by Aaron L. Friedberg and the chapter on South Asia by Ashley J. Tellis) (http://strategicasia.nbr.org/Report); S.P. Cohen, *India:*

Emerging Power, Washington D.C.: Brookings Institution Press, 2001, p. 377; Venu Rajamony, 'India-China-U.S. Triangle: A "Soft" Balance of Power in the Making', Asia Foundation, March 2002 (http://www.csis.org/saprog/venu.pdf); T.C. Schaffer, *Rising India and U.S. Policy Options in Asia*, CSIS Report, January 2002, 36 pp. (http://www.csis.org/pubs/2002_risingindia.htm); J. Sommers (Rapporteur), 'The India-China Relationship: What the United States Needs to Know', Asia Society and Woodrow Wilson Centre for Scholars Conference Report, 30 November 2001 (http://www.asiasociety.org/publications/indiachina01.html).

89. Menon, *A Nuclear Strategy for India*, p. 191.
90. Richard Weixing Hu, 'India's Nuclear Bomb and Future Sino-Indian Relations', *East Asia*, Spring 1999, pp. 61–5.
91. Indeed, the concept began to gain substance when Moscow and Beijing concluded a strategic partnership for peace, after three decades of mistrust. From the Russian perspective, the proposal aimed at seeing to what extent India was keen on joining an essentially symbolic defiance plan *vis-à-vis* the United States. Against an international context of fresh American bombings in Iraq, Moscow probably felt increasingly inclined to promote a multipolar world. Chintamani Mahapatra, 'India, China and Russia: Strategic Triangle is Possible', *Strategic Analysis*, February 1999, vol. 22, no. 11, pp. 1793–4.
92. J.W. Garver, 'The China-India-US Triangle: Strategic Relations in the Post-Cold War Era', *NBR Analysis*, vol. 13, no. 5, 2002 (http://www.nbr.org).
93. Musharraf visited China in December 2001, and the Vice-Premier Wu Bangguo went to Pakistan in March 2002. During his visit to Islamabad in May 2002, the Chinese Foreign Minister, Tang Jiaxuan, reaffirmed his country's commitment to maintaining close relations with Pakistan.

CHAPTER 10
Conclusion

Ever since the Look East policy was launched in the early 1990s, India has undoubtedly succeeded in strengthening its economic, political and strategic ties with East Asia. But while the country has begun to bind itself to the 'new Asia', it still occupies a somewhat peripheral position. The construction of an East Asian region has indeed been strengthened, and India is only partially incorporated in it. In any case, the Look East policy is a tangential and multi-dimensional process that has to be considered over the long-term and in the larger framework of the world trend towards regionalization.

INTERPRETING THE LOOK EAST POLICY IN THE PERSPECTIVE OF NEO-REGIONALISM

Originally, the Look East policy appeared as a project launched by the central government and it was essentially based on economic motivations. It aimed at creating ties with a prosperous region—East Asia—which was being structured at the time thanks to increasing economic interdependencies. However, it is of primary importance to understand that the Look East policy intended to engender a much broader process of interaction than diplomatic-economic exchanges alone. From the very start, its objectives were regionalist in nature, insofar as they intended to bind India to the East Asian region in the most diverse fields possible. This was clearly in the minds of some Indian political leaders. For instance, when New Delhi obtained the status of Full Dialogue Partner with the ASEAN, in 1996, the Minister of Foreign Affairs I.K. Gujral explained: 'What Look East really means is that an outward looking India is gathering all forces of dynamism—domestic and regional—and is directly focusing on establishing synergies with a fast consolidating and progressive neighbourhood to its East in the Mother Continent of Asia.'[1]

Then, evoking the dialogue partnership with the ASEAN, Gujral further added: 'It will involve building new constituencies—economic, political, social and cultural—in our countries. It means developing in the ASEAN tradition a degree of informality, familiarity, understanding and "comfort levels" among our political leaders, officials, business persons, academics, NGOs, media and most of all, our youth.'[2]

The spectrum of actors supposed to participate in the Indo-ASEAN dialogue was thus as broad as possible. In this sense, the Look East policy aimed at nothing less than a rapprochement between the Indian and South-East Asian civil societies, rather than just between their governments and institutions. In other words, the Look East policy was so conceived as to give an impetus to a process of regionalization that would also and essentially involve socio-economic actors. It therefore aimed to reproduce the modalities of the East Asian regionalization, which was largely driven by the activities of the private sectors.

Hence, rather than limiting the Look East policy to the foreign policy field or to the economic diplomacy argument, it should be seen in congruence with the neo-regionalism trend. It must be recalled that New Delhi forged this policy at a time when it feared being left on the periphery of a worldwide trend towards a new brand of regionalism. Briefly, there have been two waves of regionalism in recent history. The first occurred essentially in Europe, in the immediate aftermath of Second World War, until the 1960s, and it took place from the top, through states and institutions. The second wave of regionalism came in the 1980s and accelerated with the collapse of the Soviet block. While the end of the Cold War gave the impression of greater independence in several places on the planet, it also evoked a new feeling of vulnerability. In this context, the implementation of—new or more efficient—regional organizations was a way of combating the marginalization that threatened several countries in the globalization era. A major feature of this second wave of regionalism, or neo-regionalism was that it was driven by transnational actors and market forces as much as by the policies of the states. In Europe itself, neo-regionalism caught up with the first brand of regionalism, as socio-economic actors entered upon the scene. However, it is in East Asia that this new brand of regionalism came to be the most obvious, as socio-economic dynamics and market forces have been particularly prominent in structuring and uniting the region.

Indeed, markets, investment flows, trade and corporate strategies, migrations and diaspora networks have been the driving forces behind the regionalization of East Asia. In some cases, the regionalization process has even taken place irrespective of state policies.[3] However, more often than not, states have made the most out of these new socio-economic dynamics. Thus J.L. Domenach observed that the 'formation of an "Asia region"' has largely been '"directed and controlled by political leaders"' and that it is not simply '"the result of the uncontrolled interplay of transnational economic forces"'.[4] In this connection, the emergence of the 'new Asia' has also resulted from state-led strategies aimed at reorganizing a regional space along well-defined political and economic lines. All in all, the neo-regionalist trend underway in East Asia has resulted from the complex interplay of deliberate political actions on the part of the states of the region, as well as structural processes of increased socio-economic interactions. As for India, if it was indeed to bind itself to the new Asia, its Look East policy would have to reflect this new pattern of regional integration.

THE MULTIPLE DECLENSIONS OF THE LOOK EAST POLICY

Thus placed in the perspective of neo-regionalism, the 'Look East' policy can be interpreted in a wider sense, as a general trend, a multi-dimensional reorientation of India towards its eastern neighbourhood, rather than just a government policy. The entire focus of this study was precisely to pinpoint the various processes by which India could be integrated into the East Asian regionalization trends. Thus, India's Look East policy can be understood as a bunch of initiatives led by various actors, including political decision-makers from the centre, but also—and maybe increasingly—from the federated states, as well as public, semi-public and private economic actors, besides intellectuals and the diaspora in Asia. The spectrum of India's partners and interlocutors on the East Asian side has proved to be as wide and varied. Far from always being coordinated or concomitant, these various initiatives have been aimed at diverse objectives and followed various strategies, primarily commercial and financial in nature, but also touristic, cultural, political or even ideological, while also including strategic and defence objectives. In short, the Look East policy must be understood as the main axis of a more general reorientation in India's contemporary relations with the 'new Asia'.

The Look East policy has been deployed at an intermediate level between the domestic and global levels, but also in interactions with both these levels. It was born and evolved against a specific domestic context—that of India's economic liberalization and, generally speaking, its modulations have been linked to developments in internal politics, such as, for example, Indian electoral politics and the changes in government that ensued. The Look East policy could also be perceived as a strategy aimed at gaining greater access to the globalization process. In the early 1990s, integration in the Asian economic region was conceived as the best springboard to the world economy, insofar as this region was already seen as one of the most globalized regions in the world. The aim, in other words, was to accelerate the country's integration in the world market by playing the game of East Asian regionalism.

Further, to comprehend New Delhi's regionalist strategy, we must appreciate its many variations. In particular, the Look East policy has developed at diverse regional levels—the macro regional, sub-regional and micro-regional levels—that illustrate the model conceptualized by Mittelman, in which regionalism is broken down into three units.[5] In this model, macro-regions are vast spatial units with very little structuring, which also fully include states and coordinate capital flows within a given space, while providing access to the globalization process. These loose geographical units, much larger than states, also share political and cultural ties. Sub-regions are smaller formations that essentially cover the border areas of national economies, i.e. these economic zones transcend political borders, without involving national economies as a whole. Finally, micro-regions develop within the sovereign state and spearhead globalization. That is the globalized part of the national economy. At the macro-regional level, India has long aspired to integrate with the APEC and has henceforth participated in the IOR-ARC. The formation of BIMST-EC, the Kunming initiative, and the Mekong-Ganga Cooperation that involve the country's eastern part in different ways could correspond to the sub-regional level.[6] India's micro-regionalism could be seen in particular in its southern states—Andhra Pradesh, Karnataka and Tamil Nadu—that have wished to establish special ties with South-East Asia. These different regional spaces either fit together or are superimposed one on the other, but they all reinforce the overall integration of the Indian economy to East Asia.

WAYS AND MEANS TO INTEGRATE INDIA IN THE ASIAN ECONOMIC REGION: STATES AS PRIMARY ACTORS

On observing the case of the rapprochement between the Indian and East Asian economies, the states appear to have endorsed a leadership role, their objective being to give an impetus to the very process of regionalization. Indeed, in a context of opening up to the world market, Indian decision-makers became far more aware of the importance of economics with regard to external relations. They also became aware of the incredible levels of development achieved by their East Asian neighbours. Thus, the Look East policy turned into a major dimension of the economic diplomacy implemented by New Delhi in the early 1990s. In the Far East, India especially courted Japan and South Korea, who thus became its privileged interlocutors. In South-East Asia, Malaysia, Thailand and Singapore stood out from the viewpoint of their interest in the Look East policy. The concerted actions then deployed by the Indian government and its East Asian counterparts aimed at giving an impetus to interactions between the private sectors of these countries. In this respect, the study of bilateral relations between India and Singapore, the East Asian country that paid the most attention to the Look East policy, is a good illustration of the primacy of state actions with regard to external economic relations. The ties between Singapore and New Delhi also show how bilateral and regional policies can strengthen one another. Thus, this first observation highlights the continuing importance of the role of the states even in the neo-liberal context of opening up of the markets, and their capacity to mobilize support to give an impetus to the regionalization processes.

It is true that, despite the weakening of their powers in the globalization context, states have retained control over several levers. In the first place, they have retained decision-making powers concerning the main orientations to be given to economic policies and therefore, to either create or not a favourable business environment. They have established a legal framework that encourage and guide interactions between private economic actors. Moreover, states may have tried to channel the dynamics of regionalization, by drawing attention to priority sectors for national development. They have also given strong political signals by pointing their business communities in the right direction so that they would take interest in a particular market. Furthermore, there has been the whole issue of diplomatic-economic delegations aimed at creating a favourable climate overall and ensuring the development of positive collective perceptions.

Hence, this conclusion tends to show that the state has remained strong enough in India, as in a large part of East Asia, and that it still retains substantial powers with regard to initiatives in economic matters. Interestingly, the voluntarism of the Indian state to integrate the Indian economy to the East Asian regionalization has led to new partnerships with the business circles. In other words, public authorities have conferred and coordinated with the private sector to try to direct market forces in a direction they deemed desirable. On the Indian side, the strong involvement of the state has been the outcome of the country's new economic diplomacy, implemented in the context of the opening up of the economy to market forces. More than ever at the service of commercial and financial imperatives, the state therefore has entered into collaboration with the private sector in order to sustain economic growth. On the East Asian side, for instance, in Singapore or Japan, state actors have been in first line to try and take advantage of India's liberalization while playing the card of the very close ties they maintain with their business circles. In a way, the states in East Asia have adopted a pioneering role, prospecting for the opportunities offered by the vast, emerging Indian market. It also appears that government circles—notably in the case of Singapore—have tried to draw up strategies in partnership with business communities, in order to diversify investments and reduce risk-taking. These concerted approaches and the mutual support between public authorities and the private sector have aimed at a priority objective: to find new markets and sustain growth. In this perspective, the new interactions between India and East Asia have often been made more dynamic by the cross-consultations that took place between state actors and the business communities of the different parties concerned. Thus, Indian state leaders have tried to get in touch with East Asian business circles while trade organizations such as the CII have created networks within government circles in East Asia. Moreover, public or semi-public corporations have played a pioneering role in giving an impetus to economic dynamics between India and East Asia. In fact, they have undertaken some large-scale projects that have received a certain visibility in the media, and their experiences have partly shaped the perceptions of the business communities of their countries of origin.

SOCIO-ECONOMIC INTEGRATION OF INDIA IN THE EAST ASIAN REGIONALIZATION

However, state voluntarism is not enough to connect the Indian economy to the East Asian region. The actual incorporation of India in the region has to take place first of all through commercial and financial exchanges. In this regard, there has been an overall intensification of transnational flows with East Asia, in terms of trade, as well as flows of capital, ideas and people, which proves that socio-economic actors have given substance to the Look East policy. However, the 1997 Asian crisis altered somewhat this emerging dynamic. At the onset of the twenty-first century, India seems to stand right at the starting point of integrating in the Asian regionalization process.

If the total foreign direct investments during the 1991–2001[7] decade are examined, Japan was the fourth largest foreign investor in India, followed by South Korea. Malaysia was in the tenth position and Singapore the eleventh. Indeed, the flying geese phenomenon that was one of the engines of the regional integration of East Asia could be seen here too, though to a much more limited degree. Japan, which has long been the primary supplier of capital in East Asia, has not worked as a major pole of regionalization in India's case. The relative decline of Japan, both as a foreign investor and a trade partner, actually shows that India has been more on the path of globalization rather than regionalization, though these are not opposing trends. The 'secondary poles'[8] or intermediary countries, such as South Korea or Singapore, have been present too, but there again fairly modestly as compared to Western investors. Japan and South Korea each accounted for more or less four per cent of the total foreign investments approved in India between 1991 and 2001, and the ASEAN economies accounted for around 5 per cent. The East Asian economies together represented about 14–15 per cent of the total foreign investments in India. But the United States alone accounted for twenty per cent, which reveals that the integration of the Indian economy to the East Asian regionalization has been a fairly relative phenomenon.

However, the Indian case has partly reproduced the model of regional integration through transnational flows. India's comparative advantages in some sectors, especially information technologies or automobile parts, have begun to generate an economic regionalization with East Asia. Some East Asian firms have even relocated their production activities, in particular the *chaebols* that use India as a base with low labour costs and as a springboard for re-export. But these dynamics have not yet developed enough to promote high-level intra-regional and, especially, intra-branch trade, nor to incorporate the country in regional production networks. India has also participated in 'growth polygons', such as the BIMST-EC, which are theoretically based on specializations linked to the comparative advantages of each member. As for the diaspora networks in East Asia, they do exist and constitute additional ties, but often of a narrow span or difficult to quantify. These networks revolve either around political personalities or economic decision-makers who have tried to mobilize the business communities of their respective countries (especially in Singapore or Malaysia), or around a few large-scale NRI companies based in East Asia that have invested in India. But, the diaspora networks have not actually bolstered an economic integration with the East Asian region that is independent of political powers, unlike the reticular regionalism of the Chinese networks. Much to the contrary, it is state actors again that have tried to mobilize NRI networks to support the regional integration project. In any case, the mobilization of the Indian diaspora in Asia has remained limited and cannot be comparable to the role of the overseas Chinese in China's economic boom. Generally speaking, India's regional integration to East Asia has made much less progress than China's, but it has replicated some of its mechanisms, including favourable government policies, comparative advantages in relation to neighbouring East Asian economies and diaspora networks.[9]

Although they may have been rather modest, certain dynamics of regional integration have been successfully initiated. It seems that beyond state voluntarism, it would basically be a healthy Indian economy that would be the best guarantor of the continuation of its integration in the Asian region. It goes without saying that the prosperity of the East Asian economies would itself be decisive in such a development. With the worst of the Asian crisis having passed, there has been a visible resumption in trade with India that throw a ray of hope for the intensification of the regionalization processes. In this perspective, the progress in the regional integration of the Indian economy would call for more detailed research on the spatial distribution of commercial and financial flows from East Asia. This would make it possible to pinpoint the territories in India which are the most linked with the East Asian economies. It appears that the south

Indian states (Andhra Pradesh, Karnataka and Tamil Nadu) have attracted a large part of the East Asian investment projects. While the attraction effect could be attributed to geographical proximity and diasporic ties, it ensues much more from the economic dynamism of these states. Like all other foreign investors, East Asian investors have headed toward the states that have the highest economic development levels or the most attractive policies, even if they are in the hinterland (Delhi-Haryana-Punjab) or on the Western coast (Maharashtra-Gujarat).

The possible integration of the Indian economy in the East Asian regionalization would probably not, therefore, be homogeneous and would involve certain zones more than others, as the country is an immense territory with increasingly unequal development levels. India's southern part seems the most likely to benefit from such a phenomenon of regionalization, especially since the decision-makers of the south Indian states seem to practice their own Look East policy. Further, most East Asian leaders are no longer content with staying in New Delhi alone during their official travels. A number of them, since the late 1990s, have been keen to visit south India, not only to take note of its progress in the field of information technologies but also to directly network with local decision-makers. Thus, the Thai Prime Minister, Takshin Shinawatra, first stopped over in Bangalore before reaching New Delhi in November 2001, while Indonesian President Megawati Sukarnoputri and Prime Minister Mahathir chose to stay over in Hyderabad, in April and October 2002 respectively.

In other words, India's integration in the East Asian region may well be fragmentary. In the medium term, it could take place in the form of different sub-regions, more or less interlinked, that would incorporate some parts of India with various East Asian territories. This has been a fairly common economic integration process in East Asia, especially in the case of coastal China. Indeed, while Asia's economic regionalization has taken place in accordance with the logic of centralization, with Japan playing a 'structuring' role, it has also occurred through a decentralization process, with the formation of multiple sub-regional development areas, leading to the multi-polarization of the Asian economy.[10] The Asia-Pacific region can thus be conceived as a network of multiple sub-regions, which have now become interdependent with the complex division of labour and production lines. These sub-regional economic spaces often prove to be the most globalized parts of the national economy. Finally, it must be noted that while they tend to go beyond national borders, these sub-regional groupings are often promoted by the states themselves. This is especially true in India's case, where state actors are the promoters of sub-regional cooperation. The sub-region, to borrow Mittelman's terminology, therefore seems to emerge as an unavoidable unit of analysis to study the future integration of the Indian economy in the Asian region. This approach in terms of sub-regional units may be more adapted to the Indian case than models of integration through regional polarization or diaspora networks.

INDIA'S REDISCOVERY OF ITS ASIAN IDENTITY

The Look East policy has also raised questions about India's Asian identity as well as its ideological and cultural adherence to the 'new Asia' that has been under construction since the early 1990s. In a way, this policy referred to some of India's historical and cultural legacies in Asia and emanated from specific perceptions with regard to the contemporary Asian region, which were informed both by a superiority and an inferiority complex. Indeed, from the position of the leader of the Asian pack at the time of independence, India's status has fallen to that of a nation knocking at the doors of the New Asia in the 1990s. India's diplomatic discourse reflected this change: it strove to adapt itself to the sensitivities of its interlocutors in South-East Asia and proceeded with a selective reprocessing of its erstwhile pan-Asianism by shunning references that were too controversial, especially with respect to India's sphere of cultural influence in Asia. Thanks to this pragmatic approach, New Delhi made use of the notion of shared values to prop up its institutional and economic integration with the East Asian region. Only the Hindu Nationalist movement, especially its cultural organizations, continued to swear by the ethnocentric theses of Greater India. But their political wing, the BJP, proved more in favour of a discourse of consensus *vis-à-vis* East Asia while in power. The BJP government did, however, demonstrate a special penchant for the promotion of Hindu-Buddhist relations and the strengthening of ties with the diaspora, which could probably complicate relations with certain East Asian countries.

From a theoretical point of view, revisiting the Indian Pan-Asianism of the 1930s and 1940s clearly demonstrated that the idea of Asia itself is an intellectual and political exercise that is constantly reworked by different actors, in specific historical contexts. During the whole first half of the twentieth century, India enunciated the definition of Asia's identity in the larger sense and took the lead in the grand plans for regional cooperation. However, in the 1990s, the process of redefining Asia appeared to be confined to its eastern part alone, and India found it difficult to incorporate itself in a region that was being restructured without her. It is also illuminating, in this context, to recall how fluctuating geographical or regional concepts have been in Asia just over the past three decades. The metaphor of the Pacific in the 1980s was overturned by the new fascination for the Asia-Pacific during the 1990s. But the end of the decade revealed a development toward the more restrictive concept of East Asia. From an essentially 'oceanic' metaphor, based around the Pacific, the concept has become more continental, in particular because of the re-emergence of China.[11] The refocusing on the Asian landmass could be, in some ways, a good omen for India. But the regional construction process is now consolidating around East Asia itself, somewhat to the detriment of the full integration of India. The East Asian Economic Caucus (EAEC) project that the Malaysian Prime Minister, Mahathir, proposed in the early 1990s has strongly re-emerged since the 1997 Asian economic crisis. Already reinforced by ASEM, the EAEC now materializes in the 'ASEAN+3' formula (the '3' standing for China, South Korea and Japan). More importantly, this new mechanism has made it possible to re-launch regional cooperation in East Asia at a time when the ASEAN faces numerous difficulties, both in its functioning and in its identity, while the APEC—the project that was once the EAEC's competitor—seems to have stagnated.

In November 2000, New Delhi was denied participation in the 'ASEAN+3' meetings. This decision was revealing of India's peripheral position in relation to the region. In many respects, India's western border with Myanmar continued to demarcate a strong symbolic caesura between South Asia and East Asia. Nonetheless, New Delhi eventually managed to establish an ASEAN+India Summit in 2001, along the same lines as the 'ASEAN+3' mechanism and somewhat achieved parity with China, South Korea and Japan in the ASEAN partnership apparatus. In late 2004, it even signed an ASEAN-India Partnership for Peace, Progress and Shared Prosperity which sets out the road map for a long-term engagement. While the ASEAN is increasingly keen to forge a special and multidimensional relationship with India, it wants to keep its links with India as separate from the collective project of the 'ASEAN+3'. In other words, the rapprochement between India and the ASEAN continues to take place slightly in the margin of the deeper regional dynamics that are consolidating the project of an East Asian Community.

In some ways, India has not yet succeeded in taking fully part in the political and ideological construction of the Asian region. It does not yet belong to the core institutions that are structuring the regional space; it has for long not featured—or very little—in discourses on the Asian region, or even on the idea of an Asian regional identity, even while it has been a major cultural pole, as well as one of the first pan-Asianist leaders. The marginalization of India's historic role shows that the definition of a region is a discriminatory, selective and exclusive process. Those who are at the core of the regional construction deliberately highlight certain cultural and historic links, to the detriment of certain others. It must also be added that growth rates were critical in the definition of the Asian regional identity, in particular in discourses on Asian values during the 1990s. India's belated economic development and its limited trade and financial ties with the region undoubtedly constituted an obstacle to its acceptance on the conceptual level. However, it is of importance to note that the sustained dynamism of the Indian economy may well lead the East Asian nations to reconsider the position of the country in their regional construction. In addition, India has since the early 2000s proactively defended the concept of an Asian Economic Community as an alternative to the ongoing project of an East Asian Economic Community promoted under the 'ASEAN+3' mechanism.

Thus, India remains for the time being on the threshold of the 'new Asia'. From that point of view, the concept of a 'liminal state', which has been used by Higgot and Nossal to describe Australia's situation in relation to Asia, could also apply to the Indian case.[12] Indeed, this concept concerns the in-between position in which some states find themselves internationally, the best-known cases being Australia in relation to Asia, and Turkey in relation to Europe. Australia, like India, can be seen as one of these countries that 'self-consciously' and 'deliberately' tried 'to relocate' itself in international politics—economically, diplomatically and militarily'.[13] Between 1983 and 1996, the Australian labour party governments of Bob Hawke and Paul Keating promoted a policy of 'Asianization', i.e. reorientation toward Asia, breaking with the traditional identification of Australia with the Western—i.e. European and North American—world. However,

Higgott observed that by the late 1990s, Australia seemed to have 'got "stuck" in a liminal location between "two worlds", unable either to move forward to the "new" or to retreat to the "old" '.[14] In some ways, India also seems to be between 'two worlds' —between the West and the East. It has had very strong historic, intellectual and political ties with Europe and the United States, not to speak of its close friendship with the former USSR for close to twenty years. At the same time, the Look East policy launched in the early 1990s has undoubtedly marked the beginning of a return to Asia. But, as Higgott noted, while it is relatively easy to reach a liminal position in relation to a region, it is much more difficult to progress further from this transient phase. In other words, it is very difficult to cross the threshold that makes it possible to be fully integrated in a region, because the latter often builds its identity on restrictive bases: 'Any sense of common identity must be fully reciprocal. It is not enough to have one country see itself as part of a community; that sense of community must be widely shared. And without such a shared identity, one will be left, like Australia, a liminal state. . . .'[15]

This observation also applies to the Indian case, to a certain extent. While India still remains at the fringes, it nonetheless has succeeded in sensitizing its East Asian neighbourhood. The most decisive progress would perhaps take place—as in the economic sphere—at the scale of sub-regional cooperation. The launching of BIMST-EC, the MGC (Mekong-Ganga Cooperation) and the Kunming initiative testify to the opening of some East Asian sub-regions to India. As such, they reflect a change from the perspective of India's regional membership. India is no longer tangled up in South Asia. It has succeeded in projecting itself in alternative regional concepts that transcend, in fact, the symbolic border between South Asia and South-East Asia or even East Asia. The distinct metaphors of South Asia and South-East Asia could thus find themselves altered in the medium term. While India remains strongly anchored in its South Asian regional surroundings, it remains so in a less exclusive manner. It identifies itself increasingly with its eastern neighbourhood and it henceforth has multiple regional memberships. Moreover, an interesting aspect of these various sub-regional projects lies in that they highlight the historic and cultural ties between the member countries. Indeed, there is often a desire to revive once-prosperous transnational spaces (the Bay of Bengal for BIMST-EC or a part of the Silk Route for the Kunming initiative). Furthermore, these projects aim, in the first place, to initiate regionalization dynamics and primarily promote communication infrastructure and people flows. With time, the maintenance of a high growth rate and a discreet and pragmatic diplomacy, this option for sub-regional cooperation could bear fruit and increase India's integration in the East Asian region. But once again, it is important to underline that the process may be fragmentary and include just some part of the Indian territory only, probably those of the eastern coast and, maybe, the landlocked north-eastern states.

In this perspective, the capacity to consolidate the political situation and to promote the economic development of the north-eastern states stands out as a decisive factor for the Look East policy, as these territories constitute a land bridge with South-East Asia. New Delhi has understood it well, and even seems to consider sub-regional cooperation as the most viable option henceforth for the pacification of the north-east. This comes as a new approach, because, in the past, the central authorities were more inclined to handle the security issues of the north-east region by isolating it from all outside influence. However, in April 2002, India launched a trilateral process of annual dialogues with Myanmar and Thailand to develop a transportation corridor joining South and South-East Asia, via the north-eastern states. More precisely, the three states consider building a highway that would join the Indian Ocean to the South China Sea. Beyond the question of the north-east, this initiative reveals a certain desire on India's part to enhance its profile over this sub-region, where China has already made great progress and where it has supported the major project of building the 'Irrawaddy' corridor, connecting its Sichuan province to the Indian Ocean, through Myanmar. However, the profusion of transport infrastructure projects between China, India, Thailand and Myanmar is not devoid of strategic calculations. From the Indian point of view, they ensue not only from concerns related to the security and development of the north-eastern states, but also from a more general enterprise aimed at increasing India's influence in this larger neighbourhood where China is already very present.

INDIA'S ROLE IN THE ASIAN STRATEGIC ORDER

The end of the Cold War allowed for a new approach between India and the East Asian states that were more aligned with the Western block, especially the ASEAN countries and Japan. In the new international context, where dynamics of economic cooperation had become a priority, India's opening up to market forces greatly helped in improving strategic ties with many states in the Asia-Pacific. From derived relations, India and the ASEAN quickly moved on to more direct contacts. Through several confidence-building measures, New Delhi gradually inserted itself in the joint security management model proposed by the ASEAN and became part of the ASEAN Regional Forum in 1996, the only multilateral institution that discusses security issues in the Asia-Pacific at government level. However, India has not seemed to pay much attention to this cooperative approach to regional security, which in any case has been greatly affected by the Asian crisis. Apart from the fact that they diverted the attention of India's diplomacy, the recurrent tensions with Pakistan inevitably placed the country in an uncomfortable position during the ARF sessions. Indeed, New Delhi has proved to be not very at ease in multilateral fora on security such as the ARF. In any case, it seems that India's strategic positioning in Asia now depends less on the ASEAN states themselves than on the United States and China, as these two powers play a decisive role in the stability of the Asian region. Relations between India and South-East Asian states are no longer 'derived', as they used to be during the Cold War, but they continue to depend, to a certain extent, on the state of their respective links with the region's major powers, primarily the United States and China.

Furthermore, since the May 1998 nuclear tests, New Delhi has essentially tried to remodel its relations with Washington and Beijing, in order to assert its position as a major power on the Asian stage. The triangular relations between New Delhi, Beijing and Washington are therefore going to be a decisive parameter for the evolution of India's role in Asia. As things stand, the United States have more developed relations with China than with India. Perhaps one of the most difficult tasks before Indian diplomacy would therefore be to manage Sino-American relations as best as it can, so that they do not move towards either a close partnership or an open confrontation. Indeed, the relations between Beijing and Washington seem to be the axis that structures the balance of powers in Asia. On the one hand, New Delhi can only be worried about an American policy that would let China increase its military capabilities and strengthen its ambitions to emerge as the dominant power in the region, by betting on the development of a Sino-American partnership in Asia. On the other, India cannot adopt a containment strategy either, as that would place it in an awkward position with its gigantic neighbour. An alignment with the United States against Beijing would only result in complicating the security environment in the region, apart from being a high risk strategy, because the struggles of 'pro' and 'anti'-Beijing factions within the American establishment make the United States' China policy susceptible to many U-turns. In the same way, New Delhi has nothing to gain from systematically playing the game of the Chinese rhetoric to counter 'American hegemony' in Asia. This is why, in the last few years, India has tended to promote substantial political and strategic engagement with both China and the United States.

Indeed, this two-track policy with respect to the US and China is the best option available otherwise in order to intensify India's strategic relations with the other East Asian states, especially the ASEAN states. In fact, Washington's allies in East Asia are rather happy with the Indo-American rapprochement. In the same way, the ASEAN prefers to see New Delhi consolidating its relations with Beijing and, on the contrary, fears any attempt on its part to adopt an overt containment strategy against its giant neighbour. Interestingly, and to the relief of the ASEAN, the evolution of the Sino-Indian relationship is being increasingly influenced by the East Asian regional integration. As both China and India are eager to play a central and positive role in the Asian region, they have both realized that their own bilateral relations need to be stabilized. Indeed, one of the cornerstones of Chinese diplomacy since the late 1990s has been to convince its Asian neighbours that it is a benevolent and responsible power and that its formidable rise will benefit the whole region. In this perspective, the rapprochement with India—one of the countries with which it has had the thorniest bilateral relations—stands out as a case in point for its new diplomacy. As for India, it is increasingly anxious to emulate China's initiatives in terms of regional integration. For instance, India signed a framework agreement for the creation of a free trade area with the ASEAN in November 2003, i.e. just one year after China concluded a similar agreement. India also made a point of consenting to the ASEAN Treaty of Amity and Cooperation at the same time as China in late 2003. But if India wants to catch up with China in terms of regional integration in East Asia, a necessary condition is that its bilateral relations with China be stabilized. As a result, Sino-Indian relations have entered a new phase of rapprochement, featuring broad-based mutual engagement, strong commitments to normalization of the border issue and accelerated economic cooperation. Trade links have indeed developed to such an extent that in 2004, China emerged as India's second largest trading partner in the world after the United States, with a USD 12 billion in bilateral trade. In many respects, China has gained a centre-stage position in India's Look East policy. By comparison, Indo-ASEAN trade was around USD13 billion in 2004.

Thus, India is following a policy of enhanced cooperation with Beijing, even while upgrading its relations with the United States and the East Asian countries, which also have some concerns with regard to the growth of their immense neighbour. Russia, Japan and several members of the ASEAN, all have misgivings about Beijing's putative expansionist propensities and consider the affirmation of India's power along China's western front rather positively. At the same time, India and most Asian states have avoided fuelling any fears Beijing may have of being encircled, and have therefore eschewed any initiatives that could look like an anti-Chinese coalition. In the same fashion, India has striven to tone down the anti-China inflexions of its rapprochement with the United States. All in all, New Delhi's aim is first and foremost to maximize its diplomatic room for manoeuvre on the Asian stage, especially with regard to China and the United States, and to actively impose itself as a new and stabilizing pole in the emerging multipolar order in Asia. From New Delhi's viewpoint, the new approach decisively marks the conversion of its diplomacy to the precepts of pragmatism, flexibility and the pursuit of national interests. But it also emerges as a clever means of developing into a major power to be reckoned with in the new Asian strategic equations.

In this perspective, it appears that India's rise to power has to be played out on different regional chessboards in Asia. As South Asia is necessarily the foundation of its power politics, New Delhi has to reinstate a climate of confidence and cooperation in the region. Furthermore, India's inability to free itself from its conflictual relationship with Pakistan increasingly appears as the Achilles' heel of its general foreign policy. In the greater regional units of Southern Asia and the Asia-Pacific, India has to further establish itself as a stabilizing pole. While avoiding to project itself as a direct counterweight to China, India has aimed to be recognized and accepted as an indispensable player in the distribution of economic, diplomatic and strategic power in the Asian continent. In this sense, the Look East policy remains a major axis of New Delhi's overall external policy. At a third level of analysis, it appears that India's ascendancy is increasingly expressed in its bilateral and multilateral interactions with Asia's superpowers—China and the United States. Indeed, New Delhi considers the United States as its most important interlocutor in its quest for power. It has therefore tried to convince Washington that it can be a pole of stability in Asia, in particular in the Indian Ocean region and, potentially, as a counterweight to China, if that country were to engage in expansionist policies. Unless the renewed understanding between Washington and Islamabad affects India's interests directly, the strategic partnership between India and the United States is likely to continue, as the security concerns of the two states are increasingly converging in the Asian context (general balance of powers in Asia, protection of sea lanes in the Indian Ocean, the fight against terrorism, fundamentalism, drug trafficking and the proliferation of weapons of mass destruction). At the same time, New Delhi is likely to maintain its multi-dimensional policy with regard to China, which consists of actively promoting initiatives of cooperation in various fields, while reinforcing its deterrent force. Thus, the capacity of New Delhi and Beijing to manage the underlying tensions between them and to work together to build a multipolar international order, while improving their respective dialogue with Washington, becomes even more important to the future of Asia.

NOTES

1. Statement by External Affairs Minister of India, I.K. Gujral, on the occasion of the Post-Ministerial Conferences of ASEAN (7+10), 24 July 1996, Jakarta.
2. Statement by External Affairs Minister of India, I.K. Gujral, on the occasion of the Post-Ministerial Conferences of ASEAN (7+1), 24 July 1996, Jakarta, § 11.
3. N.D. Palmer, *The New Regionalism in Asia and the Pacific*, Mass.: Lexington, 1991, p. 221; Omae Kenichi, *De l'Etat-nation aux Etats-régions*, Paris: Dunod, 1996, p. 213; Kenichi Omae, *The End of the Nation State*, New York: Free Press, 1995, p. 214; R.A. Scalapino et al., eds., *Pacific-Asian Economic Policies and Regional Interdependence*, Berkeley: University of California, 1988, p. 352.
4. J.L. Domenach, 'Asie Orientale: Le Retour du Politique', in B. Badie and

M.C. Smouts, 'L'International sans Territoire', *Cultures et Conflits*, special issue, nos. 21/22, Spring/Summer 1996, p. 228. See also Peter J. Katzenstein, 'Regionalism in Comparative Perspective', *Cooperation and Conflict*, vol. 31, no. 2, 1996, pp. 123–59; and A. Gamble and A. Payne, eds., *Regionalism and World Order*, London: Macmillan, 1996.

5. James H. Mittelman, 'Rethinking the New Regionalism in the Context of Globalization', *Global Governance*, no. 2, 1996, pp. 189–213.
6. Reminder: The BIMST-EC concept was to create a region around the Bay of Bengal, and the Kunming initiative sought to promote economic cooperation between the Chinese Yunan province, India's eastern and north-eastern states, Myanmar and Bangladesh. The Mekong-Ganga Cooperation programme included the following countries: India, Myanmar, Thailand, Cambodia, Laos and Vietnam.
7. Secretariat for Industrial Approvals, *SIA Newsletter*, January 2002.
8. N. Blancher and C. Mainguy, 'Comparaison des Processus de Régionalization en Afrique Sub-Saharienne et en Asie Orientale. Revue Analytique de la Littérature', *Revue Tiers Monde*, vol. XXXIX, no. 155, July–September 1998, p. 512.
9. Xiangming Chen, 'China's Growing Integration with the Asia-Pacific', in Dirlik Arif, ed., *What is a Rim?: Critical Perspectives on the Pacific Region Idea*, Boulder, Colorado: Westview, 1993, p. 111.
10. Ibid., pp. 89–119.
11. Korhonen, *Japan and Asia Pacific Integration*, p. 188.
12. Richard A. Higgott and Kim Richard Nossal, 'The International Politics of Liminality: Relocating Australia in the Asia Pacific', *Australian Journal of Political Science*, vol. 32, no. 2, 1997, pp. 169–85.
13. Ibid., p. 169.
14. Ibid., p. 170.
15. Ibid., p. 183.

Bibliography

MONOGRAPHS

Ahluwalia, Isher Judge, Rakesh Mohan and Omkar Goswami, under the supervision of Charles Oman, *Réformes des Politiques en Inde*, Paris: OECD, 1996.

Anderson, K. and R. Blackhurst, eds., *Regional Integration and the Global Trading System*, New York: St Martin Press, 1993.

Asian Development Bank, *Asian Development Outlook, 1996–7*, Hong-Kong: Oxford University Press and Asian Development Bank, 1996.

Asian Relations, *Report of the Proceedings and Documentation of the First Asian Relations Conference, New Delhi, March–April 1947*, New Delhi: Asian Relations Organization, 1948.

Assayag, Jackie, *L'Inde : Désir de Nation*, Paris: O. Jacob, 2001.

Ayoob, Mohammed, *India and South-East Asia: Indian Perceptions and Policies*, Singapore: ISEAS & Routledge, 1990.

Badie, Bertrand and Marie-Claude Smouts, eds., 'L'International sans Territoire', *Cultures et Conflits*, special issue, nos. 21/22, Spring/Summer 1996.

Bajpai, Kanti and Mattoo, Amitabh, eds., *The Peacock and the Dragon: India-China Relations in the 21st Century*, New Delhi: Har Hanand, 2000.

Barot-Motwani, Jyoti, ed., *Global Indian Diaspora: Yesterday, Today and Tomorrow*, New York: GOPIO, 1993.

Barr, Michael D., *Cultural Politics and Asian Values: The Tepid War*, London: Routledge, 2002.

Bayly, C.A., *Indian Society and the Making of the British Empire*, Cambridge: Cambridge University Press, 1988.

Behl, R. and L.D. Mago, *India-ASEAN Trade Cooperation and Investment Opportunities*, New Delhi: Indian Institute of Foreign Trade, 1996.

Berger, M.T. and D.A. Borer, eds., *The Rise of East Asia: Critical Visions of the Pacific Century*, London: Routledge, 1997.

Boisseau du Rocher, Sophie, *L'ASEAN et la Construction Régionale en Asie du Sud-Est*, Paris: L'Harmattan, 1998.

Camroux, D. and J.L. Domenach, eds., *L'Asie Retrouvée*, Paris: Seuil, 1997.

Camroux, David, *Looking East . . . and Inwards: Internal Factors in Malaysian Foreign Relations during the Mahathir Era, 1981–94*,

Nathan, Griffith University, Centre for the Study of Australia-Asia Relations, October 1994 (Australia-Asia Papers no. 72).

Chaturvedi, Gyaneshwar, *India-China Relations: 1947 to Present Day*, Agra: MG Publishers, 1991.

Cheong, Yong Mun, and V.V. Bhanoji Rao, eds., *Singapore-India Relations: A Primer*, Singapore, Center for Advanced Studies: Singapore University Press, 1995.

Chuffrin, Gennady, ed., *Russia and Asia: The Emerging Security Agenda*, Stockholm: SIPRI, and Oxford University Press, 1999.

Cohen, S.P., *India: Emerging Power*, Washington D.C.: Brookings Institution Press, 2001.

Coleman, William D. and R.D. Underhill Geoffrey, *Regionalism and Global Economic Integration: Europe, Asia and the Americas*, London: Routledge, 1998.

De Melo, Jaime and Arvind Panagariya, eds., *New Dimensions in Regional Integration*, Cambridge: Cambridge University Press, 1995.

Dirlik, Arif, ed., *What is a Rim?: Critical Perspectives on the Pacific Region Idea*, Boulder, Colo.: Westview, 1993.

Dixit, J.N., *Across Borders: Fifty Years of India's Foreign Policy*, New Delhi: Picus Books, 1998.

———, *My South Block Years: Memoirs of a Foreign Secretary*, New Delhi: UBSPD, 1996.

Domenach, Jean-Luc, *L'Asie en Danger*, Paris: Fayard, 1998.

Dutt, V.P., *India's Foreign Policy in a Changing World*, New Delhi: Vikas Publishing House, 1999.

Faini, R. and E. Grilli, eds., *Multilateralism and Regionalism after the Uruguay Round*, London: St Martin's Press, 1997.

Fawcett, Louise and Andrew Hurrell, eds., *Regionalism in World Politics: Regional Organization and International Order*, Oxford: Oxford University Press, 1995.

Foreign Service Institute, *Indian Foreign Policy, Agenda for the 21st Century*, vol. I, New Delhi, Foreign Service Institute: Konark Publishers, 1997.

———, *Indian Foreign Policy, Agenda for the 21st Century*, vol. II, New Delhi, Foreign Service Institute: Konark Publishers, 1998.

Frankel, Jeffrey A. and Miles Kahler, eds., *Regionalism and Rivalry: Japan and the United States in Pacific Asia*, Chicago: University of Chicago Press, 1993.

Fukasaku, Kiichiro, ed., *Regional Co-operation and Integration in Asia*, Paris: OECD, 1996.

Furber, Holden, *Rival Empires of Trade in the Orient, 1600–1800*, Delhi: Oxford University Press, 1990.

Gamble, A. and A. Payne, eds., *Regionalism and World Order*, London: Macmillan, 1996.

Garver, J.W., *Protracted Contest: Sino-Indian Rivalry in the Twentieth Century*, Seattle: University of Washington Press, 2001.

Gemdev, *L'Intégration Régionale dans le Monde: Innovations et Ruptures*, Paris: Karthala, 1994.

Ghoshal, Baladas, ed., *ASEAN and South Asia: A Development Experience*, New Delhi: Sterling Publishers, 1998.

———, ed., *India and South-East Asia: Challenges and Opportunities*, New Delhi: India International Centre & Konark Publishers, 1996.

Godement, François, *Dragons de Feu, Dragon de Papier*, Paris: Flammarion, 1998.

———, *La Renaissance de l'Asie*, Paris: Edition Odile Jacob (1993).

Gole, Susan, *India within the Ganges*, New Delhi: Jayaprints, 1983.

Golwalkar, M.S., *Bunch of Thoughts*, Bangalore: Jagarana Prakashana, 1966.

Gonsalves, E., ed., *Asian Relations Conference*, New Delhi: Lancer International, 1988.

Gopal, Sarvepalli, *Jawaharlal Nehru: A Biography*, vol. 1: *1889–1947*, Delhi: Oxford University Press, 1989.

Gordon, Sandy and Ross Babbage, eds., *India's Strategic Future: Regional State or Global Power?*, London: Macmillan, 1992.

Gordon, Sandy and Stephen Henningham, eds., *India Looks East: An Emerging Power and Its Asia-Pacific Neighbours*, Canberra: Australian National University, 1995.

Gordon, Sandy, *India's Rise to Power: In the Twentieth Century and Beyond*, New York: St Martin's Press, 1995.

Grare, F. and A. Mattoo, *India and ASEAN: The Politics of India's Look East Policy*, Centre de Sciences Humaines, New Delhi: Manohar, Singapore, Institute of Southeast Asian Studies and Centre for the Study of National Security Policy, Jawaharlal Nehru University, 2001.

Grover, Verinder, ed., *Introduction to International Relations and India's Foreign Policy*, New Delhi: Deep and Deep Publications, 1992.

Gupta, Shekhar, *India Redefines Its Role*, London: IISS/Oxford University Press, 1995 (Adelphi Paper no. 293).

Gupta, Komar, *India and Regional Integration in Asia*, Bombay: Asia Publishing House, 1964.

Harris, Ian Charles, ed., *Buddhism and Politics in 20th Century Asia*, London: Pinter, 1999.

International Institute for Strategic Studies, *The Military Balance 1995–6*, London: Oxford University Press for IISS, 1996.

Jaffrelot, Christophe, ed., *L'Inde Contemporaine*, Paris: Fayard, 1996.

———, *La Démocratie en Inde, Religion, Caste et Politique*, Paris: Fayard, 1998.

———, *Les Nationalistes Hindous*, Paris: Presses de la Fondation Nationale des Sciences Politiques, 1993.

———, *The Hindu Nationalist Movement in India*, New York: Columbia University Press, 1996.

Jeshurun, Chandra, ed., *China-India-Japan and the Security of South-East Asia*, Singapore: ISEAS, 1993.

Jetley, Nancy, ed., *Indian Foreign Policy, Challenges and Prospects*, New Delhi: Vikas Publishing House, 1999.

Joshi, Vijay and I.M.D. Lttle, *India's Economic Reforms: 1991–2001*, Oxford: Clarendon Press, 1996.

Kapur, Harish, *India's Foreign Policy, 1947–92, Shadows and Substance*, New Delhi: Sage.

Karanjia, B.K., *Godrej: A Hundred Years 1897–1997*, vol. 2, New Delhi: Viking Penguin India, 1997.

Karunakaran, K.P., *India in World Affairs*, New Delhi: Oxford University Press, 1952.

Kishore, Mohammed Ali, *Jana Sangh and India's Foreign Policy*, New Delhi: Associated Publishing House, 1969.

Koh, Tommy, *The Quest for World Order*, Singapore: The Institute of Policy Studies and Times Academic Press, 1998.

Korhonen, Pekka, *Japan and Asia Pacific Integration: Pacific Romances, 1968–96*, London: Routledge, 1998.

Krishnan, R.R., ed., *The Fifth India-Korea Conference*, 22 December 1994, New Delhi: India International Center, 1995.

Lake, David A. and Patrick M. Morgan, *Regional Orders: Building Security in a New World*, University Park Pa.: Pennsylvania State University Press, 1997.

Leifer, M., *The ASEAN Regional Forum: Extending ASEAN's Model of Regional Security*, London: IISS/Oxford University Press, July 1996, (Adelphi Paper no. 302).

Leur, J.V. van, *Indonesian Trade and Society*, The Hague: W. van Hoeve, 1955.

Levi, Werner, *The Challenge of World Politics in South and South-East Asia*, London: Prentice-Hall, 1968.

Mahbubani, Kishore, *Can Asians Think*? Singapore: Times Books International, 1998.

Majumdar, R.C., *Ancient Indian Colonies in the Far East, Champa*, vol. 1, Lahore: The Punjab Sanskrit Book Depot, 1927.

———, *Ancient Indian Colonies in the Far East, Suvarnadvipa*, vol. 2 Calcutta: Modern Publishing Syndicate, 1938.

———, *Hindu Colonies in the Far East*, Calcutta: Firma K.L. Mukhopadhyaya, 1944, 2nd edn., 1966.

Mansingh, Surjit, ed., *Nehru's Foreign Policy: Fifty Years On*, New Delhi: India International Center and Mosaic Books, 1998.

Maull, Hanns, Gerald Segal and Jusuf Wanandi, eds., *Europe and the Asia Pacific*, London: Routledge, 1998.

Meng, T.T., L.A. Meng, J.J. Williams and R. Zutshi, eds., *Business Opportunities in India*, Nanyang Business Report Series, Singapore: Prentice Hall, 1997.

Menon, Raja (Rear Admiral), *A Nuclear Strategy for India*, New Delhi: Sage Publications, 2000.

Mills, James, *The History of British India and Orientalism*, Oxford: Clarendon Press, 1992.

Murthy, P.N.M., *India and Japan: Dimensions of their Relations: Historical and Political*, New Delhi: JNU, ABC Publishing House, 1986.

———, *India and Japan: Dimensions of their Relations: Economic and Cultural*, New Delhi: Lancers Books, 1993.

Nag, Kalidas, *The Discovery of Asia*, Calcutta: The Institute of Asian African Relations, 1957.

Nehru, Jawaharlal, *The Unity of India: Collected Writings, 1937–40*, London: Lindsay Drummond, 1941.

———, *An Autobiography*, Bombay: Allied Publishers, 1962.

———, *The Discovery of India*, New Delhi: Jawaharlal Nehru Memorial Fund and Oxford University Press, 1991. (First published in 1946 by Signet Press, Calcutta.)

Omae, Kenichi, *The End of the Nation State*, New York: Free Press, 1995.

Oman, Charles, *Les Défis Politiques de la Globalisation et de la Régionalisation*, Paris: OECD, 1996.

Ong, Aihwa and Donald Nonini, *Ungrounded Empires: The Cultural Politics of Modern Chineses Transnationalism*, New York: Routledge, 1997.

Palmer, N.D., *The New Regionalism in Asia and the Pacific*, Mass.: Lexington, 1991.

Panagariya, A., M.G. Quibria and N. Rao, eds., *The Global Trading System and Developing Asia*, Oxford: Oxford University Press, 1997.

Panikkar, K.M., *The Future of South-East Asia*, London: MacMillan Company, 1943.

———, *India and the Indian Ocean: An Essay on the Influence of Sea Power on Indian History*, London: George Allen & Unwin, 1945.

Postel-Vinay, Karoline, *Le Japon et la Nouvelle Asie*, Paris: Presses de Sciences Po, 1996.

Prasad, Bimla, *The Origins of Indian Foreign Policy—The Indian National Congress and World Affairs: 1885–1947*, Calcutta: Bookland Pvt Ltd, 1960.

Prasad, Birendra, *Indian Nationalism and Asia*, Delhi: B.R. Publishing Corporation, 1979.

Pye, Lucian, *Asian Power and Politics: The Cultural Dimensions of Authority*, Cambridge, Mass.: Harvard University Press, 1985.

Rana, Kishan S., *Inside Diplomacy*, New Delhi: Manas Publications, 2000.

Reddy, Narendra, et al., *P.V. Narasimha Rao—Years of Power*, New Delhi: Har-Anand Publication, 1993.

Roy-Chaudhury, Rahul, *Sea Power and Indian Security*, London: Brassey's, 1995.

Sandhu, K.S. and A. Mani, eds., *Indian Communities in South-East Asia*, Singapore, ISEAS, 1996.

Scalapino, R.A., et al., eds., *Pacific-Asian Economic Policies and Regional Interdependence*, Berkeley: University of California, 1988.

Scalapino, R.A., *The Politics of Development, Perspectives on 20th Century Asia*, Cambridge (Mass.): Harvard University Press, 1989.

Sharma, R.C. and K. Dalchoong, eds., *Korea-India Tryst with Change and Development*, New Delhi: Khama Publishers, 1993.

Singh, Deepak, ed., *NRIs Directory, Hong-Kong, Japan, Singapore, Malaysia, Thailand, Philippines, Taiwan*, New Delhi: NRI Welfare Society of India, 1997.

Singh, Jasjit, ed., *Asia's New Dawn: The Challenge to Peace and Security*, New Delhi: Knowledge World and IDSA, 2000.

Singh, Ravinder Pal, ed., *Arms Procurement Decision Making*, vol. 1, Stockholm: SIPRI and Oxford University Press, 1998.

SIPRI, *SIPRI Yearbook 1999, Armaments, Disarmament and International Security*, Stockholm: SIPRI and Oxford University Press, 1999.

Smith, Chris, *India's Ad Hoc Arsenal: Direction or Drift in Defence Policy?*, Stockholm: SIPRI and Oxford University Press, 1994.

Smouts, Marie-Claude, ed., *Les Nouvelles Relations Internationales : Pratiques et Théories*, Paris: Presses de Sciences Po, 1998.

Sondhi, M.L. and Prakash Nanda, *Vajpayee's Foreign Policy: Daring the Irreversible*, New Delhi: Har-Anand, 1999.

Sridharan, Kripa, *The ASEAN Region in India's Foreign Policy*, Aldershot, England: Darmouth Pub. Co., 1996.

Srinivasan, A.V., *Japanese Management: The Indian Context*, New Delhi: Tata McGraw-Hill, 1990.

Srinivasan, T.N., *Developing Countries and the Multilateral Trading System: From the GATT to the Uruguay Round and the Future*, Boulder: Westview Press, 1998.

Tagore, Rabindranath, *Nationalism*, London: MacMillan & Co., Ltd (1917), reprint London: Papermac, 1991.

Tan, Joseph L.H., *Singapore's Foreign Direct Investment in Indochina and Myanmar: Opportunities and Challenges*, New Delhi: RIS, 1997 (RIS Occasional Papers no. 50).

Tanham, G.K., K.P. Bajpai and A. Mattoo, eds., *Securing India: Strategic Thought and Practice in an Emerging Power*, New Delhi: Manohar, 1996.

Thakur, R., *The Politics and Economics of India's Foreign Policy*, New York: St Martin's Press, 1994.

Thakur, Ramesh and Carlyle A. Thayer, *Soviet Relations with India and Vietnam*, London: MacMillan, 1992.

Thammasat University and Information Department, Ministry of Foreign Affairs of Thailand, *Seminar on Thai-Indian Relations in the Present Decade and Prospects for Cooperation in the Future*, 30 July–1 August 1997, Bangkok: Ministry of Foreign Affairs of Thailand, 1997.

Thapar, Romila, *Ancient Indian Social History—Some Interpretations*, New Delhi: Sangam Books Ltd, 1984.

The Japan Foundation, *Dimensions of India-Japan Relations*, New Delhi: The Japan Foundation, New Delhi Office, 1997.

The National Institute for Defence Studies, *East Asian Strategic Review 1998–9*, Tokyo: NIDS, 1999.

Verghese, B.G., *Reorienting India: The New Geo-Politics of Asia*, New Delhi: Konark Publishers, 2001.

Vohra, N.N. and J.N. Dixit, eds., *Religion, Politics and Society in South and South-East Asia*, New Delhi: India International Center and Konark Publishers, 1998.

Wolters, O.W., History, *Culture and Religion in South-East Asian Perspectives*, Singapore: Institute of South-East Asian Studies, 1982.

World Bank, *Economic Development in India: Achievements and Challenges*, Washington D.C.: World Bank, 1995 (A World Bank Country Study).

———, *India's Five years of Stabilization: Reform and Challenges Ahead*, Washington D.C.: World Bank, 1996 (A World Bank Country Study).

———, *The East Asian Miracle Economic: Growth and Public Policy*, Oxford: Oxford University Press, 1993 (A World Bank Policy Research Report).

Zhang, Ming, *China's Changing Nuclear Posture: Reactions to the South Asian Nuclear Tests*, Washington D.C.: Carnegie Endowment for International Peace, 1999.

CONTRIBUTION TO COLLECTIVE WORKS

Ahluwalia, Isher Judge, 'L'ouverture de l'Inde aux Echanges et aux Investissements', in I.J. Ahluwalia, R. Mohan and O. Goswami, under the supervision of Charles OMAN, *Reformes des Politiques en Inde*, Paris: OECD, 1996.

Ahmed, A.F. Salahuddin, 'Bangladesh—A Bridge between South Asia and South-East Asia: Utopian Dream or Present-Day Imperative?', in N.N. Vohra and J.N. Dixit, *Religion, Politics and Society in South and South-East Asia*, New Delhi: India International Centre, Konark Publishers, 1998.

Anwar, Dewi Fortuna, 'Indonesia's Role in ASEAN: An ASEAN Perspective', in Baladas Goshal, ed., *ASEAN and South Asia: A Development Experience*, New Delhi: Sterling Publishers, 1998.

Asher, M.G. and R.S. Rajan, 'Singapore-India Economic Relations: Exploring Synergies for Mutual Benefit', in Y.M. Cheong, V.V.B. Rao, eds., *Singapore–India Relations: A Primer*, Singapore: Center for Advanced Studies, Singapore University Press, 1995.

Asrani, A., 'India-Japan Relations', in FSI, *Indian Foreign Policy: Agenda for the 21st Century*, vol. II, New Delhi: FSI, Konark Publishers, 1998.

Bajpai, Kanti P., 'State, Society, Strategy', in G.K. Tanham, K.P. Bajpai and A. Mattoo, eds., *Securing India: Strategic Thought and Practice in an Emerging Power*, New Delhi: Manohar, 1996.

Banerjee, U.K., 'Role of Cultural Diplomacy', in FSI, *Indian Foreign Policy: Agenda for the 21st Century*, vol. I, New Delhi: FSI, Konark Publishers, 1997.

Bhagwati, Jagdish, 'Regionalism and Multilateralism: An Overview', in Jaime De Melo and Arvind Panagariya, eds., *New Dimensions in Regional Integration*, Cambridge: Cambridge University Press, 1995.

Bhattacharyya, B., 'India's Foreign Economic Policy: Evolving Context and Tasks', in FSI, *Indian Foreign Policy: Agenda for the 21st Century*, vol. I, New Delhi, FSI: Konark Publishers, 1997.

Bouissou, J.M., 'Le Japon Peut-il donner sens à l'Asie?', in Laidiz Z, ed., *Géopolitique du Sens*, Paris: Desclée de Brouwer, 1998.

———, 'Penser l'Autre en se Pensant Soi-même : le Japon Face à l'Asie', in D. Camroux and J.L. Domenach, eds., *L'Asie Retrouvée*, Paris: Seuil, 1997.

Camroux, D., 'Malaisie: Retour vers un Futur Oriental', in D. Camroux and J.L. Domenach, eds., *L'Asie Retrouvée*, Paris: Seuil, 1997.

———, 'Des Nations Imaginées à la Région Rêvée', in D. Camroux and J.L. Domenach, *L'Asie Retrouvée*, Paris: Seuil, 1997.

Chattopadhyaya, D.P., 'Lifeworld, Science and Technology: An Indian Perspective', in N.N. Vohra and J.N. Dixit, eds., *Religion, Politics and Society in South and South-East Asia*, New Delhi: Konark Publishers and India International Centre, 1998.

Chen, Xiangming, 'China's Growing Integration with the Asia-Pacific', in Arif Dirlik, ed., *What is a Rim?: Critical Perspectives on the Pacific Region Idea*, Boulder, Colarado.: Westview, 1993.

Chung, Tan, 'Nehru's Dreams of an Eastern Federation', in Surjit Mansingh, ed., *Nehru's Foreign Policy: Fifty Years On*, New Delhi: Mosaic Books.

Coussy, Jean, 'Causes Economiques et Imaginaires Économiques de la Régionalisation', in B. Badie and M.C. Smouts, eds., 'L'International sans Territoire', *Cultures et Conflits*, special edition, nos. 21/22, Spring/ Summer 1996.

Dasgupta, Arun, 'Intellectual and Academic Cooperation between India and South-East Asia', in Baladas Ghoshal, ed., *India and South-East Asia: Challenges and Opportunities*, New Delhi: Konark Publishers, 1996.

De Souza, Walter E., 'Experience of Korean Economic Development and Its Implications for the Indian Economy', in R.R. Krishnan, ed., *The Fifth India-Korea Conference*, 22 December 1994, New Delhi: India International Centre, 1995.

Doxit, J.N., 'Culture as an Instrument of Diplomacy', in FSI, *Indian Foreign Policy Agenda for the 21st Century*, vol. I, New Delhi: FSI, Konark Publishers, 1997.

Domenach, J.L., 'Asie Orientale : Le Retour du Politique', in B. Badie and M.C. Smouts, eds., 'L'international sans Territoire', *Cultures et Conflits*, special issue, nos. 21/22, Spring/Summer 1996.

———, 'L'Asiatisme, une Idéologie pour l'Asie ?', in D. Camroux and J.L. Domenach, *L'Asie Retrouvée*, Paris: Seuil, 1997.

Dubey, Muchkund, 'APEC and Open Regionalism', in B. Ghoshal, ed., *ASEAN and South Asia*, New Delhi: Sterling Publishers, 1998.

Ghosh, Suchita, 'Thailand's Foreign Policy towards Vietnam and Cambodia and ASEAN Reactions. Some Observations and an Example for SAARC', in B. Ghoshal, ed., *ASEAN and South Asia*, New Delhi: Sterling Publishers, 1998.

Ghoshal, B., 'India, ASEAN and APEC', in N. Jetley, *India's Foreign Policy, Challenges and Prospects*, New Delhi: Vikas Publishing House, 1999.

Gipouloux, François, 'L'Asie Orientale: un Nouvel Atelier Nippon?', in GEMDEV, *L'intégration régionale dans le monde*, Paris: Karthala, 1994.

Gordon, S., 'India and South-East Asia: A Renaissance in Relations?', in S. Gordon and S. Henningham, eds., *India Looks East: An Emerging Power and its Asia-Pacific Neighbours*, Canberra: Australian National University, 1995, p. 276.

Gupta, Ranjit, 'Indo-Thai Relations', in Thammasat University and Information Department, Ministry of Foreign Affairs, *Seminiar on Thai-Indian Relations in the Present Decade and Prospect for Cooperation in the Future, 30 July–1 August 1997*, Bangkok: Ministry of Foreign Affairs of Thailand, 1997.

Habib, Lt. Gen. (Rtd) A. Hasnan, 'South-East Asian Perceptions of India's Strategic Development: An Indonesian View', in Ross Babbage and Sandy Gordon, *India's Strategic Future: Regional State or Global Power*? London: Macmillan, 1992.

Higgott, Richard, 'Libre-échange et Régionalisme Asiatique', in D. Camroux and J.L. Domenach, *L'Asie Retrouvée*, Paris: Seuil, 1997.

Hook, Glenn, 'Japan and the Construction of Asia Pacific', in Agamble and Apayne, eds., *Regionalism and World Order*, London: MacMillan, 1996.

Jaffrelot, C., 'L'Inde et l'asiatisme', in D. Camroux and J.L. Domenach, *L'Asie Retrouvée*, Paris: Seuil, 1997.

Keenleyside, T.A., 'Diplomatic Apprenticeship: Pre-Independence Origins of Indian Diplomacy and Its Relevance for the Post-Independence Foreign Policy', in Verinder Grover, ed., *Introduction to International Relations and India's Foreign Policy*, New Delhi: Deep and Deep Publications, 1992.

Kesavan, K.V., 'India and Japan', in FSI, *Indian Foreign Policy Agenda for the 21st Century*, vol. II, New Delhi: FSI, Konark Publishers, 1998.

Kile, Shannon, 'Appendix 2. Chronology of Principal Defence and Security-related Agreements', in G. Chuffrin, ed., *Russia and Asia: The Emerging Security Agenda*, Stockholm: SIPRI and Oxford University Press, 1999.

Lamb, Alastair, 'Indian Influence in Ancient South-East Asia', in A.L. Basham, ed., *A Cultural History of India*, London: Clarendon Press, 1975.

Leong, Stephen, 'The East Asian Economic Census (EAEC); "Fomalised" Regionalism Being Denied', B. Hettne, et al. *The New Regionalism, vol. 3: National Perspectives on the New Regionalism in the South*, the New Regionalism Series, London: Macmillian, 2000.

Limaye, Satu P., 'Sushi and Samosas: Indo-Japanese Relations after the Cold War', in S. Gordon and S. Henningham, eds., *India Looks East: An Emerging Power and Its Asia–Pacific Neighbours*, Canberra: Australian National University, 1995.

Mac Cargo, Ducan, 'Bouddhisme et Identité Asiatique: de Nouveaux Mandalas pour la Puissance Régionale Thaïlandaise', in D. Camroux and J.L. Domenach, *L'Asie Retrouvée*, Paris: Seuil, 1997.

Madhok, Balraj, 'India's Foreign Policy—the Jana Sangh View', in Verinder Grover, ed., *Introduction to International Relations and India's Foreign Policy*, New Delhi: Deep and Deep Publications, 1992.

Malik, J. Mohan, 'Sino-Indian Relations and India's Eastern Strategy', in S. Gordon and S. Henningham, eds., *India Looks East: An Emerging Power and its Asia-Pacific Neighbours,* Canberra: Australian National University, 1995.

Malik, P.M.S., 'The Changing Face of India's Economic Diplomacy: The Role of Ministry of External Affairs', in FSI, *Indian Foreign Policy Agenda for the 21st Century*, vol. I, New Delhi: FSI, Konark Publishers, 1997, p. 113.

Mansingh, Surjit, 'India as a Global Power: Capacity, Opportunity and Strategy', in FSI, *Indian Foreign Policy: Agenda for the 21st Century*, vol. I, New Delhi: FSI, Konark Publishers, 1997.

Mattoo, A., 'Raison d'Etat or Adhocism', in G.K. Tanham, K.P. Bajpai and A. Mattoo, eds., Securing *India: Strategic Thought and Practice in an Emerging Power*, New Delhi: Manohar, 1996.

Mehta, Rajesh, 'The Role of ODA', in Japan Foundation, ed., *Dimensions of India-Japan Relations*, New Delhi: Japan Foundation, New Delhi Office, 1997.

Mohan, C. Raja, 'India's Security Challenge', in N. Jetley, ed., *India's Foreign Policy, Challenges and Prospects*, New Delhi: Vikas Publishing House, 1999.

Moskalenko, Vladimir and Shaumian, Tatiana, 'Russia's Security and the Geopolitical Situation in South Asia', in G. Chuffrin, ed., *Russia and Asia: The Emerging Security Agenda*, Stockholm: SIPRI and Oxford University Press, 1999.

Muni, S.D., 'Nehru's India in Asia: Anatomy of a Blurred Vision', in S. Mansingh, ed., *Nehru's Foreign Policy: Fifty Years On*, New Delhi: Mosaic Books, 1998.

Oza, B.M., 'Observations on Indo-Korean Relations: Past, Present and Future', in R.R. Krishnan, ed., *The Fifth India-Korea Conference*, New Delhi: India International Center.

Pelkmans and Fukasaku, 'Evolving Trade Relations between Europe and Asia: Towards an "Open Continetalism?" ', in Küchiro Fukasaku, ed., *Regional Cooperation and Integration in Asia*, Paris: OECD, 1996.

Prasad, Chakravati Ram, 'Culture and Complementarities: Implications of the Singapore-India MOU on Culture, Heritage and the Archives', in Y.M. Cheong and Bhanoji V.V. Rao, *Singapore-India Relations: A Primer*, Center for Advanced Studies, Singapore: Singapore University Press.

Ram, A.N., 'Challenges to Economic Diplomacy', in N. Jetley ed., *Indian Foreign Policy, Challenges and Prospects*, New Delhi: Vikas Publishing House, 1999.

Rana, K.S., 'Promoting India's Economic Objectives Abroad: The Main Tasks Ahead', in FSI, *Indian Foreign Policy: Agenda for the 21st Century*, vol. I, New Delhi: FSI, Konark Publishers, 1997.

Ranganathan, C.V., 'India-China Relations—Retrospect and Prospects', in FSI, *Indian Foreign Policy: Agenda for the 21st Century*, vol. II, New Delhi: FSI, Konark Publishers, 1998.

Ray, H.P., 'Trade and Contacts', in R. Thapar, ed., *Recent Perspectives of Early Indian History*, Bombay: Popular Prakashan, 1995.

Roy-Chaudhury, R., 'The Limits to Naval Expansion', in George K. Tanham, Kanti P. Bajpai and Amitabh Mattoo, eds., *Securing India: Strategic Thought and Practice in an Emerging Power*, New Delhi: Manohar, 1996.

———, 'The Role of Naval Diplomacy in India's Foreign Policy', in FSI, *Indian Foreign Policy: Agenda for the 21st Century*, vol. II, New Delhi: FSI, Konark Publishers, 1998.

Sahni, Vasun, 'Just Another Big country', in George K. Tanham, K.P. Bajpai and A. Mattoo, eds., *Securing India: Strategic Thought and Practice in an Emerging Power*, New Delhi: Manohar, 1996.

———, 'India as a Global Power: Capacity, Opportunity and Strategy', FSI, *Indian Foreign Policy: Agenda for the 21st Century*, vol. I, New Delhi, FSI: Konark Publishers, 1997.

Satha-Anand, Chaiwat, 'Thailand: The Layers of a Strategic Culture', in Ken Booth and Russel Trood, eds., *Strategic Cultures in the Asia-Pacific Region*, London: Macmillan Press, 1999.

Selth, A., 'The China-Burma-India Triangle', in S. Gordon and S. Henningham, eds., *India Looks East: An Emerging Power and its Asia Pacific Neighbours*, Canberra: Australian National University, 1995.

Shantakumar, G., 'Human Resources Complementarities between Singapore and India: Formulating Strategy for a Win-Win Situation', Y.M. Cheong and V.V.B. Rao, eds., *Singapore–India Relations: A Primer*, Center for Advanced Studies, Singapore: Singapore University Press, 1995.

Shastri, Satya Vrat, 'Hindu Culture in Thailand', in N.N. Vohra and J.N. Dixit, eds., *Religion, Politics and Society in South and South-East Asia*, New Delhi: India International Centre, Konark Publishers, 1998, p. 252.

Shirk, Susan L., 'Asia-Pacific Regional Security: Balance of Power or Concert of Powers?', in David A. Lake, and Patrick M. Morgan, eds., *Regional Orders: Building Security in a New World*, University Park Pa.: Pennsylvania State University Press, 1997.

Sen, Keshab Chandra, 'Asia's Message to Europe', in Kalidas Nag, ed., *Greater India*, Calcutta: Brahmo Mission Press, 1960.

Shukla, Vinay, 'Russia in South Asia: A View From India', in G. Chuffrin, ed., *Russia and Asia: The Emerging Security Agenda*, Stockholm: SIPRI, Oxford University Press, 1999.

Singh, Jasjit, 'An Indian Perspective', in S. Gordon and S. Henningham, eds., *India Looks East: An Emerging power and its Asia Pacific Neighbours*, Canberra: Australian National University, 1995.

Singh, K.R., 'India and the Indian Ocean', in FSI, *Indian Foreign Policy Agenda for the 21st Century*, vol. II, New Delhi: FSI, Konark Publishers.

Singh, Surendra, 'India's Economic Reform and Regional Cooperation', in K. Fukasaku K., ed., *Regional Co-operation and Integration in Asia*, Paris: OECD, 1996.

Sridharan, Kripa, 'India-ASEAN Relations: Evolution, Growth and Prospects', in C. Jeshurun, ed., *China-India-Japan and the Security of South-East Asia*, Singapore: ISEAS, 1993.

———, 'The Evolution and Growth of India-Singapore Relations', in Y.M. Cheong and V.V.B. Rao, eds., *Singapore—India Relations: A Primer*, Center for Advanced Studies, Singapore: Singapore University Press, 1995.

Suryanarayan, V., 'India and South-East Asia: Shared Destiny', in N. Jetley, ed., *India's Foreign Policy, Challenges and Prospects*, New Delhi: Vikas Publishing House, 1999.

Swearer, Donald K., 'Centre and Periphery: Buddhism and Politics in Modern Thailand', in Ian Harris, ed., *Buddhism and Politics in Twentieth-century Asia*, London: Pinter, 1999.

Tang, Ming, 'Asian Economic Co-operation: Opportunities an Challenges', in K. Fukasaku, ed., *Regional Co-operation and Integration in Asia*, Paris: OECD, 1996.

Tanham, Georges K., 'Indian Strategic Thought: An Interpretative Essay', in G.K. Tanham, K.P. Bajpai and A. Mattoo, eds., *Securing India: Strategic Thought and Practice in an Emerging Power*, New Delhi: Manohar, 1996.

Thakur, Ramesh, 'Between East and West, from South to North', in S. Gordons and S. Henningham, eds., *India Looks East: An Emerging Power and its Asia-Pacific Neighbours*, Canberra: Australian National University, 1995.

Venkataraman, R., 'India's Foreign Policy', in Verinder Grover, ed., *Introduction to International Relations and India's Foreign Policy*, New Delhi: Deep and Deep Publications, 1992.

Vicziany, Marika, 'Regionalism, Sub-regionalism and APEC: The Case of India', in John Ingleson, ed., *Regionalism, Sub-regionalism and APEC*, Clayton, Victoria: Monash Asia Institute, 1997.

Wadhwa, C., 'India-South-East Asia Economic Partnership in the 1990s', in Baladas Ghoshal, ed., *India and South-East Asia: Challenges and Opportunities*, New Delhi: Konark Publishers, 1996.

Wah, Chin Kin, 'Regional Perceptions of China and Japan', in C. Jeshurun, ed., *China-India-Japan and the Security of South-East Asia*, Singapore: ISEAS, 1993.

Wanandi, Jusuf, 'Asia-Pacific Security Forums: Rationale and Options from the ASEAN Perspective', in D. Ball, R.L. Grant and J. Wanandi, eds., *Security Cooperation in the Asia-Pacific Region*, Washington, D.C.: Center for Strategic and International Studies, Significant Issues Series no. 5, vol. XV, 1993.

ARTICLES AND PAPERS

Acharya, Amitav, 'Ideas, Identity and Institution-building: From the "ASEAN way" to the "Asia-Pacific Way"', *The Pacific Review*, vol. 10, no. 3, 1997.

Acharya, Amitav, 'Realism, Institutionalism, and the Asian Economic Crisis', *Contemporary South-East Asia*, vol. 21, no. 1, April 1999.

Agarwal, Manmohan, 'Implications of Economic Liberalization for India's Foreign Policy', *International Studies*, vol. 30, no. 2, April–June 1993.

Asher, M.G. and R.S. Rajan, 'India and Singapore: Forging Economic Linkages in the Post-Cold War World', *Asian Survey*, vol. 35, no. 10, October 1995.

Ariff, M., 'Anatomy of Economic Reform Process: Regional Perspectives, Opportunities and Strategies', RGIS paper No. 6, *India South-East Asia and the USA: New Opportunities and Prospects for Cooperation*, Bangalore Conference Papers, 9–10 August 1995.

Ayoob, Mohammed, 'Nuclear India and Indian-American Relations', *Orbis*, Winter 1999.

Baldwin, Richard E., 'The Causes of Regionalism', *World Economy*, vol. 20, no. 7, 1997.

Bhat, Taranath P., ' Trade Blocs and Global Trade Prospects', *Foreign Trade Review*, Quarterly Journal of Indian Institute of Foreign Trade, vol. 31, no. 4, January–March 1997.

Bhattacharyya, B., 'Currency Turmoil in South-East and East Asia: Its Impact on India's Exports', *Indian Institute of Foreign Trade*, Occasional Paper, no. 12, 1998.

Blancher, N. and C. Mainguy, 'Comparaison des Processus de Régionalisation en Afrique Sub-Saharienne et en Asie Orientale. Revue Analytique de la Littérature', *Revue Tiers Monde*, vol. 33, no. 155, July–September 1998.

Bowles, Paul, 'ASEAN, AFTA and the "New Regionalism"', *Pacific Affairs*, vol. 70, no. 2, Summer 1997.

Bridge, Nick, 'India and the Asia-Pacific Region: Flying by Some Nets', *Strategic Analysis*, February 1995.

Brzezinski, Zbigniev, 'The New Challenges to Human Rights', *Journal of Democracy*, vol. 8, no. 2, 1996.

Camroux, David and Christian Lechervy, 'Close Encounter of a Third Kind? The Inaugural Asia-Europe Meeting of March 1996', *The Pacific Review*, vol. 9, no. 3, 1996.

Carpenter, Ted Galen, 'Rolling Asia: U.S. Cosiness with China Upsets the Neighbours', *Foreign Affairs*, November–December 1998.

Chaudhuri, M.D., 'Liberalization without Reform', *Seminar*, no. 437, January 1996.

Chellaney, Brahma, 'La Sécurité de l'Inde après les Essais Nucléaires', *Politique Etrangère*, no. 3, Autumn 1998.

Chisthi, Sumitra, 'Regionalism, Multilateralism, and the Developing Countries since the End of the Cold War', *International Studies* (New Delhi), vol. 32, no. 4, 1995.

Chong, Alan, 'Analysing Singapore's Foreign Policy in the 1990s and Beyond: Limitations of the Small State Approach', *Asian Journal of Political Sciences*, vol. 6, no. 1, June 1998.

Conseil pour la Cooperation Europe-Asia, 'Europe–Asie: renforcer le dialogue informel', *Les Cahiers de l'IFRI*, no. 19, 1997.

Copley, Gregory, 'South-Asia: Zone of the New Great Powers', *Defence and Foreign Affairs*, 17 (May–June) 1989.

Cordonnier, Isabelle, 'Asie-Pacifique : Une Région Politique en Devenir', *Etudes Internationales et Stratégiques*, Summer 1994.

Coussy, Jean, 'L'Inde face à la Régionalisation de l'Economie Mondiale', *Les Etudes du CERI*, no. 23, February 1997.

Das, Gurcharan, 'East Asian Boom Slows Down', *World Focus*, vol. 18, no. 6.

Delpech, Thérèse and d'Andurain, Arnaud, 'L'avenir Nucléaire se Joue-t-il en Asie?', *Critique Internationale*, no. 1, Autumn 1998.

Delpech, Thérèse, 'Les Conséquences Stratégiques des Essais Indiens et Pakistanais', *Politique Etrangère*, no. 3, Autumn 1998.

———, 'Une victoire éclatante et fragile', *Politique Etrangère*, 'Dissuasion et non-prolifération après la conférence du TNP', vol. 60, no. 3, Autumn 1995.

Devesh, Kapur, 'Indian in 1999', *Asian Survey*, vol. XL, no. 1, January–February 2000.

Dibb, Paul, D. David Hale and Peter Prince, 'The Strategic Implications of Asia's Economic Crisis', *Survival*, vol. 40, no. 2, Summer 1998.

Domenach, Jean-Luc, 'Asie: de la Crise Monétaire à une Crise de L'autorité', *Critique Internationale*, no. 1, Autumn 1998.

Dubey, M., 'The WTO and India', *Mainstream*, 25 January 1997.

Dupont, Alan, 'Is there an "Asian Way"?', *Survival*, vol. 38, no. 2.

Elliot, John, 'India and China—Asia's New Giants: Stepping Stones to Prosperity', *RGICS Paper*, no. 26, 1995.

Emmerson, Donald K., '"Southeast Asia": What's in a Name?', *Journal of South-East Asian Studies*, vol. 15, no. 1, 1984.

Faizal, Yahya, 'Singapore-India: a Confluence of National Interests', *Asian Studies Review*, vol. 19, no. 2.

Freeman, M., 'Human Rights, Democracy and Asian Values', *The Pacific Review*, vol. 9, no. 3, 1996.

Funabashi, Yoichi, 'Tokyo's Depression Diplomacy', *Foreign Affairs*, November–December, vol. 77, no. 6.

———, 'The Asianization of Asia', *Foreign Affairs*, vol. 72, no. 5.

Godement, François, 'Comment Sortir de la Crise Asiatique ?', *Politique Etrangère*, no. 2, 1998.

Gordon, Sandy, 'Indian Defence Spending: Treading Water in the Fiscal Deep', *Asian Survey*, vol. 32, no. 10, October 1992.

Ghoshal, B., 'Indian Diaspora in South-East Asia and The Emerging Relations between India and ASEAN: An Economic Perspective', working paper for the Workshop co-organized by Centre fo Study of National Security Polices, JNU and centre de Sciences Humaines, New Delhi in Collaboration with Institute of South-East Asian Studies (Singapore), *India-ASEAN Economic Relations*, New Delhi, 17–18 March 2001.

———, 'East Asian Miracle and India', World Focus, vol. 18, no. 6, June 1996, p. 12.

Ghoshal, U.N., 'Progress of Greater Indian Research during the Last Twenty Years (1917–42)', *The Journal of Greater India Society*, vol. 9, no. 2, July 1942.

Gurmeet, Kanwal, 'China's Long March to World Power Status: Strategic Challenge for India', *Strategic Analysis*, vol. 22, no. 11, February 1999.

Gyohten, Toyoo, 'The Development of Asia-Pacific Economies and India's Role in It', *RGICS Paper*, no. 9, 1994.

Harris, Stuart, 'Asian Multilateral Institutions and Their Response to the Asian Economic Crisis: The Regional and Global Implications', *The Pacific Review*, vol. 13, no. 3, 2000.

Hermann, Wilfried A., 'Conventional Arms Proliferation in East/South-East Asia', *Current Politics and Economics of Asia*, vol. 7, no. 3, 1999.

Higgott, Richard A. and Kim Richard Nossal, 'The International Politics of Liminality: Relocating Australia in the Asia Pacific', *Australian Journal of Political Science*, vol. 32, no. 2, 1997.

———, 'Mondialisation et Gouvernance : L'émergence du Niveau Régional', *Politique Etrangère*, Mondialisation et Dynamiques Régionales, no. 2, Summer 1997.

Hu, Richard Weixing, 'India's Nuclear Bomb and Future Sino-Indian Relations', *East Asia*, Spring 1999.

Hugon, Philippe, 'Les Séquences Inversée de la Régionalisation', *Revue Tiers Monde*, no. 155, July–September 1998.

———, Introduction, 'La Régionalisation Comparée en Afrique Sub-Saharienne et en Asie de l'Est', *Revue Tiers Monde*, no. 155, July–September 1998.

Hwee, Yeo Lay, 'The Bangkok ASEM and the Future of Asia-Europe Relations', *South-East Asian Affairs*, 1997.

Jaffrelot, Christophe, 'Du Nationalisme Hindou au Nationalisme Nucléaire', *Etudes*, October 1998, no. 3894.

———, 'Le Syncrétisme Stratégique et la Construction de L'identité Nationaliste Hindoue', *Revue Française de Sciences Politiques*, 42 (4), August 1992.

———, 'La Fin d'un "Parti-Etat"? : Le Congrès et la Démocratie Indienne', *Les Etudes du CERI*, no. 6, September 1995.

———, 'Inde : La Politique Introuvable', *Sociétal*, no. 19, May 1998.

Jha, G., 'India's Vietnam Policy in Regional Perspective', *Strategic Analysis*, January 1996.

———, 'A Brief Survey of India-Indonesia Relations', *Contemporary South-East Asia*, vol. 17, no. 4, March 1996.

———, 'ASEAN and India: Dawning of a New Partnership', *The Indonesian Quarterly*, vol. 25, no. 2, 1997.

Jones, Rodney W., 'Old Quarrels and New Realities: Security in Southern Asia after the Cold War', *Washington Quarterly*, Winter 1992.

Katzenstein, Peter J., 'Regionalism in Comparative Perspective', *Cooperation and Conflict*, vol. 31, no. 2, 1996.

Kausikan, Bilahari, 'Governance that Works', *Journal of Democracy*, vol. 8, no. 2, April 1997.

———, 'East and South-East Asia and the Post-Cold War International Politics of Human Rights', *Studies in Conflict and Terrorism*, vol. 16, 1993.

Keenleyside, T.A., 'Nationalist Indian Attitudes Towards Asia: A Troublesome Legacy for Post-Independence Indian Foreign Policy', *Pacific Affairs*, vol. 55, no. 2, Summer 1982.

Kelegama, Saman, 'Can Open Regionalism Work in the Indian Rim Association for Regional Co-operation?', *ASEAN Economic Bulletin*, vol. 15, no. 2, August, 1998.

Korhonen, Pekka, 'Monopolizing Asia: The Politics of a Metaphor', *Pacific Review*, vol. 10, no. 3, 1997.

Kumar, Nagesh, 'East Asian Economic Crisis and South Asian Growth Prospects: A Note', *RIS Digest, Special Issue on East Asian Economic Crisis*, September 1998.

Kux, Dennis, 'India's Fine Balance', *Foreign Affairs*, May–June 2002.

Leifer, M., 'The ASEAN Regional Forum: Extending ASEANs Model of Regional Security', *Adelphi Paper no. 302*, July 1996.

Limaye, Satu P., 'The Japan-India Encounter', *RGICS Paper*, no. 38, 1997.

Mahapatra, Chintamani, 'India, China and Russia: Strategic Triangle is Possible', *Strategic Analysis*, vol. 22, no. 11, February 1999.

———, 'Indo-American Relations after the Cold War', *Asian Strategic Review 1995–6*, New Delhi, IDSA, 1996.

Mahbubani, Kishore, 'Go East, Young Man', *The Washington Quarterly*, Spring 1994.

———, 'The Pacific Impulse', *Survival*, vol. 37, no. 2, Spring 1995.

Mahmood, Cynthia Keppley, 'Rethinking Indian Communalism: Culture and Counter-Culture', *Asian Survey*, vol. 33, no. 7, July 1993.

Malik, J. Mohan, 'India Goes Nuclear: Rationale, Benefits, Costs and Implications', *Contemporary South-East Asia*, vol. 20, no. 2, August 1998.

Manor, James and Gerald Segal, 'Taking India Seriously', *Survival*, IISS Quarterly, vol. 40, no. 2, Summer 1998.

Mehta, Rajesh, 'Trade Policy Reforms, 1991–2 to 1995–6: Their Impact on External Trade', *Economic and Political Weekly*, 12 April 1997.

———, 'Establishment of Free-trade Arrangement among BIMST-EC Countries', *RIS Discussion Papers*, no. 2, 2002.

Menon, V. Shalini, 'Milan 97—An Eyewitness Report', *Strategic Digest*, vol. 27, no. 6, June 1997.

Mishra, S.N., 'Indo-Japan Intellectual Cooperation', *The Japan Foundation Bulletin*, New Delhi Office, no. 12, March 1997.

Mistry, Dinshaw, 'Diplomacy, Sanctions, and the U.S. Non-proliferation Dialogue with India and Pakistan', *Asian Survey*, vol. 39, no. 5, September–October 1999.

———, 'India's Emerging Space Programme', *Pacific Affairs*, vol. 71, no. 2, Summer 1998.

Mittelman, James H., 'Rethinking the New Regionalism in the Context of Globalization', *Global Governance*, no. 2, 1996.

Muni, S.D., 'The Emerging Cold War in Asia', *Strategic Analysis*, March 1997.

Nag, Kalidas, 'India's Abroad', *The Modern Review*, April 1930.

Naidu, G.V.C., 'India and ASEAN', *Strategic Analysis*, vol. XIX, April 1996.

———, 'Navies of Asian Major Powers and Security of South-East Asia', *Strategic Analysis*, vol. 19, no. 12, March 1997.

———, 'Post-Cold War Pacific Asian Security: Indian Perceptions and Options', IDSA, *Delhi Papers*, no. 1, September 1994.

———, 'India, ASEAN and the ARF', *Strategic Analysis*, vol. 19, no. 6, September 1996.

———, 'Navies of Asian Major Powers and Security of South-East Asia', *Strategic Analysis*, vol. 10, no. 9, December 1996.

———, 'The Manila ASEAN Meetings and India', *Strategic Analysis*, vol. 22, no. 8, November 1998.

———, 'India and ASEAN', IDSA, *Delhi Papers*, no. 8, 1998.

Nicolas, Françoise, 'Mondialisation et Régionalisation dans les Pays en Développement: Les Deux Faces de Janus', *Politique Etrangère*, Mondialisation et Dynamiques Régionales, no. 2, Summer 1997.

Noda, Eijora, 'A Common Cultural Heritage', *India International Centre Quarterly*, vol. 20, nos. 1–2, Spring–Summer 1993.

Ollapally, Deepa M., 'India and the New "Asian" Balance of Power', *Strategic Analysis*, July 1998.

Palaha, Satinder and H.L. Sharma, 'Towards Economic Integration through Regional Trade Blocs', *Indian Institute of Foreign Trade Occasional Paper*, no. 4, 1996.

Panda, Rajan, 'India and Japan: Perceptions and Misperceptions', *Indian-Japan Relations*, New Delhi: The Japan Foundation, 1997, p. 47.

Park, K.Y. and W.H. Lee, 'The Financial Crisis of 1997–8 and Its Impact on Security Relations in East Asia', *Asian Perspectives*, vol. 23, no. 3, 1999.

Pohit, Sanjib and Chadha, Rajesh, 'Should India Join a Free Trade Bloc?', *Foreign Trade Review*, vol. XXXI, no. 4, January–March 1997.

Prabhakar, H.S. 'North-East Asia and India', *World Focus*, vol. 18, no. 6, June 1997.

Racine, J.L., 'Identité Nationale et Realpolitik: Entre Chine et Occident, l'Inde de 1989 Face au printings de Pékin', *Hérodote*, L'Inde et la Question Nationale, no. 71, October–December 1993.

———, 'La Transition Indienne', *Futuribles*, no. 258, November 2000.

Ramanathan, K., 'Hinduism in a Muslim State: The Case of Malaysia', *Asian Journal of Political Science*, vol. 4, no. 2, December 1996.

Robinson, R., 'The Politics of Asian Values', *The Pacific Review*, vol. 9, no. 3, 1996.

Rodman, Garry, 'The Internationalization of Ideological Conflict: Asia's New Significance', *The Pacific Review*, vol. 9, no. 3, 1996.

Root, Hilton L., 'A liberal India: The Triumph of Hope over Experience', *Asian Survey*, vol. 38, no. 5, May 1999.

Roy-Chaudhury, R., 'India's Security Policy', *Strategic Analysis*, May 1996.

———, 'The Indian Navy: Past, Present, and Future', *Asian Strategic Review 1995–6*, New Delhi, IDSA, 1996.

———, 'Maritime Surveillance of the Indian EEZ', *Strategic Analysis*, vol. 12, no. 1, April 1998.

Ruland, Jürgen, 'ASEAN and the Asian Crisis: Theoretical Implications and Practical Consequences for South-East Asian Regionalism', *The Pacific Review*, vol. 13, no. 3, 2000, p. 236.

Sachwald, Frédérique, 'La Mondialisation Comme Facteur d'Intégration Régionale', *Politique Étrangère*, Mondialisation et dynamiques régionales, Summer 1997.

Saravanamuttu, J., 'Malaysia's Foreign Policy in the Mahathir Period, 1981–95: An Iconoclast Come to Rule', *Asian Journal of Political Science*, vol. 4, no. 1, June 1996.

Segal, Gerald, 'Asianism and Asian Security', *The National Interest*, Winter 1995–6.

Sen Gupta, Bhabani, 'In Search of a Foreign Policy', *Seminar*, no. 472, December 1998.

———, 'India in the Twenty-first century', *International Affairs*, vol. 73, no. 2, 1997.

Singh, Jasjit, 'Introduction', *Asian Strategic Review, 1995–6*, New Delhi, IDSA, 1996.

———, 'Future of Sino-Indian Relations', *Strategic Analysis*, March 1994.

———, 'La Non-prolifération Nucléaire au XXIe Siècle', *Politique Etrangère*, 1996.

———, 'Trends in Defense Expenditure', *Asian Strategic Review 1995–6*, New Delhi, IDSA, 1996.

Singh, Jaswant (interview with), 'India in a Changing World', *World Affairs*, vol. 4, no. 2, April–June 2000.

———, 'Against Nuclear Apartheid', *Foreign Affairs*, vol. 77, no. 5, September–October 1998.

Singh, Ravinderpal, 'Indian Ballistic Missile Developments: Possibilities and Potentialities', *Strategic Analysis*, vol. 13, no. 10, January 1991.

———, 'Post-Cold War Dual-Use Technology Transfer Order: Policy Implications for India', *Strategic Analysis*, vol. 16, no. 10, January 1992.

Singh, Swaran, 'Sino-Indian Ties: Need for Bold Initiatives', *Strategic Analysis*, vol. 22, no. 11, February 1999.

———, 'Sino-US Defence Ties: Whys and Hows of Their Recent Engagement', *Strategic Analysis*, vol. 22, no. 1, April 1998.

Singh, Uday Bhanu, 'Evolution of the ASEAN Regional Forum', *Asian Strategic Review, 1995–6*, New Delhi, IDSA, 1996.

———, 'Growth of Military Power in South-East Asia', *Asian Strategic Review, 1994–5*, New Delhi, IDSA, 1995.

Siwei, Mao, 'China and the Kashmir Issue', *Strategic Analysis*, March 1995.

Sridharane, E., 'Coalition Politics', *Seminar*, no. 437, January 1996.

———, 'The 'Problem', *Wooing Japan*, *Seminar*, no. 397, September 1992.

Sridharan, Kripa, 'India and ASEAN: The Long Road to Dialogue', *The Round Table*, no. 340, 1996.

Steinberg, D.J., 'Myanmar as Nexus: Sino-Indian Rivalries on the Frontier', *Terrorism*, vol. 16.

Stobdan, P., 'China's Forays into Burma: Implications for India', *Strategic Analysis*, vol. 16, no. 1, April 1993.

———, 'Myanmar: Breaking out of Isolation', *Strategic Analysis*, February 1995.

Stubbs, R., 'ASEAN+3: Emerging East Asian Regionalism', *Asian Survey*, vol. 17, no.3, May–June 2002.

Subrahmanyam, K., 'Nuclear India in Global Politics', *World Affairs*, July–September, vol. 2, no. 3, 1998.

Mansingh Surjit, 'The United States, China and India: Relationships in Comparative Perspective', *China Report*, vol. 35, no. 2, April–June 1999.

Suryanarayan, V., 'Overseas Chinese in South-East Asia: A Comparative Study', *Strategic Analysis*, December 1995.

Tan, Joseph L.H., 'Singapore's Foreign Direct Investment in Indo-China and Myanmar: Opportunities and Challenges', *RIS Occasional Paper*, no. 50, 1997, pp. 29–32.

Tanham, G., 'Indian Strategic Culture', *Washington Quarterly*, Winter 1992.

———, 'Indian Strategic Concerns in the 1990s', *RGICS Paper*, no. 28, 1995.

Tankha, Brij, 'India–Japan and the Coming Century,' *Seminar*, no. 472, December 1998.

Varshney, Ashutosh, 'Strategy in Industrial Development: India and South Korea', *India International Centre Quarterly*, vol. 20, no. 4, Winter 1993.

Viswam, S. 'India Looks East', *World Focus*, vol. 18, no. 6, June 1997.

Wesley, Michael, 'The Politics of Exclusion: Australia, Turkey and Definitions of Regionalism', *The Pacific Review*, vol. 10, no. 4, 1997.

Wilson, Dick, 'The Asian Security Management Challenge: A Future "Trinity" of China, Japan and India', *RGICS Paper*, no. 10, 1994.

Yamazawa, Ippei, 'APEC's New Development and Its Implications for Non-member Developing Countries', *The Developing Economies*, vol. 34, no. 2, June 1996.

Zakaria, Fareed, 'Culture is Destiny: A Conversation with Lee Kuan Yew', *Foreign Affairs*, vol. 73, no. 2, March–April 1994.

Zins, M.J., 'Le Parti du Congrès et l'Identité Nationale Indienne', *Hérodote*, L'Inde et la Question Nationale, no. 71, October–December 1993.

SOURCES AVAILABLE ON THE INTERNET

Friedberg, Aaron L., 'Introduction', in National Bureau of Asian Research, *Strategic Asia 2001–2* (http://strategicasia.nbr.org/Report).

Garver, J.W., 'The China-India-US Triangle: Strategic Relations in the Post-Cold War Era', *NBR Analysis*, vol. 13, no. 5, 2002 (http://www.nbr.org).

Harding, Harry, 'The Bush Administration's Approach to Asia: Before and after September 11', Hong Kong Asia Society, 12 November 2001 (http://www.csis.org/saprog/venu.pdf).

Hirabayashi, Hiroshi, 'South Asia and Its Neighbours,' 19 April 1998 (http.//www.japan-emb.org.in/lectures).

Limaye, Satu P., 'U.S.-India Relations: Visible to the Naked Eye', *Comparative Connections*, 4th Quarter 2001 (http://www.csis.org/pacfor/cc/0104Qoa.html).

Rajagopalan, R.P., 'Indo-US Relations in the Bush White House', *Strategic Analysis*, July 2001 (http://www.idsa-india.org).

Rajamony, Venu, 'India-China-U.S. Triangle: A "Soft" Balance of Power in the Making', *Asia Foundation*, March 2002 (http://www.csis.org/saprog/venu.pdf).

Schaffer, T.C., *Rising India and U.S. Policy Options in Asia*, CSIS Report, January 2002 (http://www.csis.org/pubs/2002_risingindia.htm).

Sommers, J. (Rapporteur), 'The India-China Relationship: What the United States Needs to Know', Asia Society & Woodrow Wilson Centre for Scholars Conference Report, 30 November 2001 (http://www.asiasociety.org/publications/indiachina01.html).

Tellis, Ashley J., 'South Asia', in National Bureau of Asian Research, *Strategic Asia 2001–2* (http://strategicasia.nbr.org/Report).

BIBLIOGRAPHICAL SOURCES

Reports by Chambers of Commerce and Industry

A. *Association of Chambers of Commerce (ASSOCHAM) & Federation of Indian Chambers of Commerce and Industries (FICCI)*

ASSOCHAM & Indian Merchants' Chamber, *Sponsored Business Mission to Thailand, Malaysia, Indonesia, Singapore, A Report*, 26 March–5 April 1992.

ASSOCHAM, FICCI, *Fourth Meeting of India-Malaysia Joint Business Cooperation Committee, a Report*, 10 April 1995, Kuala Lumpur.

ASSOCHAM, FICCI, *A Report on the Nineteenth Joint Meeting of the India-Japan Standing Committee*, 18 April 1996, Hakone, Japan.

ASSOCHAM, FICCI, *Report on the 27th Joint Meeting of the India-Japan Business Cooperation Committee*, 13 November 1996, New Delhi.

ASSOCHAM, FICCI, *Third Meeting of India-Singapore Joint Business Council, a Report*, 7 September 1998, Chennai.

FICCI, *Second Meeting of India-Thailand Joint Business Council*, 24 June 1996, New Delhi.

FICCI, *20th Joint Meeting of the India-Japan Standing Committee*, 8 May 1997, Nagoya, Japan.

FICCI, *South-East Asian Crisis: Lessons for India*, New Delhi, 1998.

FICCI, *India-ASEAN Trade Relations*, New Delhi, 1999.

B. *Confederation of Indian Industry (CII)*

CII, *CEOs Mission to Japan: A Report*, 30 May–2 June 1994.

CII, *Proceedings of the Partnership Summit: CII Centenary 1895-1995*, 4–6 January 1995, Calcutta.

CII, *Workshop on Asia Vision 2000*, 15–26 May 1995.

CII, *Seminar of India-Korea Economic Cooperation, Proceedings*, New Delhi, 18 July 1995.

CII, 'CII Delegation Meets Prime Minister of Singapore', *CII Communiqué*, no. 29, December 1996.

CII, Chandrasekhar Sharma, *Visit to South Korea, 12–20 November 1996, A Report*, CII, 1996.

CII, *Twelfth Indian Engineering Trade Fair in Retrospect*, 9–15 February 1997, New Delhi.

CII, 'Moving to the Market: Sustaining Reforms in India and Asia', *CII Communiqué*, no. 9, March 1997.

CII, *CEOs Mission to Japan: A Report*, 8–11 June 1997.

CII, 'CII Core Group Meets Singapore Prime Minister', *CII Communiqué*, no. 41, December 1997.

CII, 'CII Manufacturing Mission to Japan and South Korea', *CII Communiqué*, special issue no. 40, December 1997.

CII, *The Partnership Summit, 1998: Networking Global Partnerships: A Retrospective.*

CII, *IETF'99 In Retrospect*, 12–17 February 1999, New Delhi, India.

CII, *Trade Fair Times*, no. 1, April 1999.

C. *World Trade Centre*

World Trade Centre, *India and ASEAN: Partners in Progress*, Mumbai: MVIRDC, 29 April 1993.

World Trade Centre, *The Association of South-East Asian Nations and India: A Bridge to the New Asia*, MVIRDC, Mumbai, 1993.

World Trade Centre, *A Report on South Korea*, July 1993.

D. *Singapore Indian Chamber of Commerce and Industry (SICCI)*

SICCI, *Draft Minutes, ASEAN-India Business Council Round Table*, 21 September 1995, Singapore.

SICCI, George Abraham, *Report of the Proceedings of the ASEAN-India Business Council—ASEAN Section Meeting*, 9 April 1996, Jakarta, Indonesia.

SICCI, *Global Indian Entrepreneurs Conference—India: The Uncaged Tiger*, 19-20 June 1996, Summary of Proceedings.

SICCI for ASEAN-CCI, *Report of the Proceedings of the ASEAN-India Business Council*, 14–15 November 1996, New Delhi.

SICCI, *Meeting of the ASEAN Chambers of Commerce and Industry (ASEAN-CCI), Report on the Proceedings of the ASEAN-India Business Council (AIBC), ASEAN Section Meeting*, 10 March 1997, Jakarta.

SICCI, *Report on the Proceeding of the ASEAN-India Business Council Meeting*, 14 October 1997, Singapore.

E. *India-ASEAN Economic Cooperation Committee (IAECC)*

IAECC, *Report of the Proceedings of the ASEAN-India Business Council Meeting*, New Delhi, 16 February 1995.

IAECC, *India-ASEAN Commercial Directory*, compiled and published by Amarjit Singh, MBE, Advisor, the ASSOCHAM for the IAECC, 1st edn., New Delhi, 1996.

IAECC, *India-ASEAN Economic Cooperation Committee Meeting*, 8 August 1997, New Delhi.

IAECC for AIBC, *ASEAN-India Business Council Meeting*, 14 October 1997, Singapore.

IAECC, *India-ASEAN Commercial News*, September–October 1997,
IAECC, *India-ASEAN* Commercial News, November–December 1997.

STUDIES CONDUCTED BY CONSULTANTS, COMPANIES OR RESEARCH CENTRES

S.R. Baltiboi & Co. and Ernst & Young Pvt. Ltd., *Pattern of Japanese Investment in India*, November 1996.
Tata Group, *Tata Airline Facts*, Mumbai, 1998.
Parameshwara Holdings Ltd., *Report on Investments in India* (to the Shareholders), 10 July 1997.
Centre for Policy Research, *Report of the CPR Delegation to Taiwan*, September 1994.

STATISTICAL SOURCES

A. *Monthly Sources*

Secretariat for Industrial Approvals, Ministry of Industry, *Newsletter*, Mumbai, SIA, [http://indmin.nic.in/vsindmin/publicat/newslttr/].
Indian Investment Center, *Monthly Newsletter*, New Delhi, IIC [http:/iic.nic.in/].
Indian Institute of Public Opinion, *Blue Supplement of the Monthly Opinion Surveys*, vol. XLII, no. 5–6, February–March 1997.
Centre for Monitoring Indian Economy, *Monthly Review of Investment Projects*, Mumbai: CMIE.

B. *Annual Sources*

Reserve Bank of India, *Annual Report*, Mumbai: RBI [http://www.rbi.org.in/].
Handbook on Statistics on Indian Economy, 8 January 2002.
Centre for Monitoring Indian Economy, *Foreign Trade and Balance of Payments*, Mumbai: CMIE [http://www.cmie.com/]
United Nations Department of Economics and Social Affairs, Statistics Division, *International Trade Statistics Yearbook*, New York: United Nations, 2003.
World Tourism Organization, *India—Top Destinations*, 1998.
World Trade Organization, *Annual Report. International Trade Statistics*, Washington D.C.: Bernan Press.

OFFICIAL SPEECHES

A. *Indian Political Leaders*

P.V. NARASIMHA RAO, PRIME MINISTER

P.V. Narasimha Rao, 'India and Japan', Speech at the banquet hosted by Prime Minister Miyazawa of Japan, Tokyo, 23 June 1992, in P.V.

Narasimha Rao, *Selected Speeches*, New Delhi: Ministry of External Affairs, 1997.

———, 'India and Japan', Address to the Japan Institute of International Affairs, on the occasion of the fortieth anniversary of the establishment of diplomatic relations between India and Japan, Tokyo, 23 June 1992, *Selected Speeches*.

———, 'Shared Democratic Values', Address to the Japan Institute of International Affairs, Japan, 24 June 1992, *Selected Speeches*.

———, 'Non-Aligned Movement and Global Issues', Speech at the tenth summit of the non-aligned countries in Jakarta, Indonesia, 2 September 1992, *Selected Speeches*.

———, 'India and Thailand', Speech at the banquet hosted by Thailand Premier, Chuan Leekpai, Bangkok, 7 April 1993, *Selected Speeches*.

———, 'Centre of Indo-Thailand Interaction', Speech while accepting an Honorary Degree in Liberal Arts Conferred by Thammasat University, Bangkok, 8 April 1993, *Selected Speeches*.

———, 'Common Indo-China Approach for Asian Resurgence', Speech at Beijing University, China, 9 September 1993, *Selected Speeches*.

———, 'Indo-Korea Relations', Speech at the banquet hosted by the Korean President, Seoul, 10 September 1993, *Selected Speeches*.

———, 'Challenges before the ESCAP', Speech at the inaugural fiftieth session of ESCAP, New Delhi, 5 April 1994, *Selected Speeches*.

———, 'Enormous Scope in India for NRI Investment', Address to the Indian community, Singapore, 7 September 1994, *Selected Speeches*.

———, 'India and the Asia-Pacific—A New Relationship', Speech on 'India and the Asia-Pacific: Forging a New Relationship', at the Institute of South-East Asian Studies, Singapore, 8 September 1994, *Selected Speeches*.

———, 'India and the Asia-Pacific—A New Relationship', *The Singapore Lecture Series*, Institute of South-East Asian Studies, Singapore, 1994.

SHEEL KANT SHARMA, JOINT SECRETARY AT THE MINISTER OF FOREIGN AFFAIRS

Sharma, Sheel Kant (Joint Secretary, Ministry of External Affairs), 'Indo-Malaysian Relations', *Strategic Analysis*, April 1994.

I.K. GUJRAL, MINISTER OF EXTERNAL AFFAIRS

Statement by External Affairs Minister of India, I.K. Gujral, on the occasion of the Post-Ministerial Conferences of ASEAN (7+10), 24 July 1996, Jakarta, MEA, XP Division.

Statement by External Affairs Minister of India, I.K. Gujral, on the occasion of the Post-Ministerial Conferences of ASEAN, (7+1), 24 July 1996, Jakarta, MEA, XP Division.

I.K. Gujral, 'Comprehensive Test Ban Treaty, Statements in Parliament', 31 July 1996, in I.K. Gujral, *A Foreign Policy for India*, New Delhi: MEA, 1998.

———, 'Comprehensive Test Ban treaty, Statement in Parliament', 11 September 1996, I.K. Gujral, *A Foreign Policy for India.*

———, 'Role of the ASEAN-India JCC', First Meeting of the ASEAN-India Joint Cooperation Committee, New Delhi, 14 November 1996, in I.K. Gujral, *A Foreign Policy for India.*

Speech by the External Affairs Minister I.K. Gujral, 'Essential Tenets of Indian Foreign Policy' on the occasion of the Inauguration of the Indian Association for International Affairs, New Delhi, 15 January 1997, MEA, XP division, 1997.

———, 'Areas of Common Concern in the Asian Region', Asian Media Convention, 24 February 1997, in I.K. Gujral, *A Foreign Policy for India.*

P. CHIDAMBARAM, MINISTER OF FINANCE

Statement of P. Chidambaram, Finance Minister of India, on the occasion of the Post-Ministerial Conferences of ASEAN (9+1) Session, Kuala Lumpur, 29 July 1997, MEA, XP Division, New Delhi, 1997.

Statement of P. Chidambaram, Finance Minister of India, on the Occasion of the Post-Ministerial Conferences of ASEAN (9+10) Session, Kuala Lumpur, 28 July 1997, MEA, XP Division, New Delhi, 1997.

SUDHIR DEVARE, SECRETARY, ECONOMIC RELATIONS, MINISTRY OF EXTERNAL AFFAIRS

Statement by Shri Sudhir Devare, Secretary of Economic Relations, India, on the occasion of the Second ASEAN-India JCC, Singapore, 28 April 1998.

JASWANT SINGH, DEPUTY CHAIRMAN OF THE PLANNING COMMISSION, MINISTER OF EXTERNAL AFFAIRS

Statement by Deputy Chairman Planning Commission of India, Jaswant Singh, on the occasion of the ASEAN Thirty-first Post-Ministerial Conferences (PMC 9+10) Session with India, 30 July 1998, Manila [http://www.asean.or.id/].

Statement by Deputy Chairman Planning Commission of India, Jaswant Singh, on the occasion of the ASEAN Thirty-first Post-Ministerial

Conferences (PMC 9+1) Session with India, 29 July 1998, Manila [http://www.asean.or.id/].

Statement by Minister of External Affairs, Jaswant Singh, at the ASEAN Thirty-second Post-Ministerial Conferences (PMC 10+10) Plenary Session, Singapore, 27 July 1999 [http://www.asean.or.id/].

Statement by Minister of External Affairs Jaswant Singh at the ASEAN Thirty-second Post-Ministerial Conference (PMC 10+1) Session with India, Singapore, 28 July 1999 [http://www.asean.or.id/].

B. *Asian Political Leaders*

S. JAYAKUMAR, MINISTER OF FOREIGN AFFAIRS, SINGAPORE

Opening Statement by His Excellency Prof. S. Jayakumar, Minister for Foreign Affairs of the Republic of Singapore, at the ASEAN Post-Ministerial Conference, Kuala Lumpur, 1997.

Opening Statement at the Second ASEAN-India Joint Co-operation Committee Meeting in Singapore by the Minister for Foreign Affairs, Prof. S. Jayakumar on Tuesday, 28 April 1998 [http://www.asean.or.id/]; [http://www.gov.sg/mfa/speeches/].

Opening statement by H.E., Prof. S. Jayakumar, Minister for Foreign Affairs of Singapore at the 1998 Post-Ministerial Conference (9+1) Session with India, 29 July 1998, Manila [http://www.asean.or.id/].

Opening Statement by H.E. Prof. S. Jayakumar Minister for Foreign Affairs, Singapore, at the Post-Ministerial Conference (10+1) Session with India, 29 July 2000, Bangkok, Thailand [http://www.asean.or.id/].

GOH CHOK TONG, PRIME MINISTER OF SINGAPORE

Closing Address by Prime Minister Goh Chok Tong at the Global Indian Entrepreneurs Conference (GIEC) on 20 June 1996, in SICCI, *Global Indian Entrepreneurs Conference. India: The Uncaged Tiger*, 19–20 June 1996, Summary of Proceedings, Annex D.

Goh Chok Tong, *Asian Economic Crisis: Singapore's Response*, Keynote Address by Goh Chok Tong, Prime Minister of Singapore, at the Official Opening Dinner of World Economic Forum's 1998 East Asia Economic Summit, 12 October in Singapore.

GEORGE YEO, MINISTER OF INFORMATION AND ARTS AND
VICE-MINISTER OF COMMERCE AND INDUSTRY, SINGAPORE

BG (NS) George Yeo, Minister for Information and the Arts and Second Minister of Commerce and Industry, 'Good Long-Term Climate for Economic Reform in India', *A Bimonthly Selection of Ministries*

Speeches, March–April 1997, Singapore: Ministry of Information and the Art.

LEE HSIEN LOONG, DEPUTY PRIME MINISTER OF SINGAPORE

Keynote Address by Brigadier-General (NS) Lee Hsien Loong, Deputy Prime Minister, 'Integrating the Indian Economy into the World: A Singapore perspective', in SICCI, *Global Indian Entrepreneurs Conference. India: The Uncaged Tiger*, 19–20 June 1996, Summary of Proceedings, Annex B.

MAHATHIR BIN MOHAMAD, PRIME MINISTER OF MALAYSIA

Speech by the Prime Minister of Malaysia, Dr Mahathir Bin Mohamad, at the ASEAN-India Lecture Series in New Delhi on 21 December 1996, MEA, XP Division, New Delhi, 1997.

KIM YOUNG SAM, PRESIDENT OF SOUTH KOREA

'New Partners for Common Prosperity', President Kim Young Sam's Visits to India and Singapore and Participation in the Asia-Europe Meeting, 24 February–4 March 1996, The Republic of Korea: Korean Overseas Information Service, Seoul, March 1996.

ALI ALATAS, MINISTER OF FOREIGN AFFAIRS, INDONESIA

Statement by Ali Alatas, Minister for Foreign Affairs of the Republic of Indonesia, at the fifty-first Session of the United Nations General Assembly, New York, 30 September 1996. Department of Foreign Affairs of the Republic of Indonesia [http://www.dfa-dcplu.go.id/].

Inaugural Address by Ali Alatas, Minister for Foreign Affairs of the Republic of Indonesia at the Opening of the ESCAP/UNCTAD/UNDP Meeting of Senior Officials to Assist in Preparation for the first WTO Ministerial Meeting, Jakarta, 4 September 1996 [http://www.dfa-deplu.go.id/].

C. *US Political Leaders*

Wolfowitz, Paul, U.S. Deputy Secretary of Defence, 'The Gathering Storm: The Threat of Global Terror and Asia/Pacific Security', *The First IISS Asia Security Conference: 'The Shangri-La Dialogue'*, Singapore, 31 May–June 2002.

Official Documents

A. *Indian Ministry of External Affairs*

Ministry of External Affairs, *India and ASEAN Dialogue Partnership: Friends and Neighbours*, New Delhi: MEA, 1996.

Ministry of External Affairs, *India in IOR-ARC, Towards a New Partnership in the Indian Ocean Rim*, New Delhi: MEA, 1997.

Ministry of External Affairs, 'India and G-15: Recharging South-South Cooperation and Global Dialogue', *Strategic Digest*, vol. 28, no. 2, February 1998.

Ministry of External Affairs, *India Means Business: Perspectives*, New Delhi: MEA, Investment Promotion and Publicity Division & Arthur Andersen, 1998.

Ministry of External Affairs of India, *Annual Report*, New Delhi: MEA, XP Division (From 1992–3 to 2001–2).

Foreign Affairs Record, New Delhi: MEA (From 1994 to 1999).

B. *Asian Regional Organisations*

ASEAN

Joint Press release, *The First ASEAN-India Joint Cooperation Committee Meeting*, New Delhi, 14–16 November 1996, [www.asean.or.id/].

Joint Communiqué of the Thirty-First ASEAN Ministerial Meeting, Manila, Philippines, 24–25 July 1998, *Strategic Digest*, vol. 28, no. 10, October 1998.

Statement of the Chairman of the Fifth ASEAN Regional Forum, Manila, 27 July 1998, *Strategic Digest*, vol. 28, no. 10, October 1998.

IOR-ARC

Resolution on the Adoption of the Charter of the Indian Ocean Rim—Association for Regional Cooperation, First Ministerial Meeting, Mauritius, 5–7 March 1997, *Strategic Digest*, April 1997.

BIMST-EC

Concept Paper, *Bangladesh-India-Sri Lanka-Thailand Economic Cooperation (BIST-EC)*, 5 June 1997.

Declaration on the Establishment of the Bangladesh-India-Sri Lanka-Thailand Economic Cooperation (BIST-EC), Bangkok, 6 June 1997.

Report of the Special BIST-EC Senior Officials Meeting, Bangkok, 19–20 December 1997.

Joint Statement of the BIMST-EC Ministerial Meeting, 22 December, 1997, Bangkok.

C. *The Kunming Initiative*

'The Kunming Initiative for a Growth Quadrangle between China, India, Myanmar and Bangladesh', 14–17 August, 1999', *China Report*, vol. 36, no. 3, 2000.

D. *Indian Diplomatic Representations in Asia*

Embassy of India in Seoul, *Monthly Round-up on Indo-Korean Economic Relations*, January 1996.

High Commission of India in Malaysia, *Malaysian Joint Venture in India*, March 1998.

E. *South-East Asian Government Institutions*

Singapore Trade Development Board, *India: New Opportunities*, Singapore: STDB, 1998.

Singapore Tourist Promotion Board, *Tourism in Brief*, June 1997.

Ministry of the Arts, *Singapore 1997*, Singapore: Ministry of the Arts, 1998.

Tourism Authority of Thailand, 'International Tourist Arrivals to Thailand by Nationality', in *Thailand Tourism Statistics*, 1997.

F. *Government of the United States of America*

White House, *The National Security Strategy of the United States of America*, Washington: September 2002.

POLITICAL PARTY PUBLICATIONS

Bharatiya Janata Party, *Election Manifesto '98*, New Delhi, BJP, 1998.

PERIODICALS

A. *Indian Dailies Referred to*

Business Standard; Indian express; *The Asian Age; The Economic Times*; *The Hindu*; *The Times of India*.

B. *Weekly, Bi-monthly and Monthly Magazines*

Business India; Frontline; India Today; Indian Recorder, a weekly of events & happenings; Strategic Digest, Far Eastern Economic Review, World Focus; Organiser.

Index